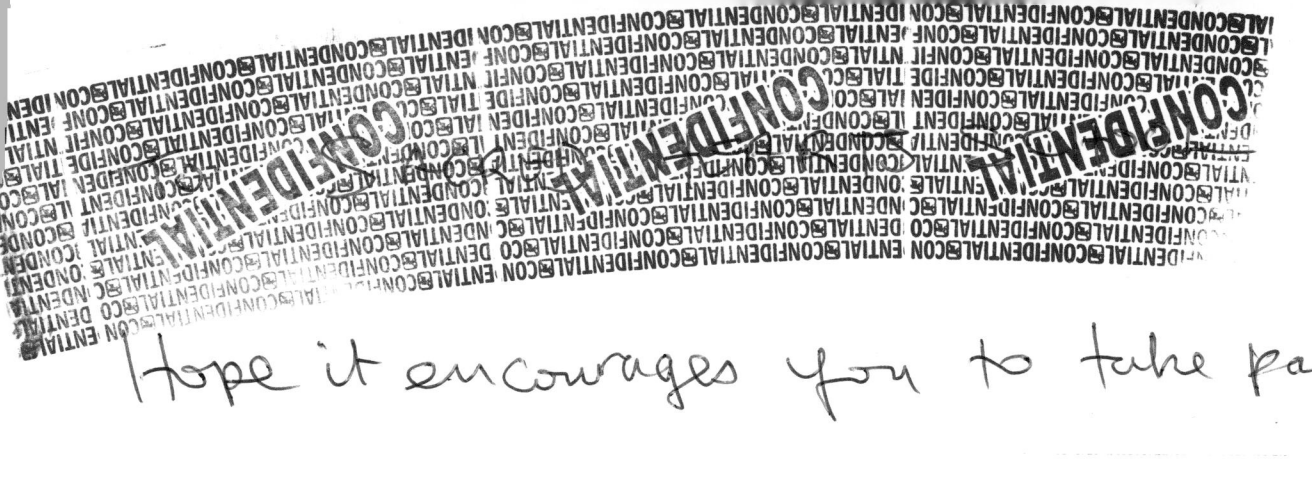

Hope it encourages you to take part.

Mike Kensey

London's New River in Maps

Robert Mylne's 1775-1809 Survey

Portrait of Sir Hugh Myddelton, Baronet: 1722 George Vertue engraving of the Welbeck Abbey 1632 replica ((MWB > TW) 12, p26). The likeness painted a year after his death. **Probably NOT knighted**, but created a Baronet in 1622 when excused the normal charge of £1,095.

Probable original 1628 oil painting by Cornelius Jansen in the Baltimore Museum of Art.

1631 (Date on Frame)/1632 replica oil painting by Jansen in Court Room, Goldsmiths' Hall, London.

1632 replica oil painting by Jansen in Duke of Portland's collection, Welbeck Abbey.

Jansen's replica copy in the NRC's offices Blackfrairs was destroyed in a 1769 fire (12, p27).

There are also reputed other versions.

London's New River in Maps

Volume 1, Part 1

c.1600 to 1850 (Ware to Enfield Flash)

Robert Mylne's Survey

by

Michael F. Kensey

Published by M.F. Kensey
London
2012 (MMXII)

To the memory of my late mother Edith Cook (> Mrs Kensey widow > Mrs Canfield widow), and to my loving daughter Alexandrina Ross-Kensey lost to me by divorce.

First published 2012
by the author M.F. Kensey, Cheshunt, Hertfordshire, EN7 6HG.

© Copyright Michael F. Kensey, 2012.

ISBN **978-0-9572240-0-1**

All rights reserved. No part of this publication may be reproduced, stored in a retrieval system, or transmitted, in any form, or by any means, electronic, mechanical, photocopying, recording or otherwise, without the prior permission of the publisher and copyright holder.

Michael Frederick Kensey hereby asserts the moral right to be identified as the author of this work.

Front Cover Illustration: May 1830 New River Company Balance Engine ((Thames Water Plc) London Metropolitan Archive; MFK photo).

Inside Front & Back Cover: 1835 Map of New River before most of the Former Loops were Bypassed ((G.E. Madeley litho) 7G, p60).

Typesetting and origination (including the jacket) by Michael F. Kensey using Microsoft Word 2007, Photoshop 7, Acro Software Cute PDF Writer, & Serif PagePlus X6.

Photos taken with a FujiFilm FinePix F11 & FujiFilm FinePix S1000 fd.

Printed in the United Kingdom by
Henry Ling Limited, at the Dorset Press,
Dorchester,
Dorset,
DT1 1HD.

Contents	i

Preface	iii
Acknowledgements	iv
400-year Celebrations	v
List of Illustrations	x

Chapter 1   Birth & Development of the Artificial Gravitational New River **1**

Early Water Supply	1
Colthurst & Myddelton constructing the Original New River	2 – 16
Original Costs of New River	16 – 19
First line of NRC wooden pipes	19
1616 Myddelton's 21-year Tenant Water Agreement	20 – 21
1617-1631 Mining Silver in Wales	21 – 23
1619 Incorporation of NRC & its Seal	23
1619 Tapping the River Lee	25
1620-1622 Reclaiming Brading Haven	26
1622 Myddelton's Baronetcy	27
Royal Moiety or King's Shares	29 – 32
1631 1st Sir Hugh Myddelton's Death	32 – 38
Great Fire of London 1666	39
NRC Shares regarding Poll Tax, Land Tax, Local Rates/Poor law & Income Tax	40
NRC Wooden Pipes & Pipe Boring	41 – 42
Death of Sir Hugh Myddelton Bart. of Hackney & Twickenham (Separate Baronetcy)	42
Henry Mill, NRC Surveyor	43 – 45
6th Baronet, the last to hold Sir Hugh's Title	46
Pre-1769 NRC Records	47
NRC Office Fire 1769, Bridewell Precinct	47 – 48
Intense Competition (1806-1818)	49
New River Poem	50 – 52
Additional NRC Reservoirs	54 – 56
Various Acts of Parliament	56 – 58
1904 Metropolitan Water Board	58
1904 NRC Limited	59
NEW RIVER PATH	60 - 61
New River Company Main Sites, Modern Autogrates & Pumphouses	62 - 63
New River Company Main Sites (Continued) & New River Company Takeovers	64 - 65
New River Company Former Headquarters	66 - 73
NRC Dividends 1633-1903	73 - 77
NRC Governors, Officers etc. 1619-1903	78 - 84

Chapter 2   Historical Features along the New River   **85**

2.1 **When Constructing the New River**	85
(Pumps/Dams; Plugs; Piling & Wharfing; Puddled Clay)	
2.2 **Under the New River**	88
(Drainage Pipes & Brick Culverts)	
2.3 **Over the New River**	88
(Bridges, Surface Water & Purity, Flashes/Troughs & Frames/Boarded Rivers)	
2.4 **Along the New River**	93
(Islands, Cistern Houses, Tunnels, Easements, Piped/Culverts, Aqueducts, Filtration/Chlorination, Pumping Waterwheels, Pumping Stations, Modern Pumphouses, Water-level Gauges, Major Sluices/Weirs, NRC Stone & Iron Boundary Markers, Stealing NR water, Illegal Bathing & Washing, Poachers Fishing, Watch Boxes/Houses, Cast-Iron Cattle Troughs fed by NR, Water-weed cutting, Weed Grates, Python Rigs/Davits/Boat Hoists, Punts/Boats, NRC inscribed Seats, Cutting the grass banks, Walksmen & Gate Keys, Fencing, MWB notice boards, NRC Street main valve-plates, Water Purity & Wildlife)	
2.5 **Gradient, Width & Length**	107
Fall/Gradient/Level	107
Width	107
Original Length	108
Reductions & Increases in Length	109 - 111

2.6 Map Overlays (Used in later Volumes)	112
2.7 Terminus (New River Head)	112
2.8 The Myddelton Name, Artists & Verse	113 – 129

Chapter 3   Robert Mylne's 1775-1809 Survey   **131**

Robert Mylne NRC Surveyor/Engineer	131
Turnpike Trusts/Roads/Toll Bars	132
3.1 TEXT on Robert Mylne's Survey	132 - 156
3.2 Robert Mylne's 1775-1809 Plans	157
Ware, Herts.	158
Balance Engine	161 - 164
Chadwell Spring	167
Old Gauge & New Gauge (aka Marble Gauge)	168 - 171
Chronological Sequence at the Source of New River	172 - 173
NRC Boundary Stone, N of White House Sluice	175
NRC Boundary Stone before White House Sluice & Gauge/Capstone SW-side of WHS	176
White House Sluice & Weir Date Stones	177 – 179
1773 plan around Chadwell Spring	180
Chadwell Spring	182 – 185
Marble Gauge	181
1793 & c.1810 Chadwell Spring	186
Chadwell Spring Main Monumental Stone	187
Other Chadwell Spring Stones	188
Amwell End	192 - 199
Ware Mill & Lock	200 - 206
Crane Mead (River Lee), Ware	208 - 212
Amwell End, Ware to Lower Road, Great Amwell	211
Amwell End	212
Red House	213
Great Amwell	218
Overlay of Original Island > Two Islands	220
Stanstead Loops	228
Stanstead to Hoddesdon	231
Hoddesdon	238
Broxbourne	244
Broxbourne High Road	252
Wormley Loops	255
Wormley 'High Road' Loop	258
Wormley, 1844 NRC plan	259
Wormley-Turnford Loop	260
Wormley Flash	263
Cheshunt Flash	270
Bury Green Loop	279
Theobalds	282
1826 Note on Cheshunt Flash	288
Theobalds Brook/Park	290
Theobalds Loop	292
Original location of 1st Capel House, Mystery Shortening, possible earlier course	295
Bullsmoor Loop	297
Whitewebbs Loop, Enfield	300
Elizabeth Myddelton & John Grene's property at Turkey Street, Enfield	302 - 310
Bowling Green House (> Myddelton House)	312
Former Deer Park > Forty Hall estate	325
Dickinson's Trough	326
Flash Lane/Road, off Clay Hill, Enfield	328

Continued in Vol. 1 Part 2

Bibliography, see Volume 3.

Index (Vol. 1, Part 1 & 2)	Index-01

Preface

- This not as such a history of London's New River from its inception, my version of this is still a work in progress.
- Vol. 1 of this book is based on the first-known reliably-accurate plan of the complete course of the New River (approx. 40-miles), drawn 1775-1809 by the famous architect and New River Company Surveyor Robert Mylne.
- Vol. 2 covers the period c.1850-1900, and Vol. 3 post-c.1900, all three volumes embellished with other such plans etc. of the same & later periods.
- The later part of these books also have a more practical purpose, that of a companion guide when following today's New River Path, where you might occasionally dwell awhile and romance about its former history and loops, and in appropriate places trace it through today's streets where it once flowed.

Being a fully HNC examination qualified Mechanical Engineer (part-time 1957-1968 Enfield & N.W. Kent, Colleges of Technology), my prime interest in history is as an Industrial Archaeologist, my training in field archaeology itself consolidated on a 1969 Summer School at the Roman excavations at Corbridge, Northumberland. In 1968 on behalf of the Enfield Archaeological Society, I led the team of members exposing the 1820 Cast-Iron Aqueduct at Flash Lane, and in 1971 supervised the excavation of a timber aqueduct at Bull Beggars Hole, Whitewebbs, both in Enfield. In later years to avoid the manual labour of field archaeology, have converted to for the want of a better term 'Carto(graphic)-Archaeology' for uncovering the hidden past. In fact the last thing I 'dug up' was from dusty shelves, the Robert Mylne plans the main subject of Vol. 1.

This hasn't been just about writing a book. It has been an exciting 40-year journey of discovery that included fieldwork, research, the responsibility for two archaeological excavations, walking and photographing most locations, and visiting virtually every archive from Hertford to the City of London, and many other places. Whenever I went for a walk, there was invariably a purpose in mind, to firm-up or confirm details on a local historical feature.

This has resulting in amassing:
- At least thirty-two A4 lever arch files & various books, some original editions.
- Perhaps the largest officially-obtained multi-archive collection of illustrations (historic prints etc.) & MFK photos of historical features along the New River & London's Water Supply (78,890 files, 147GB June 2011), plus typed text documents.

Perhaps this is the time to throw down the gauntlet to a far younger person (with staying power), to find even more gold nuggets (especially going through the original NRC Mins., and vast collection at the LMA), and maybe prove that some of my nuggets may have been fool's gold.

Due to space considerations & and in some cases costs, sadly have had to leave out many previously unpublished illustrations. I have an insatiable appetite for old prints of the New River, and am always glad to hear from anyone with interesting information, prints or photos etc. of the New River. Any material offered, if later used will be acknowledged.

Note that any errors in this book are mine, and should not be attributable to others. Some of the individual sheets throughout have been written at different times, such that there might be minor differences in details. Since this is the first edition there are bound to be some errors, that if notified will be corrected for any subsequent version/s.

Also note that **29 Sept. 2013 is the 400-year anniversary of the completion of the New River**, and like all 100-year anniversaries should be honoured with great celebrations, a list of those parties that might be interested follows later.

Bryan Hornby for all those 'field walks' years ago, gathering knowledge on the physical remains of local history.

The late Roger Eddington for sharing his passion for the New River, so ably assisting me in undertaking two archaeological excavations of the New River in Enfield (and all those other EAS members too many to name individually), and for permission to use his superb drawing of the NRC Cast-Iron Aqueduct.

Guido Bitter for accompanying me on so many field walks of discovery over 15-years along the New River.

The late G.C. Berry, archivist of the former MWB who greatly helped me with research in the early days. To the late Dave Allkins of Thames Water Plc who I first met at the Science Museum Library, for his dedicated enthusiasm, expansive knowledge and help on the history of water supply, such that parts of this book were greatly enhanced and are rightly dedicated.

Robin Winters (since retired) & Matthew Wood of Thames Water Plc, for their help when researching at the Abbey Mills Archive; also for Matthew Wood's permission to publish Thames Water Plc. material.

John & Dave Liddard of Thames Water Plc for permissions to visit and photograph some of the New River sites. Also to Bob Collington of Thames Water Plc who pointed me in their direction. Valerie Hicks for kindly loaning me her copies of 'Thames Water News' etc.

Mr & Mrs Sally Carr for permitting me to photograph their delightful island/garden aside the New River at Broxbourne. Brian Hewitt & Andrew Turvey of the Lee Valley Regional Park Authority for help & illustrations on Myddelton House, Enfield.

Enfield Grammar School for permitting me to photograph the old course of the New River through its grounds. Bush Hill Park Golf Club (Lee Fickling, Director of Golf, his ground staff and the lady players on Wednesday's Ladies Day) similarly for permitting me to photograph the former course of the New River through its grounds.

Of the many archives on route, staff at HALS (Hertfordshire Archives & Local Studies) & Susan Flood the County Archivist for permission to publish their material, Ware Museum, Lowewood Museum Hoddesdon, Enfield Local Study Centre & Archive (David Pam, Graham Dalling, today's John Clark, Kate Godfrey & recent assistant). John Griffin & Val Munday (both since moved on) for help with the historic images held by the Enfield Museum Service. Bruce Castle Archive (BCMA) volunteer Bill Rust for his enthusiastic & most knowledgeable help, Valerie Crosby, Clare Stephens, Renata Pillay, and Deborah Hedgecock. Hackney Archives (for their superb images), Islington Local History Centre (Isl. LHC) former staff Lorraine Lees, Christopher Sweeney, Caroline Ward, Elizabeth Highfield; afterwards Allie Dillon, Nicola Feggetter, & Mark Aston the current Local History Manager for permission to publish their material; and the staff of the London Metropolitan Archive (LMA).

Enfield Local Study Centre & Archive (former ELHU) for permission to publish various prints & illustrations etc., each one individually identified within the text of this book.

Stephen Sellick for permission to publish his photos of the former New River through Enfield.

Bryce Caller ex-MWB architect staff & volunteer archivist at Kew Bridge Steam Museum for his help on the history of London's water supply.

Staff at the Science Museum Library (Mandy Taylor and others), London; The Royal Society for permission to publish two 1767 drawings of John Smeaton's Fire Engine at New River Head (JS/3/14 & /15); the British Museum for their declared permission to publish some of their copyright prints.

Graham Levins for his enthusiastic interest in Sir Hugh Myddelton's Welsh Silver mines.

Clive West-Bulford over the years for repairs to my computers and currently Peter Frost of P.FixIT, Cheshunt, Herts., on which this book was compiled. In the early days fraught with loss of data and time-consuming reconstructions of lost information, but today not such a problem that youngsters have it so easy, as also with 'instant' digital cameras. With this my first self-publish venture, thanks for the help of Andrew Hunter, Tim Hine & the Technical Dept. at my printers Henry Ling Limited at the Dorset Press.

The following works (from which I have greatly drawn) must also be acknowledged as adding much to the knowledge of Sir Hugh & the New River: Samuel Smiles ('Lives of the Engineers'), G.C. Berry (Archivist at former M.W.B., who unearthed the Original Account Books), J.W. Gough (detailed biography of Myddelton), Bernard Rudden (full legal treatise on New River), Michael Essex-Lopresti (popular NR handbook), Mary Cosh (popular NR Islington Walk), 'New River News' of the New River Action Group (NRAG) & Robert Ward (popular NR history).

The list could go on and on, and if you think I have missed you out (certainly not intentionally), write to jog my dulling memory, for a possible inclusion in any reprint or further publication.

3 Oct. 2010 & since updated.

Sir Hugh Myddelton (Goldsmith) completing London's New River 29 Sept. 1613.

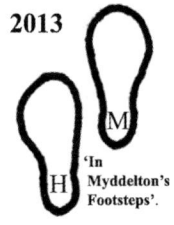

2013

'In Myddelton's Footsteps'.

'In the Footsteps of Sir Hugh Myddelton'
400-year Anniversary 29 September 2013.

Celebration of Sir Hugh Myddelton & London's Water Supply: All 100-year anniversaries should be honoured with great celebrations, probably starting 2-years before which gives adequate time to organise some worthwhile events, including budgets for displays, exhibitions, updating fact sheets, local histories etc.

One previous comprehensive exhibition on the New River providing valuable original source material:
'An Exhibition of Historical Records ['Prints, Documents, Photographs, Photostats, Paintings and Books'] relating to the New River in Hoddesdon & the surrounding district' held at the Public Library, 'Lowewood', Hoddesdon, 4 – 9 Oct. 1954, admission free. Introduction by E.W. Paddick, Branch Librarian. Light-green covered catalogue priced $2^{d.}$ Copy at Enfield Local Study Centre & Archive (628.1 (1) New River), and at Islington Local History Centre.

Hugh Myddelton born c.1560, said to be in a house at Galch-Hill Denbigh (and still there), plus a monumental brass of parents & children in porch of Whitchurch or St Marcellus, Denbigh. Hopefully involve his birthplace (Denbigh, and Ruthin & Oswestry), such as via their Library & Art Gallery (rose.mcmahon@denbighshire.gov.uk).
Apprenticed 1576 as a goldsmith, 1604 & 1605 Warden of the Goldsmiths Company, 1610 & 1624 Prime Warden, in 1611 headed the jury at the Trial of the Pyx. For the Goldsmiths see later.

1. Late-April 1609 to 29 Sept. 1613 (Michaelmas Day) constructed London's legendry New River, providing the City of London with abundant clean drinking water.

"To the memory of Sir Hugh Myddelton the **inhabitants of London should have raised a statue in gold**", 19 July 1794 'Morning Chronicle' (6D, p341; 15D, p3).

"... and the New River consumers when they drink a glass of water ought to consider that they are toasting a great and glorious past, coupled with the names and associated with the memory of the old New River Company (root and branch) and Sir Hugh Myddelton. Nor would it seem to be frivolous or illogical to suggest that those who prefer **stronger vintages should nevertheless favour the same great toast on Michaelmas Day** - the anniversary of the completion of Myddelton's great adventure" (15D, p5).

EVERY-100 YEARS (MINI-PAGEANT) ROUND POND: Every 100-years a mini-pageant (or Son et Lumiere sound & light show) **SYMBOLISING WATER POURING INTO THE ROUND POND. Too late for most of us to wait another 100-years!** Sadlers Wells Theatre is alongside, do they have any members willing to dress up for such an occasion!

The original idea for the New River was **NOT Myddelton's**, c.1600 Capt. Edmund Colthurst of Bath proposed the bringing of water from springs in Herts. & Middx. to London. Contact webmaster@cityofbath.co.uk.

Colthurst by Feb. 1605 claiming to have brought the river forward by 2-3 miles, but had run out of money, hence financed by Myddelton (& later by James I).

16 Aug. 2010 – March 2011 early celebrations such as the Guildhall Art Gallery's '400 years of the New River' exhibition, good but resurrecting basement material (http://www.cityoflondon.gov.uk/Corporation/LGNL_Services/Leisure_and_culture/Museums_and_galleries/Guildhall_Art_Gallery/Exhibitions/current_exhibitions.htm).

The Public Record Office at Kew has the **NINE original 'New River Account Books**, 20 Feb. 1609 to 1632', under Ref. L.R.2/27-34, plus other records (020 8876 3444; no apparent generic e-mail address).

National Portrait Gallery, 1637 portrait of Sir John Backhouse, showing first known picture of New River Head (possible contact hcorcoran@npg.org.uk).

Science Museum London (has Myddelton portraits) and G.C. Berry Archive (New River records), but the bulk of their records & artefacts probably now held at their Swindon site

(SMLWroughton@sciencemuseum.org.uk).

Kew Bridge Steam Museum (Water Supply Museum), volunteer archivist Bryce Caller (brycecaller@waitrose.com).

LOCAL ARCHIVES: Many of the local archives & historical societies along the 40-mile long New River possibly getting together for producing displays, from N to S:

- Hertfordshire Archive & Local Studies (HALS, at hertsdirect@hertscc.gov.uk).
- Ware Museum (curatorial_team@ware-herts.org.uk).
- 'Amwell Society' near Ware (Chairman, Mr David Hardy 01920 870526). 25 June 1806 the New River Company presented Robert Mylne (of Gt Amwell) with a Silver Cup for his dedicated service. Locally are they still in contact with the family, **such that the cup may be put on display locally?**
- **Ring the church bells along the New River:** Starting as Myddelton did from Great Amwell.
- Hoddesdon History Unit at Hoddesdon Library (Tel: 0300 123 4049).
- Lowewood Museum, Hoddesdon (www.lowewood.com/contact-us; or Neil Robbins at museum.leisure@broxbourne.gov.uk).
- Myddelton House, Bulls Cross, Enfield (bhewitt@leevalleypark.org.uk). In 1785 the New River Company presenting Daniel Garnault with a Silver Cup for his dedicated service as Treasurer; and in 1902 a similar Silver Cup to the last Governor H.C.B. Bowles. If the Lee Valley Park Authority are still in contact with the family, **could these two cups be put on display locally for the 400-year celebrations?**
- John Clark of the Enfield Local Study Centre & Archive (john.clark@enfield.gov.uk) has expressed an interest. Enfield Museum Service has a collection of various paintings (John Griffin recently retired, such that contact John Clark).
- St Andrew's Church Enfield where his granddaughter was interred (editor@st-andrew-enfield.com).
- All Saint's Church, Edmonton where some of Sir Hugh's family was buried (fr.stuart@gmail.com).
- Edmonton Hundred Historical Society (EHHS at edmontonhundred@freeukisp.co.uk).
- Hugh Myddelton was also one of the original trustees of Latymer's Charity, does this still exist!
- Enfield Archaeology Society (EAS at michaeol@haydens.uk.com); and Enfield Society (newsletter@enfieldsociety.org.uk).
- Former New River Company Whitewebbs Pumping Station, now the Whitewebbs Museum of Transport (info@whitewebbsmuseum.co.uk).
- Hornsey Historical Society (archivist@hornseyhistorical.org.uk).
- Bruce Castle Museum Archive (deborah.hedgecock@haringey.gov.uk).
- Hackney Archives (archives@hackney.gov.uk).
- Islington Local History Centre (local.history@islington.gov.uk). Amwell Society, Islington (info@amwellsociety.org).
- Other local libraries, photographic societies, wildlife societies, and local schools such as Enfield Grammar School, the New River winding through its grounds (enfgrammar@aol.com); Hazelwood Lane Schools, Palmers Green & Broomfield School, Southgate etc.) where they could **stretch a line of pupils along the former course** and photograph from an upper window.
- Sadler's Wells Theatre (Rosebery Avenue, London, EC1) long associated historically with the New River itself (even at one time pumping its water to the stage for epic dramas), might be persuaded to incorporate a performance associated with the New River. Contact Britannia Morton, Director of Visitor Services & Estates, Interim General Manager, Sadler's Wells, Rosebery, Islington, London, EC1R 4TN, Tel. 020 7863 8199.

Thames Water inherited the property and records of the New River Company. London Metropolitan Archives have the bulk of Thames Water historical archives (ask.lma@cityoflondon.gov.uk), their online Catalogue at http://search.lma.gov.uk/OPAC_LMA/login.html Thames Water's Matthew Wood (matthew.wood@thameswater.co.uk) if given a budget might organise a small exhibition at Abbey Mills Pumping Station. Also for Thames Water John.Liddard@thameswater.co.uk their Recreation & Amenity Coordinator.

Oak Room, New River Head: Thames Water should also be requested to open their historic Oak Room at New River Head for the weekend, such as they did at the Sept. 2012 London Open House Weekend.

Opening-Up the Closed Sections on Specified Days: Request Thames Water to open up all the closed sections on different days (and even all the NRC Pumping Stations/Reservoirs), perhaps at a nominal charge of say £3-5 per person that could be donated to a charity such as Water Aid.

New River Action Group (NRAG, John Polley at metromodels@yahoo.co.uk), & local history groups, might be interested in organising some walks along the FORMER LOOPS of the New River, such as the Manifold Ditch, Stanstead, Broxbourne, [Wormley is private land], Cheshunt, Theobalds, Enfield Town, [Enf. to Bush Hill is private Golf Course], Hamilton Crescent, Southgate, Edm.-Tottenham, Hornsey Village, Haringey, Holloway, Highbury, Clissold Park & Aden Terrace, Canonbury, and Horse Shoe Point.

TV Documentaries/Dramas: Regarding documentaries etc., contacting the BBC, ITV & Sky etc. is not made easy via their websites (if you have any contacts in this type of media, please pass a copy of this document to them). There are two existing novels on Hugh Myddelton and the New River:

'**The New River: a Romance of the Time of Hugh Myddelton**' by E. Fitzgibbon (pseudonym of S. Gibney), published 1885.

'**Water for London**' by Agnes Ashton. An adventure history for older children on the building of the New River. Published 1956 by the Epworth Press (Frank H. Cumbers).

Both are mainly historically accurate, and include dialogue.

2. From 1617 for the rest of Hugh Myddelton's life (d. 7th Dec. 1631) mining Silver from lead-ore in Cardiganshire, North Wales.

Near Aberystwyth, his Cardiganshire mines at Cwmsymlog (variously spelt by C17th Englishmen as Coomsumlock, Coomsumblock, Cumsumlock, Consumlock, and Consomlogh), Cwmerfin, Goginan, Cwmystwyth, and Allt-y-Crib near Talybont. Aberystwyth Museum (museum@ceredigion.gov.uk); and also archives@ceredigion.gov.uk Plus the National Library of Wales cat@llgc.org.uk

In 2011 Graham Levins, Secretary of the Welsh Mines Preservation Trust, offering to arrange a Heritage Weekend with guided walks around mines that Sir Hugh Myddleton was involved with, and an evening of talks about his involvement in mines in the area at a venue near Aberystwyth (graham.levins@btinternet.com & WMPTsecretary@welshmines.org 01293-510567 & 07880-817370).

3. 1620-1622 Hugh Myddelton Reclaiming Brading Haven/Harbour, Isle of Wight. Possible involvement of the Isle of Wight (customer.services@iow.gov.uk).

In 1600 Hugh Myddelton presenting a silver gilt cup (1599 hallmark) to William Myddelton the head of his family at Gwaenynog (the one presumably purchased by the Goldsmiths Co.), also in 1616 presenting a silver gilt cup to Denbigh, and other cups to the corporations of Ruthin & Oswestry (said to still exist).

Hopefully the **Goldsmiths Co.** (the.clerk@thegoldsmiths.co.uk) might be interested in organising an exhibition of their portraits of Sir Hugh, Lady Myddelton (or family), displaying the Silver Cup purchased by the Goldsmiths 1922, and exhibiting records of the New River share bequeathed in charity to the Goldsmiths' Company. Contact David Beasley, Librarian, Tel. 020 7606 7010.

19 Oct. 1622 Baronetcy, gratis of the usual charge. Might the **'College of Arms'**, P.L. Dickinson Richmond Herald, Queen Victoria Street, London EC3V 4BT be interested in the celebrations, although they are financed by professional fees and not supported by public funds. Or the various **Family History websites** undertaking a promotional Myddelton family tree?

1623 the Lord Mayor of the City of London presented Myddelton with a diamond encrusted gold chain and jewelled pedant with the City's Arms worth £219. 15s./200-marks (as shown on many of his portraits), left in his will to his wife, then most worthy son, probably long broken up and lost.

Would the Goldsmiths' Co. (or any other craft body) have any interest in **making a repro. of his 'Great Jewel'**? If made it could afterwards be lodged with the Goldsmiths as a specimen of their craft, or put on permanent display at the Museum of London. They could also sell a limited edition of 10 or 20; even replica's of Lady Elizabeth's thumb-ring?

Would the City's Lord Mayor of London (**tableaus on Lord's Mayor's Day**) or other guilds have any interest in such celebrations?

Died 7 Dec. 1631 (Sir High Myddelton): London Metropolitan Archives (online Catalogue at http://search.lma.gov.uk/OPAC_LMA/login.html) also hold the **City of London Record Office archives**, such as for collecting information on St Matthews Church, Friday Street, Faringdon, where Sir Hugh was buried 10 Dec. 1631 (he was living at Bashishawe Street, now Basinghall Street, aside the Guildhall), the church rebuilt after the Great Fire of 1666, demolished 1883 when no trace of his remains were found, any remains transferred to Ilford Cemetery.

Also the Museum of London (info@museumoflondon.org.uk); and Guildhall Library (guildhall.library@cityoflondon.gov.uk).

London & National Celebration?: There is also no reason why it should not be a country-wide celebration of London's & the nation's water supply.

IDEAS (Food for Thought) for Commemorating Local New River Events (Following the NR) But first some dates that various communities on route might wish to celebrate (fol. text section © M.F. Kensey since to appear in a publication):

Late-April 1609 Myddelton Starts Actual Work on New River From Amwell, but later WIDENING BACK TO CHADWELL SPRING

Last Week April to 5 May 1609 (First Wages Paid): Myddelton surveys his course 3-times and each time from **Amwell** not Chadwell Spring, so it is likely that Colthurst had brought the first part of the river to near the village of Gt. Amwell. Myddelton having to widen Colthurst's 6 ft. cut to 10ft. as specified in the City's Acts. But not until 15 May 1613 the men **cutting the trench 4ft. wider at the top & 1½ ft. wider at the bottom from Chadwell to Amwell** costing £15. 0s. 0d. (15J, p46).

So many various dates given for when Myddelton started actual digging **(MYTHS & Prob. TRUTH) but probably the last week in April** since the first wages paid 5 May 1609 (11, pp36-37 first page of 1st Account Books/p38; 7G6, p3 May 1609; 7K3, p5 began 20 Feb. 1608/p192).

2 Dec. 1609 had reached **Spital Brook**, Hoddesdon (8, p33).

16 Dec. 1609 had reached **Broxbourne Church**, the sexton for 3d. lending a bell rope to pull down a tree (8, p33; 11, p57).

23 Dec. 1609 the sluice at **Amwell spring** given a pin & padlock (8, p33).

c. Jan. 1610 - Nov. 1611 (Great Hold-Up or Standstill for 23-Months)

MYTH & Prob. TRUTH (NOT at Enfield but the Wormley Loop): The number of workers falls to 17 on W/E 27 Jan. 1610, but work limited to maintenance (8, pp24-25; 15J, pp35-40 the Great Disruption). Work was stopped whilst they negotiated the first great loop at Wormley (border with Cheshunt), apparently entirely due to being obstructed by local landowners, not engineering problems or London water-carrier opposition (Tom Mason's cuttings, 'reached as far as Bush Hill'; all other early commentators say Enfield, but G.C. Berry (8, p25) the first to thoroughly study the actual accounts says Wormley; 11, p46; 7K1, p19 stopped after 10-12 miles at Enfield after Myddelton had spent £3,000, nearly all his money; 7K3, p5 had reached Enfield).

Nov. 1611 the **highway bridge built at Broxbourne** ((Original Account Bks.) 8, p33).

11 Jan. 1612 (Wk. Ending): **Windmill field Wormley, Brookefield Cheshunt**, and a week later **Cheshunt Park** (8, p33).

11 Feb. 1612 **Killsmores**, Cheshunt (8, p33). 7 March 1612 **Aldbury**, Cheshunt (8, p33; 11, p52 early-1612 through Cheshunt).

11 April 1612 **Theobalds** and **Northe field Enfield** (8, p33; 11, p52 April & May reached Theobalds & Enfield). Aug. 1612 reaching Theobalds Park (15J, p40). 25 April 1612 **Hatchmore Grove** (8, p33); possibly Moor Hatch meadow (1803 Enf. Encl. map) near Flash Lane, Clay Hill Enfield. 16 May 1612 **Churchbury field** Enfield (8, p33).

13 June 1612 **Butts Farm Edmonton** (8, p33; 11, p52 Edmonton), near today's Firs Lane.

11 July 1612 **Mynceing Wood Southgate** & 25 July **Wood Green** (8, p33). July 1612 Southgate & Wood Green (11, p52).

6 March 1613 had reached **Hornsey highway**, and the fol. week **Newington** (8, p33).

20 March 1613 **Holloway** (8, p33). March 1613, cutting the channel 6ft. deep at Hornsey bowling alley, and excavating at Stroud Green the same month, the channel at this time being bottomed & tidied (15J, p40).

10 April 1613 had reached the **Mantells** where they were to build the Round Pond (8, p33; 11, p57).

April - Sept. 1613 (Terminus Reached) New River Head: Reaching the terminus at the Ducking Pond (named after the pastime of duck-shooting) 80ft. above the Thames which they turned into an open reservoir called the Round Pond (> New River Head), Islington. Constructing a Water House with a cistern beneath on the S-side of the Round Pond, from which water was piped through wooden mains (mainly elm) to the streets of London.

The forward 'guard' digging & reaching these places as stated, with a rear 'guard' following to consolidate & finish the river itself.

It is important for the fol. Councils to rope in the **SCHOOLS** on the former & today's route of the New River.

Ware/Hertford: Thames Water (TW) could erect an 'interpretation board' at the site of the former Balance Engine/Gauge, Ware/Hertford.
Great Amwell: Thames Water could erect an interpretation board at Great Amwell islands, the spot where Hugh Myddelton started digging his New River. **Even a symbolic cutting of the turf?**
St Margarets, Stanstead: At St Margarets the locals could erect an interpretation board for the former Stanstead Loops.
Turnford/Wormley: TW could erect an interpretation board for the Turnford/Wormley Loop aside the New River at Turnford, and Broxbourne Council might even be able to get the old course, or Wormley Flash itself (the last surviving New River Flash) accredited as listed before its presence becomes obliterated (or even get it excavated **by C4's 'Time Team'** before it disappears). Even an Int. Board for the former Theobalds Loop (N-limb still there filled with water), N-side of the M25 Motorway.
Enfield: Enfield Council the custodian of the best remains of the New River (of which they have little awareness), might best get the last part of a circular walk opened up (short section between Archery Wood & start of Whitewebbs Golf Course), that as such would allow walkers to follow almost the complete former Whitewebbs Loop (create the **only 'NR Heritage Trail'**, since as such the **only surviving unique public Mecca for following a former NR Loop** that needs proper sign posting), that also **needs to become listed as a scheduled monument** (since they will only realise its important significance, after it becomes eventually obliterated). They could also erect an interpretation board at Bull Beggars Hole (former New River 'Aqueduct'), and just as important give back the road Bull Beggars Hollow its original name (it was never called Beggars Hollow that has quite a different meaning). Regarding Enf. Town Loop, since there always seems to be a shortage of water, I'm amazed that they don't **re-circulate the water** by using a pump powered by solar/wind & local electricity, through the latest flexible (so can be raised & lowered for any local repairs) butyl pipe sunk in the middle of the river back to the start of the loop? If not in one length, then in overlapping sections?

TW could erect an interpretation board aside the New River near Sir Hugh Myddelton's house Bush Hill/& or one nearer the site of Bush Hill Frame (**longer & older than Highbury Frame**).
Enfield Council could mark out the former course through Arnos Park with **sunken slabs** in the grass, erect an interpretation board at the site of Wild's Flash (W-end of park) to commemorate the former Southgate Loop, now filled-in on council land.
Haringay (Hornsey & Tottenham): Haringay Council could erect an interpretation board near the former Flash/Loop at Hornsey/or near the extremity of the former Tottenham Loop at the green aside New River House, Devonshire Hill Lane.
Stoke Newington: Hackney Council could erect an interpretation board near the site of the often forgotten 'Stamford Hill' Loop (that actually entered Hackney itself)/or Highbury Sluice/Highbury Frame/or near the former giant New River Loop at Holloway.
Islington: Islington Council could erect an interpretation board near the site of the long forgotten Horse Shoe Point Loop near Canonbury Villas.

It's a matter of creating momentum no matter how small, for the ball to really start rolling!

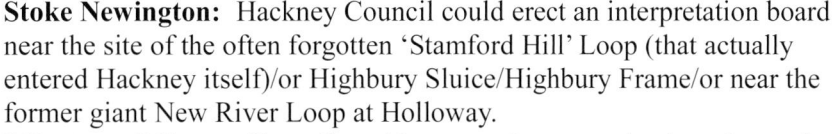

CENTRAL (INFORMATION ONLY) POINT? Believe it is better for locals to get on with their own creative ideas for a celebration (not bogged down by a global organising body) with just a central point for informing of overall activities elsewhere (if there are to be any, and stop dates clashing), and until this is arranged I can be contacted at **michael.kensey@ntlworld.com**
Regards,
Mike Kensey. Responsible for two E.A.S. archaeological excavations of the New River in Enfield.
TOP photo (1968) New River 1820 Cast-Iron Aqueduct, Whitewebbs. **BOTTOM photo** (1971) New River timber 'trough' at Bull Beggars Hole, Clay Hill (Both photos Enf. Gaz. & Obs., ELSC&A).

P.S. Please pass a copy of this 400-year celebration document to any party/ies that you think might be interested.

Large portrait of Sir Hugh Myddelton	Frontispiece
Hugh Myddelton's Family Tree	xiii
Whitchurch, & Myddelton memorial brass	xiv
Denbigh District map & Myddelton's house Galch Hill, Denbigh	xv
Small portrait of Sir Hugh Myddelton	3
'The Myddelton Arms' public house, Ruthin	4
1609-1613 'Working Day Average' (Monthly) of workers constructing the New River	7
X-Section of New River led along hillsides	8
Small portrait of James I.	11
2 May 1612 'Royal Investment', photo of deed with Myddelton's signature	11
Another Myddelton signature	12
Depiction of the New River Opening Ceremony, Michaelmas Day 29 Sept. 1613	14
'Chart of Mines in North Wales'	22
'Plan of Myddelton's Silver Mining Works at Cwmsymlog'	22
1619 New River Company Seal	24
Bronze roundel of King James I falling into New River 1622	26
Sir Hugh Myddelton's Coat of Arms	27
'Map of Brading Haven, Ordnance Survey'	28
View of Brading Haven	28
Small portrait of King Charles I	29
1772 plan showing location of St Matthews Church	33
1812 St Matthew Church, Friday Street	33
Graphic chart of rising New River share prices	58
Metropolitan Water Board, Coat of Arms	58
New River Path Signpost	61
1850 map of locations of the Metropolitan Water Companies	68
1667 map showing NRC sites on N-side of River Thames	69
c.1750 NRC Bridewell Precinct Office & Pipe Wharf	70
c.1770 plan of NRC Dorset Stairs Offices & Bridewell Precinct	71
1771 NRC Office/s, Dorset Stairs, Blackfriars	72
1872 map showing NRC Engine House, Broken Wharf	73
Portrait of Robert Percy Smith, NRC Governor 1827-45	78
John White (1658-1741), NRC 'River Surveyor' sketch of his tomb in Enfield Churchyard	86
Wooden NRC boundary marker	98
New River Waterweed Cutting Boat	101
New River Punt/boat.	101
NRC-style single & double bench seats	102
MWB-style New River gate lock	103
Large keys for MWB-style New River gate lock	103
MWB cast-iron Notices/Boards	105
New River 'N.R.' valve-plate for street mains	105
Carp in New River	107
'Hugh Myddelton' Railway Steam Engine	113
'My banks they are furnished'	125
Piscator	127
Small portrait of Robert Mylne	131
1857 Toll Bars	132
Mylne plans 1775-1809, **Ware**	158
Crane Mead, Ware, 1842	163
Balance Engine	164
Mylne plans 1775-1809, Ware.	165
Old Gauge	168
Location of Old Gauge	171
Manifold Ditch	174
NRC Marker Stone, N-side White House Sluice	175
NRC Marker Stone, W-side White House Sluice, and 'Gauge Stone' aka 'Capstone'	176
White House Sluice (1746)	177
Sluice Gate within White House Sluice (1854)	178
Weir behind White House Sluice	179
New River near Chadwell Spring, 1773	180

Marble Gauge (May 1830)	181
Chadwell Spring	186
Main monumental stone, Chadwell Spring	187
Boundary & other Marker Stones, Chadwell Spring	188
c.1811 NRC land Chadwell Spring & Hill	189
c.1811 NRC land in Chadwell Mead	190
c.1811 NRC land in Barrow Common Field & Broad Mead	191
1773 Amwell End	192 - 193
1782 Mr Prior's Dwelling House, Amwell End	195
c.1800s Amwell End?	199
Ware Mill 1775-1809 & c.1830-40	200
Ware Lock 1840	201
Ware Lock & Mills 1898 OS map	202
Ware Lock & Mills 1923/38 OS map	203
River Lee, Ware Early-1800s	204
Ware Bridge 1841	207
Crane Mead, Ware, 1775-1809	208
Crane Mead, Ware, 1898 OS map	209
Amwell End to Lower Road, Great Amwell, 1775-1809	211
Red House, 1775-1809	213
London Road to Great Amwell, 1775-1809	214
Great Amwell to Stanstead, 1775-1809	216
Great Amwell, 1775-1809	218
Overlay at Great Amwell Islands	220
Amwell Grove (Front Elevation) & Washer-women (c.1770s)	221
Late-C18[th] Amwell & 1794 Thorpe's Farm	222
Lower (1807) & Upper (c.1836) Amwell Islands	223
Amwell Marsh, NRC land 1839	225
St Margarets, Stanstead, 1775-1809	227
Stanstead Loop/s, 1775-1809	228
Stanstead to Hoddesdon, 1775-1809	231
Rye Common Field, Early-1800s?	232
Rye Common, 1834	235
Rye Common Field, 1847	236
Hoddesdon, 1775-1809	238
Hoddesdon to Broxbourne, 1775-1809	243
Broxbourne, 1775-1809	244
Broxbourne, NRC land 1834	248
Broxbourne Church, 1775-1809 plan	249
Broxbourne Church, 1794	250
Broxbourne High Road, 1775-1809 plan	252
Wormley Loops, 1775-1809 plan	255
Hide Common Field, 1775-1809	257
Wormley 'High Road' Loop	258
Wormley, NRC land 1844	259
Wormley-Turnford Loop	260
Wormleybury House, 1806 & 2004	261
Monuments Wormley/bury Church	262
Wormley Flash, NRC land c.1834	264
Water Lane, NRC land 1841	265
Cheshunt Flash, 1775-1809	270
Church Lane, Cheshunt, 1775-1809	273
Cheshunt Church (1800) & Theobalds House (1806)	277
Monuments Cheshunt Church	278
Bury Green, 1775-1809 plan	279
Theobalds, 1775-1809 plan	282
Theobalds Park Wall (1620-23)	284
Theobalds Palace	286
Cedars Park Gates	289
Old Palace House (Cedars Park) at demolition	289b

Capel House (1804)	296
Bullsmoor Loop	297
Whitewebbs Loop, Enfield	298
John Grene's House, Turkey Street, Enfield	309 - 310
1754 plan of Bowling Green House	313
Family Tree, Garnault & Bowles of Bowling Green House > Myddelton House, Enfield	316
Myddelton House (1821) & Front Porch Bell (1969)	317
Bowles family portraits	318
1773 location of Bowling Green House	319
1775-1809 location of Bowling Green House	320
1818 Bowling Green House > Myddelton House	321
1818 location of Bowling Green House	322
Optimum location of Bowling Green House	323
1773 plan of Forty Hill estate	325
Dickinson's Trough	327

Continued in Vol.1, Part 2.

Abbreviations Used for Copyright Owners
For brevity of lengthy repetitive text appearing on illustrations (and in many cases where there is a real shortage of space on the page), the following abbreviations have been used to identify copyright owners of illustrations appearing within this book.

BCMA (Bruce Castle Museum Archive) has the full official title of '**Bruce Castle Museum (Haringey Culture, Libraries and Learning)**'.

Brit. Mus./British Museum has the full official title of '© **Trustees of the British Museum**'.

Enf. Gaz. & Obs. has the full official title of '**Enfield Gazette & Observer**' newspaper.

Former **ELHU** (Enfield Local History Unit) now has the full official title of '**Enfield Local Studies Centre & Archive**' (ELSC&A).

Enf. Mus. Service/Forty Hall Museum Collection has the full official title of '**Enfield Museum Service**'.

Hackney Archive has full official title of '**London Borough of Hackney Archives**'.

HALS has the full official title of '**Hertfordshire Archives & Local Studies**'.

Isl. LHC has the full official title of '**Islington Local History Centre**'.

KBSM/Kew Bridge Steam Museum has the full official title of '**Kew Bridge Engines Trust & Water Supply Museum Ltd.**'.

LMA has the full official title of '**London Metropolitan Archives**' where also as custodians some appropriate item copyright is retained by Thames Water Plc.

O.S. Maps: Crown copyright on Ordnance Survey maps lasting for 50 years from end of year in which published '© **Crown Copyright [Year of publication]**' such that 2012 pre-1962 maps included in this book said not to need a licence.

Soane Museum has the full official title of '**By courtesy of the Trustees of Sir John Soane's Museum**'.

The Royal Society has the full official title of '© **The Royal Society**'.

TW has the full official title of '**Thames Water Plc**', who also retain the copyright of a multitude of items held by the London Metropolitan Archives.

There are also others just as important that have been individually identified on specific pages.

HUGH MYDDELTON'S FAMILY TREE ((1842 Lewis's 'History of Islington' facing p430, XIII) ELSC&A; MFK enhanced).

The family of Myddelton is said to have descended from Porth Vlaydd, lord of Penlyn, in Merionethshire; whose descendant, Riride, married Cicily, sister and heiress of Sir Alexander Middleton, of Middleton, county Salop; and was father of Riride, whose great grandson was

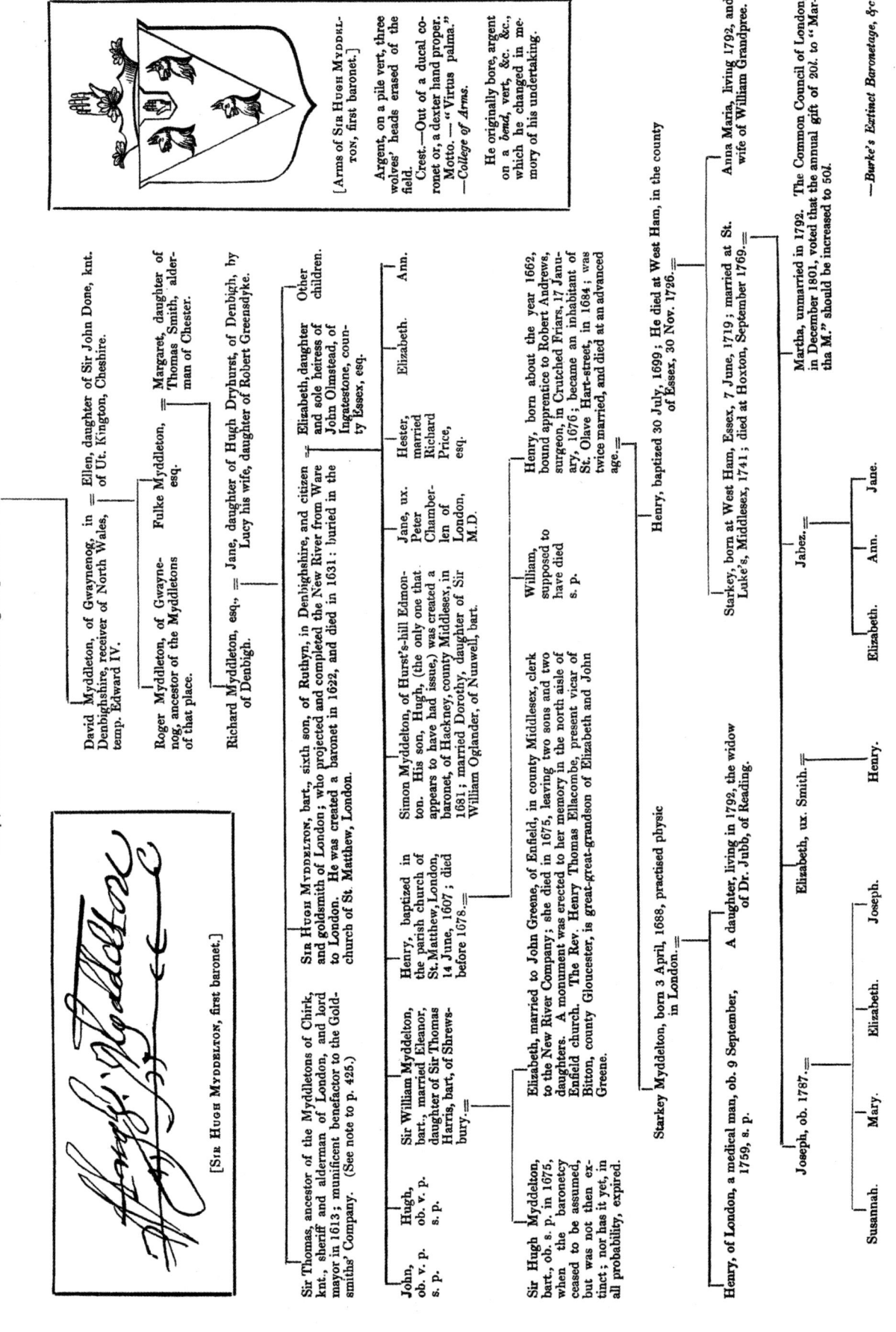

[Sir Hugh Myddelton, first baronet.]

[Arms of Sir Hugh Myddelton, first baronet.]

Argent, on a pile vert, three wolves' heads erased of the field.
Crest.—Out of a ducal coronet or, a dexter hand proper. Motto.—"Virtus palma." —*College of Arms.*

He originally bore, argent on a *bend*, vert, &c. &c., which he changed in memory of his undertaking.

David Myddelton, of Gwaynenog, in Denbighshire, receiver of North Wales, temp. Edward IV. = Ellen, daughter of Sir John Done, knt. of Ut. Kington, Cheshire.

Roger Myddelton, of Gwaynenog, ancestor of the Myddletons of that place.

Fulke Myddelton, esq. = Margaret, daughter of Thomas Smith, alderman of Chester.

Richard Myddelton, esq., of Denbigh. = Jane, daughter of Hugh Dryhurst, of Denbigh, by Lucy his wife, daughter of Robert Greensdyke.

Sir Thomas, ancestor of the Myddletons of Chirk, knt., sheriff and alderman of London, and lord mayor in 1613; munificent benefactor to the Goldsmiths' Company. (See note to p. 425.)

Sir Hugh Myddelton, bart., sixth son, of Ruthyn, in Denbighshire, and citizen and goldsmith of London; who projected and completed the New River from Ware to London. He was created a baronet in 1622, and died in 1631: buried in the church of St. Matthew, London.

Elizabeth, daughter and sole heiress of John Olmstead, of Ingatestone, county Essex, esq.

Other children.

John, ob. v. p. s. p.

Hugh, ob. v. p. s. p.

Sir William Myddelton, bart., married Eleanor, daughter of Sir Thomas Harris, bart, of Shrewsbury. =

Henry, baptized in the parish church of St. Matthew, London, 14 June, 1607; died before 1678. =

Simon Myddelton, of Hurst's-hill Edmonton. His son, Hugh, (the only one that appears to have had issue,) was created a baronet, of Hackney, county Middlesex, in 1681; married Dorothy, daughter of Sir William Oglander, of Nunwell, bart.

Jane, ux. Peter Chamberlen of London, M.D.

Hester, married Richard Price, esq.

Elizabeth.

Ann.

William, supposed to have died s. p.

Henry, born about the year 1662, bound apprentice to Robert Andrews, surgeon, in Crutched Friars, 17 January, 1676; became an inhabitant of St. Olave Hart-street, in 1684; was twice married, and died at an advanced age. =

Sir Hugh Myddelton, bart., ob. s. p. in 1675, when the baronetcy ceased to be assumed, but was not then extinct; nor has it yet, in all probability, expired.

Elizabeth, married to John Greene, of Enfield, in county Middlesex, clerk to the New River Company; she died in 1675, leaving two sons and two daughters. A monument was erected to her memory in the north aisle of Enfield church. The Rev. Henry Thomas Ellacombe, present vicar of Bitton, county Gloucester, is great-great-grandson of Elizabeth and John Greene.

Henry, baptized 30 July, 1699; He died at West Ham, in the county of Essex, 30 Nov. 1726. =

Starkey Myddelton, born 3 April, 1688, practised physic in London. =

Starkey, born at West Ham, Essex, 7 June, 1719; married at St. Luke's, Middlesex, 1741; died at Hoxton, September 1769. =

Anna Maria, living 1792, and wife of William Grandpree.

Martha, unmarried in 1792. The Common Council of London, in December 1801, voted that the annual gift of 20*l*. to "Martha M." should be increased to 50*l*.

Henry, of London, a medical man, ob. 9 September, 1759, s. p.

A daughter, living in 1792, the widow of Dr. Jubb, of Reading.

Elizabeth, ux. Smith. =

Jabez. =

Joseph, ob. 1787. =

Joseph.

Henry.

Elizabeth.

Ann.

Jane.

Susannah.

Mary.

Elizabeth.

—*Burke's Extinct Baronetage, &c.*

ABOVE: 'Whitchurch, or St Marcellus, Denbigh' ((E.M.Wimperis, after an original sketch) 13, p106).
BELOW: 'Facsimile of the Myddelton Brass in Whitchurch porch' (13, p96). Shows Richard Myddelton (d.1575, Governor of Denbigh Castle, & father of Hugh Myddelton) with 9-sons behind, & Jane Dryhurst (d.1565) his wife with 7-daughters behind.

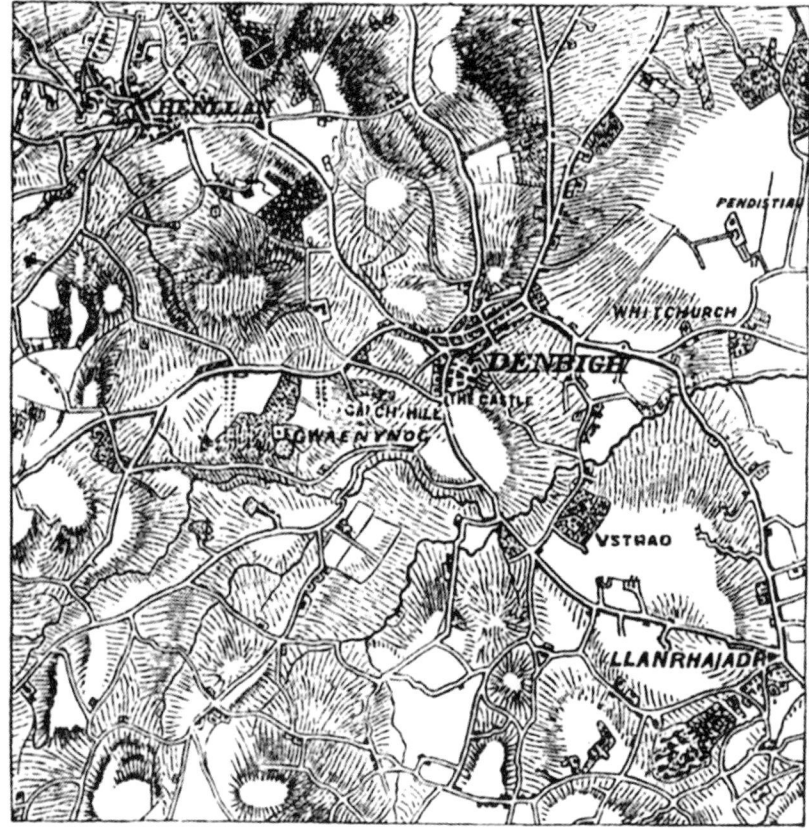

ABOVE: **'Myddelton's native district'** ((c.1862 Ordnance Survey) 13, p94).

BELOW: **'Myddelton's house at Galch-Hill, Denbigh'** where he is said to have been born ((E.M. Wimperis, after an original sketch) 13, p95); said today to be part of Galch Hill

Chapter 1

Birth & Development of the Artificial Gravitational 'New River'
Supplying Drinking Water to London
(From its inception aka Myddelton's Water)

After the Romans left Britain their drainage & water schemes fell into disuse, until new schemes were created from the early-C12th mainly by monks for their own monastic establishments, followed from the C14th by some provincial towns.

Since ancient times those without direct access to local water relying on Water Carriers aka Water Bearers.

> The poor water-bearer first recorded 1276 when Henry Grene drowned in the Thames when filling his 6-gal. (1562) or a 3½ gal. minimum tankard (1680), and that W.H. Overall's 1871 statement that a Water-bearers Co. existed by 1276 has not been substantiated by primary records (7K4-1, p6). From 1496 the brotherhood or fraternity of Saint Christopher of the Water Bearers, dissolved 1553, 1562 newly approved City ordinances for Water-bearers, in 1568 selling their Waterbearers' Hall (site of Nos. 143 & 144 Bishopsgate Street Without > Liverpool Street Station), in 1591 meeting at a house in Whitecross Street. From 1562-1666 the fraternity with rulers and at least 500 members, probably with a shelter near a particular City conduit with its free water for human use, supplying regular customers, until the 1666 Great Fire devastated the conduits, not all rebuilt, and houses built over the pipes ((City Records, Rep. 13/1/63.b.) 8A1, 3/3-2); 1M1, pp62-3; 7K4-1, p9/12/16/19/20/21/69).
>
> **C19th MYTH that Water Carriers were called Cobs (Created from Clifford's Footnotes):** Cobb's Court did not lead down to the Thames, Oliver Cob did not live in Blackfriars, and **no evidence has been found to substantiate William Clifford's** (C19th editor of Jonson's works) **claim that Cob's Court in Blackfriars was named after water-carriers** ((Corres. in reply to query, dated 3 Feb. 1958) 8A1, 2-8; ((Cob's Court did not lead down to the Thames) Typed sheet headed 'The London Water Bearer') 8A1, 2/5 Vol. N-S; both sources G.C. Berry archivist/historian at MWB; (7K4-1) 7J1, p30 no evidence called Cobs; 'Sweet and Wholesome Water – Five Centuries of History of Water-bearers in the City of London' by E.W. Flaxman & E.W. Jackson, 2004, 7K4-1, pp25-26/70).

Due to London's desperate shortage of pure water, then mainly supplied by **streams, shallow wells, springs** (that began to dry up or became polluted) **& gravity fountain heads aka conduits** (from 1236, 1285 the Great Conduit bringing water by leaden pipes from suburban springs, ultimately reaching 15-16 but becoming inadequate & threatened by urban development) there were various schemes.

- 1543/4 Act's powers for using Hampstead springs at first unsuccessful when attempted 1589, and not implemented until 1692 by the Hampstead Water Company (7K4-1, p57 1692 for fine of £200 & £80 a year; 7K3, p191 1543 Act 35 Edw. I).
- In 1580 Russell's abortive scheme for bringing water from the River of Uxbridge (KJ1, p47; 7G5, p42; 7K3, p191).
- The London Bridge Waterworks established 1579 by Peter Morris/Morice pumping water from the Thames. 1593-5 Bevis Bulmar erecting a horse driven chain pump at Broken Wharf also for pumping water from the Thames (KJ1, p41/pp45-47; 4, p9 LBWWs est. 1581; 7G5, pp16-18; 7K3, p191 1582), at the time both only capable of pumping locally, and the water from the Thames far from pure, often called **turbid and foul**.
- Gianibelli/Genebelli getting approval for a Tyburn waterworks scheme using a fountain head windmill to increase the supply, but abortive (7K3, p191 1591).
- In 1591 completion of Drake's Leat at Plymouth, a later model for the New River.
- Pre-1609 Edward Wright trying to raise Thames' water at Botolph's Wharf (13, pp90-92 Plymouth Leet; 8, p24; 15J, p18).

1604/1609-1613 London's 'New River': The New River an artificial stream, waterway or canal, a **man-made gravity fed water channel** constructed to supply London with fresh drinking water from far away springs.

> An "**'artificial' river** – for artificial it is, its whole course being **dug out by hand** long before

excavating machinery was dreamt of" (15).

In fact a man-made tributary of the River Lee with over 40-miles of 400-year old history!
An unrivalled engineering achievement of its time, and still in use today supplying approx. 8% of London's Water, although much altered and shortened.

Birth of London's New River
c./1560 Hugh Myddelton born at Galch Hill (Henllan), near Denbigh, North Wales. Born 1560 (according to being aged 68 on the 1628 Cornelius Johnson painting) the 6th son of Richard Myddelton, Governor of Denbigh castle, and said to be descended from the Rhirid Flaidd medieval nobility of North Wales (11, p1 Rhirid Flaidd/p21 or Blaidd = wolf; 8, p22; 13, p94 Blaidd/p98 born c.1555).
Surviving Cottage & House (Myddelton's Birthplace): His father Richard Myddelton's surviving c.1500 gale-ended rubble-constructed cottage with exterior chimneys, Galch Hill, Gwaynynog, Denbighshire (SJ 0441365419), and whitewashed 2-storey rubble-constructed 2-storey house with timber-framed upper storey & end gables (((Os495 card, 08.10.02, J. Wiles) Royal Commission on the Ancient & Historical Monuments of Wales) www.coflein.gov.uk).
Myddelton's Family Tree: Pedigrees etc. of Myddelton family members ((Reprint from The Cheshire Sheaf, 'Notes on the Myddelton Family & their Pedigrees' by W. Duncombe Pink, Chester, 1891; 'Pedigree of the Family of Myddelton etc.' by W.M. Myddelton, Horncastle, 1910; 'Miscellanea Genealogica et Heraldica' by G. Milner-Gibson-Cullum, 3rd series, 1897, Vol. ii, parts 7 & 8; Dictionary of Welsh Biography, A.H. Dodd/Welsh Biography Online; family members within footnotes, W.M. Myddelton edited 'Chirk Castle Accounts 1605-66, St Albans, 1908) 11, p1-3).

c./1600 (Edmund Colthurst's Revolutionary Proposal) to Bring Water from Herts. & Middx: Combining ideas from the schemes of Russell c./1580 (Colne aka River of Uxbridge to the N-side of London) & Frederic Genebelli 1591 (water from the Thames to the City for cleansing the ditches, providing wholesome clear water, and for quenching house fires), c.1600 Capt. Edmund Colthurst of Bath, came up with the revolutionary proposal to bring water from springs in Hertfordshire and Middlesex to London (Genebelli probably the Gianibelli above).

> **MYTH:** Lyson in 1811 wrongly stating that Hugh Middleton 'first projected the scheme of bringing New River water to London' (1AA, p495).

18 April 1604 (Colthurst's Letters Patent) 2 Jas. I, part 25: Colthurst getting Letters Patent from King James I to bring springs (unnamed, but the place-names mentioned on route fol. the line of the later New River) in a trench not exceeding 6 ft. in breadth from Hertfordshire and Middlesex to London and Westminster and the work to be **completed within 7 years** ((18 April 1604 Letters Patent, box 79 Strongroom B30, TW; NR copy deed B/184; 1603-10 CSPD 93; 'Stuart England' by J.P. Kenyon, 1978 pp14-15) 15I, p9; 11, pp27-28; 8, p19; 15J, pp19-21).
Summer/Autumn 1604: Colthurst's likely start date.

Colthurst's First 2-3 Miles prob. reaching Amwell Springs
26 Feb. 1605 (Colthurst) First 2-3 Miles Costing £200+ > £700+ > In all approx. 2-3 miles for £1,000 which included his Patent: Colthurst said to had brought the river forward three miles, but had soon got into difficulties after expending **over £200**.

> Possibly starting from the W-side of Amwell End, since the channel back to Chadwell Spring may have been created earlier by monks.
> Dismayed at the City's competing venture in gaining their Jan. 1606 Bill (see fol.) stopping work, and whilst away working on Hobson's Brook at Cambridge in April 1606, claiming he had spent **£700** (or over) on the **first 3-miles of the New River**. Colthurst also claiming later in 1610-11, that he had spent **about £1,000** (but this included the cost of his original patent) for bringing the stream two miles or thereabouts (11, p28/29; 8, p19 brought forward 3-miles; 15J, p21/p29 1605 letter requesting to cut through Viscount Cranborne's land, and mention of springs near Hertford/p45). He had run out of funds, and not until 1608 managing to find backers, but the City awarding their backing to Hugh Myddelton.

City of London Acts

1st NEW RIVER ACT 1605–1606 (3 James I c. 18): City of London's first Act for bringing water from springs at or near Chadwell & Amwell (no mention of using the River Lee), increasing the width of the channel from **6ft. to 10ft.** Carried by 60 to 49 and only talk of compensating Colthurst (15I, p9/10/pp251-254 Appendix A has full text of 1605 Act).

City's Survey: Soon after £5. 6s. 0d. paid by the City to Richard Staper for surveying the springs and the course of the river (8, p20; 15J, p29 paid Sept. 1606).

2nd NEW RIVER (AMENDMENT) ACT 1606-1607 (4 James I, c. 12): After a study by William Inglebert of the engineering problems involved, the City of London's second Act for including provisions for inclosure in a brick or stone trunk or vault, in the earth or upon arches (15I, pp254-255 Appendix A has full text of 1606 Act; 11, pp32-33; 8, pp20-21; 15J, pp21-22).

MYTH: John Aubrey wrongly crediting Inglebert as the originator of the NR scheme, seen later as a poor almsman in a rug-gown at Parliamentary Stairs (15I, p10; 11, pp32-33). 14 Oct. 1606 petition by Inglebert to bring the river forth in a trench or trenches of brick, that was referred, with no action; and wrongly said to have been started by Edward Wright - but this was only a survey of the route see later ((City Journals) Smiles, p90; ('Canal' art. in addenda to 'Mathematical & Philosophical Dictionary' by Hutton) Smiles, p90) 14B2, pp444; 15J, p22 another petition by Ruddell to raise Thames' water abortive/p23).

22 Dec. 1606 (Parchment Map of New River) Stolen: A map of the new cut for bringing water from Amwell to Theobalds worth £15, stolen from Robert Boothe when waylaid by two London butchers who were sentenced to hang (15I, p9; 15J, p22/(Rep. 27/265 11 Sept. 1606)/p29).

Jan. 1609 to July 1610 (Plague at Enfield on the Intended Route): A minor outbreak of the plague returned to Enfield from Jan. 1609 until July 1610, but luckily it had disappeared before they reached Enfield after the great hold up (B10, p94).

COLTHURST > MYDDELTON: In Oct. 1608 Colthurst seeking permission to proceed, which was agreed by the City without opposition, but in Feb. 1609 upon requesting that the two above Acts be transferred to him & his partners, they instead were transferred to Hugh Myddelton (a London Goldsmith) probably because of the funding (11, pp33-34; 8, p21/23; (6 James I 'Records of the City of London') 13, p93 March 1608 Colthurst petition; 15J, p23).

'no one was found bold enough to attempt it' until 'The **dauntless Welshman stept forth and smote the rock, and the waters flowed into the thirsty Metropolis**' (13, p109; C4, p131; ('Tours in Wales' by T. Pennant, 1784, ii. 29) 11, p33 Note 2). "**Yet he was not an engineer, or even an architect, nor a builder**" (15).

ORIGINAL NR ACCOUNTS: The original NR Accounts (**kept as a result of the King's involvement from 1612**) passing through various offices of state, until pre-1948 unearthed by G.C. Berry (of the MWB) at the Public Record Office.

1609-1630 (Original NR Accounts) £18,524. 19s. 0d. Total Disbursements: 9-books of disbursements, 9-books of income from March 1614, plus drafts, fair copies etc., half of the disbursements £9,262. 9s. 6d. (24 Feb. 1625/6) although 6½d. short, the total thereafter given as £18,524. 19s. 0d., a detailed summary of Myddelton's accounts and mention of four leather-wrapped parchment membranes of Myddelton's clerk William Lewyn's accounts formerly kept at the NRC Ltd offices ((PRO) 15I, pp16-17; 15J, p68 described).

The New River at First Funded by Hugh Myddelton
Funded from his profits as a City Goldsmith & from other enterprises.

28 March 1609 (City Accepting Hugh Myddelton's Offer & made their Lawful Deputy)
To start within 2-months, & given 4-Years (Later Amended to 7-years)

Portrait based on the one at Goldsmiths' Hall (ELSC&A).

The New River "Known at its inception as **Myddelton's Water/s**" (C4, p126; (Camden's 'Brit.', by Gibson, vol. i., 319, 320) 13, p110; Sir Henry

Chauncy the Hertfordshire historian writing in 1700) E1, p8; B9, p40).

'... Hugh Myddelton, by whom the original work was supervised, if not actually designed' (7K1, p17). Promising to bring the river to a convenient place near Islington within 4-years, having already Feb. 1609 employed the famous mathematician Edward Wright to survey its intended course, and the **foresight to employ Edmund Colthurst as overseer of the work**. As compensation on 8 May 1612, Colthurst was **assigned free of charge a life interest in 4 of the subsequent 36-Adventurers' shares** (at his death two shares to Myddelton, and 2 shares to his estate in fee simple), but he died circa Aug. 1616 never having received any dividends (15I, p19/20; 11, p37 4-shares; 15J, p25/p61 Colthurst's 4-shares).

Such that the New River mainly constructed 1609-13 by Hugh Myddelton a London citizen & goldsmith.

Note that his name is invariably wrongly spelt in many ways (often called Middleton), with him normally signing as Myddelton (as did his grandson Sir Hugh Myddelton of Hackney).

Born 1560 at Galch Hill (Henllan) the 6th/youngest son of Richard Myddelton (Governor of Denbigh Castle etc.), 1597 the first Alderman of Denbigh, 1604-11, 1614, 1621-22, 1624-25, 1626, & 1628-29 their M.P. in Parliament (11, p9 MP from 1603-1628/pp16-19 undistinguished parliamentary career/p20; 12D, p6; 11C, p2 & 11E, p58 1603 M.P. for Denbigh; 13, p107 from 1603).

c.1583 (Hugh Myddelton's 1st–known London Address) Cheapside: 1576 went up to London where apprenticed to Thomas Hartop (no specific location given), c.1583 granted the freedom of the Goldsmiths' Company and living above his goldsmith's workshop in Cheapside (Info. supplied by Prof. A. H. Dodd) 11, p4/13 Note 3).

c.1585 (Hugh Myddelton's First Marriage) to Anne Edwards, nee Anne Collins: Shortly after returning to London from Antwerp, Hugh married the first of his two wives, a much older widow called Anne, the daughter of Richard Collins of Lichfield, with his brother Thomas paying for 'his wyffes gowne cloth against his wedding' £2. 15s. ((Thomas Myddelton's ledger dated 5 Nov. 1585) 11, p5; 15I, p12 nearly 20-years older than himself). Anne died childless on 11 Jan. 1597 aged 54 (11, p5).

1590 (Hugh Myddelton) Admitted to Guild of the Goldsmiths Company: (11B, p2; 11, p5 & 11C, p1 1592 became liveryman of Goldsmiths Co.). 1604 & 1605 Warden of the Goldsmiths' Co., and 1610 & 1624 the Prime Warden of the Goldsmiths' Company (11, p5; 15I, p11 Warden 1604). Myddelton supplying pearls to Queen Elizabeth, gilt bowls to Gerard Malynes, and a diamond pendant to James I for his queen (11, p6; 15I, p11; 14B2, p461; 13, p108; 15J, p24). 1611 Hugh Myddelton headed the 16 jurors in the 'Trial of the Pixe'/testing of the coinage (11, p8).

'The Myddelton Arms', Ruthin with plaque 'Sir Hugh Myddelton, who bought this house in 1595, provided London with its first supply of fresh water' (From two 2011 Nigel Chapman photos, via Graham Levins); owning this house another myth or fact!

1598 (Hugh Myddelton's Second Marriage) to Miss Elizabeth Olmstead: In 1598 Hugh Myddelton married his much younger second wife, the heiress Elizabeth Olmstead, whom brought to the marriage a valuable addition of property (11, pp8-9; 15I, p12 twenty years younger than Myddelton, his brother Thomas's stepdaughter).

c.1604 to c.1615 (Hugh Myddelton's 2nd–known London Address) Wood Street: Letters from

Ruthin in the early 1600's were addressed to Myddelton's Wood Street house. Wood Street ran from Cheapside to London Wall, with him still living there some ten years later since he was paying rent for his piped New River water ((Ruthin Castle Letters, Nos. 924, 925 (5 March 1604), N.L.W.) 11, p13 Note 4/p14 Note 1; (Stow in 1598/1603 lists a Great Wood street, Little Wood street, and Wood street all in Cripplegate ward; and a Wood street in Faringdon ward) 1F1, p260/265/281). Myddelton's 1616 tenant's agreement confirms his address as being at Westcheap. 1620 Hugh Myddelton recorded as living in a house at Little Wood Street (15J, p76 first address at Little Wood Street).

By Jan. 1627 (Myddelton's Business Moved, 3rd–known London Address) to 'Bassishaw': Had moved his business to 'Bassishaw' Street (now Basinghall Street, aside the Guildhall), and not before as implied by Samuel Smiles and other biographers ((Cal. S.P.D., 1627-8, p20) 11, p13 Note 2; 14B2, pp467 1627 letter dated from Bassishaw-street; 13, pp148-149; 15J, p76). In those days they lived over their work addresses.

Prob. TRUTH (Failed to find Coal): c.1600 Hugh Myddelton failed in an attempt to find coal near Denbigh/Vale of Clwyd (DWB). Authorised by his father to find & supply coal to Denbigh Castle (failed probably because of lack of reserves), after which became involved with the Mines Royal (11E, p54/101; 8, p22; 13, pp105-106 Myddelton himself referring to seeking coal). **MYTH** that whilst residing at Denbigh Myddelton attempted to 'sink for gold' ('The New River its Story & its Builder' Enf. Gaz. & Observer, 13 Jan. 1939; presumably referring to Myddelton seeking coal).

'**there was no good memoir extant of Myddelton, all being overlaid by a mass of inaccuracy and downright fable**' until Smile's 'Lives of the Engineers' was published 1861-2 ('Book of Days' undated, p390, Islington LHC). Even in modern times writers still propagating mistruths, such as the 'Hugh Myddelton, Citizen and Grocer' (**MYTH**), there being no such evidence of him having been a grocer, probably his brother ('The New River' by John Boyes, A.R. Hist. S., 'Metropolitan', Vol. 16, No. 2, Jan. 1994, pp62-66). '**Unfortunately, so much fiction has been mixed up with the facts recorded of this remarkable man,** ...' (7K1, p17), that the following is an attempt to separate the truth from the myths.

MYTH & Prob. TRUTH (NOT a Pioneer Pipe Smoker): Hugh Myddelton romanticised as a pioneer pipe smoker, but this probably mistaken identity for his cousin the sea-captain William Middleton (11, p19).

MYTH & Prob. TRUTH (NOT a Clothmaker, Nor Merchant Adventurer of England): Not a Clothmaker as so often quoted, or as such a Merchant Adventurer of England viz. merchant who engages in the export trade or exports from a major port (11, p19; KJ1, p48/51; 13, p102 prob. from being called one of the 'Merchant Adventurers of England' in 'Ancient & Modern Denbigh' by Williams), although he was involved with his brothers who were trading or Merchant Adventurers and in one case buccaneering (11, p6). This probably also arising because shares in the New River were called Adventurers' Shares. As such Myddelton should be called a **New River Adventurer & Mines Adventurer** (see later).

Sir Hugh Myddelton died 7 Dec. 1631 & was buried 10 Dec. 1631.

Until 1752, Jan., Feb. & Most of March was in the Previous Year.

14 Sept. 1752 (Changing to the Gregorian Calendar): The 1752 Act of Parliament for England and the British Colonies accepting the Gregorian calendar (called the New Style (N.S.) changing from the Julian Old Style (O.S.), such that the day after 2 Sept became the 14 Sept. 1752, to get into synchronisation losing 11 days between 3-13 Sept., they did not exist.

Pope Gregory XIII (1502-1585) Pope from 1572, under his papal bull Inter Gravissimas 24 Feb. 1582 introduced the Gregorian calendar to give an accurate date for Easter, where a century leap year is only relevant if the year was divisible by 400. By 1582 the Gregorian calendar had been implemented by most Catholic countries, but because Britain was mainly Protestant, it took far longer to accept something that had a Catholic tag to it (R4 Making History 31/12/01; ('Past and Present', no. 149, Robert Poole, Nov. 1995) 1G1, p182/329).

Jan. 1752 Also Becomes English New Year: At the same time the old New Year day of Lady Day, 25

> March was changed to 1 January. Contrary to some reports, there were no riots just that Christmas took a long time to settle down to the revised date. In Scotland it had been changed to 1 Jan. from 1600 (ia, p113). Under the 1750 Calendar Act, the day after 31 Dec. 1751 becoming the 1 Jan. 1752 (10-3, p6). **Prior to this Jan., Feb., and March had been in the previous year**, with some people quoting two years so that you could relate it to the Catholic year in Europe where they had converted to the Gregorian calendar from 1582 e.g. "February 22 1747/8" was put on a small tombstone to Mrs Ann Reeves in Cheshunt Church (Broxbourne Borough leaflet).
> The above, the probable reason for the often differently quoted year of the start date!

Pre-1752 New Year of 25 March from 1752 becoming 1st January. The following dates based on a 1st January New Year, as we know it today.
2 Jan. 1609 (Wayleave) Amwell: Free passage given for New River through church grounds at Amwell by the vicar Thomas Hassall (15I, p265 text of grant).
27 Jan. 1609 (Passage through Ground) in Wormley: 20s. to William Manton for the NR to pass through his [illegible] Wormley grounds (15I, p265 text of Receipt).
16 March 1609 for the first survey paying 11s. 7d. for horse hire at Waltham [Cross] (8, p23).
21 April 1609 City formal agreement with Myddelton (('London & the Kingdom' by R.R. Sharpe, ii, 21, 1894) 11, p34; 12, p16). 28 March 1609 Myddelton offer & 21 April 1609 Indenture (14B2, p444; 13, p110; 7K3, p5 my copy has typo of 1 April 1606).

Late-April 1609 Myddelton Starts Actual Work on New River
  From Amwell, but later WIDENING BACK TO CHADWELL SPRING
Last Week April to 5 May 1609 (First Wages Paid): Myddelton surveys his course 3-times and each time from **Amwell** not Chadwell Spring, so it is likely that Colthurst had brought the first part of the river to near the village of Gt. Amwell. Myddelton having to widen Colthurst's 6 ft. cut to 10ft. as specified in the City's Acts.
  But not until 15 May 1613 the men **cutting the trench 4ft. wider at the top & 1½ ft. wider at the bottom from Chadwell to Amwell** costing £15. 0s. 0d. (15J, p46).
So many various dates given for when Myddelton started actual digging **(MYTHS & Prob. TRUTH) but probably the last week in April** since the first wages paid 5 May 1609 (11, pp36-37 first page of 1st Account Books/p38; 7G6, p3 May 1609; 7K3, p5 began 20 Feb. 1608/p192).

SURVEYING the LINE OF MYDDELTON's NEW RIVER (Edward Wright > Edward Pond)
  Effectively following what we call today the 100ft. Contour.
The famous astronomer & mathematician **Edward Wright** (1558-1615) of Garveston, Norfolk was employed to survey and direct the original line of the New River. Wright said to have used a perspective glass (telescope) to directly read open-sighted levels. A spot level attained using a single graduated staff/rod, or a line of levels using a pair of rods as with the notch & foresights of a musket, the length between the two sights based on what was convenient to walk, shout or signal.
  For a line Wright claiming 1s. 0d., and for a board for a gauge £1s. 2d., and on 12 Sept. 1612 Mr Wright's bond (surety) sued to judgement and execution, such that there might have been irregularities in the compensation paid to landowners (15J, p29).
Since after the great holdup, in 1611 when resuming work, for some reason Wright was replaced by the mathematician **John Blagrave** (of Reading who d. Aug. 1611) & his mathematician friend **Edward Pond** (compiler of a well-known almanac, d.1629) who kept his level in a tent carried by two men, set via a water-level, plumb-line level, or suspension of the whole instrument (11, p38 Edward Wright; 8, p24/30).
  'To Mr. Ponde for his weekes enterteynment' £2. 6s. 8d. a week, from Dec. 1611, to Oct. 1613, **for setting out a channel with a fall of only 3 inches to the mile** (3, p8). 'ffor 4 Ells of Canves att xvid the Elle for to make a Shellter for Mr. Pondes leavell 00:05:04' (3, p8).

WORKFORCE (Maximum just Over 300 per day): Not 600 men as often previously quoted, this probably referring to the different men employed over 4-years **(MYTH & Prob. TRUTH)**, the

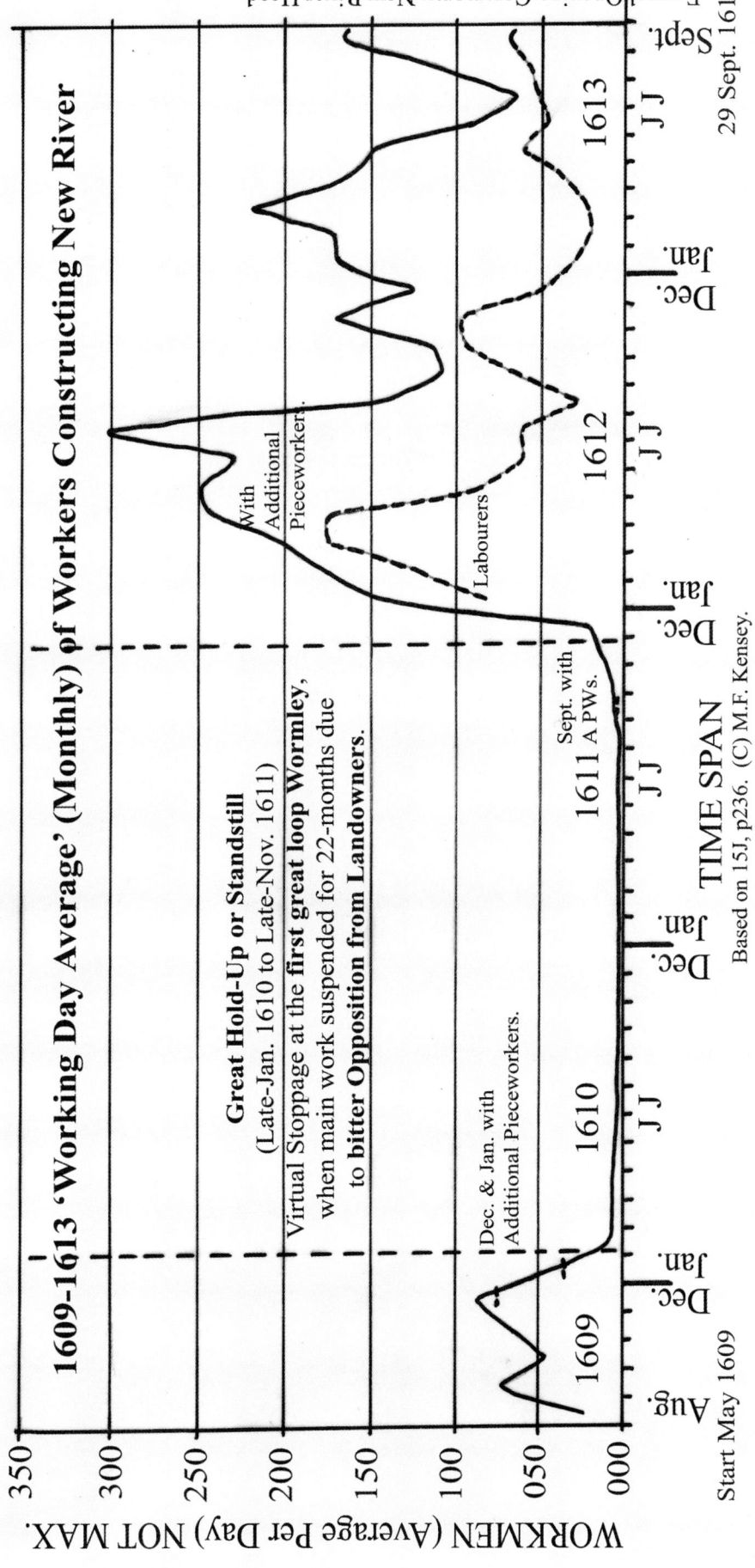

maximum daily number of men employed reaching **just over 300 per day during July 1612**. Robert Ward estimating it cost approx. 10d./cubic yard to dig the original New River channel, using an **average of 128-workmen digging 6-days per week for 30-months** (the max. number one day reached just over 300 and using 50-months less the 20-month standstill), or **progressing at 90-yards per working day** (15J, p70/71). According to the accounts, the workforce was **nearer 250**, rather than the 1,700 quoted in a Bodleian Library manuscript regarding the great holdup; 50 to 100 employed in second half of 1609 (15I, p14/20; 14B2, p445 'upwards of six hundred labourers'; 7J1, p41 600). Some workers paid for 6-days (**only Sunday being a day of rest**), but some for only 5 days, 4 or less (11, p39; 15J, p27 **paid on Saturdays**).

Colthurst employed as the overseer of the work and paid 14s. per week (8, p23; 15J, p28).

Entirely Dug by Manual Labour: Not using Dutch workmen, many in fact Welsh or from Hertfordshire families (8, p38; 15J, p26 all the workers named), using **shovels/spades, crowbars, & wheelbarrows**. There are records of baskets to carry the earth, and hods for the earth where the wheelbarrows cannot go; beetles (hammers) to drive piles, and iron crowes for pinning piles; lime to fill cracks in the banks, and horse dung to mend the banks; and timber used for wharfing the banks (11, p53).

"ffor a Dosen & a halfe of **Basketts** toe carrie earthe uppon the Bancke   00 : 05 : 06".
"ffor xii **hoddes** toe carrie earthe where the wheele Barrowes cannot goe   00 : 18 : 00".
"ffor carrieng upp Water into the newe Bancke by nighte to make itt fitt to work the next daye
                                                                                  00 : 04 : 00".
("To Mr. Ffordam) for his **two horses** fower daies to tread the bancks   00 : 08 : 00".
"ffor xi loades of **horse dunge** att Amwell to mende the Bancke att 4d ye load - : 3 : 8".
"Molle trapps" and wages "To a moll catcher for takeing molles", also "ffor killing of moules"
((All from Orig. NR Accts.) 3, pp8-9 brackets on source; 11, p53 baskets & hods/p57 moles, horse dung; 15J, p35 moles). As today mole holes near the River resulting in leaks.

Probably Sealed with Puddled Clay (Known used Later): An impervious lining created from puddled clay, the traditional method for lining a pond, whereby humans or horses pound the wet clay to remove any air bubbles.

The Accounts show purchasing tools such as spades, an iron-spade, shovels, a shod 'scavell', hand/wheelbarrows, dragge, baskets, hoddes, rakes some iron, staves, rammers, crowbar, Essex axe, hatchet, saw, knife & old scythe to cut waterweeds, and horses normally hired but one nagg purchased plus its running costs (15J, p31).

The labourers **earning 10d. a day**, plus an extra 2d. a day if working in water. Individual excavators or gangs paid **piecework**, first based on gauges ('single gauge' approx. 18-inches at 1s. 2d. the rod, 'double gauge' & 'treble gauge'), then at so much a pole or rod. The banks wharfed and bridges erected by **carpenters** at 1s. 4d. a day. The occasional brick bridge by **bricklayers** at 1s. 6d. a day (11, p56; 8, pp36-37 for labour costs, piecework, gauges, overwork/overtime; 15J, p27 some cart bridges erected by landowners who were reimbursed at the rate paid to contractors/p30 wages of labourers, pieceworkers, carpenters, tradesmen & contractors/p33 bridges).

Original New River X-Section: By the original charter limited to 10 feet wide, such 'that it could not have been more than 4 feet in depth' (13, p121; B2, p255), such that originally no more than a large ditch.

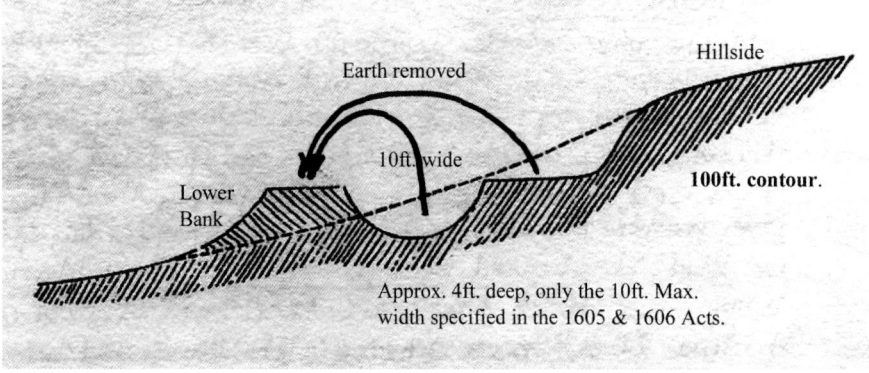

X-SECTION of New River led along hillsides, on level ground spoil thrown either side (13, p121; MFK version).

BED OF THE RIVER (Still Belonged to Landowner): The inheritance or 'fee simple' of the bed of the New River retained by the local landowner, the NR as such with a 'public-law easement', later purchasing parts of the bed & other land, but since held as 'undivided shares' (tenant in common in land, a unique type of share, fixed by number not value) it became legally decided that the investors not the company owned the land (15I, p4/5/10; 15J, pp21-22).

Right of Easement for Cleansing & Repairs: There was sufficient land procured on either side of the river, so that horses and carts could pass along either bank for the purpose of cleansing and repairs (13, p121).

The New River probably completed in sections, first by a **vanguard digging a trial trench** close to the 100ft. contour, often having to fill in the first cut and making a new one. The forward work was then followed by the **main body of workers** removing trees & their roots, especially at Enfield, deepening or bottoming as applicable, the spoil used to spread and raise the banks (15J, pp32-33 raising & with horses treading the banks, and removing obstructing trees). Any drains or channels inserted beneath the bed (for draining traverse land waters, preventing the flooding of adjacent fields), before clay puddling to make the channel watertight, followed by (or later) the building of bridges. The section dammed off and filled with water, controlled by sluices & floodgates. Likely leaving gaps where there were structures such as small wooden troughs over opposing streams, flashes (similar but able to tap the opposing stream) or the Bush Hill Frame (circumventing a valley), that were joined up when completed, prior to the final consolidation of the entire route. Occasionally collapsing banks (cave-ins) needed repairing, raising and strengthening with piles and clay, and leaks repaired with wet clay & lime ((NRC Books) 8, p33/38 cave-ins; 15J02, p4).

Outside Capital

Unspecified Date (Divided into 36-Adventurers' Shares) held by 29 Persons: After the work had begun, Myddelton divided the venture into 36 transferable Adventurers' Shares (regarded as an Inheritance), by 1619 held by 29 persons. One such transaction recorded 8 May 1612 (see later). The Adventurers' shares later much **divided into fractions**, and from a 1711 decree holders of two or more fractional parts of a share might jointly depute a person to represent them on the board (14B2, p450).

County Vote (NRC Shareholders in 2-Counties): From 1429, confirmed by the 1832 Reform Act (and until 1918) certain freeholders had the right to vote, in the case of original NR shareholders or part shareholders, in the two counties that the river ran through (15I, p236).

5 May 1609 paying Mr Wright £20. 3s. 0d. for three different surveys to Amwell and back to Islington, and on the same day for **600 boards (& their carriage) for the spring head**, William Parnell (principal supplier of timber for the NR works) paid £2. 18s. 0d. (8, p24; 15J, p29 Wright's surveys lasting 20-days, on 1st survey accompanied by Myddelton).

A week later Wright made Myddelton's 'Arts man' when paid a £40 advance, and from Sept. 1609 paid £2 per week (8, p24; 15J, p29).

Local Help for Myddelton & Compensation Commission

10 July 1609 letter from the Lord Mayor to the Privy Council requesting that the J.P.'s for Herts. & Middx. help Myddelton, and a **Commission set up 2 Aug. 1609 for settling compensation to landowners** as laid down in the 1606 Act (11, pp38-39; 8, p24; 15J, p34 various claims for compensation).

From 11 Aug. 1609 the NR accounts are kept weekly by the first Clerk, Edward Hughes, and by the end-Aug. over 50-named labourers are employed, and by the end-Sept. over 130 (8, p24).

Oct. 1609 – March 1610 (Giant Plough): Using a **17-horse 'Ingen'** probably a Giant Plough or 'Drag Scraper' that kept breaking down so was jettisoned ('Brief Lives' by John Aubrey, edn. by O.L. Dick, 1949, p198; 15I, p20; 11, pp53-54; 8, pp35-36 lists costs for Ingen; 15J, p32 Ingen).

2 Dec. 1609 had reached **Spital Brook**, Hoddesdon (8, p33).

16 Dec. 1609 had reached **Broxbourne Church**, the sexton for 3d. lending a bell rope to pull down a tree (8, p33; 11, p57).

23 Dec. 1609 the sluice at **Amwell spring** given a pin & padlock (8, p33).

26 Dec. 1609 (The Only Death Recorded): Records the only death, 2s. being paid 'for the buriall of Tho. Trenson the Scottishman' (11, p39 Note 2).

1609-10 (Rival Scheme) Abortive: A competitive attempt by the Chelsea School to forestall

Myddelton's project, by bringing water to London on a commercial basis from the River Lee at Hackney (7K1, p19; 11, p45 Chelsea, but also adds Edward Hayes applying to Lord Salisbury for waterworks better than Amwell; 7G5, p42).
20 Feb. 1609 to 29 Sept. 1630 Abstract of NR Accounts (15I, pp39-40).

c. Jan. 1610 - Nov. 1611 (Great Hold-Up or Standstill for 23-Months)
MYTH & Prob. TRUTH (NOT at Enfield but the Wormley Loop): The number of workers falls to 17 on W/E 27 Jan. 1610, such that the work is limited to maintenance (8, pp24-25; 15J, pp35-40 the Great Disruption). Work was stopped whilst they negotiated the first great loop at Wormley (border with Cheshunt), apparently entirely due to being obstructed by local landowners, not engineering problems or London water-carrier opposition (Tom Mason's cuttings, 'reached as far as Bush Hill'; all other early commentators say Enfield, but G.C. Berry (8, p25) the first to thoroughly study the actual accounts says Wormley; 11, p46; 7K1, p19 stopped after 10-12 miles at Enfield after Myddelton had spent £3,000, nearly all his money; 7K3, p5 had reached Enfield).

>**MYDDELTON'S OPPONENTS:** The formidable organised campaign against Myddelton, led by **William Purvey of Wormley** and **Dr Henry Atkins of Cheshunt** (both Royal Servants), **plus another landowner** (11, p40 Note 1: Bodl. Tanner MS. 98, f. 113/p47; 15I, p14 Purvey Auditor of the Duchy of Lancaster and two others/p47; 15J, p35 Purvey & 2-others, plus arguments of objectors). See their later monuments.

>**MYTH: King James could NOT have seen** the New River being constructed through Theobalds before the Great Hold-Up, as it had NOT reached there, as recorded by Smiles and others (13, pp115-116; 7J1, p39; KJ1, p49 as he watched it being built from his windows at Theobalds).

April 1610 appeal by the City to the Privy Council, and an 18 May 1610 Bill to repeal the two New River Acts resulting July 1610 in ten members of Parliament to review the works, but Parliament was dissolved Feb. 1611 (and not recalled until 1614), such that despairing Myddelton applied to and was granted a further 5-years extension of time by the City (('The Effects of a Bill to Repeal the Acts 3 & 4 Jac, I, for bringing the New River into London' etc., Record Office) 7K1, p18; 15I, p15 May 1610 reached the Commons; 11, pp40-45; 8, pp25-27; 12, p16 20 June 1610 Bill; (28 March 1611 agreement granting Myddelton a 5-year extension, but not yet able to continue ((Journals 28, f. 176 verso) 11, p45; 8, p27 **7-years from fol. 21 April [1611]**; 14B2, p445 Bill introduced 20 June 1610, after a year's delay getting a 5-year extension, and the fol. year extended to 7-years; 15J, p37-38 completion dated extended for 5-years i.e. April 1618; 12, p17 28 March 1611 Indenture).

>**MYTH (Did NOT at this time Apply for Loan):** 'It is usually said that he applied to the Corporation of London for a money grant, but there does not seem to be any truth in this statement, which is given on no reliable authority, and has been copied from one book to another' (7K1, p19; 13, p114 'Londinium Redivivus' by Malcolm says the City refusing aid to Myddelton, but this not borne out in the Corporation's records; KJ1, p48 refused a loan by City).

Mid-Summer 1610 (First NR Walksmen): Employing and paying the first four of the Walksmen (John Allen, Robert Essex, Thomas Stone & Edward Toaler) and according to G.C. Berry part-time (11, p39; 8, p25).
1610 (Myddelton's 1st Term as Prime Warden) of Goldsmiths' Co.: In 1610 Hugh Myddelton served as Prime Warden of the Goldsmiths' Company for the first time, and again in 1624.
c.1610 Hugh Myddelton's House (1993 SITE OF > Halliwick Gate) Bush Hill, Enfield, Middx.: c.1610 Hugh Myddelton acquiring a house at Bush Hill (possibly called Red Hills/Ridge/House > Bush Hill House > Halliwick House) from which he is said to have superintended the construction of the New River, after which became his country house, sold by his youngest son Simon pre-1650 (Various general sources with varying dates). Much later erroneously called 'the Nurses' Home (Myddelton Hall), said to be the site of the house occupied by Sir John Myddelton, when laying out the canals of the New River, ...' ((Series of articles 'The Churches of Enfield', 'Enfield Gazette' 1922) B2B1, p45). In Jan. 1969 MFK visited Halliwick House, but **after 360-years found no identifiable remnants from the time of Hugh Myddelton**, although felt proud that had walked where he had once lived, the house demolished in 1993 and replaced by the modern residential Halliwick Gate on which there is a Blue Plaque.

28 March 1611 (Statutory Powers Transferred to Myddelton) to COMPLETE WITHIN 7-YEARS:
The earlier arrangements superseded by an indenture transferring the Statutory Powers to Myddelton, the completion within 4 [sic.] years amended to completion within 7-years (15I, pp256-264 Appendix B has full text/p256 **'fower years'**/p258 **'seaven years'**; 12, p17 28 March 1611 Indenture).
But the work on the New River **remaining at a standstill for many more months**.

King James I, Half the Costs for Half the Profits (Later 36-King's Shares)
c. July 1611 > 5 Nov. 1611 Formal Agreement > **2 May 1612 Indenture with King James:** Negotiations from Summer-1611 to 1 Nov. 1611 then a 2 May 1612 signed agreement (8, p29). The

king to be a silent partner with no voting rights, and contribute half the expenditure (past as well as future) for one half of the anticipated profits, and agreed that Myddelton could provide a free 'quill' of water to the poor people about St John's Street & Aldersgate Street. The king commanding his subjects **not to molest or hinder Myddelton in his work**, also permitting Myddelton to **cut the river through the King's lands without any payment** ((NRH; 2-parchment membranes with Great Seal, formerly framed) Acc 2558/NR13/35/1A-C, LMA); also c. 2 May 1612 with title of previous reference ((NRH) Acc 2558/NR13/35/2, LMA; (Within bundle) LR 2/34, National Archives, Kew; Copy (14ff, C 66/1952, full text published in 'The New River, a Legal History' by Bernard Rudden, pp268-273) LR 2/34/1, National Archives, Kew; 11, pp47-48; 15J, p39 Sept. 1611 mention in Accounts Books, and May 1612 agreement; 12, p17 2 May 1612 Deed).

MYTHS & Prob. TRUTH: Said that Myddelton's wealth was almost exhausted, King James took advantage of him etc., but the agreement probably had mutual benefits to both. The king's involvement also provided the added benefit that all expenditure was recorded in the **New River Account Books**, now lodged at the PRO, Kew (11, pp48-49 9 Account Books described).

ABOVE: 2 May 1612 'Royal Investment' with Sir Hugh Myddelton's Signature & Seal (TW, Abbey Mills Archive; MFK revamp of original with inset enlarged signature).

BELOW: Another & larger signature of Hugh Myddelton (1809 'London' by Hughson, p360,

ELSC&A).

21 Aug. 1611 end of the first book of NR Accounts, the 1st four pages in Myddelton's handwriting, every page signed by him, this book kept by Edward Hughes (who probably died soon after), at the end a sworn statement by Myddelton of the total sum. The other 7-books are signed by Myddelton & Miles Whitacres (representing the King, Whitacres succeeded by Edward Ball), the books kept by William Lewyn (8, p28). Aug. 1611 became known that Myddelton was not taking the river to Moorfields, but to a pond between Islington & Clerkenwell (15J, p38).

Work Resumed (After Great Holdup)
28 Sept. 1611 Colthurst's allowance resumed and £1 paid to Mr Wright (Myddelton's 'Arts Man' d.1615) for trying the level at Cheshunt Park, but the last mention of him since on 30 Nov. 1611 another mathematician Edward Pond (& his friend John Blagrave of Swallowfield also a distinguished mathematician who prob. d.1612) paid £2. 6s. 8d. per week for plotting the level between Cheshunt & Theobalds (11, p49-51; 8, p30/31).
   Sept. 1611 (Another Rival Scheme): Edward Hayes applying to Lord Salisbury to continue with his waterworks proposal better than the Amwell waters ((S.P. Dom. 1611-18) 14B2, p446; 11, p45).
Oct. 1611 £60 advance for bridges paid to William Parnell the master of the timberwork (11, pp49-50 the 1st Account Book last page recording the timber, & works constructed by Parnell).
   Workforce (2 > 300-Workers): From March 1610 an average of 2-workers employed until Oct. 1611, rising to 16 by Nov. 1611, 200 by March 1612, approx. 250 by late-May 1612, and just above 300 July 1612 at its peak (15J, p40).
Nov. 1611 the **highway bridge built at Broxbourne** ((Original Account Bks.) 8, p33).
11 Jan. 1612 (Wk. Ending): **Windmill field Wormley**, **Brookefield Cheshunt**, and a week later **Cheshunt Park** (8, p33).
11 Feb. 1612 **Killsmores**, Cheshunt (8, p33).
7 March 1612 **Aldbury**, Cheshunt (8, p33; 11, p52 early-1612 through Cheshunt).
21 March 1612 spending 14s. on a **drum to summon the men to work**, and also mention of 'Davie Gryffethe' the trumpeter (8, p31/37; 11, p57; 15J, p31).
11 April 1612 **Theobalds** and **Northe field Enfield** (8, p33; 11, p52 April & May reached Theobalds & Enfield). Aug. 1612 reaching Theobalds Park (15J, p40).
   18 April 1612 (Elm Trunks > Pipe-borers' Wharf) > Wooden Water Mains: John Bartholomew (pump maker of Ware) paid 10s. for going to Berkshire to choose elm trees for use as London water mains, on 6 March 1613 Sir Henry Neville of Billingsbear Park paid £67.
      Richard Parkes chief pipe-borer (later Avery Lacey), and pipe-borer John Bartholomew boring pipes of **3, 4 & 6-inches bore** using augers powered by men or horses, and **iron collars** used at joints when laying in the streets, with brass ferules aka 'quills' driven into the pipe on which were soldered the tenant's leaden pipes into their houses. The poor had a water butt, the rich a cistern that was filled two or three times a week (sometimes not for over a week & more), when the turncock for the district turned on the supply for just long enough to fill the receptacles, before moving on to the next district (11, p61 1613 costs of boring & costs of iron hoops/p62 materials used to prevent leaks; 15J, pp52-54).
      Intermittent Supply > 1899 NRC Constant Supply: The above called an intermittent supply, and it was not until 1899 that the NRC's area achieved an overall constant supply.
Also searching for elms in Bucks. (Maidenhead), Middx. (Staines), Essex (Walthamstow & Northfleet) & Kent (Dartford & Faversham), that were shipped on the Thames for storage at the **City's Green Yard store near the Tower at Bear Quay**, or landed at **Pipe-borers' Wharf, Bridgehouse yard** (8, p39/p40 iron hoops; 15J, pp51-52 also searching for elms, Bear Quay, Green Yard, Tower Wharf, Bridge House).

25 April 1612 **Hatchmore Grove** (8, p33); possibly Moor Hatch meadow (1803 Enf. Encl. map) near Flash Lane, Clay Hill Enfield.

8 May 1612 (Two NR Shares): Sir Henry Nevill of Billingsbear, Berks. had previously paid £200 for two $1/_{36}$-shares with a call on further money if needed, a probable £189 in calls giving a £289 par value/price per share (15I, p18/58-67 traces the 1612-1904 Neville holdings/pp274-278 full text of 8 May 1612 Indenture; 11, p72; 8, p30; 15J, pp24-25 calls them £100 down payment for shares/p61 details of 8 May 1612 deed; 4, p10 each Adv. subscribed £500).

9 May 1612 £40 paid to Thomas Springfeild & Robert Nottingham for **lime & bricks for bridges** & other uses, 7 Nov. 1612 their work inspected, and more thoroughly Feb. 1613 (11, p56).

16 May 1612 **Churchbury field** Enfield (8, p33).

13 June 1612 **Butts Farm Edmonton** (8, p33; 11, p52 Edmonton). Butts Farm by 1591 to the N of Fords Green ((M.R.O., Acc 241/8) V.C.H. Middx., Vol. 5), **near today's Firs Lane**. 1775-1959 Firs Lane Estate & Gibraltar Cottages, Winchmore Hill, and Butts Farm, Edmonton ('19', ACC/1953/C/0688, LMA).

11 July 1612 **Mynceing Wood Southgate** & 25 July **Wood Green** (8, p33). July 1612 Southgate & Wood Green (11, p52).

 The previous work then being consolidated, sometimes the original cut was not successful and another cut had to be made (8, p33). As recorded 5 Sept. 1612 & 19 June 1613 using clay & piles to raise & strengthen the banks ((LR. 2/27 & 2/28, 2nd Accounts Book, P.R.O.) 8, p38).

xiijth Dec. 1612 (Compensation): 5s. to Thomas Collyns of Edmonton for two years damage to grass, after a trench for the NR filled in again (15I, p265-266 text of Receipt).

In 1612 constructing a large trough at Haw/Hawe Mores reinforced with 20ft. long oak piles, this having to be rebuilt & caulked Jan. 1615 for £26 (15J, p44), possibly in Cheshunt?

6 March 1613 had reached **Hornsey highway**, and the fol. week **Newington** (8, p33).

20 March 1613 **Holloway** (8, p33). March 1613, cutting the channel 6ft. deep at Hornsey bowling alley, and excavating at Stroud Green the same month, the channel at this time being bottomed & tidied (15J, p40).

10 April 1613 had reached the **Mantells** where they were to build the Round Pond (8, p33; 11, p57).

xxijth April 1613 (Compensation): £5. 5s. paid to William Hollyday for damages caused by the trench cut through his land in the parish of Islington (15I, p266 text of Receipt).

 Not until 15 May 1613 the men **cutting the trench 4ft. wider at the top & 1½ ft. wider at the bottom from Chadwell to Amwell** costing £15. 0s. 0d. (15J, p46).

 15 May 1613 at Islington town end Steven Boone constructing an 18ft. wide Great brick bridge for which he was paid £7. 3s. 6d. (15J, p42).

 May 1613 for £1. 10s. Robert Handes **making the fences** between Stroud Green & Islington (15J, p42).

 28 Aug. 1613 the channel cleared and bottomed between Theobalds Park and the Trough at Gyrton Park (Little Enfield Park, Whitewebbs), and in Nov. 1613 altering the Cutt in John Gyrton's Parke for the King ((J.W. Gough p44, 1964) EAS News No. 33, June 1969; 11, p52; 8, p38; 15J, p42 adds and at Rye Field making 80 pole, 1ft. deeper & 3ft. wider).

 March 1615 bank at Watery Lane breached in floods & needed repairing (15J, p45); probably Wormley-Cheshunt border.

 July 1615 bottoming the river at Ring Cross Holloway (15J, p44).

 Aug. 1615 renewing the flash at Newmans Grove (15J, p45), on former Southgate loop.

After approx. 48-miles (today reduced by half) reaching the terminus.

April -Sept. 1613 (Terminus Reached): Reaching the terminus at the Ducking Pond (named after the pastime of duck-shooting) 80ft. above the Thames which they turned into an open reservoir called the Round Pond (> New River Head), Islington. Constructing a Water House with a cistern beneath on the S-side of the Round Pond, from which water was piped through wooden mains (mainly elm) to the streets of London.

Formal Opening Ceremony of New River
Afternoon, Michaelmas Day, 29 Sept. 1613: The jubilation romantically depicted in a later 1772 engraving by George Bickham of the water issuing into the NRH basin (1772 G. Bickham engraving,

Thames Water; 7K3, p192 my copy has typo of 1619). As follows.

Public Pageant & Parade: The colourful opening celebrations consisting of a notable public Pageant & Parade, as recorded by Anthony Munday (Editor of 'Stow') thus: "Being brought to the intended Cisterne, but not (as yet) the water admitted entrance thereinto; on Michaelmas day in Anno 1613, being the day when Sir Thomas Middleton, Knt., (brother to the said Hugh Middleton), was elected Lord Maior of London for the yeere ensueing, in the afternoone of the same day, Sir John Swinerton, Knt., and Lord Maior of London, accompanied with the said Sir Thomas, Sir Henry Montague, Knt. and Recorder of London, and many of the worthy Alderman rode to see the Cisterne and first issueing of the River thereinto; which was performed in this manner" ((Stow's Survey, 1638) 12, pp17-19; KA20, p13; 12, p17).

March or Parade: "A troop of Labourers to the number of 60 or more, well apparelled and wearing greene Monmouth Caps, all alike, carried Spades, Shovels, Pick-axes and such like instruments of laborious imployment, marching after Drummes twice or thrice about the Cisterne, presented themselves **before the Mount**, where the Lord Maior, Aldermen, and a worthy company beside, stood to behold them; and one man (in behalfe of the rest) delivered this Speech" ((Stow's Survey, 1638) 12, p19; B2, p241; KA20, p13). "… marched round about the cistern to the martial music of drums and trumpets" (13, p124).

Metrical Speech: Composed by the English dramatist Thomas Middleton (c.1570-1627) and read aloud, "The speech at the Cisterne, according as it was delivered to me:-
'Long have we labour'd, long desir'd & pray'd,
For this great work's perfection; & by th'ayd
Of Heaven, and good men's wishes, 'tis at length
Happily conquer'd by Cost, Art and Strength,
And after five yeeres deare expence in dayes,
Travaile and paines, beside the infinite Wayes
Of malice, envy, false suggestions,
Able to daunt the spirit of mighty ones
In wealth and courage: this a worke so rare,
Onely by one man's industry, cost and care,
Is brought to blest effect, so much withstood,
His only aim the Citie's generall good,
And where (before) many unjust complaints
Enviously seated, caus'd oft restraints,
Stops and great crosses, to our Master's charge,
And the Works hindrance; favour now at large
Spreads itself open to him, and commends
To admiration, both his paines and ends,
The King's most gracious love (12, p19; C4, pp129-130).
    "Perfection draws
Favour from Princes, and (from all) applause,
Then worthy Magistrates, to whose content,
(Next to the State) all this great care was bent,
And for the publike good (which grace requires)
Your loves and furtherance chiefly, he desires,

To cherish these proceedings, which may give
Courage to some that may hereafter live,
To practice deeds of Goodness, and of Fame,
And gladly light their Actions by his Name (7H2, p88).
Clarke of the Worke, reach me the Booke to Show,
How many Arts from such a Labour flow" (C4, p130; KA20, p14).
 All this he readeth from the Clerk's Book.
First, here's the Overseer, this tride man,
An ancient Souldier and an Artisan;
The Clarke; next him the Mathematician;
The Maister of the timber-worke takes place
Next after these; the Measurer in like case;
Bricklayer, and Engineer; and after those
The Borer, and the Pavier. Then it showes
The Labourers next; Keeper of Amwell-head;
The Walkers last; - so all their names are read.
Yet these but parcels of six hundred more,
That (at one time) have been imployed before;
Yet these in sight and all the rest will say
That all the weeke they had their Royall pay" (C4, p130; KA20, p14; 15J, p43 quotes last part; 7G5, pp35-36 last part; 7H2, p89). Smiles quotes this section in full as being expressive of the character and sentiments of the workmen employed in the undertaking (13, p125).

Edmund Colthurst as Overseer came first, probably at Myddelton's insistence because of his respect for Colthurst as the instigator of the New River, it was his idea and he was its overseer, then William Lewyn the Clerk, the Mathematician Edward Pond, bricklayer Stephen Boone, Engineer unknown presumably Myddelton, the carpenter William Parnell, the Borer Richard Parkes, the Pavier Thomas Horne (15J, p43 suggests that Howell Jones possibly the Measurer).

Floodgates Thrown Open: "At the opening of the Sluice:
"Now for the fruits then:- Flow forth precious Spring
 So long and dearely sought for, and now bring
 Comfort to all that love thee; loudly sing
And with thy Chrystal murmurs strook together
Bid all thy true Well-wishers Welcome hither" (7H2, p89; 11, p58 described).

Version 1: 'At which Word, the Sluices being opened, **the Stream ran plentifully into the Bason**, under the Sound of Drums and Trumpets, the Discharge of divers Chambers, and loud Acclamations of the People' ((Biographia Britannica) 1AA, pp495-6; 12, p19; C4, p130; B12C, pp16-17 full text; (Mund. Ed. Stow Sur.) 1A1, p1270; KA20, p15). Around 39 lines of poetical speech, 'Biographia Britannica' under Notes on Middleton (H4); the opening ceremony 'mentioned at length in the Biographia Britannica (Article Middleton, in the Notes, where the poetical speech spoken on the occasion is given at length consisting of 48 lines)' (5-sheets headed 'CPR, Beauties of England & Wales (Middx.)' by Rev. Joseph Nightingale, p595 Vol. III, 1815; also 'Vide ante, Part I p68') 8A1, 4/1-3).

Version 2: "At which words the Flood-gates flew open, **the streame ranne gallantly into the Cisterne**, Drummes and Trumpets sounding in triumphall manner and a brave Peal of Chambers gave full issue to the intended entertainment" ((Stow's Survey, 1638) 7G, pp49-51 gives full text; 12, p19 chambers or miniature mortars; B2, p241; C4, p130; C7, p34-35; 11, p58 Note 5: chambers small pieces of ordnance; (Original Stow, not later 1636 version) 14D4, pp162-164; KA20, p15).

Loud Huzzas (Cries of Joy): "… amidst loud huzzas, the firing of mortars, the pealing of bells, and the triumphant welcome of drums and trumpets" ((Smiles) 13, p125).

Additional Notes: Sir Thomas Middleton elder brother of Hugh Myddelton and one of the Adventurers. Sir Thomas Myddelton wrongly called a goldsmith of Basinghall Street. He was a Grocer (1K1, p404). Sir Henry Montague, Knt. and Recorder of London also an Adventurer. Flat round Monmouth caps formerly worn by soldiers and sailors (11, p58 Note 2). The dramatist Thomas Middleton no relation to Hugh Myddelton, also "wrote a Pageant called 'The Triumphs of Truth' in honour of Sir Thomas Myddelton's inauguration as Lord Mayor" for the ensuing year (12, p20 not said whether part of above or separate). He was also " … the author, amongst other plays, of 'A Mad World, my Masters', and 'The Roaring Girl'. He occasionally wrote in conjunction with Beaumont and Fletcher, and other poets of the time" (13, p124-125; Francis Beaumont (1584-1616), John Fletcher (1579-1625)). He also wrote 'Women Beware Women' (BBC Radio 3 30/3/03). 1613 published article of opening of New River by 'T.M.' likely Thomas Myddelton ((Guildhall Library) 15I, p70).

> **MYTHS:** 'The New River was completed after eight years of work. The length of the canal was 60 miles; it was crossed by 800 bridges, and five years were spent in the construction; the people were slow in taking their water from the new supply, probably because they detested changing their ways'. 'The completion of the New River in 1620 was a great boon and blessing to the people, but the greatest benefit to trade in the reign of James I was the improvement of the navigation of the upper part of the Thames by deepening the channel, ...' (1K10F, p9/195).

MYTH & Prob. TRUTH (NOT KNIGHTED): There is no evidence that he was knighted upon completion of the New River (as said by various commentators), but awarded a baronetcy in 1622 (11, p21 knighthood erroneous; 7G6, p3 'knighted on its completion'); also erroneous that Sir Hugh Myddelton 'was on this elected Lord Mayor of London' (7K3, p6).

Accidental Drownings & Suicides: For over 400-years the New River's purer water supply saved a multitude of lives, but we should not forget that it has taken 100s of lives due to accidental drownings and suicides.

> **1788 (Attempted Suicides) All Women:** 'Yesterday as a gentleman and lady were walking by the side of the New River, near Sadlers Wells' upon seeing a floating bonnet then a hand move underwater, the gentleman with great difficulty raising an unfortunate women onto the bank, who was taken to a public-house to recover. Because of abuse by her husband, she was attempting suicide. In the same year 'Last Wednesday night about eleven o'clock' two young girls (one 17, the other nearly 20) with their arms tied together, attempting suicide in the New River near Sadlers Wells, after hearing terrible shrieks the 17-year old pulled out 'perfectly sensible', the older one resuscitated by one of the Faculty ((Two printed cuttings with inked '1788') Islington LHC). The Faculty probably referring to some rescue stations (aka Drag Stations that kept rescue equipment incl. long hooked poles) voluntary set-up on the New River, one near Colebrooke Row. In the 1770s Dr William Hawes son of the innkeeper of the Thatched House Tavern (aside the NR at Islington), had developed resuscitation techniques for reviving drowned persons, giving rewards for runners to alert voluntary doctors that could rush to the scene and attempt resuscitation, at which they became extremely successful. Said to have evolved into the Royal Humane Society (15J, pp200-202 NR drownings).

Complete MYTH on New River Expenditure
1) The New River Company Always in Denial Regarding the Original Costs
Robert Mylne from 1771-1810 NRC Surveyor, aware of the **£7,856** figure (King's half of costs) but calls it the cost of a single share which he multiplies by 36 (number of shares), then doubles to **£565,632**, and is aware that in the 'History of London' a share being about **£6,347** (Acc 2558 NR13/188, LMA; ('books in the Exchequer') 'Hist. of London' by Maitland, 1739, p619; (1751) 11D; (Hughson, 1811) 1A2-4, p19 typographical error of a sub-total £[2 when should be 1],034. 7s. 6½d. of £6,347; printed pp18-21 'London' annotated Hughson vol. IV, p19 with same typographical error, Isl. LHC; 14B3, p335 same error).
In 1812 a NRC leaflet stating it had cost Myddelton **£500,000** to build the river and that it was absurd that his shares had only cost £100 each (2½-sided printed document, Isl. LHC; 15J, p73 15 March 1812 Min./p164 letter to water tenants penned by NRC Gov. Robert Smith). The NRC always in denial regarding the original costs, W.C. Mylne their Engineer preferring in 1815 to state that the then capital engaged in the works was £846,640. 7s. 0d. (probably reliable regarding the then current valuation), and at Christmas 1820 was £968,868. 13s. 0½d., in 1828 was £1,038,725 (the original records said lost in the 1769 fire), in 1833 was £1,116,964 (15I, p148 1814-5, Xmas 1820; 'L5.723' Handwritten 6pp MS, Islington LHC, fully detailed 1815 & Xmas 1820 capital; (Typed sheet Headed 'PLW, Appendix No. 4 to the Report from the Select Committee on the Supply of Water to the Metropolis, 1828') 8A1, 2-8 1828 capital; 14D6-I, p428 1833 capital; 12, p23 1828 capital; 4, p11 1815 capital £750,000).

> **1845 NRC Suppress Book on Original Costs:** In 1845 the NRC paying £50 to suppress a handwritten book ('History of the New River', 1844) probably compiled by NRC Collector

Alexander Wilkinson, containing early published sources, with **accurate costs & income of the NRC up to 1632** ((Acc 2558/NR13/304, LMA) 15J, p72).

Referred to a Committee, Mr H. Berens and Mr Miles report recommending that Mr Wilkinson should be given £50, upon giving up the books and papers from which they were compiled, and **not pursuing his enquiries any further**.

Oct. 1939 (Manuscript & Docs. Resurface): A 'History of the New River' manuscript (dated 1844 with initials 'A.W.') and other documents, collected from the home of Mr J. Mackworth Wood. Evidently A.W. being Alexander Wilkinson, in 1841 appointed a NRC Collector, retiring in 1877 (8A1-N1, pp3-4).

In 1851 the capital invested said to be £1,421,717 (('LRS, Minutes of Evidence taken before the Select Committee on Metropolis Water Bill') 8A1, 2-8; (Parliamentary Paper 1851 xv, Q's.11708-16, pp661-663) 15J, p74).

MYTH £500,000(+/-) Repeated Since 1734: Tracing back this nebulas £500,000 figure, it appears 1734 in Mottley's or Seymour's Stow, 1739 Maitland said to have considerably under-estimated the costs, but £500,000 repeated 1756 (& 1772) by Maitland, 1761 J. Entick, 1811 Nelson, 1819 Robinson, 1835 (Entick) Thomas Cromwell, 1835 William Matthews £100,000 to £200,000, 1835 published poem 'The Origin of the New River' **£800,000**, 1840 £500,000 again by Robinson, 1862 (various writers) Samuel Smiles then equivalent to £2m, 1873 Ford & Hodson (£504,000 using Entick's figures, Myd's 8-Shares costing £56,000, or from Parl. evidence £428,420 or about £6,000 per share), again £500,000 1911 Witaker, 1937 William Kent, 1975 Roberts, Christopher Trent about £500,000, 1980 Patricia Braun.

2) End-Nov. 1614 (Costs of New River) INCLUDING DISTRIBUTION PIPEWORK
The more accurate costs (including the more realistic) normally associated with the New River are those included up until the end of Nov. 1614 as follows:

    1784 Pennant only £7,200 for whole costs.

    1806 £6,347 or £7,856 for King's Half.

    1832 Edmund Lodge £6,347 King's Half.

    1862 Samuel Smiles (later Sir) near-correct total (because of misprint):
- i) Expenditure to the end of 1612 was £4,485. 18s. 11d. (2 x £2,242 19s. 5½d.).
- ii) Expenditure to the end of Nov. 1614 and a further payment from the Treasury was £4104. 5s. 6d.
- iii) Further & Final Payment to April 1616 (from the Domestic State Papers) was £2262. 9s. 6½d.
- iv) Smile's 1862 Total (2 x £8609. 14s. 6d.) being £17,219. 9s. 0d. (13, p119).

    1876 'The Builder' £9,430. 4s. 3d. x 2.

    1911 W. R. Scott: Total of both moieties £18,524. 19s. 0d.'

    1925 F.W. Drake's Estimate of Costs: For the actual formation of the river £17,219 9s., "But before May 1610, **Myddelton had expended above £3,000**, to which must be added a further sum of at least £4,000, for the following 16 months previous to 1611, making a total of £24,219. 9s.

    1930 Meyers Brooks total £18,000.

    1939 Near Correct Figure of £8,609. 14s. 6d. x 2 = £17,219. 9s. 0d. (15; probably taken from Smiles).

1948-9 First Accurate Assessment by G.C. Berry of MWB: The total expenditure between 20 Feb. 1609 and 26 Nov. 1614 was **£18,525. 0s. 1d.**, which includes a considerable amount of main-laying (3, p7; 8, p41; 9, p223). £18,524. 19s. 0d. a figure often quoted since 1948? (15J, p68).

1960 King's contribution nearly £9,000.

1964 G.C. Berry's Figures confirmed by J.W. Gough: In 1964 Gough's book confirms Berry's assessment of the costs to the end of Nov. 1614 as **£18,525. 0s. 1d.**, two-thirds of this spent in 1613 & 1614 (11, p64).

    £18,525 EQUIVALENT IN TODAY'S MONEY (INCLUDES DISTRIBUTION PIPEWORK)
    Multiply **x 1,000** for an approx. today's value = **£18.525m** (15J, p27), but presumably for greater accuracy the fol.:

    Estimate 1. 1614 (£) > 2009 (£): £18,525. 0s. 0d. from 1614 to 2009 is worth:
    £ 2,490,000.00 retail price index.
    £43,900,000.00 average earnings ((Current data was only available till 2009)
    http://www.measuringworth.com/ppoweruk/?redirurl=calculators/ppoweruk/).

    Estimate 2. 1610-1970 ('Old money to new') until Decimalisation: £18,525 > £1,813,227.

Then (1971-2005 > Today) but only lets you enter 1975 and doesn't show end date, such that presumably 1975-2011 = x 5.57 (x 1,813,227) = **£10,099,674** (www.nationalarchives.gov.uk/currency/).

£18,525 equivalent to **£20 million** (Malcolm Tucker text for NR Exhibition, 'London Canal Museum', June 1996 with illustrations from an earlier Finsbury Library exhibition, and GLIAS photos).

1989 Elain Harwood of English Heritage: Suggesting that "The New River cost £30,663. 2s. 4d., of which £2,500 was Myddelton's fee", this probably including the costs for the London distribution pipes ((No source quoted) 15E, p3).

Estimated Cost of Original New River Channel Itself (Approx. £9,750)
    (or £11,050 if including the Distribution Pipework)
<u>UP TO SEPT. 1613</u> **(Cost of Original New River Channel):** Adapting Robert Ward's summarised costs attributed to digging the New River Channel up to the 29 Sept. 1613 opening of NRH (15J, pp69-71):

New River Costs	£	NRH & Pipe Costs	£
Compensation to Landowners to 26/9/1613*	848.	New River Head	268.
Legal Fees	189.	Elm Trunks & boring	1,033.
H. Myd., Colthurst, Surveyors & Clerks etc.	1,092.	into wooden mains.	
Pieceworkers	2,713.	**Sub Total**	**1,301** (B)
Daily Labourers & Carpenters	2,030.		
Bridges	664.		
'Ingen'	29.		
Horses	427.		
Trapping Moles	14.		
Timber (mainly from William Parnell)	1,404.		
Tools, Lime & Bricks etc.	204.		
Walksmen ('Quarterage')	138.		
*Some also paid later. **Myd's. Sub Total £9,752** (A)		Myddelton's TOTAL (A+B) £11,053.	
PLUS Colthurst's Original Costs	700.	i.e. for first 2-3 miles, later widened by	
		Myddelton from 6ft. to 10ft.	
GRAND TOTAL	**£10,452.**		

N.B. Does not include the City's costs for their two Acts, nor Colthurst's (approx. £1,000 minus **£700** = £300 for his Letters Patent). Myddelton paying a total of £341. 2s. 0d. compensation to over 300 landowners etc. ((MS 4883/9, Guildhall Library) 15I, p14).

1. £9,750 EQUIVALENT IN TODAY'S MONEY (MYDDELTON'S NEW RIVER ONLY)
Estimate 1A. 1614 (£) > 2009 (£): £ 9,750. from 1614 to 2009 is worth:
£ 1,310,000 retail price index
£23,100,000 average earnings ((Current data was then only available till 2009)
http://www.measuringworth.com/ppoweruk/?redirurl=calculators/ppoweruk/).
Estimate 1B. 1610-1970 ('Old money to new'): £9,750 > £954,330. Then (1971-2005 > Today) but only lets you enter 1975 and doesn't show end date, such that presumably 1975-2011 = x 5.57 (x 954,330) = **£5,315,618.10** (www.nationalarchives.gov.uk/currency/).

2. £10,450 EQUIVALENT IN TODAY'S MONEY (COLTHURST'S & MYDDELTON'S NEW RIVER ONLY)
Estimate 2A. 1614 (£) > 2009 (£): £10,450. from 1614 to 2009 is worth:
£ 1,410,000 retail price index
£24,800,000 average earnings ((Current data was only available till 2009)
http://www.measuringworth.com/ppoweruk/?redirurl=calculators/ppoweruk/).
Estimate 2B. 1610-1970 ('Old money to new'): £10,450 > £1,022,846. Then (1971-2005 > Today) but only lets you enter 1975 and doesn't show end date, such that presumably 1975-2011 = x 5.57 (x 1,022,846) = **£5,697,252.20** (www.nationalarchives.gov.uk/currency/).

Prob. £5.5m approx. (for the New River itself): Whatever money conversion you prefer, a **lot of money for one man's knicker-pocket** (there being no local banks then) to have personally provided in today's equivalent value from 1609-1613.

For cartage of the heavy money 'portage of viij C li, 2s. 6d. the hundred £1.' (8, p38).
It should be remembered that when the New River was originally constructed, virtually all of its route was through virgin open countryside, where land values were at their lowest, and where he could have been easily robbed of his money.
The cost of the wooden pipes and the laying in London's streets, eventually cost more than the New River itself.

Jan. 1614 Completion of 1st Line of Wooden Pipes:
NRH > St John Street > West Smithfield > Pie Corner > Newgate where branches to:
First branch to Cheapside.
Second branch to Old Bailey > Ludgate.
Soon after a branch to Holborn conduit at Snow Hill > Holborn Bars & from Ludgate to Temple Bar (by Oct. 1614).
1616 main from Cistern House to Gray's Inn (15J, p54).
1617 2nd Line of Pipes: Down Goswell Street, Foster Lane too narrow, so laying a leaden pipe.
And other pipes laid in the side streets to above, with brass ferrule 'quills' soldered to the customer's lead pipes. Using wooden & sometimes brass stopcocks for controlling the flow in the pipes (8, p40/41; 11, p63 Jan. 1614 had reached Cheapside; 15J, pp54-55 first lines of pipes, street costs).
Sept. to March 1622-23 (Wooden Pipes through Shoreditch): 'Boring and jointing 162-yards of 3-inch pipe at 7½d. a yard to lay new pipes through Shoreditch' ((30+ typed foolscap sheets 'Draft Lecture NRC', p25) 8A1, 4/1-1).
In 1656 the existing 6-mains from NRH inadequate so running another main to Ludgate (15J, pp55-57).
Four mains called Soho Main, Grosvenor Main, Oxford Main & Portland Main (12, p48).
From NRH the water was distributed through the main thoroughfares in 3 to 6-inch internal diameter wooden pipes. To tap off the water, bronze ferrules driven into the pipes, onto which were sweated lead 'quills' of ½-inch bore for carrying the water into the yards of houses.
20 Feb. 1614 (Land near Source) Ware: A piece of land acquired near the NR source at Ware by Hugh Myddelton, Samuel Backhouse plus two other NR Adventurers ((C/266, NRC Ltd offices) 15I, p47).
Midsummer 1614 only 37 tenants [customers] taking NR water, Michaelmas 175, and Xmas 351 (11, p66).
6 Sept. 1614 (Myddelton's £3,000 Loan) from the City: Myddelton petitions the Corporation of London for a loan of 3000*l.* for three years at six percent, which is granted 'entering into consideration of the great benefitt this Citty is likely to receave and enioye by bringing of his water to this citty and of the reasonableness of his request' (('City of London Corporation Records', 6 Sept. 1614) 13, p128; B2, p249; 8, p41 Note 69: City Records Repertories, 31-2/396; 11, p65; 7K1, p20 not less than £3,000). Not repaid until 1634 after his death, when reduced by £1,000 because of the breaches made in the pipes to put out fires (7K1, p20; 11, p83 1635 £1,000 allowed by City if rest paid off).
2 July 1614 (FOGWELL SPRING > HUGH MYDDELTON) Smithfield: Hugh Myddelton purchasing Mr John Darge's small waterworks at Fogwell Spring/Pond, Smithfield that supplied the City of London (11, pp63-64 for further details; 8, p18; 7G4, p156 500-year lease obtained by Henry Shaw; 15J, p231).
xxxth June 1615 (Compensation): £3. 6s. 8d. paid to Edmund Niccolsonne of Bushe Hilles for damages caused by the trench passing through his grounds (15I, p267 full text of Receipt).
Aug. 1615 for a fortnight cutting weeds in the river from Chadwell Head to Amwell Spring for 14s. ((LR. 2/29, 2nd Accounts Book, P.R.O.) 8, p38).
5 Sept. 1616 (Silver Cups): Hugh Myddelton presents a silver cup to Denbigh Corporation (> Goldsmiths' Co.); and similar cups to the corporations of Ruthin (and Oswestry) still in there possession, having in 1600 presented a silver-gilt/gold cup to William Myddelton the head of his family at Gwaynynog, near Denbigh (hallmarked 1599, in 1922 purchased by the Goldsmiths' Co.) (('Ancient & Modern Denbigh' 1856, pp156-157; 'Archaeologia Cambrensis', No. 1 second series, 1850, pp134-136) 11, p10; 13, p146 Denbigh & head of family).

By Lady Day 1615 (Tenants): 384 water tenants, and for his known 1616 tenant agreement (21-year supply for a ½-inch quill or branch of lead with swan-necked cocks, called a 'watercourse') Myddelton probably adopting the wording from a Broken Wharf Waterworks document ('Aquarius', F.W. Drake, p570, KBSM; 15I, p23; 15J, p57).

Myddelton's 21-Year Supply Agreement (Leases with New River 'Tenants')
  ½-Inch Quill on Branch of Lead aka Watercourse
'**AD 1616.** This indenture made, etc., between Hugh Myddelton, citizen and Goldsmith of London on the one party and A. B. and C. his wife on the other party, witnesseth, That the said Hugh Myddelton for and in consideration of the some [sic.] of **twentie six shillings and eight pence** of lawful money of England to him in hand at upon the sealing and delivery hereof by the said A. B. and C. hath demised and granted, etc., a **quill or branch of lead containing halfe an inch of water** or thereabouts the said branch to be taken from the maine pipe that lyeth in [BLANK] Streete, and from thence to be convaied in the aforesaid pipe of lead by **tooe of the smallest swan-necked cockes** for that purpose already imployed into the yarde and Kichnie of the now dwelling house of A. B. and C. his wife and at their or one of their owne proper costs and charges. To have and to hould the said branch and watercourse unto the said A. B. and C. his wife, and to the longer liver of them two from the feast of the natyuitye of St John Baptist next enseweing the date of these presents unto the end and terme of **twenty and one yeares** from thence next ensuing and fully to the complete and ended time of needful reparations and of mischance and casualty by fire only excepted if they the said A. B. and C. or either of them shall so long dwell and continue in the said house wherein now they do and use no other trade then now they do for the greater expences of water. Yeilding and paying therefore yearly during the saide term unto the said Hugh Myddelton his heires and assignes **twentie-six shillings and eight pence** of lawful mony of England at the feast of etc., by even and equal portions the first paiment to begin at etc. That the sayde A. B. and C. his executors or assignes shall pay to the said Hugh his heires or assignes at the feasts aforesaid yearly during the said terms or within one and twenty daies after at the said **dwelling house of the said Hugh in Westcheap** London. And the said Hugh Myddelton for him his heires and assignes doth covenant and grant to and with the said A. B. and C. by these presents, That they the said A. B. and C. shall peaceably and quietly enjoy the said quill or branch of water according to the tenor and true meaning of these presents needful reparations and casualties by fire excepted. Provided alwaies and the said A. B. and C. for them and either of them do covenant promise and grant to and with the said Hugh his heires and assignes or his or their officers or servants shall or may peaceably and quietly come into the house of the said A. B. to view the said cocke and pipe for the said water course or any other pipe or branch that shall be derived into any other house from their the said A. B. and C. his wife's branch by the consent of the said Hugh Myddelton or his assignes and to see that the said water shall not run at wast[e], and further that the said A. B. and C. his wife and either of them shall repair and maintain the cockes and so much of the pipe serving for the said watercourse belonging to this the said A. B. his said house at his or their owne proper cost and charges by the oversight and direction of the said Hugh his heires or assignes or his or their officers appointed for that purpose. And the said A. B. and C. his wife do further covenant, etc. That neither the saide A. B. and C. his wife nor either of them shall suffer any currant or other disposing of the said water from their said cockes or pipe other than for the service only of the said A. B. his said house and only for so long time as their lease shall remain in force. Neither shall without the agreement and consent of the said Hugh Myddelton his heires and assignes first had and obtained alter or remouve or cause to be altered or remouved the saide pipe or cockes otherwise then as the same are now at the first made and set up. Nor in the end of the said terme or other ceasing of this present lease shall disturb the saide Hugh or his assignes in cutting the said lesser pipe from the saide maine pipe or any other pipe or branch that shall be derived into any other house from the said branch of the said A. B. and C. his wife as aforesaid for the ceasing of the said water course. Provided alwaies that if the said yearly rent of twenty-six shillings and eight pence shall be behind or unpaid in part or in all contrary to the tenor and true meaning of these presents being by the said Hugh his heires or assignes or his or their servants or officers for that purpose lawfully demanded at the said dwelling house of the said A. B. at any time in the day before the end of the said one and twentie daies or if the said rent or any part thereof shall be behind or unpaid after one and twenty dayes ended or if the said A. B. and C. his wife or either of them or any other by their permittance shall suffer the said water to run at wast, except in time of frost, a quarter cocke and shall not for every such wast at the finding thereof by the saide Hugh his heires or assignes or his or their

officers or servants within six daies next after his or their reasonable request pay or cause to be paid to the said Hugh Myddelton at his said house the summe of two shillings sixpence *nomine pene* or if the said pipe or cocke shall be altered or taken away or any other water course out of the said pipe or cocke suffered by the said A. B. and C. or either of them or by their or either of their assignes or by any other person by their or any of their procurement contrary to the true tenor and meaning of these presents; That then this present graunt and demise and all covenants and graunts therein contained which ought to be performed on the part of the saide Hugh shall cease, bee voyde, and clearly frustrate; and the saide terme shall cease and no longer indure (sic); any such thing in these presents contained to the contrary, notwithstanding. And it is condescended and agreed by and between the saide parties to these presents That if the saide A. B. and C. his wife or either of them shall directly or indirectly give or contract to give to any person or persons any money or reward more than the fine and rent agreed upon which shall be expressed in this present demise, except the fee to the Clarke for engrossing this present demise that then he the saide A. B. and C. his wife shall have their aforesaid pipe and branch cut off and the officer to lose his place that taketh or consenteth to the taking and receiving any such reward. And lastlie the said Hugh Myddelton for him his heires and assignes doth further covenant promise and grant to and with the said A. B. and C. his wife by these presents that if the said A. and C. his wife or either of them shall happen to be unserved with water into their pipe through the default of the saide Hugh Myddelton by reason of any let or impediment in the maine pipe and shall not be amended within one weeke after notice given; Then it shall be lawful for the saide A. B. and C. his wife to detaine and keepe to their owne uses the next quarters rent and alwaies after till the fault be amended without any forfeiture of the demise or grant made to the saide A. B. and C. his wife as aforesaid. In witness whereof the parties to these presents have interchangeably put their hands and seales the day and yeare above written. [Signed] **HUGH MYDDELTON**' (((Hughson's 'London' Vol. VI, 1809, p358) 'JG, NRC Water Supply Agreement 1616') 8A1, 3/3-2, also 8A1, 2-8; 15; (Hughson's 'London' vol. VI, p358) 14D4, p167; (ELSC&A) 1A2-6, pp358-361 lengthy specimen document; 'Aquarius', 'The NRC' by F.W. Drake, 2nd Article continued, pp484-5, KBSM; ('Natural History & Views of London & its Environs' ed. by C.F. Partington, Vol. 2, 1835) 10-3, pp30-31; (D. Hughson, London (1809), vi. 358 n., plus elsewhere) 11, p 63 Note 1; 7F, p1600 repeats the 26s. 8d. cost; (Nelson's 'Hist. of Islington') 7G, p73; '1616 the sum of £1. 8s. 8d.' 'What London Drinks' '3062', BCMA; 15J, pp57-58 mentioned with conditions of supply, and trade supplies).

Similar 30 Dec. 1669 NRC Waterlease to Robert Chevill, Sadler, from the main at Fleet Street, printed in full (15I, pp302-305).

June 1615 (Vandalism) Privy Council Open Warrant: To arrest those cutting the banks of the New River and letting out the water, casting in filth & dead dogs, letting in fowl & sewer water, breaking down and carrying away bridges, and wholesale stealing of water & branch cocks (15I, p23).

MINING SILVER from Lead Ore, North WALES
MYTH & Prob. TRUTH: That his copper or silver mines funded the building of the New River, whereas it replenished his dwindling resources after building the New River and help fund further development.

1617-1631 (Hugh Myddelton Mining Silver) N. Wales: Under a lease from the Mines Royal Company, from 1617 Hugh Myddelton for the rest of his life, after at first finding no copper, mining silver from lead-ore near Aberystwyth, Cardinganshire, in North Wales. His first lease for copper, but 3-months later changed to any ores or metals covered by the Society of the Mines Royal, and renewed 1625, for which he **employed mining experts to work five North Cardiganshire mines** viz. the most important probably being **Cwmsymlog**, plus **Allt-y-Crib** near Talybont, **Cwmystwyth, Goginan,** & **Cwmerfin**. At Cwmsymlog installing two pumping engines possibly invented by Thomas Russell (11, p114; 13, p141 Smiles says principally at Cwmsymlog & the Darren Hills/p143 using pumping machines of his own contrivance to drain the mines).

8 Sept. 1623 the King authorising the Council of Wales to apprehend persons encroaching upon the Cardiganshire mines of Sir Hugh Myddelton; 2 July 1624 to complete the contract with Thomas Russell for his invention; 21 Feb. 1625 confirming Myddelton's Co. of Mines Royal mining lease & 30 April 1625 renewal grant; in 1625 Wm. Gomeldon seeking to work mines in Cardiganshire not worked by Myddelton ((S.P. Dom. 1623-25 James I, & 1625-26 Charles I) 14B2, pp462-463; ('History of Cardiganshire' by Sir S.R. Meyricke, introduction pp ccx,12-14)

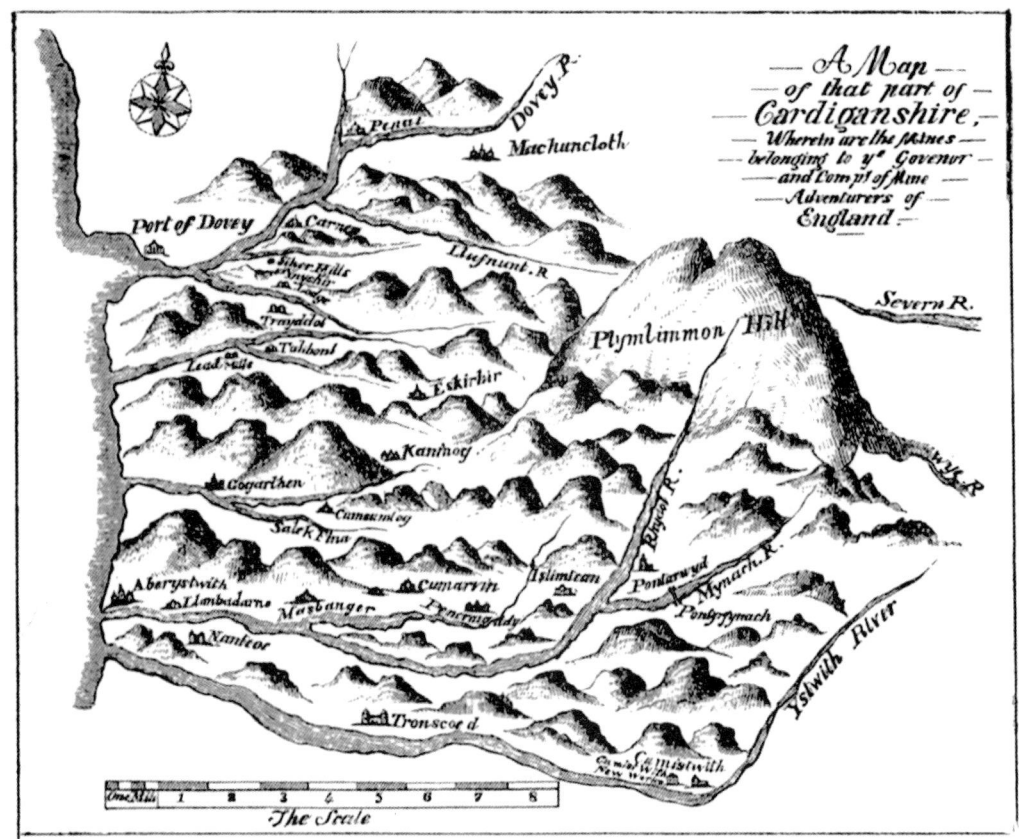

ABOVE: 'Chart of Mines in North Wales' ((From an old Brit. Mus. print) 13, p142).
BELOW: From Pettus' 1670 'Fodinae Regales' (13, p145). From 1617 for the rest of his life, Myddelton mining silver from 5-mines near Aberystwyth, Cardinganshire.

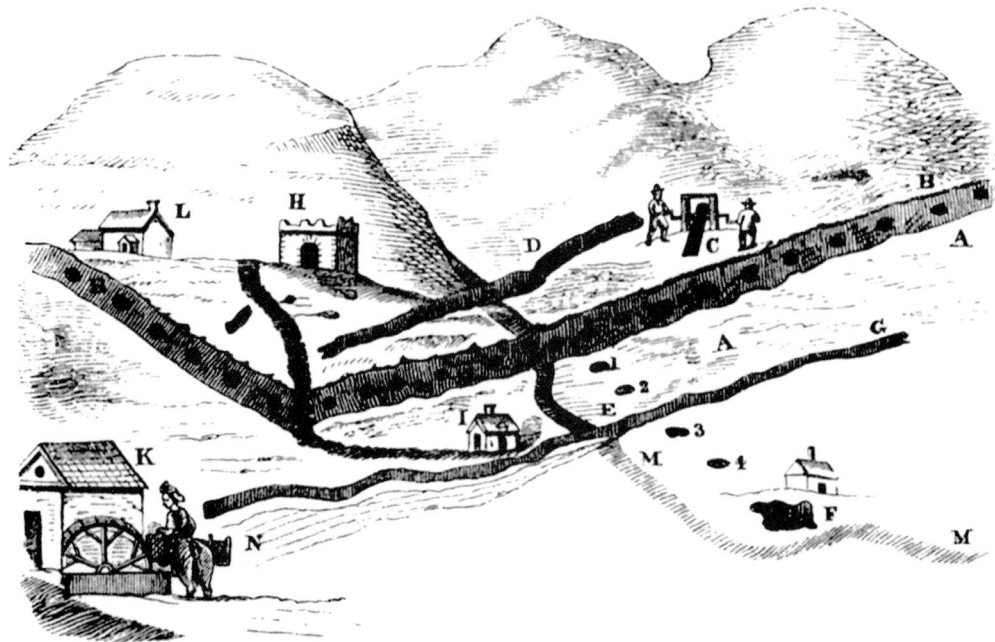

PLAN OF MYDDELTON'S SILVER MINING WORKS AT CWMSYMLOG

A. The old works of Myddelton and Bushell.
B. The round holes are the shafts of the mine.
C. Windlace to wind up ore from the shafts.
D. A new vein.
E. Sir H. Myddelton's adit.
F. A new adit.
G. Adits to drain works.
H. Myddelton's decayed chapel.
I. Old stamping-house.
K. The smelting mills, supposed six miles from the hill.
L. Unwrought ground.
M. The brook that divides the hill.
N. The stream which drives the mills.

13, p144 when confirming the lease waiving all claim of the royalty on silver to the Crown).
In a 1623 trial in front of umpires, Hugh Myddelton defeating Levin/Lewin van Hack/Hake's claim that he could produce twice as much lead from the ore by using pit/sea coal instead of charcoal, proving Hake an imposter (11, p109/110/113/p114 5-mines, but as with the Myddelton **myths this number of mines probably trebled by the general histories**/pp118-122 Hake trial, but does not name at which Myddelton mine, presumably Cwmsymlog). Welsh silver bore the Welsh feathers and from Sept. 1623 was to be coined separately (11, pp127-128).

'First Ever Mines Adventurer in Britain': Hugh Myddelton called the first ever Mines Adventurer in Britain, some 250-years before John Taylor a renown famous 1850's mine engineer (11E, p58). Sir Bevis Bulmer (1536-1615) called the 'first successful English mining engineer' (7J1, p66).

Estimated Profit to Myddelton of £2,000 Gross per month: Myddelton said to have 'cleared monthly the summe of £2,000' ('Fodinae Regales' by J. Pettus, 1670), and Bushell Myddelton's successor at his mines claiming Myddelton had sent £50,000 worth of silver to the Mint, probably an exaggeration (11, p127), that over 14-years would be equivalent to £3,571 per annum. But based on the silver from the Hake trial probably for silver grossing approx. £1,500 per month, such that for all the mines £2,000 does not seem excessive, but minus the operating costs that are impossible to estimate (11, p127).

Myddelton's Welsh Mines > 1631 Lady Myddelton > 1636 Thomas Bushell. But Bushell defaulting on his rent July 1641 when being sued by Lady Myddelton, his tenure shortened by the outbreak of the Civil War (11, p113/128).

9 March 1618 the King trying to find out what yearly pension the New River Adventurers would accept for delivering their shares up to the king, but it came to nothing, and by Michaelmas 1618 there were over 1,000 tenants taking NR water (11, p66/70; 15J, pp64-65), but by 1619 over 1500.

21 JUNE 1619 (NEW RIVER COMPANY) INCORPORATION: In 1619 the 29 NR Adventurer's 36-shares (later only 24 remaining whole and not subdivided) were incorporated by Charter, the first Governor Hugh Myddelton, a position he held until his death. The lengthy Patent Roll 17 Jac. I No. 2214/67, Letters Patent under the Great Seal (fully recited in 'The London Water Supply' by R. Sisley, pp161-171; and 15I, pp279-291 full text of Incorporation) was **forgetfully for 118-years not enrolled, only spotted when finally endorsed 28 March 1737** (7G5, p35; 15I, pp290-291; 11, pp70-72 lists the original shareholders etc.; 15J, pp61-63 details with costs/p64 list of original shareholders, some trustees for Myddelton).

1619 (NRC Incorporation) No Trees within 5 yds of NR: Landowners along the river were prohibited from planting elms, willows or sallows within 5-yards of the New River (14C, p162; sallows = a low shrubby willow tree).

The NRC's capital assets & future profits held in socage tenure, leading to the view that the **shares in these profits must be realty** (real property, that could not be distributed to shareholders), since the profits were held in tenure. Although never tested, because NR shareholdings were realty it was assumed they could recover pieces of land in several counties, such that documents were sealed in Herts., Middx. & London (**fines & recoveries in each county**), as in 1833 '10 messuages 100 acres of meadow 20 acres of pasture 160 acres of land covered with water ... etc.', and even adding the name of parish churches as new London streets were opened up & given piped water (15I, p29/48-49/54/62/215).

NRC (Land & Water Co.): Over the years until 'it possesses a large quantity of land, and is, as a matter of fact, a land company as well as a water company' (7K1, p25).

28 Oct. 1619 (King's Moiety) > Trustees: The NRC granting half of the profits etc. of the company to Sir Henry Cary, Sir Robert Naunton, Sir Foulk Grevill, Sir Julius Caesar & Sir Giles Mompesson, to hold in trust for the King, who legally took no part in its management, only having an observer called the 'Surveyor of the New River' (Edward Ball for life & given £100 p.a. when later taken over by Myddelton that could attend meetings and inspect the accounts; and a joint 'surveyor of the profits' one Sir Giles Mompesson who in 1621 fled the country in disgrace (KA20, p18; E8-2, p7; ((Within bundle) LR 2/34, National Archives Kew; Copy of Indenture, bargain & sale (6ff, & f6v with later rates of payment) LR 2/34/2,

ABOVE: THE NEW RIVER SEAL - OBVERSE & REVERSE (12, p38).

From 1619 the New River Company were to "have and enjoy a common seale".
On the reverse side (the back surface) of the old New River "Governor and Company" seal, is the wording spiraling inwards from the perimeter:

"THE SEAL OF THE COMPANY OF THE NEW RIVER BROUGHT FROM CHADWELL AND AMWELL TO LONDON".

On the observe side (the one with the main device), there is a scene whose symbolism represents:
- Rain descending from "an open hand upon a City" (all water comes from the clouds), with an outer perimeter motto of "Et plui super unam civitatem" ("and on another city I will not rain"). "The hand of Providence, issuing from clouds, and distributing water over London" (6E, p358; 15C, p8 translated as "and I caused it to rain upon one City"; B2, p247; 10, p8; 10-3, p10 print of seal; KA20, pp21-22).
- Below which there is a scene of St. John's Gate and old St. Paul's Cathedral (without a wooden steeple since it had been burnt down in 1561 and was never re-erected) that was destroyed in the 1666 Fire of London.

The motto has been taken from the Latin Vulgate, the Fourth Chapter of Amos, part of verse 7 as following:
"7. Ego quoque prohibui a vobis imbrem, cum adhuc tres menses supressent usqe ad messem, et plui super unam civitatem, et super alteram civitatem non plui; pars una compluta est, et pars super quam non plui, aruit" ((Amos-Pars Altera, Sermo II. "Biblia Sacra juxta Vulgate") A.C. Fillion, Paris, 1887).

The English translation being:
"7. Also I withheld from you the rain three months before the harvest; and I will rain upon one city, and on another city I will not rain; one part shall be rained upon, and the other part on which I shall not rain shall be dried up". From 'The Septuagint Version from the Vatican Text, translated by Sir L. C. Lee Brenton, Bart., 1884', being the best literal translation available (12, p37-38; KA20, p22).

LEFT: Larger more graphic detail of the observe side of NRC Seal (TP No. 4, Thames Water Plc).

National Archives, Kew; 11, p72; 13, p130 Mompesson; 15J, p60 Mompesson; 7H2, p92).
2 Nov. 1619 first meeting of NRC attended by 21-Adventurers at Sir Henry Montague's chambers, Serjeant's Inn (15I, p30; 11, p72 meetings also held at Myddelton's house).

Tapping the River Lee (Prob. from 1613, but a 1619 Agreement)
Soon after the NR was completed, its spring supply was augmented by tapping the Old River Lee at Chalk Island, Ware. Also in the early days every opportunity was taken to tap subsidiary streams etc. on route (see the 1775-1809 plans), but as local streams etc. eventually became polluted, local surface waters were excluded. Possibly even before 1619, unofficially tapping the River Lee.

1619 (Agreement) Augmenting Water Supply: May 1613 mention of dams being remade by Parnell at Ware for £100, Oct.-Nov. 1618 Commission, with Sept. 1619 agreement for tapping the River Lee, June 1620 a dam built in the Lee to turn the water into the New River, often pulled down by the bargemen and then rebuilt ('Abstraction from the River Lee') 8A1, 3/3-2). Oct. 1618 Commission costs, Nov. 1618 scouring the ditches for taking water from the Lee, Sept. 1619 the King signing the articles of the agreement, and warrants delivered to the county Sheriffs ((NRC Mins.) 15J, pp47-48).

16 Jas. I (1618-19) Commission 'which reported that a **20-inch extraction pipe would not make a discernible abatement in the River Lee**' ((3-sheets headed 'New River Deeds') 8A1, 3/3-2).

June 1620 (Dam at Ware) for Tapping the River Lee: NRC augmenting the Chadwell Spring supply by tapping the River Lee at Ware, this causing disputes until 1670 (15I, p32; 11, p74 making a dam at Ware; 15J, p48).

Manifold Ditch (Ancient or New?): A 1632 plan showing the New River up to today's Lee Navigation (12 Dec. 1632 Kings Meads, B. Hare Col. copy D-EHx P7 prob. Acc 2425, HALS), such that it would appear that the NRC were by then using the Manifold Ditch (from today's New Gauge in a 'U' to the later Black Ditch which was probably part of the Old River Lee), until the old River Lee as such **bypassed 1658 by Ware Mill Stream with Ware Lock (1st)**, when a dam put up for Lord Viscount Fanshaw (probably across the start of today's Black Ditch), such that the NRC using the Manifold Ditch to retain the supply to the old River Lee and its dam at Chalk Island.

1660 (Tapping the Lee), Ware: "The River Lee was only a few hundred yards from the New River below Chadwell Spring, and in 1660, under an order of the King in Council, the Company were empowered to take a certain quantity of water out of what was the former navigable River Lee, afterwards called the Manifold Ditch. This arrangement gave rise to a great deal of trouble between the Corporation of the Borough of Hertford and the Town of Ware and the inhabitants of the Towns" (6L, p438; 10, p11 1660 Act; 15C1, p6 1660 cut from River Lea; A, p66; 4, p11 suggests that 1660 first time used).

1667 the dam tore down by bargemen, 28 Aug. 1669 the dam was to be replaced by two jetties with fourteen feet of water being left between the pipes so that boats could pass (('Extracts from the Books of the Mayor and Aldermen of Hertford', p22) A-A2, p12). In 1669 it agreed that the NRC's **Great Pipes ('Thrice as Big' or 17-inch & 12-inch) be replaced by 2-Lesser Pipes of 8-inch & 6-inch bore** (('NRC, The Bargemen of Ware and abstraction from the River Lee') 8A1, 3/3-2; (1892 Commission, Lee Conservancy Board p6, KBSM; (3-sheets headed 'New River Deeds') 8A1, 3/3-2; (Acc2558/NR13/7 p199) 15J, p49; 10-2, p11).

1670 (NR Restricted to the then 'Outtake'): An Order in Council of Charles II, appointing a Committee to look into the complaints of the Lee bargemen, and after a Sir Robert Murray & Christopher Wren survey of the river, reporting that the NRC pipes at Ware, only drew off $^1/_{30}$ of the navigation resulting in just a ½- inch drop in water level, that the New River itself was well maintained, and that it was the millers who were causing the problems to navigation, then making its general recommendations, for the NRC limiting it to its then outtake, later confirmed by 1738/9 Act of Parliament ((Wren's Report, R. Mylne's commonplace book, LMA) 15I, p32; 15J, p48).

1733 (Balance Engine & Separately Located Gauge): 1733 balance engine & gauge constructed by NRC Engineer Henry Mill for controlling the amount of water drawn from the River Lee, legalised by later 1738-9 Acts, the balance engine **rebuilt 1770** under Henry Mill & Robert Mylne but the old gauge replaced **1776** by the 'New Gauge' aka Marble Gauge, **both replaced 1856 by 'New Gauge'** (15J, p49/pp143-145 says balance engine built 1741 **but this was Ware Lock**; KJ1, p79 erroneously dates Marble Gauge 1739; 7K1, p28 Bal. House built 1732).

1737 Byde Act (Private), 11 Geo. II, c.32 (Infant > NRC): The NRC securing an advantage on tapping the River Lee and for the first time getting its corporate existence recognised by Parliament (15I, p31/108).

1737 Act for the NRC to purchase Ware Mills the property of the minor Thomas Plumer Byde, **transferred 20 June 1738** at a perpetual rent charge of £400 per annum (D20B, p128; (HL/PO/PB/1/1737/11 G2 n53, Parliamentary Archives; 7H2, p94 NRC Acts of 1738 & 1739).

In 1876 £400 per annum 'now less land-tax of £40. 8s. … A family who had held it for a century sold it this present year for £8,640, …' ('The Builder' Sat. 22 Jan. 1876, 'The New River' p68, Isl. LHC).

1738/9 River Lee Act, 12 Geo. II, c.32: 1738/9 Act gave the NRC statutory recognition and the power to litigate, millers were to supply water for barges, and certain locks were to be maintained by the NRC for which they could collect tolls. The supply from the River Lee was confirmed, and the **Manifold Ditch made part of the new River**, although the rights of the landowners remaining as per the 1605 Act, on which contention remained until 1855 (15I, p35; 7H2, p94 1738 & 1739 Acts).

1738 (£350 p.a. > £650 p.a.) NRC > Lee Trustees: For extracting water from the Lee, for decades pre-1900 assessed at £650 payable to the Lee Trustees (15I, p130). They appear to have originally paid £2,500 plus £750 in first year, then £300 plus £50 (£350) annually (12, p22; 12D, p13; 6L, p438; 14C, p161; 15M, Acc. 2558/NR13/188, difficult to read handwritten note in ink, signed on back W.C. Mylne with wax seal; An. probably meaning Annuity; Typeset copy of Act pp590-606) 15M, Acc. 2558/NR13/188; pp590-602 1854 printed copy Ref. 346.628, Hackney Archives).

A silly anecdote that soon after 1738 the NRC **paying double** for a pipe twice the size and getting squares of their diameters or **4-times the water** ((Oct. 1814 'European Magazine') 14B2, p453; 12, p22).

1900 (£3,830 p.a.) NRC > Lee Trustees: £3,180 added to the £650, that after a Court of Appeal ruling was upheld ((1901 NRC v. Hertford Union) 15I, p130).

1741 (NRC Rebuilt Ware Lock): (15J, p49/pp143-145 calls erecting the balance engine).

In 1620 Hugh Myddelton paid £800 a year to manage the River but not for extensions or inspection parties. In Sept. 1622 raised to £900 p.a., and from 1623 £1,000 p.a., this also paid to Lady Myddelton after his death in 1632 (11, p75; 15I, p41 1622 £1,000; 8, p43; 15J, p71).

1620-1622 (RECLAIMING BRADING HARBOUR): Using his own 2 July 1621 Patent method for draining land, Hugh Myddelton reclaims 700-acres (hearsay magnifying to 2,000-acres) of land at Brading Haven or Harbour, Isle of Wight, this time **using Dutch workmen**, and costing £7,000 to £8,000 when completed 1622. Sept. 1624 sold to Bevis Thelwall and due to neglect on 8 March 1630 Myddelton's embankment was breached (said because resting on foundations of sand) resulting in Thelwall sueing Myddelton. Finally embanked 1874-1882 (11, pp88-100/p92 patent; 13, p133-140 Embankment of Brading Haven). After which Sept. 1625 declining to embank Traeth Mawr & Traeth Bychan for Sir John Wynn of Gwydir North Wales (13, pp147-148); later in 1812 3,000-acres embanked by William Alexander Madocks and finally reconstructed late-1814.

1621 NRC Bill's failure before first reading to get recognised by Parliament (15I, p31; 11, p75 7 May 1621; 15J, p63).

LEFT: MFK 2002 designed bronze roundel for new front gates to Cedars Park, Cheshunt (1603 added by Brox. Council & refers to the first year of King James' reign).

9 Jan. 1622 (When his Horse Stumbles, King James I thrown into New River) & Nearly Drowns: John Nichols in his 'The Progresses, Processions and Magnificent Festivities of King James the First (1828), IV. p749, and other contemporary writers record how James I:

" … had gone out one winter's day after dinner to ride in the park at Theobalds accompanied by his son Prince Charles; when, about three miles from the palace, his horse stumbled and fell, and the King was thrown into the river. It was slightly frozen over at the time, and the King's body disappeared under the ice, nothing but his boots remaining visible. Sir Richard Young rushed in to his rescue, and dragged him out, when 'there came much water out of his mouth and body'. He was able to ride back to Theobalds, where he got to bed and was soon well again' (13, pp125-126; 11, p43). John Chamberlain recording, "if there had not been present help at hand, a miserable mischance might have followed ...." (8A, p23; 6A, p4 "On Wednesday ..."; 6D, p340; B2, p240 9th Jan. 1622 letter from Joseph Meade to Sir Martin Stuteville; C4, p135 "about half a mile west of the site of the Royal Palace", and recorded in a 11th Jan. 1622 letter from Joseph Meade to Sir Martin Stuteville, 'Ellis's Letters'; 13, p125). Although James loved horse riding, he was a poor horseman, even having a saddle made with a high front and back to stop him falling off (C6, p23). It is said that the King was to in rather strong terms, attribute his accident to the neglect of Myddelton and the Corporation of London in not taking measures to properly fence the river, reminding the Lord Mayor (Sir Edward Barkham when he was knighted at Greenwich in June 1622) and his brethren of his recent mischance in "Myddelton's Water" ((Smiles) 13, p126; 11, p76 Note 1: Supposition by Smiles, there being no evidence for this, in Cal. S.P.D. 1619-23, p409 was told to 'attend to Middleton's water' being the King telling the Lord Mayor to exert pressure on Londoners to pay for the New River water).

New River Prob. Already Fenced in Dangerous Places?
'The river was in the first place unfenced', the King after falling in said, "**to cause it to be fenced at all dangerous places with all speed**" (12D, p9 not quoting any source).
May 1622 Royal Commission for James I to buy out the NR Adventurers, 20 Dec. 1622 report that the Adventurers were evading a reply, 13 Feb. 1622/3 report that the Adventurers would have to sell at a great loss, but the king could help raise the dividends, such that the Commission advising James I not to use the power of proclamation (15I, p37; 11, pp76-77).

19 Oct. 1622 (SIR HUGH MYDDELTON) BARONETCY: For the New River, Brading Haven & Welsh Mines, awarded a Baronetcy and not charged the usual cost of £1,095 (11, pp20-21/78; 13, p143; 15J, p65; 12, p25).

LEFT: Sir Hugh Myddelton's Coat of Arms, presumably as altered by him for the occasion ('Visitation of London' 1883, ELSC&A); 11, p21 Coat of Arms described, his motto 'Virtus palma'). Myddelton's wolf's head later used in the crest of the coat of arms for the Company of Water Conservators, who also hold an annual Myddelton Lunch (7J1, p43).

12 Nov. 1623 (Great Jewel) Gold Chain & Jewel: In 1623 the Lord Mayor of the City of London presented Sir Hugh Myddelton with a diamond encrusted gold chain & jewelled pedant with the City's Arms worth £219 15s./200-marks (as shown on many of his portraits), left in his will to his wife, then most worthy son, probably long broken up and lost. Said awarded to him because of the New River being used to put out fires, and that Sir Hugh supervised the making of the jewel (15I, p41; 11, pp78-79 13 Nov. 1623/p131).

1624 NRC Bill to get the NRC recognised by Parliament, only reached the Committee stage, Sir Edward Coke pronouncing it prevents the great mischief 'nimia potatio; frequens incendium' (15I, p31; 11, p75; 15J, p63).

In 1625 the plague in London denting the number of New River customers (11, p79; 15J, p65).

March 1627 & 1631 (Another Rival Scheme) Abortive: Springs at Hoddesdon promoted for bringing water to London, resurrected Feb. 1631 as a brick or stone aqueduct, a lottery organised c.1639 but soon in difficulties with Edward Forde's scheme to tap the River Colne, opposing pamphlets published 1641, but faded away (11, pp79-80/p80a woodcut map; 14B2, p452 Edward Ford 1641; 'A Design for bringing a Navigable River from Rickmansworth in Herts. to St Giles's in the Fields' by Sir E. Forde, 1641; 'An Answer to Mr Forde's Book', and 'A Proposition for the serving & supplying of London with water from Hoddesdon' both by Sir W. Roberts, 1641; 15J, pp65-66; 7G5, pp43-44).

In 1630 Sir James Weston ordered by Charles I to examine the NR accounts, such that 5 Nov. 1631 the amount due to the king is discharged (because of debts & arrears of rent), since the reliability to the royal income is not more than £300 a year (15I, p38/191). Jan. 1630 & 17 April Commission into fees

'View of Brading Haven, temporarily reclaimed by Sir [later] Hugh Myddelton, as seen from the village of Brading', after Percival Skelton's original drawing ((Publ. 1862) 13, p84).

Reclaimed 1620-22 by Hugh Myddelton, using his own 2 July 1621 Patent method for draining land, breached 1630 due to neglect of new owner, finally embanked 1874-82.

'Map of Brading Haven [Isle of Wight], Ordnance Survey' ((Publ. 1862) 13, p134).

owing to Myddelton, 4 Oct. 1631 letter that from 1612-1617 a £9,262. 9s. 6d. constat, 17 Oct. constat of sums received by Myddelton, and 4 Nov. warrant to remit Myddelton arrears of £1,290. 0s. 4d. ((S.P. Dom. 1629-31 & 1631-33) 14B2, pp449-450).

18 Nov. 1631 (Royal Moiety > Myddelton) called 'King's Shares' (aka Crown Clogg/Clog): The New River originally not financially successful, so from 1618 King James attempting to purchase the Adventurers' shares, not resolved until 1631 when King Charles I sold the Royal Moiety (half the profits for half the costs) to Sir Hugh Myddelton for £500, and a perpetual rent charge of £500 p.a., plus a life annuity to Edward Ball (15I, pp292-301 full text of the Tripartite Indenture; 11, pp81-82; 14B2, p450 Edward Ball original grant 19 Jan. 1618; 15J, p66; 7K3, p6 my copy typo 'Nov. 18, 1636'/p192 1636). Myddelton divided this into a **further 36-shares called King's shares**, most of which were burdened by the rent charge called the Crown Clog/Clogg, **later because of land tax reduced to £400**, continuing to be paid until redeemed by the Metropolitan Water Board in 1956 for £8,230.

The £500 per annum (giving an approx. 5% yield) to the Sovereign forever, the 'fee-farm' a personal obligation on Myddelton & his heirs, post-1631 paid by the company (**although the obligation never officially transferred**), not redeemed until 1956 by the MWB (15I, p5/38/44). To his heir Sir William by intestacy who transferred them 1646 by a trust to his brother Henry for the settler's heir Sir Hugh Myddelton, who June 1657 sold 14 King's shares Crown Clog free for £7,000 to William Bishop married to Flower (daughter of William Backhouse, the later Lady Cornbury). But also in 1657 uncle Simon (Simon Myddelton, 1st Sir Hugh's youngest son), in breach of the trust, persuading his nephew (Sir Hugh Myddelton, the eldest son of Sir William Myddelton, the heir of the first Sir Hugh) to convey him the whole of the King's moiety for £15,100, probably never fully paid for, since in 1675 a debt remaining in the nephew's will, and the transaction causing 1658-1671 lawsuits with the Clarendon family, resulting in 14-shares being conveyed to Lady Cornbury, and that $^7/_8$'s **of the £500 rent charge be borne by the remaining 22-shares** (1671 Chancery decree) with 29 King's & 2 Adventurers shares long burdened with the Clog, 1904 Act (15I, p196 for details; 11, p82 on $29^1/_8$ King's shares & 1½ Adventurers' shares by mid-C18th). The King's shares also allowing Simon Myddelton to become the NRC Treasurer (15J, p76 1649), but was dismissed for detaining profits on some shares, in 1665 Charles I recommending that he be given the lower position of NRC Clerk ((S.P. Dom. 11 April 1665) 14B2, p451) but this was refused ((S.P. Dom. 17 April 1665) 14B2, p451 reasons for refusing, and 22 April Simon's answers, and same date details of company meeting on the matter; 15J, p79). Simon married four times (his 2nd wife Mary Soame; by his second wife 4-children Hugh, Sarah (married Robert Harley who became the 1st Earl of Oxford), Hannah, & Anne; by his third wife four children Elizabeth, Rebecca, Benjamin & Hezekiah an unmarried infant drowned 1688) who died 1680 aged 67 seised of 17 of the 36 King shares, leaving 10-shares to Hugh (also a leasehold house in Hackney) with 3 of these shares burdened with paying the Crown Clog devised to his full sisters, and 1-share subject to the Clog to each of his four children of the third marriage. Anne settled a $^1/_5$ part of Hezekiah's share on her family (future husband Bennet Swayne & heirs, but died childless), such that in 1693 Benjamin Middleton v. Swayne a decision that upon Anne's death the entitlement ended, so passing to Hezekiah's rightful heir, his brother Benjamin (15I, p44/49/68/74-78 Harley papers have lots on affairs of NRC/p188/195; 11, p82 1657/p136 Simon Myddelton & King's moiety etc./p138 the 14-shares/p148 Mary Soame).

BENEFIT of Clog Rent:

31 Dec. 1799 ('Opinion of Mr Mitford on Mr Adair's Case'): 'On the incorporation of the New River Compy. the King James 1st having sustained one full & equal moiety of the disbursements, was intitled accordy. to the true intent & meaning of the sd. Letters patent, to take from time to time one full moiety or half part of the profits resulting from the sd. Water Works. The Govr. & Compy. of the N. River in accomplishment of the intent & meaning of the sd. Charter did by Indre., grant bargain & sale, at the nomination of the sd. King James 1st & for the use & benefit of him, his Heirs & successors unto Heny. Visct. Falkland & five then being named, In Trust for sd. King, his heirs & assigns, one full & equal whole moiety of the profits resulting from the sd. Water Works upon Trust for the profit & commodity of the sd.

King Jas. 1ˢᵗ his Heirs & successors forever. By Indre. Triptite made between King Chas. of 1ˢᵗ part – The sd. Visct. Falkland & the other trustees of the 2ⁿᵈ part – The sd. Govr. & Compy. of the N. River & Sir Hugh Middleton Bart. of the 3ʳᵈ part – The sd. King Chas. for the considerations therein expressed did give & grant, & by his command the sd. Visct. Falkland & the other trustees did grant assign & set over, unto the sd. Hugh Middleton his heirs & assigns – the sd. Indre. dated 28ᵗʰ Oct. 17ᵗʰ of Jas. 1ˢᵗ & sd. moiety of all the profits benefits & granted to the Trustees as aforesaid to hold unto & for the use of the sd. Sir H. Middleton & his heirs forever ----- provided nevertheless, & the sd. Sir H. Middleton did by the same Indre. promise & covenant for himself & his heirs to pay unto the sd. King Chas. 1ˢᵗ or the King's Receiver General for the City of London for the time being the yearly rent or sum of £500 ----- On looking into the enrollt. of this last mentioned deed, it appears that Chas. 1ˢᵗ covenanted wh. Sir H. Middleton, that the sd. rent of **£500 shd. always remain vested & never be alienated from the Crown** & yet on the 23 July 13ᵗʰ Chas 2ⁿᵈ the King did by his letters patent for the consideration therein expressed, give grant & assign, & also command & authorise the sd. Sir H. Middleton to pay unto John Buckworth of London Mercht. the sd. rent or sum of £500 to hold **unto the sd. Buckworth**, his Exors. administrators & assigns from the Christmas then last for the term of 31 yrs. rendering to the King 5 marks [One mark = 13s. 4d.] yearly & on Novr. 21ˢᵗ of Chas. 2ⁿᵈ by other letters patent, the King granted the sd. rent of £500 to **Silvester Dennis** Mercht. for 41 yrs. to commence from the expiration of the lease to Buckworth under the like rent of 5 marks pr. anm. On the 12ᵗʰ May the 9ᵗʰ of Wm. 3ʳᵈ the King by his letters patent granted & demised the sd. rent of £500 to **Dennis Cooling** Gent. together wh. the reserved rent of £3. 6s. 8d. to hold unto him & his heirs forever, as of his sd. Majesty's free gift & Royal bounty. The sd. Dennis Cooling did by a deed under his hand & seal declare the sd. grant of £500 pr. anm. to be in Trust, & for the proper use &c of the **Earl of Albermarle**, as appears by a copy of a minute of the N. River Bd. whereof they directed the Treasurer to take notice. **Some & parts of some of the King's shares do not now pay anything towards the sd. rent, & others do not pay in equal proportions & one share & a half of the proprietors moiety contribute towards the rent, but not in equal proportions**. How or for what reason these arrangements were made, or whether the owner of the rent concurr'd in them does not appear. It has been the practice of the Compy. ever since the yr. 1769, but how long before cannot be ascertained, as the Books of the Compy. were destroyed by fire in that yr. to pay the rent of £500 pr. anm. for such of the Proprietors of shares in the King's Moiety, & the share & a half in the Adventurers' Moiety as are liable thereto, & to make the necessary deductions for that purpose out of their respective shares of profits & upon paying such rent to the owner, & has uniformly allowed Land Tax thereon at the full rate of that Tax for the time being, but in this transaction the Compy. considered themselves as having acted as Agents only & not that they are in anyway ... to see the paymt. of the sd. rent, the same being no charge on the Compy. but merely a covenant of Sir H. Middleton affecting the King's moiety & therefore the Co. think ..., the owner is obliged to seek for payment from the holders of such moiety. It appears from an entry in the Company's Books in the yr. 1770, that the sd. rent of £500 pr. anm. **came to Wm. Adair by lease & release in the yr. 1736**. The sd. Wm. Adair by his will devised his real estate to Trustees in Trust to raise £2000 a yr. as an accumulating fund to be laid out in land to increase his real estate for his Nephew Alexr. Adair wh. remr. over. The sd. Wm. Adair was pd. the sd. rent by the Compy. as appears by their Books from the yr. 1769 until his death in 1783 & the same was probably [was] so paid to him from the time of his purchase in 1736. Since Wm. Adair's death the Compy. have paid the rent to the **sd. Alexr. Adair**, with the privity of his Trustees up to Lady day 1798. Both Wm. & Alexr. Adair always allowed the Land Tax out of the rent at the full rate, so that when the tax was 3/- in the pound, they received £425, & when at 4/- only £400 pr. anm. for the rent. **Mr Adair now disputes allowing the full Land Tax for the future**, alleging the props. are not rated to the full extent of their profits, & that he ought only to allow the tax in the same proportion, the Compy. or proprietors of shares pay, after reciting various sections & clauses of the Land Tax Act for the service of the yr. 1798 (wh. is now made perpetual) as applicable to the present question particularly the 50ᵗʰ & 31ˢᵗ in the former it is enacted that "any person or persons claiming by any grant or purchase from or under the Crown, shall allow 4/- for every pound of the sd. rents" & by the latter it is "declared, that the fee farm rents for which a deduction or allowance of 4/- in the pound is intended to be made by the sd. Act, are such fee farm rents only as are answerable to his Majesty, or have been purchased from the Crown by virtue of two made 22ⁿᵈ & 23ʳᵈ of Charles 2ⁿᵈ". The charge for the Land Tax remained the same for many yrs. together, but in 1793 the Commiss's. thinking the Compy. was rated too low, they set a considerably higher rate, at which it has continued ever since, tho' still not amounting to 4/- in the pound upon the profits (Footnote 'x'. The assesst. the 22nd May 1797 "upon all & every person or persons, having shares or interest in the New River at £18000 pr. Anm. £3600").

Your opinion is desired –
Whether under all the circumstances of the case, Mr Adair is not bound to allow the Land Tax out of his rent charge, in the same manner that he always used to do, & if he will not accept the rent in that manner. Whether the Compy. may not properly refrain the paymt. & refer him to the props. of the King's Moiety, to recover the same of them in such way as he shall think fit? Or do you think Mr Adair has any & what remedy against the Compy. for his rent, & if not what remedy has he agst. the props. of the King's Moiety for the same? But if you are clearly of opinion that Mr Adair ought to have any abatement of the Tax, may the Co. safely make it without the danger of being involved in disputes with the proprietors of the King's Moiety who are liable to the paymt. & are very numerous? And if Mr Adair's claim is doubtful & the proprietors of the King's Moiety are willing to put it in a way of being decided, what method will it be most advisable to take for that purpose. By the letters patent of the 17th Jas. 1st the Corporation was created, & the property vested in that Corporation, subject to an Acct. for a moiety of the profits to the King. By the **subseqt. Deed of the same yr. which I presume was enrolled**, the Corporation granted to Trustees for the King a moiety of the profits, in performance of the intent of the prior Instrumt. This in trust in a moiety of the profits, wh. could only be enjoyed by acct. with the Corporation was granted by King Chas. 1st to Sir Hugh Middleton subjt. to a covenant for paymt. to the King's Receiver & ... for the City of London or into the receipt of the King's Exchequer at Westr. for the use of the King, his heirs & successors of the yearly rent or sum of £500. This yearly sum was aliened for yrs. by Chas. 2nd & granted absolutely by King William to a trustee of the Earl of Albermarle; & the grant authorised the paymt. to the Grantee his heirs & assigns, instead of the paymt. to the King's Receiver, or into the Exchequer, & the King also authorised the receiving of the rent in the name of his Majesty his heirs or successors, or in the name of the Grantee his heirs or assigns. As an assign of his Grantee Mr Adair claims. & is title is to the paymt. of £500 a yr. out of a moiety of the clear profits of the Compy. for wh. the Compy. are accountable to the props. of the shares of what is called the King's Moiety. The Land Tax Acts authorise these props. to make a deduction out of this paymt. in respt. of the Ld. Tax payable by them on their moiety of the clear profits; & this deduction must be made in proportion to the sum pd. for that moiety, unless this can be deemed a rent answerable to his Majesty, within the meaning of the Ld. Tax Acts; for it is clearly not a rent sold under ... ... Act of Chas. 2nd. I think it cannot be deemed a rent still answerable to his Majesty, nor do I conceive that the Letters patent of King Wm. could authorise the Grantee to use prerogative process for recovery of the rent; or that after paymt. made to the Grantee it could have been at the election of either party that it shd. be pd. to the King's Receiver Genl. or into the ... of the Exchequer; & I apprehend this special privilege & advantage is one of the special privileges & advantages, which the preamble states could not well be transferr'd without the aid of Parliamt. Upon the whole therefore I think Mr Adair is not bound to allow 4/- in the pound out of the £500 a yr., but only a sum proportioned to the value of the Moiety of the profits answered to the proprietors of the King's Moiety. As however the allowance of 4/- in the pd. has constantly been made hitherto, & the Co. in payg. Mr Adair act only as agents of the props. of the King's Moiety, I conceive they are not warranted in altering the allowance, without the consent of those props. I conceive Mr Adair's remedy is agt. those props. In what manner he can have remedy, I am much at a loss to say, the interest of those props. being in the profits only, so that in effect, they can only have acct. agt. the Compy. accordg. to the statemt. of the Deed of the 28th Octr. 17 Jas. 1st & the claim of Mr Adair under his grant seems also to be persl. agt. those props. as there is nothing upon wh. he can distrain, supposing this rent to be one, to wh. power of distress wd. otherwise have been given under the 4 of Geo. 2. I apprehend therefore he is without remedy unless he can have relief by a Bill in Equity to wch. all the props. of shares in the King's Moiety ought to be parties. Signed John Mitford, Lincoln's Inn, 31st Decr. 1799 –

Mr Adair laid his case also before Sir John Mitford – not so fully & clearly stated as the above, the opinion not so long, but in substance the same' (J. Walker's Commonplace Book, p474-471 page Nos. downwards, Zc1, ELSC&A; 11, p82 June 1661 to John Robinson, then John Buckworth, after which Eleanor daughter of Sir Edward Villiers; 14B2, pp450-451 John Robinson, John Buckworth, Eleanor Villiers). **Then held by the Adair family until 1956 when redeemed by the MWB**.

Summarised: 1660 grant of rent cancelled and reissued to John Buckworth, in 1664 to Eleanor Villiers after current term for 41-years, 1691 expiry of first grant, 1697 for ever to the first Earl of Albermarle. 1735 conveyed to 2nd Earl, 1737 to the Adair family (1805 Adair v. NRC action dismissed, the NRC to continue deducting the rent from the King's shares) and held by them until purchased by the MWB in 1956 for £8,230. At first the MWB not paying but in 1908 [Sir Shafto] Adair v. NRC & MWB confirming the payment (15I, pp192-207).

7 Dec. 1631 (Death of Sir Hugh Myddelton): Died 7 Dec. 1631 ((Sloane MSS 866, Richard Smith obituary, B.M.) 11, p23/83; 8, p45/46 d. 7th buried 10th).

Thus died "**a man full of enterprise and resources, an energetic and untiring worker, a great conqueror of obstacles and difficulties, an honest and truly noble man, and one of the most distinguished benefactors the City of London has ever known**" (13, p152).

Buried 10 Dec. 1631 at St Matthews Church, NW-side of Friday Street (See separate site plan & print). The church destroyed in the Great Fire 1666, rebuilt 1685, taken down 1883, all burial remains transferred to Ilford Cemetery, none identified as being those of Sir Hugh Myddelton or of his family, probably removed at the 1685 rebuilding by Wren.

When living in London, Hugh had worshipped here, and where from 1598-9 & 1599-1600 he had served as churchwarden, and for several years audited the accounts ((St. Matthew's Churchwardens' Accounts, Guildhall Library) 11, p23 Note 2). It was where five of his daughters and six of his sons were baptized, and where his first wife and those of his children who died young (including his eldest son) were buried.

Just SE of St Paul's Cathedral:

"This church stood on the **west side, at the northern end close to Cheapside** and was taken down in 1881" ("London City Churches" by A.E. Daniell, 1907).

Just N of Fulham Palace 'St Peter's, in Reporton Road, which contains a pulpit that might make more ancient churches proud, for it is of carved oak, and is supposed to be the work of Grinling Gibbons [1648-1721]. It came from St Matthew's, Friday Street' (1K10, p24). 1881 Mission District, 1883 St Peter's Anglican church, Filmer Road/Reporton Road, Fulham, **still open** (GENUKI website). The reredos said to be in the hall of Polesden Lacy, Gt. Bookham, Surrey; the communion table at St Vedast-alias-Foster, Foster Lane; the font & pulpit at St Andrews-by-the- Wardrobe (Wikipedia). After WW2 bombing that part of Friday Street was built over in the 1950s by **New Change Buildings [presumably Bank of England Offices], the courtyard being the site of St Matthews**, but once again is being redeveloped (Wikipedia).

Sir Hugh Myddelton's Will (21 Nov. 1631): Made out his will on 21 Nov. 1631, which was proved on 21 Dec. 1631 (11A, p4). Sir Hugh made out his will on the 21 Nov. 1631, three weeks prior to his death, being "sick in bodie" but "strong in mind" for which he praised God (13, p149; B75-1, p93 20 Nov. 1631 dated will; 7H2, p93 20 Nov. 1631). Following is the text of his 21 Nov. 1631 will:

"In the name of God, Amen. The one and twentieth daie of November, in the yeare of our Lord God according to the computacion of the Church of England one thousand six hundred thirty and one, I, SIR HUGH MIDDELTON, barronett, and cittizen and gouldsmith of London, being (though sicke of bodie) of good and perfect mind and memorie (thankes be to Almightie God therefore), doe make and ordaine this my last will and testament, hereby revoking and makinge void all former wills whatsover. First, therefore, I comende my soule into the handes of Almightie God my Creator, Redeemer, and Sanctifier; and my bodie to the earth in hope of a joyful resurrection. And I appoint my funeralls to be accordinge to the discrecion of myne executrix hereinafter named. And it is my will and desire this my bodie be buried in the parish church of Saint Matthewe in London, where I was sometimes a parishioner, and a monument to be sett upp there for me at the discrecion of my executrix. And touchinge the disposicion of my personall and reall estate wherewith it hath pleased God to blesse me, I will that all my debtes which I shall owe at the time of my decease, with the charge of my funeralls, shalbe first paid and satisfied, and then I give and bequeath to my deare and loving wife Dame Elizabeth Middelton [Note 3: Elizabeth, daughter and heiress of John Olmstead of Ingatestone, Essex] all the chaines, rings, jewells, pearles, bracelettes, and gould buttons, which shee hath in her custodie, and useth to weare at festivalls. And also the deepe silver bason, the spout pott and maudlin cupp of silver, and the smale bowle, all which were given her. And whereas I have already given to my sonne William Middelton [Note 4: Succeeded his father as Baronet, for his descendants see Gents. Mag. lxii, p784] his full porcion which I intended to him out of my personall estate; I doe hereby give and bequeath to my said sonne William the some of one hundred poundes, and to my daughter in lawe his wife the some of tenn poundes to buy her a ring. And whereas my daughter Jane

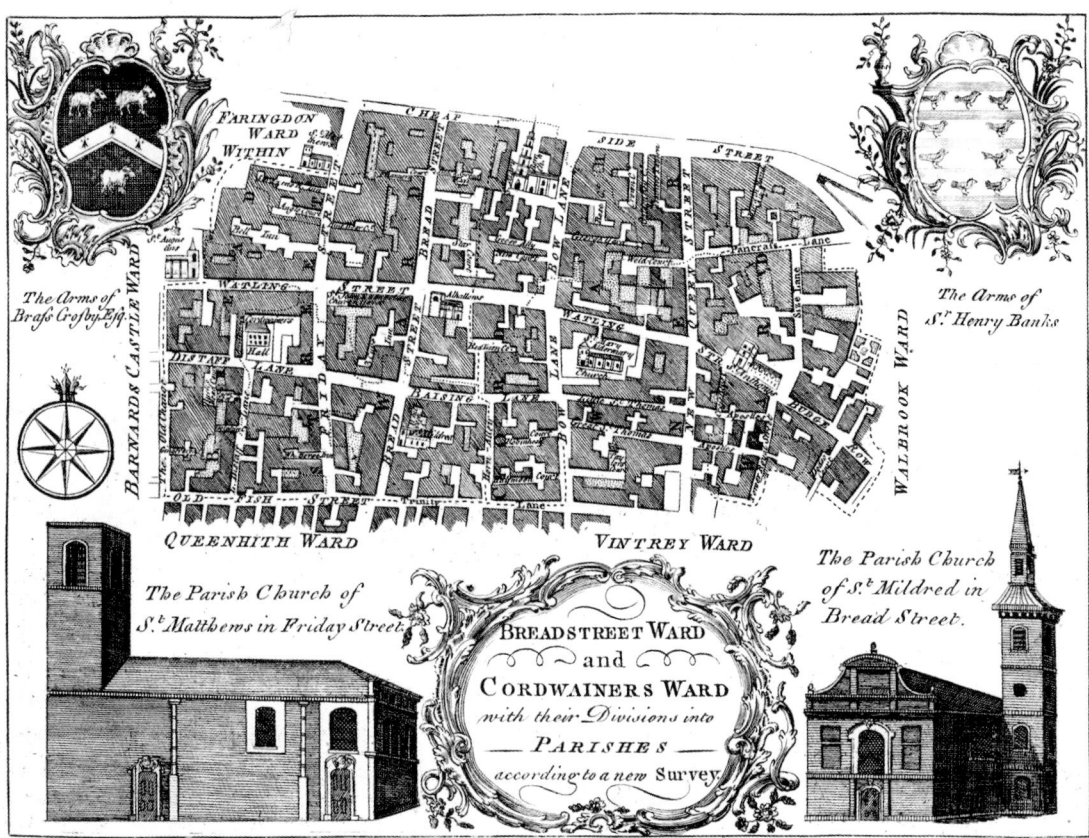

ABOVE: 1772 plan showing St Matthews Church **(SITE OF)**, Friday Street, **very Top-L** (AN904305, © Trustees of the British Museum).

BELOW: 1812 St Matthews Church, Friday Street. **Sir Hugh Myddelton buried here 10 Dec.1631**, church destroyed 1666, rebuilt 1685, removed 1883, all burial remains to Ilford Cemetery ((G. Shepherd) AN737518, © Trustees of the British Museum).

hath also had her full portion, upon her marriage, I give to her husband Doctor Chamberlaine [Note 5: 'Peter Chamberlaine, M.D., born 8 May 1601, died 23 Dec. 1683 ... had 11-sons & 2-daughters, and at his death a very numerous posterity. ... buried at Woodham Mortimer, Essex. See Morant's 'Hist. of Essex', i., 342, and the octavo History vol. v., p293'] and my said daughter Jane the severall somes of ten poundes to buy each of them a ringe. And whereas also my daughter Hester [Note 6: 'Married to Richard Price'] hath had one thousand poundes in part of her porcion of nynetenne hundred poundes, and the other nyne hundred poundes are deteyned till the articles on the parte of the Ladie Price are performed which were agreed on for and on the behalfe of her grandchild Richard Price, Esquier, being within age at the time of the marriage of the said Hester, I give over and above the said nyne hundred poundes remayninge to be paid to my said sonne Richard Price and Hester his wife the severall somes of tenn poundes a peece to buy each of them a ringe. Item. I give and bequeath to my sonne Henry Myddelton [Note 7: '... baptised at St Matthews's, Friday-street, 14 June 1607. For his posterity see Gents. Mag. Aug. 1792, p698'] the some of fower hundred poundes. Item, I give to my sonne Simon Middelton the like some of foure hundred poundes. Item. I give and bequeath to my daughter Elizabeth Middelton the some of five hundred poundes. Item, I give and bequeath to my daughter Ann the like some of five hundred poundes. Item, I give and bequeath to the poore of the parish of Henllan, where I was borne, the some of twentie poundes; and to the poore of the towns of Denbigh, in the countie of Denbigh, I give the like some of twentie poundes. Item, I give and bequeath to the poore of the parish of Amwell in the countie of Hartford the some of five poundes. Item, I give and bequeath to my nephew Captaine Roger Middelton the some of thirtie poundes. Item, I give to Richard Newell the some of thirtie poundes, to the end he shall continue his care in the workes of the Mynes Royall wherein he is now ymployed. Item, I give to Howell Jones the some of twentie poundes, to th'ende he shall alsoe continue his care in the Water-Workes, wherein he hath benne and still is imployed. And my will and meaninge that my executrix hereafter named shall have two yeares tyme next after my decease to make payment of all and everie the legacies in this my will mentioned, except shee cann sooner raise them out of my personall estate.

And for the better payment of my debtes and legacies in this my will bequeathed, I doe hereby give to myne executrix hereafter named full power and authoritie to bargayn and sell all the messuages, landes, tenementes, and hereditamentes whatsoever, with their appurtenances, mentioned in an indenture of mortgage dated the nyneteenth of March, in the yeare of our Lord one thowsand six hundred and thirtie, made betweene me the said Sir Hugh Middelton and my sonne William Middelton of th'one part, and Sir Thomas Middelton Knighte and Alderman of the cittie of London [Note A1: '... Lord Mayor in 1613, was Sir Hugh's elder brother'], Rowland Heighling, and others of the other part, as by the said indenture appeareth, desiring my said executrix and my nephew Roger Middelton to doe their best endeavours to sell the said messuages, landes, and tenementes to their best value. And if it shall happen that my said executrix dye before shee shall have made sale of the said messuages, landes, and tenementes, then I give full power and authoritie to my two sonnes William Middelton and Henry Middelton to make sale of them and to sell them to their best value for the payment of my debtes and legacies aforesaid. And my further will and meanings is that all my partes and shares in the Mynes Royall in the principallitie of Wales shalbe also sould for the better payment of my debts and legacies by myne executrix hereafter named. AND FOR AND CONCERNING all my partes and shares of and in the New River and waterworkes brought from Chadwell and Amwell in the countie of Hartford to the city of London, my will and meaninge is, and I doe hereby give and bequeath all my said partes and shares in the said waterworkes, together with the rentes, arrerages of rentes, and proffites of them, and every of them, to my saide lovinge wife Dame Elizabeth Middelton, to have and to hould for and dureinge her naturall life; and if the moneys arisinge out of the sale and proffitts of the messuages, landes, and tenementes appointed to bee sould, and the Mynes Royall aforesaid, and all my other personall estate, shall not prove sufficient to pay all my debtes and legacies, then my further will and meaninge is, and I doe hereby give full power and authoritie to my executrix hereafter named, to sell fower of the said partes and shares, or soe many of the said fower shares as shalbe sufficient to raise moneys sufficient to make payment of the residue of my debtes and legacies which shall soe happen to be unpaide; and after the decease of my said wife Dame Elizabeth I give and bequeath one part and share of the said river and waterworks to my sonne William Middelton and his heires; and one part and share of the said river and waterworkes I give to my sonne Henry Middelton and his heires; and one other part and share of the said river and waterworks I give to my sonne Simon Middelton [Note A2: 'Said to have been father of Sir Hugh, created a baronet in 1681 See Gents. Mag. vol. lxii, p900'] and his heires; and one other part or share of the said river and waterwourkes I give to my daughter Elizabeth and her heires; and one other part or share of the said river and waterwourkes I give to my daughter Anne Middelton and her heires; and one other part or share of the said river or waterwourkes I give and bequeath to Richard Rogers, - Terry, Walter Merrell, John Williams, John Hawes, Richard Millard, John Gravett, William Cuttes, John Acton, and Robert Hooke, cittizens and gouldsmiths of London, and their successours assistants of the Company of Gouldsmithes, London, forever; upon trust and confidence that the profittes of the said part and share shalbe by them disposed and disbursed in manner and forme followinge, that is to say: every halfe yeare after the decease of my said wife in weekly portions of twelve pence a peece to the poore of the said Company of Gouldsmiths of the said citty, by the discretion of the wardens and assistantes of the said company for the tyme being or the greater number of them, and especiallie to such poore men of my name, kindred, or countrymen as are or shalbe free of the said companie [Note A3: Long note on distributing its income]; and for the better declaracion of what partes are here ment and intended to be devised as aforesaid, I doe hereby declare that the one halfe of the water wourkes are devided into sixe and thirty partes or shares, **thirteene of which partes or shares are to my selfe belonginge** and are in the name of my selfe and other feoffees in trust to my use and the proffettes by me receeved, and therefore my meaninge is that the six severall partes or shares hereby devised and given are sixe of the partes and shares of my said thirteene partes and noe other. AND MY FURTHER WILL and meaninge is and I doe hereby devise and give to my said wife Dame Elizabeth my house and landes at Bush hills in the parish of Edmonton in the county of Middlesex, with all the household stuff and furniture therein, to have and to hould the same to her owne use forever duringe her naturall life; and after her decease my will is that my youngest sonne Simon Middelton shall have and injoye the same to him and his heires. And alsoe my will and meaninge is that my said wife shall have the keeping and wearing of that great jewel [Note A4: 'This jewel is shown upon Sir Hugh's breast in his portrait'] which was given unto me by the Lord Maior of the cittie of London and the aldermen of the same, and that she doe give and leave the same after her decease to such one of my sonnes as she shall thinke most worthy to weare and enjoye the same. Item, I give to my brother Robert Bateman the some of twentie poundes to buy him a ringe. Item, I give to Peter Hinde and his wife twentie poundes to be devided betweene them, desiringe the saide Peter Hinde to continue his care in the workes I have ymploied him in. Item, I give to Mr. William Lewyn the yearly some of twenty poundes to be paid unto him every halfe yeare out of the rentes and proffittes of the said Water-works, by equall porcions, for and duringe his naturall life, to the end that he shall doe his best endeavor for the advancement of the said Water workes. Item, I give and bequeath to all my men servants (except the boy in kitchen) to each of them the some of five poundes which shalbe dwelling with me at the tyme of my decease. And to the said boy and Elizabeth my maidservant to each of them fortie shillinges. And I doe make and ordain; nominate and appoint, my said lovinge wife Dame Elizabeth Middelton my full and sole executrix of this my last will and testament. And I doe make my nephew Sir Thomas Middelton Knight, my brother Bateman, my nephewes Roger Middelton and Richard Middelton, overseers of this my last will and testament; praying my said executrix and overseers to see this my last will and testament trulie performed. Item, I give to any nephewe Sir Thomas Middelton twenty poundes, to my nephewe Timothie Middelton the some of tenn poundes. Item, I give to Mr. William Lewis fiftie poundes. Item, to my nephewe John Chambers and his wife to each of them five poundes a peece to buy each of them a ringe. Item, to Robert Berners esquire I give five poundes to buy him a ringe. In wittnes whereof I have hereunto sett my hande to everie sheete the daie and yeare first within written, and sealed the same with my seale. And my further will is and I doe give to my nephewe Richard Middelton and his wife five poundes a peece to each of them to buy each of them a ringe. Item, to Richard Trihurst tenn poundes; and soe I doe declare this to be my last will and testament. **HUGH MIDDELTON**".

"Theis eight sheetes of paper before annexed contayne the last will and testament of Sir Hugh

Middelton, baronett, and were by himselfe subscribed and sealed and the same by him published and declared to be his last will and testament in the presence of us, this one and twentith daie of Nov., 1631. Roger Mydl, Robert Berners, Will. Lewyn, Mathewe Hobman, William Jones, William Graie, Richard Dryhurst. "Proved at London before Sir Henry Marten, LL.D. on the 21st Dec., 1631, by the oath of Lady Elizabeth Middelton relict of the deceased, and executor in the above will named" (('Wills from Doctors'-commons' Vol. lxxxiii, p92, Camden Society) 14B2, pp463-465; C6, p137 condensed version). Comments on Myddelton's will (11, pp130-132).

Goldsmiths' Share 1631-1904 (15I, p71 details). The company not exactly complying to the terms of his will, the NRC share held by them until 1904 when converted to MWB stock (11, pp133-134).

Sir Hugh's 15-Children: '... issue of Sir Hugh and Elizabeth [Olmstead] is recorded as follows:

Thomas	**Born**	1598	**Died**	1600.
Elizabeth M.		1600		1605
Hugh		1601		1630 [?; see page xiii].
William		1603		? [2nd baronet, and descendants Gents. Mag. lxii, p784].
Jane		1604		? [married a Dr. Peter Chamberlaine; also see page xiii].
James		1605		1620
Henry		1607		? [baptised 14 June 1607, and descendants Gents. Mag. Aug. 1792, p698; also see page xiii].
Elizabeth		1608		? [see page xiii].
Anne		1610		1635 [see page xiii].
John		1611		1623 [see page xiii].
Hester [or Ester]		1612		1651 [married a Richard Price; as page xiii].
Mary		?		Buried at Edmonton Church
Simon		?		Buried at Edmonton Church.
Robert		?		?
Bartholomew		?		?

Of the foregoing 15 children, it is clear in Sir Hugh Myddelton's will that only three sons and one daughter were then living' ('The Enfield Gazette & Observer', 13 Jan. 1939, p8 Continued, ELSC&A).

Inaccuracies in Number of Children (Needs Modern Research?) Prob. 9-Sons & 6-Daughters: Leaving a widow, and of his 15 children [7-sons & 8-daughters], just 3 sons and 5 daughters surviving him, with 7 of his children having died before him (13, p150 surviving three sons & five daughters; C6, p137 of his 15 children, just 3 sons and 1 daughter were still living; 11A, p5 Myddelton had ten sons and six daughters; 11, p130 surviving daughters Jane, Hester & Elizabeth/p132 left NR shares to William, Henry & Simon, & Elizabeth & Anne/p134 7-sons (3-surviving) & 8-daughters/pp135-136 surviving sons William, Henry & Simon).

Thomas: Bap. Jan. 1599 buried May 1600, **Hugh** bap. Sept. 1601 died post-1623 (11, p16).

William: His heir inherited the baronetcy & Ruthin estate, married Eleanor Harris and d.1652 (13, p150; also see page xiii).

Mary & Anne (('History of Shoreditch' by Ellis) 14B2, pp467).

Simon: Born c.1612 (15J, p117; also see page xiii).

Simon Myddelton's daughter Elizabeth married John Lane, son Myddelton Lane born 7 March 1685/6 ('The Visitation of London begun 1687' ed. by T.C. Wake & C.P. Hartley, London, 2004). Another Mrs [sic] Elizabeth Myddelton of Nottingham eldest daughter of Sir Hugh Myddelton [? Bart] d. aged 43, 6 Jan. 1725, according to an inscription on the N-wall of the tower at old St James church, Clerkenwell (14B2, p467). Nephew Captain Roger Middleton remembered in his will.

MYTH & Prob. TRUTH: '... Middleton died in reduced circumstances, unable to pay a loan which the City had advanced him on the progress of the work' (1K10F, p9). He did not die a poor man, according to his will with considerable wealth, his widow paying back an amount reduced by the City, and William his successor, presumed to have paid back some other outstanding debts (11, p130 did not die a poor man). The confusion that he died poor, probably a mistaken identity with the separate baronetcy of Sir Hugh Myddelton of Hackney, who died later in reduced circumstances (15I, p42).

Tributes to Sir Hugh Myddelton

19 July 1794 (Statue in Gold?): A 'Morning Chronicle' writer stating that: "To the memory of

Sir Hugh Myddelton the **inhabitants of London should have raised a statue in gold**" (6D, p341; 15D, p3; (19 July 1794 'Morning Post') 15J, p202; 14B2, p465).
1806 (Described): Regarding the construction of the New River '.., which in the then state of knowledge of canal-making, **may be justly styled immense:** …' (1K9, Vol. 4, p51).
1764 & 1801 ('History of Commerce') by Adam Anderson: "suitable to the power and grandeur of ancient Rome **in its zenith of glory**" (14D6, p132; 1K9, Vol. 4, p389; first published 1764, 1801 edn., and 1967 facsimile of 1801 edition in 4 vols.).
1835 (Extract): The Christian Patriotism and benevolent activity of Sir Hugh Myddelton 'will ever be considered as one of the noblest monuments of our country, **worthy of a comparison with the aqueducts of ancient Rome**, …' ((Printed extract from 'The Christian's Penny Magazine' publ. every Sat., No. 143 (possibly Vol. IV), Feb. 28, 1835, p65) Islington LHC).

Portraits of 1st Sir Hugh
Original Johnson Portrait: The original 1628 Jansen (via Sir Hugh's daughter Jane) thought to be in the Mary Frick Jacobs Collection, Baltimore Museum of Art, Maryland, USA.
Replica painted by Johnson: A similar version (via Sarah daughter of Simon Myddelton) in the Duke of Portland's collection at Welbeck Abbey, **in 1722 engraved by George Vertue** the painting attributed with 'C.J. fe[it]. 1632' as confirmed by the NPG is probably a replica copy.
Nov. 1633 a portrait of Sir Hugh attributed to Cornelius Johnson/Jansen sent by Lady Myddelton to the Goldsmiths' Company, possibly the one still there with a 1631 date (probably referring to his death) on the frame (11, p147).
> Simon Myddelton in 1673 presenting a portrait of his father to the Goldsmiths' Co. but appears to have been lost. This copy said **engraved by E. Scriven for 'Portraits of Illustrious Persons of Gt. Britain'** by Edmund Lodge (11, p137/146/147).

Replica Painted by Johnson or Later Copy?: Lady Myddelton's original possibly destroyed in the 1666 Great Fire may have been replaced by Simon Myddelton's copy, the original frame said with an 1644 inscription (thought post Lady Myddelton's death benefaction), the present frame c./post-1725 presumably with 1631 date (11, pp146-147).
Prob. Johnson Replica (via Simon Myddelton): In 1866 owned by the Rev. J.M. St. Clere Raymond of Belchamp Walter, Essex, then in possession of the founder of the White Star Line one T.H. Ismay, sold 1908 when ascribed by 'C. Jansen' for only 50-guineas, via several owners to Mr & Mrs R.S. Frankel of Woodside, California (11, p148).
New River Company's Jansen Copy: Destroyed in the 1769 fire at their offices in Bridewell Precinct, having a copy of the Goldsmiths' version painted in 1773 by Nathaniel Hone for £42, presumably today with Thames Water (11, p148; 12, p27 re-gilt 1821).
Chirk Castle Jansen Copy: Source unknown but likely purchased in an 1859 London sale; the copy of Sir Hugh at Chirk Castle ascribed to Anthonisz bears no resemblance and is unlikely to be Sir Hugh ((NPG note) 11, pp148-149).
NPG's Jansen Copy: Said formerly at Gwaenynog (William Myddelton's family) in possession of the Rev. Robert Myddelton who in the 1870s sold it to a Chester dealer, and purchased by Major Cornwallis-West, sold by his son Major G.F.M. Cornwallis-West of Ruthin in 1928 at Christie's, when purchased by the National Portrait Gallery for £50 ((Based on 16 Jan. 1929 statement by R.F. Myddelton of Colne Mead, Rickmansworth) 11, p148).
> **Science Museum Library Copy (Unlikely Sir Hugh):** In c.1600 dress but unlike other portraits such that if a Myddelton could be another member of the Myddelton family (11, p149).
> **Another Copy (Unlikely Sir Hugh):** At the 1878 death of Sir Thomas Myddelton-Biddulph of Chirk Castle obtained by Francis Morgan of Romsey, Hants., but again unlike other portraits such that if a Myddelton could be another member of the Myddelton family ((Details via a G.C. Berry photo of the portrait) 11, p149).
> **Not a likeness (Sir H. Myddelton's Head Sign) 'Evening' by Hogarth:** (11, p149), his engraving not very accurate at all, also locating Sir H. Myddelton's Head on same side of the New River as Sadlers Wells.

LADY MYDDELTON: The Goldsmiths Co. in 1897 purchasing a portrait of Lady Myddelton said to be by the same artist (with 1643 on the frame prob. referring to her death; thought of earlier c.1610-15 date because of her dress) from Belchamp Hall, Essex.

Simon Myddelton's 2nd wife Mary Soame through which he acquired Goldingham Hall (under a mile from Belchamp Hall) becoming the residence of his son Hugh, the same Sir Hugh Myddelton of Hackney who died destitute under the name of Raymond, such that via him or his estate to the Raymonds. The portrait in 1803 at Belchamp Hall the residence of the Rev. Samuel Raymond, 1866 owned by the Rev. J.M. St. Clere Raymond of Belchamp Walter, Essex, at whose 1894 death the portrait **sold 1897 to the Goldsmiths' Co.** (11, p132/pp147-148).

Later Statues erected to Sir Hugh Myddelton
1800 memorial urn erected by Robert Mylne on S-island at Amwell Pond on New River ((Gents. Mag. 1802, Vol. lxxvii, part 2, p988 described) 14B2, pp465-6).
1845 statue by Samuel Joseph high up on side of Royal Exchange, London (14B2, pp466 by Carew; 15J, p202 adds the right hand renewed 1999).
1862 imposing marble statue of Sir Hugh Myddelton by John Thomas, on S-corner of Islington Green (14B2, pp466-7 details).
Former 1869 Bronze Statue of Sir Hugh on Holborn Viaduct, destroyed by enemy action in WW2 (15J, p202 demolished 1950s).
c.1925 a nearly life-size Statue of Sir Hugh in the yard at NRH, badly damaged when hit by a van, such that buried under the floor of the Old Windmill, New River Head (6D, p341/359; 15J, p202 mention), at least it had a reverential burial.

1633 (First NR Dividends) 24-years from Start: Because of the costs of laying down the wooden pipes, and making repairs and improvements, the New River was not in profit until 1622 (it seems with just the King being paid his share), the first dividends apparently being paid in 1633 (£11. 19s. 1d.), 14 years after incorporation
1633 (Purchase of Chest) for NRC Charters: A 3-lock chest purchased and kept at the Governor's house (in an area destroyed by the 1666 Great Fire), with keys to separate locks kept by the Governor, Deputy Gov. and Treasurer (15J, p76); but charters known to have survived.
1634 (Rival Scheme): City petitioning to bring water from the Roundhead near Tyburn for the Conduits (7K1, pp19-20). 1812 Tyburn Springs disposed of by the Corporation to the Bishop of London (7K3, p192).
1637 Middleton v. Backhouse (15I, p80).
3 May 1642 NRC's third Bill also unsuccessful on eve of Civil War to get recognised by Parliament (11, p75; 15I, p31 c.1640; 15J, p63).
19 July 1643 (Death) of Lady Myddelton: Died aged 63 (11, p132).
19 July 1644 (Sir William) Seeks Warrant: Sir William Middleton, Bart., Governor of NRC, petitions the Lords of the Council for a warrant to apprehend persons who cut or spoil the banks, bridges, or wharves of the Co. (HL/PO/JO/10/1/171 Main Papers, Parliamentary Archives).
1644 (Vandalism on the New River): There was more vandalism on the New River, since 'sundry ill disposed and disaffected persons' had 'dammed up the passage of the river, cut the banks', &c. ((H.M.C. 6th Report, p18b) 11, p67 Note 2).
Fri. 9 Nov. 1649 (NRC Courte): At Symon Myddelton's house, Paule's Churchyard, London.

Sir William Myddelton, Governor.	Henry Borlase.
Issac Jones, Treasurer.	Nichas Backhouse.
Sir John Thorowgood.	Symon Myddelton.
Richard Neville.	William Cuddrington.
Bennett Hoskins.	Henry Harewell.
Henry Myddelton of Lovesgrove.	Thomas Thyn.
William Backhouse.	Wm. Thorowgood.

'John Stanseby came to this court and requested that his claim might be entred to ye 36th parte of ye New River wch Sir John Backhouse purchased off Edward Colthurst the youngest (?) Sonne of Edmond Colethurste, wch clayme is made in the right of his wife Margery daughter and heire of Henry Colthurst ye eldest Sonne of ye said Edmond wch clayme is entered accordingly. The **Committee appointed last**

Courte for ye frame at Highbury or any foure of them, whereof the Governor or Deputy or Trear to be one, are desired by this Courte to **advise and order ye making of ye River in an Arch of brick through ye upper parte of Islington** and put ye same in execucon when and how they shall think fitt and direct, And Mr Trear is desired to issue out such monies therefore as they shall appoint' (('The Tunnel at Islington (Essex Road)') 8A1, 3/3-2). At this meeting Simon Myddelton appointed Treasurer (15J, p76).

Post-1652 Sir Hugh Myddelton's Granddaughter's 4-Shares: At the 1652 death of Sir William Myddelton (1st Sir Hugh's heir), his daughter Elizabeth inheriting 4-NRC shares & marrying John Grene, who via these shares became Clerk to the NRC. At her death 1673/5, settling the shares on their children. But in the fol. year marrying Joanna his servant and having 4-more children, such that by 1685 deeds tried to avoid the trust, but the deeds set aside by the Lord Chancellor. Entering into a deed of variation in 1694 with his son William, then promoting a private bill to reclaim the power of disposition over the shares, but nothing more heard after a mention in a 1697 Select Committee. John Grene d.1705, William filing a bill to set aside the variation, but upheld by the House of Lords. The shares after Joanna's & William's death by entail to his only daughter Jane, who married the Rev. Richard Ellicombe/Ellacombe of Stoke Canon, at some time selling two of the shares but retaining 2 until the 1904 takeover, allowing Canon H.N. Ellacombe the vicar of Bitton near Bristol a seat on the NRC Ltd board and d.1916 aged 96 (15I, pp68-70; 11, p141 Ellicombe; 14B2, p467 Elizabeth d. 1675).

1664 (NRC Meetings): NRC meetings at the Treasurer's (Simon Myddelton's) house at St Paul's Chains ((Acc 2558/NR13/7, LMA) 15J, p76).

   Simon Myddelton NOT Reinstated as NRC Treasurer: Simon Myddelton (1st Sir Hugh's youngest son) after being dismissed as NRC Treasurer bringing a *mandamus* to get himself reinstated, but was unsuccessful ((Three manuscript & 3 printed reports) 15I, pp101-103).

11 April 1665 (5-years New River Maintenance) by John Grene: 'For bringing the water from the springhead at Chadwell to the Round Pond at Islington for £500 an audit. To be for five years as from 25 March last',

   "Excepting out of this proposall the brick Arch which runs through Islington underground yo/r not having been at any chardge thereabouts for many years, and i(t …)s may be daily feared which whenever it should … happen the chardge will be greater to mend it then (to turn) the Ryver into its antient Channel" (('From John Grene & Gregory Hardwick's proposal') 8A1, 3/3-2), probably charged twice a year.

For 5-years up to 25 March 1670 retaining existing workers as long as they do their duty, maintaining all country troughs, flashes, and bridges, in 1670 renewed for 3-years at £1,000 per annum (15J, p72).

1666 New River Water Turned Off at Height of Great Fire?: "The main of the New River at Islington was, it is said, shut down at the time of the Great Fire of London in 1666; and it was believed by some, who pretended to the means of knowing, that the supply of water had been stopped by Captain John Graunt, a papist, under whose name Sir William Petty published his observations on the bills of mortality - Burnet's 'Own Times', ed. 1823, Vol. i., p. 401" (13, p128 quote). At this time most of London's water supply was on the intermittent basis, so probably as such was turned off.

In times of fire, regulations had provided for pumps (early form of fire hydrants) to be inserted into the pipes at regular intervals, this forgotten about, such that streets were torn up to puncture the pipes, and the water pressure became non-existent (1G2, pp9-10), and useless for fighting fires.

   MYTH regarding Capt. John Grant (Fire of London): Maitland Vol. I, p435 referring to Burnet pp155-156, 'In order to inform myself in respect to Bishop Burnet's Relation regarding Dr Lloyd, the Countess of Clarendon and Mr Graunt, I applied to the Governor and Company of the New River who generously ordered Mr Jasper Bull, their Clerk, and Mr Henry Mill, their Engineer to let me have such Accounts belonging to the Company as were proper to be published. Whereupon I had recourse to their Minute-Book, wherein I found, that a general Court of the said Company was held at Mr Clifton's in Covert-Garden (a Tavern, I suppose, because the Company's Courts were long before and after kept, at such House) on the twenty-fifth of Sept. Anno 1666; at which Court John Grant was first admitted a member of the said NRC, (in the room of Alexander Broome deceased) in Trust for one of the Shares belonging to Sir William Backhouse … who dying in the Year 1669, Dame Flower Backhouse (I suppose his relict) became possessed of nine of his shares, and, on 12th Nov. in the same Year, she appointed the said Mr Grant as one of her trustees in the said Company: Whereby 'tis manifest that the above-recited Relation, which the Bishop had of Dr Lloyd and the Countess of Clarendon, **has not the least foundation**.

For by what has been said it is evident that **Mr Grant was not admitted into the Government of the NRC till twenty-three Days after the Breaking-out of the Fire of London**, and then put in trust by the above-named Sir William Backhouse …' (('John Graunt') 8A1, 3/3-2; ('London' by Maitland, p291, 1739) 8A1, 4/1-1; also see (Bur. Hist. Vol. I, p229/230 & 231; and Maitland Lon. p291, edit. 1739) H4-01, p431).

1666 (Cesar, knight, Hatcher, Masters & Levingston v. NRC Governor et al & Middleton): (Six Clerks Office, Court of Chancery, C 10/471/30, National Archives, Kew).

SIR EDWARD FORD'S WATERWORKS > Dec. 1667 NRC: Ordered to remove a water tower in grounds of Somerset House, but gets a licence for 3-new waterworks at Wapping Wall, Durham Yard & Marybone, Dec. 1667 taken over by the NRC. The Wapping undertaking granted by moiety to James Hayes & Thomas Toogood, 1665 Letters patent, and a short time after conveyed to Hartupp & Clayton, divided into 25-shares, 5-shares held by Hartupp & Clayton and 10-shares by Toogood, **in 1667 purchased by the NRC for £6,100** (15I, p36/p113 says purchased 1657; 15J, p231 further details; 7G5, pp18-20).

1670 Backhouse v. Middleton (15I, pp74-78).

1670-1684 (Audited Treasurer's Books) Abstracts: NRC with over 3,000 tenants, seven rent collectors and supplying St James's Palace & the Fleet prison (15I, p35).

1671 Cornbury v. Middleton (15I, pp74-78/195-196/206).

1685 (1686, 1689, 1704 & 1716) Royal Proclamations on the merits of the NR (15I, p107; 15J, p67 1689; 12, p20 1689).

28 Oct. 1687 NRC receipt for 16s. water rent of the Churchwardens of St Stephens Walbrook signed by turncock Aquila Garfield ((Guildhall Library) KJ1, p50; 7J1, p43 poor copy).

1688-1698 (Poll Tax/Income Tax) on NR Shares: Poll tax (assessed directly on income) of 2s. in every 20s. payable on rents or profits from New River shares, collectable from the shareholder's abode, but later like Land Tax collectable initially by the company and deducted (15I, pp120-121).

1689-1963 (Land Tax on NR Shares) 1 Will. & Mary, c.20: Every New River shareholder shall pay 1s. for every 20s. (later increasing to 2%, 3%, then up to 4% with fixed quotas for districts) of the clear yearly value, collectable initially by the company deducted from the next dividends. Post-1689 deducting 4s., such that **Clog shareholders received £400**, the £100 deducted by the company offset against the land tax assessment for the company's shareholders. In 1692 assessed at £3,600, but just below this during most of the C18th, post-1769 £3,300, from 1794 always £3,600, but rising at NRC takeovers, in the 1850s £3,627. Unless earlier redeemed, from 1794-1904 the NRC deducting £50 from each shares annual dividend, and also against the £3,600 assessment deducting £100 from the £500 p.a. Clog that was contested as unfair in 1805. In 1798 Land Tax made perpetual but redeemable (most of the company's liability for land under this tax redeemed post-1798, but not for the bed of the New River), from 1802 redeemable by NRC shareholders, the tax surviving until 1963. The Commandery Mantles never assessed for Middx., and most of the tax in Herts. redeemed by 1854. In 1857 a test case regarding the Herts. assessment deliberated that property (incl. the river) held in 1798 was liable only by the special section that was made perpetual, and property purchased thereafter taxable where it was located (15I, pp123-127/pp198-201).

C15th/1601-1967 (Local Rates/Poor Law): Occupiers of land taxed for the poor rate, subsequently based on annual rental value. In the 1813 legal case **R. v. NRC** found that although the land at Chadwell Spring had only an annual value of £5 they were rated at £300, which included the benefit of the NR itself, this confirmed by the court. The 1836 Parochial Assessments Act the rating based on the net annual value (15I, pp128-129).

1799-1815 & 1842 - Today (Income Tax) 39 Geo. III, c.13: At first based on income received, but from 1803 Act imposed at source, for private landowners the annual value of streams of water & watercourses charged at 1s. in the £, but if held by a company assessed as head office trade profits under Schedule D. But from 1806 Act all waterwork companies charged at 2s. in the £ under Schedule A, deductable from dividends, ending 1815. Re-introduced 1842 at 7d. in the £, companies assessed at head office on the preceding year, charged under Schedule A III, to deduct from dividends (15I, pp127-128).

1691-1723 (NRC 'River Surveyor') for Bush Hill to Ware: John White (1658-1741) buried in Enfield Churchyard (15I, p112 c.1691-1720). See later note on John White.

c.1700 John White earning £30 per annum, but on complaints of some injustice, resigning without offering to work his notice, recorded in a 23 Sept. 1723 letter to Jasper Bull. He died aged 83 in 1741 (((Jasper Bull's copy letter book Aug. & Sept. 1723) Acc 2558/NR13/9 & 188, LMA) 15J, p80).

6 March & 21 Dec. 1692-3 (NRC) Supplying St James' Palace: £20. 6s. 10d. owing to John Cocke, plumber to the NRC for work over past 4-years at St James's House, normally paid by the privy purse, referred to Sir Christopher Wren, who said it should be paid for repairing the pipes into St James's Palace, and that they had been in arrears with the NRC water rent until adjusted by the Lp$^{s.}$/Lords Comm$^{rs.}$ ((Treasury Papers, 1693, Vol. xxv., No. 17) 7K1, pp173-4).

NRC USED ELM & FIR PIPES

PROB. MYTH: For the wooden pipes "elms were planted along the river to supply wood for them" ((1947 article) 15-1).

1693, 1770, 1771-1814 & 1816 (MYTH) NRC only used Elm
> **(TRUTH) also used 'Firr' Timber for Pipes**

1656 (NRC) Lease Wharf: Part of a small wharf of Bridge House Estates leased to NRC by Alexander Hay, afterwards called 'Pipe Boarers Wharf', that may have been preceded here by a shop of the London Bridge Water Works (7G5, p31).

1667 (NRC Pumpbearers' Wharf) Pipebearers': Mention of the NRC's Pumpbearers' wharf near Bridge House (near Southwark end of London Bridge), leased from the Bridge Estates, City of London (OS3.18, p91; 1667 Mins. of Bridge House Estates Committee p91, also mentioned 1733).

"It has been stated that only elm trees were used for pipes, but I find an entry in the minutes dated as long ago as the 5 Oct. 1693, to the effect that "**This Company doth approve of firr timber with the rind on**, as sent for by Mr. Green's agreement, for which he is to pay 50/- the load, and if the merchant can afford it at that rate he may bring over more on the same terms, to serve for three and four-inch pipes", and again in a minute dated the 19 Aug. 1770, "Mr. Kinlock attended and agreed to deliver a quantity of 20 loads of firr timber at 10½d. per foot, the lighterage and delivery to be paid by the Company, and to return such as may be unsatisfactory for the Company's use". On the 27 June 1771, Dr. Grant agreed "to deliver firr timber, now in the river, at 10d. a foot, and 1/10 a yard for 3 inch, and 2/6 a yard for 4 inch pipe of firr timber, now coming from Scotland". Fir timber pipes were used as late as 1814, as shown by the following minute of 30 June 1814, "James Tracy, inspector, reported that some New River pipes were sent out of the Yard which required changing in many places as soon as put down, and R. Cheffins, Clerk of the Yard, was called upon, who stated that the firr timber in the yard was much injured in the late frost, and he was directed not to send any firr pipes to the W-end of town". In a minute dated 6 Dec. 1816, R. Cheffins, Clerk of the Yard, reported, "That Mr. Smart had offered to take the remaining old firr pipes in the Yard, from 3 to 5 inches bore, at the rate of 6d. per foot, and the 6 and 7 inches firr, with the remaining elm pipes of those sizes at 8d. per foot, and a quantity of firr spills at 3d. per bushel". This tender was accepted (6L, p441; 6, p441 annotated copy regarding 5 Oct. 1693 minute adding 'At bottom of 4a, Min. Bk. A', and payment to Dr Grant of 10 guineas, Min. B/18a, 9 Sept. 1779; ((6L, p441) Mins. 5 Oct. 1693, 19 Aug. 1770, 27 June 1771, 30 June 17[8]14) 15J, p52 mention of some of above dates).

11 Nov. 1731 (Sir James Lowther) Letter: Sir James visiting the wharf and yard on the Thames where the NRC had an office, watching small pipes being bored by men and larger by Horse Engine, most of their pipes 4-inches. The foundryman Mr Harrison producing iron pipes under an inch thick, a 7½-inch pipe weighing about 1-quarter 32 pounds per yard, used by Mr Lyddel at Newcastle (((1 July 1930 'The Times'/Mr E.L. Nanson, Somerset House, Whitehaven; B.W.A. 1930/541) Typed 'Iron Pipes') 8A1, 2-5 Vol. N-S, with added note that iron water pipes used at a **much earlier date** than supposed by Mr W.R. Rowe; (1 July 1930 'The Times', B.W.A. 1930/541) 15J, p52 part repeated).

Dec. 1752 (One Horse Engine) NRC: Decided that only a single horse boring-engine was needed for producing wooden pipes, since 3-men could cope with any emergency ((Works Committee) 15J, p53).

19 Sept. 1779 (Testing Wooden Pipes): "The wooden pipes appear to have been tested before being used, as there is a record dated 19 Sept. 1779, of the payment of 10 guineas to Dr. Grant for "the engine for trying the strength of wooden pipes in the Yard" (6L, p441; (Mins. 19 Sept. 1779) 15J, p52 repeated, adding Grant had earlier supplied the NRC with fir timber).

16 July 1801 (Mr Murdock's Pipe Boring Machine): Letter received from Mr William Murdock regarding his pipe boring machine that instead of removing wood chips leaves a solid piece of core. The Surveyor to request drawings and extra information (Min. E/152) ((Typed 'NRC') 8A1, 2-5 Vol. N-S).

14 Jan. 1802 (Drawings & Machine Part): Received drawings and a machine part, Mr Mylne empowered to make ready for using (Min. E/173).

3 April 1806 (NRC Boring Engines Out of Repair): Clerk of the Yard reporting the Boring Engines out of repair, such that Mr Mylne to prepare a report (Min. F/110).

18 Sept. 1806 (Trial of New Boring Machine): W.C. Mylne empowered to trial the boring machine on fir timber at the Head (Min. F/139).

13 Nov. 1806 (£50 Paid) to Mr Murdock: Mr Murdock for his machine to be paid £50 (Min. F/154).

9 April 1807 (Seek Out New Horse for Boring Engines) & Apply Winch to Cranes: Mr Teddere to search out a strong blind new horse for the boring engines, and for the Cranes of the two boring engines, Mr Cheffins to seek the most efficient way of applying a winch etc. (Min. F/191) ((Typed 'NRC, Extracts relating to the pipe boring machine designed by Mr Murdock' of Soho, Birmingham) 8A1, 2-8; 15J, p53 parts of above repeated).

1693 Middleton v. Swain (15I, pp49-52). 1693 a committee of the Court of Alderman to negotiate a supply of water from the main pipes of the NRC, for the relief of the Tankard-bearers whilst the City's Conduit Pipes (main Tyburn Aqueduct) was being new laid as a 5-inch pipe beneath the roads, presumably sanctioned. The London water-bearer's fraternity surviving to c.1732, thereafter as individual water-bearers, still recorded in London 1851 ((CLRO, Repertory 97, folio 322) 7K4-1, p56/61/62). In 1695 the NR capital said to be £288,000 ((Scott) 15I, p98).

1701 NRC v. Graves (15I, pp103-104). 'Receipt for water rent – Pepys the Diarist - 1701' (7H2, p230 mention 1884).

Buried 11 March 1702 (Separate Baronetcy to the 1st Sir Hugh's)
6 Dec. 1681 (Sir Hugh Myddelton, Bart.) of Hackney & Twickenham, Middlesex: This baronetcy is quite separate from that of the first Sir Hugh Myddelton's baronetcy of Ruthin, but they have inevitably been confused (('Westminster Abbey Register' by J. L. Chester, Harleian Soc. vol. x, 1876, p21 note) 11, p137 Note 7: A note that is used as the basis for the family's later history/p137; (Sheet containing a pencilled family tree) 8A1, 3/3-3 Hackney and Twickenham; (Gents Mag. Vol. lxii, p900) 14B2, p464).

This Hugh also appears to have been unbalanced like his father Simon (1st Sir Hugh's youngest son), and unworthy of the title [probably purchased]. After a most unhappy broken marriage to Dorothy, the daughter of Sir William Oglander of Nunwell, Baronet, he squandered his wealth, such that in the early-1700s it was said that this Hugh was at one time living at Kemberton in Shropshire, under the name of William Raymond, employed as a labourer paving the streets, and dying in poverty, buried at Shifnal on 11 March 1702, this separate baronetcy then becoming extinct (('Gentleman's Magazine, lxxix, 1809, p795) 11, p137 Notes 5 & 6; 13, p150). Dorothy obtained a separation and died aged 45 in 1701 and is buried in Long Melford Church, Suffolk, her wish to have an epitaph 'the unhappy wife of Sir Hugh Myddelton' not honoured by her executors (11, p97).

1708-9 High or Upper Pond (Supplying the West End)
  1708-1720 Filled by Combination Windmill & Faulty Horse-Engine Driven Pumps
  > c.1720s - c.1769 Square Horse Works Driven Pumps
Summer 1708-9 (Mantles > 1-Acre High or Upper Pond or 'New Reservoir'), site of the later Claremont Square Reservoir: Originally called the High Pond, in fields where London was viewed in the distance from a hilltop (Islington Hill), used to provide a better head of water to the higher buildings in the City of London. At 115ft. above high water mark, being 33ft. above the Round Pond (7G5, p38). Constructed to supply the newly built vicinity at Soho Square, and also by using a short line of pipes the

village of Islington (15J, p172).
1710 Grene v. Grene (15I, pp68-70).

c.1718-1767 (NRC Surveyor) Henry Mill: Henry Mill (b.1682/3, d.1770) NRC Surveyor (c.1718-1767) through a period of NRC stagnation (7G5, p40 1683-1771, appointed 1720).

> **Published 1784 (Probably from Gents. Mag.):** 'MILL (HENRY, Esq) many years principal engineer to the New-river company; a man to whom the city of London and its environs have many and great obligations, was the son of a gentleman, and nearly related to the baronet of that name: he was born in London, in or near Red-Lion Square, Holbourn, soon after the year 1680. He had a liberal education, and was for some time at one of our universities. We know by experience, that genius blazes forth at different ages, and often in so different a manner from what even parents and tutors themselves expected, as to fill them with surprise. Mr. Mill, at a very early period of life, displayed his skill in mechanics; and though we are unable to fix either his age, or the time, yet it is certain that he was very young when the New-river company engaged him as their principal engineer; in which station he continued, with the highest esteem, till his death. The almanacs tell us when the New-river was brought to London, by Sir Hugh Middleton, namely, in the year 1614 [Footnote: It was brought to Islington on Michaelmas-day 1613]; but of the chasm from Sir Hugh's death to the appointment of Mr. Mill we can say nothing. Mr. Mill has told his friends that **Sir Hugh accomplished two mains**, as they are called, and no more; **Mr Mill completed many**, as may be seen at the company's Works at Islington. His attention to the interest of his employers, and to the accommodation of the town, was amazing. His general knowledge, the fruit of constant study, was great, but in hydraulics he was probably unequalled. The company placed implicit confidence in him, and with the utmost reason: for such, through his skill and labours, was the increase of their credit, of their power, and of their capital, that a share in their property, which, it is said, was originally £100 is now worth between seven and eight thousand. Many particulars respecting Mr. Mill's assiduous attention to the service of the company, and in surmounting difficulties for the public good, are remembered by his friends; but he never boasted of his performances, contenting himself with deserving praise, without seeking it.
> For the convenience of attending the weekly boards at the New-river company's office, Mr. Mill, early in life, **took a lodging five or fix doors eastward of Somerset-house in the Strand**, where he resided till his death. He had by choice the second and third floors; and whoever occupied the house, he continued a lodger: it was usually inhabited by a milliner. From his windows, he saw the greatest part of the New-church in the Strand erected, on the spot where formerly stood a may-pole. From Mr. Mill's long continuance in the same situation he naturally contracted a fondness for it; and, even supposing it fanciful, the fancy was innocent, and it made him happy: he boasted, that, having, from his back windows, the river Thames immediately under him, beyond it the fine Surrey hills, and a vista [B footnote: The vista is Drury-Lane, opposite to Mr, Mill's lodgings. The line continued from Drury lane is Bow-street, Bloomsbury, then Queen-street, to the wall of the British Museum in Great Russel-street] leading to Hampstead and Highgate before him, he needed not a country-house. Mr. Mill's great scientific skill in hydraulics supplied the town of Northampton with water, for which he was presented with the freedom of that corporation; an honour of which he was not ambitious. He had also a taste for architecture, and frequently gave his advice on that subject to his friends.
> Many personages of rank esteemed Mr. Mill, and courted his acquaintance and company; to one in particular he was singularly serviceable, the first earl of Orford. When his lordship, while Sir Robert Walpole, had built his stately seat at Houghton [Hall] in Norfolk, he was greatly embarrassed for a commodious supply of water [Footnote C: Cibber being at Houghton, and observing the great deficiency of water in the gardens, exclaimed, "Sir Robert, Sir Robert, here is a crow that will drink up all your canal"]. It is true, he had a river near it, but that was not like the convenience of London, which requires only the turning of a cock. After many ineffectual attempts, Mr. Mill was applied to, who, by great exertion of skill, brought water to the house in great plenty, and much to the satisfaction of his honourable employer. Mr. Mill, through age, becoming infirm, and particularly by having a few years before his death a slight paralytic stroke; an assistant was taken into the company's service, (Mr, Milne, the present engineer,) but without derogation to him; on the contrary, though he ceased to take an active part, he constantly attended on the board days, his advice was asked, and his salary was continued to his death. As a proof of the esteem in which the company held him, they had his picture drawn at whole length by the late Mr. Francis Cotes, for which they gave sixty guineas, and hung it in

their **office near Black-Fryars bridge**, with which, a few years ago, it was accidentally consumed by fire. Though Mr. Mill was an old bachelor, and by his dress and manner looked like one, yet nothing testy, sour, or morose, escaped him: he was of a pleasing amiable disposition; his manners were mild and gentle, and his temper cheerful. He gradually indeed acquired some singularities, the usual attendants on age; but they were so harmless in themselves, and what he expected from others being in general rather requested than required, no one could reasonably be offended at them, or refuse complying with them. He often declined giving even his own servants trouble; for though he always kept a man and a maid, he did as many things for himself, without their aid, as he could. Mr. Mill was a member of the Church of England, and was regular in his attendance on public worship: at the same time he had no bitterness towards those of other persuasions; on the contrary, his deportment to them was friendly, and his conversation easy. He was a man of great simplicity of life and manners: in a word, it seemed to be his care to "have a conscience void of offence;" and, as far as we can see another's heart, his was wholly free from guile. His thoughts were of such a serious and elevated turn, and so just were his ideas of the Almighty, and the wonderful works of Creation, &c. that he seemed well qualified for the sacred function.

On Christmas-day, 1770, Mr. Mill dined; and sat the evening, with his landlady the milliner; and it was remarked that he was uncommonly cheerful. Among his singularities he had that of ordering his breakfast (which was usually chocolate) to be always set down at his chamber-door; and when the servant was gone, he took it in, and required no farther attendance till he rung. This signal not being given at the usual time, his servant went up to his chamber-door, and found his breakfast not taken in. Alarmed at this, and recollecting that early in the morning they had heard a noise like something fallen down, the two servants, with the assistance of the landlady, forced their way into his room, where they found him on the floor senseless and speechless. A physician was immediately sent for, and all means used for his recovery, but in vain: he died before the next morning, viz. Dec. 26, **1770**. His surviving sister, Mrs. Hubert (who, though in 1780 near 70 years of age, was then living, in full possession of her faculties), has erected a monument to his memory in the parish-church of Breemoore; near Salisbury; a tribute which several of Mr. Mill's friends have thought he justly merited from that company to which he had been so long and so eminently serviceable. We have said that Mr. Mill was one of the most valuable of men: and whether we consider him in his public capacity, labouring through a long life for the general benefit of the inhabitants of a great and opulent city, or view him in his private capacity, every way exemplary, pleasing to all, and giving offence to none, the assertion will not be denied. He was a good son, an affectionate father, a warm friend, and a kind master. But we should injure his memory if we concealed a circumstance of his life, which, though the dissolute and abandoned may disregard, the virtuous and good will esteem. Mrs. Mill, the mother of the subject of these memoirs, one day took her son aside, and thus accosted him: "My dear Harry, will you make me a promise?" "Of what kind?" says the son. "Excuse me, Harry, my declaring myself, unless you previously promise to comply with my request". "As I cannot, honoured madam", says Mr. Mill, "suppose you capable of asking impossibilities, I here solemnly promise to fulfil what you ask". "I thank you, my dear child", says Mrs. Mill. "You make me happy: and now my earnest request is, that till you shall be disposed to marry, you avoid all commerce with our sex". Mr, Mill repeated his promise, and kept it inviolably. MILLER' (15K1, 'Biographical Dictionary', 1784, pp 224-227).

Memorial Epitaph (Breamore Church) near Salisbury: Henry Mill's epitaph in Breamore Church, near Salisbury where he is buried in the churchyard, ascribes him as being a relative of Sir Hugh Myddelton, probably why c.1718 he was appointed NRC Surveyor aka Engineer (10-3, p17 1720-1771):

> "Near this Marble is interred
> **Henry Mill** Esq., eldest son of Andrew Mill Esq., and Dorothy his Wife
> He was Religious, Charitable and Friendly
> His Thoughts of the Almighty Just and Great
> His Capacity excellent in Philosophy
> In all the Branches of the Mathematicks
> and other Liberal Sciences
> His Modesty in offering his opinion and advice much to be admired
> His Temper sweet and calm his whole Behaviour affable and obliging

> He was **Engineer to the New River Company above fifty years**
> and but young when he undertook
> A new Disposition of the Water Works of his Relation Sir Hugh Myddelton
> For giving general and regular Supplies of Water
> To the Cities of London and Westminster.
> A Work before attempted in vain
> by Several of his able Predecessors in that office
> In which by his great Skill and constant attention
> He happily succeeded
> For the Utility, Security and Health of those Cities
> and the great Benefit of the New River Company
> Declining after constructing the Water Works
> at Houghton for Sir Robert Walpole
> and at Northampton
> to engage in many other Employments.
> That would have been attended with greater advantages
> Contenting himself with the Satisfaction
> of having been able to make good Use of his Talents
> For the Service of the Publick
> He departed this Life the 26th December **1770** aged Eighty Seven
> Greatly lamented by many as a General Loss
> but much more by his only Sister
> Mrs Ann Hubert
> who ever loved and esteemed Him
> and erected this Monument to his Memory
> And it is her Hope after this Life is ended
> That They shall meet again
> where Parting and Sorrow will be no more
> and with this pleasing Reflection
> she bids her last Adieu"

(12, p31; 8A1, 3/3-3 photo of his memorial tablet showing a crest with 3 Bears rampant, in London probably living at Camois? Court; 15J, p146 Robert Ward photo of tablet; 7G5, p40 died in parish of St Clement Danes).

1719 (Rival Scheme) Abortive: Proposal for bringing water from St Albans/River Colne to London, but Bill rejected (7G5, p45).

15 Jan. 1720 (Acquitted of Stealing New River Pipes): John Laurence of Holborn acquitted of stealing 4-wooden pipes of the NRC worth 20s. (G5, Old Bailey Trial).

12 July 1720 (Washing in New River): Peter Cornelius of Shoreditch had been washing in the New River, prior to assaulting Dorothy Orwell for which he was transported (G5, Old Bailey Trial).

7 Sept. 1720 (Transported for NRC Theft): Thomas Higden of St Brides transported after being found guilty of stealing 4-brass pulleys, 50-lbs lead and an iron case from the NRC worth 40s. (G5, Old Bailey Trial).

1723 (NRC Surveyor) Henry Mill Measures Length of New River as 38¾ miles & 16 poles: Confusingly this distance said to represent the original length of the New River, and erroneously adding with 200-300 bridges and 40 sluices (D20B, p124).

14 Oct. 1724 (Acquitted of Stealing) NRC Turncock's Key: William Doleman of Holborn acquitted of stealing a NRC turncock's key worth 4s. (G5, Old Bailey Trial).

Undated (Turncock's Business Card): 'W. Howes, Turncock to the NRC, 24 Pudding Lane, Eastcheap; where it is requested, in case of Fire, or any deficiency in the Supply of Water, information may be given, to which immediate attention will be paid' ((Guildhall Library) KJ1, p60; 7J1, p47).

10 July 1734 (New River Master Carpenter) Found Not Guilty of Rape: A master carpenter of the New River works was found not guilty of raping a women at a lone house on Enfield Chase (G5, Old Bailey Trial).

c.1736 - 1787 Extracts from NRC minute books, 1736–1751 pipe driving arrangements for collectors &

paviours, paving and repairing Goswell Street Road, establishment 11 Mar. 1741/2 of Committee regulating repair expenses & works to New River, and 8 Feb. 1787 order that turncocks should be elected only from labourers ((T3, RB7) Acc 2558/NR13/14/1-5, LMA).

6th Baronet & LAST TO BEAR the 1st Sir Hugh's Title (Also Called Sir Hugh Myddelton) Sir Hugh (1st Bart.), > Sir William (2nd), Sir Hugh (3rd married 3-times d.1675), > Sir Hugh (4th married a lady of property), > Sir Hugh (5th married Anne Comyne of Chigwell, Essex) > Sir Hugh (6th & Last of Ruthin).

Utter Collapse of the Family Fortunes

1723 or c./1757? Death of Last Baronet of Ruthin: 'Lysons tells us that within the memory of his own generation the last male descendent of Sir Hugh was allowed by them to become a pensioner on the bounty of the New River Company. Verily, virtue in this country is too often its own sole reward!' ((Lysons) 1B1, p350). The last Sir Hugh 'an unworthy scion', that 'could raise his mind no higher than the enjoyment of a rummer of ale; and towards the end of his life existed upon a pension granted him by the New River Company' (13, p152 Note 1; scion a descendent; a rummer is a large drinking glass). His only work and pastime 'consisted in drinking ale in any company he could pick up. Mr. Harvey took care of him, and put him to board in the house of a sober farmer at or **near Chigwell** [Essex] on whom he could depend' ((Gent. Mag. Vol. LIV, p805; 14B3, p342) 14D4, p169; (Gents. Mag., LIV, 1784, p805) 11, p139 Note 3; 14B2, pp468). A pupil from the school at Chigwell in later life, remembering him as 'a tall, thin man, very profligate and addicted to all manner of low vices', 'the report of his being in the village ... so frightened us children that we always locked ourselves up in our rooms'. He **died c./1757** 'unmarried, in extreme poverty ..., in a barn belonging to Mr. Brown, who then kept the White Hart', the parish paying for the burial of this most unfortunate man, **the last to bear the honourable first Sir Hugh's title**, although via the first Sir Hugh's fifth son Henry's descendents, the male line was not yet legally extinct ((Gents. Mag., lxii, 1792, p720) 11, p140 Note 1). At his 1723 [sic] death, the title becoming dormant [probably because too poor to claim the title] and legally extinct 1828 (Welsh Biography Online).

The 1st Sir Hugh's 5th son Henry [I], had a son Henry [II] a surgeon, who had sons Starkey [I] also a surgeon whom d.1755, and Henry [III] who had a son called Starkey [II] living in West Ham and died poor 1768. Starkey [II] had sons Joseph who d.1787 (kept a journal of their family tree, later held by Dr G.C. Myddelton of Henley-on-Thames), and **Jabez Myddelton** of Hoxton having three daughters (the last petitioned the City for a pension, d.1863) and d.27 March 1828, **thus the last male descendent**, after which the City deciding no more relief to the family (11, p140/141).

3rd Bart. married 3-times and died 1675-6, said he had no heir but had a son Hugh by his 3rd wife, that became the 4th Bart., his son Hugh the 5th Bart. a Royal Navy captain retiring to Chigwell, and his son Hugh the last/6th Bart. (11, pp137-139).

Since Family History is so popular today, it's about time we had a modern compiled family tree, now that we have Internet resources! Amazingly 2011 found some further details at: http://histfam.familysearch.org/showsource.php?sourceID=S2673&tree=Welsh

---

15 Jan. 1731 (Transported for Stealing NRC Iron Lock & Sluice Bolt): Thomas Wright of Enfield transported after being found guilty of stealing an iron lock and bolt of a sluice, property of the NRC worth 10d. (G5, Old Bailey Trial).

1756 (NRH > City) Wooden Pipes: From NRH fifty eight 7-inch NRC wooden pipes to the City ((Morris p8; Dickinson p57) 4, p15). 1767 NRC Act (7H2, p94).

1769 ('Memorial Rings to Governors of the NRC'): When Philip de la Haize d.1769 (his grave in All Saints churchyard, Tottenham) he left large bequests to Aimé or Aymé Garnault (1717-1782) and his family of Bull's Cross, Enfield, and memorial rings to Governors of the NRC ('Garnault Group of Families' by W.D. Collins, 1933, ELSC&A).

Hope the following may be of some help to those interested, although complicated:

Pre-1769 NRC Office Fire
Two Groups NRC Docs. > Acc 2558/NR13/1-316, LMA: Two groups of NRC documents have been combined as Acc 2558/NR13/1-316, LMA, since very similar in nature, and found either at:
1. NRH in 1991 (**NRH = New River Head**) found interspersed with MWB/TWA archivist G.C. Berry's correspondence & lecture notes, after the main NRC records had been listed. Some might originally be part of Acc 2558/NR2/1-734 Board Papers, others possibly from (E1-E3, E45, D13-D14 and D27) Acc 2558/NR5/8-80 Legal Papers. Rather than reintegrate with the main NRC series, they have been catalogued as a separate group.
2. Or obtained in 1992 when access was obtained to the locked tin trunks at **Surbiton Muniment Houses**.

T3 = Trunk No. 3, Surbiton
T78 = Trunk No. 78, Surbiton
T84 = Trunk No. 84, Surbiton
T85 = Trunk No. 85, Surbiton
T87 = Trunk No. 87, Surbiton
T89 = Trunk No. 89, Surbiton

RB2, 3, 4 etc. = Red Box 2, 3, 4 etc.
GB = Grey Box file

Use in conjunction with Acc 2558/NR1-12; and Acc 1953 **NRC Limited** records deposited 1984 in the Greater London Record Office (> LMA).
See also Metropolitan Water Board Clerk's Department Acc 2558/MW/C/15, **list of 'Exhibits' pages 13-41**.
Groups or bundles of documents have been **split between:**
    NRC 'Additional Records' and MWB 'Exhibits'.
Original NRC compensation receipts for constructing the New River, is catalogued as
    Acc 2558/**NR13**/226/1-284
    Acc 2558/**MW/C**/15/32, Acc 2558/**MW/C**/15/121, Acc 2558/**MW/C**/15/138/1, Acc 2558/**MW/C**/15/64-65, Acc 2558/**MW/C**/15/123, Acc 2558/**MW/C**/15/152, and Acc 2558/**MW/C**/15/262/2.
Original Hattersfield, Islington of James Colebrooke is now:
    Acc 2558/**NR13**/48/1-8,
    Acc 2558/**MW/C**/15/180, Acc 2558/**MW/C**/15/213/1-5, and Acc 2558/**MW/C**/15/268/1-3.
Original Commandery Mantles, Clerkenwell is now:
    Acc 2558/**NR13**/284-288,
    Acc 2558/**MW/C**/15/237/1-2, Acc 2558/**MW/C**/15/179/1-8, Acc 2558/**MW/C**/15/72, and Acc 2558/**MW/C**/15/298/5.
(Info. from National Archives website).

Sun. Morning 24 Dec. 1769 (Christmas Eve Fire) Destroys NRC Office at Bridewell Precinct: The NRC offices at Bridewell Precinct entirely burnt down on Christmas Eve, Sunday 24 December 1769. The day after the fire the NRC Directors (Governor, Treasurer, and two others) met at Peel's Coffee House, Fleet Street, to discuss the arrangements for continuing business, at which the Clerk reported that the Bridewell Hospital Governor/officials "had very politely offered the use of their public rooms and hall" to the Company until other arrangements could be made; so the Directors held their meetings there paying £50 for one half-year's rent, the Company's lease for the Bridewell Precinct offices being surrendered to Bridewell Hospital in 1770, since in 1771 they were to build new offices just to the W (9 April 1904 'Builders' snippet, fire 24 Nov. 1769; 12D, p14 'burned down on Nov. 14, 1769, or some say on Christmas Day that year' the Nov. date annotated with '?' and Christmas Day with 'NO'; 8A1-N1, p1 fire at Dorset Street; (Box L5.723 'NR Works') Islington LHC, 1769 fire of office in Dorset St.; 12, p51).

    1. Most of the Early Records Destroyed: Most of the early NRC records (books and documents) were destroyed in the fire, except some pages of various books, which had charred edges and water damage, in 1927 kept at the MWB Muniment Houses, Surbiton. The oldest record saved is a 1615 compensation receipt witnessed by Mr. William Lewyn the first Clerk of the Company (12, p51).

Pre-1770 (Scarce Details) Regarding the New River: "There is, of course, a long period between Myddelton's accounts and 1770 when details are scarce indeed" (MFK corres. May 1971 with G.C. Berry, MWB). "Minutes of the New River Company survive from 1768" (15E, p8).
Before the fire, keeping two series of minute books, an office & an engrossed copy. After the New River Office, Bridewell Precinct fire on 24 Dec. 1769 many of the archives were badly damaged or destroyed ((No date or ref.), LMA); for 25 Dec 1769 - 21 July 1904 minutes of the Weekly Meetings & General Courts (Acc 2558/NR 1/1-47). For 1778-1904 rough minute books (Acc 1953). Fragments of legal docs. Nos. 203-324 ((NRH; No date or ref., not available for consultation since not rebound after repair) Acc 2558, 371 series, LMA).

20 March 1951 (Report on Charred Remains): Report by Clerk of the Board (probably written by G.C. Berry) regarding the charred remains of the NRC Records:
The fragile charred records (from the 24 Dec. 1769 fire at Blackfriars) of the NRC handed to the MWB in 4-folders containing:

236 sheets of C17th Min. Books covering the first NRC meeting 2 Nov. 1619 to 1692, and fragmentary copies of Letters Patent (1742-1769).

96 fragments including Letters Patent regarding King James's share in New River; documents on Ford's waterworks purchased by NRC in 1667; fragments of Counsel's opinion and titles to NRC shares. Various information included within the charred remains:

Appointments and remuneration of Governors, Deputies, Treasurers, Auditors, Clerks and Collectors. Share transfers, admission of new Board members and meeting places.

In the early days they met at Sir Hugh's house, later at the Governor's or members houses until well after the mid-C17th. After the Great Fire of London in 1666, meeting in taverns, such as the Devil and Saint Dunstan's (of Ben Jonson fame) near Temple Bar.

At the end of the C17th transferring meetings to their **office near Puddle Dock**.

In 1620 Hugh Myddelton paid £800 a year to manage the River.

1622 negotiations with King James when he attempted to buy out the Adventurers.

In 1665 John Greene (who probably fitted out the Oak Room at NRH) agreeing to manage the 'country work' from Ware to Islington.

In 1667 the famous engraver W. Hollar was paid £20 to produce a map of the New River.

By 1689 (Weekly Meetings): Frequent mention of repairs, extensions of works, and prices of materials. Damage from leaking mains resulting in visits to properties, and sometimes compensation in remission of water rent.

Inspections of the New River starting from 7 or 8 o'clock from NRH.

1913 (Kept with Care): NRC Clerk in evidence to Royal Commission on Public Records, saying that at present time just taking care of these precious charred records, at some time hoping to have them specially treated.

1951 (Estimate for Restoration) £125: A 15 Jan. 1951 estimate obtained from the P.R.O. of around £125, that included repairing them with 'hand-made paper and silk gauze, treating with size, and guarding after repair with guard paper'. At the same time Lt. Col. G. Malet of the National Register of Archives, and Professor J.G. Edwards, Director of the Institute of Historical Research, both recommending that these documents be repaired, 'the Minute Book is unique, that it is the earliest of its kind in this country'. Awaiting instructions of the Committee, Clerk of the Board ((3-typed sheets 'MAN, Draft 20/3/51') 8A1, 2-8). c.1951 draft report on the charred NRC minute books etc. salvaged from the fire, and possibility of paying the Public Record Office for conservation ((T3, RB7) Acc 2558/NR13/1/1; & only 1-page of a 16 Mar. 1951 typescript report by the MWB Clerk, Acc 2558/NR13/1/2 LMA).
Looks like they were repaired, since Berry adds a final note regarding the sudden death of Mr T.E. Hassell, B.E.M., late Supt. of Binding & Repairs at the P.R.O., reported in 'The Times' Fri. 8 Jan. 1954; Copy of 'The Times' 8 Jan 1954 obituary of Mr T E Hassell, Superintendent of Binding and Repairs at the Public Record Office (NRH) Acc 2558/NR13/1/4). c.1953 key correlating MWB numbering of 322 fire damaged documents by the P.R.O. ((NRH) Acc 2558/NR13/1/3, LMA).

2. But All Board Minutes from 1769-1904 are Preserved: But since all Board minutes from 1769-1904 have been preserved without any breaks (12, p34/50-51; later annotated copy by G.C. Berry saying 'compensation receipts from 1609 [?] not charred').

Unearthed by Bernard Rudden
> **26 June 1686 (NRC Inventory):** 1686 inventory of NRC documents locked in their indenture chest, except very few, most of them traced by Bernard Rudden ((Guildhall Manuscripts) 15I, p92).

25 Dec. 1769 - 21 July 1904 NRC Minutes of Weekly Meetings & General Courts (Acc 2558/NR 1/1-47, LMA).

June 1770 NRC Offices Dorset Yard: Adjacent on the W-side the NRC also leasing Dorset Yard, where in June 1770 laying the first stone and using the £1,000 insurance proceeds (and withheld dividends) to build new offices, remaining here until 1819 when transferring to NRH, the lease of Dorset Yard sold 1861 (15I, p91).

1771-1810 Robert Mylne NRC Surveyor: See Chapter 3.

1775 a new main driven from 'Islington to the West end of Town toward St Mary le Bonne' (15I, p99).

1778-1904 NRC Rough minute books (Acc 1953, LMA).

1778 in a Soho street, 2ft. down finding a rotting NRC wooden main laying across a sewer such that to inform the Co. (('The London Commissioners of Sewers and their Records' by I. Darlington, Phillimore, 1970, p39) 7K4-1, p41). 1779 NRC Act (7H2, p94).

1792 rumours that the NR had been poisoned, the NRC having to publish a denial notice (14B2, p460).

In 1800 the NRC supplying nearly 55,000 houses with water, and their policy of not covering the plug holes of the mains connections justified by saying that it was **less expensive to pay now and then for an accident to a donkey's leg** (15I, p98/99).

1805 Adair v. NRC (15I, pp196-201). 1805 NRC Act (7H2, p94). Between 1805-1811 five new water companies created in the London area (9, p2).

1806-1811 INTENSE COMPETITON; 1815-1818 AGREEMENTS: From 1806-1811 competition from the new London water companies, starting with the West Middlesex Waterworks Company etc., such that the streets became a battlefield, where overnight they tore up competitors pipes, or you woke up to find you had been connected to another company's pipes. Price cutting to attract new customers was disastrous to profits, such that by 1815-1818 they agreed to draw up demarcation lines for defined territories, and not trespass on another company's area, then raising their prices by 25% such that there was public outcry ('London's Water Wars – The competition for London's water supply in the nineteenth century' by John Graham-Leigh, 135pp published 2000 by Francis Boutler) pp37-61; 15J, pp161-170 competition).

> **1810-1815 (NRC Bankrupts Holloway Waterworks):** George Pocock under his Holloway Waterworks Act 1810 (50 Geo. III) sinking a deep well at today's Eden Grove, and the NRC immediately laying pipes nearby, such that by 1815 bankrupting Pocock (15I, p138; 15J, p234 further details on HWWs; 4, p21; 7G5, p76; 7K1, p23).

In 1810 nine parallel 7-inch NRC pipes down Goswell Street/Road ((1821 Mins. W.C. Mylne) 4, p15).

1810-19 NRC (WOODEN PIPES > CAST-IRON) Enabling a Proper High Service: Converting to cast-iron pipes during a period of intense competition with the newly formed water companies, at first in 1811 & 1812 financed by loans from the shareholders, but from 1817-30 by a mortgage from the Bank of England who held NRC land as a security, the pipes mainly supplied by Fereday & Co. (7K1, p22 1810-20; 15I, p100 & p109 1811/pp114-115; 15J, p54 1810-20; 12, p48 greater part in 2-years, 'substitution occupied about 4-years', then says about 1814-16 in the NR District).

1810-1859 William Chadwell Mylne NRC Surveyor/Engineer: Under which most of the Large Loops were bypassed, and storage reservoirs & filter beds created.

1811-1853 (New River Residential Estate) Clerkenwell: With the land freed of criss-crossing wooden water mains, the NRC developing their land into the NRC Islington/Clerkenwell housing estate, many of the street names derived from those of NRC Governors, Directors etc.

1813 R. v. NRC (15I, p129/229).

In 1815 it became legal to connect house drains to sewers & streams, thus early flushing c.1770s Water Closets polluting the rivers (and tidal action not permitting it to be washed out to sea) used by the London Water Companies for their supply.

1815-1816 (W. Middx. & NRC) Failed Merger: In 1815 the W. Middx. & NR companies agreeing to amalgamate, but their 1816 Bill met great opposition so was withdrawn, from 1816-1817 agreeing on defined boundaries (4, pp55-57).

Oct. 1816 Poem: The following poem best read and appreciated, after first studying some of the history of the New River. If you read it at the beginning, remember to read it again after finishing the history.

'THE NEW RIVER;
OR,
A WALK FROM AMWELL TO LONDON.

FLOW on, thou gently winding River,
Refreshing flow'ry lawn and vale;
And may thy banks run full forever,
Thy Springs exhaustless never fail.

Clear and unruffled as thy Stream,
As free from care – as free from woe;
Oh! may our journey peaceful seem,
As down the vale of life we go.

Come, let us trace thy devious course,
And tread thy verdant banks along;
Could but my numbers, like thy source,
As sweetly flow – to aid my song.

From CHADWELL'S Spring, near sedgy LEA,
We'll pass by WARE'S fam'd malting Town;
Whence thousand quarters day by day,
To LONDON'S mart are floated down.

Thy chalky hills and opening vale,
AMWELL, once seat of Poet's song;
Matchless the view – here hill and dale,
In beauteous order spread along.

Yon rising hill, where once the Dane,
Encamp'd his rude invading hands;
His Ships, in which he cross'd the main,
Were there left dry by Alfred's plans.

Yon Church, which midway rears its fane [religious place],
That little Emerald Isle, below,
Just rising from the limpid Stream,
A Sculptur'd Urn and Tablet show:-

> "AMWELL perpetual be thy Stream,
> Nor e'er thy Spring be less,
> Which thousands drink, who never dream
> Whence flows this boon they bless.
>
> Too often thus ungrateful Man,
> Blind and unconscious lives;
> Enjoys kind Heaven's indulgent plan,
> Nor thinks of him who gives".
> [Inscribed on stone on Upper island at Gt. Amwell, **accredited to 'Nares, 1818', although this poem as such dated 1816**].

Thence to ST MARGARET'S shady grove,
To where the RYE stands on the LEA;
Delighted I could frequent rove,
Lov'd scenes of youthful joys to me.

The Angler here, with studious care,
Thro' the long day does silent stand,
With baited hook the eel to snare,
Or draws the scaly pike to land.

Now HOD'SDON'S turrets meet my view,
It's flowery meadows scent the gale;
Its Mill, its streams of glassy hue,
Enliven'd by the swelling sail.

On thy steep banks, in youthful days,
I've gamboll'd oft at morn or eve;
Or, warm'd by Sol's enlivening rays,
My limbs within thy current lav'd.

Thro' BROXBOURNE church-yard lies our way –
Here peaceful sleep the mingled throng;
Tombs, Stones, and Rails but briefly say,
To whom they never did belong.

Here let me drop Affection's tear,
Which Brothers and which Fathers shed;
One Brother and four Sisters here,
Lie number'd with the silent dead.

Two lovely Boys to me were giv'n,
Each op'ning flow'ret blooming spread;
Untimely nipt – so will'd it Heav'n,
Beneath yon turf decreed their bed.

Within these walls a Christian made,
To manhood's years I weekly trod;
Where holy texts – Religion's aid,
Taught me to know to fear my God.

Farewell, lov'd spot, tho' weighty care
Prevents my visits oft to thee;
In dreams ideal scenes appear,
Which transient pleasure gives to me.

Onward to WORMLEY let us rove,
Thro' gardens deck'd in flow'ry pride;
To HUME'S fine seat and shady grove,
Our Stream adorns the eastern side.

Thro' fertile field, and daisied lawn,
To CHESHUNT Church approach we near;
Delightful spot – which eve and morn,
A paradise of sweets appear.

To THEOBALD'S next our Stream pursue,
Once Royal JAMES'S Court and pride;
Now PRESCOTT'S mansion, hid from view,

By shady branches spreading wide.

Thy curved course we'll follow on
Till ENFIELD'S whiten'd Steeple's seen;
Encircling quite that pleasant Town,
Thy margins deck'd with lively green.

Here thy first Founder saw an end
Of all his hopes – his fortune gone;
So great the cost, all did he spend,
Yet half the work was scarcely done.

The Patriot true must ever bless
The name of him who made thee flow;
And shed a tear for his distress
Whose patriot mind was dimm'd by woe.

A CHARTER'D COMPANY thence was form'd,
Adventurers his great plan complete;
And many thousand pounds expend,
Tho' distant profit – Hopes were great.

Perfected and matur'd by years,
Success at length their wishes crown'd;
Liberal as Nature's bounteous care,
Dispensing health and blessings round.

BUSH-HILL, with lofty trees well lin'd,
The broaden'd Stream scarce seems to glide;
Which here by Sluice-gate back confin'd,
Distant appears from side to side.

Crossing the vale, the limpid flood,
In high raised banks, by art achiev'd;
Till late a timber frame long stood,
Which, lin'd with lead, the stream receiv'd.

Tho' Aqueducts of GREECE and ROME,
On marble arch and columns rear'd,
More noble in appearance shone;
Such Streams – how small, with this compar'd!

SOUTHGATE'S embow'ring shades are near,
Where titled rank and wealth reside;
See ARNOS GROVE'S fam'd seat appear,
There classic lore and taste preside.

Thy devious course we still pursue,
Round MUSWELL'S base we wind along;
HIGHGATE and HAMPSTEAD distant view,
To LONDON'S Spires – the sight prolong.

Southward the KENTISH HILLS arise,
Along yon vale broad THAMES appears;
Thence Eastward turn thy gladden'd eyes,
Nature her gayest livery wears.

To HORNSEY'S rural village come,
Where Meditation loves to dwell;
Where Friends in social converse roam,
And all its varied beauties tell.

The prudent Tradesman here retir'd,
From busy scenes and anxious cares;
Enjoys the wish so long desir'd,
To spend his few remaining years.

The thrifty Merchant here resides,
His Children breathe the purer air;
Each morn to bus'ness forth he rides,
At eve returns their smiles to share.

The speckled trout – and silvery eels,
Not long escape the Angler's snare;
Each tempting bait a hook conceals,
Success rewards his wily care.

Pursue we now our course along,
And see yon shady wood above;
Where numbers ev'ry Sabbath throng,
And thro' the mazy thicket rove.

NEWINGTON steeple's now in sight,
The Stream adds lustre to the scene;
Adorns each villa – glitt'ring white,
Contrasted by the shaded GREEN.

Our journey now draws to an end,
See HIGHBURY HILL before us rise;
Yet, ere we quit this fav'rite bend,
A public good let me devise.

Britons profess (and practice too),
Each decent, social, moral tie;
Yet here exposed Bathers shew,
Scenes which our public laws defy.

Here would I, by subscription, buy
A plot of ground, whereon to build
A Public Bath, which, walled high,
This crystal stream should keep well fill'd.

Nor longer, then, excuses should
Both law and decency defy;
By rules well plann'd and understood,
No more offend the modest eye.

To ISLINGTON at length arriv'd,
We lose awhile the aqueous store,
Which, through an arch (too small contriv'd)
Again we see it as before.

Within these ample reservoirs Constant
the flowing stream's supply;
Thence, forc'd by Steam's mechanic pow'rs

To others elevated high.

By num'rous pipes and tubes suppli'd,
Each house receives the liquid store;
Health, comfort, cleanliness alli'd,
Alike enjoy'd by rich and poor.

PARIS, with all her varied store,
Comforts like these do not supply;
There SEINE'S foul streams in fountains pour,
But gen'ral use almost deny.
Thro' subterraneous sewers (tho' foul)
Thy liquefying streams convey,
Thence refluent THAMES receives the soil,
Which to the OCEAN rolls away.

So, from this secret acting cease,

LONDON its comforts shall retain;
Pure, and as wholesome as her laws,
Its health preserves, and will sustain.

FLOW ON, THOU GENTLY WINDING RIVER,
REFRESHING FLOW'RY LAWN AND VALE;
OH! MAY THY BANKS RUN FULL FOR EVER,
THY SPRINGS EXHAUSTLESS NEVER FAIL.
      R. CHEFFINS
[NRC Clerk of the Yard]
Dorset Street,
October 1816'.

('Herts. Mercury', Sat. 23 Sept. 1905, p3 cols. 5-6) Microfilm, Herts. Archives & Local Studies, Hertford; 'Mr Cheffins, of Hoddesdon'). Annoyingly after including this version, later found a fuller/4 extra verse version ($9^{1}/_{3}$ small page bound original, SR-824 CHE, Hackney Archives).

Sights & Sounds Along the New River Over 400-Years: But let's imagine awhile and ponder on the sights and sounds that we might have encountered over the centuries travelling up & down the New River! At the time of its inception most people for protection wearing superstitious charms or signs of the zodiac, were frightened of ghosts, phantoms & by soothsayers. In 1604 still folk beliefs of demons (fallen angels) & nymphs or spirits (evil fairies - objects of terror, only in Victorian times made innocents with wings). The colourful & drab dress of the rich & poor, the less well-off with dirty bodies & rank breath, both kept going on quack medicines, and probably when met with different dialects. The mud & noise, the dung, open sewers, milestones, crosses, churches, mills, pubs & inns, pawnbrokers, cattle & horses, wagons, carriages and post-chaises, hermits, tramps, footpads, pickpockets, thieves, vagabonds & highwaymen, beggars, cripples, malformed & lepers, pedlars, the hawkers & street traders, the occasional funeral or hanging, street entertainers, performing animals, fairs & sideshows (giants, midgets & malformed) from 1800 Punch & Judy, cock-fighting, bull-baiting, horse-racing & boxing contests. No doubt you can add some others!

1817 (Michael Angelo Taylor's Act) Section 12, New Water Mains Must be of Iron Alone:
Although Non-Iron Pipes can be repaired using the same materials within 10-years (12, p46).

 1691 York Buildings Waterworks > May 1816 – March 1818 NRC: The NRC in 1818 taking over the York Buildings Waterworks established 1691 with reservoirs on the site of Charing Cross Station supplying customers in the Strand (15I, pp113-114; 15J, pp232 further details on YBWWs; 7J1, p71 YBWWs est. 1676 taken over 1818 and wound up 1829; 4, p58 May 1816–March 1818 NRC paying the YBWWs £250. 18s. 6d. per year; 7G5, pp47-49; 7K1, p24; 7K3, p7 1818 leased to NRC, YBWWs abolished 1829).

In 1821 W.C. Mylne without sight of the original NR accounts hidden away amongst the Land Revenue papers, calculating that the capital invested in the NR was:

	1630	1815
	£43,671. 4s. 4d.	£846,640. 7s. 0d.
Iron pipes to 1820		£ Not stated
257-miles of rotting wooden pipes		LESS £113,000+
Xmas 1820		**£986,868. 13s. 0½d.** ((1821 v, Appendix C

(10), Parl. Papers) 15I, p148).

1579 London Bridge Waterworks (Plus Broken Wharf WWs 1593-1703) > 1822 NRC:
LBWWs established 1579, the NRC using their Broken Wharf site (1701/c.1702 taken over by Richard Soames after he acquired LBWWs, the BW-site said discontinued due to its high running costs) for times of emergency by installing a 100 h.p. pumping engine for supplying Thames water

in times of drought or winter icing of the New River. As mentioned previously a small Thames-side WWs originated 1593 by Bevis Bulmar using a 'Forcier', passing to Thomas Parradyne who 1604 had a 489-year lease at 10s. per annum from the City. At some time becoming part of London Bridge WWs that the Morris family sold to Richard Soame, in 1822 the BW WWs site included when LBWWs were sold to the NRC. After negotiations 1924-27 with the City, the MWB selling No. 7 Broken Wharf, Upper Thames St., E.C. for £3,000 (15I, p114; 15J, pp231-232 further details on LBWWs; 7J1, p67; 4, p9 1701; 9, p292-293; 7G5, pp16-18 Broken Wharf/pp20-30 LBWWs; 7H2, p94 NRC securing LBWWs dividends for 260-years, that part of the unexpired 500-years).
1822 NRC Act (7H2, p94).

c.1825 the architect of St Paul's Charles Robert Cockerell (1788-1863): "The insurance of the magnificent cathedral, Mr Cockerell tells us, engaged his [Sydney Smith's] early attention; and the fabric was speedily and effectually insured in some of the most substantial offices in London. Not satisfied with this security, he advised the introduction of the **mains of the New River into the lower parts of the fabric, and cisterns and movable engines in the roof**; and quite justifiable was his joke that 'he would reproduce the Deluge in our cathedral'" (1K1, p260).

1828 (End of Annuities) to Myddelton's Descendants: Regarding Myddelton's descendants 'Several others of the family have enjoyed a small annuity from the [Goldsmiths'] Company till 1828' ((Printed extract from 'The Christian's Penny Magazine' publ. every Sat., No. 143 (possibly Vol. IV), Feb. 28, 1835, p65) Islington LHC). 'Another descendant, Jabez Myddelton, had a pension of £52 per annum from the Goldsmiths' Company, until his death 27 March 1828; and in July of the same year, Mrs Jane Myddelton Bowyers had £30 per annum allotted to her, - which annuity was reduced to 7s. per week in Sept., when Mrs Plummer, another of the family (since dead), also had an allowance of 7s. per week. The corporation have passed a resolution, to the effect that they **will grant no more relief to Myddelton's connexions**' (14D6-I, p430). 28 July 1818 the City voting £50 to the distressed Jabez Myddelton ((Note in back of 1613 published article of opening of NR by 'T.M.' likely Thomas Myddelton, Guildhall Library) 15I, p70).

MYTH, 2 June 1837 'Hull Packet' (Cruel Rumours) of a Fortune for Myddelton's Heirs: 'Sir Hugh Myddelton – A correspondent states that he has been informed that a sum, amounting to **£10,000**, lies in the Bank of England, or has been received by the NRC, for the descendants of Sir Hugh Myddelton, upon their clearly making out their descendants. It is also reported that the money so reserved arises from the arrears of £100 per annum rent charge, payable out of the company's shares to the heirs of the second son of Sir Hugh Myddelton, and that such arrears have been accumulating for a great number of years - Herald' (Issue 2739, Brit Library, via Graham Levins; 15J, p202 1838 newspaper reports).

No such sums of money existed, even the Goldsmiths' Company only held the one charitable share left to them by Sir Hugh; but the plight of the distressed individuals stimulated many articles on Sir Hugh and his genealogy; local histories started to summarise his works; he became widely accepted in the mid-Victorian period as a public benefactor, his will was published by the Camden Society; he was included in the Dictionary of National Biography; and statues were erected in his name (11, p143; 13, p152 footnote).

1828 (No More Relief) for Myddelton's Descendants: By the nineteenth century, since most of Sir Hugh's descendants were poor and needy, the Corporation of London after the death of Jabez Myddelton in 1828, passed a resolution stating that no more relief would be granted to members of the family ((' History and Topography of the Parish of St. Mary, Islington' by S. Lewis, 1842, p430) 11, p141 Note 4).

20 March 1862 'Morning Post' (Destitute Myddelton Descendant): A destitute starving women said to be the great-granddaughter of Sir Hugh Myddelton, and widow of a freeman of the Goldsmiths' Company being refused prompt relief from the same company (Page 3, Issue 27536, C19[th] British Library Newspapers Part II, via Graham Levins).

1828 (Screening Rubbish) > 1852 First Slow-Sand Filtration: At Chelsea Waterworks, James Simpson developing the first practical slow sand filtration (filtration used mandatory in London from 1852) that still has worldwide use today.

The New River's slow flow acting as a continuous settling reservoir, only floating debris removed approx. every 5-miles at grates, at NRH using fine screens and cleaning the chambers every 3-months (7G5, p119).

1830 NRC Act (7H2, p94).

1830s Additional Open Storage Reservoirs (Uncovered) listed in Date order.

1793 NRC Tottenham Court-Hampstead Road Reservoir, removed c.1860 **(SITE OF)** > Tolmers Square. 1793 from the Upper Pond a 16-inch iron main supplied by Booth iron-founders over 1-mile long to the Tottenham Court Road Reservoir, costs with laying £4804. 19s. 2d. (((Sht. 9 of 10pp headed 'Pipes') 8A1, 3/3-2; (Acc 2558/MW/C/15/68/1, LMA) 15J, p160 1790 cost of pipes £4,157). Their 1845 B & W engine here transferred 1870-1 to Turnford P.S. (7G5, p71).

Also the previous Hampstead Co., Kentish Town deep well, 1884 said 'not now used' (7H2, p97).

1830-33 (2-Large NRC Reservoirs) Stoke Newington: Said 1867 'two subsiding reservoirs... of 42-acres 2-roods, and a capacity of 130 m.g.' (when cleaned & deepened c.1852, finding that only 10-inches of deposits had accumulated over approx. 22-years) with 5 filter beds of 6½-acres cleaned every 6-weeks in winter and every 3-weeks in summer, the filtered water then pumped to Claremont Square, and Maiden-lane/York-road (7G6, p4/6).

Two large NRC storage reservoirs constructed at Stoke Newington, the NE-reservoir now a Nature Reserve, the SW-reservoir now owned by Hackney Council for pleasure purposes.

1830 Stoke Newington Prebendary Act (private), 1 Will. IV, c.44: The NRC constructing settlement reservoirs at Stoke Newington.

1954 Primary filters said operating at Stoke Newington (7G5, p133).

1835-37 (2-Smaller NRC Reservoirs) Cheshunt, Herts.: 'Two subsiding reservoirs of 18-acres 2-roods, ... estimated ... 75,549,375 gals.' (7G6, p4).

A small pair of NRC storage reservoirs constructed at Cheshunt, Herts., by 1897 only used for flood management not water supply, 1971 the N-reservoir leased by Cheshunt UDC for pleasure purposes (> part of Broxborne Council's Cheshunt Park), from 2005-7 the S-reservoir drained & levelled for conversion to a private housing estate.

c.1841-2 NRC Camden Park Road Open Reservoir (SITE OF). Presumably the 1867 mentioned 'Camden-square reservoir, near the Cattle Market (7G6, p5). Suggested that this reservoir belonged to the Hampstead Waterworks Co. (15J, p233); but it was a NRC reservoir that after the 1852 Act was used for storing the Hampstead & Highgate pond's non-domestic water supply. Lease not renewed 1936.

1851 Intended NRC Reservoir (ABORTIVE), NW-side of Manifold Ditch, Ware.

1852 Proposed NRC Reservoir (ABORTIVE), N-side White Hart Lane, Tottenham.

1854 Proposed NRC Reservoir (ABORTIVE), S-side Ferry Lane on River Lee, Tottenham.

c.1856 (Small NRC Reservoir) E-side Amwell End P.S., Ware, there 1938, since removed.

1859 NRC Hornsey Basin (2-Old Settling Reservoirs on New River). Said that the Hornsey open reservoir contains 39 m.g. (7G6, p4).

1896 Proposed NRC Reservoir (ABORTIVE), Enfield Chase.

1896 Proposed NRC Reservoir (ABORTIVE), S-side Barrowell Green, Palmers Green.

1896 Staines Aqueduct, Reservoirs (N & S) Joint Committee of Grand Junction, W. Middx. & NRC: (7G5, pp110-111 para. on scheme).

1897-1903 built NRC Kempton Park Open Reservoirs (W (SITE OF) & E), 12-Filter Beds & P.S. The reservoirs filled May 1902 but not then drawing the water (9, p86). 1902-1905 12 slow sand filter beds and Engine House (Lillieshall Building) etc. housing five 100h.p. Lillieshall triple-expansion steam engines, removed in the 1960s (1X2, p76). The NRC engine house not today open to the public.

Pumping for 17-miles via:

> **1897-1908 built Cricklewood Covered Balancing** Reservoirs.

> **1897-1908 built Fortis Green** Covered Reservoir (see fol.).

Oct. 1929 Kempton Park P.S. (II) under MWB: 1924-26 MWB staff constructing the 2-mile long 6ft. dia. Littleton to Kempton Park conduit on a **revised line to the Staines Aqueduct** (but never completed in duplicate as originally planned), and from Kempton Park a 48-inch main to Hampton (9, p120-122). 1924 for Kempton Park, ordering two 1008h.p. Worthington & Simpson Ltd of Newark triple expansion engines (called 'Sir William Prescott' & 'Lady Bessie Prescott'), and Paterson Engineering Co Ltd apparatus for rapid filters. 1924-26 a duplicate main from Kempton Park to Cricklewood constructed by Sir W.G. Armstrong, Whitworth & Co. Ltd. 1925 order to William Moss & Sons Ltd for constructing the Kempton Park Engine house (completed Jan. 1929), & given a 1927 order for constructing 24 open rapid gravity primary filters (allowing the existing filter beds to quadruple their throughput and not having to construct additional filter beds), the works inaugurated 24 Oct. 1929 (9, p123). In 1929 approval for a 42-inch 2¼-mile main from Kempton Park to Hampton (9, p125). Mostly completed 1953 a 60-inch 13½-mile long main from Kempton Park to Cricklewood (9, p138). 1954 Primary filters said operating at Kempton Park, for pumping filtered water using steam turbines through gearing driving centrifugal pumps (7G5, p133/139). Engines finished working in the 1960s, and the engine house since restored by a Trust for public viewing.

1904-6 (MWB Article) New River Can Now End Abruptly: "The construction of the New River was indeed a great engineering feat. It gives one some idea of the skill required in its design when we realise that **the flow of the river is so regulated that it can end abruptly in a reservoir without fear of overflowing**" (6A, p4). The endless mass of water had finally somewhere to go!

For ponds & reservoirs around NRH, see later section.

NRC COVERED Reservoirs (Constructed by NRC) listed fol. the River from N to S, constructed as a result of the 1852 Metropolitan Water Act.
c.1874 NRC Southgate/Oakwood Covered Reservoir **(SITE OF)** > Housing.
c.1884 NRC Dog & Duck Lane > Bourne Hill, Palmers Green Covered Reservoir.
1880 Crouch Hill > Stroud Green Covered Reservoirs.
c.1850 Highgate (The Grove/W. Hill) Covered Reservoir.
1845 Hornsey Lane (Archway) Covered Reservoir > Pumping Station 2001 Housing. In 1857 the Archway, Highgate site (1,180,000 gal. covered reservoir) said re-pumping with an old marine engine to the covered reservoir at Hampstead Heath (7G6, p5). Later heavy oil engine-driven centrifugal pumps at Hornsey, presumably here (7G5, p160).
1897 NRC Act - 1908 built Cricklewood Re-pumping Station & Covered Balancing Reservoirs. 1902 three triple expansion surface condensing engines by the Lillieshall Company installed at Cricklewood (7G5, pp116-117). June- July 1906 accepted tender for 42-inch iron main from Cricklewood to Fortis Green, and March 1907 for laying the main, completed 1908, and 1911 approval for **building a station next to the engine house** for supplying Cricklewood & the MWB's Kidderpore districts. In Sept. 1914 installing **three** 4-cylinder vertical diesel engines of 160 b.h.p. each at 200 revs./min., through gearing driving 3-throw horizontal ram pumps, supplied by Mirrlees, Bickerton & Day Ltd, capable of pumping 4.m.g.d. to Shoot-up Hill or Kidderpore reservoir zones. c.1914 6-engine driven pumps installed at Cricklewood (7G5, p128). 1939 & 1945 the diesels supplemented with electric pumps, and in 1951 the steam plant supplemented with electric pumps (9, p87/88/89). Earlier heavy oil engine-driven reciprocating pumps at Cricklewood (7G5, p160).
1897-1908 built Fortis Green Covered Reservoir (filled from Cricklewood) for supplying Highgate & Hampstead reservoirs, and in emergencies Hornsey Lane reservoir. 1911 approval for building a station. In Nov. 1914 installing **three** 4-cylinder vertical diesel engines of 160 b.h.p. each at 200 revs./min., through gearing driving 3-throw horizontal ram pumps, supplied by Mirrlees, Bickerton & Day Ltd, capable of pumping 4.m.g.d. to Hampstead & Highgate reservoirs. In 1935 installing four vertical oil engines from W.H. Allen & Sons Ltd. March 1947 to summer 1952 installing three electric pumps for the Southgate reservoir head and two smaller similar pumps for the Highgate & Hampstead heads (9, p88/89/90). Nov. 1927 48 & 42-inch mains layed from St Michaels Road, Willesden to Fortis Green reservoir by William Press & Sons (9, p125). Earlier heavy oil engine-driven reciprocating pumps at Fortis Green, and later centrifugal pumps (7G5, p160).
1856 Hampstead Grove Covered Reservoirs. Hampstead-heath covered reservoir described 1867 as holding 617,000 gals. (7G6, p5).
c.1854 Maiden Lane > Dartmouth Park Hill Covered Reservoirs. 1867 described as two reservoirs each 273ft. by 208ft. 22ft. deep, together containing 14,520,000 gals., in 1856 est. to have cost **£61,000**

(7G6, p7).

1834 (Thomas Telford) Report: Thomas Telford report to the House of Commons recommending that the NRC for extra water should pump it from the Lee some miles below the Government's Waltham Abbey works (see their Tottenham P.S.), route upland sewage beneath the NR, and **fence the NR to prevent cattle polluting the water when treading down the edges of the banks** (7K3, p16).

1846-1903 (Wells with Pumping Stations) on Route of NR: Additionally augmented by wells with pumping stations along its route, pumping into the New River and sometimes directly into supply. That at Betstile acquired 1871-2, Hadley Road acquired by MWB 1903. See later Schematic list, or chapter 2 for list with dates.

    1846-7 (Baths & Wash-houses Act) 9 & 10 Vic.: Water to be supplied by agreement and contract with the water company that may be without charge or at favourable terms (7K3, p180).

    1847 Water Works Clauses Act: Incorporated a clause that Churchwardens as the local authority were empowered to require water companies to **install fire-plugs** on pipes or mains at convenient intervals, at the expence of the parish. And except from unavoidable causes, must keep a **constant or sufficient supply** for cleansing sewers & drains, watering & cleaning streets, and for free or poor-rate wash-houses, baths & public pumps (7K3, p179/180).

1848 outbreak of cholera in London. 1849 Davall v. NRC (15I, pp216-217).

    1852 (Metropolis Water Act) QUALITY OF WATER > Filter Beds & Covered Reservoirs: Which required that domestic water should not come from the tidal part of the Thames (below Teddington, Chelsea Co. 1856) or River Lee after 1855, that it should be **filtered for domestic use**, and if within 5-miles of St Paul's **stored in Covered reservoirs** (4, pp103-104).

    As for all relevant London water companies, the NRC having to construct filter beds and store filtered water in covered reservoirs, hence by 1856 converting the Upper Pond to the Claremont Square covered reservoir, and constructing other filter beds & covered reservoirs with pumping facilities within the NRC district.

1852 NRC Act (Works & Bonds), 15 & 16 Vict., c. clx.: The **share capital deemed to be £1,519,958**, and to issue bonds for borrowing up to £150,000 for general purposes, and up to £250,000 for widening the river and abandoning some of Myddelton's sections, constructing reservoirs near Islington, filtration at Stoke Newington, drains at Enfield, a communicating pipe network, and a pledge to resolve the problem of **Hertford sewage** flowing into the Lee above the New River intake, their Bill on this thrown out in the next session because it failed to comply with Standing Orders (15I, p118/161-163; 12, p1852 capital; 7K3, pp164-165 NRC 1852 Act fixes their charges which are listed).

1854 NRC Act (Hertford Sewage Diversion), 17 & 18 Vic., c. xxxix: The Hertford sewage flowing into the Lee above the NR intake, to be diverted to an outlet lower down the Lee, such that no doubt that the 'East London Water Works will catch it all'. In 1857 Act said likely to cost £2,000, probably a misprint for £20,000 (15I, p118-119/150).

1854 NRC Act (Reservoirs & £20,000 bonds), 17 & 18 Vic., c. lxxii: For constructing reservoirs in Middx. and £20,000 in bonds (15I, p118).

    1855 River Lee Act: NRC authorised to take extra water from the Lee, since all river water except for navigation was vested in the NRC & ELWWs for an annual payment to the Conservators (15I, pp164-165).

1857 NRC Act (To Raise £30,000), 20 & 21 Vic., c. cxlii: To raise £30,000 on bond, or in lieu issue debenture stock at par (15I, p118/176; 7K3, p172 known as Debenture 'A'). 1857 NRC v. Hertford Land Tax Commissioners (15I, pp126-127).

c./1857 a Mr Burnell article 'Visits to the London Waterworks' published in the weekly 'Journal of Gas Lighting' includes statistical details etc. of NRC reservoirs, which might be of interest, since the NRC had always declined to contribute a paper to the Institution of Civil Engineers (7G6, p4 also adding '**The bed of the NR has been estimated to contain 117 m.g.**'), as yet not getting sight of a copy.

    1692 Hampstead Water Co. > 1856 - 1861 NRC: Originating from a 1543-4 Act (35 Hen. VIII, cap. 10), leased by the City in 1692 to the Hampstead Aqueducts Waterworks, the leasehold finally acquired by the NRC 1856-1861 for a redeemable £3,500 annuity (still being paid by the MWB in 1953). The ponds themselves leased at £80 per annum and not used for domestic water (used for street watering, cattle markets, & loco sheds etc.), the lease renewed by the MWB in 1929 but not renewed in 1936 after the City not willing to sell the freehold (15I, p114; 15J, pp233-234 further details on HWWs; 9, p293 £3,500; 7G5, pp45-46 1856 NRC takeover).

1860 NRC v. Johnston (15I, p112).

1865 Fire Brigades Act: For fires the water companies were expected to provide free water and plugs or hydrants, a constant supply in the pipes preferable, else if intermittent requires finding a turncock to turn on the water which might make it too late. A **fire-plug is a wooden stopper** that can be removed by a fireman, but not replaceable until the turncock turns off the water pressure, such that said not used on mains of the metropolis, under a 1847 Act churchwardens as the local authority were empowered to require water companies to install fire-plugs on pipes or mains at convenient intervals, at the expence of the parish, this 1865 Act transferring the responsibility to the Metro. Board of Works > L.C.C.

Hydrants were superior to fire plugs in that they are stopcocks with a fitting for connecting to firehoses, and became preferable under the following 1871 Act (7K3, pp60-61).

1866 NRC Act (To Raise £500,000 in £100 Non-voting Shares), 29 & 30 Vic., c. ccxxx: (15I, p119/164). In 1867 a Select Committee seeking to compel '**each town or place on the river Lea or its tributaries to intercept its sewage and apply it to the adjacent land**' (7K3, p26). In an 1869 report of a Royal Commission 'the engineer of the NRC, .., stated that it required **great labour and considerable expence in severe frosts to keep the NR, .., in efficient flow**', W.C. Mylne the NRC engineer also proposing 'to increase the supply of water from the basin of the river Lea, by making the drainage area better available, by collecting the streams and chalk springs into **impounding reservoirs to be formed at various places, but principally at Enfield Chase** [this scheme later aborted] which, being on London clay, would be the more favourable for the purpose than any site that could be found on the Lea proper ... The cost of these works, excluding compensation, he estimated at £1.25m' (7K3, p28/p33).

1871 Metropolis Water Act: Incorporated provisions for local or metropolitan authorities to **invoke a constant supply**, such that within 5-days of the request a copy of the notice to be published in the 'London Gazette' & two morning newspapers (7K3, p159). Not actioned until 1881 when gradually extended, after setting up waste meters for its 340-districts (15J, pp181-182). A fire-plug or fire hydrant could be requested by any works or manufactory, at the expence of the owner (7K3, p180). Also audit of water company's accounts by the Board of Trade, and the appointment of a **permanent Metropolitan Water Examiner** (7K3, p40, 7H2, pp18-20 Water Examiner's duties & info. Reports/pp21-22 foulness of using cisterns when not provided with a constant supply; 7H2, pp208-215 1871 Act regulations). This Act also enforcing outward leakage from water pipes (not inward) to **prevent contamination from ground water and sewers** (7K4-1, p94).

c.1851 North Middx. Waterworks > 1871 NRC: A well sunk at Colney Hatch/Betstile, Southgate (Deeds, ELSC&A; 15J, pp234 further details on NMWWs; 7J1, p76; 7G5, pp76-77; 7K1, p24).

1875 NRC v. Mather decided that water charges should be based on **net rateable value not gross rateable value**, in 1882 confirmed in another legal case after reversals, in 1885 confirmed by statute, said to have cost the NRC £12,000 p.a. (15I, p169).

1877 Metropolitan Board of Works v. NRC (15I, p171).

1879 NRC Act (42 & 43 Vic., c.x.): For creating further Debenture 'B' stock (7K3, p172).

1884 ('Not now Used') Hampstead Heath Well (of former Hampstead Water Co.): 5 ponds covering 11 acres holding 10.5 m.g. of surface water from the surrounding district, now **only used for street watering and trade purposes** (7H2, p96).

1884 the NRC said to have invented cistern overflow pipes draining into a water-closet or sink, and later over the back door, householders required to use water fittings passed & stamped by the NRC (15I, p134).

1884 NRC v. Barham (15I, p170); NRC v. Cole (15I, p134); NRC v. Restall (15I, p134); NRC v. Wilson (15I, p170).

c.1872 Bush Hill Park Estates Co. (Well, Water Tower & Small Reservoir) **> 1887 NRC:** Never as such used, the water tower converted to worker accommodation and sold off 1925, such that today a private residence (15J, pp234 further details on BHP Co.; 7J1, p76; 7G5, p77; 7K1, p24).

1889 Cooke v. NRC (15I, p161/pp170-172).

May 1890 'The New River – Unique Auction' Catalogue: 'By Order of the Devisee, **The New River, without doubt the choicest home investment of this year or any other age**. Particulars & Conditions of Sale of A King's Freehold Share (being a one 72nd part of the entire concern), in this Grand Historic

Corporation, producing a present & annually increasing income, which has **doubled in 20 years**, amounting to £515,481 last year, derived from land & water, with important reversions to landed estates,

for sale by Auction by Messrs Edwin Fox & Bousfield, at the Mart, Tokenhouse Yard, Bank of England, on Wed. 21 May, 1890, at Two o'clock precisely in One Lot, in consequence of the death of the late proprietor, at a low reserve', **the hammer falling at £95,100**, the catalogue filled with many interesting details on the NR (Duplicate NRC catalogue given to me by John Clark, ELSC&A; 15J, pp229-230 has details from 19 March 1879 sale catalogue; Graphic chart from Microsoft website). **In 1897 one full Adventurers Share sold for £125,500** (6, p359).

31 Dec. 1891 only 45% of NRC customers on constant supply, by April 1898 the **NRC's London area** expected to be converted by the end of 1898 (7K3, p155).

1895 NRC Bill for raising more capital without an auction clause was withdrawn after the Commons Committee insisted upon its inclusion (15I, p176).

1896 NRC Act, 59 & 60 Vic., c. ccxxix: The NRC forbidden from converting debenture stock into share capital; the 'sterilisation clause' that if to be acquired by a public authority, the 1% allowed for managing the debenture stock not subject to increasing its capital, or compensation ((s. 23 & s. 31(2)) 15I, p176/178).

1896 Staines Reservoirs Act, 60 & 61 Vic., c civ: NRC & two others, stating that they had no advantage from the Act, if acquired by a public authority within 7-years, unless by agreement ((s. 84) 15I, p178).

1897 NRC Act, 60 & 61 Vic., c. ccxxii.

1899 (Intermittent > Constant Supply) Finally Achieved in NRC Area: Prior to constant supply the water was only turned-on on alternate/weekdays, and never on Sundays, such that customers had to store water in any receptacle they had available (in the City often un-hygienically in butts without lids), the NRC area not achieving overall constant supply until 1899 (15I, p131/151; 15J, p54 achieved 1904/p182 1904).

1899 (NRC Connected to Other Company Mains): NRC mains linked to the 'West Middx. Waterworks Co. at the junction of Tottenham Court Road with Oxford Street, and at the junction of Tottenham Court Road with Euston Road. During the year 1898 a new communication was established between the Grand Junction Water Company's and the NRC's systems by means of a main extending from Oxford Street to the NRH, Clerkenwell, with a branch from the West Middx. Co's main' (7K1, pp60-61).

Water Meter Repairs & Fittings (Testing & Stamping)
1899 described as large workshop at NRH where around **50,000 taps per week** (tested to 300 lb. pressure), and ball-valves after successful testing are stamped with the Co's mark. Plus a yard containing stores (7K1, p53). In 1899 the NRC erected a water meter repair and fittings testing shop at NRH, that after 1904 was coping with an increase of work covering the north of the Thames, such that from 1922-24 extending the existing shop at NRH. A 1932 MWB Act making it compulsory for all water fittings to be tested, such that adapting the NRH buildings & erecting a temporary steel-framed building, for the extra workload taking the tenancy of a factory at Cynthia Street, Pentonville Road, Finsbury, and transferring the repair of meters to Battersea. At the outbreak of WW2 suspending compulsory testing and closing the Cynthia Street premises, and after the war proposing to erect a combined testing and meter repair shop at Barn Elms (9, pp208-209).

1902-4 (Metropolis Water Act) NRC Waterworks > MWB) & NRC Estates > NRC Ltd.: That from Midsummer Day (but 25 July 1904 for the NRC) the eight London water companies (**Chelsea, East London, Grand Junction, Kent, Lambeth, NRC, Southwark & Vauxhall and W. Middx.**) became vested in the publically owned Metropolitan Water Board whose members were appointed by the supply areas Local Authorities (15I, p181).

LEFT: Coat of Arms of Metropolitan Water Board (9, frontispiece).

NRC Compensation: For loss of office the 25 NRC Directors were awarded **£76,917. 17s. 10d.**, and for the Company awarded £6,000,534, the nominal amount being £6,534,000, such that after deducting expenses divided **£6.5m in stock to shareholders** (15I, p183/186/187; 15J, p75; 12, p24 £6,534,000 for MW 'B' Stock plus £1,258,000 for Debenture Stocks).
1902 NRC v. Hertford Union (15I, p130). 1904 NRC v. Westminster (15I, p144).

> **1904 NRC Limited (Property Company) Act, 4 Edw. VII., c. xlviii:** Developed the extensive and valuable landed estate, houses and property that were not transferred to the MWB in 1904. The NRC's entire constitution only endorsed by Parliament when it no longer held the socage tenure of the New River. With an authorised capital of £240,000 in £1 shares, but only 130,000 issued at the rate of £50 per Adventurers', King's (both to remain as land and held by the same trusts until vested or sold to someone entitled possession; and as a fixed asset all land or property forming the company shall be vested in the company) or former New share, nominally equivalent to its landed estates assets. Such that 21-directors with a near gross income of £10,000 from rack & ground rents (over 600 houses in Clerkenwell where ⅔'s of the leases were due to expire in around 10-years; and over 150 houses in the suburbs with leases due to expire in the mid-1900s), producing an approx. 5% dividend (15I, pp188-190). Company Secretary c.1904 one H. Stoddard (had died by 1917). The NRC Ltd in 1927 located at 18, Percy Circus, Kings Cross Road, W.C. (12, p24). But the gloss had gone, the Rent Acts after WW1 protecting most of their tenants, in the early-1960s collaborating with London Merchant Securities who had been acquiring loan capital and equity, in 1974 after more that 10-years of negotiations, most of their Clerkenwell estate sold to Islington Council for over £4m. In 1964 at 30 Myddelton Square, St. John St., E.C.1 (11, p70 Note 3). April 1969 - March 1970 (NRC Ltd) office & capital expenditure, new tenancies, & blocks 'A' & 'O' expenditure ((1 bundle) Acc/1953/C/0595, LMA); same for April 1970 – March 1971 ((1 bundle) Acc/1953/C/0596, LMA; same for April 1971 – March 1972 ((1 bundle) Acc/1953/C/0597, LMA). In the 1970s with property assets of £8.4m in the Angel area (14C, p172). In 1974 approx. rents of £250,000 p.a. on property worth £9m, the residential part of the Clerkenwell estate sold for over £4m to the London Borough of Islington (15J, p199).
>> **OCT. 1974 (NRC LIMITED) > LONDON MERCHANT SECURITIES Plc:** Purchasing more commercial premises that included the Angel Corner House refurbished as a banking hall & offices, their Angel site redeveloped 1980-83 as air-conditioned offices, but since redeveloped again (15I, p5/31/44/p188 s. 16 & s. 31/189-190). Mr. R.A. J. Bennett the Company Secretary, their offices at 30, Myddelton Square, Islington, closing c.1983, the early NRC records transferred to the GLRO > London Metropolitan Archives (15I, p. xii; 15J, Preface). Myddelton Place, off Rosebery Avenue, in air-conditioned offices with 100,000 sq.ft. of space (KD, p23). 33, Robert Adam Street, London, W1, near Portman Square (2002 telephone directory).

1904 (Herts. C.C. v. NRC): The Hertford County Council seeking that the NRC repair the approaches to bridges up to 300ft., as per the cases related to the 1530 Henry VIII's Statute of Bridges, but thought overridden by the 1605 NR Act, such that not necessarily to 300ft. ((20 TLR 686 & 687) 15I, p187). From 1904 called the **NR District**, and later the **Northern District** after being merged with the East London area (12, p1).

> **1909-10 (New River Football Club):** No. 3 Highfield Road the former home of Christopher Everett, who for 42-years worked for the MWB, and in the 1909/10 season played for the New River Football Club of which the family have a photo (F1E2, p24/p26 (Everett sisters) photo of 1909/10 New River Football Club, with 'NRF' on football).

1911 Adair v. NRC Ltd (15I, pp202-207).
1913 the MWB advertising for tenders for removal of Furnace Refuse etc. for 12-months from Campsbourne, Betstile, Park, Alma Road, Hoe Lane, Whitewebbs & Rye Common pumping stations (10 Jan. 1913 Enf. Gaz. & Obs., ELSC&A), the clinker probably used for filtering at sewage works or in brickmaking.

> **4 July 1913 (Drowning) Enfield:** 50-year old Miss Annie Ruth Willis a cook recently out of a situation, found drowned in the New River at 6 o'clock in the morning by a MWB worker at a grating near Maidens Bridge (11 July 1913 Enf. Gaz. & Obs., ELSC&A).

Tues. 9 Sept. 1913 (Drowning) Enfield: At about 2:30 16-year old Cornelius Harold Hill, a nursery hand of Birkbeck Road, found drowned in New River at Carrs Basin by William White of the MWB, the victim said to be exceedingly short-sighted and probably fell-in trying to retrieve his glasses. A few days ago at the same spot also called the 'Reservoir', the drowning of a horse-keeper from Winchmore Hill (12 Sept. 1913 Enf. Gaz. & Obs., ELSC&A).

6 Oct. 1913 (Attempted Suicide) Enfield: At 1:30 in the morning at Church Street Enfield, 19-year old Nellie Robertson a domestic servant of Norfolk, attempting to drown herself in the New River, but stopped by PC Mackinder No. 177 Y (17 Oct. 1913 Enf. Gaz. & Obs., ELSC&A).

1914-18 (Great War/World War One): 1915 air raids over London with bombs falling from German Zeppelin airships, and 1917-18 long range Gotha & Giant Bombers. No hits or major damage as such recorded on the New River by the MWB.

1915-20 (Oak Room of Water House > MWB's New-NRH Headquarters): The Oak Room of the old Water House incorporated into the MWB's new headquarters called New River Head build on part of the Round Pond.

3 Sept. 1939 to 7 May 1945 (World War Two) Central Control Room at NRH: During WW2 bombs falling very close to some MWB's pumping stations (within NR area, Stoke Newington, Hornsey, Cricklewood & Kempton Park) but none receiving direct hits. But the distribution pipe network was hit hard (and as such not specifically detailed), causing the mains to become charged with sewage, but luckily protective measures were already in place. The only major incident on the NR, in Oct. 1940 when the three mains that bypass the Enfield Town Loop where hit, but the supply restored within 24-hours, see appropriate section for further details (9, pp302-303); and much bomb damage to the NRC's Clerkenwell estate, such that parts rebuilt after the war (15J, p208).

1940 (Explosion) Blows Man into New River, Enfield: During WW2 there was an explosion at the nearby Waltham Abbey munitions factory, that shook windows 75 miles away, **a man on the New River hereabouts blown in**, who upon scrambling out, **was blown in again** (B11, p208).

1956 (Dog Patrol) New River: Three additional dogs to patrol the New River between Enfield and Stoke Newington (plus William Girling & King George's Reservoir) to be purchased and trained, as well as three employees as handlers, est. to cost £560 (MWB Mins 1956, p289, KBSM).

1974 MWB > Thames Water Authority, becoming one of the ten public Regional Water Authorities.

1987-1994 Officially Opened TW's 'London Ring Main': First section of tunnel completed Jan. 1991, later to which the NRH & the Stoke Newington sites were connected.

1989 Thames Water Authority > Thames Water Plc.: London's water industry becomes privatised again becoming one of the ten Water Service Public Ltd Companies, that included the New River.

2000 became part of German RWE Group.

Oct. 2006 (German RWE Group) > Australian Group Macquarie Bank (1F10-47, p167).

From 1991, Inaugurated 1995 (Artificial Recharge Pumping Stations) Modern Pumphouses: From 1991 a series of additional boreholes constructed beside the New River, enabling **treated water** to be stored in the chalk aquifer in times of surplus (winter), for pumping back into the New River when levels are low, such as in dry summers. The apparatus for these boreholes housed in **approx. 28 modern Pumphouses**, two of these said to be in the older engine houses.

NEW RIVER PATH

1992 - 2004 'New River Path' (HISTORICALLY IMPORTANT): Whilst there have been several short stretches of ancient public footpaths aside the New River, most of it was part of the NRC private estate (> 1904 MWB > 1974 TW although public authorities kept private) without public access. All this historically changing from 1992-2004 when Thames Water Plc magnificently created the New River Path, **although not a public footpath, there is full public access**, only normally closed or diverted for essential TW maintenance.

Public Access > Private > Public Access (FULL CIRCLE): The New River channel up to the C20th open to public access and unhygienic because of swimming and waste disposal. Then enclosed within fences as a private company estate with locked gates, but now again a green finger or long distance public greenway, an extended pedestrian walkway into London beside the New River, in 1988 a dream of Bob Errington of the Rambler's Association, and the late Norman King coming to fruition after his death (www.cityoflondon.gov.uk New River Head, Teacher's Pack; 14A, p14).

28 Mile/45 km Long-Distance Continuous 'New River Path' into London (1992-2004): Since 1992 "The New River Path was developed over a 12 year period at a cost of over £2 million; of this sum £1.3 million has been invested by Thames Water in the project. Throughout this time the Company has worked to overcome operational, safety and security issues in partnership with, and with the support of many organisations; including Groundwork, London's Waterway Partnership, Countryside Agency, New River Action Group, Friends of New River Walk, schools and communities, and all the local authorities along the route" (5A, p6 quote).

The first part opened the 22.4 km path between New Gauge and the M25.

By June 2004, the New River Path completed from Hertford to Islington. Much against the spirit of being a greenway, one women at the NRAG 2006 AGM, wanting parts of it covered with tarmac.

Linking the inner city to the open countryside, following as far as possible the original historic course and some later straightened and piped sections, starting at New Gauge on the River Lee between Hertford and Ware, to its original termination at New River Head in Islington, finally completed along the whole length of the river (5A, p1).

- Over 200 way-marking signs displaying the NR Path logo throughout its length.
- 19 route guide signs.
- 17 interpretation boards on route, to help your enjoyment of this historic aqueduct, that still today provides fresh water for London.

But for such pleasurable walking there are a few relevant **Safety Precautions:**
'Danger Deep Water', No Swimming', 'No Boating', 'No Fishing', 'No Cycles', 'Take Litter Home' & 'No Dog Fouling'.

Dec. 2004 (Thames Water Awarded the National Gold Award) in the Green Apple Environment Awards: For their achievement in creating the New River Path, Thames Water winning a top environmental award, the National Gold award in the Green Apple Environment Awards of the independent environment group the Green Organisation, presented to their Head of Environment at a ceremony in the House of Commons.

And as such makes this book hopefully useful in enhancing the enjoyment of any walk you might undertake today along the route of the New River Path.

SO WALK THE WALK, the NEW RIVER WALK!

NRC Main Sites (from W to E, then N to S): © Copyright M.F. Kensey.

West 1831-1855 (**NRC ownership**) Holme Mill, River **East**
Ivel, Biggleswade, Beds. > W.H. Jordan > 1972
Jordan's Cereals > Holme Mill Heritage Centre Ltd.

```
-------|----- River Lee -------------------- 1738 (NRC) Ware ---------------------------------------------------------------------|
```

West column			East column
1856 New Gauge.	Fishery, Mills & Lock		
1733-1856 'Balance House'	(Leased out) > MWB > TW.		
rebuilt 1770 (SITE OF).		c.1856 to Post-1938	NRC land aside
Manifold Ditch	1613 Tapping the Lee.	NRC Reservoir (SITE OF)	Lee. NRC's
(1739 Act - 1856)	1746 White House 1733-1776 Old Gauge (SITE OF).	between P.S. & prior to	Ware Fishery &
Bypassed by	Sluice. 1773-76 New/Marble Gauge.	Viaduct Road.	Stanstead Fishery.
'New Cut'	1609 Chadwell Spring. Broadmead P.S.	Amwell End P.S.	[Today's Amwell
1856.	(1877 Well	(1848 Well,	Magna Fishery].
	1881 Eng. Hse.).	1868 Eng. Hse.).	
		'Red House'	
		(NRC 1787, dem. c.1954).	
		Amwell Hill P.S.	
		(Well, 1847 Eng. Hse.).	
		Amwell Spring (1609-c.1873).	
		'Amwell Pond'.	
		2 Islands. 'Emma's Well'.	
		1st Island 'Nares' Inscription.	
		2nd Island Mylne Inscription.	
		Amwell Marsh P.S.	
		(1883 Well & Eng. Hse.).	
	1900 NRC pumping water to FORMER	Rye Common P.S.	
	a Res. at Haileybury College. LOOP/s.	(1882-3 Well & Eng. Hse.).	
	1954 Res. > transfer to MWB.		1838-???? (NRC)
		Hoddesdon P.S.	Stanstead Mill
		(1865-6 Well & Eng. Hse.).	(Leased out).
	FORMER	Broxbourne P.S.	R. Lee.
	Small Loop.	(1884 Well, 1887-8 Eng. Hse.).	

Wormley FLASH (rebuilt 1780 in brick & stone)
NW-extremity of former Turnford Loop.
                FORMER   1855 Turnford AQUEDUCT.
                LOOP/s.   Turnford P.S.
                          (1866 Well, 1871 Eng. Hse.).

                          Cheshunt FLASH (Bypassed 1825-6)
                               1835-37 N-RES. > Lake.
                          1836 Eng. Hse., P.S. c.1846 Well.
                               1835-37 S-RES. (SITE OF).
                          Grove House Loop, Cheshunt (Bypassed
                          c.1854-1860.
                FORMER   Small Theobalds Loop >
                LOOP/s.   c.1852-4 Embkmnt > c.1981 M25 AQUEDUCT.

                          FORMER Pre-c.1856 Bullsmoor LOOP.
                             1989 'New River Transfer Tunnel'
                             > King George's Reservoir.

Whitewebbs (1895 Well, 1898 Eng. Hse. &   **(X). (Y). (Z).**   FORMER   1857-58 Docwra AQUEDUCT.
PIPELINE) Closed 1962-64 > Transport Museum.   **(BBH).**   LOOP.
                                      (Bull Beggars Hole).

'**X**' = Enfield FLASH rebuilt 1775 in brick & stone; Enfield Flash LOOP bypassed by a surviving 1820-21 cast-iron aqueduct
('**Y**'), also bypassed 1858 by Docwra Aqueduct. '**Z**' = c. 1775 'Dickinson's/Dickenson's Trough' to the W of Myddelton
House, Enfield, presumably made of wood, used to take an opposing stream over the New River.

  [1902 (Enf. Local Board > MWB
  > TW) Hadley Road P.S.].   Hoe Lane P.S.
1896 (NRC) Proposed   [c.1854 Enf. Local Board > MWB   (1880 Well & Eng. Hse.).
Reservoir, Enfield Chase. > TW) Holtwhite's Hill Res. (1887
(NEVER BUILT).   Water Tower; Alma Rd. W-works (SITE OF)
                           & small Res. Southbury Rd. (SITE OF);
                           1913-14 Water Tower, Ridgeway > Housing].
                                      Enfield Town LOOP   BYPASS PIPES (1853, 1875 & 1912).
                                      (ORNAMENTAL).

c.1874 NRC SOUTHGATE (Oakwood) Reservoir (SITE OF) > Housing.	BUSH HILL Well, Tower & Res., (c.1875 > 1887 NRC, capped 1925) Quaker's Walk NRC Bush Hill Sluice (SITE OF). House, rebuilt 1796. c.1613 Red House (Sir H. Myddelton's Country House) > Halliwick dem. 1993 (SITE OF) > Mod. housing. 1. 1613-1788 BUSH HILL FRAME (SITE OF) > 1788 Embkmnt. 2. CLARENDON ARCH (Rebuilt 1682, Moved 1786).	
	HIGHFIELD Rd. P.S. [1896 NRC Proposed but NEVER (1885 Well & Eng. Hse.). BUILT Res. & Filter Beds]. BOURNE HILL c.1884 NRC (Palmers Green) Cov. Reservoir.	
BETSTILE FORMER SOUTHGATE LOOP. Well & PS Wilde's/Mincing Flash (abandoned 1774) & Newman's Flash (abandoned 1779). (1867, 1870 NRC) 1857-58 Pymmes Brook AQUEDUCT. FORMER TOTTENHAM c.1938 Housing 1859 Wood Green TUNNEL. LOOP, [& c.1852 Proposed Res. (SITE OF). NEVER BUILT].		R. Lee. | | (1) NOT NRC, | Tottenham Local Board Pre-1893 Longwater P.S (> 1904 MWB Park P.S > TW, Marsh Lane). | |

Then see **LANDSCAPE CONTINUATION SHEET**.

New River Autogrates MODERN (Locations):
Turkey Street (S-side), Enfield.
Southbury Road (N-side), Enfield.
North Circular/Bowes Road (N-side), Palmers Green, N13.
Lordship Road (N-side), Stoke Newington.

Post-1991 MODERN NR Pumphouses (Locations):
Probably all or mainly Artificial Recharge Pumphouses, many of them built with a hole in a 'bat brick' on the New River side, with an **internal roosting box for bats**.
2007 (Not Inscribed) Cheshunt, SW-side previous S-reservoir.
2007 (Not Inscribed) S-side M25 aqueduct, Cheshunt-Enfield border.
'1994' W-side New River, N-side of footpath, N-side of Maidens Brook , said to be the only one that pumps direct to E. London [prob. into Transfer Tunnel], all others pump into the NR (10-3, p58).
'1992' W-bank opposite Worcesters Ave., Enfield.
Hoe Lane P.S. said to have been converted, perhaps the two brick 'beehives' on W-bank, just N of P.S.
'1994' NW-side Carterhatch Lane, Enfield.
'1994' W-side Eaton Road, S-side Southbury Rd., Enfield.
Prob. 1994, NW-side Bush Hill Road.
TWO '1992' together, NW-side Ridge Avenue.
Highfield Road P.S., said to have been converted.
Date? NW-side Hazelwood Lane.
'1994' NW-side of Oakthorpe Road.
'1994' S-side of former Southgate Town Hall.
c./2007-8 (Probably Not inscribed) Pumphouse on E-bank before Autogate at Bowes Road.
Inscribed date hidden by trees, SE-side of Whittington Road.
'1994' NW-side of Myddelton Road.
'1993' NW-side Station Road, Wood Green.
1998? on N-side of Penstock path on site of disused filter bed, Hornsey.
'1994' W-bank, S-side of footbridge, Hornsey.
'1993' W-side of Hornsey Sluice House.
'1994' NW-side of Hornsey High Street.
Date? Lothair Road South.
Date? N-bank, S-side of Eade Road.
Date (Not visible from NR) N-end of E-Reservoir, on a roadway off Bethune Road.
'1992' SE-bank, SE-side of Lordship Road.
No visible date, SW-side of former 'Primary Filter House', Stoke Newington.
Unknown Date, Arlington Way, incorporated into rear of Sadlers Wells Theatre.

London's New River in Maps (Vol. 1, Part 1) by Michael F. Kensey

NRC Main Sites (from W to E):

© Copyright M.F. Kensey.

West — **East**

(4) NRC TOTTENHAM PS (1851-1905) SITE OF, S-side Ferry Lane. 1836/40 NRC Tottenham Mills, 1852 Fire. [Plus c.1854 Proposed Res. NEVER BUILT].

(2) HORNSEY Basin Res's & F-Beds (b. 1859), 3rd P.S. (1893-1960s), 2nd P.S. (1875-c.1936), 4th (1903-c.1936 > Rest.), 1st (1859, dem. c.1881).

(3) 1859 Hornsey Sluice House, 1861-62 WW supplying Wood Green. FORMER 2-Lower Hornsey LOOPS > 1886 Cut, & 1891-92 Small Tunnel.

FORMER Hornsey Village LOOP with SITE OF FORMER Sluice.

CAMPSBOURNE Well (1884) & P.S. (1887-88) by 1996 disused.

FORTIS GREEN ---> Reservoir (b.1897-1908).

CROUCH HILL (> Stroud Green) Reservoirs (b. 1880).

FORMER Stamford Hill LOOP & Tunnel.

Hornsey supply from Moselle Brook, abandoned 1790.

(5) HIGHGATE (The Grove/W. Hill) Reservoir (c.1850).

FORMER Hol. LOOP, HIGHBURY SLUICE/HM/ WW & HIGHBURY FRAME. HORNSEY LANE (Archway) Res. (b. 1845) > PS 2001 Hsg. (1854-56) > 1995 Climbing Centre, Hse. > 1996 Water Sports Centre. FORMER Eng. Hse. (1830-1902). West Res. (1830-33) & 1936 Prim. Filter & Filter Beds (1852

(6) STOKE NEWINGTON PS.

East Reservoir (1830-33),

MAIDEN LANE (> Dartmouth Park Hill) Res's (c.1854).

/1856/1867 > Housing). FORMER Clissold Park LOOP.

FORMER St Pauls Rd LOOP.

CRICKLEWOOD Bal. Res's & PS (b.1897-1903).

HAMPSTEAD GROVE Reservoir(s) (b. 1856).

[Also 1859 Hampstead Water Works/Ponds > NRC].

(7)

FORMER small Horse Shoe Point LOOP.

FORMER Thatched House Sluice & c.1650 Essex Rd TUNNEL (Both SITE OF).

Raised Wooden Trough lined with lead, 'Hollow', City Road.

CAMDEN PARK ROAD NRC Open Res. c.1841 -1939 (SITE OF).

1708-9 High/Upper Pond > Lanes Garden Cistern > 1856 CLAREMONT Sq. Reservoir. St. JOHN STREET

(1613 Round Pond *) **NEW RIVER HEAD** Reservoir (1805-1857) SITE OF. (Later Outer Pond * (> 1856-1946 3-Filter Beds); 1707-8 Windmill (*), c.1720s-1768 Horse Eng., 1768-9 1st Eng. House (*), aided by c.1779-1840s Waterwheel, then later Engines *, 1936-8 MWB Water Labs. *) SITE OF > RESIDENTIAL.

TOTTENHAM COURT- HAMPSTEAD ROAD Reservoir (SITE OF) > Tolmers Square. (1793 Res., 1837-38 Well, removed c. 1860).

DORSET GARDENS (1771-1819).

BRIDEWELL PRECINCT (1717-1771).

PUDDLE DOCK. NRC Office & Quay (By-1669 -1717).

BROKEN WHARF. Bulmer's WWs > LBWWs > 1822 NRC > MWB.

LBWWs, NRC's Pumpbearers' Wharf 1822 'Bridge House' near London Bridge, Southwark, mentioned 1667. Assets sold to NRC.

(ALL SITE OF)

N.B.
1809-15 NRC causes bankruptcy of Holloway Waterworks Co.

1896 STAINES RESERVOIRS ------>NRC KEMPTON PARK Res's, Filter Beds & PS (b.1897-1903). [N & S] JOINT COMMITTEE (Grand Junction, W. Middx. & NRC).

(2) NOT NRC, Tottenham Local Board Waterworks 1883 Downhills W-Tower & Res's (SITE OF).
(3) NOT NRC, Tottenham Local Board Waterworks, Tottenham Hale, extended 1856 (SITE OF).
(4) NOT NRC, East London Waterworks Co. c.1894 FERRY LANE (S-side) PS.
(5) NOT NRC, 1928 MWB HIGHGATE [Golf Club] Res.
(6) NOT NRC, East London Waterworks Co. c.1869 Finsbury Park Cov. Res.
(7) Kentish Town Well (N of William Ellis School), Hampstead Water Co. (> 1859 NRC).

'PS/P.S.' = Pumping Station. 'b.' = Built. 'Hol' = Holloway. 'Rest.' = Restaurant. LBWWs = London Bridge Water Works. 'MWB' = Metropolitan Water Board. 'HM' = Horse Machine. 'WW' = Water Wheel. * = Part Remains.

London's New River in Maps (Vol. 1, Part 1) by Michael F. Kensey

NRC Takeovers etc.

2 July 1614 (Fogwell Spring) Smithfield: Hugh Myddelton purchasing Mr John Darge's small waterworks at Fogwell Spring/Pond, Smithfield that supplied the City of London.
Dec. 1667 (Sir Edward Ford > NRC) Waterworks: Ordered to remove a water tower in grounds of Somerset House, but gets a licence for 3-new waterworks (**X, Y & Z**), Dec. 1667 taken over by the NRC.

1738 (NRC Housing): William Berners (NRC Deputy Governor) in trust for NRC, building houses on Hugh Marchant's (prop. of Marchant's Waterworks) former Marylebone land, 1751 Release.
1809-15 (NRC Bankrupts) Holloway Waterworks Co.: By laying pipes into area, immediately after George Pocock dug a 172ft. deep well & obtained an Act for financing a steam engine etc.
1816-18 (York Buildings Waterworks) N-bank River Thames: Taken over 1816-18 by NRC.
1822 (London Bridge Waterworks): Established 30 May 1581, in 1822 taken over by NRC, gaining their customers, but the LBWWs removed for demolishing Old London Bridge, in return given the Broken Wharf site. In 1822 the NRC sold the S-end of LBWWs to a Mr Edwards, who in 1820 had purchased the St Mary Overie water rights, uniting them under the Southwark Waterworks.
1856-1861 (Hampstead Waterworks Company): Created 1544, 1692 'Society of Hampstead Aqueducts' taken over 1856-1861 by NRC.
1871 (N. Middx. aka Colney Hatch Waterworks) New Southgate: With only 250-customers taken over by NRC in 1871.
1887 (Bush Hill Park Est.) Private Waterworks, Enfield: In 1887 taken over by NRC, sold by MWB in 1925.

Sites from W to E/N to S:

West

Bush Hill Park Co.
1872 well etc., 1887 > **NRC.**

East

City's 1544 Act, 1590 attempt
John Hart prob. unsuccessful.
1692 Soc. of Hampstead Aqueducts
> **Hampstead Waterworks Co.**
1856-1861 > **NRC.** Also 2-wells,
at **Kentish Town** & Hampstead Heath.
Water source leased until 1936.

c.1851 well > 1867 N. Middx. by
aka **Colney Hatch Waterworks**
1871 > **NRC.**

1809-15 NRC causes bankruptcy of
Holloway Waterworks Co.

Based around Oxford St./Marylebone

Described 1720 City's **Maribone** 1667-8 Sir William Smith
Conduit waters > **Leased by LBWWs.** & partners conveying Marybone
Windmill in water to Covent Garden.

Somewhere off Tottenham Court Field/
Oxford Street Rathbone Place,
(Z) Marybone N-side Oxford Street
Waterworks & at Northumberland
Sir Edward Ford Ave., Charing X Stn.
> Sir Robert Vyner **Marchant's**
Dec.1667 > **NRC.** **Waterworks**
(aka Hartshorn
Lane)
c.1696
to c.1772.
In 1738 tenements
built on the former
Marylebone land of
Hugh Marchant for
William Berners in trust
for **NRC**, 1751 release.

Bot. of Villiers   1660s   Temple Pier, N-end   North of Blackfriars Bridge   SE of St Paul's   From 1582 waterwheels
Street.   over   Surrey St. to near   supplying City of London.   Cathedral.   in arches of bridge.
York Bldgs.   looking   the Adelphi in the   c.1595 Fogwell Pond,   **Broken Wharf**   **London Bridge**
Waterworks   Gdns. of   Strand, **(Y) Durham**   Henry Shaw 500-year   1594 Bevis Bulmar's   **Waterworks**
1675 YBWWs   Somerset   **Yard Waterworks**   lease.   Horse-engine WWs.   3-horses.
with wooden   House,   Sir Edward Ford   1614 Fogwell Spring   1733 > LBWWs.   Sir Edward Ford
tower. 1816-18   **Water**   > Sir Robert Vyner   Smithfield > **NRC.**   1822 > **NRC.**   > Sir Robert Vyner
> **NRC.**   **Tower**   Dec.1667 > **NRC.**   For the rebuilding of   Dec.1667 > **NRC.**
                       filled by   London Bridge, in   In 1822 assets purchased
                       horsepower,   return **NRC** gets the   by NRC, customers to
                       Sir Edward Ford   **Broken Wharf**   **NRC**, LBWWs dem.
                       ordered to   **site.**   **(X) Wapping Wall**
                       remove it   **Waterworks**
                       Gets licence for 3-new   Prob. sold off.
                       waterworks (**X, Y & Z**).

© Copyright M.F. Kensey.

NRC FORMER Headquarters

4.
< New River Head, (1904 MWB Offices elsewhere, 1915-20 demolished
Islington/Clerkenwell. NRC Offices to build MWB NRH Offices).
1820-1904.

		River Fleet		-------------------- Other Sites ----------------------		
3.	**2.**	|	**1.**			
Dorset Gardens	**Bridewell**	|	**Puddle Dock**	**Broken Wharf**	**LBWWs**	**NRC's Pipe Borer's**
1771-1819	**Precinct**	|	**NRC Office & Quay**	Bulmer's WWs.	1822	**Wharf** 'Bridge House'
	1717-1771	|	**by 1669-1717**	> LBWWs	assets	near London Bridge
		|		> 1822 NRC	sold to	Southwark, first mentioned
		|		> MWB.	NRC.	1656.

-------------------------------|---------- **River Thames** --------------------------------

1. By 1669-1717 NRC Clerk's Office (near Puddle Dock) with Possible Quay, E of Blackfriars. Used for landing corn etc. prior to being owned by Mr Puddle ((1755 Strype, Vol. 1, p709) OS3.10, p71/222). Probably fol. a post 1656-1661 increase of rent on Bridge House wharf to £40 per annum (previously free) moving to Puddle Dock, resulting in weekly meetings Dec. 1669 at the Clerk's Office of NRC members, near Puddle Dock (15J, p90; 1F10-47, p167 by 1669). 1682 weekly meeting of NRC Members at the Clerk's office near Puddle-Dock ((Typed 'B.M. Cup. 651. e. (116)') 8A1, 2-8; B2-1, pp71-72 1685 weekly meetings; 1689 water lease, weekly meetings; 15J, p90 also adds 1687 board meeting prob. at Puddle Dock). 8 Aug. 1717 newspaper notice that NRC's Puddle Dock **office had been transferred to Bridewell Precinct** beside the Fleet Ditch ((Acc 2558/NR13/13/1, LMA) 15J, p90); that might have been because of the adjacent laystall, and possibly continuing with pipe boring here or leasing the site out. Post/1742 mention of NRC still paying rent (15J, pp90-91).
1749 (S. & N. Buck) print showing the Dock stacked with tree trunks with an **E-side laystall for street refuse which probably stank**. 1761 Dodsley calls 'Pipe Yard' Bristol Street, Puddle Dock. Later site of Mermaid Theatre ((No source quoted) 11, p73 early-C18th).

2. 1717-1771 NRC Offices & Yard, Bridewell Precinct: 1717 first building, and in 1742 a second large building with land & wharf (22 July long lease for £80 from Humphrey Ambler) at the SW extremity of where the River Fleet entered the Thames ((Acc 2558/NR13/54/1-6, LMA) 15J, p91). The former offices here burnt down 24 Dec. 1769, the site in 1770 assigned to Bridewell Hospital ((Acc 2558/MW C/46/26-2, LMA) 15J, p91).
Then adjacent on the W-side:

3. 1771-1819 NRC Offices Dorset Gardens, & Pipe Wharf, Blackfriars: W-facing frontage of NRC Headquarter Offices, Dorset Street/Gardens, aka Salisbury Square/Whitefriars, with pipe-boring works (Stables, Workshops, Mill & Sheds) alongside called Dorset Yard. The site originally leased from July 1750 but sublet to timber merchants, used after the above fire to build new offices designed by Robert Mylne when NRC Assistant Surveyor, just to the West on the site of the former Duke's aka Salisbury Court Theatre (where Shakespeare once performed, destroyed in the 1666 Great Fire) > 1671-97 Dorset Gardens Theatre dem. 1709), at right angles to the River Thames ((Acc 2558/NR13/53/1-10) 15J, p91 long lease at £140 p.a. with former Bagge's Wharf). The foundation stone laid 28 June 1770 by the NRC Governor, Mr Holford (14B2, p458). Building work by Sylvanus Hall. Using £1,000 fire insurance paid by the 'Hand in Hand Office'. After converting to Iron Pipes (mainly c.1810-18) there was no need for a pipe-boring wharf, so 1819-20 moving to New River Head, Islington. Leasing out the site, 1814 City Gas Works, 1860 sold to the City Gas Company for £47,000 > 1885 City of London School (aka Sion College Library/part Guildhall School of Music), Blackfriars (15J, pp92-93 further details).

4. 1819/20 - 1904 NRC New River Head Offices (1904 MWB, 1915-20 Replaced by NRH Offices > Housing), Clerkenwell, aka Islington: On their own land here extending the Water House to create their new Head Offices at NRH with its new Board Room (15J, p93 built by James Donaldson of Bloomsbury for £3,500). From 1767 the upper part of NRH used as private apartments for Robert

Mylne the NRC Surveyor, these apartments from 1810 used by his son W.C. Mylne, such that when rebuilt the NRC Secretary Mr Rowe having to rent a nearby house, but from 1862 the private apartments converted to offices ((Acc 2558/MW C/15/364) 15J, p93). In 1902-4 taken over by the MWB, who used offices rented elsewhere, but from 1915-20 replaced the NRC offices with a new 3-storey MWB headquarters building designed by H. Asten Hall built at a cost of £324,205, given a 4th-floor 1934-36 (15J, pp93-94 interim rented offices).

1997-8 (Offices > 129 Apartments): In 1996 after an agreement with English Heritage and Islington Council, the vast offices of New River Head sold to the developers Berkeley Manhattan and Kennet Properties (a subsidiary of Thames Water), who from 1997-8 converted the main Neo-Georgian building into 129 private two-room and duplex penthouse apartments on 6-levels, whilst inside retaining the Oak Room (available for private functions) and Board Room with gallery, and opening up the large 2-storey Revenue Hall with its glazed barrel-vaulted roof, so that it became fully viewable from the entrance hall (14A, p9 1993 TW moving to Reading/p14; 5A, until 1993 Thames Water offices).

ABOVE-R (Previous Sketch Map)
1822-1927 Broken Wharf: 1594 Broken Wharf Waterworks > 1703/33 LBWWs > 1822 NRC, the site used as a backup Pumping Station for times of drought/fire etc. until sold by the MWB in 1927.

1581 London Bridge Water Works (LBWWs): 1822 at the impending rebuilding of London Bridge, the LBWWs assets were sold to the NRC.

1656 NRC 'Pipe Borer's Wharf', Southwark, aside the Thames: Wooden pipe boring likely introduced to England c.1582 by Peter Morris of the London Bridge Water Works (LBWWs), who possibly had a workshop on the site here near the Southwark-end of London Bridge, at today's Hay's Wharf. In 1651 on the site of the Abbots of Battle, Sussex town house or inn, Alexander Hay taking a small wharf for which he paid £6 p.a. to the Bridge House Estates, of which a part 1656 was rented to the NRC on which he erected a lean-to or hanging shed for their workmen. This became known as 'Pipe Borer's Wharf', where until the latter-$C17^{th}$ wooden pipe boring was undertaken manually using tree-trunks transported from Hertfordshire, until the NRC installed a **horse-mill at Puddle Dock or Dorset Stairs** (7G5, p31; also mentioned 1667).

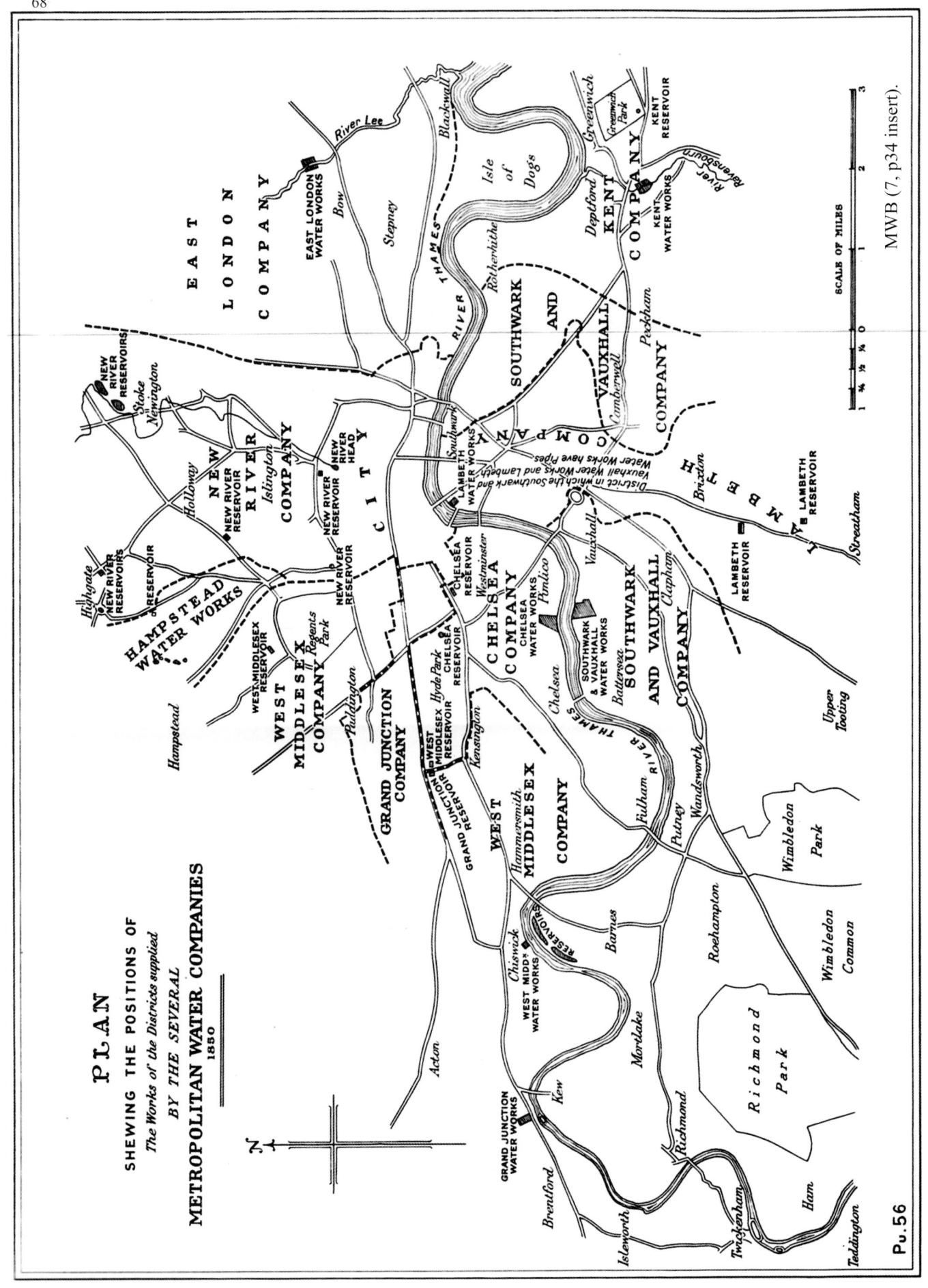

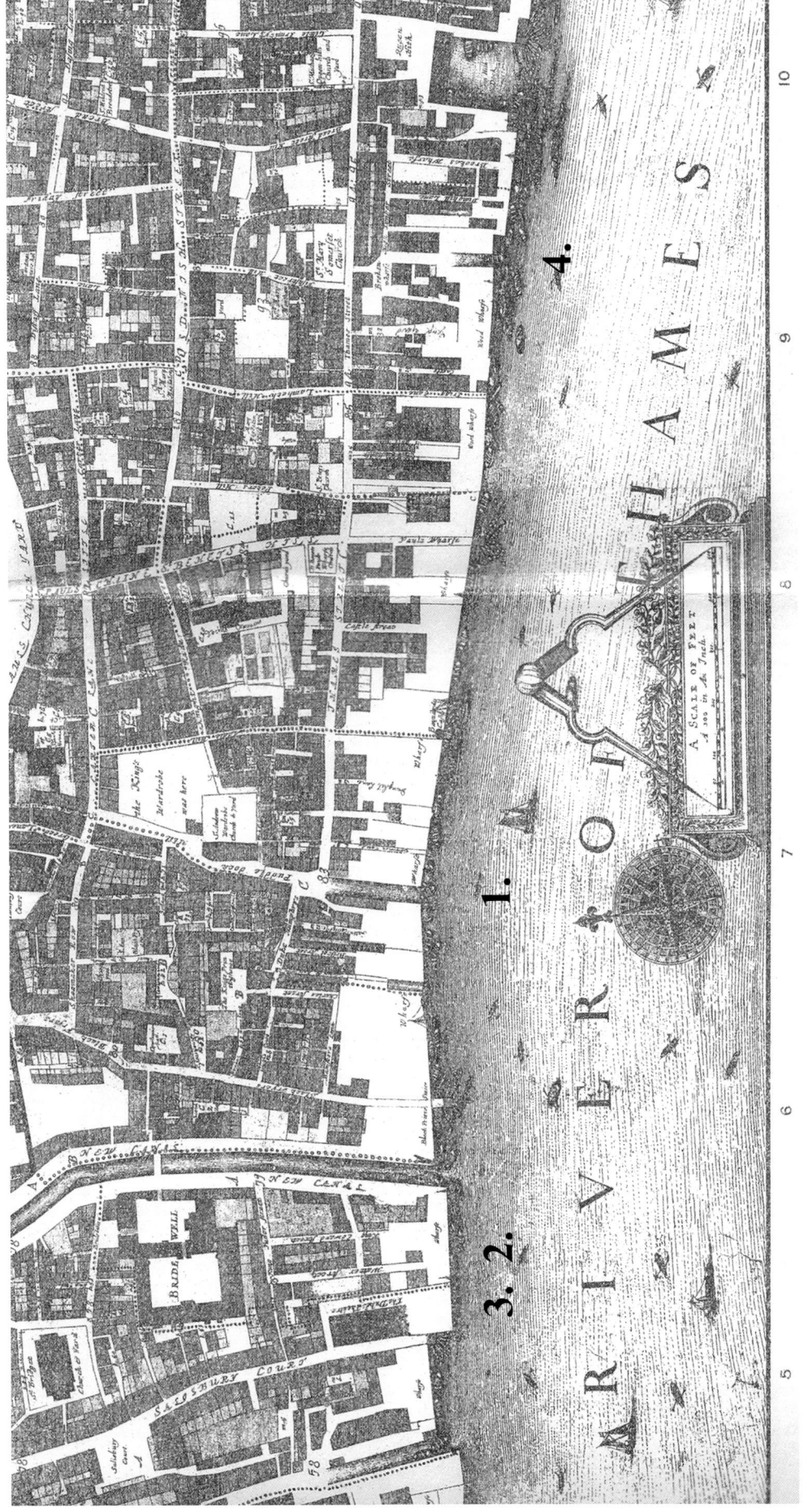

1667 Ogilby & Morgan Map of London (1K10F, endpaper). Showing SITES OF New River Company's premises on N-side of River Thames: **1. By1669-1717 Puddle Dock, NRC Office & Quay. 2. 1717-1771 Bridewell Precinct** (Destroyed by a Fire). **3. 1771-1819 Dorset Gardens** > 1820 NRH. **4.** 1594 Broken Wharf Waterworks > 1703/33 LBWWs > **1822 NRC Broken Wharf**, sold by MWB 1927.

ABOVE: Entrance of the River Fleet with Bridewell Bridge ((Pink's 14B2, p264a with date of 1756; based on a Guildhall painting of the school of/or by Samuel Scott variously dated c.1700, c.1750, mid-C18th).

  8 Aug. 1717-1771 NRC Office, Yard & Quay, Bridewell Precinct, on the W-corner of the Fleet. Moving here from Puddle Dock sited to the E, and located here until the **premises were destroyed in a Xmas Eve 1769 fire**. The property on the W-side (previous site of the 'Duke's Theatre' dem. c.1709, of which there is a Brit. Museum print) until 1750 a Timber Yard of the Company of Carpenters, from 1750 leased by the NRC and sublet, but used 1771 to build the **NRC Offices Dorset Gardens, & Pipe Wharf, Blackfriars**, moving 1819-20 to new offices at New River Head, Clerkenwell.

BELOW: Larger above, **showing the NRC Bridewell Precinct building ('X')** behind a stack of wooden water pipes.

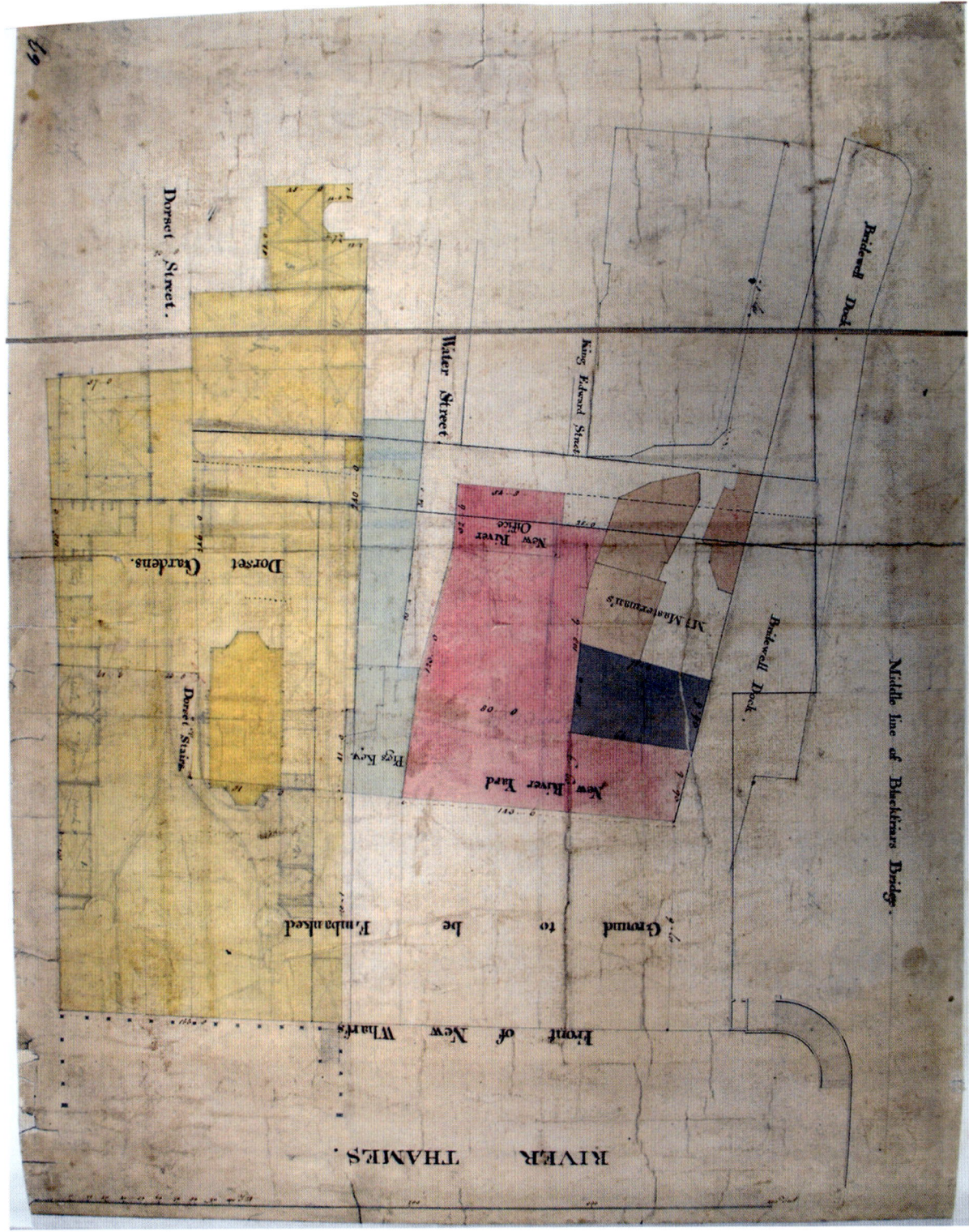

c.1770 Plan of NRC W-facing Dorset Stairs Offices (1771-1819) & Bridewell Precinct: Measured plan probably by Robert Mylne, from 1767 NRC Assistant Surveyor, 1761-69 having completing the construction of Blackfriars Bridge (see far right of plan), 1770-71 becoming NRC Surveyor (TW Archive; MFK photo). Although presumably moving out 1819-20, the Dorset lease not sold until 1866-7 for which the NRC shareholders were paid a £1,400 bonus per share.

1771 W-facing NRC Office Dorset Stairs, on N-side of Thames, Blackfriars: Designed by Robert Mylne NRC Surveyor/Engineer, following a 1769 fire at their adjacent Bridewell Precinct premises immediately to the E. Inset plan shows central part as Main Office, with ground level rear-wing extensions (12, p50; MFK enhanced & text).

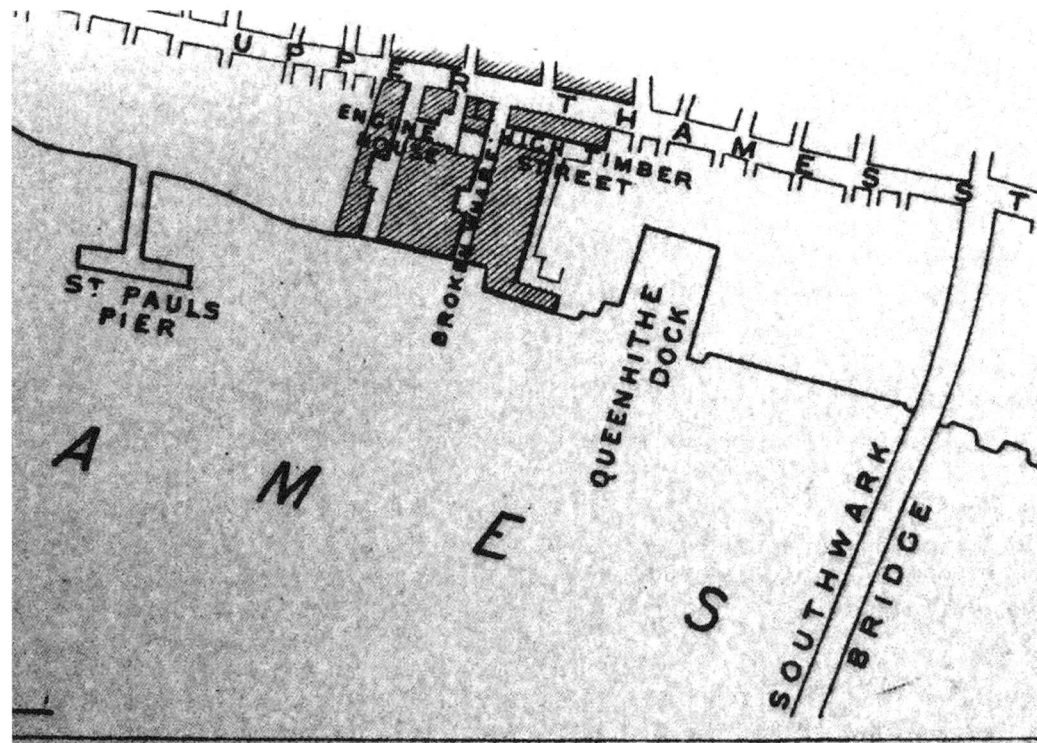

ABOVE: 1872 NRC Map of Works & Estates. NRC Engine House at Broken Wharf for use in times of drought & fires but probably never used as such. Site sold off 1927 by the MWB (TW Archive; MFK photo).

New River Company Dividends from 1633-1903

'**An Acct. of Dividends on New River Shares commencing 1633 [-1822]**.
Midsummer & Christmas.

YEAR	£ s. d.	YEAR	£ s. d.	YEAR	£ s. d.
New River originally constructed **1609-13**, but **no profits until 1633**.		1640	15. 15. 10½.	1648	19. 3. 6¼.
		1640	17. 6. 10.	1648	18. 19. 11.
		1640 A	**33. 2. 9.**	**1648 A**	**38. 3. 5.**
Midsr.		1641	14. 8. 2.	1649	16. 2. 5.
1633	**11. 19. 1.**	1641	16. 6. 5½.	1649	19. 12. 3¾.
Midsr. & Christs.		**1641 A**	**30. 14. 8.**	**1649 A**	**35. 14. 9.**
1634	3. 4. 2.	1642	14. 15. 8¼.	1650	19. 1. 8½.
[Then Midsr. followed by Christs.]		1642	17. 3. 8½.	1650	20. 17. -¼.
		1642 A	**31. 19. 5.**	**1650 A**	**39. 18. 9.**
1635	5. 16. 8½.	1643	13. 11. 3¾.	1651	18. 14. -¾.
1635	8. 17. 6¾.	1643	14. 2. 2.	1651	20. 15. 4.
1635 A	**14. 14. 3.**	**1643 A**	**27. 13. 6.**	**1651 A**	**39. 9. 5.**
1636	6. 15. 6¾.	1644	12. 12. 10½.	1652	19. 11. 3¼.
1636	12. 15. 4½.	1644	14. 17. 7½.	1652	24. 10. 11¾.
1636 A	**19. 10. 11.**	**1644 A**	**27. 10. 6.**	**1652 A**	**44. 2. 3.**
1637	10. 18. 7½.	1645	15. 19. 7¾.	1653	25. 2. 8½.
1637	12. 1. 1½.	1645	16. 3. 5½.	1653	27. 1. 4.
1637 A	**22. 19. 9.**	**1645 A**	**32. 3. 1.**	**1653 A**	**52. 4. 1.**
1638	9. 15. 2.	1646	17. 1. 4.	1654	26. 15. 1¾.
1638	16. 10. 7¾.	1646	19. 8. 8.	1654	25. 8. 5.
1638 A	**26. 5. 10.**	**1646 A**	**36. 10. -**	**1654 A**	**52. 3. 7.**
1639	15. 5. 1¼.	1647	17. 15. 4.	1655	29. 6. -½.
1639	13. 9. 3¾.	1647	20. 17. 6.	1655	25. 10. 9¾.
1639 A	**28. 14. 5.**	**1647 A**	**38. 12. 11.**	**1655 A**	**54. 16. 10.**

Year	£. s. d.	Year	£. s. d.	Year	£. s. d.
1656	18. 13.11¼.	1676	63. 1. 4½.	1695	103. 12. 9½.
1656	25. – 6¾.	1676	71. 12. 1.	1695	104. 4. 6.
1656 A	**43. 14. 6.**	**1676 A**	**134. 13. 6.**	**1695 A**	**207. 17. 4.**
1657	29. 14. 5½.	1677	70. 1.11½.	1696	103. 15. 8½.
1657	31. 14. –½.	1677	73. – 5.	1696	9. 11. 9½.
1657 A	**61. 8. 6.**	**1677 A**	**143. 2. 5.**	**1696 A**	**113. 7. 6.**
1658	28. 14. 4¾.	1678	71. 14. 9½.	1697	87. 18. 1¾.
1658	31. 9. 3¾.	1678	78. 3. 4.	1697	95. 15. 7.
1658 A	**60. 3. 8.**	**1678 A**	**149. 18. 2.**	**1697 A**	**183. 13. 9.**
1659	33. 2. 5½.	1679	80. 15. 2½.	1698	83. 9.11¼.
1659	32. 16. 5.	1679	70. 13.10.	1698	97. 9. 5½.
1659 A	**65. 18. 11.**	**1679 A**	**151. 9. 0.**	**1698 A**	**180. 19. 5.**
1660	34. 7. 5.	1680	69. – –	1699	102. 3.10.
1660	34. 7. 5½.	1680	76. 1. 8.	1699	104. 6. 5¾.
1660 A	**68. 15. –**	**1680 A**	**145. 1. 8.**	**1699 A**	**206. 10. 4.**
1661	39. 11.10¾.	1681	78. 14. 8.	1700	107. 15. 2½.
1661	41. 17. 2½.	1681	90. 7. –¼.	1700	104. 1. 4¾.
1661 A	**81. 9. 11.**	**1681 A**	**169. 1. 1.**	**1700 A**	**211. 16. 7.**
1662	37. 4. 1½.	1682	91. 3. 7½.	1701	108. – 1½.
1662	40. 8. 3¾.	1682	81. 5. 7½.	1701	100. 12. 8.
1662 A	**77. 12. 7.**	**1682 A**	**172. 9. 3.**	**1701 A**	**208. 12. 10.**
1663	29. 17. 4.	1683	83. 5. 8.	1702	101. 1. 1¾.
1663	31. 11. 9¼.	1683	85. 8. -	1702	85. 6. 9¼.
1663 A	**61. 9. 11.**	**1683 A**	**168. 13. 8.**	**1702 A**	**186. 7. 11.**
1664	32. – 1½.	1684	85. 18. 8½.	1703	79. 10. 4.
1664	38. 9. –¼.	1684	86. 5. 8¾.	1703	82. 10. 5½.
1664 A	**70. 9. 2.**	**1684 A**	**172. 4. 5.**	**1703 A**	**162. – 10.**
1665	30. 2.10¼.	1685	96. 1. 4.	1704	88. 10.11.
1665	34. 13. 9.	1685	99. 16. 1.	1704	89. 16. –½.
1665 A	**64. 16. 7.**	**1685 A**	**195. 17. 5.**	**1704 A**	**178. 7. -.**
1666	34. 13. 9.	1686	99. 8.11½.	1705	91. 10. 6½.
1666	40. 3. 2.	1686	106. 17. -	1705	91. 15. 9½.
1666 A	**74. 16. 11.**	**1686 A**	**206. 6. 0.**	**1705 A**	**183. 6. 4.**
1667	27. 5. 5½.	1687	109. 14.11.	1706	89. 8. 1½.
1667	24. 11. 5.	1687	116. 8. 8.	1706	96. 15. 3.
1667 A	**51. 16. 11.**	**1687 A**	**226. 3. 7.**	**1706 A**	**186. 3. 5.**
1668	20. 3. 5.	1688	113. 11. 1½.	1707	99. 2. 3.
1668	33. 9. –¾.	1688	117. 19. 5½.	1707	84. 8. 5½.
1668 A	**53. 12. 6.**	**1688 A**	**231. 10. 7.**	**1707 A**	**183. 10. 9.**
1669	22. – 4¾.	1689	119. 14. 5.	1708	81. 6. 9½.
1669	34. 18. 4.	1689	117. 6. 8.	1708	72. 6.10¾.
1669 A	**56. 18. 9.**	**1689 A**	**237. 1. 1.**	**1708 A**	**153. 13. 8.**
1670	23. 15. 9.	1690	112. 10. 3.	1709	81. 19. 7.
1670	46. 18. 4½.	1690	109. 19. 1.	1709	74. 5. 9¾.
1670 A	**70. 14. 2.**	**1690 A**	**222. 9. 4.**	**1709 A**	**156. 5. 5.**
1671	39. 13. 6½.	1691	108. 7.10½.	1710	77. 11. 5½.
1671	57. 15. 9½.	1691	104. 7. 4.	1710	72. 8. 6¾.
1671 A	**97. 9. 4.**	**1691 A**	**212. 15. 3.**	**1710 A**	**150. 0. 0.**
1672	47. – 5½.	1692	134. 8. 8.	1711	81. 6. 5.
1672	56. 9. 8½.	1692	120. 14. 1.	1711	76. 10. 7¾.
1672 A	**103. 10. 2.**	**1692 A**	**255. 2. 9.**	**1711 A**	**157. 17. 1.**
1673	44. 5. 6.	**Competition from Hampstead Waterworks & York Buildings**		1712	83. 6. 9½.
1673	63. 17. 9.			1712	81. 1. 7½.
1673 A	**108. 3. 3.**	1693	110. 13. -	**1712 A**	**164. 8. 5.**
1674	64. 6. 7½.	1693	106. 7. 2.	1713	92. 6. 2½.
1674	64. 17.11½.	**1693 A**	**217. 0. 2.**	1713	116. 4. 5½.
1674 A	**129. 4. 7.**	1694	96. 2. 7.	**1713 A**	**209. – 8.**
1675	60. 2. 8.	1694	103. 4. -	1714	123. 6. 5¾.
1675	67. 1. 5.	**1694 A**	**119. 6. 7.**	1714	118. 5. –¼.
1675 A	**127. 4. 1.**				

1714 A	241. 11. 6.	**1734 A**	226. 1. 5.	**1754 A**	255. 9. 6.
1715	109. 15. 1.	1735	123. 18. 1¾.	1755	141. 5. 4.
1715	119. 9. 6.	1735	117. 17.10¾.	1755	139. 6. 0.
1715 A	229. 4. 7.	**1735 A**	241. 16. 1.	**1755 A**	280. 11. 4.
1716	125. 5.11½.	1736	123. 16. 6.	1756	141. 1. 0.
1716	92. 11. 9.	1736	96. 4. –¼.	1756	138. 3. 2¼.
1716 A	217. 17. 9.	**1736 A**	220. 0. 7.	**1756 A**	279. 3. 3.
1717	116. 13. 8½.	1737	122. 1.11.	1757	134. 9. 5¼.
1717	107. 6.11.	1737	112. 1. 2¾.	1757	134. 1.10¾.
1717 A	224. – 8.	**1737 A**	234. 3. 2.	**1757 A**	268. 11. 4.
1718	122. 6. 8¼.	1738	98. 6. 5¼.	1758	128. 7. 3.
1718	107. 15. 9.	1738	91. 11. 4¼.	1758	128. – 4½.
1718 A	230. 2. 6.	**1738 A**	189. 17. 10.	**1758 A**	256. 7. 7.
[Only one ½ year quoted]		1739	105. 1. 9½.	1759	134. 14. 9½.
1719	118. 12. 3½.	1739	90. - -½.	1759	130. 15. –¼.
1719 A	217. 16. 3.	**1739 A**	195. 1. 10.	**1759 A**	265. 9. 10.
1720	111. 18.10½.	1740	84. 2. 2¼.	1760	136. 10. 3½.
1720	102. 16. 9¼.	1740	82. 6. 1.	1760	132. 2. –½.
1720 A	214. 15. 8.	**1740 A**	166. 8. 3.	**1760 A**	268. 12. 4.
1721	120. 10. 2½.	1741	88. 4. 5¼.	1761	143. 16. 4½.
1721	108. 5. 3.	1741	82. 12. 8¾.	1761	141. 9. 8¼.
1721 A	228. 15. 6.	**1741 A**	170. 17. 2.	**1761 A**	285. 6. 1.
1722	132. 6. 5.	1742	121. 16. 7½.	1762	147. – 9¾.
1722	96. 7. 6.	1742	84. 18. 9¼.	1762	141. 3. 7.
1722 A	228. 13. 11.	**1742 A**	206. 15. 5.	**1762 A**	288. 4. 5.
1723	127. 15. 2½.	1743	110. 10. 5¾.	1763	127. 9. –¾.
1723	121. 15. 5¾.	1743	88. 8. –½.	1763	133. - 1¼.
1723 A	249. 10. 8.	**1743 A**	198. 18. 6.	**1763 A**	260. 10. 1.
1724	128. 12. 2¼.	1744	104. 6. 8.	1764	135. 10. 9¾.
1724	117. 18. 6.	1744	108. 17. 5.	1764	127. 17. -
1724 A	246. 10. 8.	**1744 A**	213. 4. 1.	**1764 A**	263. 7. 10.
1725	125. 6. 5¾.	1745	108. 11. 2.	1765	139. 7. 1¾.
1725	132. 11. 1¾.	1745	107. 15. 7½.	1765	121. 9. 4½.
1725 A	257. 17. 8.	**1745 A**	216. 6. 10.	**1765 A**	260. 16. 6.
1726	129. 7. 1¾.	1746	111. 15.10.	1766	125. 6. 7½.
1726	107. 11. 7½.	1746	101. 15. 4¼.	1766	115. 1. 2½.
1726 A	236. 18. 9.	**1746 A**	213. 11. 2.	**1766 A**	240. 7. 10.
1727	122. 2.11¼.	1747	137. – 10.	1767	125. 12. 8½.
1727	92. 4. 4¾.	1747	114. – 10½.	1767	123. 5. 5¼.
1727 A	214. 7. 4.	**1747 A**	251. 1. 9.	**1767 A**	248. 18. 2.
1728	97. – 8½.	1748	127. 10.10.	1768	113. 16. 11.
1728	93. 2. 4¾.	1748	118. 4. 3¼.	1768	123. 1. 11.
1728 A	190. 3. 1.	**1748 A**	245. 15. 1.	**1768 A**	236. 18. 11.
1729	102. 19. 4¾.	1749	127. 1. 9½.	1769	132. 1. 2.
1729	86. 14. 1¾.	1749	120. 9. 9½.	1769	124. 19. 5½.
1729 A	189. 13. 7.	**1749 A**	247. 11. 7.	**1769 A**	257. – 7.
1730	109. 14.11½.	1750	124. 3. 2¾.	1770	133. 16. 9½.
1730	89. 17. 7½.	1750	120. 5. –½.	1770	121. 17. 1¾.
1730 A	199. 12. 7.	**1750 A**	244. 8. 3.	**1770 A**	255. 13. 11.
1731	101. 7. 6.	1751	128. 18. 5½.	1771	137. 8. 9¼.
1731	76. 19. 6¼.	1751	134. 13. 1½.	1771	118. 14.11½.
1731 A	178. 7. -.	**1751 A**	263. 12. 7.	**1771 A**	256. 3. 9.
1732	80. 17. 6¼.	1752	142. 4. –¾.	1772	113. 10. 7.
1732	79. 11. 7¾.	1752	136. – 9½.	1772	118. 15.10.
1732 A	160. 9. 2.	**1752 A**	278. 4. 10.	**1772 A**	232. 6. 5.
1733	108. 19. 4½.	1753	127. 17. 7¾.	1773	160. 13. 1¼.
1733	107. 17.11¾.	1753	134. 15. 8¼.	1773	137. 3.10½.
1733 A	216. 17. 4.	**1753 A**	262. 13. 4.	**1773 A**	297. 17. -.
1734	120. 1. 9¾.	1754	131. 10.10½.	1774	158. 15.11¼.
1734	105. 17. 9½.	1754	123. 18. 7.	1774	149. 9. 7¼.

1774 A	**308. 5. 7.**	**1794 A**	**431. 5. 8.**	1813	47. 9. 6.	
1775	165. 10. 4¾.	1795	231. 18. –½.	**1813 A**	**113. 18. 8.**	
1775	150. 16. 6.	1795	193. 16. 3¼.	1814	4. 13. 8.	
1775 A	**316. 6. 9.**	**1795 A**	**425. 14. 4.**	1814	18. 8.10.	
1776	145. 15. 5½.	1796	233. 2. 4.	**1814 A**	**23. 2. 7.**	
1776	139. 1. 9¼.	1796	212. 17.11½.	1815	27. 15. 1¼.	
1776 A	**284. 17. 3.**	**1796 A**	**445. - 4.**	1815	32. 7.10½.	
1777	157. 19. 1.	1797	249. 2. 3.	**1815 A**	**60. 3. 0.**	
1777	153. 17. 7½.	1797	221. 10. 5.	1816	51. 8. -	
1777 A	**311. 3. 4.**	**1797 A**	**470. 12. 8.**	1816	33. 12. -	
1778	177. 17. 4.	1798	251. 17. 6.	**1816 A**	**85. 0. 0.**	
1778	147. 5. 4½.	1798	204. 16. 7.	1817	53. 19. 2½.	
1778 A	**325. 2. 9.**	**1798 A**	**456. 11. 2.**	1817	66. 3. 4.	
1779	169. 16. 2.	1799	249. 12.10.	**1817 A**	**120. 2. 9.**	
1779	153. 1. -	1799	207. 19. 8¼.	1818	74. 18. 9.	
1779 A	**322. 17. 2.**	**1799 A**	**457. 12. 6.**	1818	81. 4. 2.	
1780	172. 6.10.	1800	243. 12. 1¾.	**1818 A**	**159. 4. 10.**	
1780	144. 8. 4.	1800	219. 19.11¾.	1819	[Blank]	
1780 A	**316. 15. 2.**	**1800 A**	**462. 12. 1.**	1819	104. 19. 8½.	
1781	190. 2. 1¼.	1801	242. 9. 2.	**1819 A**	**199. 10. 11.**	
1781	153. 3. 9¼.	1801	228. 19.10¾.	1820	115. 15. -	
1781 A	**343. 5. 11.**	**1801 A**	**471. 9. 1.**	1820	150. 8. 8.	
1782	183. 13. 6½.	1802	222. 0. 7¾.	**1820 A**	**266. 3. 8.**	
1782	155. 7. 9.	1802	207. 3. 8½.	1821	169. 10. 11½.	
1782 A	**339. - -.**	**1802 A**	**451. 4. 4.**	1821	172. 8. 2.	
1783	187. 13. 1½.	1803	244. 13. 1¼.	**1821 A**	**341. 19. 2.**	
1783	163. 6. 9½.	1803	200. 13. 1¼.	1822	196. 2. 6½.	
1783 A	**350. 19. 11.**	**1803 A**	**445. 6. 3.**	1822	206. 2. 8.'	
1784	191. 10. 1¼.	1804	197. 6. 5.	**END J. Walker's half-year entries.**		
1784	171. 16. 4½.	1804	199. 13. 4.			
1784 A	**363. 6. 6.**	**1804 A**	**396. 19. 10.**			
1785	202. 2. 7¼.	1805	234. 16. 3½.	**FROM 1822 (ANNUAL)**		
1785	188. 1.10¾.	1805	251. 3. 9.			
1785 A	**390. 4. 6.**	**1805 A**	**486. - 1.**	**1822 A**	**402. 5. 3.**	
1786	206. - -¼.	1806	236. 2. 5¾.	**1823 A**	**447. 17. 1.**	
1786	184. 13. 9.	Fol. altered figure		**1824 A**	**489. - 3.**	
1786 A	**390. 13. 9.**	1806	214. – 5.	**1825 A**	**501. 13. 8.**	
1787	194. 17. 5.	**1806 A**	**450. 2. 11.**	**1826 A**	**490. 12. 11.**	
1787	190. - 5½.	1807	195. 17. 1¾.	**1827 A**	**516. 11. 11.**	
1787 A	**384. 17. 11.**	1807	244. 16. -	**1828 A**	**536. 6. 5.**	
1788	210. 17. 7.	**1807 A**	**440. 13. 2.**	**1829 A**	**546. 17. 5.**	
1788	195. - 8.	1808	241. 11. 5.	**1830 A**	**568. 11. 8.**	
1788 A	**405. 18. 3.**	1808	230. 9. 6½.	**1831 A**	**583. 17. 10.**	
1789	212. 10. 1.	**1808 A**	**472. 1 0.**	**1832 A**	**598. 14. 11.**	
1789	197. 7. 4¾.	1809	225. 1. 9¾.	**1833 A**	**617. 15. 5.**	
1789 A	**409. 17. 5.**	1809	247. 3.11.	**1834 A**	**639. 1. 11.**	
1790	207. 17. 6¼.	**1809 A**	**472. 5. 9.**	**1835 A**	**647. 9. 6.**	
1790	192. 12. 2¾.	1810	225. 5. 1¾.	**1836 A**	**646. 8. 3.**	
1790 A	**400. 9. 9.**	1810	249. 15. 4¾.	**1837 A**	**650. 9. 10.**	
1791	212. 19.11½.	**1810 A**	**465. - 7.**	**1838 A**	**660. 9. 1.**	
1791	198. 17. –¾.	**Extra Competition from the West Middx., & Grand Junction Water Works.**		**1839 A**	**682. 16. -.**	
1791 A	**411. 17. 0.**			**1840 A**	**706. 12. -.**	
1792	226. 4. 1¾.			**1841 A**	**726. 9. 2.**	
1792	200. 1. 8¼.	1811	130. 17. 5¾.	**1842 A**	**755. 19. 1.**	
1792 A	**426. 5. 10.**	1811	141. 15. 3.	**1843 A**	**791. 5. 11.**	
1793	235. 9. 7.	**1811 A**	**282. 12. 10.**	**1844 A**	**820. 6. -.**	
1793	206. 3. 3.	1812	144. 2. –¾.	**1845 A**	**834. 8. -.**	
1793 A	**441. 12. 10.**	1812	76. 11. 2.	**1846 A**	**849. 17. 8.**	
1794	232. 9. 4.	**1812 A**	**220. 13. 3.**	**1847 A**	**864. 10. 4.**	
1794	198. 16. 4.	1813	66. 9. 1½.	**1848 A**	**873. 4. 1.**	

Year		Year		Year	
1849 A	878. 14. 10.	**1876 A**	**2,144.**	**1890 A**	**2,562.**
1850 A	847. 18. 8.	1877 W	2,110.	1891 W	2,520.
1851 A	847. 3. -.	1877 E	39.	1891 E	43.
1852 A	846. - -.	**1877 A**	**2,149.**	**1891 A**	**2,563.**
1853 A	846. - -.	1878 W	2,110.	1892 W	2,520.
1854 A	846. - -.	1878 E	39.	1892 E	44.
1855 A	846. - -.	**1878 A**	**2,149.**	**1892 A**	**2,564.**
1856 A	846. - -.	1879 W	2,201.	1893 W	2,540.
1857 A	846. - -.	1879 E	39.	1893 E	44.
1858 A	846. - -.	**1879 A**	**2,240.**	**1893 A**	**2,584.**
1859 A	846. - -.	1880 W	2,330.	1894 W	2,610.
1860 A	851. - -.	1880 E	39.	1894 E	44.
1861 A	856. - -.	**1880 A**	**2,369.**	**1894 A**	**2,654.**
1862 A	876. - -.	1881 W	2,430.	1895 W	2,610.
1863 A	896. - -.	1881 E	38.	1895 E	44.
1864 A	969. - -.	**1881 A**	**2,468.**	**1895 A**	**2,654.**
1865 A	1,150. - -.	1882 W	2,465.	1896 W	2,680.
1866 A	1,290. - -.	1882 E	40.	1896 E	44.
£1,400 bonus per share from selling Dorset lease.		**1882 A**	**2,505.**	**1896 A**	**2,724.**
		1883 W	2,520.	1897 W	2,740.
1867 A	1,300. - -.	1883 E	40.	1897 E	44.
1868 A	1,320. - -.	**1883 A**	**2,560.**	**1897 A**	**2,784.**
1869 A	1,530. - -.	1884 W	2,520.	1898 W	2,810.
1870 A	1,625. - -.	1884 E	40.	1898 E	44.
1871 A	1,625. - -.	**1884 A**	**2,560.**	**1898 A**	**2,854.**
W = water & E = estates.		1885 W	2,520.	1899 W	2,880.
1872 W	1,685.	1885 E	40.	1899 E	44.
1872 E	107.	**1885 A**	**2,560.**	**1899 A**	**2,924.**
1872 A	**1,792.**	1886 W	2,520.	1900 W	2,880.
1873 W	1,900.	1886 E	40.	1900 E	44.
1873 E	76.	**1886 A**	**2,560.**	**1900 A**	**2,924.**
1873 A	**1,976.**	1887 W	2,520.	1901 W	2,660.
1874 W	2,015.	1887 E	40.	1901 E	43.
1874 E	64.	**1887 A**	**2,560.**	**1901 A**	**2,703.**
1874 A	**2,079.**	1888 W	2,520.	1902 W	2,660.
£1,008 bonus per share from estates.		1888 E	40.	1902 E	42.
		1888 A	**2,560.**	**1902 A**	**2,702.**
1875 W	2,093.	1889 W	2,520.	1903 W	2,660.
1875 E	45.	1889 E	41.	1903 E	44.
1875 A	**2,138.**	**1889 A**	**2,561.**	**1903 A**	**2,704.**
1876 W	2,100.	1890 W	2,520.	**MWB Takeover.**	
1876 E	44.	1890 E	42.		

Half-yearly dividends ((J. Walker's Commonplace Book) Zc1, p467-461 page Nos. downwards, ELSC&A).
'**W**' = Water, '**E**' = Estates, & '**A**' Additional/Year TOTALS ((½d. rounded up, gross of land & poll tax, net of income tax) 'The New River – A Legal History' by Bernard Rudden, pp306-310 (Dividends & Prices 1633-1903). © 2011 M.F. Kensey.

ROBERT PERCY SMITH, M.A., M.P., 1770–1845.
Barrister-at-Law.   Advocate General of Bengal.   Wit, Scholar and Latin Poet.   Elder brother of Sydney Smith and father of the First Lord Lyveden.   Governor of the New River Company, 1827–1845.
(12, p29).

Called 'The Renovator' (said to have founded the NRC's financial prosperity): Jan. 1812 became a Director on behalf of his father, Nov. 1819 elected NRC Deputy Governor, until 1827 when elected Treasurer, but later that year elected Governor, until his death 8 March 1845 at his house in Savile Row. In 1822 the NRC presented him with a 200 guinea plate, in 1824 commissioned a 100 guinea portrait by Jackson, and in 1836 a 500 guinea engraving by George T. Doo of the Jackson portrait (12, p28/30).

New River Company Governors & Officers (1619-1903)

There is no complete list of Governors & Deputy Governors of the NRC, the present list **in places not consecutive**, the only reliable source the NRC Minutes, that for the early days are fragmentary ((Typed MWB corres. dated 11 May 1948) 8A1, 2-8), such that **any corrections to the fol. section are welcome**.

    1619 – 1904 (NRC Governors & Deputy Governors): 1965 G.C. Berry list to Mr Harwood, dates before 1769 hazy ((Deed Box No. 3 strong room, 2 typed sheets.) Acc/1953/C/143, LMA; ((Mr Harwood, Secretary NRC Ltd.) 8A1, 2/5 Vol. N-S; (Typed sheets headed 'OMF, NRC 1619-1904'; plus two amended typed drafts) 8A1, 2-8).

Becoming a board member of the company meant owning a full $^{1}/_{36}$ Adventurers' share. This qualified for standing as Governor, Deputy-Governor, or Treasurer, and vote for Officers, with a quorum of 7, quorum of 12 to remove them, and quorum of 5 for making bye-laws. The holders of King's shares were excluded (15I, p92). Appointed at an annual November election (15J, p78). For some early 'board' meetings held (15J, pp76-77). Attendance payments for weekly meetings (6, p393; 15J, p78).

NRC Governors
2 Nov. 1619 at their first meeting held at Sir Henry Montague's chambers, Serjeants' Inn.
'Hugh Middleton takes the oathe (before Sr: Edward Bromlye one of the Barons of the Exchequer) as the first governor:

    NRC Governor's Oath: 'You shall sweare that you shalbe ffaithfull & true to our Sov/aigne Lord the Kinge and to his heires & Successors Kings and Queenes of this Realme and all the lawfull Ordinances made and to be made, by the Governor and Company of the new Ryver …, you shall keepe and maintenye to your power, you shall well and honestly behave yo/selfe in the place of Governor of this Company, and iustly and indefferently Shall order the matters and causes of this Company – accordinge to Right and Conscience, and noe singular proffitt to your owne person doe nor take whereby the common proffitt of this Company or the perticuler benefitt of any member therof, shall or may be damaged. You shall admitt noe person into this Company nor shall refuse To admitt any into the same but according to the purport of the Kings Majesties Letters Patent to the said Governor and Company Granted and the orders and Constitutions lawfullie made and to bee made according to the same and all other thinges perteyning to your Office to the uttermoste of your power and skill, you shall well and trulie do and perform. Soe help you God'.   '19 October, 1619.
                                                                                                  Edw. Bromley'.

It was then agreed that this oath would be administered to all future Governors and deputies'.
(KA20, p16; ('The Oathe of Hughe Middleton Esquier Gov. for the Co. of the Newe Ryver brought from Chadwell& Amwell to London') 8A1, 2-8; 15I, p30). Transcriptions of 1619 oath of Sir Hugh Myddelton as Gov. of the NRC ((1964? copy; 1 folder) Acc/1953/A/001, LMA). NRC oaths (15J, p77).

Date	Name
2 Nov. 1619 - 7 Dec. 1631 (died)	Hugh Myddelton, Baronet 1622 (6, p392).
8 Feb. 1632 - Nov. 1632	Sir Thomas Myddelton, brother of Sir Hugh (15J, p78).
14 Nov. 1632 - 1651/2 (died)	Sir William Myddelton, eldest son of Sir Hugh (6, p392 1631; 15I, p74 Sir William d. 1652; 15J, p78 Nov. 1632 until c.1652).
c.1652 - 1661 (died)	Josias Berners. (6, p392 Josiah Berners, ante 1665 Governor & Clerk).
1662 - 1676 (died)	Col. Richard Nevill (15I, p59 heir of Sir Henry Neville).
9 Nov. 1676 - 8 Nov. 1687	Henry, Lord Hyde & Cornbury (1638-1709) > 1674 2nd Earl of Clarendon NRC Gov. 1682-1687 (15I, p73; 6, p392 c.1682). Brother-in-law to King James II, his second wife Flower the widow of Sir William Backhouse who owned the site of New River Head; buried in Westminster Abbey 4 Nov. 1709.
1687 - 12 Nov. 1700	Richard Nevill, son of Col. Richard Nevill (15I, p59 younger son heir at law of Richard Neville). 8 Nov. 1687 Richard Nevill becomes NRC Governor until 12 Nov. 1700 (((Copy of a Supplementary Bill filed May 1741, endorsed on back of the case

	of Lloyd v. NRC) Typed sheet in red headed 'Governors of the NRC 1676-1700+') 8A1, 2-8).
1700 - ?	Lawrence Hyde, Earl of Rochester. ?Francis Edwards? purchased the Earl of Rochester's shares for over £60,000 (Case of Ephraim Green, 111.a.64., British Library).
1728?, 1741 - 1751	Robert Holford (6, p392 1728 & 1741; 15I, p109 Robert Holford died 1753).
1763, 1770 - 12 March 1801	Peter Holford, who resigned. Ante 1769 (6, p392). 1769 Peter Holford Gov. (15I, p91/p109 Robert's son Peter also Gov.). 1770 Peter Holford Governor (14B2, p458).
12 March 1801 - 8 Nov. 1809	Charles Berners who resigned. 1801 (6, p392).
8 Nov. 1809 - 9 Nov. 1815	John Walker who declined re-election. 1809 (6, p392). 1811 John Walker (1AA, p498). c.1814 John Walker (12, p25).
9 Nov. 1815 - 17 May 1827	Charles Holford. 1845 (6, p392).
31 May 1827 - 8 March 1845 (died)	Robert Percy Smith. 1827 (6, p392). 1827-1845, in 1822 for services rendered, awarded 200-guineas worth of plate in form of Portland Vase executed by Messrs Green, Ward & Co., in 1824 commissioning Jackson to paint his portrait for 100-guineas, and in 1836 presumably for him, had this painting engraved by George T. Doo for 500-guineas (12, p28).
3 April 1845 - 31 Dec. 1846 (died)	Richard Smith Appleyard. 1815 (6, p392).
21 Jan. 1847 - March 1847 (died)	William Astell, M.P. 1847 (6, p392).
1 April 1847 - March 1859 (died)	Richard Beauvoir Berens.
17 March 1859 - Nov. 1862 (died)	Thomas Mills, M.P. 1859 (6, p392; 15I, p158 1851).
11 Dec. 1862 - 5 May 1886 (died)	John Miles of Friern Barnet. 1862 (6, p392).
3 June 1886 - 'Appointed Day' to MWB.	Henry Carrington Bowles-Bowles. 1886 (6, p392).

NRC Deputy Governors

2 Nov. 1619 - c.1628	Robert Bateman.
1628 - 1632	John Packer.
1634, 1635	Richard Bateman.
1637, 1638	William Myddelton.
1640 - 1648	Mr Packer.
c.1648 - ?	Nichas. Backhouse.
c.1654	Simon Myddelton.
1655 - c.1662	Peter Salmon, Dr. in Phisicke.
1662 - 1664	Henry Borlase.
1666 - 1669	Thomas Henshaw.
1688 - 1692	James Berners.
1692 - ?	Edward Soame (15J, p117 Edmund Soame who acquired 4 NRC shares by marrying one of Simon Myddelton's daughters).
1741 - 1751	James Colebrook (15I, p64 James Colebrooke Deputy Governor).
1763, 1770 - 28 Oct.1773	Sir George Colebrook who resigned. 1770 Sir George Colebrooke Deputy Gov. (14B2, p458).
18 Nov. 1773 - 18 Sept. 1783 (died)	William Berners.
7 Nov. 1783 - 12 March 1801	Charles Berners.
12 March 1801 - 8 Nov. 1809	John Walker.
8 Nov. 1809 - 4 Nov. 1819	Richard Benyon who declined re-election (1AA, p498 1811 Richard Benyon). c.1814 Richard Benyon (12, p25).
4 Nov. 1819 - 1 April 1827	Robert Percy Smith (12, p28 1819-1827).
26 April 1827 - 4 Nov. 1830	John Josiah Holford who declined re-election.
4 Nov. 1830 - 3 April 1845	Richard Smith Appleyard.
17 April 1845 - Jan. 1852	Major Gen. Chas. Grene Ellicombe.

4 Nov. 1852 - 5 July 1855   John Miles who resigned due to ill health.
5 July 1855 - 17 March 1859   Thomas Mills, M.P.
31 March 1859 - 8 Nov. 1860 (declined re-election). George Anderson.
8 Nov. 1860 - 11 Dec. 1862   John Miles.
8 Jan. 1863 - March 1884   Capt. Hugh Berners who resigned.
3 April 1884 - 3 June 1886   Henry Carrington Bowles-Bowles.
17 June 1886 - 'Appointed Day' (MWB). Joseph Trueman Mills.

NRC Treasurers Salaried Post (15J, p78).
Slightly different oath of Treasurers (((No source quoted) 'The First Court') 8A1, 3/3-2; (Loaned by County Record Office, Hertford) 15Q3, p8 2 Nov. 1619 Mins. of first Court of NRC, listing shareholders and number of shares they held; (Loaned by MWB) 15Q3, p10 'The first sheet of the Company's minutes recording the oaths of the Governor and the Treasurer, with transcript').

At Charter	Rowland Backhowse (6, p392).
1649 -1661	Simon Myddelton youngest son of 1st Sir Hugh (15J, p76 appointed 1649/p78 born c.1612, Treasurer 1656 (Acc 2558/NR13/7 3rd folder, LMA), until 1661 when not re-elected after failing to hand over some dividends/p117 1650s NRC Treasurer).
c.1670	William Edwards (6, p392 c.1670).
By 1681/1695	Darwin (6, p392 1696; 15I, p60 c.1694 Thomas Darwin). By 1681 Thomas Darwin, declared bankrupt 1696, the NRC losing £7,000 to £20,000 ((Portland 70341 29/2, Brit Lib.; Pw2 Hy/895, Nott. Univ. Lib.) 15J, p79/p109).
1702 & 1707	1702 Edward Allen (15J, p123). 1707 Edward Allen 'the said Allen as Treasurer of the sd. Co.' probably dead by 1711 ((8-typed sheets headed 'DJS, NRC, Abstract of title of Mary Gambier …') 8A1, 2-8). 1707 Edward Allen NRC Treasurer (15I, p62).
1737, c.1741, 1742	John Mitford (6, p392 c.1741; 6, p392 annotated copy amending c.1741 to 1737; (1742 security for becoming NRC Treasurer) DE/GH/1646, HALS).
1743	William Stratton (6, p392 1743).
1750	Henry Berners (6, p392 1750). 1770 Henry Berners Treasurer (14B2, p458).
Feb. 1782 but died.	Aime Garnault ['II'] (6, p392 Feb. 1782), d. 25 Feb. 1782. As security transferred £21,000 4% Bank Annuities worth £21,000, and the Deputy Gov. William Berners standing for another £10,000 (6, p392; 15J, p79).
March 1782	Richard Hulse (6, p392 March 1782).
8 Nov. 1804 -1827	Samuel Garnault (6, p392 1804; 12, p25 c.1814 John Walker). d. 11 March 1827, his tomb outside Enf. Church saying '… for more than 22-years he was Treasurer of the NRC'. Lysons 1811 says the present 'treasurer, 'D. Garnault Esq.' (1AA, p498; B1, p217 Daniel Garnault tomb outside Enf. Church, but this is Samuel Garnault's tomb); so probably mistaken identity since Daniel Garnault [II] d.1786 before Lysons 1792-6 1st edn., Daniel Garnault [III] d.1809. '10,000 7,000 Bk. Stock 7,000 3 pr. Ct. Consols 15,800 **Bond from his Brother Mr Jos. Garnault for £10,000** ' (Handwritten slip inserted with 1802 letter, at front of Zc1, ELSC&A; looks like an eight, and had a brother Joseph serving the East India Company).
April 1827	Robert Percy Smith (6, p392 April 1827; 12, p28 1827 but resigned to become Gov.).
May 1827	Charles Holford (6, p392 May 1827).
1839	E.W.B. Webster (6, p392 1839).
1849	C.H. Pilgrim (6, p392 1849).
1859	C.J. Fisher (6, p392 1859).
1866	H.C.B. Bowles (6, p392 1866).

1884	J.T. Mills (6, p392 1884).
1886 to transfer.	Lt.-Col. C. Walter Campbell (6, p392 1886-1904).

NRC Clerk > Secretary

1609-1611.	Edward Hughes became sick and prob. died (8, p29).
Sept. 1611.	William Lewyn.

The Clerks oath when taking office (6G, p392; 15J, p77 Clerk's oath summarised).

At 1619 Charter	William Lewyn for life until d.1638 (6, p392 at Charter; (Acc 2558/NR13/7 1st folder, LMA) 15J, p27/28/p79).
1619 - c.1630	Beneath the Clerk, beadle Adolphus Iremonger (15J, p81).
Pre-1665	Josiah Berners (6, p392 ante 1665 Clerk & Gov.; 15J, p79 then Josias Berners; 12, p24 c.1634 Josiah Berners).
	Dec.? 1660 at the death of Josias Berners, **John Widford** proposed for place of Clerk (((S.P. Dom. 29 Vol. XXV No. 131, 1660-61, p451) Typed sheet headed 'NRC, Civil War') 8A1, 2-8; (S.P. Dom. 1660-61 temp. Charles II) 14B2, p451 at death of Josias Berners petition from **John Wilford** (sic.)). April 1665 Clerk was lately dead (8A1, 3/3-2).
1665? - d.1667	Gregory Hardwicke (6, p392 1667) d.1667 (6E, p359; 15J, p80). Known from 1665 (8A1, 3/3-2).
1667-c.1697/1705	John Grene (6, p392 1668; 12, p24 1667 John Grene). 1667 at £100 p.a. (plus £1,000 p.a. for maintaining the NR) until died 29 March 1705 ((Acc 2558/NR13/12, LMA) 15J, p80).
c.1705/1711 - c.1717	Ephraim Green employed from 1682, c.1700 called NRC City Surveyor & responsible for City & NRH workers, Deputy then Clerk presumably 1705, 1711 mention of Ephraim Green as Secretary, dismissed c.1717, **one Matthew voted to be Clerk** although had confessed to defrauding the Company ('The Case of Ephraim Green, late Clerk to the NRC' by E. Green, 1717, p17, 111.a.64., British Library; 15J, p80/134/244).
c.1723- c.1750	Jasper Bull (6, p392 c.1697, obit. 1751). His name on 1737 enrolment of Charter & 1739 mentioned by Maitland. Jasper Bull letter book 1723, 1724, 1725, 1728, Clerk to become Secretary (1742 fragmentary Min.), when Clerk his house burnt down (1769 fire notes in newspaper report) (15J, p80/82). 27 March 1750 will of Jasper Bull, Clerk to the NRC, Precinct of Bridewell, City of London (PROB 11/777, Greenly Quire Numbers 47 - 93, Records of the Prerogative Court of Canterbury).
1750	Richard Holford (6, p392 1750, 1780 'elected Director'), elected Director 17 March 1780. Secretary until c.1780 (15J, p77). Holfords incl. Richard NRC Clerk ((Handwritten slip) 8A1, 2/5 Vol. N-S). 1771 Mr Holford secretary.
1780	John Rowe 1780, elected Director 1812 (6, p392). d.28 Oct.1816 (Gents Mag). '… Mr Reynolds the present clerk of the Company …' (Pages torn from Gents Mag. [22] Nov. 1784, Fifth number of Vol. LIV part II, pp803-805 Isl. LHC).
1811	John Paul Rowe 1811, former Collector (6, p392; 1AA, p498 1811 'John Row Esq.'[sic]; 15-2, p1 'J.P. Rowe Secty. 1815'; 12, p25 c.1814 John Paul Rowe).
1827-8	Frederick Inglis (6, p392 1827), Chief Clerk & Sec. 12 Aug. 1828 Fredk. Inglis writing as though the Clerk, Mr Rowe said to be retiring from London because of ill health 22 Feb.1828; F. Inglis said still to be Clerk 23 March 1849 ((4¾pp handwritten sheets in ink headed 'New River L5.72') Islington LHC).
c.1839	Charles Rivington. William Mylne's daughter Emily in 1838, marrying the NRC Clerk Charles Rivington (('The Mylnes and their work at Stationer's Hall' by Christopher Rivington, p3 of 4pp 'The Stationers & Newspaper Maker' Vol. IV No. 2, Summer 1975, typeset printed newsletter) 8A1, 3/3-3).
1841	J. Myles, Clerk (12G, 12m map).
1862	Fred. Inglis signing deed as Clerk of the NRC, and Alex. Inglis as Asst. Clerk (D296, ELSC&A).

1866   Alexander Inglis (6, p392).
1880 to transfer.   James Searle (6, p392 1880 to transfer).

NRC Surveyors > Engineers

1634	General Surveyor William Grace, but disbursements not accounted for so dismissed (15J, p80).
1691-1723	River or Country Surveyor John White, d.1741 and buried at Enfield Church.
c.1700	John White £30 p.a. as surveyor from Ware to Bush Hill, John Winch £30 p.a. as surveyor from Bush Hill to Islington, and Ephraim Green £50 p.a. as City Surveyor & also overseeing the Water House & City workers (15J, p80).
c.1718 – d.1770	Henry Mill (b.1682/3), **NRC Surveyor** during a period of stagnation (15J, p81 pre/1718/p142; 12, p30 b.1683 said to be a relative of Sir H. Myddelton, NRC Surveyor from c.1720, d.1771). In 1741 for the NRC reconstructing Ware Lock. Died aged 87/88 his memorial tablet in Breamore Church, near Salisbury, Hampshire (12, p31 d.26 Dec. 1771).
4 July 1771 - 1810	Robert Mylne, **NRC Surveyor**. Born 1733, NRC Surveyor 1771-1810, d.5 May 1811.
Nov. 1810 - 1859/61	William Chadwell Mylne, **NRC Engineer**.
1860 - 1889	James Muir, **NRC Engineer**.
1889 to transfer.	Divided into 3, the **NRC Engineers:** Joseph Francis (Supply), Edmund Leigh Morris (Pumping) & Ernest Collins (Distribution) (7J1, p39/209 post-1882 resigned 1890 John Taylor NRC Chief Engineer; 7G5, p127; 7H2, p229 1884 J. Francis NRC Engineer, John Taylor Consulting Engineer to NRC).

1904 MWB's first Chief Engineer being W.B. Bryant (7G5, p127 also lists his successors).

NRC Auditors	Appointed from shareholders (6, pp392-393; 15J, p79).
NRC Collectors	Collecting the important quarterly water rents, monitoring the street pipes, arranging connections & disconnections, chasing debtors and seeking new customers. c.1635 six (having to find two sureties), 1670 seven, eight by 1684, 1724-28 five defaulters, 1785 must carry or wear their tickets or silver plates of office and reside in their collecting area, in the early-1800s collecting at inns or coffee houses and given a candle allowance, in 1831 substituted for a pair of working trousers (15J, pp81-82).
Walksmen	At first responsible for an approx. 1-mile walk, a Walksman (looking after the upper or right bank) & labouring assistant (lower or left bank) that patrolled their section mending banks & cutting waterweeds etc. By 1859 their daylight working hours increased to 7am - 6pm and their walks to approx. 1¼-miles long (15J, pp82-83). The walksmen recorded on 1775-1809 R. Mylne's plans, see appropriate section/s.

In 1800 all river labourers & walksmen given an extra 6d. per week for bread, above their 1s. per week allowance, and turncocks an extra 2s. per week in times of high prices during the Napoleonic Wars, when labour in London was being depleted by the Press Gangs. In June 1804 the NRH workers 12s. per week, rising to 15s., after which to 17s. per week; and the paviours £1 increased to £1. 2s. 0d., NR labourers by 1814 earning 18s. per week, but in 1867 a reversal when the labourer Alfred Heath only paid 15s. per week (15J, pp84-85).

Paviours & Turncocks	8 turncocks at £20 p.a. in 1700, and paviours constantly repairing the torn up streets; 16-turncocks & 12-paviours by 1756; 1785 the turncocks reminded to wear their circular NRC identification tags; 28-turncocks in 1814 (15J, p83).
Pipe Borers	In 1756 horse engines & 20-workers paid piecework for boring wooden pipes (15J, p83).
Engine Workers	For those at NRH, a horse-engine attended by Harvey, post-1769 the first 'fire-engine' worker called Forrester, 1773 called Marley, in 1792 called Edward

Hughes and by 1802 called the steam engine worker, in 1815 nearly dismissed, reprimanded in 1824, retired in the 1830s and died 1837. In May 1816 R. Walsh accidentally killed when fixing the new steam engine, in 1823 a stoker called Joseph Hind found dead likely falling from the top of the boiler, in 1848 the stoker given £2 from the NRC poor box as two children & his wife had died (15J, pp83-84).

Chapter 2

Historical Features along the New River

"The New River has considerable interest to the industrial archaeologist studying drinking water supply. The historic buildings, the remnants of the disused parts of the original course and the currently operational course are worthy of study. The New River has also developed an interesting ecology" (C3).

2.1 When Constructing the New River

PUMPS OR DAMS (Draining Wet Land & Foundations): It is assumed that Myddelton must have used buckets, hand-pumps, or small dams, or some better form of powered crude pump to remove excess water as he was building the New River, especially when digging foundations for his culverts, pipes, troughs, boarded sections, bridges, flashes, and brick tunnels. It is known that only eight years later in 1617, Myddelton in his mines at N. Wales using pumping machines of his own contrivance.

    1927 (MWB Technical Drawing) Northern District: Mild steel **New River Dam Plates** ((Dave Allkins) TW Reading, Microfilm). Copy shown in Vol. 3.

Improvements: Whilst making improvements or changes over 400-years, they kept the New River flowing uninterrupted by using:

    Dams > Suspended Troughs > Iron Bypass Pipes, today Huge Plastic Pipes.

    c.1884/Post-1904 (NRC/MWB Technical Drawings): 3-diffent forms of New River troughs, 2-copied from c.1884 drawings wrought iron, the other mild steel ((Dave Allkins) TW Reading, Microfilm). Copy of one shown in Vol. 3.

'PLUGS' (Drain Plugs): There was also the need to drain the New River for repairs etc. One known surviving on the W-bank just N of today's Lieutenant Ellis Way, Cheshunt, where if you peer into the bed of the River you can see a **length of large dia. cast-iron pipe** (probably NRC), and hidden in the grass on the bank an **'MWB' valve-plate** that permits draining this section of the River into the adjacent side ditch.

PILING & WHARFING THE BANKS: Piling an ancient art and the mention of wharfing the banks with timber mainly to prevent erosion.

    'an **Iron Crowe** to make way for the **piles** in pynning of the heads' 4s. ((Orig. NR Accts) 11, p53).
    'for tooe **Beetles** toe dryve **pyles**   00 : 01 : 06' ((Orig. NR Accts) 3, p9).
Myddelton 1620-22 at Brading Haven, Isle of Wight, had used various skills in piling and building sluices.

    1862 (Myddelton's Piles & Sluice) Described by Samuel Smiles: "… The black piles driven into the bottom of the [Brading] haven in the process of embankment are still to be seen sticking up at low water; and only a few years since the old gates which served for a sluice were dug up near 'The Boat Houses'. … situated towards the northern side of the haven, …" (13, p139).

In 1971 the MWB had just scrapped their manually powered wooden Pile Frame (For MFK sketch see Vol. 3).

2011 (Modern): Much of the piling and wharfing (aka campshedding) today made from metal, although in places still using metal piles with wooden wharfing.

PUDDLED CLAY (Plugging Leaks in New River):

    Leaky Old 'Wrinkly': It should be remembered that the New River was an old leaky 'wrinkly' (multi-deviations of route) just sealed at critical places with puddled clay, still today in places leaks like a sieve, unless it is constantly repaired.

From its inception leaks in the River were plugged using water, clay & lime (Original NR Accounts).

    "ffor **Lyme** toe putt in the Crackes of the Newe Banck   00 : 06 : 00" ((Orig. NR Accts) 3, p9).

'Clay or marl was used extensively in keeping the channel watertight. In the account for construction of the river [Original NR Accounts] there are constant references to carting clay up to Amwell and

Ware, where it was scarce' (8A, p26 quote).
The New River had to be constantly maintained by mud panners treading puddled clay for sealing the leaks and breaches to keep it watertight.

John White (1658-1741), NRC 'River Surveyor' 1691-1723 for Bush Hill to Ware, buried in Enfield Churchyard: But his tomb long since removed.
'An inscription in the church yard at Endfield:

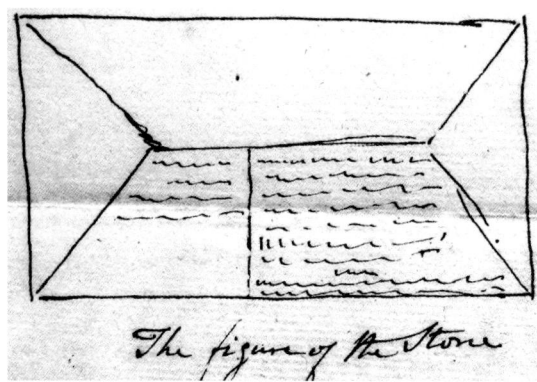

Sketch of tomb (rectangular with central peak from 4-sloping sides, with short LH inscription and larger RH inscription on longer bottom side) called 'The figure of the stone' ((TW) LMA).

'Here lies John White, who, day by day
On river works did use much clay,
Is now himself turning that way;
If not to clay, yet dust will come
Which to preserve, takes little room,
Although inclosed in this great tomb'.
'In hopes of a joyful resurrection, through the mercy of god the father and the merits of Jesus Christ and the sanctification of the Holy Ghost, Amen'
'**I served the New River Company as Surveyor from Ladyday 1691 to Michaelmas 1723**, he died April 21st, 1741 aged 83'.
'On the left hand side of the cross line:'
'Here lyes the body of
Margaret White
Late wife of Mr John White
Who died Jan. 21st 1733/4
Aged 71 years' [last line about to be lost due to deterioration of document].
On third side of document a separate handwritten note headed 'Anecdote, River Surveyor', R. Mylne calculates that **John White was Surveyor for 32½-years**, and that he was '18-years out of service till he died' ((Robert Mylne's commonplace book) 15M, Acc. 2558/NR13/188).
Under tombs listed in the churchyard, an abridged quote of epitaph (B3-2, pp75-76 1741, 'to Midsummer 1723'; 1B1, p357 to Midsummer 1723; H4-10-4, p738; 1AA, p202 footnote 127, Midsummer 1723; since the others agree on **Midsummer**, perhaps Mylne got it wrong; 15D, p14; 15C, p18 Midsummer; 15J, p80 Midsummer).
1775-1809 (Robert Mylne's Survey) Clay Pits & Claypit Field: NRC Clay Pits near Enfield Flash, and NRC Claypit Field near Bush Hill Frame.
Clay Puddling Canals (1862 Samuel Smiles): "The process of puddling is of considerable importance in canal engineering [for making canal beds watertight, with the banks generally left unprotected since in the early days un-powered craft made little wash]. Puddle is formed by a mixture of well-tempered clay and sand reduced to a semi-fluid state, and rendered impervious to water by manual labour, as by working and chopping it about with spades. It is usually applied in three or more strata to a depth or thickness of about three feet; and care is taken at each operation so to work the new layer of puddling stuff as to unite it with the stratum immediately beneath. Over the top course a layer of common soil is usually laid. It is only by the careful employment of puddling that the filtration of the water of canals into the neighbouring lower lands through which they pass can be effectually prevented" (13, p353).
Clay-puddle as used 150 years later by Brindley, one of the most brilliantly ingenious of engineers, to

make the bed of his great canals impervious to water, and to traverse boggy ground (Trafford Moss) that proved completely successful (13, p355).

When giving evidence on canal bills before Parliament, on one occasion Brindley frequently mentioned 'puddling', "describing its uses and advantages, that some of the members expressed a desire to know what this extraordinary mixture was that could be applied to so many and important purposes. Preferring a practical illustration to a verbal description, Brindley caused a mass of clay to be brought into the committee-room, and, moulding it in its raw un-tempered state into the form of a trough, he poured into it some water, which speedily ran through and disappeared. He then worked the clay up with water to imitate the process of puddling, and again forming it into a trough, filled it with water, which was now held in without a particle of leakage. "Thus it is", said Brindley, "that I form a water-tight trunk to carry water over rivers and valleys, whenever they cross the path of the canal" (('Memoir of Brindley' by S. Hughes, C.E., in 'Weale's Papers on Civil Engineering') 13, p373-4). Even as Brindley lay dying "scarce able to gasp, yet his mind was clear", it is said that when some eager canal undertakers who must have his advice since "they could not make their canal hold water". "Then puddle it", said the engineer. They explained that they had already done so. "**Then puddle it again - and again**". This was all he could say, and it was enough" (13, p475).

1926 (New River Leakage): "Passing reference may be made to the fact that the grassy banks of the New River are very well kept, and, if you follow the windings of the River, the reflection on the water is often startling - almost as if fluorescein had been added. Nearly 20 years ago [c.1906] fluorescein was actually added purposely and in large amount. There was then a suspicion that much of the water pumped out of the wells into the New River was **really water that had leaked out of the River**. One Sunday, the writer and some of his colleagues added a large dose of fluorescein (a harmless chemical) and an alkali to the New River near its source, and samples were collected, at regular intervals, of the water being pumped from the wells, and examined for green fluorescence. **The results were negative, and it was concluded that the leakage could not be great**, or the dilution enormous, as otherwise a positive result might have been anticipated. With a clear well water, less than 1 part of fluorescein in 10 million parts of water can be readily noted, even in a small bottle. The writer can recall no more fascinating sight than the New River presented on that occasion - like a glorious wide ribbon of shimmering fluorescent green extending for miles and miles towards London. It was a glorious day and many people were enjoying their Sunday walks abroad. There are many places where the New River runs close to the road for considerable distances and it was extraordinarily interesting to watch their behaviour. Most people know what water looks like after the addition of fluorescein, but all are familiar, at all events, with those yellowish green glass supports for the legs of a piano, so often seen in old-fashioned parlours. Imagine miles of that glass in liquid form flowing down a broad channel. Some gazed at it stonily, as if the sight were in no way peculiar, or, if extraordinary, in no respect more wonderful than things they had seen in their own native place of - shall we say - Peebles. Most persons, however were obviously impressed, puzzled, and a few perhaps startled. The comments of two children were as follows: "Doesn't the river look lovely, Mummie?" "Daddy, why has the river turned bright green?" As usual, the parents were unable to answer their children's questions satisfactorily. Two lovers looked at it and then in each other's eyes. To them all the colours of the rainbow were as one the colour of the eyes of his, or her, beloved. So the parents and children and lovers gazed awhile and passed on, and so indeed did the writer, who was beginning to wonder if his calculations, that the colour could not reach as far as London, were based on sound premises" (15D, p15).

Clay Puddling (1934 Morris): "… the original length was 40 miles beginning in a chalk formation and travelling over gravel beds until it reached the clay beds in the neighbourhood of Cheshunt. It was a bold project to make a river upon porous ground, because it might have leaked like a basket unless properly sealed at the bottom. This watertight lining as provided by a **thick layer of puddled clay** excavated from beds near London and conveyed to Hertfordshire (at least that is the procedure at the present day in affecting repairs to the river) and I imagine it must have been the method adopted in the first work of construction of the river more than 300 years [now 400 years] ago' (15C, p18). Archaeologists cut a cross-section through the Borrowstounness Canal that was abandoned incomplete in 1796, to reveal its clay-puddled bed (G3, p5).

2011 (Clay Puddle): Small piles of clay can still be occasionally seen today along the New River.

2.2 Under the New River

DRAINAGE PIPES & BRICK CULVERTS (beneath New River): To avoid flooding of property or the contamination of the New River, pipes & culverts provided a passage so that the surface waters or opposing streams normally crossing from West to East, could still pass under the new cut and drain naturally away, normally eventually into the River Lee (13, p122). A culvert is a drain or covered channel for water beneath a road, although in our case beneath the New River.

To prevent contamination opposing streams taken beneath the New River (I3, p5). "The intervening streams were often carried under the river in pipes and culverts but sometimes they were carried over the river in troughs. On certain streams there were flashes" (8A, p19). It would appear that only 'Dirty' water was taken beneath the New River according to Mylne's 1775-1809 Survey, the cleaner water taken over the New River at **Flashes/troughs** (see later) for augmenting the River when appropriate.

2.3 Over the New River

BRIDGES (Most of the Earlier Numbers) MYTHS or UNRELIABLE: Except from actual NRC records, invariably there is no reliable source quoted for the number of bridges (**mostly timber but some brick**), mainly never quoting the date for the number of bridges, or the same number of bridges in previous years repeated for various later dates.

> **Myddelton's Time (UNRELIABLE) 1862 Samuel Smiles:** In Myddelton's time, 'The bridges over the stream were about a **hundred and sixty** in number, mostly of timber, and they were invariably executed with a waterway under them not exceeding 10-feet' (13, p121 quote from S. Smiles; B2, p255 160 bridges repeated).
>
> **Myddelton's Time (UNSUBSTANTIATED) Morris 1934:** "… all roads running West to East that were in the way of the New River had to be accommodated by bridges and in the case of private properties being severed by the river private or occupation bridges had to be provided so that cattle or farm waggons could cross from the farm buildings to the fields or in some cases a carriage drive to a mansion had to be carried over a bridge. When the river was finished it had **157 bridges** crossing in its length of 40 miles. This is approximately 4 bridges to every mile so it can be imagined what a number of obstacles were encountered in cross roads and other obligations" ((1934 no source quoted) 15C, p6; 10-3, p9 157 bridges repeated 1997; 15Z-3, p5 repeated prob. pre-1990; I3, p5 repeated 2009).
>
> **Myddelton's Time (UNSUBSTANTIATED) Thames Water:** 'In all, some **200 bridges** were built across the river in order to maintain the "waies"' (15J02, p4).
>
> **Myddelton's Time (MYTHS) 1839:** Seldom employing fewer than six hundred workmen, and constructing **eight hundred bridges**, the number of bridges since considerably diminished (Printed article 'Biographical Sketches – Sir H.M.' with pencilled 'The London Railway Journal, Dec. 1839', Isl. LHC).
>
>> Regarding the original River, '…, and has **eight hundred Bridges** over it' ((Maitland publ. 1772) 1A1, chapter XXIX, p282/p295).
>>
>> Published 1832 '**eight hundred bridges** of various dimensions' ((Edmund Lodge, 1832) 11A, p3).
>>
>> **About 800 bridges** ((1914 published by Meyers, Brooks & Co. Ltd.) B9; 'The Story of Enfield', Meyers Brooks, 1930).
>
> **Myddelton's Time (Brick Bridges) RELIABLE:** All of the original brick-built bridges over and along the New River were built by a specialist contractor called Stephen Bone. He also built the New River Head's encircling wall, and the Water House's chimneys and other items (14C, p161 no source quoted).
>
> e.g. For a small contract:
>> "To Steeven Boone for makeinge a greate Brick Bridge att
>> Islingtonne towne end, being 18 foote wyde   07 : 03 : 06" (3, p7).
>
> The bricks probably made locally, since heavy goods did not normally travel far on unkempt C17th roads.
>
> In Henry Mills 1723 survey said to include **two to three hundred bridges & over 40-sluices** (14B2,

p454).

1772 (Maitland) 215 Bridges & 43 Sluices (POS. RELIABLE): 'This River, wherein, and over it, are **forty-three Sluices, and two hundred and fifteen Bridges**, is carried over two Vales in Wooden Frames, or Troughs, lined with Lead; that at Bushill being six hundred and sixty Feet in Length, and thirty in Height, under which, for the Passage of the Land-waters, is an Arch, capacious enough to receive the Greatest Cart, or Waggon, laden with Hay or Straw; and the other, at Highbury, is in Length four hundred and sixty-two Feet, and in Height seventeen. And over and under the said River, besides divers considerable Currents of Land-waters, a great Number of Brooks, Rills, and Water-courses have their Passage' (1A1, p1269). **215 Bridges & 43 Sluices** appears to have been repeated in the 1796 Ambulator 8th Edn., p195 (ELSC&A).

7 Nov. 1782 (226 > 196 Bridges) RELIABLE: Reduction in number of bridges since last count ((NRC Mins., LMA) 15J, p33).

1775 & 1809 (ROBERT MYLNE'S SURVEY) RELIABLE: MFK separately listed the bridges & comments shown on Mylne's NR plans, finding that his bridge numbers (1775 records 221 bridge numbers & 1809 records 161 bridge numbers) had various discrepancies (gaps in numbers, un-numbered bridges, **private bridges not included** etc.) such that having to make some slight adjustments for the resulting analysis as follows:

No. of Bridges	1775	1809
Manifold Ditch	2	2 [Kept separated from following]
Numbered	200	170 (includes 6 new)
Numbered Double bridge	1 (called 2)	1 (called 1)
Un-numbered	5	5
Private Un-numbered	25	25 (both include a 'Draw bridge')
Private Numbered	1	1
Not annotated	3	3
Mentioned	1	0
NR Total	**236**	**205** (Along original NR, Chadwell Spring to NRH).
TOTAL	238	207

Also includes a **'Draw bridge'** at Cheshunt, & the early use of a **'Cast Iron Private Bridge'** at Harringey House loop.

ONLY 10-SLUICES SHOWN: It appears that only major Sluices are recorded on Mylne's NR plans, at White House Sluice, Enfield Flash, Bush Hill Sluice House, Sluice House (taken away) Southgate Loop, Stone Sluice (taken away) before Highbury Loop, Stop Sluice Gate/Highbury Sluice, Sluice House (taken away) at start of Clissold Park Loop, Sluice House before Essex Road, Sluice into St John Street reservoir, and Sluice into the Outer Pond, NRH (Mylne 1775-1809 New River Survey).

1809 (Hughson) 200 Bridges (ROUNDED): 'The total number of bridges is **about two hundred**;' (1A2-6, p360).

1811 & 1842 (Newspaper Article) POS. RELIABLE: 'The New River is mentioned in 1811 as having **204 bridges over it and 40 sluices**. In 1842 there were **154 bridges and but four large sluices** in its course and in various parts both over and under its stream numerous currents of land water, brooks, and rivulets' ('Enf. Gaz. & Obs.' 13 Jan. 1939, p8 'The New River its Story & its Builders').

   1811 (Nelson) 200-300; or 204 Bridges (DISAGREEING): Nelson saying 'as having between **200 and 300 bridges** over it, and upwards of forty sluices' (1K, p207; (Nelson) 14D4, p166). "… mentioned in 1811 as having **204 bridges** over it and 40 sluices" (15).

1815 (NRC Capital Value) RELIABLE: '**157 brick, timber and iron bridges** ('L5.723' Handwritten 6pp MS, Islington LHC possibly the original; 6E, p358 summary).

1815 (Nightingale) About 200 Bridges (ROUNDED): 'About **two hundred bridges** cross the New River at various places; …' (H4, p597).

   INSCRIBED '1817' (THREE NRC SURVIVING CAST-IRON BRIDGES): Three NRC cast-iron bridges inscribed '1817' still surviving and in use.

c.1820 (G.C. Berry) Wooden > Cast Iron Bridges (RELIABLE): Replacing many of the wooden bridges with cast-iron, most of the castings coming from the Priestfield foundry (8A, p32 G.C. Berry, MWB Archivist).

1842 (Lewis) 154 Bridges & 4-Large Sluices (POS. RELIABLE): Lewis telling us "as having in his day **'one hundred and fifty-four bridges** over it, and four large sluices in its course, and in various parts, both over and under its stream, numerous currents of land-waters, and brooks, and rivulets'" (1K, p207; 15 repeated).

1859 BRIDGES REUSED (Old Bridges on Former Loops > Removed to New Lines of River): 'some of the Bridges were removed and placed on the New lines of River, temporary ones filling their places – That whatever might have to be expended on these loops would be, Mr Mylne trusted to be repaid by the sale of the spare Iron Bridges, ... etc.' ((NRC Min. W/117) 8A1, 4/1-2; ((Mins. pp117-118) Typed 'NS, The Loops 12 May 1859') 8A1, 2-8). This can be **confusing regarding the dating of certain sections of the River, SO BE AWARE!** There being three (probably reused/resited) NRC bridges across the former sewage ditch S-side of the Manifold Ditch, Ware.

It appears that over the years as roads became widened to take more traffic, the far narrower NRC bridges becoming major traffic restrictions, often not cured until much wider bridges built at the part expense of Toll Road & Local Authorities.

DIFFERENT X-SECTION at Every NR-Bridge: As will be seen later in these volumes, the River has a different X-section at each & every NR-bridge, dependant on angles of flow, wharfing, date they were built etc.

Official lists of bridges at some Later dates are included in subsequent Volumes.

SURFACE WATER & FLASHES/TROUGHS (Over New River) also Augmenting Supply

QUALITY/PURITY of New River Water: Was probably inferior to London's Conduit water (although this deteriorated c./1673 as the West End expanded), but superior to the polluted Thames water (7K4-1, p42/pp92-94). In 1615 reference by the Privy Council to abuses such as 'casting in doggs and filth, and letting in sewers and other fowle and unclean water, to the annoyance of the said [NR] water' ((PC Acts 1615-16, pp212-213) 11, p67).

In 1613 just a grate in the NRH Water House sifting rubbish prior to the water entering the wooden mains to the City (11, p60).

The New River's slow flow acting as a continuous settling reservoir, only floating debris removed approx. every 5-miles at grates, at NRH using fine screens and cleaning the chambers every 3-months (7G5, p119).

From 1620 the bulk of NR water from the River Lee (where upstream towns used it as a drain) not just its springs.

SURFACE WATER

c.1800 from Robert Mylne's 1775-1809 NR plans, at this time picking up any suitable water from **adjoining streams or surface water road drains** on the way to augment the New River.

Undated (Common Sewers) into New River: 'the shameful practice of common sewers running into the New River, so as, in some places, to make it look as black and thick as if hogsheads of ink were thrown into it, is so intolerable, in such an elegant town as this, that we should no longer pretend to any degree of elegancy, or even of cleanliness, if we suffer it to continue; or go on drinking or using such water in our kitchens … by so doing we in some sort fall under a curse denounced in the Old Testament to some Nations' and that unlike the Thames the New River has no Flux or Reflux to purify or purge itself (('Mundus') 15C2, page VII, Isl. LHC).

Augmenting Supply (Surface Water): Published 1899 'During the early part of its career the NRC obtained a good deal of water between Chadwell and London. This was chiefly surface water. Of late years, however, the surface water has been carefully excluded, and many channels have been made to intercept it and convey it into the River Lee below the intake of the Company', 'A former engineer to the Company estimated that at one time **something like half the amount of water which fed the river was surface water**' (7K1, p21/25).

Published 1909 'Surface water, which used to form a large proportion of the supply, has within recent

years been as far as possible excluded from the river' (1K11C, p351).
By 1853 the River Lee becoming the sewer of the Lee Valley, especially the lower part with floating dead animals (('A practical essay on water supplies to the Metropolis' by W. Burch, pp20/21) 7K4-1, p93).
1871 NR water arriving at their works called 'turbid', in 1877 after filtration at first called very pale brown and slightly turbid, and 2-months later as slightly yellow although clear and unsavoury ((F. Bolton and Professor Frankland) 7K4-1, p94).

FLASHES/TROUGHS: In some places intervening streams were carried over the New River in flashes or troughs, such that at flashes, if required this water could be tapped and further feed the New River (7, p11).

Definitions & Descriptions of a Flash
A pool, a marshy place "now local". A sudden movement of water; a splash; a breaker, c. 1713.
A sudden rush of water, let down from a weir, to take a boat over shallow places, c. 1677 (O.E.D.). A flash is to reflect light as a sheet of water would; to send a rush of water down a river, weir etc.; a body of water driven along with violence; a sluice or lock just above a shoal to raise the water while boats are passing.

Original NRC Accounts 'Shippwrights and Plummers' (Timber Chutes & Troughs): Received 2s. a day (3, p8) for making and repairing **timber chutes or troughs** for carry the River over ravines, using quantities of purchased:

"Tarre, pytche Rossen, harde Tallowe toe mingle with ye pytche, Rossen, nayles & Okeam" (3, p9).

1775-1809 (Robert Mylne's Survey) Flashes: For a list of Flashes/Troughs on New River, see fol.

1862 (Flashes Described) by Samuel Smiles: "In some cases these drainage waters were conveyed under the New River in culverts, and in others over it by what were termed flashes' Footnote: 'At each of these flashes there were **extensive swamps**, where the flood-waters were upheld to such a level as to enable them to pass over the flash, which consisted of a **wooden trough, about twelve feet wide and three deep**, extending across the river; and from these swamps, as well as from every other running stream, such apparatus was introduced as enabled the Company to avail themselves of the supply of water which they afforded, when required. Mr [W.C.] Mylne is of opinion that the river, as originally constructed by Myddelton, **obtained quite as large a supply from the grass lands along the hill-sides as was obtained from the Hertfordshire springs**' (13, p122).

The waters were probably held back by driving piles (green oak or alder) into the ground and forming a retaining bank, the boggy marsh formed with its tall reeds, rushes, flags and sedge, would have echoed to the screaming of wild fowl feeding on the swarms of fish in the meres (lakes and pools), and provided rich grazing land nearby.

1873 (Flashes) Described by Ford & Hodson: "The surface waters of the district were carried off, sometimes by a culvert under the bed of the river, and sometimes by a "flash", which consisted of a wooden trough carried over it. One of these flashes was situated at Clay Hill [Enfield], where the name is still retained" (B2, p255 probably from Smiles).

1939 (Flashes) Described: "In those places where [an] embankment was formed, provision had of course to be made for the passage of surface waters from the west of the line of works into the River Lee, which forms the natural drain of the district, in some cases the drainage waters were conveyed under the New River in culverts, and in others over it by what were termed 'flashes'. At each of these 'flashes' there were extensive swamps, where the flood waters were upheld to such a level as to enable them to pass over the flash, which consisted of a wooden trough, about **12 feet wide and 3 feet deep**, extending across the river; and from these swamps as well as every other running stream, such apparatus was introduced as enabled the company to avail themselves of the supply of water which they afforded, when required" (('Enfield Gazette & Observer' article) 15; probably based on Smiles).

1957 (Flashes) Described by G.C. Berry, MWB: "To cross the streams, the river was carried in small wooden troughs near the point where the level of the stream coincided. Sometimes the intervening stream was carried over the river by what was called a flash, the stream being confined in a trough. It must have been a very wet business, as the water level of the stream would have to be raised to the level of the trough. It was possible by means of the flash to tap the stream if necessary" (8, p35).

Published 1962: Augmenting the supply by tapping streams such as Hackney Brook on the way (K1, p70); MFK not aware at what location.

27 Dec. 1968 (Flashes) Described by G.C. Berry, MWB: "The word relates to river navigation and was applied to a sluice like contrivance for raising water over shoals. The word also means a sudden rush of water let down from a weir (See the Oxford English Dictionary). In the case of the New River, the flashes were contrivances for raising the water level of a stream over the river in a trough. This created a pool above the flash and a waterfall below it to both of which the word flash would also apply" (MFK corres. with G.C. Berry, MWB).

1970 (Flashes) Described by G.C. Berry, MWB: 'On the river he [Robert Mylne NRC Surveyor] straightened various small wrinkles and did away with three of the flashes. These flashes were constructed at various points where the New River was led to a stream crossing its path at the same level. It appears that the stream was made to rise above the level of the New River and was then carried across in a trough, the banks of the river being protected by wing walls. A pipe from the stream was driven through the bank of the river under the control of a sluice or tampin, as it was called' (8A, p27).

1989 (Flashes) Described: A flash, "in a trough of about twelve feet in width with a pool behind it and a waterfall below. Water could be drawn from these subsidiary streams into the New River if required" (('English Heritage' article) 15E, p3).

Whilst the intervening streams augmented the supply in Myddelton's time because they quickly ran short of water from the original sources, within two hundred years the increasing population and industrial revolution would turn most of those streams into open sewers, so the practice of tapping them eventually discontinued.

FORMER FLASHES & TROUGHS/FRAMES (SITES OF):
1. March 1615 the **Trough at 'Gyddinges'** rebuilt (15J, pp44-45), probably over Woollens Brook, Geddings, Hoddesdon.
2. In Jan. 1615 over 30-days rebuilding the large 1612 **Trough at 'Hawe Mores'**, and 60-loads of rubbish carted away by Edward Curtesse to Lady Cock's ground to fill where they had dug the clay £2 (15J, p44). Sir Henry Cock of Broxbournebury d.1609. **Possibly at Rags Brook, Cheshunt?**
   1 Feb. 1612: Had reached Housemores, Cheshunt ((30+ typed foolscap sheets 'Draft Lecture NRC', p14) 8A1, 4/1-1). Or possibly Halmores, Hoddesdon?
3. **Turnford-Wormley Flash** (NGR TL 358 057) rebuilt 1780 in brick & stone, NW extremity of former Turnford Loop, is the **LAST SURVIVING NEW RIVER FLASH WITH EXISTING REMAINS, and unless soon thoroughly recorded will be lost forever** (Not clearly shown on OS Explorer Map 174 but is there as is most of the dried-up channel of the New River Loop).
4. **Cheshunt Flash** (bypassed 1825-6), beneath later NRC N-reservoir, Cheshunt.
5. 1613 mention of the **Trough at Gyrton Park** (John Gyrton the keeper of Little Enfield Park, Whitewebbs) > probably 1773/5 'Dickinson's/Dickenson's Trough' to the W of Myddelton House, Enfield (shown on 1773 Breton Estates plan, ELSC&A, and Mylne's 1775 plan), presumably made of wood, used to take an opposing stream over the New River.
6. **Enfield/Chase/Whitewebbs Flash** (rebuilt 1775 in brick & stone), W of Flash Lane, off Clay Hill, Enfield.
7. Bush Hill **FRAME/Trough**. Will be described in detail later.
8. 1612-1774 **Mincing Wood/Wild's Flash** (bypassed 1774), and 1612-1779 **Newman's Flash** (bypassed 1779), both on former Southgate Loop. Aug. 1615 renewing the flash at Newmans Grove (15J, p45).
   Possible Former Flash?: Where the Muswell Stream was swelled by the Mutton Brook, Priory Brook & Cholmeley Brook before reaching the former Green Lanes, at conjunction of Southgate-Tottenham Loops.
Also 'a **pysher att Woodgreene** 25 foote longe & a foote square **toe Carried ye Land water**' costing 15s. ((15 May 1613, L.R. 2/28, First Accounts Book, P.R.O.) 8, p35).
9. **Hornsey Flash** & Grate bypassed 1790 ending the supply from the Moselle Brook.
10. Highbury **FRAME/Trough**. Will be described in detail later.
11. **Raised Wooden Trough** lined with lead (SITE OF), 'Hollow', City Road.

2.4 Along the New River

ISLANDS: Chalk Island near Chadwell Spring (not sure why named aside the Old River Lee, 1676 NRC had 50-year lease, and subsequent ownership), **Gt. Amwell islands** (1775-1809 originally only the SE-island, since two), **Broxbourne island** (c.1854), **Cheshunt island** (c.1854), **Theobalds island** (Prob. c.1854), **Enfield Town Park island** (Carr's basin, 1835), and **two islands Bowes Manor** (post-1809, after loop that on bypassed 1859, retained for some time, but long since gone).

FORMER Frames/Troughs aka Myddelton's 'Boarded River'

  1612-1788 Bush Hill Frame, aka 'Great Frame', replaced by a raised embankment.

  1619-1778 Highbury Frame, replaced by Highbury Bank (embankment).

FORMER NRC CISTERN HOUSES (Along New River) from Clissold Park SOUTH: Aside of or adjacent to New River:

  N-side Paradise Row > Church Street, Stoke Newington, S-side New River.
  Pre-1781 NRC Newington Cistern, probably shown in a pre-1871 watercolour.

Further S.
  NE-End, Essex Road.
  Pre-1765 Green Man Cistern, retained 1858, probably removed 1892-3 when Astey's Row was piped.

Further S.
  NE on (River or) Water Lane > St Peter's Street, N-end of Colebrook Row.
  1740/1 Cistern House, Hattersfield, possibly not built (Draft Conveyance).

Further S.
  S-side of City Road (opened 1761), and N-side of Goswell Road an ancient road into London.
  c.1720 'Old Street Cistern' > 1787 'Goswell Street Road Cistern'.
  1775-1809 Mylne Survey calls '**Dalby's Cistern**'.

Goswell Road.

  SE-side of New River, opposite just before Sadlers Wells Theatre, approx. halfway between St John's Street to start of Outer Pond.
  Pre-1720 to 1805-6 'Bullocks Cistern' > 1805-6 Replaced by Inlet to NRC St John's Street Reservoir.
There were many others around NRH (see appropriate section).

TUNNELS (Former & Present): Listed geographically fol. line of River.

  c.1987-9 (Modern TUNNEL) Diverting $^2/_3$'rds. of New River Flow > KING GEORGE'S RESERVOIR:
70-inch Pipe-Jack Transfer Tunnel from New River at Maiden's Brook, Enfield to N-side of King George's Reservoir. **Only $^1/_3$ of the NR's Original Volume then heading South**.

  1857-59 ($^2/_3$–Mile Long) Wood Green Brick TUNNEL: 1,100 yards long, 12 feet wide by 9 feet deep (7K1, p38; 7, p11 $^2/_3$–mile; 10-3, p17 built 1852 700 yds long by 14ft. wide.; 15J, p180 14ft./p181 1,108 yds long; (1939) 15C, p19 700 yards long and 14 feet dia., appears to be source of these dimensions). Mostly 'Cut & Cover' constructed by Thomas Docwra bypassing the former

Tottenham Loop.

1891-2 Harringay TUNNEL: Completed for £4,947, bypassing the Harringay House NE-Loop ((1939) 15C, p19 7 feet diameter; 10-3, p17 200yds long).

FORMER 'Newington TUNNEL' (> c.1828 Open New River)
   1613 - c./1724 Former 'Stamford Hill' Loop bypassed by:
c./1724 to 1799 & 1825 Newington Tunnel > c.1828 Open River: In 1799 500ft. (167 yds) of Arch removed, Robinson's 1814 map possibly showing S-end part removed, 1825 agreed to open the Old Dark Arch (probably the N-part), the name Dark Arch and its ready removal would **suggest it was 'cut & cover'**. Today a section of the NR here the **only part of the New River with brick 'wharfing'**, so possibly the foundations for the tunnel (13, p123, Newington brick tunnel).

Modern 3-km long Tunnel, from Stoke Newington to Coppermills.

2008-9 TUNNEL (TWRM Northern Extension) Stoke Newington PS to NRH: Proposed March 2007 start of a new tunnel from the TWRM (TW Ring Main) here to New River Head (near Kings Cross), due for completion 2010 (Dave Allkins, TW). After 12-months breaking through at NRH on Mon. 11 May 2009.
   1955-60 Thames-Lee Raw Water TUNNEL: Crosses beneath the New River's West Reservoir, with an Air Valve, and tunnel shaft on NE-bank (Dave Allkins, TW).

   c./1650 to Post-1851 Essex Road TUNNEL (also aka 'Dark Arch'), 'Cut & Cover': The original River along Essex Road left open, c./1650 covered by a brick arch, 1851 probably replaced by 36-inch main.

EASEMENTS (Bypass Pipes): Iron bypass pipes to prevent bank erosion at sharp bends or at restricted width bridges, also improving flow e.g. at Hoddesdon P.S., as at many other places on the River.

PIPED SECTIONS/'CULVERTING' (Bypassing or Replacing Loops): Listed geographically fol. line of River.

   1857-8 (4-Pipes of the Docwra Aqueduct), Maidens Brook Enfield (See fol.).

   1853 (48-inch), 1875 (48-inch) & 1912 (54-inch) Three Cast-Iron Mains (Bypassing Enfield Town Loop), Southbury Road to Bush Hill (8B, corres. April 1969; Post-1984/5 Map with 'Index to Bridges' New River, TW Reading Microfilm; 15J, p221 ¾-mile long pipeline).

   1971-3 Conduit (Inverted Siphon) Bowes/North Circular Road: Bowes Road widened c.1962-4, the road lowered 1971-3 after a reinforced concrete inverted siphon conduit was constructed beneath the old road.

   1851-1892 (Various Iron Pipes) Stoke Newington to NRH: Mainly culverting the New River from the Stoke Newington Green Lanes road-bridge to NRH. Said usually **three pipes laid side-by-side** (15J, p180). Their use discontinued 1945-6, the pipes said removed 1950. See further detailed sheet/s in Vol. 2.

AQUEDUCTS (Present) normally with Embankments: Listed geographically fol. line of River.

   1854-5 Turnford Aqueduct (Bypassing Wormley Loop): Constructed by Thomas Docwra.

   1857-8 Docwra Aqueduct (An 'Inverted Siphon') Bypassing Whitewebbs Loop, Maidens Brook Enfield: Carrying two large iron pipes on iron girders (covered with corrugated sheeting) **below the**

normal level of the New River, supported on brick abutments, later augmented by two pipes under the brook.
1857/8 Pymmes Brook Aqueduct (Bypassing Southgate Loop): For 100ft. above and below the new aqueduct, deepening & straightening the brook along the central arch.

NRC RESERVOIRS: For list of open storage reservoirs (see p54), & covered reservoirs (p55/56/57/58).

FILTRATION & CHLORINATION Etc. (NRC & MWB > TW)

Rye Common (S-side of P.S.)
Former 1908 No. 1 & 2 Filters (MWB > TW) > 1995 closed (when ALL Well water now pumped into the New River), the site left to decay. 1910 the well water first chlorinated before part put into local supply.

Former 1926 (MWB Ammonia Plant) N-side Bush Hill Road: Added to the New River here to prevent taste troubles. Probably long discontinued.

Former 1926 (MWB Liquid Chlorine & Permanganate of Potassium into New River) Highfield Lane: MWB known to have put liquid chlorine into the New River, usually only during the flood months, with a 2 lb. per m.g. dosage of permanganate of potassium. Probably long discontinued.

Former 1926 (MWB 'Dechlorination' Plant) before the New River disappeared under the railway line, S-side Station Road, Wood Green. Long discontinued.

1859-79 NRC > MWB > TW Modernised, Hornsey Filter Beds.
  1949 MWB installing a temporary Contact & Balancing Tank, Hornsey Works: For the dechlorination of the filtered water after superchlorination, to overcome outbreaks of taste.
  1956 MWB to purchase an Ammoniator, Hornsey Works: For adding ammonia after terminal chlorination. **At these two dates also at Stoke Newington.**

Stoke Newington > Coppermills
(i) FORMER 1852-5 to 1993 NRC (> MWB > TW) Filter Beds, Stoke Newington > 1994-1999 Mydelton Avenue Housing Estate. One of the new roads fittingly called **Colthurst Crescent**, after the pioneer who first dreamt up the idea of constructing the 'New River'.
(ii) FORMER 1936 MWB Primary Filter House > 'West Reservoir Centre'/Water Sports Centre, S-side West Reservoir, Stoke Newington: 32 m.g.d. Primary Filter House built in Rational Modern Architecture to remove algae growth interfering with the slow sand filtration (14FB). Redeveloped into a modern water sports leisure complex.
  1949 MWB installing a temporary Contact & Balancing Tank, Stoke Newington: For the dechlorination of the filtered water after superchlorination, to overcome outbreaks of taste.
  1956 MWB to purchase an Ammoniator, Stoke Newington: For adding ammonia after terminal chlorination. **At these two dates also at Hornsey Works.**
(iii) c./1993 > MWB Coppermills Primary Filter Beds (Constructed 1970-72) > Thames Water, aside the River Lee: Presumably any excess NR-water reaching Stoke Newington is today transferred by a modern transfer tunnel to the MWB > Thames Water Coppermills Primary Filter Beds, constructed mainly on the site of the former East London Waterworks Racecourse Reservoir.

Former 1855-6 to 1946 (NRC > MWB) 3-Filter Beds, Outer Pond, New River Head: Three slow sand filter beds constructed in Outer Pond for £32,000, 1913 extending the southern boundary, 1936 one taken out of use to construct the new MWB Laboratory building, March 1946 the remaining two taken out of use.

Former PUMPING WATERWHEELS on New River

Hornsey Sluice House
1859 to c.1899 Waterwheel: 1859 built Hornsey Sluice House with Poncelet-type (semi-turbine) low breastshot waterwheel (F3B, p2); the 1859 installed Messrs Watt engine at Hornsey ready to pump to Highgate. 1861-2 presumably this waterwheel first pumping to Wood Green. In 1899 called an undershot waterwheel formerly pumping to Maiden Lane.

Highbury Sluice House
Pre-1819 Horse Machine > 1819 Waterwheel with 1834 Steam Power Backup. 1837 relocated aside the Sluice House. Possibly 1841 a new Sluice House built to immediate S in centre of widened New River, with no further references to this waterwheel.

NRC WELLS/PUMPING STATIONS:

List of Wells along New River (1926): Most New River well stations did not have force pumps (they had lift pumps), since water was delivered into the river at surface level only.

	Order Sunk (*).	Depth of bore-holes Feet (max.)	Nom. Pumping capacity per 24 hours (Gals.).
Broadmead	1880	500	1,500,000
	(6) 1877 (*).		
Amwell End	1868	419	1,200,000
	(2) 1848 (*).		
Amwell Hill	1847	160	3,300,000
	(3) 1848 (*).		
Amwell Marsh	1884	392	5,600,000
	(7) 1885 (*).		
Rye Common	1883	204 (depth of well)	4,600,000
Part direct into supply after chlorination and filtration.			
	(8) 1886 (*).		
Hoddesdon	1866	385	2,300,000
	(5) 1868 (*).		
Broxbourne	1886	212	3,500,000
	(10) 1886 (*).		
Turnford	1850	1,010	4,000,000
	(4) 1867 (*).		
Cheshunt	(1) 1846 (*).	First well along route of New River (8A1, 4/1-6).	
Whitewebb's	1898	402	700,000
	(13) 1898 (*).		
Hoe Lane	1880	395	2,400,000
	(9) 1886 (*).		
Hadley Rd. (acquired)	1903	323 (depth of well)	1,000,000
Pumped direct into supply.			
Highfield	1885	371	600,000
Pumped into New River, or service reservoirs.			
	(11) 1887 (*).		
Betstile (acquired)	1871	300	375,000
Out of regular use. Not pumped into the New River.			
	(14)	'Acquired in 1872, the water from it is pumped into the service reservoir at Chase Side, Southgate'; Betstile P.S. at former Grove Road.	
Campsbourne	1887	396	1,500,000
Pumped into the New River, or used to augment Hornsey filtered water supply.			
	(12) 1888 (*).		

((1926) 15D, p6; 15C1, p8 14-wells along river). * (6L, p439 quoted c.1925). As with most historical details the figures vary (**they agree to disagree**), for more exacting dates see details regarding the site itself.

The wells typically a brick or cast-iron lined 12-15ft. dia. shaft sunk down to the chalk, where long gallery boreholes, 6ft. by 4ft. wide, are cut sideways to collect the water, raised by reciprocating bucket type borehole and well pumps, driven by steam engines, later mostly replaced by electric pumps (pumphouse electric motors driving shafting to water-level vertical-spindle, multi-stage centrifugal pumps; later using submersible electric pumps), with diesel engines as a standby. Most converted by 1955, although some steam powered pumps still operating in June 1961 according to an MWB report (10-3, p19).

Rye Common 1935 small electric pump replacing a large steam engine (9, pp221-222).

Amwell Hill 1944 small electric pump (9, pp221-222), at Amwell Hill purchased electricity driving centrifugal borehole pumps (7G5, p141).

Hoddesdon 1946 small electric pumps (9, pp221-222), at Hoddesdon submersible pumps & motors (7G5, p141).

Broxbourne 1946 small electric pumps (9, pp221-222), purchased electricity driving centrifugal borehole pumps of unique variable speed design (7G5, p141).

Turnford remodelled 1953 (9, pp221-222).

Hoe Lane remodelled 1953 (9, pp221-222).

Hornsey described 1867, the Cornish engine made at St Austell, Cornwall, transferred from Kentish Town where a 1,300ft. deep well never gave water, with a 44-inch dia. cylinder, 10ft. piston stroke, 15-inch pole with 9ft. stroke, the engine beam unequally divided, pumping to the covered reservoir at the Archway, Highgate (7G6, p5/p7 'purchased second-hand a few years ago, and now expanding from half-stroke only').

Stoke Newington electric pumps using purchased electricity (7G5, p140).

There are also other pumping stations within the NRC area/district (See '**List of Main Sites**'). When I first started on my quest, under the MWB most of the New River pumping stations with wells, were often beautifully bedecked inside with large coloured X-section diagrams of the wells themselves, but sadly these have long disappeared. Also in 1971 there were often the remains of the old **brick-built coal bunkers**, but sadly today all gone. Another reminder is the use of weigh-bridges (probably installed by the MWB) for weighing the coal & coke supplied to the steam-powered pumping stations, the lorries weighed in & out of the station, the only accurate method for determining the real quantity supplied, if they didn't fiddle the vehicle's spare wheel.

Weigh Bridges: Presumably one still remains at the former Whitewebbs P.S. (now a veteran vehicle Museum).

NRC Standpipes: Standpipes used for equalising the water pressure from the pumping engines. Former NRC standpipes at Southgate (Oakwood) Reservoir, and NRH Upper Pond. Also two remaining standpipes at NRC Hampstead Grove Covered Reservoirs.

Modern NR-PUMPHOUSES

From 1991, Inaugurated 1995 (Artificial Recharge Pumping Stations) Pumphouses: From 1991 a series of additional boreholes constructed beside the New River, enabling **treated water** to be stored in the chalk aquifer in times of surplus (winter), for pumping back into the New River when levels are low, such as in dry summers. The 'Aquifer Recharge Scheme' for storing 33-billion gals. beneath ground in the aquifer, equivalent to constructing 350 reservoirs the size of both Stoke Newington reservoirs. Costing £7m, 17 new pumping stations to be built aside the NR, making 23 south of Enfield, operational by mid-1994, filling the aquifer possibly taking up to 10-years (Historical notes in 1993 NR Celebration Concert souvenir programme). Inaugurated 25 June 1995 by the Minister of the Environment, tested 1 Sept. 1995, for use in such summers as 1997 and July 2005 (BBC Radio 4, 4 July 2005). Three 250ft. approx. deep boreholes at each pumphouse, for the pump, and two for monitoring equipment.

The Enfield-Haringay Recharge Project winning a commendation in the 1996 Civic Trust Awards (NRAG Issue No. 35, June 1996). **A list of the latest known Pumphouses incorporated into the previously shown 'List of Main Sites'**.

Pumphouse 'Bat Bricks': Most of the pumphouses built with a hole in a 'bat brick' (to a London Bat Group design, after consultation with English Nature) on the New River side, with an internal roosting box (15F, No. 26, Sept 1994, bat bricks already being installed; 15F, Issue No. 32, Sept. 1995, Bat bricks with 'upward & backward sloping entrances').

NR WATER-LEVEL GAUGES: The occasional old rusting water-level gauge (prominent on the banks of the NR), most modern ones now enclosed in large galvanised cylinders attached to wharfing.

MAJOR SLUICES/WEIRS: For controlling the level of water in the River, erected across the River, or as waste gate weirs at side of the River.

   1775-1809 (Sluices) Mylne Survey: White House Sluice, Ware, Enfield Flash, Bush Hill Sluice House, just inside today's Arnos Park, Stone Sluice (overflow) Green Lanes, Highbury Sluice, at start of former Clissold Park Loop, Thatched House Sluice, sluice into St John Street Reservoir, smaller sluice into the Outer Pond.

   1862 (NR Sluices Described) by Samuel Smiles: 'Where the fall of the ground was found inconveniently rapid, a stop-gate was introduced at such places across the stream, penning from 3 to 4 feet perpendicularly, the water flowing over such weirs down to the next level' (13, p121 quote).

   1868-9 recorded **"Coffee Pot" sluice house** (possibly still there) at start of Clissold House Loop (7K1, p41).

   1943 (Sluice Gates): "Sluice gates were also fixed at various places to regulate the flow of the water and separate the total length of the river into a series of pounds from which the water could be sent down or held back as demanded by the outflow at the London end. This followed the practice adopted in canals where locks are provided to accommodate the varying levels of the surface of the ground over which the canal is constructed. The sluice gates of the New River were originally placed and are still in existence at:

     Amwell Hill, Broxbourne, Cheshunt, Maidens Brook, Enfield, Bush Hill, Hornsey, Highbury. They are plain wooden shutters raised or lowered by a rack and wheel into which a bar or lever was inserted similar to the old fashioned waste gate in the upper pond or mill head stream of a Corn Mill worked by a wheel with the water carried over or under it. The original wooden gates have now nearly all been **replaced by modern roller sluices** which are much easier to operate, but there function is the same" (15C, p14).

   2011 (Sluices): Aside Amwell Hill P.S., before Broxbourne Church, N-side Brookfield Lane, Cheshunt, historic Bush Hill Sluice House, Hornsey Sluice House, mid-C19th Ivy Sluice House.

SMALLER SLUICES/WEIRS (Mainly Modern): There are too many to list, the first probably an old one at Chadwell Spring itself, and many others of a modern date along the River giving better water-level control.

NRC STONE & IRON BOUNDARY MARKERS: The only known LARGE boundary stones marking out NRC property boundaries are around and near Chadwell Spring. Surviving smaller $^N_C{}^R$ inscribed

stone at former W-Loop Wormley, two at the former Clay Pits, Whitewebbs probably date to c./1805. The iron markers inscribed $^N R_C$ (vertically), mainly flat but also found square $^N_{Co.}{}^R$ with bevel top (near New Gauge & other places) probably first dating from c.1830, but most probably later, 'PIPE' with vertical $^N R_C$, beneath near S-end of Wood Green Tunnel, '**NRC (or MWB) PIPE TRACK**' said remaining today on W-side of former filter beds Stoke Newington, but **lots more if you keep your eyes peeled aside today's course of the New River**. Although in nearly all places they are the later (Post-1904) $^M W_B$ (vertically) inscribed ones. They don't seem to have been used by Thames Water.

LEFT: Wooden $^N_C{}^R$ Inscribed Boundary Post (Perhaps Unique?): Interestingly in 1971 MFK dug up

the only wooden $^N_C{}^R$ inscribed marker known, at Wormley (**first noticed by Pete Manning** who manned the MWB Cheshunt Grate, removed by MFK purely for conservation purposes before it was lost forever, cutting off the rotted bottom part, mounting on board, and highlighting the inscribed NRC in green), which assumably must be at least pre-1904, and it is difficult to know why it should have been made of wood and not iron (unless it was just an expedient temporary one, forgotten to be replaced by iron), if it pre-dates iron (c.1830), then it is remarkably preserved?

STEALING NR WATER
Various methods used along the New River and in London by persons not wanting to pay for NR water. June 1614 having to pay watchers when brewers at Goswell Street stealing water, 1632 payments authorised to informants at discretion of NRC Gov., 1669 warrant for arresting persons diverting the New River, and brewers cutting the banks for water, May 1723 at Exeter Street a man with two houses only paying for water for one of them, June 1723 near Newman's Flash a Mr Tho. Nash stealing water day & night for his Physick garden, and in 1740 Mr Richard Holland at Hornsey Sluice only paying for a supply to his house, having illegally inserted a 3-inch pipe to his brewhouse (15J, p95-96).

ILLEGAL BATHING & WASHING IN NEW RIVER:
  June 1614 (Illicit Bathing) in New River: For 3-days over the Whitsun holiday two labourers paid for watching out for swimmers in the New River ((LR/2/27-33, PRO) 15J, p96).
  30 March 1616 (Illicit Bathing) in 'Pond': 2s. paid to the messenger Simpson for keeping out swimmers and dogs from the pond ((LR/2/27-33, PRO) 15J, p96). July 1728 boarders at a school in Enfield (15J, p96).
  16 Aug. 1770 (NRC Advert) Illegal Bathing & Washing in New River: From the New River Office at Bridewell Precinct, a notice that the NRC would prosecute such persons who bath & wash in the New River, such as those that recently did so in the fields between Newington & Islington, damaging property and the banks of the New River ((Acc 2558/NR2/2, LMA; text almost identical to June 1771 below) 15J, p96). Nov. 1770 Liscombe Price Jnr. let off by signing a pledge never to swim in NR again & paying the NRC's costs, the company the fol. year introducing a 40s. reward ((Add. MS. 48904, f.18, BL; Acc 2558/MW C/15/105, LMA) 15J, p96).
  Thurs. 13 June 1771 (Disorderly Bathing) in New River: 'New River Office, Bridewell Precinct, Thurs. 13 June 1771. Whereas a great number of idle and disorderly persons have assembled themselves together in the fields between Islington and Newington and the parts adjacent, and have, by bathing & washing themselves in the New River, broke down the banks, and done other damage, nuisance and annoyances to the said river, and have also in a most atrocious, indecent and illegal manner committed many other offences highly injurious to the property of this company and to the public in general, contrary to an Act of Parliament passed in the 12th year of his Majesty King George the Second: this is therefore to give notice, that the said company are determined to prosecute with the utmost severity of the law all such persons who for the future shall be found so offending: And whoever shall apprehend any person or persons guilty of such offences, shall, upon his or their conviction before any of his majesty's justices of the peace, be paid the sum of 40s. by Mr Holford, Secretary to the NRC, at their office in Bridewell Precinct, London' (Printed cutting with inked 'Public Advertiser 15/6/1771', Isl. LHC; 15C2, page X repeated; also see 14B2, pp460-461).
  4 Dec. 1776 (Bathing) in New River: As part of evidence at a trial, John Heckstall & William Catherall (sentenced to death for highway robbery) had gone to bathe in the New River (G5, Old Bailey trials). June 1781 advertising a £2 reward & to erect trespassing signs, and in 1783 problem with bathers in the NRC's recently opened West Pond such that to build a surrounding brick wall & lock for the door ((Mins. B/189) Typed 'NRC, The West Pond in the Hanging Field') 8A1, 2-8; (17 July 1783 Min.) 15J, p96).
  12 Sept. 1798 (Bathing) in New River: William Williams in evidence was at work by the side of the New River at Islington, one of the accused in the trial was on his way to bathe in the New River (G5, Old Bailey trials).
  Aug. 1801 (Two Letters) Regarding Bathing: Anonymous letter sent to the NRC requesting they ban bathing in the New River between Duncan Terrace & Colebrooke Row, that was annoying local residents, such that the Collectors were ordered to call on more respectable residents and inform them that the company would pay part of the expenses for prosecuting those named by parish officers.

Another letter a few days later signed by a Rob't Yelton, also thought anonymous. Rhodes the cowkeeper visiting Robert Mylne to make the same complaint ((Acc 2558/MW/C/15/142-8 & 105/1, LMA) 15J, pp96-97).

5 Dec 1809 (R. Mylne's Diary) Bathing: "Attended Cause at Session House on bathing etc. in the New River. Verdict – in favour of River etc. Sentence – to be imprisoned for 2 months – Newgate" (15K, p218); evidently John Tire of Islington bathing in NR and running naked near Highbury Place ((8 Dec. 1809 'Diary of Joseph Farington' editor K. Cave, 1982) 15J, p97).

1810 resolutions to prevent bathing in the New River ((Printed Sheet) 15I, p145).

July 1830 said that in 12-hours during the summer there might be up to 800-1,000 persons bathing in the NR, breaking down the banks and in one place virtually creating a 60-70ft. pond ((Acc 2558/NR13/10/13, LMA) 15J, p97).

Over the years many of the lower class washing in the New River, and sometimes coupled with references to robberies. Bathing in the New River still occasionally occurs today! In June 2005 when passing the S-side of the NR Aqueduct over the M25, about a dozen teenagers bathing in the NR. A hot day sends their brains crazy, and they became abusive when being told it was prohibited, one boy even punching me in the back of the neck. So beware, because when later reported to the police, as usual they did nothing.

POACHERS/FISHING: The NRC making up their own rights on fishing in the New River, since not covered by Myddelton's 1605 Act (15J, p97).

21 July 1785 (Poaching Fish) from New River, Bluechurch 'near Bulls Cross', Enfield: "The river meanwhile meandered slowly along its devious course, never free for long, however, from the unwanted attentions of poaching landowners, occupiers and fisherman, the trampling of cattle and bathing hordes. One fisherman, William Hart, was caught red-handed by Samuel Garnault at Bluechurch near Bulls Cross, in 1785, using a dragnet. Roach, Dace, Chubb, petch [perch], the alleged property of the company were being extracted. He claimed that he had a grant from Queen Elizabeth. How Queen Elizabeth could have granted him a right to fish in the New River I do not know, nor did the company, who sued him for trespass" (8A, p30; 15J, p97 mention). Caught on 21 July 1785 by Samuel Garnault with Chapman Salt, Under Walksman, and Abraham Cressey, River Surveyor with Wm. Collins, Walksman ((MWB 244) 8A1, 3/3.1).

11 Feb. 1813 (Walksman Fired) for Fishing on Duty: The walksman Tingey dismissed after frequent warnings of continually fishing the New River and neglecting his work ((Mins.) 15J, p98).

Former NRC WATCH BOXES OR WATCH HOUSES: A Watch House recorded 1618 at Highbury Frame, and Watch Boxes shown on Mylne's 1775-1809 Survey e.g. at & near Myddelton House. In later years becoming NR-workers huts, MFK visiting several still in use 1971, but as such not used today.

CAST-IRON CATTLE TROUGHS (Supplied from New River): We shouldn't forget that the New River was important to adjacent landowner' estates, in that it also provided a clean NRC water supply for their cattle troughs.

1970s (Approx. 7-Remaining): MFK recorded at least half a dozen cast-iron cattle troughs surviving from Bullsmoor Lane, Enfield northwards, some inscribed 'NRCo.'.

2011 (Nearly All Now Gone): All except probably two now all gone.

WATER-WEED CUTTING (To Keep the River Fast Flowing)

From its inception the River would have needed continual clearing of waterweeds and obstructing material.

1872-8 (Mowing the Water Weed): 'Bathing in the New River is entirely prohibited; and men called "walksmen" **mow the bed of the river** every week in order to keep down the growth of weeds, which are stopped by gratings placed at intervals, where the weeds are regularly removed' (('Life of Sir Hugh Myddelton', in Mr Charles Knight's 'Penny Cyclopedia') 1K5, p539).

1934 (Cutting the Waterweeds): "During spring and summer months the growth of [water]weeds, long, coarse, ribbon like tendrils, growing up from the bed of the river in the sunlight, have the effect of retarding the flow of water considerably unless they are frequently cut and removed. This is accomplished by specially shaped scythes with blades linked together and drawn to and fro in the bed of the river by a man upon either bank walking upstream so that the scythe meets the weed that is naturally trailing downstream in the current of water. The weeds float when cut and are taken out at gratings placed across the river at convenient situations, after which the weeds are carried away as quickly as possible because they have an objectionable smell" (15C, p20). In the 1970s still undertaken manually as above.

2003 (Modern Weed & Silt Removal) Thames Water: Most of this work now mechanised by using

boats that mechanically cut the weed, others that remove the silt; and using computerised mechanical removal of weed at some grates (15G).

LEFT: Waterweed cutting boat (MFK 2004 photo) with tilting blades so that can go beneath the low NR-bridges (**after cutting the waterweeds left to float down to the next grate**), moored S-side of Broxbourne P.S. For TW photos of weed cutting boats see TWA Photo Library www.waterinschools.com.newriver/main.html).

WEED GRATES (Waterweed Removal): The waterweeds & any obstructing material manually pulled out at Weed Grates.
  1775-1809 (Weed Grates) Mylne Survey: Shows Weed Grates near the Former Broxbourne Loop, near Church Lane, Cheshunt, near & at Myddelton House, Enfield, on the Former Tottenham Loop, at Former Hornsey Flash, near Former Highbury Sluice, and near Former Horse Shoe Point.
  1970s (Manned Weed Grates): Personally known manned smelly Weed Grates N-side Brookfield Lane, Cheshunt (since gone), and N-side of Docwra Aqueduct, Enfield.
  2011 (Modern AUTOMATED Autogrates): S-side Turkey Street, Enfield, N-side Southbury Road, Enfield, N-side Bowes Road/NCR, Palmers Green, and N-side of Lordship Road, Stoke Newington.

'PYTHON RIGS'/DAVITS/BOAT HOISTS (Modern): For raising & lowering boats located at various points along the River.

PUNTS/BOATS for River Maintenance
  1899 (NRC Punts): Each walk also possessing a uniform pattern 30ft. long by 2ft. deep. & 6ft. breadth punt (7K1, p26/27/29).
  1901/Post-1904/1944/1947 (NRC & MWB Technical Drawings): 4-versions of **New River Steel Punts**, riveted steel, riveted mild-steel, welded steel with aluminium, 2-pointed & 2 with flat ends ((Dave Allkins) TW Reading, Microfilm), a copy of one of these shown in Vol. 3.

LEFT: Thames Water punt moored on New River, aside Theobalds Brook, near former blockhouse (MFK 2006 photo).

2010 an old New River punt filled with soil on E-bank within grounds of Enfield Grammar School.

NRC INSCRIBED SEATS: Whilst walking the New River Path there are the occasional pre-1904 NRC inscribed seats, some 'single' & some 'double' the ends cast with the NRC logo. Although have been told that some of them are replicas, and if so are near impossible to identify from the originals!

ABOVE-L: NRC **single** seat S-side Amwell Hill Sluice with four wooden slats (MFK 2004 photo).
ABOVE-R: NRC **double** seat near Broxbourne Church with seven wooden slats, since moved farther W into park (MFK 2004 photo).

CUTTING THE GRASS BANKS

1700s (Grass Cutting with Scythes): Formal lawns of short grass with a rough finish, first kept shorn in France in the 1700s by grazing animals, or labour intensive sickles, shears or scythes, soon spreading worldwide.

1830 (Scythes > First Lawnmower Invented): Doing the work of 8-men scything, the first mechanical lawnmower was invented and patented by Edwin Beard Budding (1795-1846) of Stroud in 1830, being a cast-iron cylinder type machine inspired from nap-cutting cloth mill machines, in partnership with a John Ferrabee selling 7,000 by 1858 (Ransomes from 1832 making copies under license), and because of their weight the larger ones pulled by horses, until lighter ones were made from the 1850s, motorised petrol and steam ones from the 1890s, from 1900 mainly petrol, c.1926 tens of thousands of Atco motor mowers produced per annum, by the 1930s Qualcast selling millions to people with small lawns, then Flymos by the early-1960s (British Lawnmower Museum, Southport: www.lawnmowerworld.co.uk).
At some time the lawnmower must have been taken up by the New River Company. In my day their successors the MWB employing large numbers of river workers to mechanically cut the grass, all Pumping Stations then having or sharing a gardener who tended the **rose-beds and lawns**.

2011 (Today): Thames Water using contractors with modern tractors and appliances.

WALKSMEN (NR Workforce)

MYTH: 'walksmen probably old men instructed to patrol the banks and apprehend people committing nuisances', most unlikely since there was continual daily manual maintenance work (15C2, p12).
Some of them known to have been fired because they were missing when they should have been working (Various NRC Mins.).

1775-1809 (Robert Mylne's Survey) Walksman: All the then Walks suitably detailed on Mylne's plans, but as ever the details are not straightforward and need sorting (there are many changes), such that will have to await further analysis.

13 Oct. 1859 (Increase in Hours & Length of Walks): The labourers' daylight working hours of 7 a.m.- 5 p.m. changed to 7 a.m.- 6 p.m., extra work paid for when required to perform it, and each 1-mile walk increased to 1¼ miles (((NRC Min. W/235) Typed 'River Walks') 8A1, 2-8).

1897 (12-Walks): From 'The Lancet' 1897 when the river was longer, "The River is divided into twelve divisions or 'walks'. Each walk is under the care of two men, the senior of whom is called the 'Walksman' and the assistant the 'Walksman's Mate'. It is the duty of these men constantly to perambulate the river to keep off all intruders, man and beast, to repair the banks where necessary and to cut the grass on the walks, which extend to both sides of the greater part of the course of the river. It may be interesting to mention as a curious matter of etiquette which has lasted a long time, that it is usual for the 'Walksman' to look after the right or 'upper bank' of the river as it is called and for the 'Walksman's Mate' to look after the left or 'lower bank'. This custom is a constant one" (C4, p134).

1899 (12-Walks): Its length divided into 12-'Walks', that each have a 'Walksman' responsible for the upper or right bank & 'Walksman's Mate' responsible for the lower or left bank, plus from May to Sept. extra men that help cut the waterweeds (using 8-12 scythes shackled to a chain with ropes fixed at each end, dragged by a sawing motion & pulled from both bank); cut grass, and repair the banks. The cut waterweeds float down to the next grate, were they are manually removed and taken away usually for use as manure. At this time the Walks were numbered as follows: 1. NRH to Stoke Newington; 2. Stoke Newington to Hornsey; 3. Hornsey to Bowes Park; 4. Bowes Park to Winchmore Hill; 5. Winchmore Hill to Enfield; 6. Enfield to Turkey Street; 7. Turkey Street to Theobalds Lane bridge; 8. Theobalds Lane bridge to Turnford; 9. Turnford to Broxbourne; 10. Broxbourne to Rye House; 11. Rye House to Amwell; 12. Amwell to Chadwell (7K1, p26/27/29).

1926 (12-Walks): "For purposes of inspection, repairs, cutting of weeds, etc., the New River was originally divided into twelve so-called "walks", beginning with (1) New River Head to Stoke Newington and ending with (12) Amwell to Chadwell" (15D, p6).

1934 (River Maintenance) Waterweed & Grass Cutting, Checking for Leakage, & Operating the Sluices: "It will be realised that as a great amount of water in the New River has to be pumped into it from wells, the question of leakage from the river is of great importance, therefore constant supervision and care is necessary in keeping the banks and bed of the channel in a sound and watertight condition. The length of the river between Clerkenwell and Hertford is divided into twelve sections, or walks, as they are termed, each patrolled and **inspected daily by two walksmen, one upon either bank**, and it is their duty to search for any suspicion of a leakage and to report it at once for repair by the use of puddle or timber. The walksmen **also cut weeds in the river** so that the water can get along freely, and have to **keep the grass short upon the banks so that any cracks may be easily seen and the river generally protected from pollution or trespass**. It is also the duty of the walksmen to **regulate the flow by means of the sluice gates**, to suit the requirements of the pumping stations at Hornsey, Stoke Newington and Clerkenwell, because the consumption varies during the week, less water being required on Saturdays and Sundays due to the cessation of activities of trade" (15C, p20).

1971 (ALTERNATE NR-WALKS) HAD TWO DIFFERENT GATE KEYS UP THE RIVER: When I first walked the then private parts of the New River (with permission of the MWB), they gave me a set of mortise-lock gate keys (issued from Highfield Road when bustling with activity). For administration purposes, alternate NR-Walks used two different gate keys up the River viz. Key 1, Key 2, Key 1, Key 2 etc. I would unknowingly come to the set of gates between different Walks, and find that the key I had been using wouldn't work. For a non-employee like me, you had to put your hand through the slats of the gate and feel the back of the lock for a 'I' or 'II' raised imprint, to confirm you needed to use the key for the next Walk. After all these years, I found the set they gave me stored away with my nostalgic bric-a-brac, unknowingly they were never handed back after use, and I might add never used without prior permission. This is a spot of luck, since the locks have all since been changed/modernised, such that my surviving set must now be of historic interest!

 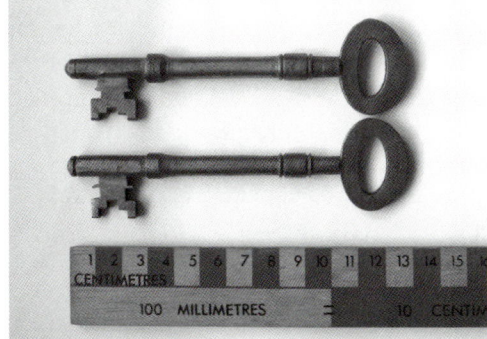

ABOVE-L: MWB New River gate mortise lock type **'II'**, N-side Bridge House, Broxbourne (MFK 2007 photo). **ABOVE-R:** 1971 MWB alternate NR-Walk Gate Keys, above No. 'II', below No. 'I' (MFK photo).

1989 (River Maintenance): "The New River is maintained today in much the same manner as it was in the C18th. New works and major repairs were carried out to the designs of the Surveyor, under whom was a River Surveyor, responsible for the maintenance of the River and the management of the walksmen. As now, the River was divided into a series of walks, patrolled and maintained by walksmen. As now, there were a **series of weed grates to catch rubbish and fallen leaves**, especially in the 'weed season' (NRC Mins., 10 October 1805) and the River was **regularly dredged of mud**. In addition the River was controlled by a **series of sluice gates** consisting of wooden shutters which could be raised or lowered by a rack and wheel. There was a tendency for the number of sluices to be reduced in the late-C18th and C19th and in the London area only four are thought to survive, of which Ivy House in Hackney are listed" (15E, p5).

FENCING

9 Jan. 1621-2 (King James I) falling into the New River near Theobalds: 'The river was in the first place unfenced', the King after falling in said, "**to cause it to be fenced at all dangerous places with all speed**" (12D, p9 not quoting any source).

New River Prob. Already Fenced in Dangerous Places? Since in those days there would seem little point in fencing every mile of pastoral countryside along **both** sides of the New River, it would have meant approx. **80-miles of fencing**. With any sense they no doubt checked the fencing near and through Theobalds after the Royal fall, since they were traversing the Park at Theobalds free of any costs. Although when the King fell in he was liable for 50% of any fencing costs, and one assumes any damages.

1834 Act (Intended Act) that Included Fencing: To authorise the said NRC '**to fence the banks of the said River with post and rail**, in fields and commons bordering thereon' and '**close iron railing where it passes through the streets**' (Printed cutting with inked 'County Press 22 Nov. 1834', Isl. LHC; also www.london-gazette.co.uk 7, 14 & 21 Nov. 1834).

Prob. from c.1840-50 (NRC Iron Railings): The very expensive process of erecting iron railings aside the New River started probably c.1840-50. Mention in 1833 of making a rough estimate for fencing both sides of the river to keep out strangers. On 16 Sept. 1840 the NRC Clerk to get official tenders for **River Railing per mile**. The remaining NRC railings (cast iron posts & wrought iron bars) having stood the test of time, and will be much on view in many sections as we journey down the length of today's river (8A1, 2-8).

1899 (2ft. 6-inches High) NRC Fencing: Aside the river the 'standard fence is 2ft. 6-inches in height, and has two wrought iron rails' (7K1, p26/27/29).

    Post-1835 NRC Iron Fencing
      > Post-1904 MWB Boarded, & Concrete Fencing
        > Post-1974 TW Tall Slatted Metal with Spikes.

Much of the old NRC 2-bar iron rural fencing surviving N of Enfield.

1923 (Secure Fencing): "Prevention of pollution of the New River forms an important branch of the work and as time goes on it is more difficult than in former years, because whereas when first constructed the stream was bounded by fields containing cattle, or used only for the growing of crops, in the present day housing estates, with gardens, footpaths and roads, are in close proximity to the river, with the result that a **securely fenced and protected boundary has had to be provided** to prevent trespass upon the banks and the depositing of undesirable rubbish in the water" (15C, p20).

2011: Fencing as such still applies today even though much of the River's length has become the public-accessible New River Path (**ONLY some parts are a public footpath**), Thames Water the owner's still need to protect their property boundaries, and close it to public access when required. Interestingly the same style railings still to be seen on the N-side of the River Lee millstream at Priory Street, Ware, from the day's when the NRC owned Ware Mills (> MWB > TW).

MWB NOTICE BOARDS

BELOW-L: Typical MWB notice used along the New River, several still remaining (MFK 2004 photo).
BELOW-R: Former MWB bridge weight restriction sign (MFK 1971 photo). One still remaining at

Amwell End.

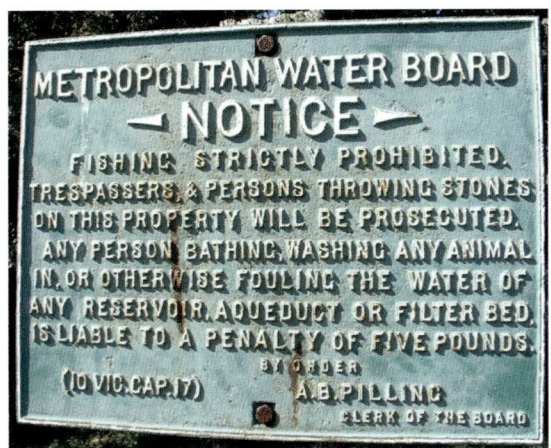

NRC (> MWB > TW) STREET MAIN VALVEPLATES (STOP VALVES)

LEFT: A typical surviving NRC cast-iron street main valve-plate (MFK 2008 photo). Mainly pre-1902/4 but stocks may have been used up after MWB takeover.

July 2010 all the fol. '**NR**' inscribed valve plates in the roads N & S of Lancaster Road, Enfield, W to E, N to S:
Two far E-end of Cedar Road, one at far W-end of Phipps Hatch Lane, another near E-end, and one S-side of SW-end of Hillside Crescent.
Cedar Park Road: Near mid-alley to Hilly Fields, TWO close together on N-side pavement & one in middle of road, & one near far E-end.
One far W-end & far E-end of Brodie Road.
Three grouped together in Brigadier Hill, S-side of W-end of Brodie Road.
Glenville Road: One in N-side mid-alley to Hilly Fields, & one in mid road.
One far E-end of Brigadier Avenue, one far E-end of Merton Road.
One far E-end of Sterling Road, one far S-end of Morley Hill.
One near E-end of White House Lane, one far W-end of Burlington Road, one far E-end of Primrose Avenue.
Two at bottom of Brigadier Hill, one opposite former Horse Trough (12 July 1970, noticed one on photo took of horse trough there), another far S-end of Woodlands Road, Browning Road, Birkbeck Road, Acacia Road, Lavender Road.
Roads S-side of Lancaster Road: One aside Hollybush Pub, Chase Side, far N-end of Laurel Bank Road, '**ND**' (prob. Post-1904 Northern District) far N-end of Lynn Street, far N-end & S-end of Walton Street, far S-end of Drake Street, far N-ends of Armfield Road & Kynaston Road.
'**HR**' (possibly Hydrant River District) at far W-end of Laurel Bank Road, and another just S on E-side of Chase Side. Two outside No. 9 Heene Road (owner says that the common sewer across his back garden needs clearing every 6-months by TW), and another far S-end of Heene Road.
Also spent a fun 29/6/2008 afternoon of who could spot them first for £1 (by the end the winnings roughly evened out) along both sides of Lordship Lane, Tottenham. The '**MWB**' inscribed ones are post-1902/4, and the '**TW**' inscribed ones post-1974.
TW Could be More Helpful!: When I offered to pay TW the scrap value of a 'NR'-inscribed valve-plate for local museums, was sadly told would have to keep a continuous watch on their impending water main replacement website, then visit the location and beg the workman for a specimen. Which as such is over-complicated, unnecessary & not acceptable!

WATER PURITY (CHLORINATION & SAMPLING)

1926 (> Purity): "Later on, it will be shown how the New River Company (by the construction of storage reservoirs, filter beds, etc.) and then the Metropolitan Water Board (by the introduction of chlorination etc.) progressively safeguarded the purity of the New River supply. It is as if all concerned had conspired to keep Myddelton's ideal of a safe water supply for London sacred forever" (15D, p6).

1934 (Purity) & Daily Sampling of New River Water: "The method adopted to ensure a safe and potable water supply for the consumer", are:
- "Purity of the source of supply.
- Prevention of contamination in the river.
- Efficient filtration through deep beds of fine sand.
- The storing of the water in covered reservoirs".

"Samples are collected daily from the New River, from various filter beds and from the mains leaving the pumping stations to the service reservoirs for examination both as to chemical and bacteriological purity in the laboratory, with the result that a continuous check and record is kept of the condition of the water during its passage from its source to the time it issues from the taps of the consumer" (15C, p20 quotes).

WILDLIFE along New River

1822 (Sclavonian Grebe): "Graves, in his "History of British Birds", records a female of this grebe, **as killed on the New River**, at Clay-hill, in 1822" (B2, p146).

Pre-1840 (The Raven or Corbie): "Bred for many years, - before 1840, - ... and subsequently in one of the group of Elms called "The Sisters", **on the banks of the New River**, below Old-park, - being the latest record of the bird's nesting in Middlesex" (B2, p142).

1869 (Common Sandpiper, or Summer Snipe): "On the borders of brooks. One was observed for ten days **on the New River**, at Chase-park 1869. Never remains to breed" (B2, p145).

1871 (Little Grebe): "Breeds occasionally at Bush-hill Park. Occurred on the water at Chase-park, in 1871" (B2, p146; Chase Park W-side of Enfield Town Park).

Autumn 1871 (Kittiwake): In Enfield, "An immature specimen, or "**Tarrock**", was picked up dead on the **banks of the New River**, in the autumn of 1871" (B2, p146).

1893 (Wildlife) Stoke Newington Reservoirs: Article by H. Chipperfield in London Guardian ((`Off the tracks, New River', 'Islington's People' 12 Feb. 1987) Isl. LHC).

29 Aug. 1907 (Record 18 lb. Trout): 2 ft. 6/10-inch long Grey or Lake trout caught by a Mr J. Briggs in the New River at Hornsey (C. Herman photo, BCMA; 8 Aug. 1907 'Tottenham Herald').

1926 (Grebe (P. auritus) Stoke Newington Reservoirs: "The reservoirs are much beloved by fishermen, and wild fowl, some of them of the rarer sort, may be seen there in large numbers. The great crested grebe, a lover of solitude, nests here and may sometimes be seen swimming about on the water carrying the young grebes, most beautiful objects, on her back.
Of the grebe (P. auritus) it has been written:
> "P. auritus when in its full nuptial attire presents an extraordinary aspect, the head (being surrounded, as it were, by a nimbus or aureole, such as that with which painters adorn saintly characters), reflecting the rays of light, glitters with a glory that passes description" (15D, p24).

c.1994 article 'Birds on the Reservoirs' (Stoke Newington) by Richard Steenhuis (15F, Issue 27, June 1994, pp13-15).

1989 'The Aquatic Flora of the New River' by S.J. Smith, 'London Naturalist' No. 68, 1989, pp35-48 (v7254933, Guildhall Library; copy at HALS).

2004 (New Biodiversity Action Plan?): In 2004 Thames Water appear to have evolved a new biodiversity action plan, namely a new policy for cutting grass around water and sewage treatment works that favours and protects wildlife, by permitting some areas of grass to grow longer, this helping the distribution of flower seeds and promoting more species to eventually create flower-rich grasslands, that will help support many varieties of bugs, butterflies, moths, bees, and hence encourage voles, shrews, bats, nesting birds, owls, and birds of prey ('Newwave', Spring 2004, Issue 7).

BELOW: Approx. 2ft. long carp in New River, N-side Bullsmoor Lane, Enfield (MFK 2005 photo);

one of many other photos I have of large fish occasionally seen in the New River.

In 2008 a heron residential on the New River in grounds of Enfield Grammar School. In 2008 an Adder snake swimming across the NR on S-side of M25 aqueduct trying to get out on opposite bank, one of about three snakes see in the New River by MFK over about 5-years.

2.5 Gradient, Width & Length of New River

MYTH or Hearsay until c.1850: Probably only NRC authenticated sources are reliable, since older histories mostly repeat earlier facts confusingly related to the later date.

FALL /GRADIENT/LEVEL of New River
1862 (S. Smiles) About 2-inches in the Mile: 'The stream originally presented a fall of **about 2-inches in the mile**, and at its City end was at the level of about 82 feet above what is known as Trinity high water mark. Where the fall of the ground was found inconveniently rapid, a stop-gate was introduced at such places across the stream, penning from 3 to 4-feet perpendicularly, the water flowing down to the next level' ((1862) 13, p121; (1873) B2, p255 apparently repeating Smiles except on length; 15J20, p112 based on the **fol. 18ft. drop**, the 3 to 4ft. probably an exaggeration).
Pre-1872-8 (Sisley) Quoting: 'The fall of the New River is **three feet per mile**, which gives a velocity of about two miles an hour. The average width is **about twenty-one feet, and the average depth about four feet in the centre**; so that, taking it at about half that depth, there is a section of forty-two square feet of water flowing into London at the rate of two miles an hour' (('Life of Sir Hugh Myddelton', in Mr Charles Knight's 'Penny Cyclopedia') 1K5, p539).
1934 (Morris, MWB) Doesn't Allow for Sluices: "reduction in level of only **18 feet** in a total length of 40 miles (5½ -inches per mile)" (15C, p5; **IS THIS THE FIRST MENTION OF 18ft. DROP**).
1956 (G.C. Berry, MWB) Between 2 and 3 inches a Mile: "The total fall between these two points is **about 18 feet**, which gives an average fall of about 5 inches per mile. But the course was intercepted by sluices, e.g. at the [Chadwell] spring head, at Amwell, Broxbourne, and [not to MFK's knowledge] Theobalds, which produced drops of varying depths so that the fall between sluices was very much less, **between 2 and 3 inches a mile**. The maintenance of this near level course accounts for its many twists and turns" (8, p34; (30+ typed foolscap sheets 'Draft Lecture NRC', p20) 8A1, 4/1-1).
1989 (English Heritage): "the total fall was only **eighteen feet**, and sometimes as little as two or three inches in a mile" (15E, p3).
CHALLENGE (For an Accurate Gradient Measurement): For someone to use a modern GPS/electronic map device to record the levels at Chadwell Spring & New River Head, MFK has such a device but never had the free time.

WIDTH
10ft. > 25ft. WIDTH of New River (Not incl. Adjacent Private Estate Embellishments): Originally by statute 10ft. wide (by approx. 4ft. deep). "From time to time land was acquired in order to widen the river, and the banks were raised in order to increase the capacity of the channel where possible" (15C, p14). Post-1855 NRC Act the 'New River was widened from its original ten feet to about twenty feet wide' (15E, p5). In 1867 'varying width and depth, at places **28ft. wide**, while in many parts it is hardly half that width' (7G6, p4). 'There are no references in Acts of Parliament relating to changes in width, except for an Act of 1896 (59-60 Vict, cap. ccxxix) relating to the widening of certain bridges in Enfield' (15E, p4).
1899 (17-25ft.) Wide: Width of the river varying from 17 - 25ft. (7K1, p26/27/29).

1903 (Avge. approx. 24ft. by 4 to 6ft. deep) Width & Depth: 'average width of about 24 feet, with depths in the middle varying from 4 feet to 6 feet' ((NRC) 12E1, p28).
And as such approx. 25ft. wide today.

c.1900 CONCRETING PARTS of New River Bed
c.1900 (Bed Lined with Concrete): Published 1903, 'portions amounting altogether to **about one mile and three quarters in length**, have during recent years been lined with concrete' which also permitted a broader X-section area ((NRC) 12E1, p28). Today implemented at sections where there have been persistent leaks.
c.1925 Concrete River Bed: Written in 1934, "Of late years it has been the practice to reconstruct the river channel when necessary over bad ground or for other reasons, in concrete. It makes a stronger channel, is easier to keep clear of mud or weeds and contains more water than the old half round section of the river. Of course, the water must be kept flowing whilst the river bed is reconstructed, so a system of temporary troughs is adopted, supported from timbers placed across the river and dammed off at either end of the section to be dealt with. The timbers are placed in position, the troughs are suspended by bolts, the dams are driven into the bed of the river and made watertight by an apron of clay outside them, then the water is pumped out of the intervening space, if it has not already leaked out of its own accord. The old river bed and sides are excavated to the depth and width determined, timber shuttering is erected and concrete walls constructed with substantial footings, then a concrete bottom is put in to complete the section. Ladder irons are provided at intervals, because if a person fell into the river from one of the concrete walls, it would be difficult to get out again" (15C, p19).

ORIGINAL LENGTH of New River
   FACT: As the crow flies approx. 20-miles from Chadwell Spring to NRH, but the original length of the New River having to deviate to circumvent opposing streams etc., thus at least twice this length. Compared to the distance as the crow flies, 'the stream must have a serpentine circuit of nearly double that length, …' ((Printed extract from 'The Christian's Penny Magazine' publ. every Sat., No. 143 (possibly Vol. IV), Feb. 28, 1835, p65) Islington LHC).
   MYDDELTON FOLLOWED THE 100FT. CONTOUR: This was a gravitational river, such that it was necessary for Myddelton to effectively follow what we call today the 100ft. contour. At first plotted by Edward Wright, but after the great hold-up, from 1611 by Edward Pond (& John Blagrave). As far as possible, Myddelton would have needed to avoid deep cuttings in high ground and having to form high embankments in low ground. To avoid the many opposing streams, **traversing westwards along the contour of the N-side of the opposing valleys, to a point where the valley could be crossed, then turning back eastwards along the contour of the S-side, until he could again make his SPINAL THRUST SOUTHWARDS.**

   Main OPPOSING STREAMS: The main opposing streams located as follows from N to S:
      Unknown-Name Brook at small valley, at later Rye Common P.S.
      Woolens Brook (> Very Short River Lynch > River Lee), at later Hoddesdon P.S.
      Spital Brook, at later Broxbourne P.S.
      Wormleybury Brook (> Turnford Brook > R. Lee), at former Wormley Flash, & within a short distance, **Turnford Brook**/Valley (> R. Lee).
      Rags Brook, at former Cheshunt Flash (later Cheshunt N-reservoir).
      Minor brook alongside S-side of, College Road, Cheshunt.
      Theobalds Brook, Theobalds Lane, Cheshunt.
      Former Shire Ditch (> County Brook), at former Theobalds Loop.
      'Carr Brook' (1754 Rocque map), today with c.1856, 15 to 18-inch dia. cast-iron pipe under NR on present course near SW-side of former Bullsmoor Loop.
      At the former major Whitewebbs Loop, Enfield:
         Unknown-Name Brook (on my modern A-Z sourced by a feeder, also to Theobalds Brook), at former Trough, Gyrton Park (> Dickinson's Trough), W-side Myddelton House.
         Cuffley Brook (> Turkey Brook), at former Enfield Flash, Whitewebbs, Enfield.

Turkey Brook (> River Lee), at former Bull Beggars Hole, Whitewebbs, Enfield, joins Cuffley Brook as main Turkey Brook.

At the former major Enfield Town Loop:

Mystery stream, near today's Enfield Town Police Station.

Saddlers Mill Stream, within grounds of today's Enfield Grammar School.

Drain beneath (at significant deviation of NR), Bush Hill Golf Course/Enfield Town Park.

Brook at arched drain, 'Bush Hill Park' Mansion.

Salmon's Brook/Valley, major with the Great Frame/Bush Hill Frame.

Brook at brick arch, Fords Green, Winchmore Hill.

Brook at arched drain, Barrowell Green.

Common sewer under NR (at significant fair-size deviation of NR), at former Hamilton Crescent Loop.

At the former major Southgate Loop:

Pymmes Brook/Valley, major with 4-brick arches & adjacent 3-brick arches under NR, near former Wild's Flash/Southgate Loop.

Bounds Green Brook, considerable since Strawberry Vale Brook, Coppetts Brook & Pages Hill Brook all swelled Bounds Green Brook, before it reached the former Newman's Flash/Southgate Loop.

Muswell Stream, considerable since Mutton Brook, Priory Brook & Cholmeley Brook all swelled the Muswell Stream before it reached Green Lanes (**also the possible site of a former Flash**), at conjunction of Southgate-Tottenham Loops.

Over two water courses at far E-end of Clay Hill/White Hart Lane, former Tottenham Loop.

Moselle Brook, swelled by the Mutton Brook, Priory Brook & Cholmeley Brook before it reached former Horsey Flash.

Stonebridge Brook, at former Haringay House Loop.

Hackney Brook and source brooks, at the major former Holloway Loop > former Highbury Frame (Have not had time to research source brooks).

Large iron pipe beneath NR (at significant deviation in NR), at former St Paul's Loop, Canonbury.

A pipe under the NR, at former Horse Shoe Point Loop.

'This was no Roman aqueduct; it was more like Chesterton's rolling English road' ((G.C. Berry) 8, p33). On several of the older New River maps the outline sometimes looks like the left-half outline of a 'Circum-Terrestrial' Christmas tree, spreading wider as it reaches further south, especially when reaching the former Holloway Loop.

MYTHS on Length: As always with the New River, there are just as many myths about its length!

'It is strange that every writer we have seen should have stated this length to have been under forty miles', then states W.C. Mylne's 1852 length of 48-miles ((1873) B2, p254).

'Not less than 38¾-Miles in Length' ((1872 S. Smiles) 13, p124)

40-Miles Long? (Inscribed Chadwell Spring): 'Conveyed 40 miles' (assumed as original length) referring to the date inscribed on the Chadwell Spring stone (6L, p439). One of the associated stones repaired 1728. The pedestal/stone rebuilt in 1883 and again in 1922 (15D, p5).

42-Miles Long? (Inscribed Stone, NRH): An old stone inscribed '42' in the arch of the bridge over the entrance to the Round Pond, in 1925 in the wall of the Round Pond (facing W-side of NRH offices), thought to be the original length of the New River (6L, p439; 15J, p180 1920s).

1810 (48-Miles Long?): W.C. Mylne the NRC Engineer saying 48-miles long, see following.

1927 (About 40-Miles?): 'total length, as first made, of about 40 miles' ((MWB) 12, p22).

Lengths with Related Dates: If the length of the River isn't related to a date, it's not of much use!

REDUCTIONS (& Increases) IN LENGTH of New River

Less river to maintain means less expence in leases, bridges & workforce etc. A straighter course also resolved the then icing at bends in winter, and created a more even flow, taking less time to reach London (15E, p5). They couldn't straighten the River unless they could **obtain the land by lease or purchase**, sometimes enforced by obtaining Acts of Parliament.

The original distance over the ensuing years being greatly reduced as following.

YOUR INVOLVEMENT REQUIRED? (SADLY NO PRIZES): There just hasn't been time for me to use the Overlays (that are based on the more accurate OS maps in **Vol. 2 & 3**), to calculate a more reliable original length of the New River. So unless there is a further edition of this book, would suggest that any enthusiasts out there accept the challenge to compute their own figure using the later Vols. scaled Overlays of the bypassed loops.

USE $1/10^{th}$-Miles: For ease of calculation below using $1/10^{th}$-miles e.g. 0.75 for ¾-mile. If undertaking your own calculations on the shortened lengths of the river, **don't forget to add back the length of the New Cut that bypasses the Old.**

From Chadwell Spring or New Gauge? Probably best to do both, to the centre of the Round Pond, NRH!

1619 (>) Former Holloway Loop: Shortened by 2.75-miles when the Holloway Road loop bypassed by the 'Boarded River' (15J, p180 2¾-miles). **Most authors would NOT have been aware of this early Loop**, probably why the lengths vary.

1618 (INCREASE) Tapping Old River Lee: Channel to augment Chadwell Spring: **ADDS ?-Miles**.

1723 (38.75-Miles) PROB. UNRELIABLE: As measured by Henry Mill (('Hist. of London' by W. Maitland, 1739, p630) 11, p85 1723 survey just over 38¾ miles long **after about 2-miles of loops had been cut out**; 15J, p180 1722). Pos. BENCHMARK, **but see 1852**.

> **1728 (Minus 2-Miles) Shortenings, Exact Locations NOT KNOWN:** The New River also called Middleton's Water 'ran formerly two miles farther about, near Enfield and Hornsey **[both at unknown specific locations]**, which is now saved by finding a more commodious channel' (('History of Herts.' by N. Salmon, 1728, p20) 8A1, 2-8; **may have been included** in Henry Mills 1722 measurement of river; (Salmon 1728) 15J, p180 Enfield & Hornsey improvements).

1733 (INCREASE), 1739 Statutory Authority, Manifold Ditch: ADDS ?-Miles.

c./1742 'Stamford Hill Loop' bypassed by tunnel. **Decrease of ?-Miles**.

NO CHANGE IN LENGTH (Tunnel > Open River): Former c./1724 to 1799 & 1825 'Newington Tunnel' (> Today's Open River).

1775-1809 (Kinks Straightened) Amwell Close, Bush Hill, Edmonton: **Miniscule saving in length**. Also post-1809 straightening S-side Park Avenue, Palmers Green (see Part 2, pp425-427).

1790 (Hornsey Flash) Bypassed: Small decrease in length.

1810 (48-MILES LONG) PROB. RELIABLE: Evidence given by W.C. Mylne (length referring to the date he was appointed to NRC) at 1852 Metropolis Water Act (6L, p439).

1820-21 (Cast-iron aqueduct) bypasses Enfield Flash, short saving in length.

1822 (Horse Shoe Point Spur) Bypassed: Faden's 1822 map shows the former short Horse Shoe Point Spur with new bypass channel (14D7-2, p21). 199-yd. spur loop shown truncated to 70yds. (12G/31), as such a minor saving in length.

1825-6 (Cheshunt Flash) Bypassed: Cheshunt Flash cut out when H. Rogers of Cheshunt constructed three brick water courses beneath an embankment built on a shorter line (8A, p33; ((F212) 8A1, 3/3.1 'See Committee 2 Feb. 1825').

1835-7 (Cheshunt South Reservoir) PLUS slight Increase in Length: Re-routes line of New River around reservoir with a probable **slight INCREASE in length** of River.

6 MAY 1852 (MIN. OF EVID.) PROB. RELIABLE: Mr. [W.C.] Mylne in answer to "2700 - What is the measured distance of the New River, as constructed?". "It was 48 miles when I was appointed [1810], but we have taken off some of the contours nearer London, and it is reduced to 38 miles". Since 1852 the length has been still further diminished, and it is now only about 28 miles" ((1873) B2, p254).

'Originally nearly 39 miles Long' (June 1852) W.C. Mylne: To Select Committee of the House of Lords, but suggested that this refers to the 1852 length, after small $C18^{th}$ & early-$C19^{th}$ loops had been bypassed (15E, p3, this doesn't agree with (1873) B2, p254).

W.C. Mylne shortened the length of the New River from **38.8 miles to 27 miles** ((Pam, quotes no source) B10, p105).

1852 (38-MILES LONG) RELIABLE: In evidence given by W.C. Mylne at 1852 Metropolis Water Act (6L, p439).

c.1852-4 (Stanstead W & E-Loop) Bypassed: Former Stanstead Loops bypassed.

c.1852-4 (Broxbourne P.S. W-Loop) Bypassed: Former Spital Brook-Broxbourne Loop bypassed.

Broxbourne Church (Straightenings): c.1841 (Pos.) Minor straightening SW–side Broxbourne Church and **1861** slightly larger straightening at Churchyard N-side of Broxbourne Church.

c.1852-4 (Bury Green W-E Loop) Bypassed: Straightening of small curve before College Road, Cheshunt, and bypassing of former Bury Green W & E Loop/s.

1853 (35-Miles Long) but from Marble Gauge to Stoke Newington: W.C. Mylne intending to improve the flow by increasing the width to 18ft. and depth to 5ft. and reducing the length from 35 to 22-miles by bypassing loops with embankments at Turnford & Hornsey, a tunnel at Wood Green (from Myddelton Road to Station Roads), and in places by easements using three side-by-side 4ft. to 5ft. dia. iron pipes (15J, p180). In the 1850s reduced to about 27-miles by bypassing several of the large devious loops.

1854-55 (Wormley-Turnford Loop) Bypassed: Former Wormley-Turnford Loop bypassed (15J, p180 Wormley Aqueduct saving **1,370 yds.**).

1856 (Most of Manifold Ditch) Bypassed: Bypassing most of Manifold Ditch, Ware.

1856 (DECREASE) MINUS ?-Miles if ADDED Above.

1859 (Minus 7.75-Miles): Whitewebbs Loop at Enfield Chase, Southgate Loop, Clay Hill Edmonton-Tottenham bypassed by 1857-59 Wood Green tunnel ((W.C. Mylne report) 15J, pp180-181 14ft. brick WG tunnel 20ft deep 1,108 yds long, the loops **saving 7¾-miles**).

1859 (Hornsey Village Loop) Bypassed: In addition 1859, after slippage awaiting the settlement of the embankment aside the railway at Hornsey before bypassing the Horsey Village Loop ((W.C. Mylne report) 15J, pp180-181). Bypassed 1859 by Thomas Docwra & Son, but the old Hornsey Loop not abandoned until 1862 ((MWB answer to corres. 21 Dec. 1956) 8A1, 2-8). Jan. - May 1862 (NRC 1852/4 Acts) Negotiations for sale of Hornsey Loop ((NRH) Acc 2558/NR13/77/1-5, LMA).

1868-69 (Highbury Bank) Bypassed: Using 4ft. dia. iron pipes along Green Lanes, from Stoke Newington to Clissold Park. c.1872 piped from Stoke Newington filter beds to Clissold Park (15E, p3; 15J, p181 1865-68).

1873 (28-Miles Approx.) POS. RELIABLE: "now only about 28 miles" long ((1873) B2, p254).

1886 (Hornsey Station Loop): New Cut bypassing W-limb aside railway before Haringay House.

1891-92 (Haringay House/Park Loop): Bypassed by tunnel.

1903 (27-Miles Long): ((NRC) 12E1, p28). 26-Miles long at 1902-04 transfer to MWB (6L, p439).

1927 (27-Miles Long): 'from time to time have reduced this to 27 miles, much of the stream being now culverted' ((MWB) 12, p22).

1933-4 (Enfield Town Loop) Bypassed:

Pipe Track: Three Cast-Iron Mains 1853 (48-inch), 1875 (48-inch) & 1912 (54-inch). Complicated as such, since 1933-4 the Enfield Town Loop conveyed to Enfield UDC, after the pipe-track was bombed in WW2 re-opened Oct. 1940 (re-excavating the filled-in section SE-side of Enfield Town Park), so 1941 re-conveyed back to the MWB, the re-excavated section filled-in again Oct. 1945, finally Sept. 1953 re-conveyed back to Enfield UDC and becoming **an ornamental loop**.

1945-6 (Shortening) from Stoke Newington Green Lanes road bridge to NRH:

Nov. 1945 to June 1947 (MWB Abandonment of Clissold Park Loop), Stoke Newington: Because it had become a liability, the MWB deciding in Nov. 1945 to abandon the NR in Stoke Newington. Agreeing June 1947 to transfer the open portions free of cost, parts to Stoke Newington Borough Council & the L.C.C. S-section in Clissold Park filled-in 1955-1968.

c.1872 piped from Stoke Newington filter beds to Clissold Park (15E, p3).

1945-6 (New River) Terminating at Stoke Newington: The various **1851-1892** pipes (mainly culverting) from the Stoke Newington Green Lanes road-bridge to NRH said removed 1950.

Don't forget to include the bits & bobs (where the end of one section doesn't match exactly the start of the next) not included above.

2.6 MFK MAP OVERLAYS: All of the above earlier historical shortenings of the New River have been graphically represented as accurately as possible on more accurate later OS maps (see Vols. 2 & 3), using the following manual techniques, since I have never mastered the skills of using computer software translucent 'Layers':

'Best Fit' (Optimum) Map Overlays: Note that the later enclosed map overlays were produced without making unfounded adjustments. Photocopies were created to the same size/scale and a tracing of one optimally position over the other, retaining common alignment markers for you the reader to judge its accuracy.

>**Earliest 1860s OS Maps (25-ins to Mile) used for Accuracy & Detail:** Except for the detail of the 1775 Mylne map, accuracy can only be achieved by using the earliest OS map of the section of the New River being followed; most other earlier maps are not up to the job.

All Maps Have Tolerances & Inaccuracies: Maps are drawn to various accuracies, even Ordnance Survey. Users should therefore make an allowance for mapmaker's tolerances and other minor inaccuracies. In many cases adjacent OS map sheets do not line up exactly, or may have been surveyed in a different year showing different features. At some of the archives visited, it was like trying to extract blood out of a stone to get the exact copy maps required!

>**Working with Photocopies of Maps:** The results were achieved by using photocopies of original maps. All photocopiers create very minor discrepancies and will only reduce or enlarge to a minimum of ± 1%. This across a 4-5ft. map can generate a ¼-inch difference, whilst appearing major, is no more than considering the former course as following the line of adjacent properties. Found out much later, that probably better to produce overlays for individual 'sections' of maps, then joining these together to form a larger map.

>>**Don't Mix Portrait & Landscape Photocopies:** If joining photocopies of maps, best not to mix portrait & landscape photocopies, since most photocopiers will create noticeable minor distortions!

Using Camera Copies (e.g. 1775 Mylne Map): The earliest accurate course of the New River is shown on the 1775 Mylne map that for practical purposes had to be copied using a digital camera. Most cameras create 'parallax'-type errors that cause a subtle distortion. Note that the **New River is often shown much narrower, it was continually widened over the following centuries**.

Adjustments (Best Diagonal): You can make horizontal adjustments, but as I found late in the day that this also affects the depth, so wiser to adjust or optimise across the diagonal to maintain the accuracy of OS maps.

The Ordnance Survey themselves could be of great help to historians by providing an Overlay Service, that could be especially applicable for further volumes of this book, if they could use their specialised computer Mapping software to generate more accurate quality overlays.

Localised Areas on Older NOT-TO-SCALE Maps (Can be Amended Both Vertically & Horizontally): Because not to scale, can use computer software to adjust at different ratios vertically & horizontally, for a best fit to match known boundaries on later OS maps.

For Maximum Accuracy use Site-Specific Details: For maximum accuracy at a specific location, always compare site specific plans, deeds etc. where available.

CHALLENGE (Check Your Property Deeds): If you live near the New River shown in the overlays, check your property deeds, since you might be able to help more accurately track the former course of the New River.

2.7 TERMINUS New River Head & Surroundings

For the Round Pond & Upper Pond much will be said later. Of the other main features:

FORMER NRC Cistern Houses (NRH): For the former NRC Cistern Houses near/around New River Head see later section. For others on the New River from Clissold Park south, see page 93.

FORMER New River Head Pumping Windmill, Horsemill & Waterwheel): See later section.

NRC Drinking Fountains: Not aware of any still surviving. Previously known at NW-corner of Claremont Square Res., grand version with lion's head S-side of former NRC NRH, and cast-iron canopied one at Clerkenwell Green, plus others shown on earlier OS maps around streets at NRH.

2.8 The 'MYDDELTON' NAME, ARTISTS, & VERSE/LITERARY MENTIONS

'Myddelton' Name: On route from Ware to London, the name of Sir Hugh Myddelton immortalised in the name of many **roads, schools** etc., and in the heyday of steam, even **railway engines**.
Public houses such as the 'Myddelton Arms' in Ruthin, Wales, the 'New River Arms' Turnford, the 'Myddelton Arms', Canonbury Road, Islington.

The Hugh Myddelton Primary School, Gloucester Way, almost opposite New River Head, and passing a dozen more plus with different names aside the former & present course of the New River.
With the New River passing so many schools, it is an ideal opportunity for them to '**Adopt a S-t-r-e-t-c-h**' of the New River to study its history, flora & fauna, bridges & features etc.

LEFT: Said to be possibly the only photo of No. 1536 aka '**Hugh Myddelton**', a Webb 2-2-2-2 three-cylinder compound locomotive photographed on the slow line pulling five wooden-topped six-wheelers, just west of Colwyn Bay towards Mochdre, her name not visible but the photographer recording her number. Another 'Hugh Myddelton' said to have been a 'John Hick class built 1894 www.lnwrs.org.uk/PassLocos/PassLoco.php?loco=09'; and another of a later class also called Experiment (Robert Ireland & Graham Levins researches).

Artists: The New River a popular subject for some artists over the years, and just a few names fol. of those that painted several views.

Engravers such as **Wenceslaus Hollar** (1665 NRH), **Hogarth** (1738 New River at Sadlers Wells although not an accurate representation), **Canaletto** (c.1750 NRH), **& Cruikshank** (1796 New River at Sadlers Wells).

C.H. Matthews: Worked c.1820-1850 his NR sketches included looking towards Highbury Sluice House (1836), Canonbury prob. looking SW towards Willow Bridge (Isl. LHC; calls c.1800 but could be later), Colebrook Row (1841), City Road (1841), Lady Owens School (1839 & 1840) & the former Sir Hugh Myddelton Tavern (undated) (1902 British Museum catalogue of artists working in Great Britain Vol. III by Laurence Binyon).

Thomas Hosmer Shepherd: c.1825-40 sketches of Highbury Sluice, anglers at Sadlers Wells & Sir Hugh Myddelton's Head, from 1842-51 living aside the New River at No. 2 Colebrooke Row.

H.H. Bingley: c.1933 painting many watercolours of the NRC cottages etc. around Stoke Newington reservoirs (Hackney Archives).

Verse & Literary Mentions of the New River

29 Sept. 1613 (Michaelmas Day): Rhythmic speech at opening of sluice at the Cistern, New River Head, see previous text.

1613 Play 'Wit at Several Weapons' by Beaumont & Fletcher: Act 4 '… direct him and his horses toward the New River by Islington, there shall they have me, looking upon the Pipes, …'; Act 5 '… I have been 7 mile in length along the New River; I have seen a hundred sticklebacks … .., I will go walk by the New River… I shall be found angling, for I will try what I can catch' (10-3, p29).

1635 'Hollander': 'This Cup was as deepe as Fleet-street Conduit. Sound me my lo, I ha' made a new River in my Belly, and my guts are the Pipes' (10-3, p29).

1639 Comedie 'Wit Without Money': '… till Waterworks, and rumours of new Rivers rid you again …' (10-3, p29).

1699 Verse 'A Walk to Islington':
'… …
Took a walk in the Fields, with my wife.
We sauntered about New River head
We rambled about till we came to a gate
To gaze at the ladies amidst of their revels
As fine all as angels, but wicked as devils' (('A Walk to Islington' by Edward Ward) 'Growth of Stuart London' by B.G. Brett-James, 1935, p465; 15J, p205 tediously long verse quoting a line about a 'lady of pleasure ... enjoyed at leisure').

1728 (Prob.) 'New-River, a Poem by William Garbott' *Otium, non Negotium*, London:

'Destructive Wars some may delight to sing,
And think they to their Hero Glory bring,
Where Brother Brother, father slays the Son
What Nature shocks, can Glory thence be won?
Man, Man to help the Great CREATOR made;
Man, Man to butcher now's become a Trade.
Nature recoils, affrighted at the Act,
And splendid Infamy attends the Fact.
Others may sing, th' unconstant Fair to please,
And melt their Hero into Love and Ease;
Who whilom from his Steed, at ev'ry Blow
Assured Death did deal unto the Foe:
What after-times will scarce believe, is true;
Thro' thickest Squadrons did his Passage hew,
Whose mighty Arm was not to be withstood,
But turn'd the Field into a Sea of Blood;
Who, like Destroying Angel, laid about
Until h'ad put the Foe to total Rout.
This mighty Chief, who all these Feats has done,
So many Thousands slain, such Battels won,
Him now they place on bended Knees, before
A Women Fair and Fickle, to adore:
Tell me but One that's true! no more I ask,
That One to find will prove an endless Task.
At the Jilt's Feet the Victor vanquish'd kneels,
Swears by her Eyes, such scorching Flames he feels
As will his Constant Heart to Ashes burn,
To quench those Flames, begs she'l a Smile return:
She smiles, is caught, by her own Arts ensnar'd,
He gains his Point, she has her Just Reward:
For fresh Game now his Tackle he prepares,
Make use of all his Arts, both Nets and Snares,
With solemn Vows, and fair deluding Lyes,
He lures them to, then snares them by surprise.
His Stomach's cloy'd, can't always one Dish eat,
But must be fed with sev'ral sorts of Meat.

A constant Lover in a MAN's as rare
As in a WOMEN to be just and fair.
They both will lye, Vow break, both false will prove:
I speak not here of Wedlock's sacred Love,
Which oft is Chaste and Constant as the Dove.
But Lust I mean, that Irreligious Flame,
Which both the Laws of GOD and Man do blame,
And both severely punish too the same.
Of Mars or Venus they may sing that will,
Flames, Rapes, and Blood flow thence, and all that's ill.
Those dire Effects the famous Troy did feel,
Where Greek and Trojan fell by mutual Steel.

A Theme that serves Mankind is my delight;
That I could muse all Day, That dream all Night.
Thus, diff'rent Poets diff'rent Fancies lead;
I sing NEW-RIVER, and its Chrystal Head;
From its first Source, unto its Basons, down
From thence unto Great-Britain's chiefest Town.
Assist me, Muse! its Virtues to rehearse;
And with thy Aid, thus I begin my Verse.

IMMORTAL MIDDLETON! Glory of thy Age!
Thou, Thou the Wonder shall be, I presage,
Of Future Times, which Thou hast made thy Own
By this Unequal'd Work which Thou hast done.
Let Bards no more their mighty Herc'les boast,
His Labours twelve all in thy One are lost.
Fictitious they, thy mighty Toyl is true;
But what's so great thy Genius can't subdue?
Augusta fair is fond of thy Great Name,
So long as She shall stand, shall stand thy Fame.
Thrice happy Thou, to see this Work of thine

To be compleat (short space) in five years time!
In Sixteen-hundred-eight it was begun;
In Sixteen-hundred-thirteen it was done.
Six hundred Hands Thou daily didst employ
To speed thy Work, the Glory to enjoy.
Great was thy Thought, great the Performance too,
Surmounting all but thy Great Self to do.
Thy Courage, equal to thy vast Design,
Doth shew the Undertaking must be Thine.

The Sources whence this River doth spring
(As first in order) them I first shall sing.
Chadwell and Amwell, Springs in Hertfordshire,
Whose Crystal Streams to view you wou'd admire.
In them the Ladies may their Beauties see,
And their Defects, if any in them be.
Nature's true Looking-glass, that doth declare
Not what they would be, but just what they are.
Twenty Miles off, if by the Road you ride,
But Forty Miles, if by the River side.
These two fair Springs this River's Parents are,
Beautiful Issue of two Fountains fair!
From whence in wanton windings he does rove,
And as the Ground admits, doth gently move:
Sometimes a Hill his Passage smooth doth stop,
Then Great Sir HUGH steps in and lifts him up;
With Lead'n Cisterns rears his drooping Head,
Hard to believe! but may with Truth be said:
Between the Heav'n and Earth he makes him flow,
And glide Triumphant o'er his conquer'd Foe.
O sacred Muse! I pray to me impart
What Force, what Pow'r, can resist the Art
Of him that can make Rivers Hills o'erflow.
What is it his resistless Art can't do?
Sure he can make them likewise backwards run,
Or, Joshua-like, cause to stand still the Sun.
Eight hundred Bridges o'er this Stream are laid,
As in Authentick Story it is said,
The most of Timber, some of Brick, some Stone;
The Charge too weighty to be bore by One:
Of LONDON'S Chamber he desir'd Supply,
But LONDON'S Chamber did his Suit deny.
The Monarch viewing well what Work was done,
At his own Charge resolv'd to carry't on, K. Ja. I.
Under the Conduct of the Great Sir HUGH,
Who had the whole Design at once in view:
That the King knew, to his immortal Praise,
The Solomon esteemed of his Days.

And now the Pickaxe, Barrow, Spade, Hands all
Unto their former Work with Courage fall:
The Great Attempt with Vigour now goes on,
Which otherwise would never have been done:
The King his F.at [?] gave, inspir'd by GOD,
And All-commanding Gold obey'd his Nod.

Thro' divers Towns this stream transparent flows,
On Man and Beast his Favours he bestows.
In greatest Droughts, what greatest Benefit To thirsty Cattle, than to drink of it!
When all the Ponds, as well as they, are dry,
He them supplies with Water constantly,
Else they wou'd pine away with Thirst, and die.
In Forty Miles, tho' some will say Threescore,
Full Thirty thousand Cattle, if not more,
Besides the Vills and Towns he floweth by,
Doth he with Water constantly supply:
So that, if Beasts could speak as well as Men,
Live Sir HUGH's Name, they'd cry, Amen, Amen.
But Man he finds with Liquor, and with Meat;
Liquor good Ale to brew, good Fish to eat;
Such as the Finny Inmates of his Flood,
Which are more rare than Flesh, and full as good.
The pretty little Gudgeon is fine Fare;
The Fin-back'd Perch, by some esteemed rare;
The Silver Eel, so mellow, firm, and fine,
A Prince may like a Prince upon it dine!
Boil'd, Potted, Roasted, Broil'd, is good all ways,
The Silver Eel is worthy of all Praise.
The greedy, cruel Tyrant of the Flood,
The Pike, who preys on other Fishes Blood,
Who ev'n his own Species does not spare,
Those less than he by him devoured are:
Wicked, when swimming in the Silver Stream,
But good, when swimming (in good Sauce I mean)
At His dread fight the little Fish will fly,

As trembling Birds do, when the Hawk is nigh.
All but the Perch, who doth (let him know,
Tho' to the rest he's such a dreadful Foe,
He values not his cruel Tyranny,
Nor will he as the rest, who fear him, fly)
Erect his Finny Back, his Armour shows;
The Pike, tho' hungry, dares not with him close,
Suffers all this, altho' he's so provok'd,
And dares not seize, afraid of being choak'd.

As the Great Pikes the smaller do devour,
So acts the Rich Man when he grinds the Poor.
The Pike, less cruel, at one Gorge doth kill,
But Man kills Man by piecemeal, greater Ill!
Pike preys on Pike, and Man doth prey on Man,
The diff'rence then? Pray tell me if you can.
As Fish on Fish in Brooks and Seas do prey,
So Man on Man, in a more cruel way.
Eel, Pike, Carp, Tench, Fish of Repute and Fame,
With many more, which here I shall not name,
Of this our Flood the Finny Natives are,
With Noble Crawfish, which makes Soup so rare.

Thro' Cheshunt Park and Theobalds he glides;
Thro' both the Enfield Parks he gently slides;
And as he thro' them wantonly doth roam,
Well pleas'd that he is drawing near his Home,
The thirsty Deer of him do drink their fill,
The noble Stagg too drinks there at his Will,
And as he's drinking in the limpid Stream,
Beholds his branched Horns, grows proud of them,
Shakes his Brow-Antlers, and defies his Foes,
And struts majestic ev'ry Step he goes.
But hark! The Dogs are out, their Cry he hears,
To listen then he pricks up both his Ears:
But not approving the ungrateful Noise,
He bounds at first, and then away he flies,
Takes to his Heels, and now begins the Sport,
Reserves his Weapons for his last Effort.
The BLOODY Fatal Chase is now begun,
To the Doggs fatal, not the Stagg alone.
The Stagg runs swift, to fly impending Doom,
But all in vain, his latest Hour is come:
The Doggs run swift, to meet their unseen Fate,
Which did they know, they wou'd as swift retreat;
The Man rides swift, hot in pursuit of Game,
And leaps at all, and sometimes comes off lame;
The Fool courts Dangers, which his Beast wou'd shun,
Who wou'd avoid such Leaps, unless spurr'd on;
Let not this Man then of his Reason boast,
Who buys his Pleasure at so dear a Cost.
His share of Reason here appears the least,
Either of Stagg, or Dogg, or his poor Beast.
Least, did I say? In this he shews h'as none,
But by Irrationals he's far outdone.
Learn then, O Man! so to pursue thy Game;
Avoid all Dangers, Beasts will do the same.

BUT to our Sport return we now again,
To take the Pleasure, and avoid the Pain:
The Stagg now spent, his Fate he doth bewail,
And lets fall Tears, but Tears will not avail;
With hungry Hounds his Tears are of no pow'r,
They want his Blood and Carcase to devour.
To his own Herd he then for Refuge flies,
But his own Herd his humble Suit denies,
Shun him as one that's pointed out for Doom,
And amongst them they'll not admit him room
They know by Instinct he's design'd for Death,
And will not risque their own to save his Breath.
He now looks out, to find the fittest place
To make a stand, resolv'd the Foe to face;
No more to flee, no longer now to shun,
But stand the Bloodmouth'd Hounds when they come on.
A lofty Oak, whose Head aspir'd so high,
And grew so proud, it rival'd with the Sky,
Whose mighty Limbs projected such a Shade
As cool by them the ambient Air was made:
Whose Body was of that circumference
That wou'd behind him be a sure Defence:
Thither he shapes his Course, full bent to fight
The fell invet'rate Foe with all his Might;
Takes Courage from Despair, resolves to fall
Aveng'd on some, if not aveng'd on all,
Contented then he quietly could die,
So that he could some of the Foe destroy.
And now the Horn with Musick strikes his Ear,
Which not long since struck it with Pannick Fear:
The Doggs, full Cry, are just now coming on,

As eager he doth for their coming long:
The swiftest Hounds of all the bloody Pack
Are now come up, and see the Prey they lack.
He ready to receive them stands, prepar'd
And arm'd with Resolution, on his Guard;
Displays his branched Weapons, lets them see,
If they attack, what their Reward shall be.
Thus they hold him, and he holds them at Bay,
To try the Combat; if they please they may.
But they, like Cowards, make a mighty Cry,
Dare not attack without a fresh Supply.
The others hear, and swiftly they push on,
With greedy Jaws about the Victim throng.
Thus reinforc'd, some bolder than the rest
Attempt his Head to seize, and some his Breast.
Too late they found the Danger, to their Cost,
For in the bold Attempt their Lives they lost.
Here Rockwood, Ringwood, Jowler, Ruler fell,
And trusty Bowman, O! it grieves to tell!
But when the Huntsman saw the best Doggs fall,
His Piece he fir'd, loaded with double Ball,
Which put an End unto the fatal Strife:
So dy'd the Doggs, so lost the Stagg his Life.
Thus fell the Glory of Brow-Antler's Race,
Of late the Pride and Monarch of the Chace
He fell, but how? Not by a common Death,
The Doggs put not a Period to his Breath,
But, like a Soldier fighting in the Field,
Who scorned unto the Enemy to yield,
With Glory fell, just by that River's side
In which Himself he oft beheld with Pride;
That River, which for LONDON was design'd,
Could she have mov'd, sh'ad met her Lover kind.
With eager Joy he flows to her Embrace,
And she expects him with a Joy no less.
All Creatures greet him as he glides along;
The Feather'd Choir chant forth his Nuptial Song.
And thro' Hornsey Town he floweth on,
And waters healthful, airy Newington
Thro' Islington then glides my best-lov'd Theme,
And Miles's Garden washes with his Stream:
Now Forcer's Garden is its proper name,
Tho' Miles the Man was who first got it Fame:
And tho' it's own'd Miles first did make it known,
Forcer improves the same, we all must own:
There you may sit under the shady Trees
And drink and smoak, fann'd by a gentle Breeze,
Behold the Fish, how wantonly they play,
And catch them also, if you please, you may;
With Finny Oars they cut the silver Stream,
Which to the Eye gives a diverting Scene;
Each pushes on, to win the fatal Prize,
For his Reward the swiftest Racer dies,
With eager Mouth gorges the gilded Bait,
And then repents, but then it is too late.
The Harlot so displayeth all her Charms,
And under them conceals her fatal Harms,
Takes the unwary Youth with gilded Snares,
Who oft for good and sound, buys wrotten Wares.
Beware, my Youth, avoid that Fair and Foul,
Or she'll destroy Purse, Body, and thy Soul.
How thou shalt know the Syren I will tell,
That thou may'st shun this Firebrand of Hell.
Her Eyes are Rovers, and her Airs so free,
As far exceed the Sex's Modesty
Honey upon her Tongue you'd think did dwell,
But underneath lurks Poyson, Poyson fell,
That will thy Soul and Body poyson too,
Fly, fly, my Youth, have not with her to do.
If Rich thou art, she'll surely make thee Poor
And (may be) beg thy Bread from door to door.
If thou art Strong, canst mighty Pillars shake,
She soon will make thee Impotent and Weak.
Of thee (if Wife thou art) she'll make a Fool
What art thou else, if thou'rt a Harlot's Tool?
She, Serpent-like will poison by Embrace;
Then sad, and full of Woe, will be thy Case:
Her forked Bane will thro' thy Liver go,
Like Arrow poyson'd when shot from the Bow,
Thus by degrees, tho' late, yet too too sure
Thy Blood may be infected beyond cure:
A ling'ring Death then art thou doom'd to die:
Now drops a Nose, and after rots an Eye
A Nusance then thou art become to Man,
And all avoid and shun thee, if they can:
Life unto thee at last a Burthen's grown,
Thou Death invok'st, but Death then shall not come:
On thy Condition none shall Pity have,
But piecemeal rot before thou'rt in the Grave.
The Harlot too shall share the self-same Fate,
And die the Object of all People's Hate.
Beware, my Youth, avoid that Fair and Foul,
Or she'll destroy Purse, Body, and thy Soul.
Again I give this my before Advice,

Because it is Youth's Fav'rite – Fatal Vice.

On this vile Women we'll no longer dwell,
The Devil's Agent, Fact'ress-Chief of Hell,
Our former Theme we now shall re-assume,
And to the GARDEN and NEW-RIVER come [Sadlers Wells Theatre].

Two noble Swans swim by this Garden side,
Of Water-fowl the Glory and the Pride,
Which to the Garden no small Beauty are;
Were they but black, they would be much more rare;
With Ducks so tame, that from your Hand they'll feed;
And, I believe, for that they sometimes bleed.
A Noble Walk likewise adorns the Place,
To which the RIVER adds a greater Grace:
There you may sit, or walk, do which you please'
Which best you like, and suits most with your Ease.
All things conspire to please the best they can,
Walks, Waiters, River, Liquor, and the MAN.
Who would not go where Pleasure does invite?
Walks shady, silver Stream, the Eye's Delight;
Ducks feeding from your Hand, and Snow-white Swan,
Balsamick Ale, and most-obliging Man,
So good it is, it's prais'd by all Mens Tongues,
Healing as Balm of Gilead to the Lungs.
Miles in his Way obliging was, we know,
Yet F-----rs Language doth the softer flow,
Behav'our far genteeler of the two,
By Birth a Gentleman, and Breeding too.
OXFORD, for Lib'ral Arts that is so fam'd,
(Inferior all, none Equal can be nam'd)
His Alma Mater was, it is well known,
And Grey's Inn Learned gave to him the Gown.
Called he was from thence unto the Bar,
And pleaded likewise as a Barrister.
Another Bar he uses now, we know;
Where most is got, the Councel there will go:
Altho' his Fees may not so large be there
Greater the number of his Clients are,
Which makes the Gain to be the greater far.
He's Judge, he's Jury, and sole Pleader there,
A thing that is unknown at Westminster.
Invested with this Pow'r, not Insolent,
But unto ev'ry one he gives Content.
Whom Wealth, and Pow'r, and Pleasure too doth call,
And will not go, must have no Brains at all.
Rome's Emperor, Titus Vespasian,
Rais'd Money from (O strange!) the Piss of Man:
He us'd to say, Gold always sweet did smell,
Come it from what it wou'd, come but, 'twas well.
Of Profit too this Consequence is plain,
Greater it is, the sweeter is the Gain.
Monarchs have Money rais'd from Subjects Smoak,
And thought they did not less majestick look,
Then who can blame if, by his Care and Pains,
F------r doth Money raise from Barley-Grains?

Now to the Show-Room let's a while repair,
To see the active Feats performed there:
How the Bold Dutch-man on the Rope doth bound,
With greater Air than others on the Ground,
What Capers does he cut! how backward leaps!
With Andrew Merry eying all his Steps.
His Comick Humours with Delight you see,
Pleasing unto the best of Company.
The great D'Aumont has been diverted there,
With divers Others of like Character,
As by their gen'rous Guifts [sic.] they made appear.

The Famous TUMBLER lately is come o'er
Who was the Wonder of the other Shore:
France, Spain, and Holland, and High-Germany,
Sweden, and Denmark, and fam'd Italy,
His active Feats did with Amazement see,
Which done by Man they thought could never be:
Amongst the rest, he falleth from on high,
Head foremost, from the Upper-Gallery,
And in his Fall performs a Somerset [sic];
The Women shriek, in dread he'll break his Neck,
And gently on his Feet comes to the Ground,
To the Amazement of Beholders 'round.
So have I Seen Birds wanton in the Air,
Now falling on their Backs you'd think they were,
Now up they'd mount, then down Head-foremost go;
Downwards he can, but upwards can't fly so.
In this strange Feat he doth the Birds outvy,
Without their feather'd Wings they cannot fly,
But fall they must, and by the Fall must dye:

But he, without Wings, to the Ground doth fall
Gently, and comes unto no harm at all.
Black Scaramouch, and Harlequin of Fame,
The Ladder-Dance, with Forty I could name
Full as diverting, and of later date,
You may see there, at much a cheaper rate
Than at THE HOUSE, as well performed too,
You only pay for Liquors, not the Show,
Such as Neat Brandy, Southam Cyder fine,
And Grape's true Juice as e'er was press'd from Vine.
Return we now to our First Theme again,
A Nobler Subject, and a Nobler Strain!
But this same Place did lie so in our way,
We could not less than what we have done say:
He is a Neighbour to our present Theme,
His Ducks, Swans, Geese, and Walks adorn our Stream.

And now the RIVER'S near his Journey's End,
The Citizens go out to greet their Friend,
Their Folly blame, applaud the Great Sir HUGH,
Extol then Sov'reign, as they ought to do,
Look on their Guest with the same Art and Pride
As Bridegroom doth on his approaching Bride.
At last the Work is to its Period brought
Which was before Impracticable thought,
Where are two deep and ample Basons made,
And These are what they call NEW-RIVER-HEAD.

These two fair Basons must not be forgot,
The CITY did them honour, Shall I not?
So soon as ever they were made compleat,
The then Lord-May'r gave a most noble Treat,
Invited all the Citizens of Note,
And was resolv'd to have a merry Bout.
The Treat was cold, but this I dare to say,
There wa'n't a Man but what went warm away.

From Hall call'd Guild they in their Coaches rode,
And when come to the Bason's side, they stood;
Then each alighting, gently did descend,
And ev'ry Man was glad to see his Friend
In Place so odd, Occasion too so rare,
And all the Beauties of the City there,
To see the Sight went, and attend the May'r.
The Sun, asham'd to see their brighter Eyes,
Drew in his Rays, and quite forsook his Skyes;
But from their Beauty broke a brighter Ray,
And in his absence made it more than Day.
Ages to come may not the like produce,
To see a River finish'd, of such Use,
To serve a Place so fam'd for Wealth and Trade;
The WORLD'S Chief Port, it may be truly said.

Merry to be they all resolved were,
And to regale themselves with such good Cheer
As did then Tables sumptuously adorn,
Such Wines the Devil never drew, or Horn
With Eatables embellish'd, of the best;
Pontac himself, or Brawn, ne'er better dress'd.
Grace being said, they then fell to their Work
With Stomachs keen as Scymitar of Turk;
What Wounds they gave the Fierce Westphalian Boar!
But he, they knew full well, was slain before:
Had he been living, they had not come near,
Much less had cut and slash'd him so severe.
He soon had made them all to quit the Place,
Lest all their Cheer, and said no after-Grace.
Poor harmless Chickens too no Quarter have,
But Ham and Poultry buried in one Grave:
Neats-Tongues and Udders share the self-same Fate,
More Mercy would they shew the Foe they hate.
Innocent Tongue, who never told a Lye,
Why should'st Thou then be us'd so cruelly?
Thou never flatter'd, or thy Friend betray'd,
I wish of Man's that could be truly said:
Tho' form'd by GOD to praise his Holy Name,
We too too often do prophane the same.
Cease we to lye, to swear, our Friend betray,
And with our Tongues to sing His Praise, and pray,
O! that wou'd lead us to Eternal Day
Then wou'd the Golden Age again return,
Plain Truth and Honesty no longer mourn,
Which from Our Sphere too long have Exiles been,
And, till we mend, they'l not return again.

After Repast, the then Lord-May'r began
The King's Health, which was drunk by ev'ry Man.

The next a Bumper was, to Great Sir HUGH,
And that was drank by all with Good-will too,
The City-Musick playing all the time
As they carouzing were the noblest Wine.
But now this RIVER must baptized be;
Forgive the term, if it may seem too free.
My Lord himself it was who gave the Name,
And Sound of Trumpet did proclaim the same.
Then each Man with his Bottle in right Hand,
Glass in his left, such was my Lord's
Command:
Fill all, [they fill'd] oft with it, said my Lord;
And off they drank it, and obey'd his Word:
Bottle and Glass he then threw o'er his Head,
Each Man the Signal readily obey'd,
Be thou New-River call'd, my Lord then said.
Trumpets, Drums, Shouts then fill'd the
Hemisphere,
Highgate and Hampstead in the Joy did share,
And back again the grateful Noise rebound;
And Hornsey-Wood danc'd at the joyful
Sound.
Let's now survey the AQUEDUCTS of Rome,
Built by the Heathens, and by Christians some,
And then compare which best do serve their
Town,
To Ours the Conquest they must justly own.
The first were rais'd by mighty Emperours;
The Charges infinitely more than Ours;
And others by succeeding Popes were made;
Of those departed nought but good be said,
I shall not rail at them, for they are dead.
Well then may Rome her Aqueducts so boast,
And tell us of the vast Expence they cost,
Tell us, they rear'd their tow'ring Heads so
high,
As if they meant to pierce the very Sky;
And spar'd no Charge the same to beautifie.
This they did do, to celebrate a Name,
And recommend it down to future Fame,
More than for Use or Service of the same;
For most of Rome's great Emp'rours were
vain.
Of these fam'd Conduits sev'ral Builders
were,
At distant times, one from the other far:
Great are the Works, much greater wou'd
they seem
If by a Subject they had raised been,
Who had begun, and liv'd to finish them
But these were built by Potent Emperours,
And Consuls too, all Men of mighty Pow'rs,
Who Money had, and She can all things do,
Can level Mountains build great Cities too.

What is it Dame Pecunia cannot do?
To Conq'ring Rome all did a Tribute pay,
All the Victorious Eagle's Arms obey,
And the whole World to her became a Prey.
To her the Riches of the World did flow;
When she commanded, who durst then say
No?
Thus into her Ærarium all was hurl'd,
And Rome became the Great Bank of the
World.

OUR HERO wanted Gold to carry on
His Great Design, which was so well begun;
And he a Subject was, a Tradesman too,
But what was that his Spirit dar'd not do?
And live he did to see his Great Work done:
O Glorious! O Immortal MIDDLETON!
Thy Aqueduct was finish'd in Five Years;
As many Ages they were building theirs:
Unite them all, they can't with thine compare,
No more than Tyber can with Thames so fair.
Tho' ancient Bards of him so loudly sing,
Tyber unto the Thames is but a Spring
So are Rome's Conduits, when compar'd to
thine,
Like to broad Thames as is our narrow Tyne.
In this thy Work, they can't come near to
Thee,
No more than Thames can to the boundless
Sea
Let Heathen Rome then, let the Christian too,
Own themselves conquer'd by the GREAT Sir
HUGH.

Vast is the Charge the Company doth bear,
To keep this RIVER in its due Repair;
Which not long since was plainly made
appear,
But They, in Spirit like their Great Sir HUGH,
The Publick Good have alwaies in their view.

THRO' Pipes of Elm he does his Water throw,
And makes it to the highest Garrets flow
By Pipes of Lead, which into them are laid,
Of those at Rome the like cannot be said.
Ready he is to quench the dreadful Fire,
Combats with Joy that Element most dire:
The Foe, tho' hot, yet coolly doth he fight;
At first you'd think he'd beat our RIVER
quite,
He cracks and roars, and makes a dreadful
noise,
And threatens Conflagration to the Skies:
But Ours fights cool, and gives a gentle

Check,
Which doth in part his Rage and Fury break;
And finding that, pursues so close the Foe,
Until extinguish'd, will not let him go.
The Fire, but now which made the Skies afraid,
By this our Stream dead on the Ground is laid.
Victorious Stream! immortal be thy Fame;
To Thee, O LONDON! Precious be its Name.

FROM Basons large the Water is convey'd
By Pipes, which thence into the Town are laid.
Had I but Skill, how sweetly could I play
Upon thy Pipes, Sir HUGH, a Roundelay!
O Glorious Theme! Equal unto the Pen
Of Dryden Great, or Matchless O Rare BEN!
Unthinking Men! to leave Thy Song unsung;
Had they once thought on Thee, they'd Justice done;
Thee they had sung in their exalted Lays
Worthy of Thee; Thou worthy of their Praise.
If I fall short, accept of my Good-will,
The Fault impute unto my Want of Skill.
By Thee Fair London long has served been;
Long has thy Water kept Her sweet and clean.
Chelsea, the Bridge, and York, those Upstarts three,
Tho' all combined, could not come near to Thee;
By Art and Nature Thou, above them plac'd,
With all the Gifts House-water can be grac'd,
To serve Augusta feated art the best,
And with Contempt look'st down upon the rest. **FINIS**'.

(11, p86 dated from the three rival 'upstarts' undertakings it mentions; 1K, p291 c.1725; 15J, p244 'New River a Poem' by W. Garbott, 1750; 14D4, p165 'a poem, called "The New River", 8vo, 'sans date', was written by William Garbot; 'Brit. Topog.' Vol. I, p428'; 14B2, p414 c.1725 by voluntary subscription; H4-10-7 mentioned in book list at end; ('Brit. Topog.' Vol. i, p428) 14D6-I, p28; Undated doggerel verse published in 8vo; (Garbott's Poem,' The New River', p18) 14E1, p6; British Library copy '[1728]', 38pp reproduced by ECCO (Eighteenth Century Collections Online) Print Editions, my copy purchased 2011). Note that unfair comparison is made between the New River and the 50-mile Roman aqueduct, to which there is little resemblance (this being built by the might of the Roman Empire in a far hotter climate that was desperate for water).

1739 'The New River Head' by E. Dower: A part follows:
'Tired with Books and reading on the Bed
I walk'd one Evening to the River Head
There patient Anglers do the Fishes teize,
And Dogs are wash'd to clean them from the Fleas;
From thence, you hear the noise of jangling Bells,
Or the Soft Italian Tunes from Sadler's Wells:
There Citizens tell each other who is the winner,
And Clergy boast of what they had for Dinner:
The love-sick maid from Death will not refrain,
- Plunges in there, and laughs at future Pain.
Some walk there to get Appetites for their meat,
And others, like me, that has no Food to eat,
From the verdant Fields comes a fragrant Smell,
Whilst the gay Town looks like the Mouth of Hell.
- I thought of Woods, Palaces and Springs,
Riches, Poverty, and the Pomp of Kings.
Whilst th' Royal Swans for Food did seem to weep,
I lean'd upon my Staff and fell asleep'.

((2-copies typed 'FB, "New River Head" by E. Dower' attached to 'Salopian Esq. or The Joyous Miller, 1739, p74') 8A1, 2-8; 15J, p200 quotes 2-lines). Published 1763 [sic.] a tale 'The New River Head' 4to., London (14B2, p457).

1751 ('The Morning Walk or City Encompassed') by W.H. Draper (a poem in blank verse), London:
'But what ascending water meets my eyes
Which cleanses th' ordure of polluted streets,
Or checks some conflagration growing horrors
Tis Middleton! Thy gift: O! wond'rous man!
Whose bright inventive mind, with useful art
Could thus afford what nature had denied,
And spread this elemental good thro' tubes,
Of cleanness, and of blooming health the source
Just as the sanguine tide in purple streams
Through all the microcosms still circling glades
Mysterious spring of animated pow're
Ah! Had the country's voice forestall'd thy fate

I could have viewed thy works with more delight
I thence return with spirit refresh'd warm health
—
To hear thee, Doughty!
[footnote: Rector of St James's Clerkenwell]
from thy hands receive
(Handwritten, Islington LHC).

The heavenly banquet
O! let me last in philosophic thought!
Wander fair Islington's delightful scenes
Or Newington's: then to some height repair,
And view the varied blooming prospect round'

1775/6 'Amwell, a Descriptive Poem' by John Scott of Amwell, which scornfully mentions Myddelton and extols the early Roman aqueduct and the River Lea's diminished water (although is more realistic about its engineering magnificence):

"… Of Chadwell's azure pool. From Chadwell's pool
To London's plains **the Cambrian artist**
brought [Welshman Hugh Myddelton].
This ample aqueduct; suppos'd a work
Of matchless skill, by those who ne'er had heard
How from Preneste's heights and Anio's banks
By Tivoli to Rome's imperial walls
On marble arches came the limpid store,
[referring to the 50-mile Roman aqueduct]
[6-lines]
Not sordid lucre [financial profit or gain], but the honest wish
Of future fame, or care for public wheal,
Existence gave; and unconfin'd as dew
Falls from the hand of Evening on the fields,
They flow'd for all. **Our mercenary stream,**
No grandeur boasting, here obscurely glides
O'er grassy lawns or under willow shades.
As thro' the human frame, arterial tubes
Branched every way, minute and more minute,
The circulating sanguine fluid extend;
To pipes innumerable to peopled streets
Transmit the purchas'd wave. Old Lee, meanwhile, …" (D20B, pp147-148; E1, p15 'Amwell' poem published 1775; E8-2, p21 published 1776; 11, p86 'Amwell, a Descriptive Poem' written by John Scott published in 1766).

1775-1834 (Charles Lamb) Essays & Letters: The famous Essayist and Critic, and his authoress sister Mary, lived in houses aside the New River at Colebrooke Row then Enfield, hence includes many mentions of the New River in his writings.

At Newington "those bathing excursions to the New River, … …. How merrily we would sally forth into the fields and strip under the first warmth of the sun, and wanton like young dace in the streams getting us appetites for noon. … … How faint and languid finally we would return towards nightfall to our desired morsel" (Z20-1, pp29-30 when a schoolboy at Christ's Hospital, Hertford).

Nov. 1776 (Poem) 'Genius of Chadwell Spring' (New River) by Richard Gough: His attempt to emulate better known poets on the New River with Classic analogies (4-handwritten sheets with numerous second thoughts) best left to historical enthusiasts (D1624 No.18, ELSC&A; MFK typed transcription deposited at ELSC&A).

c.1804 'Rhyming Reminiscences' by Thos. Greenwood:
'ATTRACTION was needed, the town to engage,
So Dick emptied the River, that year, on the stage; [1804 Sadlers Wells]
The House overflow'd, and became quite the ton,
And the Wells, for some seasons, went swimmingly on'.

Oct. 1816 (Poem) on New River: 'The New River: A walk from Amwell to London' by R. Cheffins, 'Dorset-street, Salisbury-square' ('Herts. Mercury', Sat. 23 Sept. 1905, p3 cols. 5-6) Microfilm, HALS; 9 small-page longer version (SR-824 CHE, Hackney Archives). **For full text see Chapter 1**.

1818 (Nares' Verse): "AMWELL! Perpetual be thy Stream , …" etc. inscribed on a stone on the small upper island at Amwell Pool.

1821 (Verse), Reprinted 1865: 'Apostrophe to the New River' by A. Heraud (11, p87 Note 1: Gentleman's Magazine, 1821 (xci, part 2, pp.65-67)/2, Part II (1821 Vol. XCI), pp65-67; reprinted in W. J. Pinks, History of Clerkenwell (1865), p468; ('Gents. Mag.' 1821, vol. xci, part 2, pp65-67) 14B2, pp468-471) the fol. from Pinks:

'Apostrophe to the New River
Stream of the Cambrian artist! – hail, all hail
Even thus distant from thy fountain vale
Amwell, renown'd of Bards, for there a Bard
Dwelt, and enrich'd it with his song's regard,
Planted his garden, edified his grot,
Hallowing to Taste and Sentiment the spot.
But here, e'en here, the unlimited free Muse,
That o'er the Universe extends her views,
Mounts to the sun, or dives beneath the sea,
Or revels in the shades of phantasy,
Where nothing hath a being and a name,
A heart of passion, and a tongue of flame,
In Infen's lovely pastures, fancy-fond,
May trace thy far-off source, and pass beyond,
E'en on his native mountains, to survey
Thy mighty Master in his infant day.
Now, in her waking vision, she beholds
Thee, patriot HUGH, invested with the folds
Of shadowy mist, and seated on the throne
Of cloud-swath'd rock, and everlasting stone;
There, yet a Boy, didst thou imbibe the strength
Of the high elements, till such at length
Thy spirit grew, and became firm to dare
The writhen bolt, and lightning's purple care;
Grapple with storm, and darkness, and the night,
And bide the wild winds in their hour of might!
What wonder then, that such appear'd thy soul,
So full of nerve and energy the whole,
When Fate proclaim'd the task for thee prepar'd,
Which none besides, save Hercules, had dar'd?
Men shrunk from it – the men who felt of need
The spur that urges weakness unto deed –
The mighty and the wealthy of the land
Who thirsted for the fresh stream pure and bland
Shrunk from the task. And sordid souls there were
Who yielded to their own the general care,
Oppos'd their profit to the public good,
And what they should have strengthen'd, still withstood,
Leering on prudence with phlegmatic eyes,
Who should have swell'd the tide of Enterprise,
And triumph'd in his triumphs, - they were rife,
In heartless opposition and blind strife,
Till royal favour on his labour shone,
Speeding the mighty work of patriot Middleton.
Bright smile of Royalty! on such works as these,
Should be thy glory to award increase –
ere there of other virtue not a gem
To enhance the lustre of his diadem,
That King deserves the honours which the Muse
Around the brow of Merit doth diffuse,
Who aided with his power the Patriot
Who chose harsh poverty's severest lot,
So might he but complete his mighty plan,
The benefit of universal man!
Immortal work! since none may nearer rise
To the first essence, which is Deity's,
Than he who peril'd, scorn'd, and lost all wealth
In the great cause of Piety and Health –
Such is, oh, Hugh, with evergreen embrac'd
Thine Epitaph on marble tablet trac'd,
A monumental pile,
Girt with thine own pure flood in Amwell's em'rald Isle.
Deciduous shrub, with evergreen, is there,
Fit emblems both! – of such who must appear
At the dark bar of death, but leave a name
Never to perish from the scrine of fame.
Matter endures but for a season – Mind
Leaves an immortal memory behind,
And is itself immortal! – Such are thou! –
While they who knitted on thee the stern brow,
O'er eyes that had no speculation in them,
Fall like the shrub, and let oblivion win them.
But thy perennial name is like the Spring,
Whereof I seek to sing;
The Spring whence thou deducedst the ample stream,
The Poet's and Historian's theme,
Trenching thy mighty aqueduct a way,
'Till as the humble plains, the aspiring hills obey.

Muse! hence again, devolve the stream of verse,
And be this spring our Helicon to thee;
Drink of its Master's spirit; and rehearse
Its pleasant wanderings manifold, and be
The Minstrel of his Mind and Memory:
So may thy flower be with his wreath entwined,
And in the gentle murmuring of its course
Thy name may mingle musical, and find
A dulcet offering at its crystal source.
Arise! thou gently winding River,
**From Chadwell's spring, and sedgy Lea,
Arise, and fill thy banks for ever**,
Flow on, and plenty be with thee!
Through shady grove and flowery mead,
A paradise of sweets,
In thy fertility proceed,
And lave the rural streets.
And in thy clear blue mirror glass
The angler on thy banks,
Whose song upon the dewy grass
Shall trill his morning thanks.
But thricely welcome to the verdant marge
Of pleasant Infen! Lengthen and enlarge
Thy course and current! rise, ye Naiads, rise!
Advance your sway – but, how - ! – these tearful eyes!
These heart-consuming suspirs? – these soft moans,
Echoingly gurgling 'mid the bedded stones?
"Our Founder is in grief! his heart's best vision
Of perfect joy, and Hope's sublime Elysian,
Is darken'd – and a dread and heavy weight
Trammels his spirit, like the hand of fate:
Want shuts the hand, and doth confine his act,
Limit his labour, and our course contract!
Oh, we had laid the promise up at heart,
'Till of our being it becomes a part,
That we from our full urns should pour the wave,
And London's plains with lymph salubrious lave –
But Want, the Gorgon, petrifies our flow,
And says – 'Thus far –enter ye, no further go!'
And here, last eve, the PATRIOT came – to view,
Within his River's breast, Heaven's mirror'd blue! –
No! – in strange mood, he sought as if to number
The inverted stars repos'd in wat'ry slumber;
And then he wept; and mutter'd something wild
Of the world's cowardice – then inly smil'd
Superior to its utmost malice – then
Uprush'd, e'en like a lion from its den,
His spirit to his lips – and then away! –
Haughtily sped –".
Muse! wither wouldst thou stray!
Why through the backward vestibule of years
Travell'st to trace the Hero's hopes and fears?
Another burthen have the Naiads now,
For Royal Bounty gave their urns to flow:
And in their unseen cell they have a shrine,
Round which, with triumph, and with song divine,
They celebrate their Founder; - and each Nymph
Carols her lay, and purifies the lymph.

"Flow on! River of our toil,
    Flow, thou gentle River,
And whatever land thou coil,
    Health attend thee ever!

"May she bathe within thee oft,
    Nature's buxom daughter;
And a pleasant breeze aloft
    Revel with thy water.

"May she medicine the cup
    That dips in thee its brim;
And he who drinks the blessing up
    Repay thee with a hymn!

"Through shady grove and flowery mead,
    A paradise of sweets,
In thy fertility proceed,
    And lave the rural streets!

"Flow on! River of our toil,
    Flow, thou gentle River,
And whatever land thou coil,
    Health attend thee ever!"

And then there was an old man – now no more,
Whose port was lofty, though his head was hoar;
And his delight was in his garden centr'd,
And sternly chid he, if 'twas rudely enter'd,
His flower-beds trodden, and destroy'd their hue,
Or the fruit rifl'd – ere 'twas ripen'd too!
He was my Grandfather! And then there was
The village Governess, I must not pass,

Who urg'd the little ones in learning to excel,
And taught to lisp the monosyllable. –
Alas, indeed! if we are warp'd too far,
For what we may become, from what we are,
And but exalted, o'er the crowd, to be
A surer mark for Fortune's archery.
And I, of other past delights might speak,
But that the traces of those things are weak
Which chanc'd, ere memory kept a register,
Or thought had language wherewith to confer;
Yet with the dim reality I blend
Imagination, as an ardent friend,
To colour up the outline, 'till I can,
Each several feature of the picture scan,
And in each spot, and about every place,
The hill, lane, field, the river, and the chase,
The haunt and home of early pleasure trace:
And in the very gale there is a voice,
Lingering o'er infancey's evanish'd joys,
Which with thy name, sweet Infen, like a spell,
Winds round the heart – the soul of this farewell!
A. HERAUD'.

(Does seem to go on a bit and tells us little about the New River, but it shows how some became so enraptured by Myddelton's achievement!).

1822 ('Julia', Letter iii, Luttrell):
'Now the New River's current swells
The reservoir of Sadler's Wells,
And in some melodrama of slaughter
Floats all the stage with real water' [Sadlers Wells].

25 March 1827 (Verse) 'The New River':
'Thou pleasant river! in the summer time
    About thy margin I delight to stray,
Perusing Byron's captivating rhyme,
    And drinking inspiration from his lay
For there is something in thy placid stream
    That gives a keener relish to his song,
And makes the spirit of his numbers seem
    More fascinating as I move along:-

There is besides upon thy waves a moral,
With which it were ridiculous to quarrel;
For, like the current of our lives, they flow
Thro' multifarious channels, till they go
Down into darkness, and preserve no more
The "form and feature" they possessed before!
Islington, March 25, 1827'

(Printed cutting possibly Gents Mag, Isl. LHC; another copy without annotation, Isl. LHC).

1828 ('Walton Redivivus. A New-River Eclogue' by Thomas Hood: An idyll or pastoral poem containing dialogue by a poet and humorist of Scottish descent (pp88-95 included in 'Whims & Oddities in prose & verse etc.' by Thomas Hood, London, 1828; available at Google e-books). But first:

'My old New River has presented no extraordinary novelties lately. But there Hope sits, day after day, speculating on traditionary gudgeons. I think she hath taken the Fisheries. I now know the reasons why our forefathers were denominated East and West Angles. Yet is there no lack of spawn, for I wash my hands in fishets that come through the pump, every morning, thick as motelings - little things that perish untimely, and never taste the brook' (From a Letter of C. Lamb). [10 Aug. 1824 Lamb letter to Hood].

[Piscator is fishing, **- near the Sir Hugh Middleton's Head**, without either basket or can. Viator cometh up to him, with an angling-rod and a bottle.]

Via. Good morrow, Master Piscator. Is there any sport afloat?
Pis. I have not been here time enough to answer for it. It is barely two hours agone since I put in.
Via. The fishes are shyer in this stream, than in any water that I know.

LEFT: Print of **"My banks they are furnished"**. Said to be representing the New River Head/NRC.

Pis. I have fished here a whole Whitsuntide through, without a nibble. - But then the weather was not so excellent as to-day. This nice shower will set the gudgeons all agape.

Via. I am impatient to begin.

Pis. Do you fish with gut?

Via. No - I bait with gentles.

Pis. It is a good taking bait; though my question referred to the nature of your line. Let me see your tackle. Why, this is no line, but a ship's cable. It is six-twist. There is nothing in this water but you may pull out with a single hair.

Via. What, are there no dace, nor perch?

Pis. I doubt not, but there have been such fish here in former ages. But, now-a-days, there is nothing of that size. They are gone extinct, like the mammoths.

Via. There was always such a fishing at 'em. Where there was one Angler in former times, there is now a hundred.

Pis. A murrain on 'em ! - A New-River fish, now-a-days, cannot take his common swimming exercise without hitching on a hook.

Via. It is the natural course of things, for man's populousness to terminate other breeds. As the proverb says, "The more Scotchmen, the fewer herrings". It is curious to consider the family of whales growing thinner according to the propagation of parish lamps.

Pis. Aye, and, withal, how the race of man, who is a terrestrial animal, should have been in the greatest jeopardy of extinction by the element of water; whereas the whales, living in the ocean, are most liable to be burnt out.

Via. It is a pleasant speculation. But how is this? - I thought to have brought my gentles comfortably in an old snuff-box, and they are all stark dead!

Pis. The odour hath killed them. There is nothing more mortal than tobacco, to all kinds of vermin. Wherefore, a new box will be indispensable, though, for my own practice, I prefer my waistcoat pockets for their carriage. Pray mark this:— and in the meantime I will lend you some worms.

Via. I am much beholden: and when you come to Long Acre, I will faithfully repay you. But, look you, my tackle is still amiss. My float will not swim.

Pis. It is no miracle - for here is at least a good ounce of swan-shots upon your line. It is overcharged with lead.

Via. I confess, I am used only to killing sparrows, and such small fowls, out of the back-casement. But my ignorance shall make me the more thankful for your help and instruction.

Pis. There. The fault is amended. And now, observe, - you must watch your cork very narrowly, without even an eye-wink another way;— for, otherwise, you may overlook the only nibble throughout the day.

Via. I have a bite already ! - My float is going up and down like a ship at sea.

Pis. No. It is only that house-maid dipping in her bucket, which causes the agitation you perceive. 'Tis a shame so to interrupt the honest Angler's diversion. It would be but a judgment of God, now, if the jade should fall in! [Minus Print of "Vot a Burnin' Shame"].

Via. But I would have her only drowned for some brief twenty minutes or so - and then restored again by the Surgeons. And yet I have doubts of the lawfulness of that dragging of souls back again, that have taken their formal leaves. In my conscience, it seems like flying against the laws of predestination.

Pis. It is a doubtful point;— for, on the other hand, I have heard of some that were revived into life by the Doctors, and came afterwards to be hanged.

Via. Marry! 'tis pity such knaves' lungs were ever puff'd up again! It was good tobacco-smoke ill wasted! Oh, how pleasant, now, is this angling, which furnishes us with matter for such agreeable discourse! Surely, it is well called a contemplative recreation, for I never had half so many thoughts in my head before!

Pis. I am glad you relish it so well.

Via. I will take a summer lodging hereabouts, to be near the stream. How pleasant is this solitude! There are but fourteen a-fishing here, - and of those but few men.

Pis. And we shall be still more lonely on the **other side of the City Road**. - Come, let's across. Nay, we'll put in our lines lower down. There was a butcher's wife dragged for, at this bridge, in the last week.

Via. Have you, indeed, any qualms of that kind?

Pis. No - but, hereabouts, 'tis likely the gudgeons will be gorged. Now, we are far enough. **Yonder is the row of Colebrooke**. What a balmy wholesome gust is blowing over to us from the cow-lair!

Via. For my part, I smell nothing but dead kittens - for here lies a whole brood in soak. Would you

believe it, - to my phantasy, the nine days' blindness of these creatures smacks somewhat of a type of the human pre-existence. Methinks, I have had myself such a mysterious being, before I beheld the light. My dreams hint at it. A sort of world before eyesight.
Pis. I have some dim sympathy with your meaning. At the Creation, there was such a kind of blind man's bluff work. The atoms jostled together, before there was a revealing sun. But are we not fishing too deep?
Via. I am afeard on't! Would we had a plummet! We shall catch weeds.
Pis. It would be well to fish thus at the bottom, if we were fishing for flounders in the sea. But there, you must have forty fathom, or so, of stout line; and then, with your fish at the end, it will be the boy's old pastime carried into another element. I assure you, 'tis like swimming a kite! –

LEFT: Print of **'Piscator'**.

Via. It should be pretty sport - but hush! My cork has just made a bob. It is diving under the water! - Holla ! - I have catch'd a fish!
Pis. Is it a great one?
Via. Purely, a huge one! Shall I put it into the bottle?
Pis. It will be well, - and let there be a good measure of water, too, lest he scorch against the glass.
Via. How slippery and shining it is! - Ah, he is gone!
Pis. You are not used to the handling of a New River fish; - and, indeed, very few be. But hath he altogether escaped?
Via. No; I have his chin here, which I was obliged to tear off, to get away my hook.
Pis. Well, let him go:— it would be labour wasted to seek for him amongst this rank herbage. 'Tis the commonest of Anglers' crosses.
Via. I am comforted to consider he did not fall into the water again, as he was without a mouth, - and might have pined for years. Do you think there is any cruelty in our Art?
Pis. As for other methods of taking fish, I cannot say: but I think none in the hooking of them. - For, to look at the gills of a fish, with those manifold red leaves, like a housewife's needle-book, they are admirably adapted to our purpose; and manifestly intended by Nature to stick our steel in.
Via. I am glad to have the question so comfortably resolved; - for, in truth, I have had some misgivings. Now, look how dark the water grows! There is another shower towards.
Pis. Let it come down, and welcome. I have only my working-day clothes on. Sunday coats spoil holidays. Let everything hang loose, and time too will sit easy.
Via. I like your philosophy. In this world, we are the fools of restraint. We starch our ruffs till they cut us under the ear.
Pis. How pleasant it would be to discuss these sentiments over a tankard of ale ! - I have a simple bashfulness against going into a public tavern; but I think we could dodge into the Castle, without being much seen. [Probably the **Castle Inn tea-gardens, Colebrooke Row** (H2-8, p47); or near Upper Street the Castle on S-side of Cross Street by 1610, 1683, by 1788 demolished (H2-8, pp45-46)].
Via. And I have a sort of shuddering about me, that is willing to go more frankly in. Let us put up, then. - By my halidom! here is a little dead fish hanging at my hook:- and yet I never felt him bite.
Pis. 'Tis only a little week-old gudgeon, and he had not strength enough to stir the cork. However, we may say boldly, that we have caught a fish.
Via. Nay, I have another here, in my bottle. He was sleeping on his back at the top of the water, and I got him out nimbly with the hollow of my hand.
Pis. We have caught a brace, then;— besides the great one that was lost amongst the grass. I am glad on't, for we can bestow them upon some poor hungry person in our way home. It is passable good sport for the place.
Via. I am satisfied it must be called so. But the next time I come hither, I shall bring a reel with me, and a ready-made minnow, for I am certain there must be some marvellous huge pikes here; they always make a scarcity of other fish. However, I have been bravely entertained, and, at the first holiday, I will come to it again' [END].

c.1835 'The Origin of the New River', 'by a descendant of Sir Hugh Myddelton' from a 28 Feb. 1835 Publication:

'All honour to thee! Patriot rever'd!
Justly by noble deed thy name's endear'd:
True, Time has sped his way in ceaseless race,
Since thou, by his sole lock, restrain'd his pace;
Since, in those olden days, thy praise was sung
By many an ancient bard and grateful tongue;
Yet once again we'll search th' historic page,
Where lives thy gen'rous worth from age to age,
And joy to cast a wild flow'r on thy tomb,
Which steals from thee its value and perfume.
Say, in that glorious hour what wak'd thy zeal,
What thought of high emprize? Thy country's weal
[further 44 lines of generalities]
   London, revive! thy benefactor's near,
He comes with kind intent thy heart to cheer;
With soul to plan, and wealth to give thee aid,
Lo! **MYDDELTON** forsakes th' inglorious shade
There might his latest offspring yet possess
The rich domains by fortune's favours blest,
[further 33 lines of generalities]
   London, arise! thy wish'd-for dawn survey.
The welcome pledge of scientific day:
He comes, the stranger-friend, he sees thy want,
With his own hands prepar'd thy suit to grant,
[further 3 lines of generalities]
The first bold conqueror of the subject stream:
Through subterranean caves and depths profound,
Dangers and difficulties scowling round!
With untir'd patience an industrious few,
Each obstacle o'ercome, their work pursue;
And where the soil most unpropitious proves,
Vast leaden troughs th' impediment removes.
Through woods and wilds they bend its devious maze,
Wherein no triton dives or naiad plays;
[further 5 lines of generalities]
The sounding pickaxe scooping out the green,
Whilst hoe and mattock in the lab'rers hands,
Handmaids of science prove, for he commands;
The half-scar'd rustic, starting with surprise,
Near his lone hut beholds a stream arise,
Whence gently gliding o'er the verdant plain,
It owns **'NEW RIVER'** as its lowly name.
Here wild meanderings the progress stay,
As though the truant had forsook its way,
Averse to quit fair Hertford's flowery meads,
[further 11 lines of generalities]
Ah! from that source, a well-spring of all ill,
[further 3 lines of generalities]
   But see, emerging from th' alluring shade,
No longer tempts the pleasant hill and glade;
Through towns and hamlets on the current flows,
And higher swells, nor let nor barrier knows;
Two hundred bridges span the silvery wave,
Where finny tribes in shoals disportant lave;
Eight hundred thousand pounds the cost immense,
No spare of skill, of labour, or expense.
Five circling years the noble work complete,
Then Britain cheers her patriot hero greet –
And far beyond the treasures of a mine,
Those cheers, which spoke a nation's suffrage thine;
Thy name distinguish'd by a sovereign's voice,
Dear as the echo of his people's choice'.

(To be concluded next week)' such that have as yet not found a copy of the last part ((Printed extract from 'The Christian's Penny Magazine' publ. every Sat., No. 143 (possibly Vol. IV), Feb. 28, 1835, pp67-68) Islington LHC).

1836 & 1841 ('Pickwick Papers' & 'Barnaby Rudge') by Charles Dickens: 'The Pickwick Papers are our New River Head; and we may be compared to the New River Company. The labours of others have raised for us an immense reservoir of important facts. We merely lay them on, and communicate them in a clear and gentle stream …'. The New River Head also mentioned in 'Barnaby Rudge' regarding the Gordon Riots of 1780 (('Pickwick Papers' and 'Barnaby Rudge' both by Charles Dickens, 1836 and 1841) 10-3, p30/34; (Dicken's Search Engine) www.victorianlondon.org).
'Barnaby Rudge' 1841 Chapter 4 '… Fields were nigh at hand, through which the New River took … winding course, and …'; Chapter 67 '… A numerous detachment of soldiers were stationed to keep guard at the New River Head …' ((Dicken's Search Engine) www.victorianlondon.org

'David Copperfield' 1849-50 Chapter 25 "… considering. 'The ouse that I am stopping at – a sort of a private hotel and boarding ouse, Master Copperfield, near New River ed - …'" ((Dicken's Search Engine) www.victorianlondon.org; ouse = house and ed = Head).

Autumn 1888 (Verse): Composed by Miss Henrietta Cresswell:

'A Lay of the Suburbs'
'…
Then we cross a dreamy river
Looking weird beneath the twilight,
Bearing water to the City,
(F1B, p118).

To the slums, and dens, and hovels
Of the toilers in the smoke-land,
From the breezy healthful country.
…'.

c.1890s > 1906 (Verse): Scottish poet J.L. Davidson when living in Park Ridings, Hornsey, using early 1890s prose to write the following in early-1906:

'LABURNUM AND LILAC
Where the New River strays,
Eddying in olive green
And chrysophrase,

And briefly seen
In traffic-troubled ways,
Laburnum showers', … …'

The rest regarding lilac and laburnum in London during the spring (('A Random Itinerary' by J.L. Davidson, 1894, London) thanks to Dr. Andrew Turnbull of Tain, Ross-shire, who published a printed treatise on J.L. Davidson for his doctorate, the quote presumably from this).

Undated (Doggerel) Ode to the New River: Twelve 4-line verses and 2-line repeat refrain between.

'Our glorious citizens have not been slow
Their sense of his greatness most fitly to show
For his statue of stone any day may be seen
In bold relief standing near Islington Green.
Flow on! O, flow on! O'er thy soft sandy bed,
To finish thy course in the New River Head'
(((By B.S.C. (oupe), B.M. 1870 d.l. (140)) Typed 'MEM, Ode to the NR, Doggerel') 8A1, 2-8).

(Verse 9).

Chapter 3

Robert Mylne's 1775-1809 Survey of the New River

1775-1809 (Plans) of New River: The early maps of the New River used in this volume, are those created 1775-1809 by Robert Mylne, Surveyor to the New River Company (Thames Water Archive, Abbey Mills). They are the earliest most accurate & complete plans of the New River, from its source on the Hertford/Ware border, covering the whole 40-mile (approx.) journey south, to its destination at New River Head, Islington. Have no doubt the accuracy of his plans when compared to others of the time, is extremely amazing, near Ordnance Survey quality.

Robert Mylne (b.1733-1811) NRC Surveyor 1771-1811: Robert Mylne, F.R.S., the famous Scottish architect, born 4 Jan. 1733 in Edinburgh from a family of 'Master Masons of Scotland'. 1754-59 taking the European 'Grand Tour'. Whilst in Rome during 1758, winning two silver medals (for best 'prova', & best design) for architecture and soon after elected a professor of the Academy of St Luke. His winning design in a competition used by him 1761-69 to construct the 1st Blackfriars Bridge, using 9-elliptical river arches. First contact with NRC possibly in 1762, their Bridewell Precinct Offices & Yard were nearby. His own diary states 26 Nov. 1767 'Appointed joint surveyor to the New River Company' at a salary of £200 p.a.; **but as such Assistant Surveyor to the aged Henry Mill NRC Surveyor** (There are many varying dates quoted, such as 1752, 1762, 1768, 1771 etc., but his own diary should be the most reliable; 7G5, p40 1771; Portrait, MWB Aquarius Mag., p415; 15J, pp148-151 R. Mylne's early life; also see 'Robert Mylne Architect and Engineer 1733-1811' by A.E. Richardson, P.R.A., F.R.I.B.A. 220pp published 1955 by B.T. Batsford, which incorporates Robert Mylne's pocket diary; 12, p34 c.1762, 1767 his official title Assistant Surveyor). In 1767 Robert Mylne installing **Smeaton's Fire Engine (atmospheric 'steam' engine) at New River Head** to pump water to the Upper Pond, although never found to be completely successful.

At Henry Mill's death (Dec. 1770) Robert Mylne on **4 July 1771 becoming NRC Surveyor (afterwards this title altered to Engineer)**. 1774 moving from either Arundel St. or Bridge St (both near Blackfriars Bridge) or from Croydon, to the NRC Water House at NRH where he mainly lived for the rest of his life.

　　Robert Mylne built his own residence in Little Bridge-street with a medallion and his crest inscribed 'R.M., MDCCLXXX' [**1780**], the later York Hotel (14B2, p439).

In 1770 when aged 37 and earning £1,000 p.a., marrying 22-year old Mary Home (1748 - d.1797 aged 49 and interred at Gt. Amwell) at St Martin-in-the-Fields, London, having 9-children (Maria, Emila, Harriet, Caroline (1775-1844, 1797 married Col. William Duncan of the East India Co. at St James's Church, Clerkenwell), Robert (d.1798 aged-18 at sea on way to Gibraltar for military career), William Chadwell Mylne (succeeded his father as NRC Engineer), Thomas (d. at 3-months 1782), Charlotte (1785, post- 1811) & Leonora (1788, post-1823), only 1-son & 4-daughters surviving him.

From 1776-78 Robert Mylne **replacing the trough at Highbury Frame** with a clay embankment. The Highbury Frame aka Boarded River, completed 1618-19 to bypass the even earlier former Holloway Loop, said to have been lined with lead in the mid-C17th.

From 1784-87 Robert Mylne similarly **replacing the trough at Bush Hill Frame** with a clay Embankment. This Great Frame or Boarded River completed May 1612, in 1650 lined with lead, the arch there rebuilt 1682, in 1725 the Frame raised 1ft. higher.

Later also purchasing a 'summer-estate' at Gt. Amwell, near Ware, aside the New River. From 1794-97 building a 2-storey house with 31-windows called 'The Grove' (aka Amwell Grove, survives but much altered & enlarged) at Great Amwell, Herts., aside one of the New River's original source springs. At the time, the Mylne's owning approx. 250-acres in the parish incl. several other houses.

25 June 1806 the NRC presented Robert Mylne (of Gt Amwell) with a **Silver Cup** for his dedicated service. During his NRC tenure, constantly journeying up and down the New River by horse, normally in

a post-chaise, via the relatively expensive turnpike roads, or various alternate lengthier highways, his expenses paid by the NRC.

Under a Tudor Act parishes responsible for upkeep of roads & bridges within their area, local roads in the C18th in poor condition (B75-11, p14).

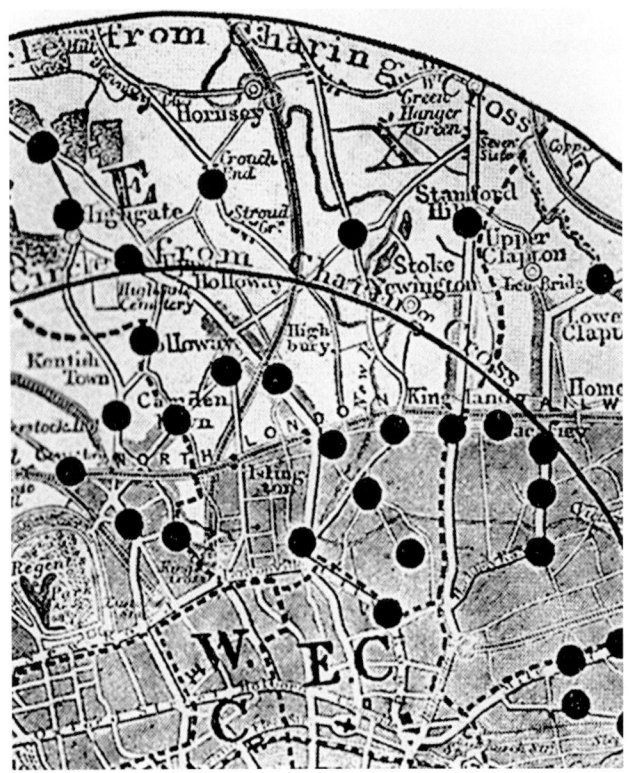

Turnpike Trusts & Toll Roads: First 1663 local Act for turnpike roads, 1700-1730 individual trusts for London's radial roads, 1706 local Act, 1773 General Turnpike Act, surge in 1770s of connecting roads (Internet). With the dominance of steam railways, Turnpike Trusts abolished in 1863, but roads remaining subject to toll not freed until 1872 (H5D1, p5).
In Robert Mylne's case mainly only affected by the Stamford Hill, Green Lanes Turnpike Trust.

LEFT: 1857 Toll Bars (1T3, p172a).

Although never his full-time job, with NRC permission he took leave when undertaking private architectural commissions throughout Britain. Robert Mylne retiring Nov. 1810 on a NRC pension, and preferring to live at NRH, where he died Sun. 5 May 1811 aged 78, and is buried in the crypt at St Paul's Cathedral, near the tomb of Sir Christopher Wren.

His Son
William Chadwell Mylne (b. 6 April 1781 - d. Xmas Day 1863 aged 83) NRC Engineer (1810-1859)
F.R.S., F.R.I.B.A., M.I.C.E.: For 3-years NRC Assistant Engineer to his father, from 1810/11-1859 NRC Engineer, retiring 1859 such that after 88-years the last Mylne to live at NRH (12, p34 1804 Assistant Engineer, 1811 Chief Engineer, 1859-1861 Consulting Engineer). Also finding time to undertake much private work. At the later rebuilding of Blackfriars Bridge, an obelisk beside the old bridge built by his father removed to the gardens of (Lea Court >) Flint House, Amwell, built 1842-44 by W.C. Mylne for his wife (nee) Mary Smith Coxhead.

His Grandsons
   1st-**Grandson: Robert William Mylne** (1817 – d.2 July 1890), F.R.S., devoted 10 years (c.1843-1853) assisting his father William Chadwell Mylne developing and managing the New River. He became an expert on wells and wrote the then award winning paper 'The Sinking of Hampstead Road Well' (12, p37; 15I, p113 succeeding as trustee for NRC copyhold land).
   2nd-**Grandson: William Chadwell Mylne (2nd)**, after 30 year's service (c.1845-1875) was River Surveyor when pensioned in 1875 (12, p37; 15I, p113).

1775-1809 Robert Mylne's Survey following the New River (Geographically)

3.1 TEXT (R. MYLNE'S SURVEY) Since some detail might NOT be Readable on Copies of Plans
Following is the text that appears on the 1775-1809 Mylne plans, later followed by the plans themselves. The numbers are MFK consecutive numbers fol. the New River, not on the plans themselves.

Large Plan 1 (1775-1809): Balance Engine (River Lee) to Broadmeads approaching Amwell End.
The accompanying text detailed as follows:
   Above River Lee: 'Part of Ware Park, Tho. Plumer Byde Esqr.'

Road, 'From Hertford to Ware'.
'Tho. Plumer Byde Esqr.'
'West end of the Company's **Fishery**'. 'River Lee'.
At W-end of '**Black Ditch**', with N-side 'NRC's, 5 : 1 : 13' part of 'Cow Bridge Mead'.
'... ... Roods, N.R. Company's, ...'.
'**Balance Engine**'.
W-side: 'Ranger Mead', '**Manifold ditch**'.
                              E-side '3 Roods Company's 0 : 2 : 18',
                              'formerly George Harrison Esq.',
                              '2 Acres NR Company 2 : 0 : 36',
                              'John Smith formerly John Stout'.
W-bank small stream joins.
Right angle bend.
'**Bridge No. 1**', 3-bends, 'Parish of Little St. John's Hertford'.
W-side: 'Morgan Esqr. formerly Sr. Tho. Clark Kt.', aside Manifold Ditch '3 Roods N.R. Company's 0 : 3 : 33', 'Manifold ditch' with 'Foot way from Hertford to Ware'.
W-side: Joined by '**Black Ditch**'.
        N-bank River Lee: 'Tho. Plumer Byde Esqr.'.
        'A. This piece is not now the property of the Company being exchanged for Long
        Acre'. 'A. Monks Mead N.R. Company's 1 : 1 : 19'.
        'Cow bridge' across River Lee.
'**Bridge No. 2**', S-bank **2-Streams join**, N-side Cow Bridge Mead ('New River Company' with **3-streams joining**):
'3 : 3 : 37, 3 Acres 3 : 1 : 4, 2 Acres 1 : 3 : 19, **S-bank stream joins**, field with just 'New River Company', **N-bank 'Tumbling bay'**, 'N. Rivr. Company 2 Acres 1: 3 : 37', 'Mr John Roberts'.
SW-side: 'Little St John's Parish', 'Wildes Marshes alias Stouts Marshes'.
    'formerly Stouts ditch', '... ..... 1 : 1 : 32', 'Beckford Esqr. formerly Fowlers', '7
    Roods 1 : 3 : 39'.
        E-side: 'Mr Dunster's ditch lately on Lease to the Company'.
            'Lady Mead', 'N. R. Company's 4 : 3 : 17', '**Stone**'[still there today],
            'Mr John Roberts'.
    Chadwell Mead: 'Tho. Jeeves formerly Smart', '3 Acres 2 : 3 : 20', 'Beckford Esqr.
    formerly Fowlers', '1 Acre 1: 1 : 24', **Ditch**, 2 Acres ...'.
At E-bend:
                            '**The Old River**'.
    '**Chalk Island**, T. Plumer Byde Esqr.', 'Edwd. Dunster' ('Esqrs. Land' on S-side) with
    feint 'N.R. Co.'
White House Sluice.
    SW-bank **Capstone**.
        '**Old Gauge**', '**New Gauge**' (aka Marble Gauge), then N-bank stream with two branches
        to 'The Old River' (probably an overflow).
    Diagonal ditch across '3 Acres 2 : 3 : 39'; 'Lady Townsend'.
    N-bank **stream joins**.
At Chadwell Spring: 'Bridge', & '**Gauge**'.
'**Chadwell Spring**', 'Bridge No. 3 taken away'.
'**Stone**', 'Edwd. Dunster Esqr.', 'Chadwell Hill'.
'Road from Hertford'.
  Isolated strip of land: '3 Roods 0 : 2 : 24'.
    NW-bank diagonal ditch joins New River. E-bank ditch joins.
After the two streams join (from Manifold Ditch & Chadwell Spring) 'Little St John's Parish Hertford'.
    N-side: 'Broad Mead', 'NRC 0 : 2 : 5'.
    S-side: '... ... ...' with inlet on S-bank, 'Corporation Post'.
N-side: 'Long Acre 0 : 3 : 37', N of which 'Mr Fearman', 'Col. Brown', 'Glebe Land', 'Col. Brown',

'Mrs Hadsley', 'Col. Brown', 'Great Amwell', **'Bridge No. 7 > 3'**, **after the bridge the New River appears to be far narrower**.
'Little Amwell … ', 'Note the dotted lines divide the different Parishes'.
   'New River'.
S-side: 'Road from Hertford to London', 'Corporation Post', 'Boundary Post between Great Amwell Parish & Little St John's Hertford'.
Block of text: 'The Company's **Freehold lands are Coloured Green**. The **Copyhold Lands Red**; and the **Leasehold Orange**. The lands coloured Yellow, together with the Mill, Fishery, Weir, and Fishing house, became by an Act of Parliament, Anno 1738 the property of the Company, and were formerly part of the Estates of the Byde Family'.
'The Leases of the Lands coloured Orange have expired, and the **Lands have been given up**'.

Large Plan 2 (1775-1809): Amwell End to today's Lower Amwell Road. The accompanying text detailed as follows:
   N-side: 'Walkman', **Inlet/Outlet** with bridge, 'house and garden', small square area with '**Gauge**'.
   '**Ware Bridge No. 8 > 4**'.
   L-bank small watering place.
   Bridge 'No. 9 > 5'.
   'Bridge No. 10, taken away'.
      'Horn Mead, Lady Townsend'.
   Bridge 'No. 6'.
      'William Squire'.
   '**Walk No. 19 begins Cooper Walksman**'.
   'Double [stroked through] bridge No. 11 > 7'.
      'Mrs Sarah Stout'.
   SW-bank 'a. The Property of the Company' [**Red House**].
   'Double bridge No. 12 > 8'.
   '20 Miles Stone from London'.
   Small kink in River.
   'Bridge No. 14, taken away'.
      'NRC's 6-acres, 5 : 3 : 2' area coloured green.
   'Bridge No. 15 > 9'.
   'Bridge No. 16 > 10'.
                                   E-bank small watering place.

Large Plan 3 (1775-1809): To Start of Amwell Hill
   Noticeable kink in River with 'Wooden trunk under the River' to clear drainage from road.
   Start of Amwell Hill. 'Common Field'.
   'Stop Gate house taken away'.
   SW-bank watering place, 'Hannah Browns Property'.
   'B. Lake Esq.'

Large Plan 4 (1775-1809): Great Amwell to St Margarets
   'Chamberlayne Esq.'
   'Bridge No. 17 > 11'.
   SW-side: NE-side:
                           'Tho. Glinister's Property'.
   'Dowell Chessy's Land'.
   '**Robert Mylne's Property**'.
   'Bridge 18 > 12'.
   NE-bank pipe to small pond with pipe outlet into Amwell Pond.
   '**Amwell Pond**', only the SE-island shown 'b. Monument erected in the Memory of Sr. Hugh Middleton by Robert Mylne Ano. 1800' (also 'a. Amwell yard the Company's Property' but doesn't

appear to be marked on plan) with SE-footbridge to island, and SE-watering place.
　　'Two Springs' flowing to the River Lee. **Probably Amwell Spring & Emma's Well**.
'Footbridge No. 19 > 13'.
'Bridge 20 > 14'.

SW-side:	NE-side:
'Chamberlayne Esqrs. Land', 'Parsonage'.	**'End of Stanstead Walk Tho. Sutton Walksman'**.
'Bibye Lake Esqr.'	'Amwell Marshes'.
	'Amwell Glebe'.
'Bridge taken away'.	
'William Cooper Esqrs. Property'.	'The Company's Property 1 : 0 : 38',
	'Amwell Marshes'.
'Old Chalk Pits'.	
	Amwell Lane turns SE.
	'William Cooper Esqrs. Property'.
'Walk No. 18 begins Hide Walksman'.	
'Bridge No. 22 > 15'.	'From Hertford Etc.', 'Bounds of Great Amwell & St Margarets Parishes', 'Stanstead Therl'.
W-bank tree.	E-side tree & 'Crown Alehouse'.
'William Cooper Esqrs. Land'.	'William Cooper Esqr.'
	E-side 'Chapel'.
	'Pipe to serve the Farm'.
W-bank tree then watering place.	
'Bridge No. 23 > 16'.	

Large Plan 5 (1775-1809): FORMER Stanstead Loop/s (LATER Bypassed by Embankment)

'Bibye Lake Esqr.' either side of River.	
	E-side 'a. Pipe to serve the fountain'.
	'b. ditto to serve the house'.
	'Mr. Lakes house'.
'Garden'.	
'Private foot bridge'.	
	SE-side 'B. Lake Esq.', 'Farm house Etc.'.
'Bibye Lake Esqr.' either side of River.	
	'Garden'.
'Bounds of St Margaret's & Great Amwell'.	
'Private bridge'.	
'12" Iron pipes [Trunk stroked through] under the River'.	
'Bibye Lake Esqrs. Land' either side of River.	
S-side 'Poor Croft Common Field'.	
'Bridge No. 26 > 17'.	
S-side 'B. Lake Esqr'.	
	E-side 'Bibye Lake Esqr'.
'Bridge No. 27 > 18'.	
'Rye Common Field' either side of River.	
'Bridge No. 28 > 19'.	
'Bounds of Great Amwell and Hoddesdon Parishes'.	'An arched drain under the River'.
'Rye Common Field' either side of River.	
	'Keeling Esqrs. Property'.
	'Rye bridge, Road to Hockerill Etc.'
'Bridge No. 29 > 20'. **'Walk No. 17 begins Scrivenor Walksman'**.	

Large Plan 6 (1775-1809): Hoddesdon
　'**Rye Common Field**'.

Bend SW.
'Bridge No. 30 > 21' at kink in River. **End of Hoddesdon Walk Jonathan Dunn Walksman**, Old Walk not among the present ones'.

'Furlong'.
'Marsh'.
'Lord Salisbury's Land'.   'Mr Gregory Borcham's Property'.
Today's Hoddesdon PS 'Loop'.

'Marsh gate house'.
S-bank 'b. Slip of ground the Company's Property'.
N-bank 'Gravel pits'.
'Bridge No. 31 > 22'.
'a. **Brick arch** under the River' for stream that fills Mill Pond at the Lynch.
'Lord Salisbury's Property'.
'Lampits Common Field'.   'Chamberlayne Esqrs. Property'.
'Gravel Pit'.   'Mill pond', 'Lince Mill'.
'Bridge No. 32 > 23'.
'Leechman Esq.'   'Chamberlayne Esqrs. Property'.
W-bank tapered watering place into River.
'Foot bridge No. 33 > 24'.
'Chamberlayne Esqrs. Property'.
W-side an Avenue of trees to River with wider bank at narrower River.

Large Plan 7 (1775-1809): Broxbourne
'Peare Williams Esqr.' either side of River.
'Bridge No. 34 > 25'.
'Bridge No. 35 > 26' at **Marsh Lane**.
'William Plumer Esqrs. Land' either side of River.
'Lord Salisbury's Property' either side of River.
'Bridge No. 36 > 27'.
'Mr Thos. Turks Land' either side of River.
Sharp S, SW turn into **FORMER W-side Broxbourne Loop (LATER Bypassed by Embankment)**
'Walk No. 16 begins Tingay Walksman'.
'Bridge No. 37 > 28'.
'A **large brick Arch** under the River called Spittle brook Arch' for ditch water. 'This ditch divides the Parishes of Hoddesdon and Broxbourne'.
'Robt. Akers Property' either side of River.

W-bank '**Watch Box**'.

LEFT: Presumed 1818 representation of Watch Box (Robinson's 'Tottenham' 1st edition, ELSC&A).

'Bridge No. 38 > 29' & '**Weed Grate**'.
W-side '**Formerly the Course of the Supply from Spittle brook Springs**'.
W-side 'Broad common Field'.
'Bridge No. 39 > 30'.
River turning back S.

'formerly Gravel pits'.
'Court common Field' either side of River.
'Gravel pits'.
'Bridge No. 40 > 31'.
W-bank '**Watchbox and Grate**', 'removed to Bridge No. 29'.
'Bridge No. 41 > 32'.
'Bishop of London' either side of River. River bends W.

FORMER Small S-Loop Broxbourne Church (LATER Realigned)
'Foot bridge maintained by the Parish, taken away'.
'Bridge No. 42 > 33'.
'Foot bridge No. 43 > 34'.   **'Broxbourne Church'**.
                                               'Parsonage'.
'Bridge No. 44 > 35' at Mill Lane. 'Pipe to serve Mr Lurchin's house a.' on S-side of lane.
'Lord Monson's Property' both sides of River.
 'Bridge No. 45 > 36'.

Large Plan 8 (1775-1809): Past Broxbourne High Road
'Lord Monson's Property' both sides of River.
'Ashcroft Common Field' both sides of River.
'Bridge No. 46 > 37'.
Later **Broxbourne Island**. N-side 'Thomas Jeeve's Land'.
'Lord Monson's Property' both sides of River.
'Bridge No. 47 > 38' with '**Brick arch** under the River', at **Broxbourne High Road**.
    '**Walk No. 15 begins Bennett Walksman**'.
'Lord Monson's Property' both sides of River.
W-side small rectangular pond with channel into New River.
'Bridge No. 48 > 39'.
'Bridge No. 49 > 40' at Lorvens Lane, today's **Cozen Lane West**.
'Lord Monson's Property' both sides of River.

Large Plan 9 (1775-1809): Through Wormley
'Lord Monson's Property' both sides of River.
'Hide Common Field' both sides of River.
'Bridge No. 50 > 44 [sic, should be 41]'.
'Bounds of Broxbourne and Wormley Parishes'.
W-bank 'The Company's Property, 0 : 1 : 14'.   E-side 'Sir Abraham Hume's Land'.
                                                      'Mr Cundalls Land'.
                                                      'Ditch kept clean by the Company'.
                                                      'Sir Abrm. Hume'.
'Bridge No. 51 > 42' at 'White horse Lane' (**today's Church Lane, Wormley**) with '**Brick Arch** under the River'.
W-bank watering place.
'Wormley common Field'.   'Sir Abrm. Hume'.
Turns SE into **FORMER E-Loop Wormley (LATER Bypassed by Embankment)**.
'Sr. Am. Hume's Property' either side of River.
Sharp E then S turn.
'Mr Homerton's Land'.   'Sir Abrm. Hume'.
                                                    'Mr Homerton's' house.
'Bridge No. 52, taken away'.   Narrow passage to main road.
'Bounds of Cheshunt and Wormley Parishes'.
                                                    'Capt. Bateman's Ld.'
'Wormley Common Field' both sides of River.
Kink, sharp W turn.
'Foot bridge No. 53 > 43', then sharp S-turn and W-turn.
FORMER W-Loop Wormley (LATER Bypassed by Embankment & Aqueduct)
'Bridge No. 54, taken away', then kink.
SW-side 'The Company's property, 0 : 0 : 30', NW, W.
'Bridge No. 55, taken away' at SW-bend.
Stream over River from **Wormley Flash**.
W-bank '**Turnpin to turn the water out of the brook into the River occasionally**'.

SE, then 'Bridge No. 56, taken away'.

'Love down hill Common'.
'A **Brick Arch** under the River' for a stream.

FORMER W-Loop 'Turnford' (LATER Bypassed by Above Aqueduct & Embankment)
Sharp W-turn at '**Water Lane**'.
'Bridge No. 57 > 44' at S-bend.
'Mr Jas. Barbar's Land'.
'A **Brick Arch** under the River' for a stream.

SE, then 'Common Field' either side of River.

'Love down bottom'.

NE-side 'Ditch to take away Waste water'.
'Common Field'.

'Mr Frans. Lee's property'.

'Mr Francis Lee's Land'.

Large Plan 10 (1775-1809): Turnford into Cheshunt
'Half Hide Common Field' either side of River.
'Bridge No. 58 > 45' then turns SW.
'A **brick Arch** under the River'.
'Miss Cromwell's property'.
'Sr. Abraham Hume' land either side of River.
'Bridge No. 59 > 46'.
W-side 'Brook field House held on lease by the Company of Sr. Abm. Hume, **occupied by John Parish Walksman**', then bends SE.
'**Brook Common Field**' either side of River.
'A **brick Arch** under the River'.
'Bridge No. 60 > 47'. '**End of Cheshunt Walk Will: Bates Walksman**', 'Old Walk not among the present ones', then turning SW.
'Bridge No. 61 > 48'. '**Walk No. 14 begins Dye Walksman**'.
NW-side 'Two Springs running into the River'.
'Miss Cromwell's Property' either side of River.
'Bridge No. 62 > 49'.
'**Cheshunt Flash**' with stream over River.
> **1825-6 (Cheshunt Flash) Bypassed:** Later added pencilled handwritten note with circle 'O' & dot '.' in middle: 'This shows the alteration of the River nr. Cheshunt Flash ordered at the Inspection of the River in 1825. It was visited by the Committee of Inspection on 14 June 1826 & found completed as shown upon the line A, C, B, & is now the course of the River at this point instead of the line A, A, B. At C. there are three brick water courses under the River in place of the old Flash at A and the two bridges above the old line done away. 'Initials?' 15 June 1826'.

S-bank 'c. **Turnpin to let the Water into the River occasionally**'.
N-side 'a. b. Two foot bridges maintained by the Company' over brook.
N-side 'd. A board to let off Waste water'.
'Bridge No. 63 > 50' then turning SE.
'Brook Common Field' either side of River.
'Bridge No. 64, taken away' then small kink in River.
'Bridge No. 65, taken away', 'Foot way to Cheshunt Street'.
NE-bank '**Pipe** to serve Mr Lewin in Cheshunt Street'.
'Killsmore (sic) common Field' either side of River.

Large Plan 11 (1775-1809): Church Lane to S of College Road, Cheshunt
'Bridge No. 66, taken away'.

W-bank tapered watering place.
'Mr John Hooper' either side of River.

E-side '**Pipe** to serve Mrs Saunders in Church lane'.
'Mr Chas. Gillam'.
'**Pipe** to serve the house and ponds'.

'Bridge No. 67 > 51' and '**Brick Arch** under the River' at **Church Lane**, Cheshunt.
              '**Grate for Weeds, and Watchbox**' (W-bank).
'Church common Field' either side of River.
'Bridge No. 68 > 52'
'Bridge No. 69 > 53' at kink, 'Church foot path'.
'Foot bridge No. 70, taken away'.
'Lord Monson' either side of River.
W-side 'Mr Rd. Wright'.
W-side 'Mr James Bishop', large channel & watering place.
W-side 'Mrs Henshaw', small rectangular 'Pond no Communication with the River'.
              E-side 'Mrs Shaw'.
'**Draw bridge**' across a narrowed River.
'Mrs Henshaw's Land' either side of River.
W-bank '**Summer house**'.
W-bank 'Pond served by the River'.
'Mrs Sarah Groilt's property' either side of River.
W-bank 'a. **Pump** to serve the house', 'Private bridge'.
W-side 'Jno. Delemar' at bend.
W-side 'Orchard, Miss Webb'.
'**Walk No. 13 begins Parker Walksman**'.
'Bridge No. 71 > 54' to 'Tanners hill Etc.' (today's **College Road**).
'**brick Arch** under the River' as there is today.
'Bridge No. 72, taken away'.
'Jno. Ashfordby Esqr.' either side of River.
              E-bank 'Waste trunk'.

FORMER W-Loop Bury Green, Cheshunt (LATER Bypassed by Embankment)
Sharp NW-turn, then 'Private bridge'.
N-bank 'a. b. **Two pipes** to serve the house & offices' of Jno. Ashfordby's premises.
Sharp turn S.
'Mr Ashfordby's Gardens' either side of River, the pronounced kink and again S.
              E-side 'Aldborough common field'.
'Mrs Shaw's Property'.
SW bend.   E-bank '**Pipe** to serve the Canal'.
'foot br: No. 73, taken away', SW, S.

Large Plan 12 (1775-1809): Theobalds, Cheshunt
'George Prescott Esq.' either side of River.
W-bank 'Ditch to keep off the Land Waters'.
'Foot bridge No. 74 > 55', then bends S.
'**Brick Arch** under the River'.
'Private Bridge' (E-side 'To Waltham Cross Etc.') then SE.
'Bridge No. 75, taken away' then E.
              E-bank '**Pipe** to serve Mr Bernes at Theobalds'.
SE.   E-bank '**Pipe** to serve Keck Esqr. and Mr Mellison at Theobalds'.
W-bank '**g**'.   'George Prescott Esqrs. Property'.
S, SW, 'A **brick arch** under the River'.
'**f**', S, SW.
'**e**'.   'NB. Mr Prescott has widened the River from **a. to b.** 3 feet, and in some places four; from **c. to d.** about 8 feet; from d. to e. about 3 or 4 feet; from **e. to f.** about 12 feet; from **f. to g.** about 3 feet.
W-side 'Mr Prescott's House', W-bank pond.

'd.'
W-side '**Theobalds Park George Prescott Esqr.**'
'**c**' river narrower.
'Formerly a bridge at the end of the lane'.   E-side '**Beldams Lane**'.
'**b**' river narrower. '**End of Bulls Cross walk John Griffis Walksman**'.
W-side '**Stables Etc**'.
S.   'George Prescott Esqrs. Land'.
SW into **FORMER W-Loop Theobalds (LATER Bypassed by Embankment > M25 Aqueduct)**.
'**a.**'.
NW-bank 'Land ditch'.
'George Prescott Esqr'. either side of River.
'**Walk No. 12 begins Cook Walksman**'.
'Foot bridge No. 76 > 56' then SE.
'**Arch's drain under the River**' for '**The Shire ditch which divides the County of Herts. & Middx., and also the Parishes of Cheshunt & Enfield**'.
Sharp bend NE.   SE-bank small rect. '**Pond** serv'd by the River'.
E, SE.   NE-side 'Robt. Jacomb Esqr'.

Large Plan 13 (1775-1809): Bullsmoor Lane to Dickenson's Trough, Enfield
W-side 'Common Field'.
W-side 'Mr Charles Bottom's' house, W-bank small pond.
'Bridge No. 77 > 57' at today's Bullsmoor Lane. 'To Waltham Cross Etc'.
'**Brick arch** under the River'.
SW into W-part of **FORMER E-Loop Bullsmoor (LATER Bypassed by Embankment)**.
'Robert Jacomb Esqr.' either side of River.
W-side 'Capt. Barnes' then SE.
W-bank watering place.
'Bridge No. 78, taken away'.
'Robert Jacombs Esqr.' either side of River.
'Mr Jacomb's House' to W.
W-bank square pond with island and '**Pipe** under the River' into W-E ditch.
Sharp turn W and sharp turn S.
W-side 'Land ditch' and small pond.
'under the River' into W-E ditch.
                                                    E bank '**Pipe** to serve Mr Kendrick's house & ponds'.
                                                    E bank '**Pipe** to serve Mr Willis's house & ponds'.
                                                    'Mr Willis's Property'.
Tapered watering place into River.
'Bridge No. 79 > 58' at today's **Turkey Street**.
                                                    E bank '**Pipe** to serve Mr Jno. Foster'.
                                                    E-side 'Rt. Jacombs Esqr'.
'**A. Weed grate removed** from Mr Garnault's Land'.
                                                    E-bank '**Watch-box**'.

Turns W, then NW.

FORMER Large W-Loop Whitewebbs
    (LATER Bypassed by Embankment & Docwra's Aqueduct)
'Mr Garnault's Garden'.   NE-side 'Robt. Jacombs Esqr'.
'**Cards Bridge** No. 80 > 59' at today's Bulls Cross.
    '**e.**' S of Cards Bridge.
'Private bridge' in grounds of Bowling Green House (> **Today's Myddelton House**).
N-bank '**b.**'   **a. b. c. Three ponds** serv'd by the River.
S-bank '**c.**'   **d.** Lead pipe under ditto.
'**d.**'   **e.** A **pipe** to serve Abrm. Frays house.
N-bank rectangular pond presumably '**a.**' (not marked).
'Private bridge No. 81'.

N-bank **oval watering place** connected to River.
'Aime Garnault Esqr.' N & S of River.
N-bank '**Grate bridge, removed to A.**' see previous.
S-bank '**Watchbox, removed**'.
N-side long pond.
N-side small pond.
S-side two avenues of trees with 'Bridge No. 86' (sic) between, 'taken away'.
S-bank 'Waste gate'.
W, kink, NW to Dickenson's Trough.
N-bank '**Pipe** thro the bank to take the water out of the ditch into the River'.
'**Dickenson's Trough**' (**FORMER Small N-spur**) taking the opposing stream over the River.
Pencilled circle with central point, referring to a now illegible long pencilled note.
Pencilled truncation of spur.
'Bridge No. 82, taken away'.
SW, then N-side 'Withy bed'.
S-bank '**Pipe** to serve Mr Breton's ponds granted to him Gratis in Lieu of some Springs which run into the River on the upper side'.

Large Plan 14 (1775-1809): Former Whitewebbs Loop
N-bank kink.
'Foot bridge No. 83, Bridge taken away'.   N-side 'Foot way to White Webbs'.
'Bridge No. 84 > 60'.
    '**Walk No. 11 begins Gladman Walksman**'.
'Bridge No. 87 [**jump in bridge Nos.**] > 61 immediately before 'Clay Pits'.
N-side '1 : 1 : 21, **Clay pitts**'. No dwellings shown (later site of 2-NRC cottages).
'The Property of the Company' that includes part within the loop here and a narrow strip to S.
S-bank '**Tumbling bay**'.
'**Enfield Flash**', trough over New River with footbridge or weir.
W-side 'Sluice' into New River.
'Bridge No. 88 > 62'.
S-bank '**River Gauge**'.
S-spur at Flash Lane, S of which land of 'Willm. May'.
Curve of later **Crescent Lake** (constructed 1820-1 for Edward Harman).
SE-turn, then E.
S-side 'Eliab. Breton Esqr.' then sharp S, SE turn.
'Foot bridge No. 89 > 63'.
'**Brick Arch** under the River'.
'Bull Bakers' (possibly from Bakers well field to far E; W.C. Mylne's later 1822 plan calls **Bull Beggars Hole**).

Large Plan 15 (1775-1809): Bull Beggars Hole to Tenniswood Road
W-side 'Road from Clay hill'.
S-side '**Pipe** to serve a Pond in Mr Weston's Gar^n'.

S-side 'foot way' and 'E. Breton Esqr.'
SE, 'Enfield Poor' either side of River, S of which 'Robt. Oram'.
S-side **small inlet**, then 'Eliab Breton Esqr'.

N-bank '**The high banks**' at the short straight kink.
N-side 'Eliab Breton Esqr'.

S-side 'James Percy Esqr'.

N-bank watering place before turning SE.

SW-side double gate.

N-side avenue of trees almost parallel to River, E- side 'E. Breton Esqr'.

SW-bank 'Brick Arch' to **large rectangular pond**, 'Draper's Company'.
W-side buildings 'Jas. Percy Esqr'.   E-side 'Mr Gough' (**Richard Gough the antiquarian**).
SW-side aside road 'From Clay hill & Moors hatch'.

Formerly called **Patten's/Pettin's Ware Lane** (E-part of today's Clay Hill): Probably named after a demolished Weir, a former house here called Pattensweir. Invariably using different spellings, also called Pettin's Ware. 1700 map calls 'Peters ware'. Mentioned 1686/1771, 1699, 1706 & 1823.

NE-bank '**Pipe** to serve a pond' but no pond shown.
SW-bank under road 'a.' '**Pipes** to serve Mr Winbolt's Ponds'.
NE-bank to small square pond 'd.' '**Pump & Cistern** to serve Mr Gough's house'.
'Foot bridge No. 91 [**jump in bridge Nos.**] > 64'.
SW-bank under road 'b.' 'Drain under the Road from the ditch to the River'.
'Bridge No. 92 > 65'.

NE-corner of bridge 'c.' '**Pipe** from the ditch to the River'.

'Walk No. 10 begins Liberty Walksman'.
SW-bank 'a.' '**Pipes** to serve Mr Winbolt's Ponds'.
SW-side 'Mr R. Winbolt'.   NE-side 'Charles Scherber Esqr'.
                                   NE-bank '**Pipe** into the pond'.

'Private bridge'.
'Charles Scherber Esqr.' either side of River.
'Foot bridge No. 93 > 66'.
'Stone pipe under the River'.
W-side 'foot way', then turn SE.
SW-side 'Draper's Company'.   NE-side 'Charles Scherber Esqr.'
At SW dip:
'Land Ditch'.   'Lord Lisbourne', 'Mr James Jarvis'.
'Lord Lisbourne's Property' either side of River.
Turns S.

London's New River in Maps (Vol. 1, Part 1)   Chapter 3   143

> **Pre-Mylne SHORTENING (MYSTERY LOCATION) near Enfield**
> **1728 (Minus ?-miles) Shortenings:** The New River also called Middleton's Water 'ran formerly two miles farther about, near Enfield and Hornsey **[both at unknown specific locations]**, which is now saved by finding a more commodious channel' (('History of Hertfordshire' by N. Salmon, LL. B., 1728, p20) 8A1, 2-8; may have been included in Henry Mills 1722 measurement of river; 15J, p180 (Salmon, 1728) Enfield & Hornsey improvements). Awaits finding maps of Enfield with reliable further information.
>
> **Prob. c.1769 (Abortive Attempt) to Bypass Enfield Parish:** 'About the same time another report prevailed in ye neighbd. [neighbourhood] the proprietors of ye New River had for contemplation a scheme for shortening its course in ye parish of Enfield wch had it been carried into executn. wd. **have deprived ye town of their greatest benefit**' ((Handwritten letter of the antiquary Richard Gough) D1624 No. 8, ELSC&A).

Large Plan 16 (1775-1809): Tenniswood Rd. to Enf. - Bush Hill, Edm. Boundary
                                                         'Miss Carter's Property'.
SW-kink.
W-bank 'Land ditch'.   'Eliab Breton Esqr'.
S, SE.
'Highway bridge No. 94 > 67' with 'foot path to Enfield highway'.
    'End of Enfield Walk, Joseph Aylett Walksman', 'Old Walk not among the present ones'.
S, 'Churchbury Common Field' either side of River.
'Land ditch'.
SW.
'**Brick Arch** under the River'.   'Eliab Breton Esqr.'
'**New Cut bridge** No. 95 > 68' N-side of **Southbury Road**.
    NOTE REFERENCE TO NEW CUT!
FORMER E-Loop Enfield Town (LATER Bypassed by Pipes)
W, then S-bank watering place.
S of Southbury Road 'Eliab Breton Esqr'.
S-side 'b. **brick drain empties into the River**' from property of 'Thomas Mills Esqr'.
S-side 'a. **Pipe** to serve the house & garden' of Thomas Mills.
'Foot bridge No. 96, taken away' on NW bend at Enfield Town.
W-bank properties:
'John Hoare'.
'Rob: Grant'.
'Will: George'.
'John Hughs' two properties.
'Mrs Reb^a. Jefferies' three properties the 1st with '**Pipe** to serve the house'.
'Mr Cuthberton' two properties.
'John Hughs' two properties.
'Bridge No. 97 > 69' today's **Churchbury Lane**. E-side 'Eliab Breton Esqr'.
'Charles Hunt Esqr.'
'Sam Wybott'.
'John Cameron' at W-bend.
N, E-side 'E. Breton Esqr.' either side of **possible FORMER course. Possibly referring to shortening mentioned above. Needs further research**.
'Pipe under the River'.
Un-numbered footbridge.
                  E-side 'Two ponds **late part of the River**' with a separate watercourse.
Or possibly tapping a Stream here!.
'Bridge No. 98 > 70' at **N-end of Silver Street**.
   Into the grounds of today's **Enfield Grammar School**.

W, 'Foot bridge No. 99 > 71'
N-side 'Eliab Breton Esqr.', S-side 'Mr John Smith'.
S-side '**Tanyard**'.
N-side Inlet.
N-bend corner S-side '**Pipe** to serve the Yard' where there is a pond.
W-side 'Messrs. Naylor and Wade'.
W-side watering place.
W-side watering place.   'Eliab Breton Esqr'.
'Private Bridge'.
'E. Breton Esqr.'   'Mrs Russell's property'.
                                                         '**Pipe** to serve the Canal'.

Turns W (N-side '**Parsons Lane**'), then SW.
'Eliab Breton Esqr.' either side of River.
'Foot bridge No. 100 > 72' at footpath.
NW-bank water into River.
NW-bank 'Mr Dowbeggin'.
NW-bank 'Mr Lepier'.
'1. Foot bridge No. 101 > 73'.
W & E-sides 'Mr John Davis' that includes the '3 Horseshoes Alehouse' today's **Crown & Horseshoes** pub.
'2. Private bridge'.
W & E-sides 'Mr John Sheffield'.
W-bank '10. **Pipe** which brings Water from the Chase to the River'.
W & E-sides 'Mary & Sarah Darton'.
'3. Private bridge'.
                                      E-bank '7. **Pipe** to serve Mrs Capener's house'.
W & E-sides 'Mrs Capener'.
W-side '10. **Pipe** which brings Water from the Chase to the River'.
       '4. Foot bridge No. 102 > 74' at today's **Gentleman's Row**.
W-side 'Mr. Barnevelt's Property'.   E-side 'Mr. Barnevelt'.
'5. Private bridge'.
W-side '8. **Brick drain** empties into the River'
            '9. **Pipe** to serve Mr Barnevelt's house'.   E-side 'Mrs Barnes'.
                                                          'Mrs Archer'.
                     E-bank '11. **Pipe** to serve Mr Dowbeggin's house' and '12. **Pipe** to serve Pond'.
'6. Foot bridge No. 103 > 75'.
E-bank '13. **Pipe** which serves Mr Barnevelt's four houses'.
W-bank '10. **Pipe** which brings Water from the Chase to the River'. E-bank '14. **Pipe** which serves
                                                                 Mr Clarkes house'.
W-bank '10. **Pipe** which brings Water from the Chase to the River'. E-bank '15. **Pipe** which serves
                                                                 Mrs Morey's house'.
                                                               E-bank '16. **Pipe** which serves Mr Cotton's
                                                                  boarding School'.
'Bridge No. 104 > 76'. Today's **Church Street**, Enfield.
   '**Walk No. 9 begins Tingey Walksman**. NB. Here begins the Walks of the upper District of the River'.
W-side 'Mr Sam[l.] Webb'.   E-bank '17. Brick Arch under the River'.
'Samuel Clayton Esqrs. Property' either side of River.
                                            '**Pipe** to serve the house'.
'Pond no Communication with the River'.
                                            '**Pipe** to serve a Canal'.
'Bridge No. 105 > 77'.
Drain under the River, then sharp turn SE.

'Bridge No. 78'.
'Bridge No. 106, taken away'.

Large Plan 17 (1775-1809): Bush Hill to S-side of Ridge Avenue
SW-side 'Samuel Clayton Esqr'.
NE-bank 'The Seven Sisters'.
'Bounds of Edmonton & Enfield Parishes'.
S-kink.
'1.'
SW-side 'Part of Enfield Park, Sam. Clayton Esqr'. NE-side 'Kitchen Garden, Jos$^{h.}$ Mellish Esqr'.
FORMER Small S-kink & N-side Loop
'2.'.
'Old Course of the River' (with small S-bank watering place) and the 'New Cut' (with central S-bank watering place). 'Nos. 1, 2 & 3 **Three pipes** ¾-inch bore to serve the Garden and Ponds'.
SW-side 'Joseph Mellish Esqr'. '3.'
'Bridge No. 107 > 79' at the road called '**Bush Hill**'.
N-bank watering place, 'Waste gate' with stream northwards, '6.' (see later note), Stone '9-Miles from London', 'The Company's Property 0 : 3 : 28', 'on Lease to Mr Mellish'.
'c. Arch'd drain under the River'
'b'. **Pipe** 'thro the Privy'.
NE-bank semicircular watering place.
'a. **Pipe** to serve the House'
'Private bridge'.
'Mr Mellish's House & Garden'.
Scimitar-shaped lake '**Bason** on Lease to Mr Mellish'.
'Joseph Mellish Esqrs. Property' either side of River.
Text 'Private bridge' but no bridge shown.
W-side 'Miss Parker'.
W-side 'Late Jno. Frame Esqr.' and rectangular pond.
'William Clarke Esqr. Property' either side of River.
Bush Hill 'Sluice House' with 'a. The Company's Property'.
'Bridge No. 109 [**jump in bridge Nos.**] > 80' at '**Bush Hill Road**'.
'Private foot bridge'.
Turning in circle to W.
'Private foot bridge, taken away'.
Bush Hill House.
N-side house of 'Will. Clarke Esqr.' his name also either side of River.
   After removal of the Frame, the property of Jebson Esqr. amended to Jephson.
To the NW:
   'A. **River Surveyor's House & Garden**'.
   '1. Claypitt Field, The Company's Property, 5 : 0 : 6'.
   '2. Rabbet Field, Company's prop$^{y.}$ 1 : 3 : 12'.
Sharp turn SW.
'Private foot bridge'.
'b. A small drain from the Corner of Mr Clarke's Garden'.
'a. A **large brick Arch** under the Road, Frame Etc.'
'c. **Tumbling bay out of the frame**'.
From a 'Cesspool', 'd. Brick drain the Company's Property'.
'**House occupied by the River Surveyor**, removed to A.' (see above).
W-bank '3. The Slope, The Company's, 0 : 1 : 21'.

     Bush Hill Frame.   E-bank, '4. 1 : 0 : 0'.
W-side 'Mr Penfold's Property'.   E-side 'W. Clarke Esqr'.
End of Frame.
W-bank 'Turnpin', then S.
'River Field, 1 : 3 : 36' either side of River.
 'Reference to the Company's Property at Bush Hill'
  1. Claypitt Field, Walksman's house and garden 5 : 0 : 6
  2. Rabbet Field 1 : 3 : 12
  3. The Slope 0 : 1 : 21
  4. House, Garden, Frame & Ground adjoining 1 : 0 : 0
  5. River Field 1 : 3 : 36
       [S/Total] **10 : 0 : 35**
  6. Slip of Ground by Mr Mellish's house 0 : 3 : 25
       [Total] **11: 0 : 20**'.
'Bridge No. 110, taken away'.
'Stop gate house'.
'Bridge No. 111' at today's **Ridge Avenue**.
 To the left a plan of the **'Present State of Bushill Cut 1809'**.
W-side **'Green Dragon Alehouse**, removed to a.' [to SW].
SE, then 'A Common Field' either side of River.
'Bridge No. 112, taken away' then S.   **'Section of the Frame'**.
          E-bank 'a. A **two Inch bore** to serve Mr Rooke
          of Edmonton'.
'Bridge No. 114 > 81', at today's **Firs Lane**.
'b. A brick Arch under the River'.
W-side 'Mr William Simmans [sic]'.
SW, then sharp W, then S.

Large Plan 18 (1775-1809): Fords Green to Hedge Lane
 S, SW.
'Mrs Sarah Tashmaker's Property' either side of River.
Just after bend **'Wooden Trough under River'**.
W-side 'Mans Lane' & W-bank right-angled bend Inlet.
S, then 'Bridge No. 115 > 82'.
'Private bridge' & 'brick Arch under the River'.
'Bridge No. 116 > 83' road 'To Edmonton Church' at **Fords Grove**.
 'Walk No. 8 begins Page Walksman'.
SW.
W-side **'Fords Green'** with 'finger' on rect. Pond. E-side 'John Skinners Property'.
'Bridge No. 117 > 84' at today's **Farm Road**.
W-bank watering place.
         E-side 'Manor house'.
         E-bank watering place.
'12 in. Iron-pipe under River'.
W-side 'Russells Green', 'Mrs Tashmakers Property' either side of River.
'Arthur George Karr's' land either side of River.
         E-bank 'An **Inch bore** to serve Jno· Porter
         Felmonger'.
'a. Brick Arch under the River' presumably for road drainage.
'Bridge No. 118 > 85' at 'High Field Row' today's **Highfield Road**.
W-side 'Mr Day's Property'.
Curving SW then S (two bends).
         E-side 'High Common Field'.

'Bridge No. 119 > 86'.
FORMER Channel 'Old Course of the River' (S then E) & 'New Cut' (SE) with land between 'The Company's 0 : 3 : 12'.
'From Winchmore Hill', 'Bridge No. 120 > 87', '**To Barrow Well Green**'.
    E-bank 'A **two Inch bore** to serve Lady Leeke's House'.
'A brick drain under the River'.
'Miss Hucksley's Land' either side of River.
'Scotch Common Field' either side of River.
'Bridge No. 121, taken away'.
'John Skinner' either side of River.
'Peter Gallier Esqrs. Land' either side of River.
W-side 'Miss Hucksley's Land'.   E-side 'Mr Day's Land'.
'Miss Hucksley's Property' either side of River.
To Palmers Green, 'Bridge No. 123 [**jump in bridge Nos.**] > 88', 'To Tanners End & Edmonton' today's **Hedge Lane**.
'Miss Hucksley's Property' either side of River.
'A Wooden pipe under the River'.
'Miss Hucksley's Property' either side of River.
Turns E then SE.

Large Plan 19, Part 1 (1775-1809): Hazelwood Lane to Oakthorpe Road
    SE, S.
'Miss Hucksley's Property' either side of River.
'Bridge No. 124 > 89'.
'Miss Hucksley's Property' either side of River.
Turns SW.
'Fox lane Bridge No. 125 > 90'.
'Bridge No. 126' **without new number**, at today's **Hazelwood Lane**.
SW, 'Miss Hucksley's Property' either side of River.
'Bridge No. 127 > 91'.
N-side 'King Field Miss Jackson's'.
FORMER Hamilton Crescent Spur
NW, then sharply S.
'Common sewer under the River'.
'Miss Jackson's Property' either side of River.
Gradually SW, W-bank 'Ditch to keep off the Land Water'.
'Bridge No. 128 > 92' (with kink in River) at Chequers Lane, today's **Oakthorpe Road**.

Large Plan 20 (1775-1809): Former Southgate/Arnos Park W-Loop
    Heading W.
'M$^{s.}$ Hucksley's' either side of River.
'Hadley Esqrs. Property' either side of River.
'Bridge No. 129 > 93'.
'Clarke Esqrs. Property' either side of River.
'Bridge No. 130 > 94' at Green Lanes with 'The Nightingales Alehouse' to N.
    '**Walk No. 7 begins Fisher Walksman**'.
FORMER Southgate Loop (LATER bypassed by Embankment & Pymmes Brook Aqueduct)
Heading W, 'Miss Hucksley' N & S-side, then N-Kink.
'Miss Sarah Jackson's Property' either side of River.
'Bridge No. 131 > 95'.
'Bridge No. 132 > 96' (at pronounced N-spur with two small inlets) at today's **Powys Lane**.
'Bridge No. 134 [**jump in bridge Nos.**] > 97'.
'Browne Esqrs. Property' either side of River.

Just inside E-end of today's Arnos Park
S-bank 'Tumbling Bay' with '**Sluice Hous**e, taken away' over S-side drainage channel.
'Private Bridge'.
    N-bank: Site of **former Summer House** marked by depression in the ground, and shown in 'the temple' photo at ELSC&A (EAS Bulletin No. 160, March 2001, p9); photo not now to be found.
W, two kinks, NW, then turning sharply S.
'4-Brick Arches under the River' at Pymmes Brook.
W-side 'John Bareing Esq. Land'.
    Probable SITE OF FORMER Wild's Flash.
SE, '3-Brick Arches under the River' for a Pymmes Brook Relief Channel.
NE-bank 'Tumbling Bay', SE.
'Private foot bridge', SE.
'Browne Esqr.' either side of River.
N-side 'Browne Esqr.' & S-side 'Miss Jackson'.
'Private Bridge' at today's SE-end of **Seafield Road**, then S.
1. FORMER Channel (Newman's Flash) 'Old Course'.
SW, 'Bridge No. 136' with number stroked through, at Bowes Road.
SW, 'Old Course of the River', SW, W-side 'Miss Jackson'.
'A brick drain under the River' for Bounds Green Brook.
'**Newman's Flash done away**' over New River, sharply turns NE.
W-side 'Hobbs Mead, 'Miss Jackson', 'Old Course of the River', E-side 'Miss Jackson'.
'Bridge No. 137' with number stroked through, NE.
                                          E-side 'Sr James Pennyman'.
'Bridge No. 138' with number stroked through at Bowes Road.
2. 'New Cut' (Bypassing Newman's Flash).
'2-Brick Arches under the River' for Bounds Green Brook, then in **large semicircular arc** ('Browne Esqr.' either side of River).
'Bridge No. 139 > 98', N-side Bowes Road, 'Pipe under the River' and Bowes Road for drainage of pond on S-side of Bowes Road.
NE, SE (**Small humped loop**), 'Sr. James Pennyman' either side of River.
'Brick drain under the River' incl. Bowes Road & Powys Lane for pond on S-side of Bowes Road.
'Bridge No. 140 > 99', at Powys Lane, eastwards.
'Miss Burton' either side of River.
'Joseph Girdler Esqrs. Property' either side of River.
'Bridge No. 141 > 100'.
'Miss Burton's Property' either side of River.
'Bridge No. 142 > 101'.
Kinks SE at 'Bridge No. 143 > 102' **Bowes Road**, then S.
    NE-side '**Pipe** thru the bank to serve Mrs Miller's house at Bows Farm', 'removed lower down'.
End of FORMER Southgate Loop.

FORMER (1612 - 1859) Edmonton-Tottenham Loop
    (Bypassed by Embankment & Wood Green Tunnel)
S, W-side 'Sr James Pennyman', E-side 'Jos^h Girdler Esqrs. Land'.
Then E 'step' a SW/SE backward curve turning E, 'Sr James Pennyman' either side of River.
At a sharp S-bend (site of **later 2-islands**), E-bank '**Pipe** to supply Bow's Farm'(**Bowes Farm**).
    [**2-islands** shown on 1864 OS map:
    Private bridge to 1st post-1809 island.
    Private bridge from 1st to 2nd post-1809 island].
S then another E 'step'.
Southgate-Wood Green Boundary.
SE, 'Sr James Pennyman' either side of River.
'Bridge No. 103'.

S, 'Sr James Pennyman' either side of River.

Large Plan 21, Part 1 (1775-1809): Sidney, Wood Green High & Woodside Roads
S, then sharp turn N (today's Sydney Road-Wood Green High Road).
Straightening (2 Small Kinks)
1. **'Old Course'** (N).
'Bridge No. 146' (crossed thru) [**jump in bridge Nos.**], 'rebuilt partly at the expense of the Road Trust'.
 'End of [stroked through] **Tyle Kiln Walk, John Lucas Walkman'** amended to **'No. 6 begins, King'**.
2. **'New Cut'** (S).
Old Course (N) & 'New Cut' (S) of straightening.
Then N.

Large Plan 19, Part 2 (1775-1809): Edmonton & Tottenham
'Mr Thos Millers Property' either side of River.
NE.
'Bridge No. 147 > 104'.
'Bounds of Edmonton & Tottenham Parishes' the New River part of the boundary.
NE, sharp turn NW, then curving NE.
'Sr. James Pennyman's Property' either side of River.
'Foot bridge No. 148', 'taken away'.
NE, 'Mr Thos. Miller' either side of River, at **rectangular field** between River.
E, 'Foot bridge No. 149 > 105'.
'Bridge No. 150 > 106', N-side 'Sr. James Pennyman'.
E, 'Bridge No. 151 > 107', at N-end of Wolves Lane.
NE, 'Richd Eaton Lee Esqrs. Land' either side of River.
'Bridge No. 152' > '**Weed Grate** No. 108'.
NE, 'Mrs Shaw's Property' either side of River.
NW-side '**Tile Kiln Green**'.
NE, 'Double bridge No. 153 > 109'.
NE, 'Foot bridge No. 154 > 110'.
NE, 'Stephen Germaine Esqr' either side of River.
NE, 'Bridge No. 155 > 111'.
NE then SE, 'Stephen Germaine Esqr' either side of River', '**Toads Hole**' to N.
SE, 'Foot bridge No. 112', 'Foot way to Tanners End &c.'
SE, 'George Beauchamp Esqr.' either side of River.
SE, 'Bridge No. 157 > 113'.
SE, 'George Beauchamp Esqr.' either side of River.
 E-bank '**Two pipes** thro the bank which serve Mr. Briggs and Doctor Clarke at Tottenham'.
'Bounds of Edmonton and Tottenham Parishes', then S.
'Charles Hornsby Esqrs. Land' either side of River, S.
 E-bank '**Two pipes** thro the bank which serve Mrs. Horne, Mr. Smith & Geo. Beauchamp Esq. at Tottenham'.
'Bridge No. 158 > 114' at **Clay Hill**, 'Road to Tottenham'.
SW, W-side inlet from NR to small oblong pond.
 E-side, '**Clay hill house**, C. Hornsby Esq.'.
'Private bridge'.
SW, S, N-side 'Garden C. Hornsby Esqr', S-side 'Charles Hornsby Esqr'.
S-side small widening of NR, W.
'Bridge No. 159 > 115'.
S-bank small semicircular watering place.
N-side '**Clay hill Green**', S-side 'Stephen Germaine Esqr'.

NW to 'Foot bridge No. 160 > 116', N-side '**Clay hill Farm**'.
SW, 'Duke of Northumberland' either side of River, then kink.
SW, 'Bridge No. 161 > 117'.
'Chas. Hornsby Esqrs. Lands' either side of River.
SW, 'Mrs Sarah Jackson's Land' either side of River.
'Bridge No. 162 > 118'.
SW, 'Bridge No. 163 > 119'.

See **1818 print of New River bridge at Clay Hill** (> Devonshire Hill Lane), Tottenham.
'Duke of Northumberland' either side of River, SW.
NW-bank 'The Dock' drainage E-side of Wolves Lane into NR.

Large Plan 21, Part 2 (1775-1809): Wolves Lane (S-end) to Wood Green
'Bridge No. 164 > 120' at **Wolves Lane**.
SW, 'Duke of Northumberland' either side of River.
Curving SE.
'Bridge No. 165 > 121' at **White Hart Lane**.
SE, 'Bridge No. 166 > 122', E-side 'Francis Bowyer Esqr'.
SW, 'Francis Bowyer Esqrs. Land' either side of River.
SW, 'John Sawbridge Esqrs. Property' either side of River.
FORMER NW-side Kink Straightened
1. '**Old Course**' NW-bank.
2. '**New Cut**' SE-bank.
'Bridge No. 167' (Number stroked through) at Jolly Butchers Hill, 'rebuilt partly at the expense of the Trust'.
   '**Start of Hornsey Walk No. 5 begins Jackson Walksman**'.
NW-side '**Three Jolly Butchers Alehouse**', 'Mrs Francis Cooper's Property', SE-side '**Wood Green**'.
SW, 'Mrs Harris's Property' either side of River.
'Bridge No. 168 > 123'.
'Bridge No. 169 > 124', 'Tottenham Glebe' either side of River.
'Francis Bowyer Esqrs. Land' either side of River.
'Bridge No. 170 > 125'.
SE-side building shown close to the River.
Sharp turn S.
End of FORMER Edm.-Tottenham Loop.
The course of the New River is clearly shown on 1798 Wyburg Survey (Facsimile, BCMA), 1818 Parish of Tottenham from an actual survey (Robinson's 'History of Tottenham' 1st Edn. 1818), and 1844 Tottenham Tithe Map (BCMA).

> **Pre-Mylne SHORTENING (MYSTERY LOCATION) Hornsey**
> **1728 (Minus ?-miles) Shortenings:** The New River also called Middleton's Water 'ran formerly two miles farther about, near Enfield and Hornsey **[both at unknown specific locations]**, which is now saved by finding a more commodious channel' (('History of Hertfordshire' by N. Salmon, LL. B., 1728, p20) 8A1, 2-8; may have been included in Henry Mills 1722 measurement of river; 15J, p180 (Salmon, 1728) Enfield & Hornsey improvements). Awaits finding maps of Hornsey with reliable 100ft. contour.

Large Plan 22 (1775-1809): Former Hornsey Village W-Loop
FORMER LARGE W-Loop Hornsey (LATER Bypassed by Embankment)
'Bridge No. 171 > 126'.
SW, 'Wood Green' either side of River.
S, W-bank watering place.
Wood Green > Hornsey Boundary.

'Francis Bowyer Esqrs. Property' either side of River.
SE, 'Bridge No. 172 > 127'.
E-bank: 'Waste Gate, taken away' to overspill channel flowing east.
S, 'Samuel Meade Esqrs. Property' either side of River.
SW, small inlet NW-bank.
'Bridge No. 173 > 128'.
Small inlet SE-bank, SW, SSW.
'Mr Richard Gould's Land' either side of River.
'Bridge No. 174 > 129'.
W-side 'Mr John Mahew's Property'.
S, E-side 'Mr Rich$^{d.}$ Gould'.
SSW, 'Bridge No. 175 > 130'.
'Mr Mahew's Land' either side of River.

FORMER SW-Spur

1. 'Old Course of the River' (SW, NE).
'Hornsey Stop gate, taken away', 'Sr. Meade Esqr.' either side of River.
'Hornsey Flash & Grate, both taken away', the Campsbourne or River Moselle shown over the New River.
NE-side of Hornsey High Street, sharp turn SE under Hornsey High Street at end of 'New Cut'.

2. 'New Cut' (SE).
'2 Brick Arches' beneath New River.
NE-bank '**Pipe** to serve Mr Gould'.
SE, 'Bridge No. 176 > 131' at **Hornsey High St.**, W-side 'Road from Finchley, Colney hatch & Muswell hill'
SE, 'Foot bridge No. 177, taken away', SE.
SE, 'Ralph Hopper Esqr.' either side of River.
'Private bridge'.
E, 'Bridge No. 178, taken away'.
E, 'Bridge No. 179 > 132'.
'Hm$^{y.}$ Everetts Property' either side of River.
NE, 'Com^n. Sewer under the River', beneath road.
'a. Bridge No. 180 > 133'.
NE, 'b. Bridge No. 181 > 134', 'Mr Everetts Land' either side of River.
  NW-bank '**Pipe** to serve the Moated House', 'Um^{y}: Everetts L$^{d.}$'.
SE-bank '**Well & pipe** to serve the house'.
NE, 'c. Bridge No. 182 > 135', 'Mrs Sarah White' either side of River.
'd. Bridge No. 183 > 136'.
'e. Bridge No. 184, taken away'.
NW-side 'Hornsey Poor'.
NE, E, NE, small watering place W-bank, 'Glebe' either side of River.
NE, 'Foot br: No. 185 > 137'.
E-side road drainage tail into River.
'Bridge No. 186 > 138' at **Hornsey High St.**
'Foot bridge' No. 187' stroked through, N-side Hornsey High St.
N, NE, NW-side 'Mr John Carter', SE-side 'John Wilmott'.
SE-side 'Mr John Carter'.
'Bridge No. 139'.
NE, bend, 'Private bridge'.
'Bridge No. 189 > 140', E.
'Mr George Wrights Property' either side of River
SE-kink, E.
'Bridge No. 190 > 141'.
N-bank 2 watering places, then 'Susana Crofts?'
SE, 'Bridge No. 191 > 142'.

Large Plan 23 (1775-1809): Former Hornsey Station & Haringay House E-Loops
  FORMER E-Loop Hornsey Station
  'Bridge No. 191 > 142'.
     After Hornsey Village, shown on 1815 Hornsey Encl. map.
  E, SE, 'Mr Thomas Wilcocks Property' either side of River, N-bank watering place, SE.
  'Bridge No. 192 > 143', S, 'Mr Thos Wilcocks' either side of River.
  'Bridge No. 193 > 144', SW.
  'Hornsey Poor' either side of River.
  Sharp turn SE, 'An Arch drain under the River', SE.
  'Bridge No. 194, taken away'.
  'John Osborne's Land' either side of River.
  Sharp turn NE. 'Hilly field bridge No. 195, taken away'.
  'Mrs Cousin's Property' either side of River.
  FORMER E-Loop Harringay House
  Turning in a large semicircular N-loop at later site of **Haringay House**.
     Haringay House loop shown on 1815 Hornsey Encl. map.
  'Cast Iron Private Bridge'. Which shows that **cast iron was used at this date for bridges**.
  S, curving SE, 'Mrs Cousin's Property' either side of River.
  'Bridge No. 196, taken away', curving SE.

Large Plan 24 (1775-1809): Finsbury Park, & Stoke Newington
  SE, kink, 'Mrs Dawes Property' either side of River.
  'Harts bridge No. 197 > 145'.
     'End of boarded River Walk, John Nickolls Walksman'.
  Kink, SE, 'Robert and Thomas Saunders Property' either side of River.
  'Bridge No. 198 > 146', E, 'Robt and Thomas Saunders Property' either side of River.
  SW-side 'Hornsey Wood'.
  'Bridge No. 199 > 147' at **Green Lanes**, N-kink, E.
  'Bridge No. 200, taken away', 'Lady Abney's Property' either side of River, NE.
  'Ambrose Paines bridge a foot bridge No. 201, taken away', NE.
  'Lady Abney's Property' either side of River, S-side 'Ditch empties itself into the River'.
  S-bank ditch channel emptying into River, NE.
  FORMER E-Loop 'Stamford Hill'.
  N-bank narrow channel to 'formerly the Old Course of the River' a wide circular E-Loop almost reaching **Stamford Hill**. Mylne shows this heading more NE, than on the 1863-71 OS map which presumably should be more accurate.
  Two dotted lines curving SW, showing River as '**The Arch where the River runs under Ground**' in **fact a TUNNEL**.
  Short open stretch SW, SE-side showing a tiny narrow piece of where the 'Old Course of the River' formerly rejoined, SW.
  NW-side 'Ditch to keep off the Land Water', SE-side 'Ditch under the bank'.
  'An Iron pipe under the River', S.
  Kink at 'Bridge No. 202 > 148', SW.
  Pronounced NW-kink, small kink, SW, 'Lady Abney's Property/Land' either side of River.
  SE, 'Bridge No. 203, taken away', SE.
  'A pipe under the River', turns SW.
  SE-bank '**Stone Sluice** for Waste Water, taken away'.
  'Bridge No. 204, rebuilt partly at the expense of the Trust' at Green Lanes.
  NW-bank '**Water Mark**', '**The Dock**' a long finger aside road draining into River.
  FORMER W-Loop Highbury
  SW, 'Robert and Thomas Saunders Property' either side of River.
  'Bridge No. 205 > 149'.

Large Plan 25 (1775-1809): Highbury, & Clissold Park to Canonbury
    SE, then turning sharply SE.
    W-side 'The Old King's head Public House'.
    Pre-Mylne W-Loop Holloway (See later Vols. for sketch plans etc.)
    '**Weed Grate**', probable bridge then '**Stop Sluice Gate & House**' aka **Highbury Sluice**
        Part of Highbury Sluice shown on 1815 Hornsey Encl. map.
    'Mr Wilcocks Property' either side of River, then E-bank watering place.
    'Bridge No. 207 > 150', SE.
    River narrows at **Highbury Frame** (> **Highbury Bank**).
    SW-side 'Crown Land', SW-bank 'Company's Gate'.
    'a. The Part coloured Yellow is the Company's Property'.
    SW-bank 'A drain'.
    'c. A Stable & Yard, Copyhold, held of the Manor of Brownswood'.
    SW-bank 'Manor Post'.
    Not mentioned but clearly shown on plan, a drain under the River.
    'b. The Part coloured Green Mr Dawes Property', SE.
        Sketch to Left of Highbury Bank (after **Frame replaced by Embankment**) showing NE-side
            'Pond' with drain from road, 'Bridge No. 151' and 'Sewer under River'.
    'John Dawes Esqr.' either side of River.
    'Bridge No. 208, taken away', turning NE.
    S-side 'Mrs Mezier's Land', E.
    'Bridge No. 209, rebuilt partly at the expence of the Trust' at **Green Lanes**.
    Ditches on N & S-banks draining into River.
    'Bridge No. 210, taken away'.
    '**Sluice House, taken away**'.
        FORMER E-Loop Clissold Park (Part Remaining Today)
        Clissold Park section shown on 1815 Hornsey Encl. map.
    NE, 'Rob.t and Tho.s Saunders Land/Property' either side of River.
    Turning E, then SE.
    NE-bank '**Pipe** to serve a Canal in the Garden'.
    NE-side 'Mrs Conaway and Mr Geo. Green's Property' then old 'Newington Church'.
    Turns SW, '**New Cistern and main to serve part of Stoke Newington**'.
    SW down W-side of Church Lane, at 'Paradise Row'.
    SE-bank 'a., b., c., d., e. & f: **Pipes** out of the River to serve the Houses in Paradise Row'.
    SE-side house of 'Walker Esqr' at f.
    At sharp turn SE two watering places.
    'Bridge No. 211 > 152' at today's Church Lane, turning sharply S at today's **Aden Terrace**.
    'Pulteny Esqrs. Land' either side of River.
    'Bridge No. 212 > 153'.
    'Drain under the River'.
    'Bridge No. 213, rebuilt as above' (at **Green Lanes**) probably meaning partly at expence of Trust.
    S, E-kink with **pencilled straightening**.
    'Bridge No. 214 > 154'.
    E-bank watering place.
    E-bank '**Newington green Cistern One Main**'.
    'Mrs Mezier's Property' either side of River.
    E-bank just before bridge a watering place.
    'Bridge No. 215 > 155', then E-side '**Newington Green**'.
    W-bank inlet just after bridge.
    S, then E-kink, S, SW.
        FORMER W-Loop St Pauls Road
    NW-side 'Land ditch', bend SW.
    SE-bank 2-trees called '**The two Sisters**'.

Large Plan 26 (1775-1809): Canonbury to Essex Road
    SW, turning sharply SE, 'A 16 in. Iron pipe under the River', E.
    'Bridge No. 217 [**jump in bridge Nos.**], taken away', River then slightly widens at '**The Gap**', SE.
    'Mrs Mezier' either side of River.
    'Bridge No. 218 > 156' at 'Green Lane' > **St Pauls Road**, joined by 'Road to Hackney' > **Balls Pond Road**, with 'Toll Gate'.
    'Bridge No. 219 > 157'.
    'Earl of Northampton' either side of River.
    SW, E-side watering place, SW, E-side watering place.
    NW-side 'Drain empties into River' with finger into River.
    'Bridge No. 220 > 158' probably at **Willow Bridge Road**.
    SW, E-side watering place.
    NW-side 'A Spring runs into the River' at **pronounced NW-kink still there today**, SW.
        FORMER Small W-Loop 'Horse Shoe Point'.
        Pencilled lines show it bypassed.
        'A pipe under the bridge, and over the River, removed to a.'
        SW, 'a.', then very sharp turn E at 'Horse Shoe Point'.
        '**Grate to Stop the Weeds**, removed to A.'
    SE, 'Bridge No. 221 > 159'.
    '**Weed Grate, A**'.
        E-bank 'A Main'.
    '**Green Man Cistern**'.
        E-bank 'A Main'.
    W-side 'Pleasant Row' then E-side 'Asty's buildings'.
                          E-side '**Thatched House**' aside Essex Road.
    Sluice House over River coloured orange.
    River then dotted down Essex Road '**Course of the River under ground**' (Essex Road).
    W-side 'Stone 7 feet'.
    W-side 'Stone'.
    W-side 'Stone 8 feet'.
    W-side 'Stone 9 feet'.
    W-side 'Stone 6 feet'.
    Turning into **N-end of Colebrook Row**, with E-side 'Stone 6 feet'.
    Just South of St Peters Street then **again an open River**, SE, SW down Colebrook Row.
    Bridge shown but not numbered, probably at today's **Camden Walk**.

Large Plan 27 (1775-1809): Colebrook Row to New River Head
    S, Bridge shown but **not numbered**, possibly at end of today's Charlton Place.
                            E-side strip of land 'The Company's Freehold 0 : 1 : 19, 671 Feet'.
    W-side 'Eliz: Pullen', E-side 'Jerod Noel Edwards Esqr'.
    'Bridge No. 160' (**two previous bridges not numbered**).
    'Brick drain under the River'.
    W-side **Oval pond with dotted line to River**.   E-side 'Sam: Pullen'.
    W-side smaller **Oval pond with dotted line to River**, E-side tiny pond, 'S$^{l.}$ Pullen' either side of River, SW, bends S.
    Beneath City Road (opened 1761).
                E-bank '**Dalby's Cistern**' from which curves a '12 in. Iron Main' down City Road.
    Beneath Goswell Road.
    S down **Owens Row**, E-bank watering place.
    SW **beneath St John Street**.
    S, E-bank outlet & 'Sluice' into **St John Street 'Reservoir'**.
        With S-side dotted lines to small circular '**Cistern**' into '**19 in. Iron Main**'.
    W-side '**Sadlers Wells**' theatre.

SW, 'Bridge No. 161' probably at today's **Arlington Way**.
           E-side 'S^r· **H. Middleton's head Alehouse**'.
NW-bank sluice into the 'Out Head'.
           E-side '**Islington Spaw or Tunbridge Wells**'.
E-bank watering place with square.
Un-numbered bridge.
River into '**Round Pond**'.
 Round Pond with NE, W & SW-sides 'Out Head' aka **Outer Pond**.
 Outlet channel from Outer Pond in SW-corner with SE watering place at 'Mill Yard', and underground pipe to small round pond in centre of road, with NW 'Brick arch' to another small pond, from which a '24 in. Iron Main heads W to another small pond'.
 NW-side of outlet channel, **FORMER Windmill** & probable **Horse Engine house**, and **Engine House**.
 SE-side probable **Cistern House** although untitled.
 S-side of Round Pond, New River Head house, S of which is 'Pipe Yard'.
Beware of some of the dates on prints depicting New River Head, because **many of the earlier prints were reissued at later dates as copies**.

Around New River Head:
 N-side of NRH from N to S:
  'Pennies Folly', 'Foot way to **White Conduit House**', '**Dobney's**', 'Angel Inn'.
  'New Road', 'One Mile from the Standard in Moorgate'.
  S-side New Road a 'Pond', and another pond.
  Field '0 : 1 : 4'.
  '**Cow Layer**, 0 : 3 : 27' with pond, '**Goose Yard**, 1 : 0 : 10'.
  '**Upper Pond**, 1 : 2 : 0', with N-side circular pond/fountain, S-corner '16 in. Iron Main'; '**Smock Field**, 2 : 0 : 18'.
  'Tent Field, 7 : 1 : 4', '**Iron Main from Fire Engine to Upper Pond**', '**Butchers Mantles**, 8 : 1 : 39', '**Sadlers Wells Field**, 4 : 3 : 33'.
 W-side of NRH from N to S:
  '**Hanging Field**, 9 : 3 : 10', '**Mill Field**, 3 : 3 : 3'.
  '12 in. Iron Main', very tiny semicircular pond, larger pond, '24 in. Iron Main', small pond etc.
  'Tyle Kiln'.
  '**Bagnigge Wells**', 'Bull in the Pound'.
 SE-side of NRH from N to S:
  'Pipe Yard', 'Kings Arms & Coach & Horses'.
  '**Merlin's Cave**' an alehouse, **Waterhouse Field**, 8 : 2 : 12', 'Laystall', 'St John Street Turnpike'.
  '**Northampton Field**, 15 : 2 : 25', '**Old London Spaw**', '**Low Pond**' fed from a stream from NE without any source shown, '**Cattle Field**, 7 : 3 : 35'.
   '**Low Pond**': Small rectangular pond with inlet on NE-corner, the source stream down its SE-side with a short NW-branch probably to a Cistern House, the SE-branch with a N-side inlet, then SW, shown ending at a road.
  'Briants Row', field '0 : 2 : 15'.
  'The Vineyard'.
  'Small Pox Hospital'.
  '**Cold Bath Fields**'.

3.2 MYLNE'S 1775-1809 PLANS: Following are copies of the 1775-1809 Mylne plans, interspersed with other historical notes, and associated plans, prints etc. to c.1850.

Probably the First Accurate Number of River Bridges: Start with the 1775-1809 Mylne plans, before this the details are most unreliable, except if they can be found in the NRC records themselves and can be accurately dated.

Having said this even Robert Mylne's plans needed further study for accurate bridge numbers, since he **leaves out some private bridges** in his numbering system, and **often leaves gaps**.

Note that road bridges were normally far narrower than the width of the road. The then far lower density of traffic was one-way across road bridges, which were mainly built to take farm carts or wagons. Originally only needing to span 10ft., but as the River was widened over the years to today's 25ft. they were gradually widened. Narrow with open railings, they had a steep gradient either side. Many c.1881 were considered dangerous to children, so the sides were boarded up, and additional modern safer footbridges were also added alongside ('Southgate's Bridges' by Tom Mason, newspaper cutting 5/12/1947, ELSC&A).

1775-1809 Mylne Survey records a **Drawbridge** on the New River N of College Road, Cheshunt.
1775-1809 also recording a **cast-iron** private bridge on the River near Haringay House, when **most of the earliest cast-iron NRC bridges are c.1820-30**.
1870 Painting: Shows an occupation **swing-bridge** on the new course of the New River before Myddelton Road ('Donated by C. Yardley of Wood Green, 1938', No. 38 or 'ldbcm:inv:42', BCMA).

Before we start on our journey south.
Augmenting Supply: c.1800 as you will note from the 1775-1809 plans, at this time picking up any suitable water from **adjoining streams or surface water road drains** on the way to augment the New River. Compared to other London water companies New River water thought mainly purer, but they also had their critics.

Local Ponds (Some Supplied by the New River): Note also that in days of yore there was a multitude of local ponds, essential for watering vegetable gardens, cattle & horses.

Note also that on the way to London, **pipes from the River supplied water to the local wealthy residents & landowners**, probably also why they needed to augment the supply.

1811 (New River) Described: 'The New River, which has been noticed by topographers at almost every village that it visits in its meandering course, …' ((Nelson) 14D4, p160).

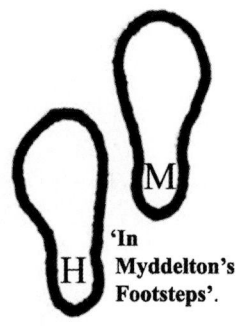

Hold on tight as we take a historical journey down the New River, **treading in the footsteps of Sir Hugh Myddelton**. Not to dwell in the past, but for a short while to savour its many bygone delights.

'In Myddelton's Footsteps'.

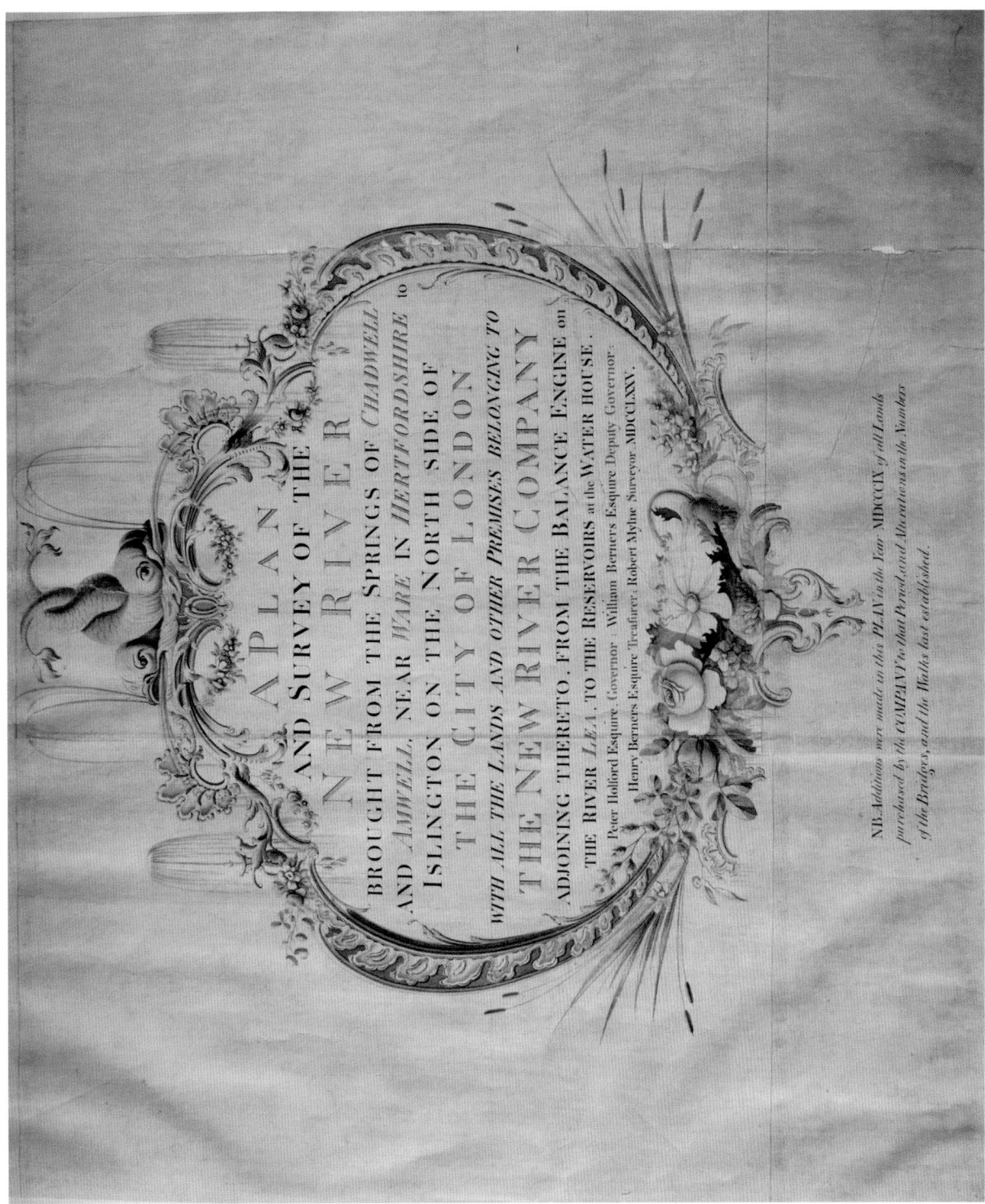

Front sheet of Robert Mylne's (New River Company Surveyor, aka Engineer 1771-1810), 1775-1809 coloured plans of the New River from the Balance Gauge (Hertford-Ware) to New River Head, Islington.
  'N.B. Additions were made in this Plan in the Year MDCCCIX [1809] of all Lands purchased by the Company to that Period, and Alterations in the Numbers of the Bridges, and the Walks last established'.
The earliest known accurate plans covering the whole length of the New River (TW, Abbey Mills Archive; MFK photo).

158

Robert Mylne 1775-1809 **New River Plan 2, to AMWELL HILL,** Herts. (TW Archive; MFK photo & join).

Robert Mylne 1775-1809 **New River Plan 1, WARE,** Herts. (TW Archive; MFK photo).

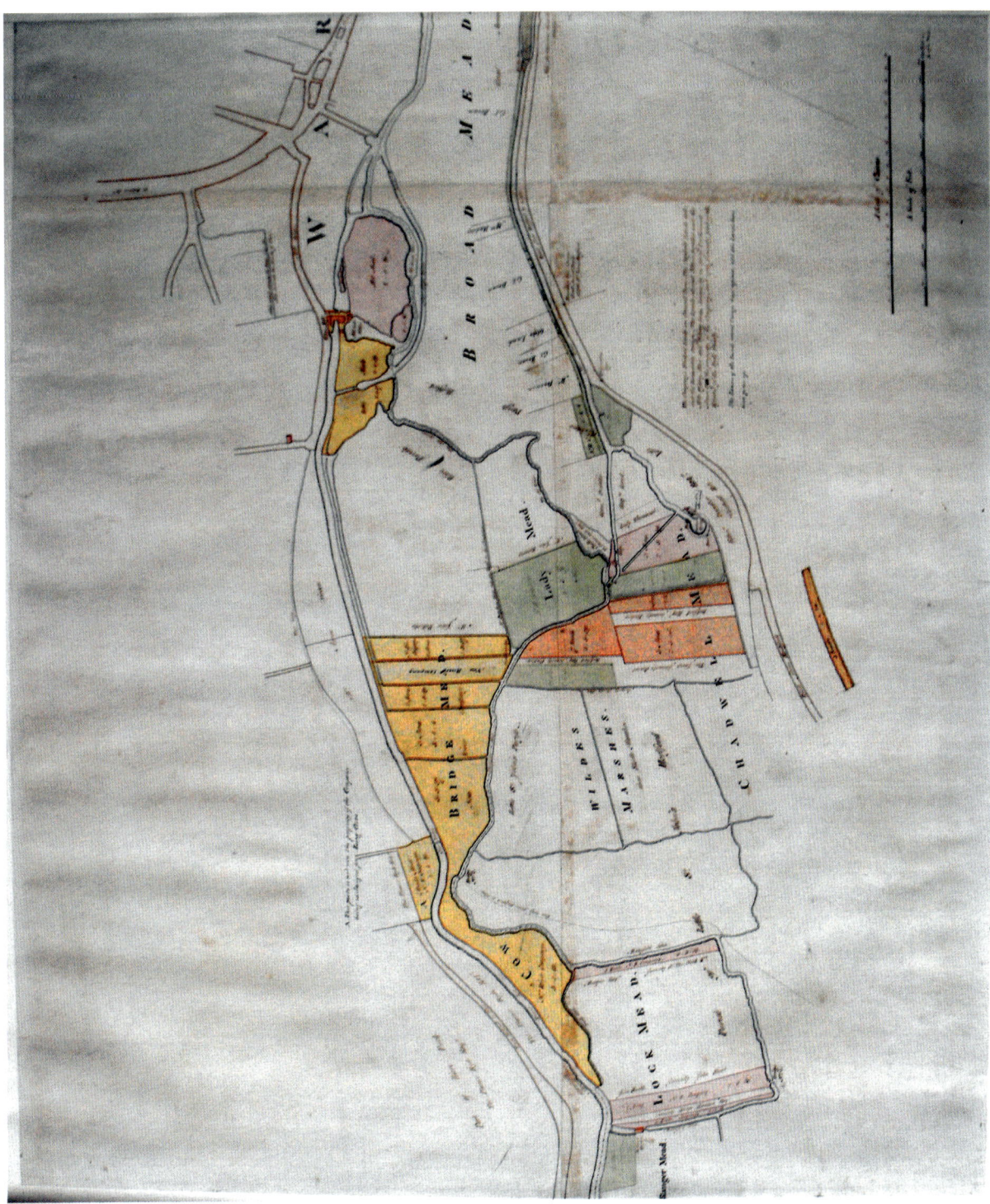

1775-1809 Robert Mylne **Plan 1: New River, Balance Engine to Broadmead** (TW Archive; MFK photo).

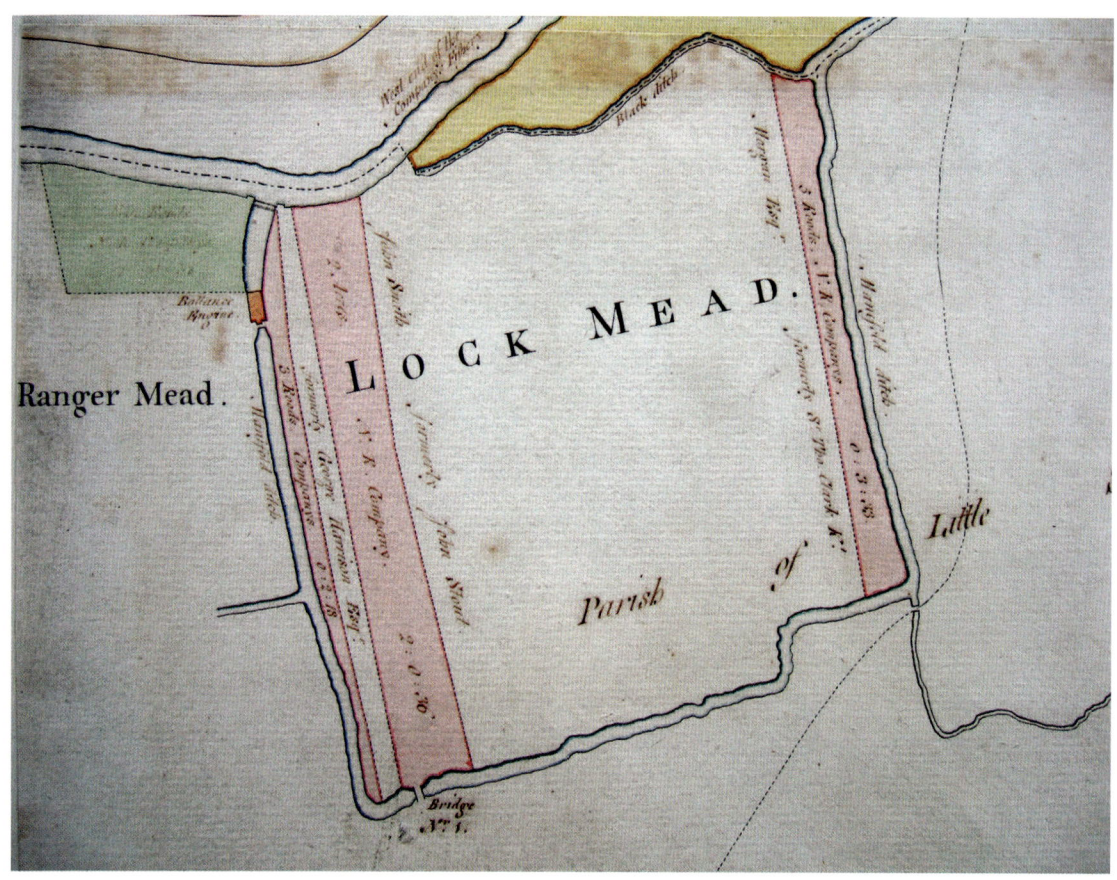

Part of 1775-1809 Plan 1 (TW Archive; MFK photos).
ABOVE: Lock Mead. **BELOW:** Cow Bridge Mead.

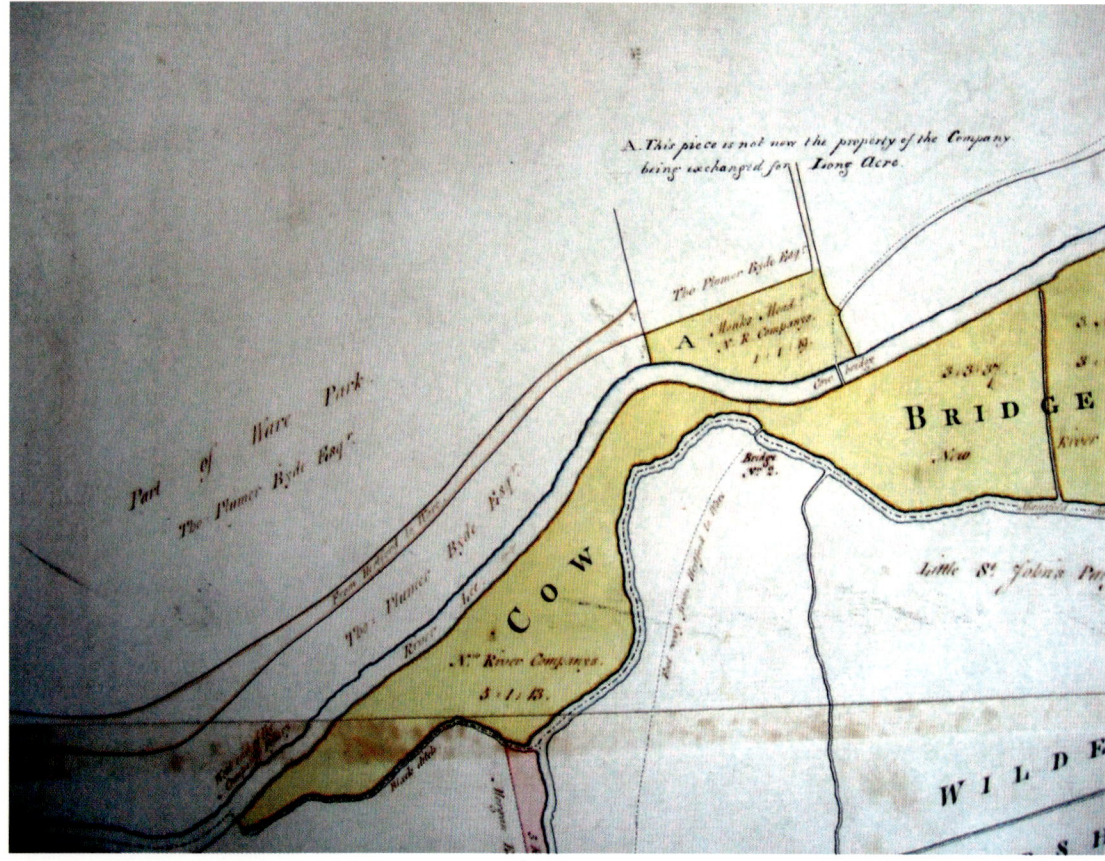

1733 Balance Engine & Separately Located Timber Gauge & Trough

Constructed by NRC Engineer Henry Mill. All previous histories do not clarify that they are in two separate locations as follows:

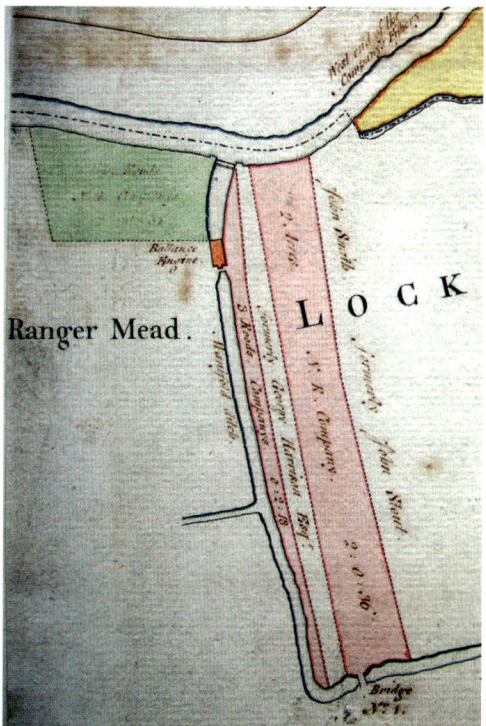

1. **Balance Engine**, at beginning of Manifold Ditch.

2. **Separate Timber Gauge/Trough**, located SE of White House Sluice (TW Arch.; MFK photos).

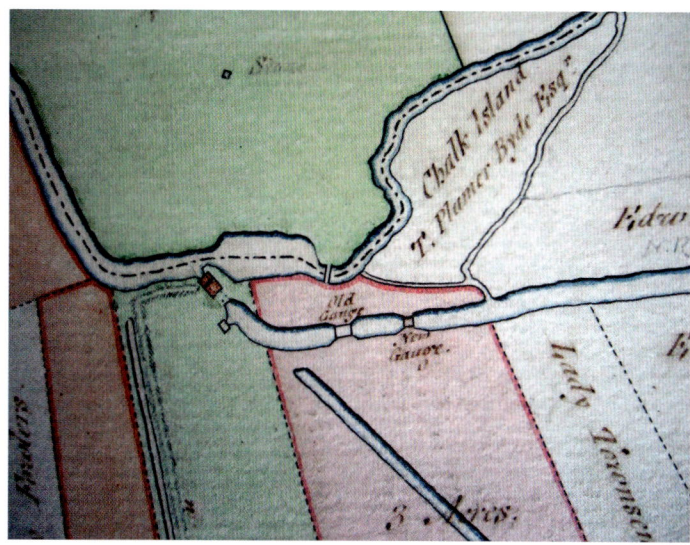

For descriptions both legally mentioned soon after in 1739 Act.

Legally Effective from 24 June 1739 (River Lee Act, 12/13 Geo. II, c.32), the Manifold Ditch extending the length of the new river.

p591 'Anno duodecimo, George II Regis, An Act for ascertaining, preserving, and improving the Navigation of the River Lee', then for brevity continued from p594 '… it shall and may be lawful to and for the said Governor and Company of the New River, at all times for ever hereafter, to have, receive, and take from and out of the said River Lee into the said New River, and to hold, use, and enjoy a **quantity or body of water constantly to issue from the said River Lee, at or near the mouth or opening of Manifold Ditch aforesaid, through the Balance Engine there lately erected** by the said Governor and Company, and to pass and run along and through the said Manifold Ditch, to the **ancient Turnpike or Sluice** of the said Governor and Company, **now standing cross the same ditch, near a small piece of land called Chalk Island**, and from the said ancient turnpike or sluice **in and along a cut or trench made from thence into the said New River, through the present Timber Gauge or Trough, there lately placed by the said Company;** … [then described at its separate location, see later].

p595 '… and at all times hereafter, as need or occasion shall require, maintain and keep open the mouth of the said Manifold Ditch, on the side of the said River Lee, and remove all soil lying before or about the same, and cleanse, scour and maintain the watercourse through the said ditch, for conveying the said water to the said New River; they making satisfaction to the owners or occupiers of the lands adjoining thereunto, for all damages which shall be done thereby, in manner as herein after is mentioned; and shall and may for ever hereafter maintain and support the said Balance-engine, or device, erected near the said mouth or opening of the said ditch next to the said River Lee, …'. p596 'that it shall and may be lawful to and for the said Governor and Company to erect, build, and continue or cause to be erected, built, and continued, over or upon the Balance-engine, or device, for the time being, standing at or near the mouth of the said Manifold Ditch, **any building or covering requisite for the preservation of the same**, or otherwise; and also to erect, build, and continue, or cause to be erected, built, and continued near or adjoining to such Balance-engine, or device, **a dwelling house or habitation for one or more servant or servants**, officer or officers of the said Governor and Company, who shall from time to time be employed to take care of such Balance-engine, or device, and buildings thereunto belonging; the said

Governor and Company making satisfaction to the owners or occupiers of the soil in such place or places whereon such dwelling house or buildings shall be erected and built, in manner as is herein after also mentioned. ... , and from time to time to **repair and amend the same; ... have free entry and passage with their men, horses, carts**, or other carriages, by, over, or through any ground or land, in places, and at times meet or convenient to and from such Balance-engine or device, dwelling house, or habitation, and buildings, gauge or trough, turnpikes, sluices or tumbling bays, or to do or perform any thing necessary or requisite for the making, building, erecting, repairing, maintaining, preserving, or amending the same, or any part thereof, they the said Governor and Company making satisfaction for all such damages as shall be done thereby; ...' p597 '**to be ascertained by the trustees nominated and appointed**, or to be nominated and appointed by or in pursuance of this Act, or any Ten or more of them, in case the parties cannot agree. ... to see and inspect the aforesaid Balance-engine or device, gauge or trough, turnpike or tumbling bay, and the several conditions and repairs thereof, to the end that no more water shall or may be taken out of the said River Lee, or Manifold Ditch, through the aforesaid gauge or trough. ... within six months after notice shall be given in writing to them, or to any of their servants employed to look after the same, of such defects or wants of repairs, shall from time to time well and sufficiently make good such defects, and repair the same, ...; and in **default thereof the said trustees, or any ten of them, shall and may do, or cause the same to be done, and be paid by the said Company the reasonable charges thereof**; ... **Manifold Ditch, and the water running through the same to the said New River, shall for ever hereafter be deemed to be a part of the said New River** ...' p598 'their respective rights of passing as usual through or over the same Ditch at the **usual ford**, ... **no new mill, lock, or weir, shall hereafter be erected** on the said River Lee, or any branch thereof, between the mouth of Manifold Ditch and Ware-mills, or on the said Manifold Ditch. ... no person or persons shall at any time or times cast or put into the said ... Manifold Ditch, or the said cut between same, and the said New River, or into the New River .... **any filth, rubbish, soil, dead dogs, dead cats, dead carcasses, carrion, or other unwholesome thing; or wash or clean therein any wool, hemp, flax, or other noisome thing; nor hinder, let, stop, draw off, turn, or divert the said water**, or the current or passage thereof, by any device, art, contrivance, or means whatsoever, ... ; **nor do any damage, nuisance, or annoyance** to the said lock or cistern, weir or jetty, gauge or trough, turnpikes or tumbling bays, or other buildings or erections aforesaid, or to the said watercourse or ditch, or to the said cut between the same and the New River, or to the said New River, ...'

'Water to be supplied from Ware Mills for cleansing the town of Ware' (p598 Summary column).
'New River Company empowered to prosecute & c.' (p599 Summary column).
'Trustees nominated' and names listed (p599 Summary column).
'Trustees when and where to meet' (p600 Summary column).
'If there not to be Ten at any meeting, the same to be adjourned till that day 4 weeks' (p600 Summary column).
'... the several sums of **two thousand five hundred pounds**, and **seven hundred and fifty pounds** .... On the nine and twentieth day of September 1739; and yearly and every year for ever ..., the several **yearly sums of £300, and £50** ..., by two equal half-yearly payments, ...'
'Sums to be paid by the New River Company, to such persons as the Trustees shall appoint' (p601 Summary column).
'The same, on non-payment, recoverable by distress' (p601 Summary column).
'Application thereof' (p601 Summary column).
'... the sum of one thousand pounds, part of the said £2,500 shall be paid to George Hathaway, John Docwra, Anthony Fage, Humphrey Ives, Thomas Fletcher, Ambrose Proctor, and Wayte Hampson, ...' (p602).
'Vacancies of Trustees how to be filled up' (p603 Summary column).
'Trustees empowered to sue out Commissioners of Sewers' (p604 Summary column).
'Penalty on vessels carrying nets & c. for destroying fish' (p604 Summary column).
'Saving to all persons their respective rights' (p604 Summary column).
'Public Act' (p605 Summary column).
'Limitation of Actions' to be commenced within twelve Calendar months (p605 Summary column).
'General Issue' (p605 Summary column).
'Full Costs' (p606 Summary column, last page). 'Finis' ((Typeset copy of Act pp590-606) Acc. 2558/NR13/188, LMA; (Typed sheet 'AJ, Lee Abstraction') 8A1, 2-8 has first part).

1770 Balance Engine Rebuilt & Covered.

The Old Gauge part (separate from the Balance Engine) replaced by the 1776 'New Gauge' aka Marble Gauge.

See appropriate pages for illustrations of the Balance House; and the actual Balance Engine (Acc/2423/P/0681, LMA; 'Plan & Section of Balance Engine' & 'Plan & Section of … Boat', 12G, Nos. 1 & 2 **both MISSING**, TW Abbey Mills Archive).

Post-1830 plan calls the Balance House the 'Red House' (Herts. Boro. Recs. Vol. 43, D/Ex827/P1, HALS). 1855 Act under section 21, the **old balance engine & marble gauge to be replaced by another gauge (AGAIN called the New Gauge)** between Hertford & Ware, permitting the NRC to draw off the first 22½ m.g.d. (9, p156 quote; 7, p8/9).
In 1856 William Chadwell Mylne constructing the official 'New Gauge', limiting 22½ m.g.d. to be drawn from the River Lee at the intake, Hertford, given official Ordnance approval 1857 (8A, p35).
The unused Balance Engine House sadly bombed in WW2 thus **(SITE OF)**.

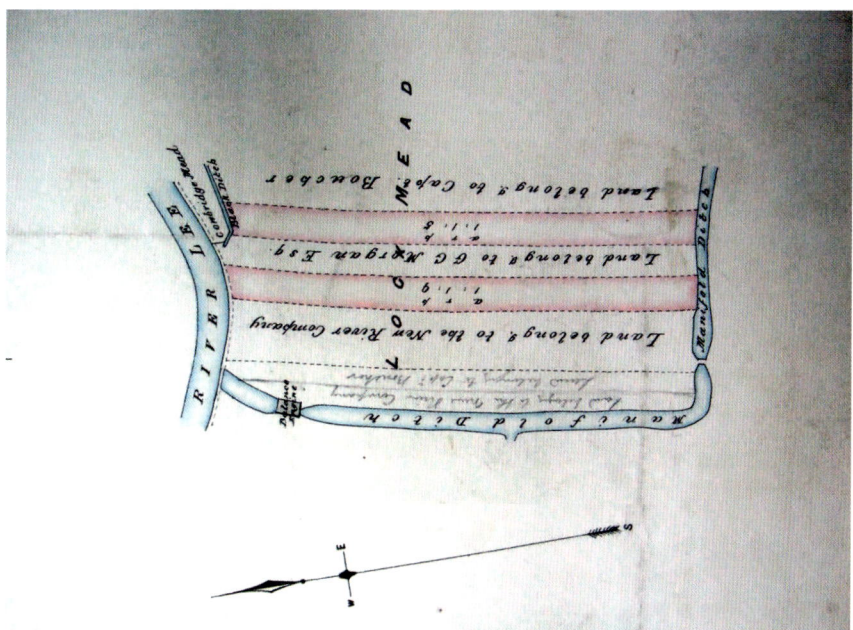

Prob. early-1800s (Undated) NRC Plan: **2-pieces of Lammas Land Lockmead** (TW Archive; MFK photo).

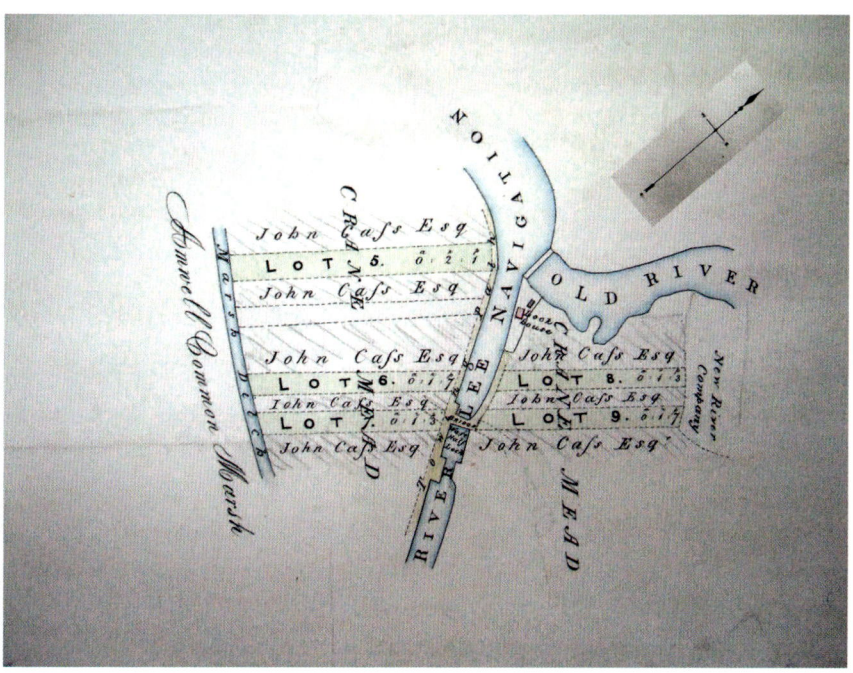

31 May 1842 Auction: **NRC purchase of 5-pieces of Land in Crane Mead**, Amwell from the Cobhams (TW Archive; MFK photo & added approx. N). See page 208 for location.

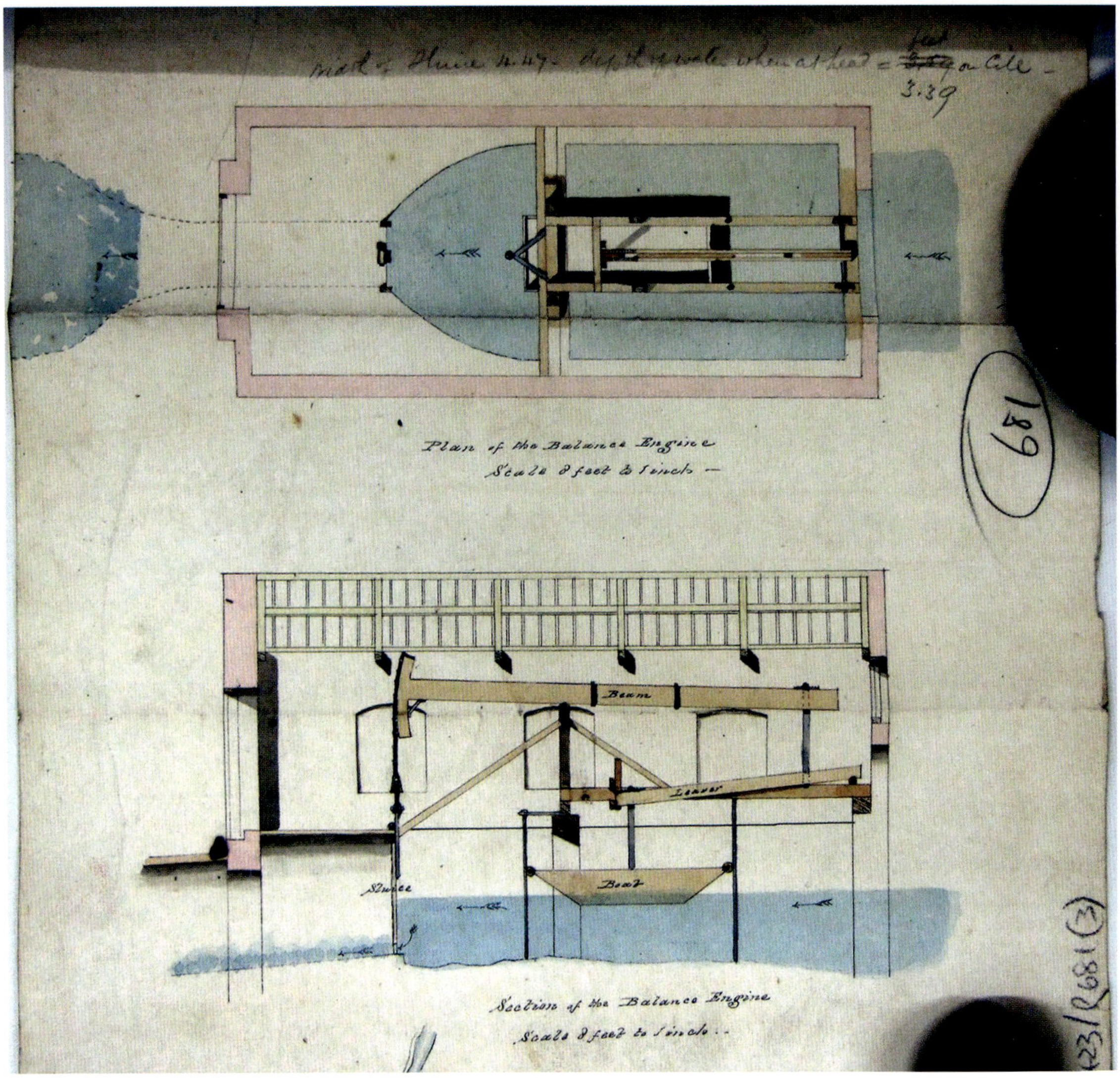

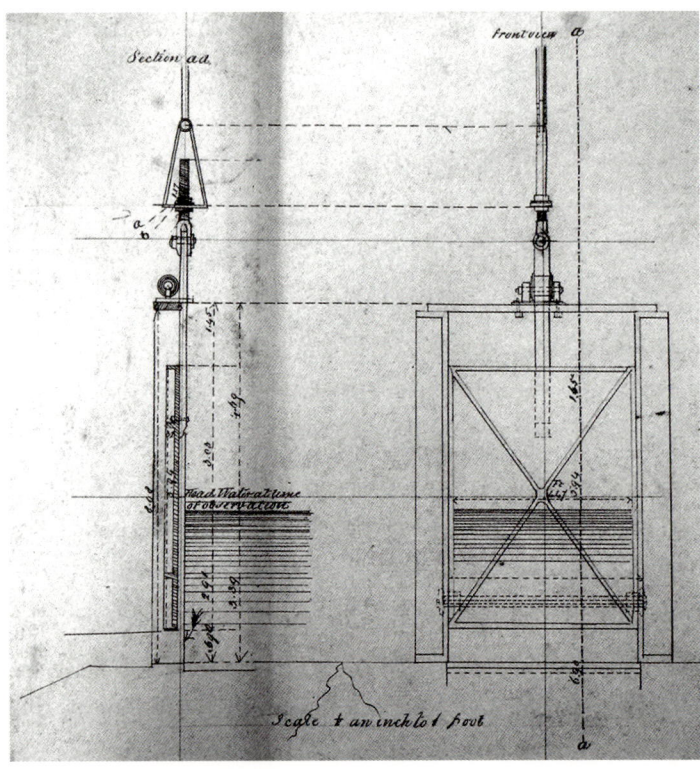

ABOVE (May 1830): Balance Engine originally constructed 1733 by Henry Mill (NRC Surveyor), made statutary by 1739 Act. Rebuilt and covered 1770 by Henry Mill & Robert Mylne. Penciled text at top, 'Width of Sluice 4.47, depth of water when at head = 3.39 feet'. Replaced 1857 by 'New Gauge', the Balance House sadly bombed in WW2 (Acc/2423/P/0681(3), LMA; MFK photo). **EXCLUSIVE, probably the first time ever that a diagram of the Balance Engine has been published**.

BELOW (c.1854): Details and dimensions of the Sluice Gate of the above Balance Engine (Acc/2423/P/0681(1), LMA; MFK photo).

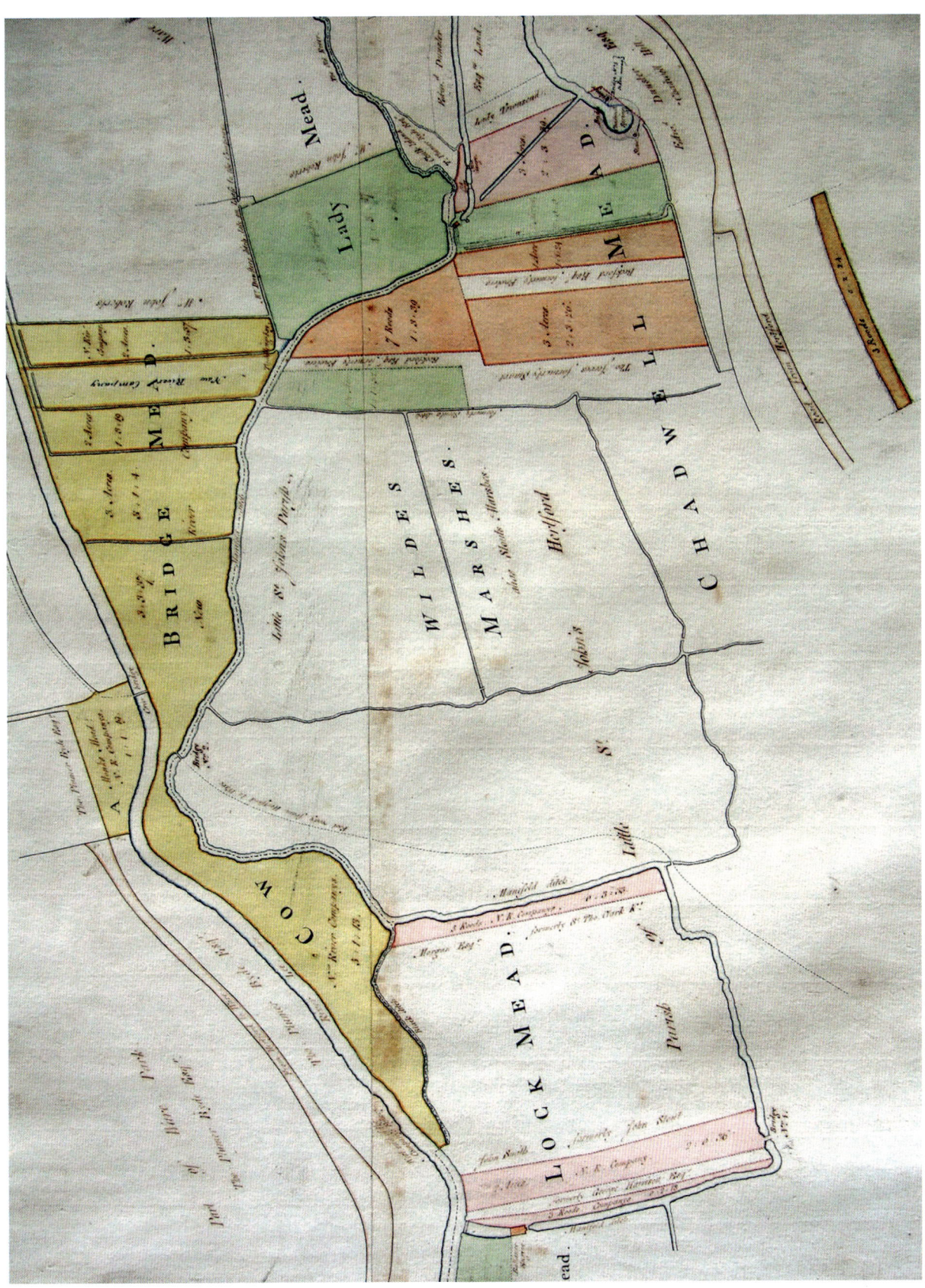

1775-1809 Plan 1: **Wildes Marshes** (TW Archive; MFK photo).

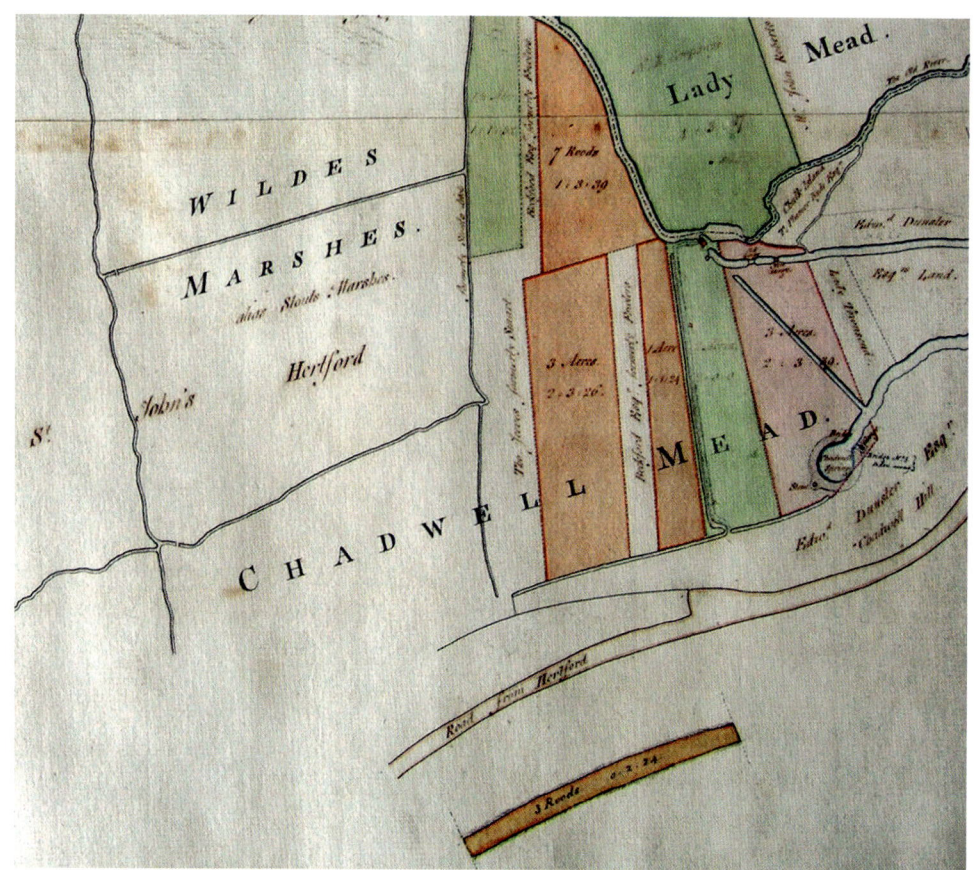

1775-1809 Plan 1. **ABOVE:** Chadwell Mead. **BELOW:** Wildes Marshes (TW Archive; MFK photos).

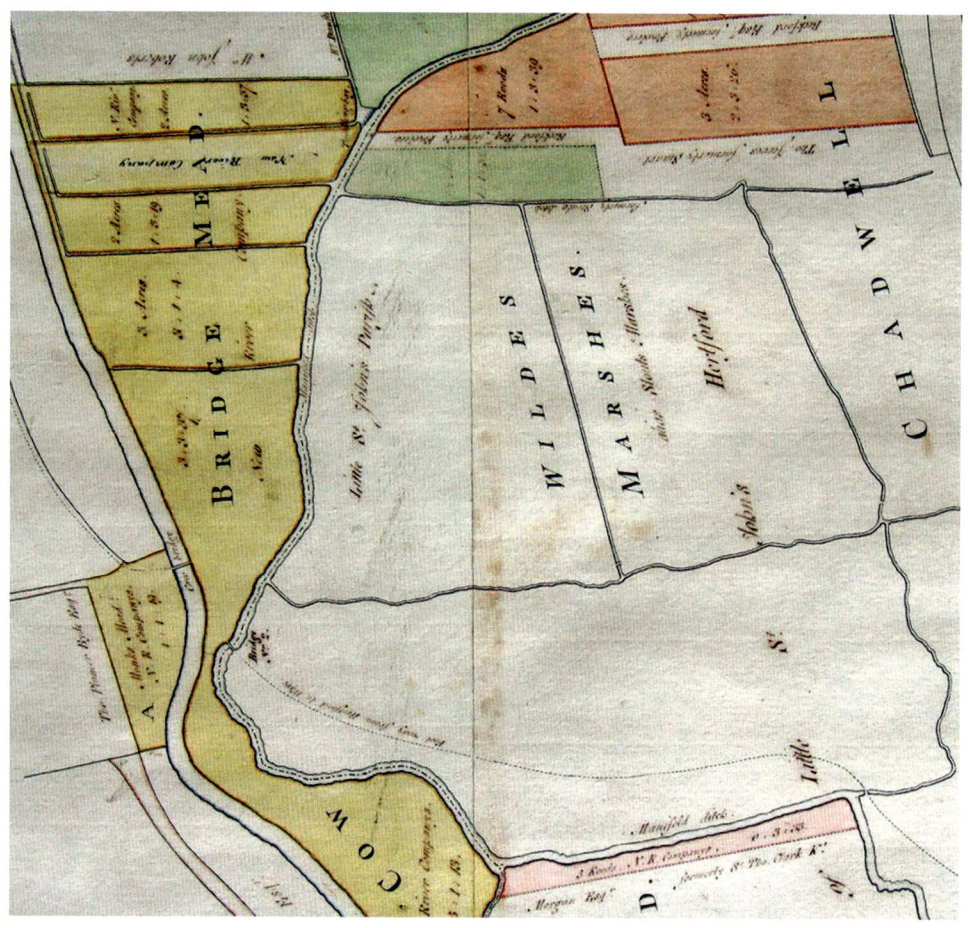

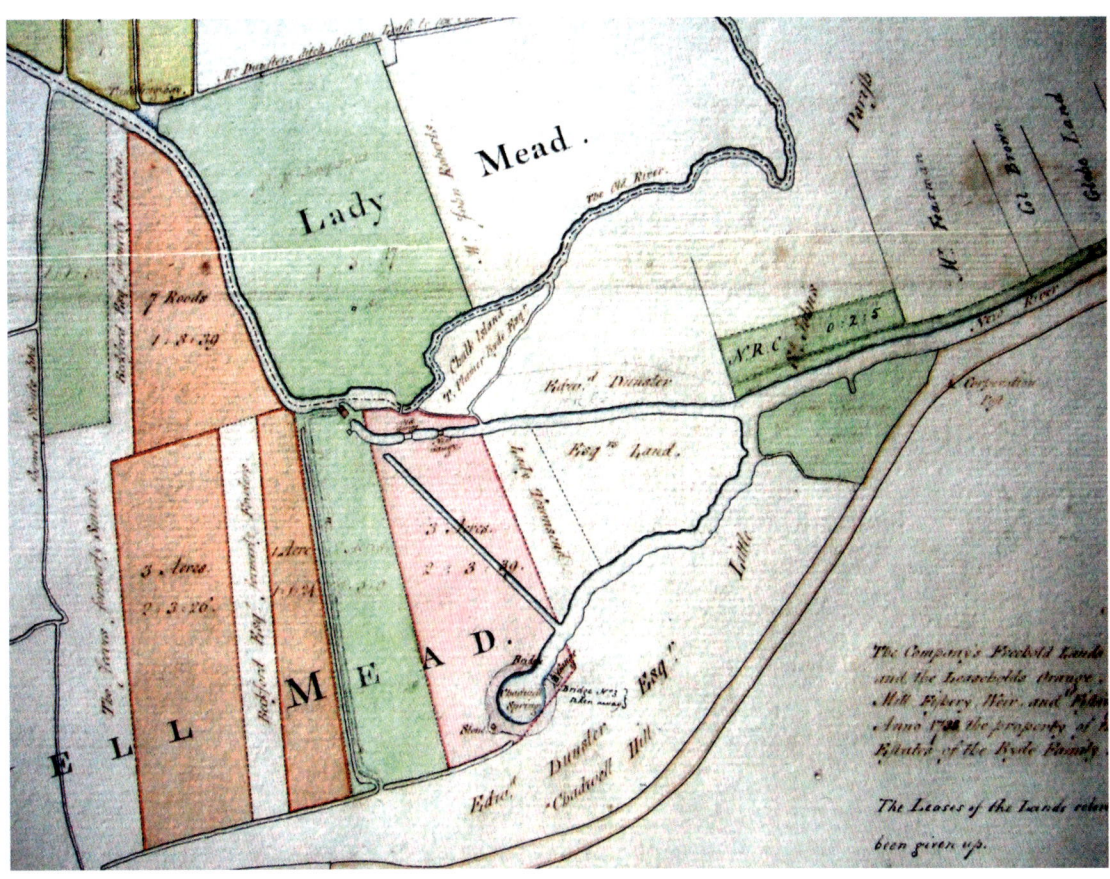

1775-1809 Plan 1. **ABOVE:** Chadwell Spring. **BELOW:** LARGER (TW Archive; MFK photos).

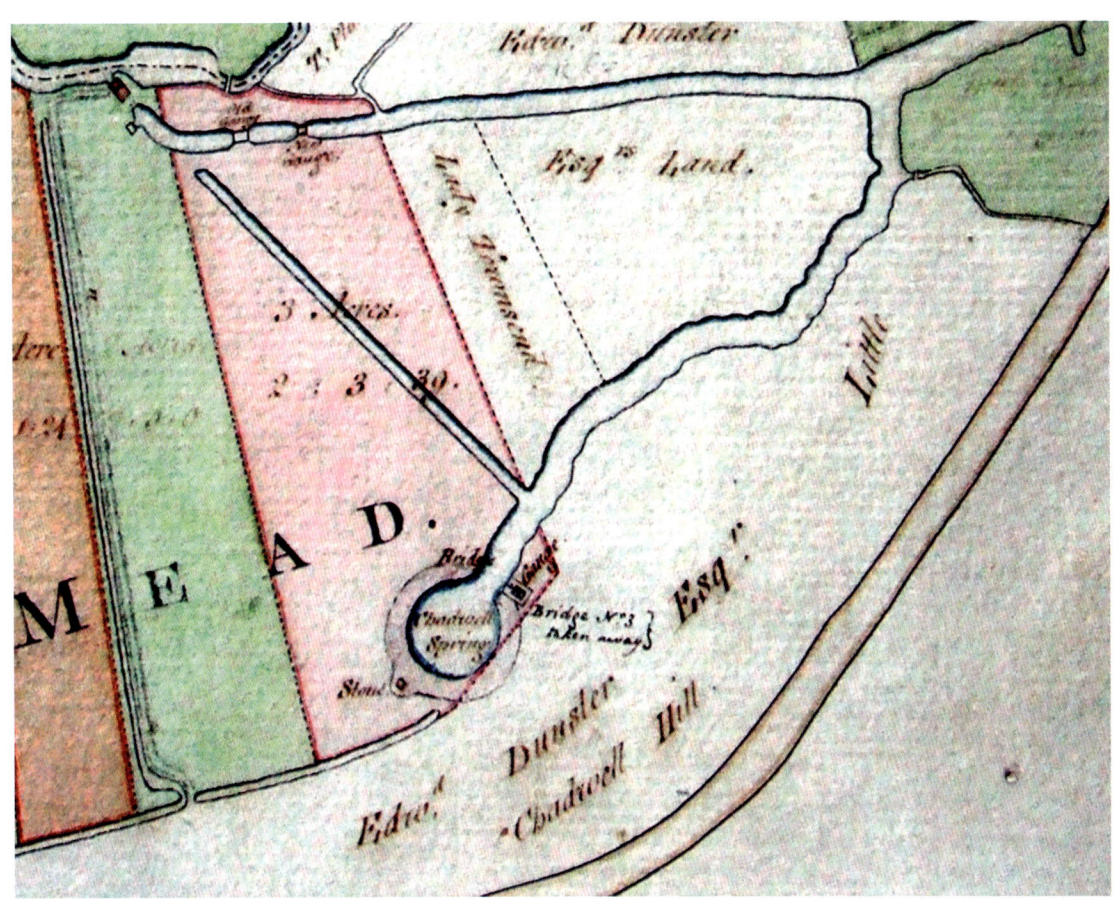

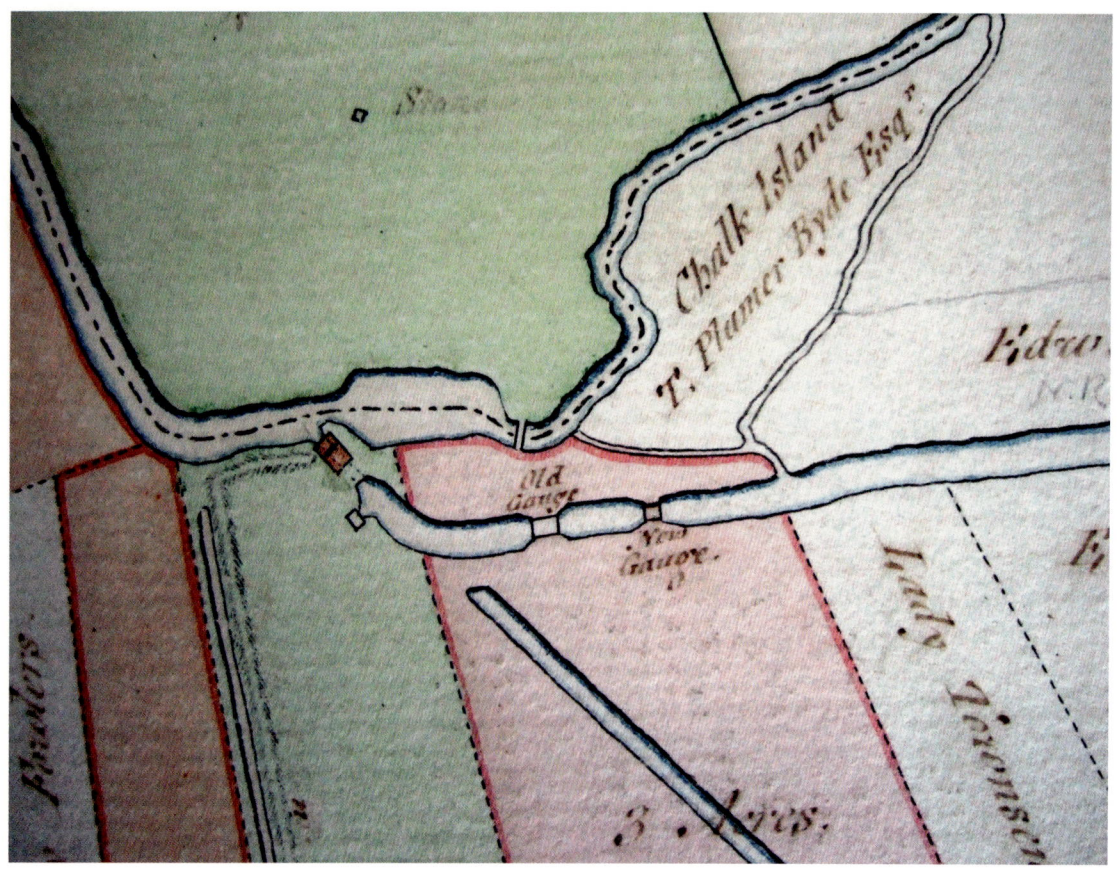

1775-1809 Plan 1 (TW Archive; MFK photos).
ABOVE: 'Stone' shown feint N of 1733 Old Gauge (Timber Gauge) & 1773-6 New Gauge (aka Marble Gauge). **BELOW:** Broad Mead.

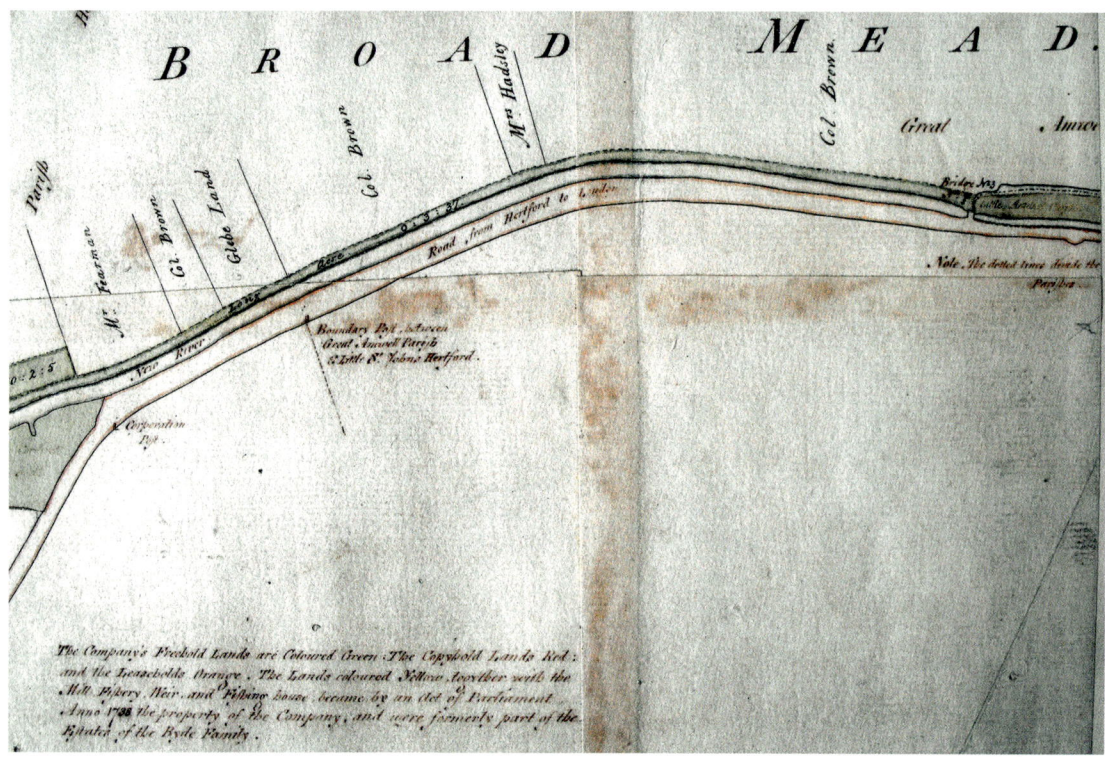

Old Gauge & New Gauge (aka Marble Gauge)

1. 1733 - 1776 'Timber Gauge or Trough' (6ft. wide by 2ft. deep by 14ft. long) > 'Old Gauge' (SITE OF): Described soon after its erection in 1739 Act as follows.

1739 Act (Lee Navigation): p594-5 'which gauge or trough is of the **clear dimensions within the same, of six feet in width or breadth, two feet in depth, and fourteen feet in length**, and is to be continued of the same and no greater dimensions for ever hereafter in **Brick, Wood, or Stone**, as the said Governor and Company shall think most proper and useful, between the **Brick Arch** standing near the said turnpike and the said New River, and not be placed perpendicularly higher or lower than the present gauge now is, to the intent that the said Governor and Company shall for ever hereafter be supplied with a constant quantity or body of water of the dimensions aforesaid, and no more, to run and pass from the said River Lee into the said New River in a natural course, and **without any pen at the said Gauge or Trough**; and that it shall not be lawful to or for the said Governor and Company, at any time or times hereafter, to take any more, or other, or greater quantity of water than as aforesaid, out of and from the said River Lee or Manifold Ditch aforesaid, between the towns of Hertford and Ware, by or through any other passage, ditch, or cut, or in any other manner than as in this Act is mentioned. And to prevent any greater quantity of water than as aforesaid, at any time or times, passing from the said River Lee, through the said gauge or trough, into the said new River; be it further enacted by the authority aforesaid, that the said Governor and Company shall at **their own costs and charges, forever hereafter, maintain the turnpike or tumbling-bay** now fixed and standing cross Manifold Ditch **just below the mouth of the said new Cut** leading from thence to the New River, and all other tumbling-bays or turnpikes by the said Governor and Company hereafter to be erected, of the same height and breadth, and no higher or narrower than the present turnpike now is (which is 14 feet wide) and so low as to keep or reduce the head of water flowing down the said ditch, to be upon a level with, and not higher than the top or uppermost part of the said gauge or trough, in the said cut, and the **two adjacent capped stones placed as Standards, the one near the said brick arch, and the other near Chadwell Spring**, now are; so that **all superfluous water, more than can with a natural current pass through the said gauge or trough, may run over the said Tumbling-bay or bays, and fall again through the present channel, below the said ancient Turnpike into the said River Lee**' ((Typeset copy of Act pp590-606) 15M, Acc. 2558/NR13/188).
   Note that it mentions two capstones, one at White House Sluice (Brick Arch), and one at Chadwell Spring.

For the location of the former Old Gauge, **see Overlay plan (p171) which shows:**
A. SE-end of Manifold Ditch (original extension of New River).
B. E-end of the 1856 Cut.
C. Former Hertford Sewage Ditch.
   Note that a projection of the overlaid 1775 course of the New River roughly aligns with the end of the Manifold Ditch shown on 1880 OS map.
NRC Stone to N of White House Sluice.
On the S-bank bend before White House Sluice, the existing NRC boundary stone roughly aligns with later course of New River.
D. White House Sluice.
E. Position of existing 'Gauge Stone' aka 'Capstone' (p180) aligns quite accurately.
F. '**Old Gauge**'. Location can now be scaled accurately by anybody using an OS map. In 1776 the Old Gauge was replaced by the Marble Gauge (just E of 'Old Gauge'), shown as dotted 'Old Gauge' on 1773 Plan, W of Marble Gauge.
G. Marble Gauge. On the N-side immediately past Marble Gauge there is another existing NRC boundary stone.
H. Old River Lee.
The Gauges (Old & New) using restricted orifices, that **controlled the maximum volume that could be extracted** from the River Lee. To prevent overflowing at Marble Gauge, the water level controlled from White House Sluice (see fol.), where any excess would overspill the weir on the NE-side, such that it falls back into the Old River Lee.

1733-1770 the Old Gauge working in conjunction with the former Balance Engine.
1770-1776 working with the Rebuilt Balance Engine.

2. 1773-76 'New Gauge' aka 'Marble Gauge' Never Inscribed (Existing but NOT Operational since 1856): The New Gauge or Marble Gauge also working similarly in conjunction with the Rebuilt Balance Engine.

Marble Gauge said by most authors to have been built 1770, but this is when the Balance Engine was rebuilt. Marble Gauge was probably built 1773-76 ((R. Mylne's Diary) 15K, p95; (A/138) 8A1, 3/3.1). Matthews says that in 1770 the Marble Gauge 'was covered with a building' (7G, p63). Robert Mylne in fact covering Marble Gauge architecturally with a huge sarcophagus-type monument, at water-level the gauge itself probably made from marble for durability, the rest likely hollow with a stone/cement-faced, brick-built outer shell.

1806 (Marble Gauge) 'Ambulator': 'A man is constantly employed to raise or lower the flood- gates, according to the fullness of the water below; and that he may not err in the given quantity, a gauge, consisting of a stone of immense bulk, is placed across the sluice, palisaded round, appearing from the road like a tomb, under which all the water passes; so that by this simple contrivance it is perfectly easy to regulate the current' (Undated printed pages pp161-164, 'New River' part of an alpha-sequence list of places, Isl. LHC; 1806 edn. of the 1796 Ambulator 8th Ed. pp193-195 almost identical text & extra details; 1806 'The Ambulator' very short article on New River (reprinted in 18 Aug. 1888 'Herts. Mercury' article, Microfilm, HALS).

3. 1856 (Marble Gauge) > Today's 'New Gauge': Marble Gauge replaced 1856 by 'New Gauge' located at the start of the Manifold Ditch, such that Marble Gauge bypassed when given additional easement pipes on both sides to increase throughput.

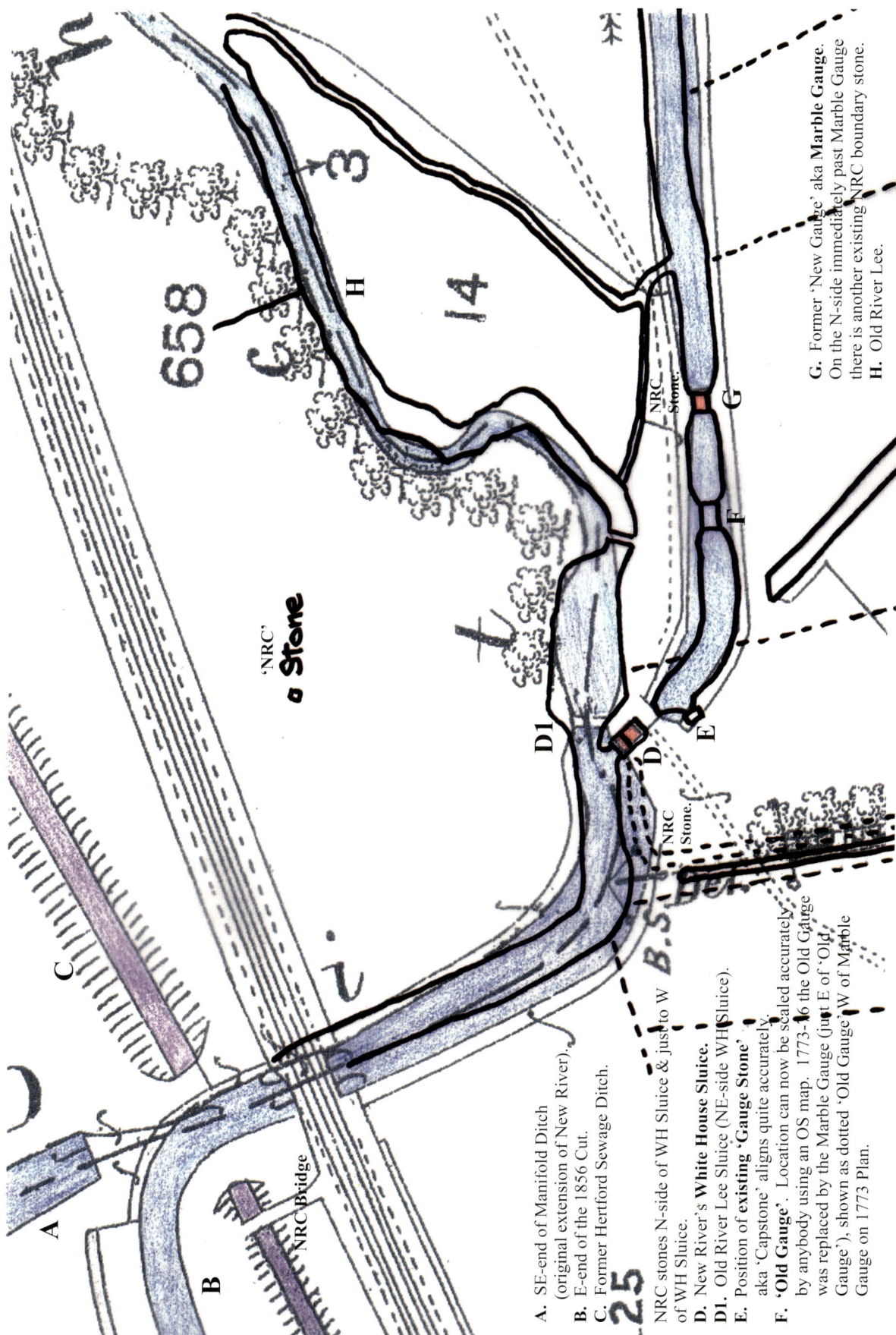

A. SE-end of Manifold Ditch (original extension of New River).
B. E-end of the 1856 Cut.
C. Former Hertford Sewage Ditch.
  NRC stones N-side of WH Sluice & just to W of WH Sluice.
D. New River's **White House Sluice**.
D1. Old River Lee Sluice (NE-side WH Sluice).
E. Position of **existing 'Gauge Stone'** aka 'Capstone' aligns quite accurately.
F. **'Old Gauge'**. Location can now be scaled accurately by anybody using an OS map. 1773-16 the Old Gauge was replaced by the Marble Gauge (just E of 'Old Gauge'), shown as dotted 'Old Gauge' W of Marble Gauge on 1773 Plan.
G. Former 'New Gauge' aka **Marble Gauge**. On the N-side immediately past Marble Gauge there is another existing NRC boundary stone.
H. Old River Lee.

LOCATION of FORMER 'Old Gauge' (SITE OF): At '**F**' between White House Sluice ('**D**') & Marble Gauge ('**G**'). For relationship to known scale, 1775-1809 Mylne map overlaid on 1880 OS map (TW Archive; HALS). See accompanying text for further details. Location also shown dotted on 1773 NRC plan.

Chronological Sequence at the Source of New River

Note that originally the NRC Governors undertook an Annual Survey of the New River, always starting from Islington, but for convenience here following the course of the New River from its source. Before following the New River, there is need to clarify the various changes made over many years at the main source of the New River, the following numbered headings marked on the following map.

1. **1604, 1609-13 Original Source (Chadwell Spring, the 1st of 2-headsprings):** See p182 for prior use.
   1604 (Chadwell Spring to Amwell) first Cut by Colthurst
   > May 1613 Colthurst's Cut widened by Myddelton.

2. **From 1618 – c.1733/1739 Augmenting the Chadwell Spring Supply (OLD RIVER LEE INTO THE NEW RIVER)**
   Great Pipe(s) > Lesser Pipes, & Dam > Tumbling Bay?
   1618-1620 (20-inch Extraction Pipe) from Old River Lee, Chalk Island: Soon after the New River was opened (Sept. 1613), a 1618 Commission agreeing in principle to a 20-inch extraction pipe from the Old River Lee, near 'Chalke Ayland toe lett in ye back Wallter', adjacent to today's White House Sluice. A 1620 erected Dam (to raise the head of water for gravitational flow through the pipe) pulled down by Ware Bargemen, but re-erected.
   c.1658 construction of Ware Mill Stream, that included Ware Lock [I], so presumably also taking the Barge traffic.
   1660 (Order in Council): In 1660 an order of the King in Council empowering the NRC to take water directly from the Old River Lee (aka Old Barge River). The dam 1667 again pulled down by Ware bargemen, with NRC pipes recorded of **9 & 16-inch bores**.
   1669 (> 8-inch & 6-inch Bores): In 1669 agreed that the NRC's 'great Pipes now lying in the River Lee' be replaced by 'two lesser Pipes, the One of **Eight, and the other of Six Inches Bore**', and if the river does not rise enough to fill the pipes, permitted to erect a moveable 'Turne Pike, Jettye' (replacing the Dam). The level of water 7-inches higher than the Spring via two pipes into a short channel connecting to the other channel from the spring.

3. **(2-Pipes) > c.1733 Balance Engine near Mouth of Manifold Ditch, & Timber Gauge or Trough. 1739 Statutory Authority.**
   For controlling the quantity of water passing from the Lee, c.1733 the NRC constructing:
   a) Balance Engine: Constructed during the tenure of the NRC Surveyor Henry Mill, near the mouth of the Manifold Ditch. Since the Balance Engine was approx. 100yds S of the Lee, it must have been used in conjunction with adjusting the tumbling bay on the Old River Lee itself.
   The Balance Engine covered when rebuilt 1770.
   b) Timber Gauge or Trough: 6 ft. wide by 2 ft. deep by 14 ft. long, immediately SE of the Tumbling Bay, a long distance away from the balance engine. Within a short walk from the Gauge, they could presumably raise or lower the tumbling bay to manually adjust or regulate the flow, until the Balance Engine was readjusted to agree with the Gauge e.g. at times of floods.
   c) Two Capstones or Standards: One just S of the Tumbling Bay, the other at Chadwell Spring. Both mentioned in 1739 Act (Lee Navigation) so might be older than first thought, unless replacements.
      d) Pre-1733 did they first use the SSE diagonal ditch? Ditch to just E of Chadwell Spring, see Mylne's 1775 plan. It aligns with the bend in today's River and would have been an easier route to augment Chadwell Spring.
      The 1733 Whittenburg map adds to this confusion in that it shows:
      '**v.** Mouth of the new Cut wch. carries the Water out of the Old Barge River into the New River'.
      '**w.** The Turnpike that stops the Old Barge River & **turns ye Water down ye New River Cut x into ye New River**'. **The plan puts 'x' on LHS of what appears to be this later Ditch.**
      '**y.** Chadwell Spring or New River Head'.
      Additionally the plan appears to show today's channel but with gap near the Turnpike. Possibly he has marked the wrong channel 'x'. Called a 'Ditch' on 1852 NRC plan.

e) **Another Pre-1733 Ditch?:** Similarly the ditch from the old River Lee to N-side of 'New River' on E-side of 'New Gauge'/Marble Gauge (1775-1809 Mylne plan) probably an overflow channel rather than a pre-1733 channel filling the 'New River'. Called a 'Ditch' on 1852 NRC plan, and not shown on 1935 OS map.
I await evidence from further maps etc. **For now will assume they only used the fol. channel.**
f) **Wider channel possibly constructed for the 1733 'Old Gauge' taking more water & also with the later 1773-76 New/Marble Gauge:** The wider N-channel we know today!
ADDS ?-miles to length of NR.

1738-9 (Manifold Ditch Legally becomes part of the New River): In 1738-9 the Manifold Ditch legally became part of the New River, the NRC having purchased Ware Mills and confirming that the mill-stream branch of the Lee would become the undisputed right of way for navigation (thus bypassing the Manifold Ditch/Old River Lee).

1738 (£350 p.a. > £650 p.a.) NRC > Lee Trustees: For extracting water from the Lee, for decades pre-1900 assessed at £650 payable to the Lee Trustees (15I, p130). They appear to have originally paid £2,500 plus £750 in first year, then £300 plus £50 (£350) annually (12, p22; 12D, p13; 6L, p438; 14C, p161; 15M, Acc. 2558/NR13/188, difficult to read handwritten note in ink, signed on back W.C. Mylne with wax seal; An. probably meaning Annuity; Typeset copy of Act pp590-606) 15M, Acc. 2558/NR13/188; pp590-602 1854 printed copy Ref. 346.628, Hackney Archives).

1900 (£3,830 p.a.) NRC > Lee Trustees: £3,180 added to the £650 (total £3,830), that after a Court of Appeal ruling was upheld ((1901 NRC v. Hertford Union) 15I, p130).

ADDS ?-miles to length of NR.
Why didn't they use the Black Ditch access into the Old River Lee? This would have saved them ?-miles of channel! Was it a matter of land ownership, such that at the time they could only acquire the circuitous Manifold Ditch! Perhaps we will never know!

4. **1746 White House Sluice (S-side of Tumbling Bay):** Probably the often mentioned 'Brick Arch', likely covered by the White House Sluice built 1746.
Dam > Jetty or Ancient Turnpike (Movable Dam), Sluice or Tumbling Bay > 1746 & 1823 repaired (Weir) Overspill into Old River Lee: The 1738-9 Act calls it a Tumbling Bay **14ft. wide.** Water not required through White House Sluice overspills a tumbling bay/weir on NE-side, today the N-side inscribed **'1746'**, and S-side inscribed **'REPAIRD 1823'**.

5. **1773-76 (1733 Old Gauge > 1773-76 Marble Gauge):** In 1773-76 the Old Gauge was replaced by the Marble Gauge (just E of 'Old Gauge'), shown as dotted 'Old Gauge' W of Marble Gauge on 1773 Plan (15K, p95 1773 'set out the work of gauge'; (A/138) 8A1, 3/3.1, 1776 gauge completed and enclosed by circular iron railing). Confusingly Matthews says the Marble Gauge in 1770 'was covered with a building' (7G, p63). Marble Gauge itself replaced in 1856 by New Gauge. Such that 1899 described as **only the base formed of marble** with a 6ft. wide by 2ft. deep opening, now bypassed by 24-inch dia. easement pipes either side (7K1, p30); the same size as the 6ft. wide by 2ft. deep & 14 ft. long former old timber gauge.

6a. **1856 'New Cut' (Bypassing part of Manifold Ditch/Old River Lee):** Most of the Manifold Ditch/Old River Lee bypassed by a 'New Cut'.
DEDUCTS ?–miles from length of NR.

6b. **1856-7 New Gauge (Replacing Balance Engine & Marble Gauge) TQ 340 138:** A more modern unique gauge replacing both the Balance Engine & Marble Gauge in 1856-7. Shown in a unique perspective sketch (1X2, p62).

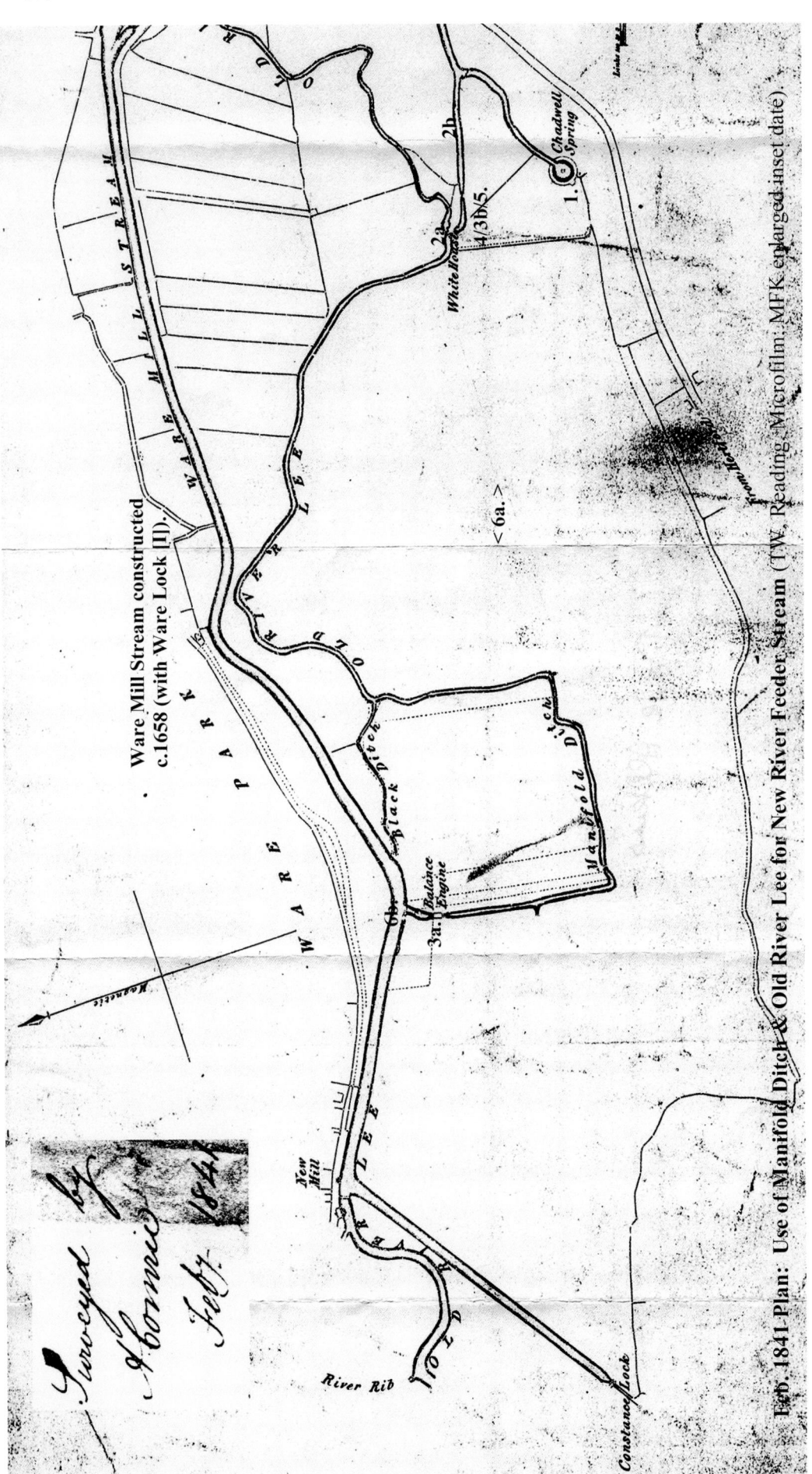

Fb.1841-Plan: Use of Manifold Ditch & Old River Lee for New River Feeder Stream (TW. Reading Microfilm; MFK enlarged inset date).

1. 1604, 1609-13 Original Source, Chadwell Spring the 1st of 2-headsprings.
2a. 1620 Chadwell Spring supply augmented from Old River Lee. Great Pipe(s) > Lesser Pipes, & Dam > Tumbling Bay.
2b. Presumed original connecting channel.
3a. 2-Pipes > **Balance Engine (& Gauge) built 1733**, 1739 becomes Statutory Authority (which included use of Manifold Ditch & Old River Lee), was **covered when rebuilt 1770. Replaced 1857 by 'New Gauge'** (so called, but incorporates a bal. engine), the Old Bal. Eng. House itself bombed WW2.
3b. The related 'Old' Gauge sited approx. 100 yds past the (later) White House Sluice. **'Old' Gauge replaced by Marble Gauge 1773-76**.
4. 1746 White House Sluice (S-side of Old River Lee Tumbling Bay).
5. 1773-76 Marble Gauge (Replaces Old Gauge).
6a. 1856 'New Cut' (Bypassing part of Manifold Ditch & Old River Lee). NOT SHOWN ON THIS PLAN.
6b. 1856-7 New Gauge replacing Balance Engine & Marble Gauge.

LEFT: 'This Belongs to New River Company, 453 Feet, NORTHWARD'.

BELOW: 'EAST WARD, 274 Feet'.

ABOVE: 'This Belongs to New River Company, SOUTH WARD, 180 Feet'.

BELOW: 'WEST WARD, 254 Feet'.

(C) MFK 30/5/2010 photos.

NRC Marker Stone: Virtually North of White House Sluice, approx. 30 ft. S of railway line.

ABOVE: NRC Boundary Stone **'This Belongs to New River Comp[any EASTWARD]'**, S-bank, just before White House Sluice (MFK 2009 photo; Stone 'h' on 1773 NRC Plan).

BELOW: **'Gauge Stone' aka 'Capstone'**, in recess of SW-bank at outlet from White House Sluice (MFK 2009 Photo). Shown as 'Gauge Stone' on 1773 NRC Plan, cut-out in SW-bank on 1775-1809 R. Mylne plan, described as 'Chalk Island Capstone' (Square base with circular rim) Nov. 1828, cut-out in SW-bank on 1852 NRC plan. No reason to suppose it is not the original.

ABOVE: White House Sluice (Built 1746), W-side. From L to R, Depth Scale on far bank, Footbridge across Overflow Weir into Old River Lee, Broadmead PS in background, White House Sluice (weather-boarded with tiled roof), additional c.1856 Iron Inlet for side-channel increasing throughput, Measuring Instrument, Marble Gauge in background, and bottom right corner partially buried NRC Marker Stone 'This Belongs to New River Company' aside the NR Path. Previous mentions of a 'Brick Arch' here, so possibly covered in this remote location for joint use of the NR Walksmen. c.1767 map records 'Turnpike turning the water down the New River'; Pre-1852 Map NRC's Turnpike or Jetty, Dam, Weir or Tumbling Bay' (MFK 2004 photo).

BELOW: Inside of White House Sluice, showing the Iron rack & pinion, Vertical Sluice. Note the drawbridge floor that can be lifted to get access below, and the timber-framed walls infilled with bricks; roofing felt beneath the tiled roof (MFK 2007 photo; with thanks to Dave Liddard, TW).

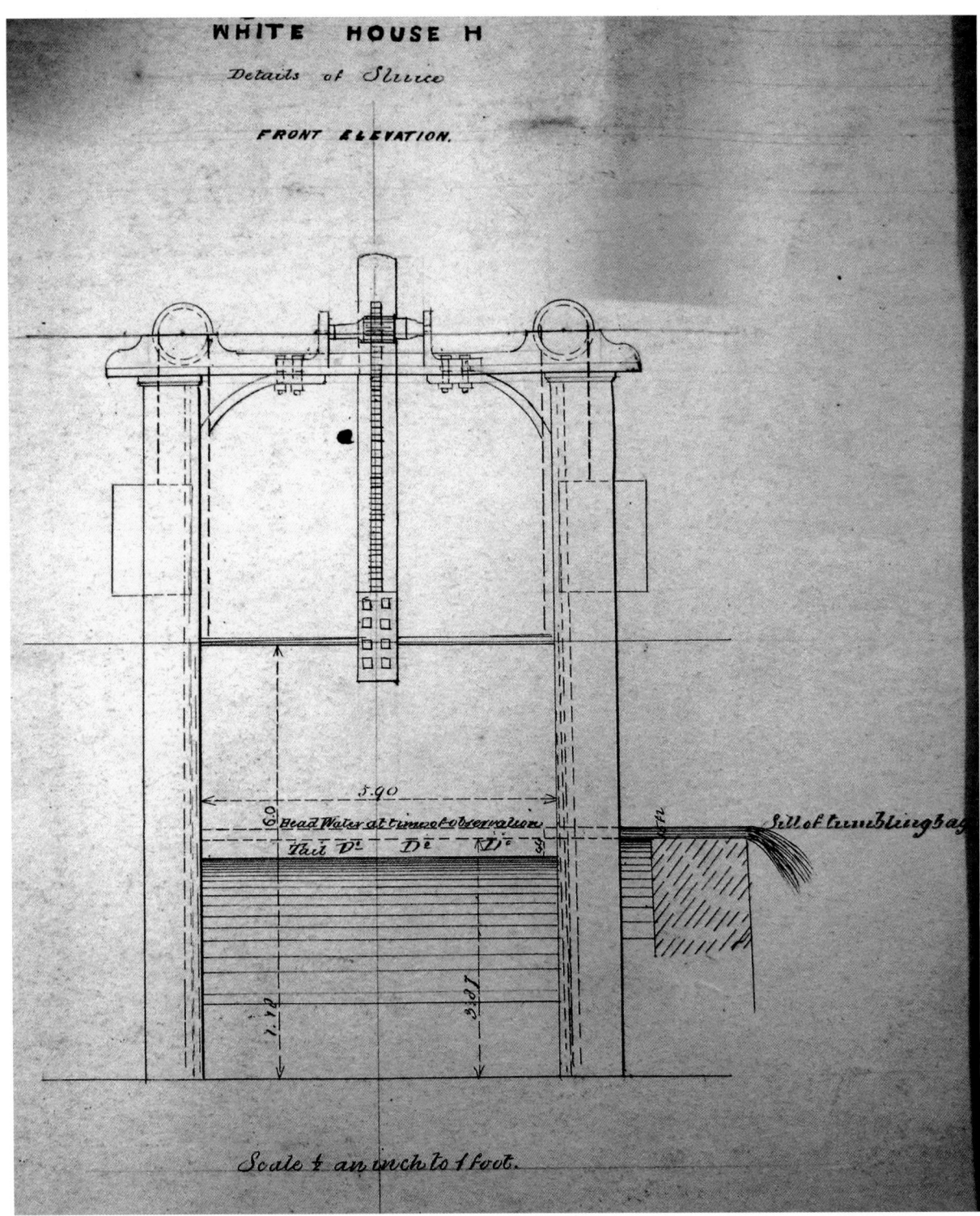

1854 front elevation of **Sluice Gate within White House Sluice** ((Trustees River Lee v. NRC) Acc 2423P0681(1), LMA). 1899 called 'spoke & pocket' (7K1, p29). Looks more like a 'rack & pinion'.

Weir & Footbridge (NE-side White House Sluice): N-side '**1746**' inscribed stone, and S-side '**REPAIRD**' flat on ground & '**1823**' vertical face (MFK 2007/9 photos).

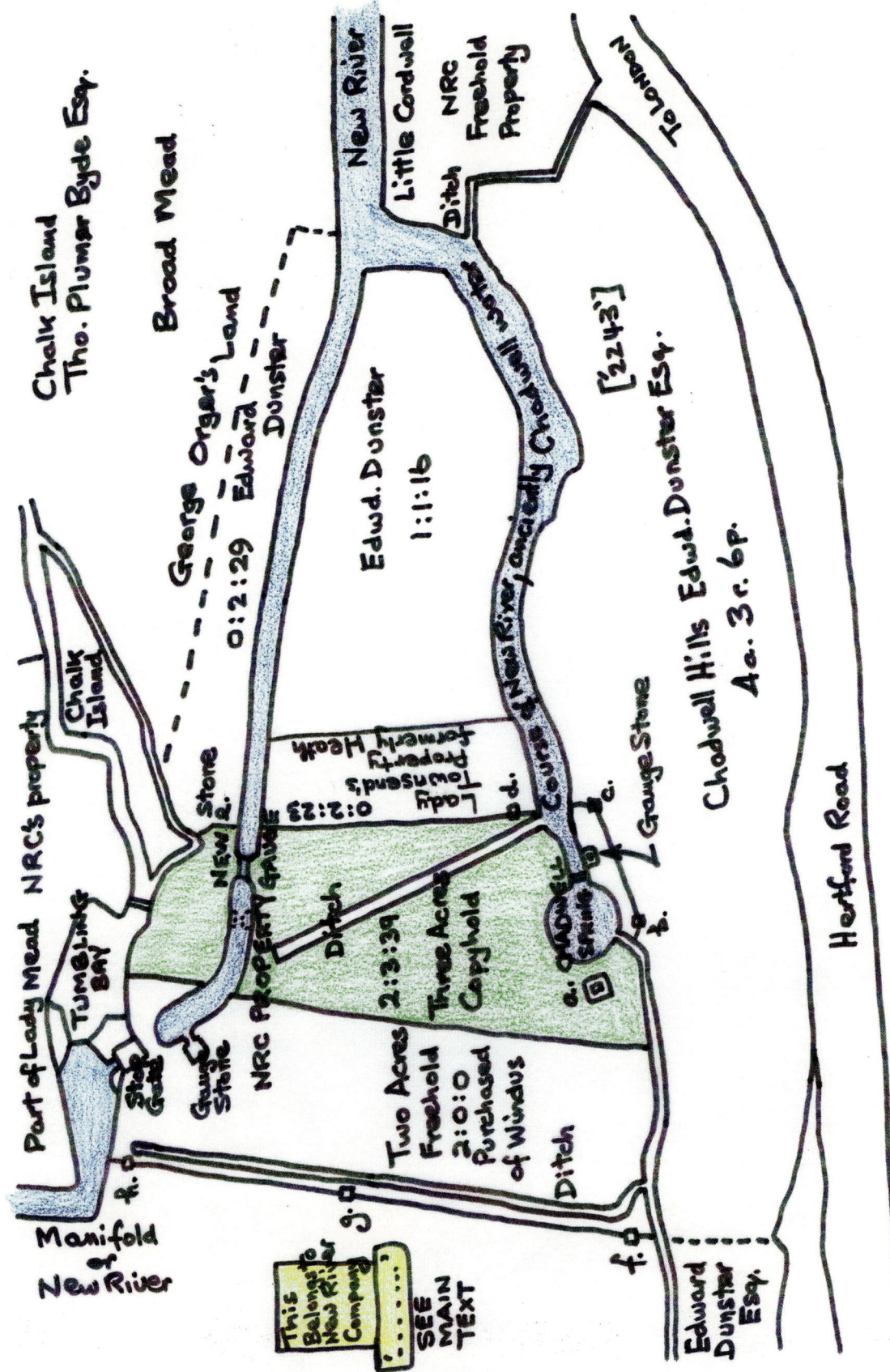

1773 NRC Plan: New River near Chadwell Spring ((Original probably at TW collection, LMA) 'Photostat' SM Lib.; NOT to scale MFK Sketch, original coloured Blue & Green, MFK Yellow Stone). See main text for information on NRC boundary stones.

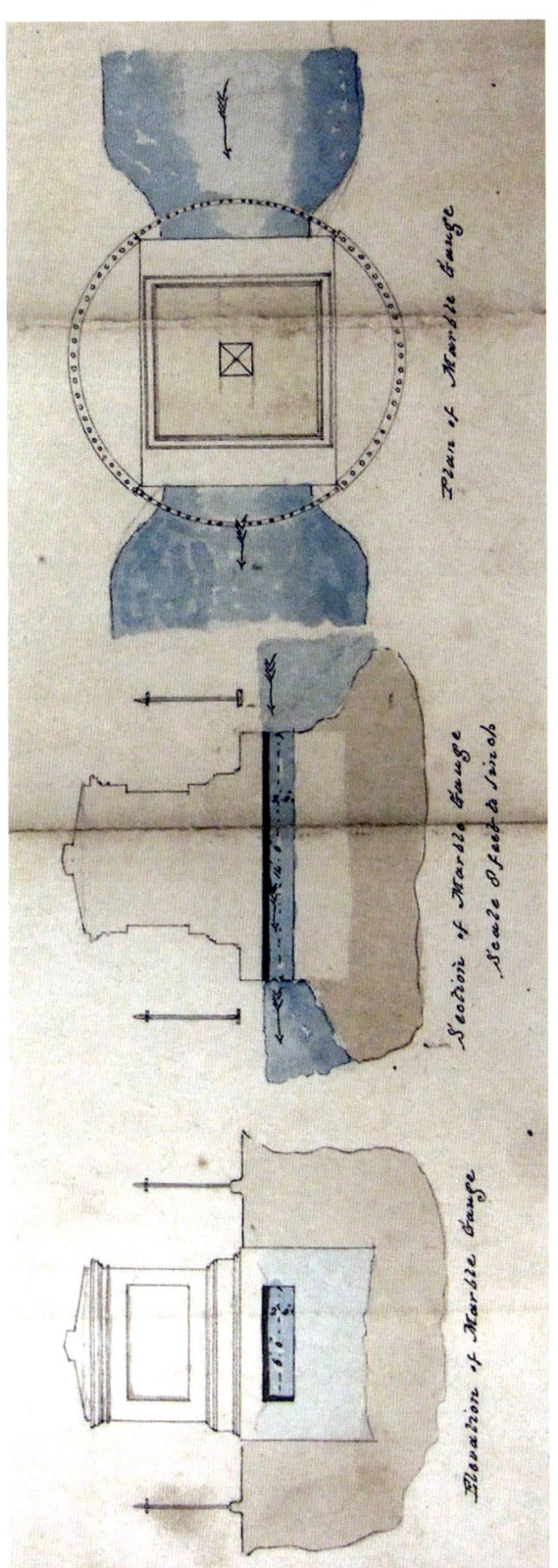

ABOVE (May 1830): 1773-76 constructed Marble Gauge (confusingly called New Gauge on 1775-1806 plans), as seen by the public from the New River Path itself. LHS aperture sizes 6ft. by 2ft.; middle 14ft. by 2ft. (1854 R. Lee Trustees v. NRC, Acc/2423/P/0681(3), LMA; most say built 1770; MFK photos). Originally had circular railings, but in 1856 when replaced by 'New Gauge' given additional side pipes to increase the throughput (can be seen in NR-bed), the railings altered to those you see today, only on one side, beside the NR Path.

Pipes > 1733 'OLD GAUGE' (timber gauge or trough) shown on 1775-1806 plans, also with a 6ft. by 2ft. restriction, & appears to have been far larger in plan than Marble Gauge. **BELOW (May 1830):** Same but flipped horizontally, if following the flow of the river on maps etc.

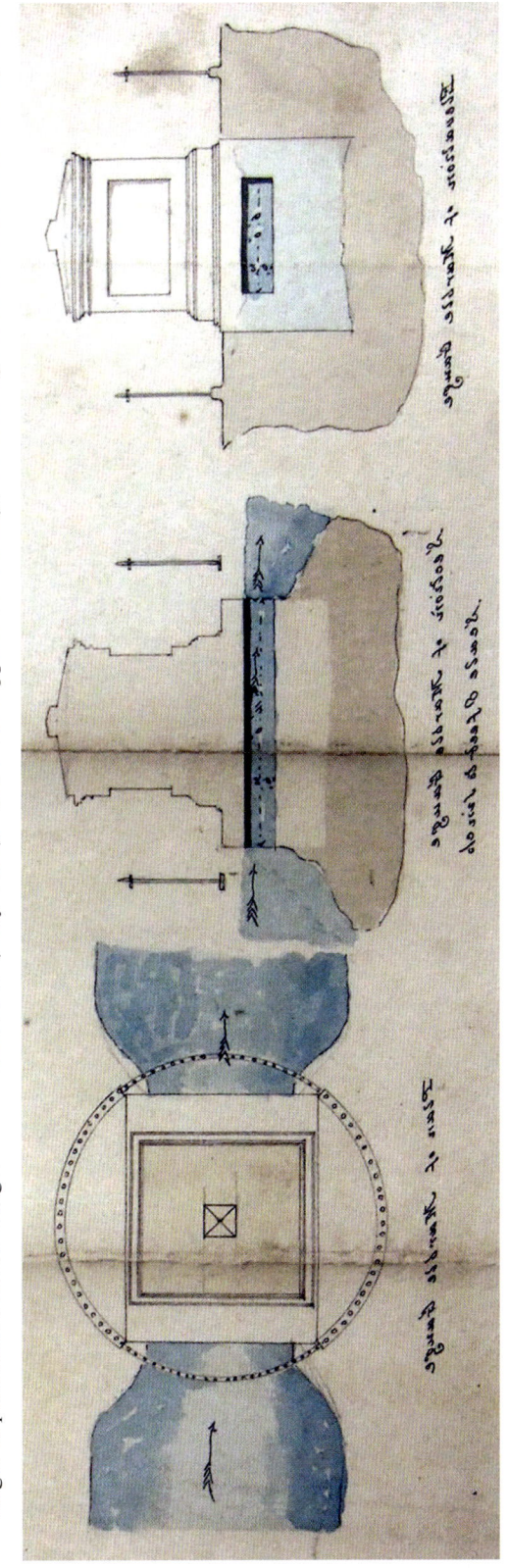

20 Nov. 1613 (Amwell Land) > 1635 NRC: In Amwell parish an acre of freehold land acquired by Hugh Myddelton & others, Sir William his son in 1635 releasing it to the Adventurers ((Feoffment) 15I, p108).
1670-1 for three acres of copyhold land in Little Amwell, John Grene paid £80 as trustee for the NRC, and also in 1670 leasing Lady Mead near Ware from John Leonard for 800-years (**expires in 2470**); and in 1699 2-acres in Chadwell Mead conveyed to John Grene also as trustee for the NRC (15I, p109).

Chadwell Spring (Called the Banjo because of its shape**),** near Ware.
    Chadwell Spring, 'at the base of Bushy Dell Nature Reserve' a chalk grassland slope with 'cowslips, bird's foot trefoil, salad burnet and the rare grass broom rape' (East Herts Council leaflet, quote). Chadwell Spring 'bestowing its blessings on mankind' for thousands of years, is supposed to have derived its name from St. Chad, the patron saint of the blind, an early English Bishop of Lichfield who died of the deadly contagious pestilence in 673 (B2, p237). The springs of this and similar names were supposed to possess a curative power for diseases of the eye.
$C13^{th}$ Supplying Local Needs: In the $C13^{th}$ the monks of Waltham were persuaded by Philip of Hertford to improve the springs at Chadwell so that the water could be supplied for local needs ((Harl. MS 4809, fol. 167) VCH Vol. 3, p409; W3A, p71). Possibly flooding beneath the hill so fed to Ware.
    E-side of Amwell End road: The dock near Victoria Malting said by Mr Croft to be the original outlet of Chadwell Spring into the Lee. The New River aside London Road past Amwell House, known by old inhabitants in 1946 as the 'Mill Brook'; then joined by a spring from 'Springfield' or 'Hog's Close' (presumably the later NRC Amwell End PS), then joining the Lee. The low-lying ground from the railway station to the back of the Mill (Domesday Survey > J.W. French) beside 'Mill Brook' just E of Ware Bridge, invariably flooding when the level of the Lee rises, supposed to have been chosen for a water supply (E3B, p154).
LINE OF NEW RIVER (Chadwell Spring to Amwell End, Ware) PROBABLY ALREADY THERE: If so in 1604 Colthurst would have had an easier task in cutting his 6ft. channel as far as Great Amwell.
1589/90 (Chadwell Spring): Twenty years before the New River was built, 'A Tale of Two Swannes' by William M. Vallans (printed in London) records the legend attached to this spring, as it follows the state progress of 'fortie swannes' headed by their king and queen, along the Lee and its tributaries:
    "A place there is not farre from hence,
    A Chalkie hill; beneath the same a hole,
    Cal'd Chadwell Head, whence issues out a streame
    That runnes behind broad Meade that you see here.
    A tale there is deliver'd unto us
    From hand to hand, how that a hunted ducke
    Diving within this Chadwell head or hole
    Was forced underneath the hollow ground
    To swimme along by wayes that be unknowne,
    And afterward at Amwell spring (they say)
    Was taken up all featherless and bare.
    The King and Lordes took pleasure at the tale,
    And so made haste quite through the arche'd bridge
    To Amwell, where they easilie did spie
    The spring and rill that comes out of the hill,
    And is supposed to rise at Chadwell Head" (E1, p10; also see C4, p32; 1B1, p560 reprinted 'in extensor' at the beginning of Mr. J.E. Cussans' 'History of Hertfordshire').

FIRST/ORIGINAL SOURCE OF NEW RIVER
1604 'Earlier Channel' (Chadwell Spring to Amwell) FIRST 'Cut' by Colthurst >
    1613 Widened by Myddelton
'an earlier channel was started in 1604' probably meaning Colthurst's Cut from Chadwell Spring, the original 1609 source of the New River (NR Path Info. Board). 1613 widened by Myddelton **from 6ft. to 10ft.**
    15 May 1613 the men **cutting the trench 4ft. wider at the top & 1½ ft. wider at the bottom**

from Chadwell to Amwell for £15. 0s. 0d. (15J, p46).

1631 (Chadwell Spring) Described by Master Hassall Rector of Amwell: 'Chadwell, the remotest of these two springs, lieth at the foot of a hill, near unto Ware, in a meadow called Chadwell mead, but whether it gives the name to the meadow or the meadow to it, tradition determineth not, - this Spring is not more commendable in respect to the pureness of the water, than admirable both in regard to the strangeness of her birth, issuing out of a hole of incredible depth, as also in respect of the richness of her current, which of itself instantly grows into a River of about twenty feet in breadth, yet ever, hereto fore, emptied her wasted waters into the River of Lea, running along by Ware, **until now being taught a new course, runneth along the highway full a mile in length, and pouring her rich spoils into the bosom of her sister (Amwell) and so, hand in hand, coming along with her to London**' ((Howes Chronicles, Ed. 1631) 15C3, pp7-8).

c.1728 NRC marker stones (most still existing) probably erected when Chadwell Spring or its monument was repaired in 1728. The pedestal/stone rebuilt in 1883 and again in 1922 (15D, p5). Also see the 1773 plan details fol.

11 May 1769 (Christening in Boat) Chadwell Spring: 'A few days ago as some gentlemen were surveying the New River, near this place, news was brought them that the wife of Thomas Sutton, one of their workmen, whose dwelling is on the bank of the stream, was at that instant safely delivered of a boy. Mr Mills [Henry Mills, NRC Surveyor c.1720-1771], a Welch gentleman, who is a bachelor near 100-years of age, being present, insisted that the child should be christened on the river at his expence, in honour of Sir Hugh Middleton [sic], the founder, and accordingly the ceremony was performed on Monday last in a boat, on that fine pool called Chadwell Spring. Two Welch gentlemen & ladies answered for the child, who was named Middleton Mills Chadwell. There was a fine band of music, and there were upwards of 2,000 spectators, to whom plenty of liquor was given. We hear Mr Mills also gave a handsome sum of money to the parents – W.N.' (((21 July 1769 newspaper) note of 18 Aug. 1888 printed 'Herts Mercury' 6 April 1889; with handwritten 11 die May, probably the actual date ceremony took place) Islington LHC; also copy on Microfilm, HALS). Different version by Richard Gough written some years previous to 1776 (D1624 No. 8, ELHU), that inspired his 1776 poem 'Genius of Chadwell Spring' (New River), in entirety best left to historic enthusiasts because heavily amended, a short quote follows below (D1624 No. 18, ELHU).

1773 Plan (Scaled in Chains & Feet): See associated plan.

Diagonal Ditch (from the Stopgate to the NE of Chadwell Spring): Have always thought that this was the earlier channel from the Lee; else just used to collect surface water into the New River.

Regarding the marker stones has the following text:

On stone marked 'a' at Chadwell Spring:

N-side.	S-side.	E-side.	W-side.	
		This	This	'These stones were put down
629	43	Belongs to	Belongs to	about 46 years ago, answering
Feet.	Feet.	New River	New River	to the date of **1728**'.
		Company	Company	
		178 Feet.	270 Feet.	
OPENED	Conveyed	CHADWELL	REPAIR'D	
1608.	40 MILES.	SPRING.	1728.	

On stones 'b' & 'c':	On stone 'd':	On stone 'e':	On stone 'f', 'g' & 'h':
This	**This**	**This**	**This**
Belongs to	**Belongs to**	**Belongs to**	**Belongs to**
New River	**New River**	**New River**	**New River**
Company	**Company**	**Company**	**Company**
NORTHWARD.	**WESTWARD.**	**SOUTHWARD.**	**EASTWARD.**
	'2: n'. on S-side.	6:5 Westward.	
		2:9 Eastward.	
		This stone was underground,	
		till lately, as was in 1773 placed,	
		so that the Inscription could be read.	

((Original possibly at LMA; Photostat Map of area covering Chalk Island, Chadwell Spring and connecting channel 'MDCCLXXIII' 1773) 8A1, File 8, 1/17).

1776 'Amwell' a Descriptive Poem by John Scott the Quaker Poet (b.1731-d.1783): A lengthy poem that includes references to both the River Lee & New River. The following is an extract regarding Chadwell Pool, Scott's view being that the New River was a 'mercenary stream' depriving the Lee of water:

> '**Of Chadwell's azure pool**. From Chadwell's pool
> To London's plains the **Cambrian artist**[1] brought
> His ample aqueduct[2]; suppos'd a work
> Of matchless skill, by those who ne'er had heard
> How from Preneste's heights and Anio's[3] banks,
> By Tivoli[4], to Rome's imperial walls,
> On marble arches[5] came the limpid store,
> And out of jasper rocks in bright cascades
> With never-ceasing murmur gush'd; or how
> To Lusitanian Ulysippo's[6] towers,
> The silver current o'er Alcantra's[7] vale
> Roll'd high in air, as ancient poets feign'd
> Eridanus[8] to roll thro' Heaven; to these
> **Not sordid lucre**[9], but the honest wish
> Of future fame, or care for public weal[10],
> Existence gave; and unconfin'd as dew
> Falls from the hand of Evening on the fields, They
> flow'd for all. Our **mercenary stream**
> No grandeur boasting, here obscurely glides O'er
> grassy lawns or under willow shades.
> As, thro' the human form, arterial tubes Branch'd
> every way, minute and more minute, The
> circulating sanguine fluid extend;
> So, **pipes innumerable to peopled streets**
> **Transmit the purchas'd wave**. Old Lea, meanwhile,
> Beneath this mossy grot o'erhung with boughs
> Of poplar quivering in the breeze, surveys
> With eye indignant his diminished tide[11]
> That laves yon ancient priory's wall[12], and shows
> In its clear mirror Ware's inverted roofs. … … etc'.

[MFK Notes: 1. Hugh Myddelton born Denbigh, Wales. 2. The 'New River'. 3. The Anio river joins the Tiber N of Rome. 4. Tivoli an Italian town. 5. Referring to the 50-mile Roman aqueduct. 6. Ulysippo the ancient name of Lisbon. 7. District of Portugal. 8. Large Italian river into the Adriatic at Po. 9. Lucre = financial profit or gain. 10. Weal = welfare. 11. Main part of New River water sourced from the Lee. 12. Ware Priory]. (D20B, pp147-148 quote/pp142-161 full length version of 'Amwell, a descriptive poem' by John Scott, that says little about Amwell; full copy at www.archive.org); extracts of above (ELSC&A) 1A2-6, pp362-363; ((Copy sent to MWB by E.J. Cox of Highbury) Typed 'EM, On the NR') 8A1, 2-8; A, p66, E1, pp10-11/15; 14E1, p8).

Nov. 1776 '**Genius of Chadwell Spring**
> whose limpid streams revive ye mead
> where flows ye genial flood
> That bounteous Middleton call'd forth
> The raptured trembling Muse presumed to sing
> Proud to recount each generous deed
> And found ye entire incitement to do good
> From gen'rous Mills's worth. … …'.

(D1624 No. 18, ELSC&A), referring to Henry Mill, NRC Surveyor. 4pp poem from the historian Richard Gough's miscellaneous papers, probably written by him but with masses of revisions & mythological references.

9 July 1778 (Renew Rails & Mud Pan Centre of Spring): To renew the rails round the stone at Chadwell Spring, since they are decayed and gone, and mud pan the middle of the spring-head (((Mins. B/3) Typed 'Chadwell Spring, Ware') 8A1, 2-8).

17 Sept. 1806 (Robert Mylne's Diary): 'Opened monument at Chadwell Spring' (15K, p207). Probably made available for public viewing.

'The pedestal was **rebuilt in 1883 and again in 1922**' (15D, p5).

Summer 1898 (Chadwell Spring) Ceasing to Flow: After previous dry years then a drought, Chadwell Spring temporarily ceasing to flow, such that pumped dry and cleared of mud, its flow gradually resuming by Autumn (11, p84). Sept. 1898 photo of repairs at Chadwell Spring (HALS).

Chadwell Spring ceased to flow again in June 1933 ('2684' 10/1/1934 photo & un-numbered 20/6/1934 photo, TW A-Mills Archive) but probably cleaned and shown flowing again 17/1/1935.

Jan. 1995 (Chadwell Spring) New Revetment: New-year completion of new revetment around Chadwell Spring (15F, Issue No. 29, Dec. 1994).

Feb. 2006 (Chadwell Spring) Cleaned & Re-wharfed: Contractors J. Browne had just completed cleaning and re-wharfing the spring in timber. Many thanks to John & David Liddard of Thames Water, who arranged for me to photograph the spring and its marker stones.

ABOVE: 1793 'The New River Head - with part of the town of Ware'. Drawn by R.M. Batty & Engraved by F. Jukes (Batty & Jukes Collection No. 1, HALS).

Today called the 'Banjo' because of its shape. Although geographically was the New River Head, this title was used to name its destination at Islington, since this was from where London was supplied with water.

BELOW: 1806-1813 print called 'New River Head' looking down on Chadwell Spring (((Drawn by Schnebbdies & Engraved by Warren) 'Description of London' by David Hughson) ELSC&A).

Pre-1728 Main Monumental Stone, SW-side Chadwell Spring (MFK 2006 photos; thanks to Dave Liddard, TW). Marked 'a' on 1773 Plan scaled in Chain & Feet (Berry Archive, SML, Swindon).

N-side.	S-side.	E-side.	W-side.
629 Feet.	**43 Feet.**	**This Belongs to New River Company 178 Feet.**	**This Belongs to New River Company 270 Feet.**
OPENED 1608.	**Conveyed 40 MILES.**	**CHADWELL SPRING.**	**REPAIR'D 1728.**

There are TWO other NRC Boundary Stones, not shown in Volume 1:

1. **SE-side of NE-part of Manifold Ditch**, only accessible if prepared to cross low fences on the marshy mead.
2. **NE-side of Marble Gauge**, visible from the New River Path. For photos of both see Vol. 3.

RIGHT:
'WESTWARD' Stone 'd' on 1773 Plan. RHS has inscribed '2.JJ' prob. 2:11. N-side immediately upstream of Chadwell Spring.

ABOVE: Probably the **'Gauge Stone'** shown on 1773 Plan. S-bank immediately upstream of Chadwell Spring. Called 'Capstone' on pre-1856 Plan.

RIGHT: 'NORTHWARD' Stone 'c' on 1773 Plan. SE-side of Chadwell Spring. Top has Iron Peg seated in Lead.

BELOW:
'NORTHWARD' Stone 'b' on 1773 Plan. S-side of Chadwell Spring.

ABOVE:
Probably a **Modern Gauge Stone**, within S-bank of Chadwell Spring itself.

Boundary & Other Markers at Chadwell Spring (MFK 2006 photos; thanks to Dave Liddard, TW).

1773 Plan shows site of NRC Property or Boundary Stones.

'a' Main Chadwell Spring Stone, see separate photos.

'b', 'c' & 'd' on this page.

'e' just E of Marble Gauge, see separate photo.

'f', 'g' & 'h' ('This Belongs to New River Company, EASTWARD') follows the W-side of N-S embankment (Needs further research as to when embankment built, but **prob. these stones no longer exist**).

c.1811 NRC Plan: **Chadwell Spring & Hill**, showing 4a. 3r. 9.5p. purchased 1811 from the Dunster Family (TW Archive; MFK photo).

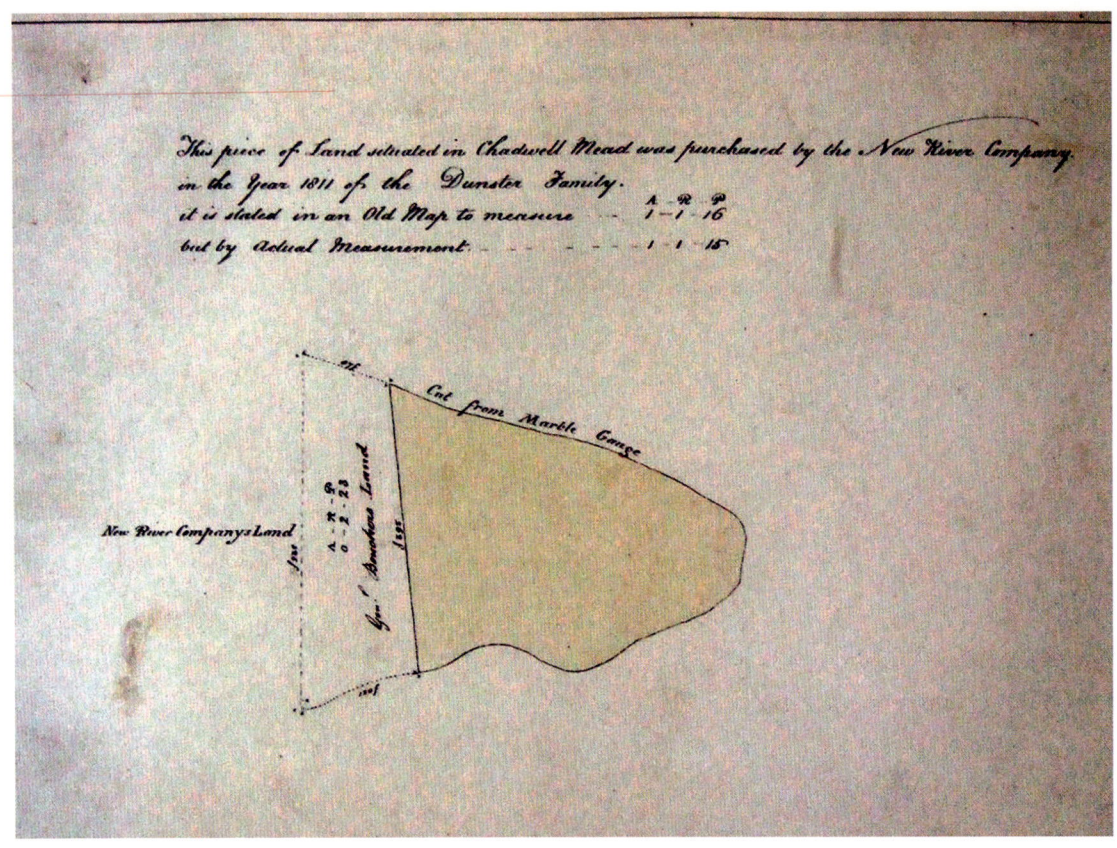

c./1811 Land purchased by the NRC from the Dunster Family (TW Archive; MFK photos).

ABOVE: c.1811 in Chadwell Mead (Truncated Plan).
BELOW: 1811 'The Slipe' near Chadwell Spring (Truncated Plan).

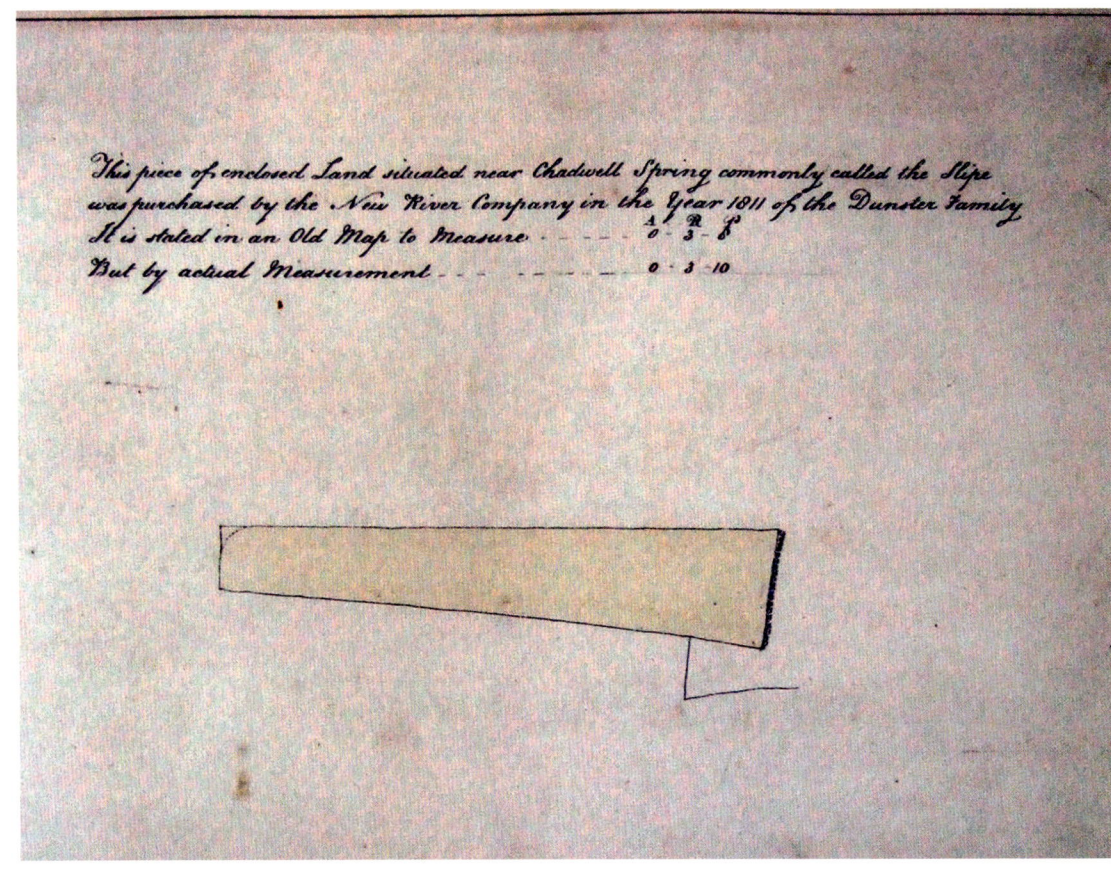

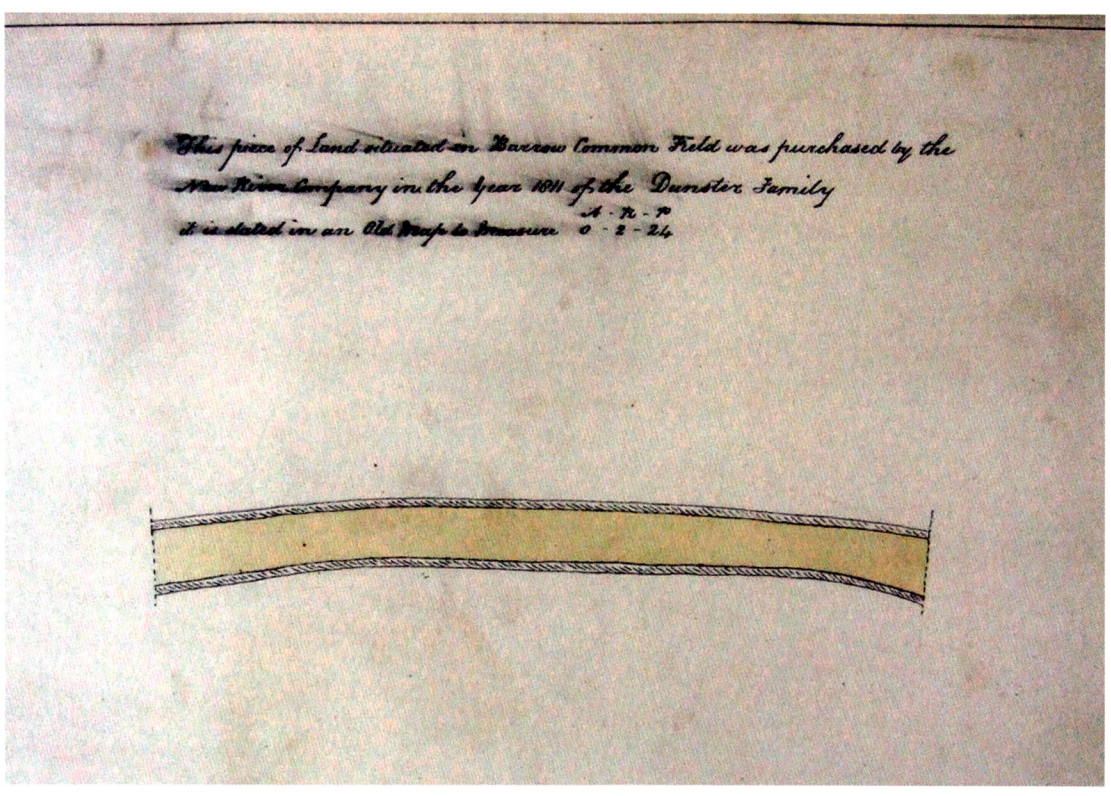

Purchased 1811 by the NRC from the Dunster Family (TW Archive; MFK photos).
ABOVE: Barrow Common Field (Smudged original, MFK truncated).
BELOW: Broad Mead near Chadwell Spring (MFK truncated).
Part 'C' (Blue part) below purchased 1809 from Mr Fearman.

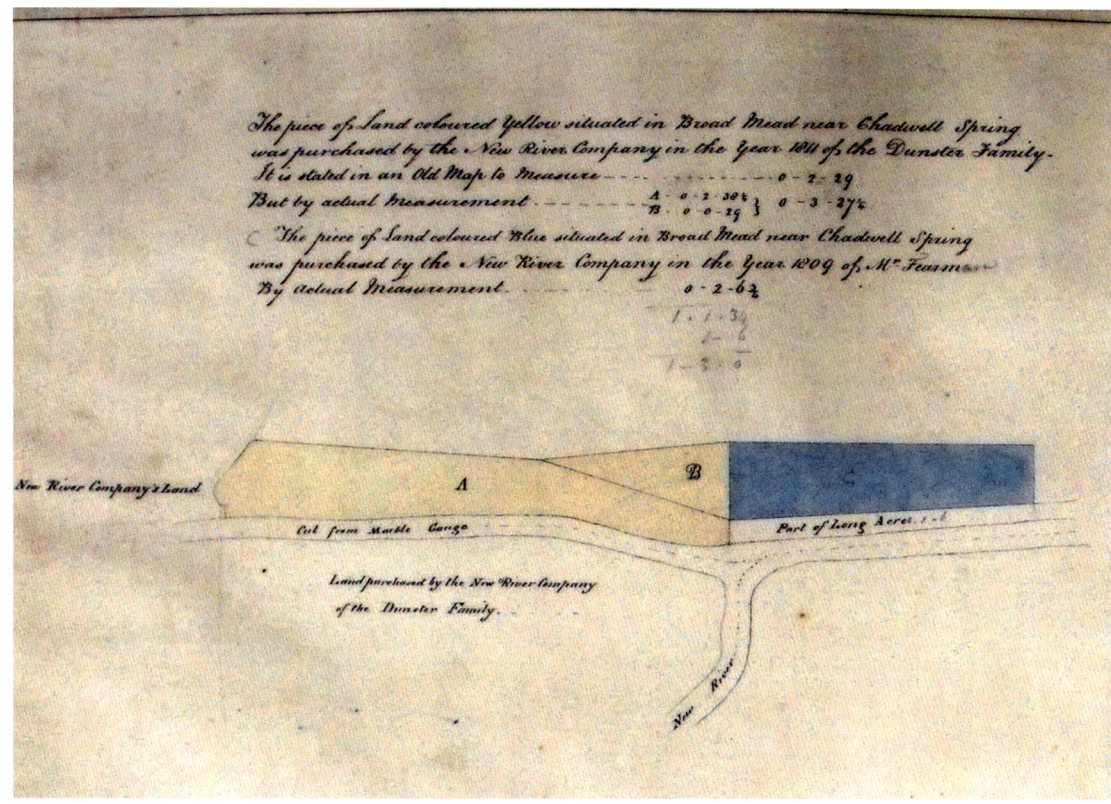

1773 Plan: New River at Amwell End ((Original Much Deteriorated) TW, Abbey Mills Archive; MFK photo). Probably that used by R. Mylne for his 1775-1809 plans of the New River. Text: **Chadwell Water**; Waste, Content including the River 0a. 2r. ?9p.; **Walkman's House & Garden** 0.a. 2r. 9p., NRC's Property; Parish of Little St Johns Hertford otherwise Little Amwell; New River; Road from Hertford; Mr Scotts. New River; To London. This could be where the pre-New River overflow from Chadwell Spring ran to waste into the Ditch then River Lee. **If so, up to this point only deepened & widened**.

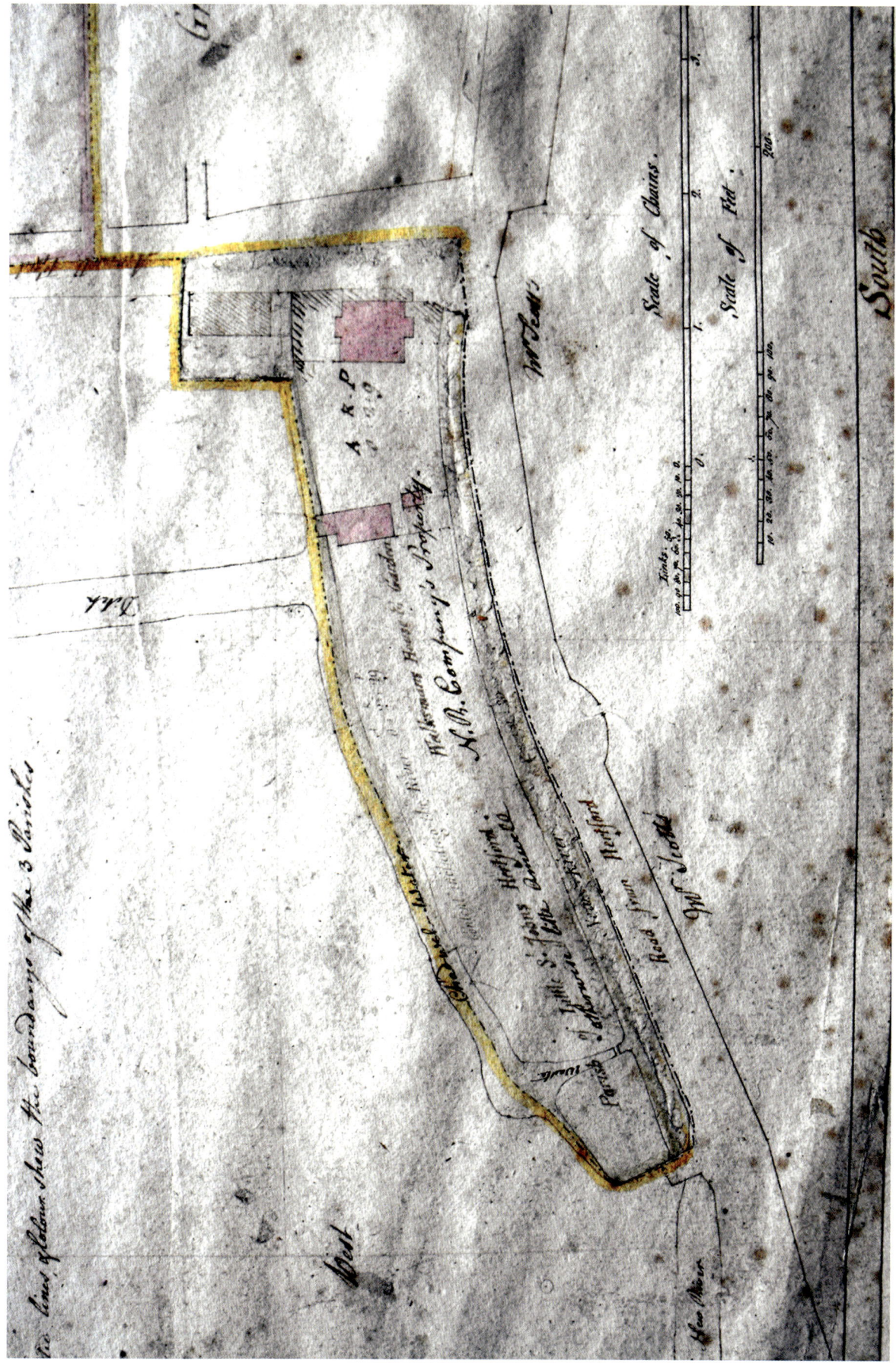

LARGER Part of 1773 Plan: **New River at Amwell End** (TW, Abbey Mills Archive; MFK photo).

1775-1809 Plan 1 & 2 Joined: New River at Amwell End (TW Abbey Mills Archive; MFK photos joined to best fit). 'Bridge No. 3' 'Little Amwell Parish. Walkmans house and Garden', 'Guage'. 'No. 7' [Struck through]

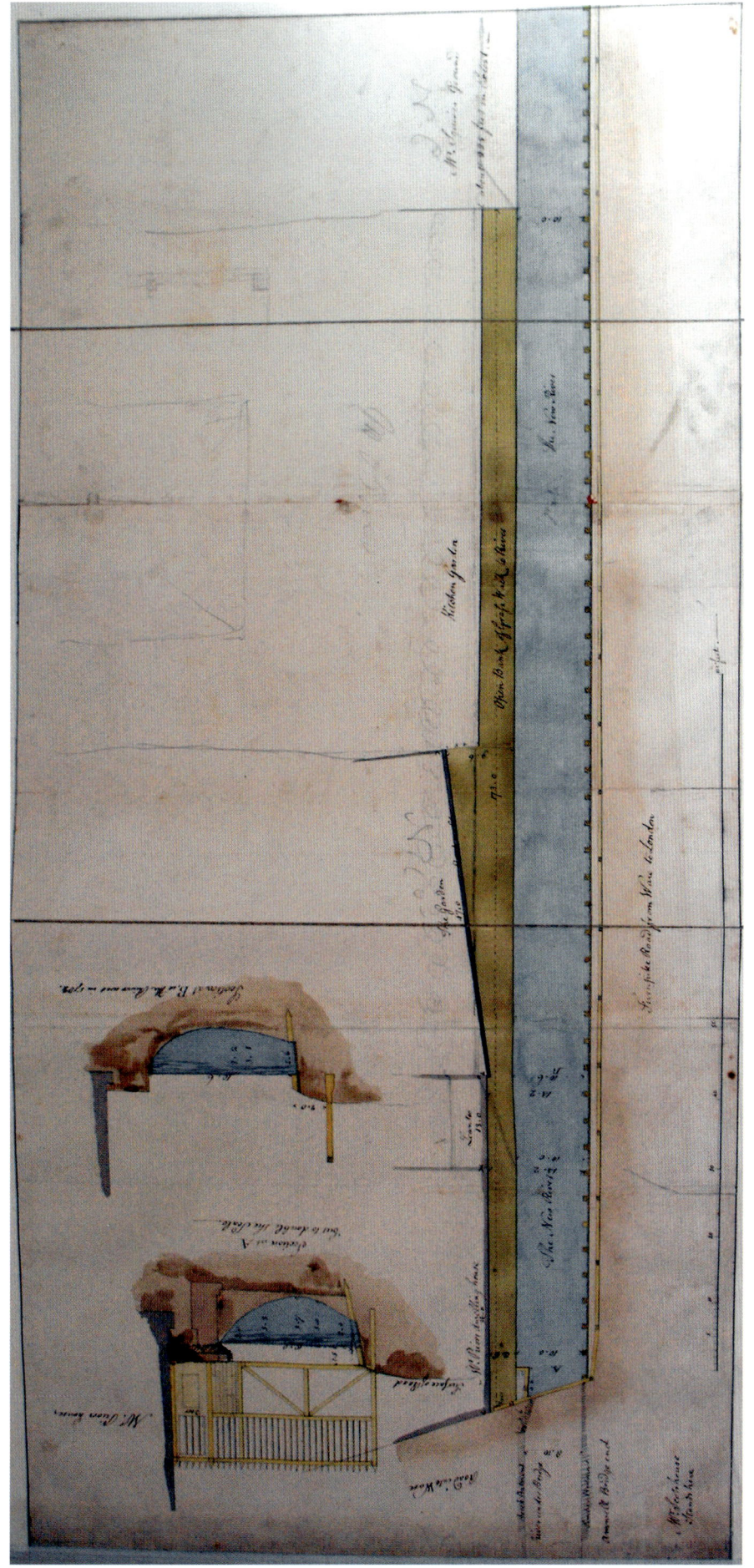

1782 New River at Mr Prior's Dwelling House, Ware. 'At Amwell Bridge end' opposite Mr Scot's House. New River then only 10ft. - 10ft. 6ins. Wide (TW Archive; MFK photo).

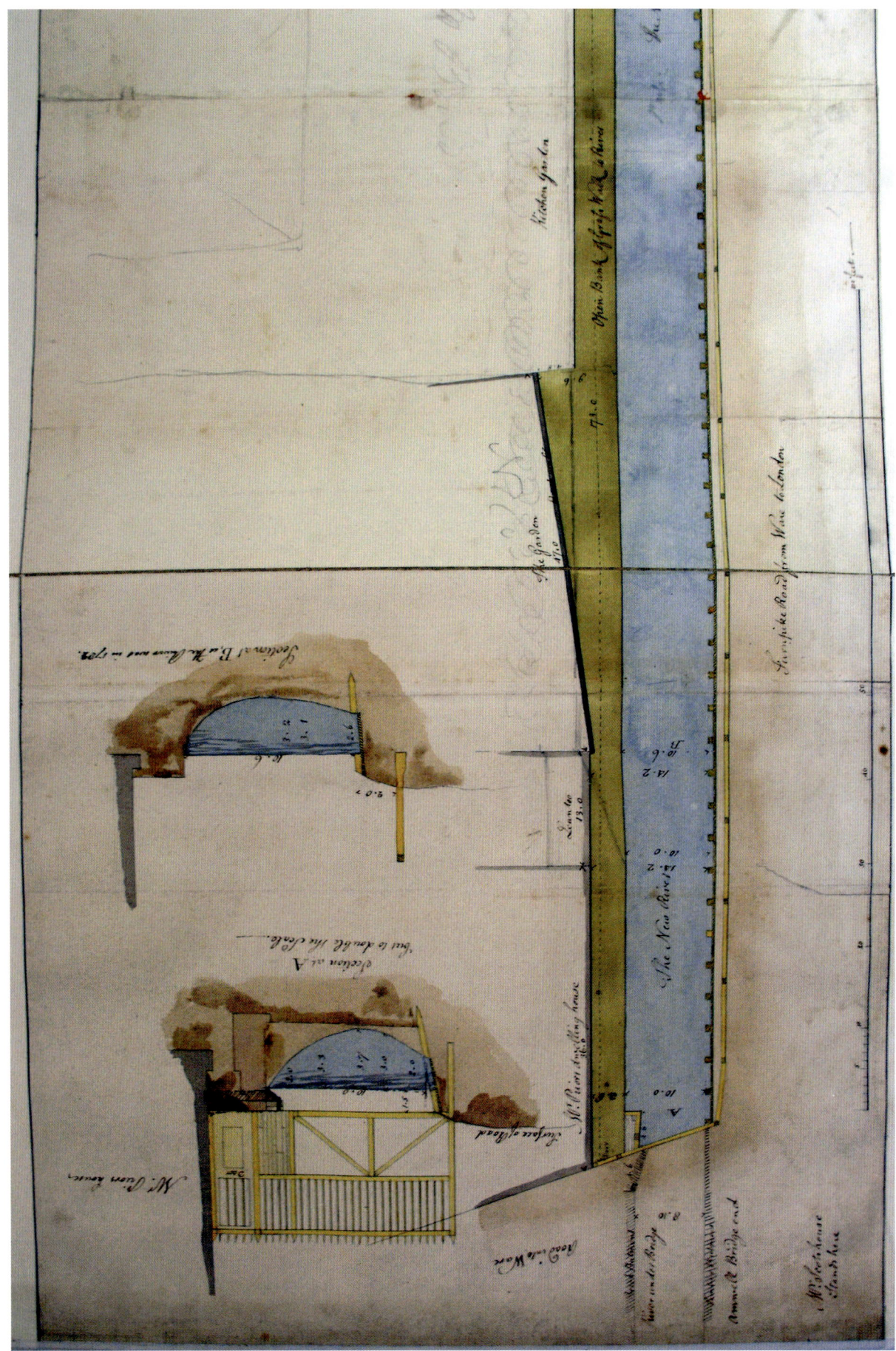

LARGER 1 of 2: **1782 New River at Mr Prior's Dwelling House**, Ware (TW Archive; MFK photo).

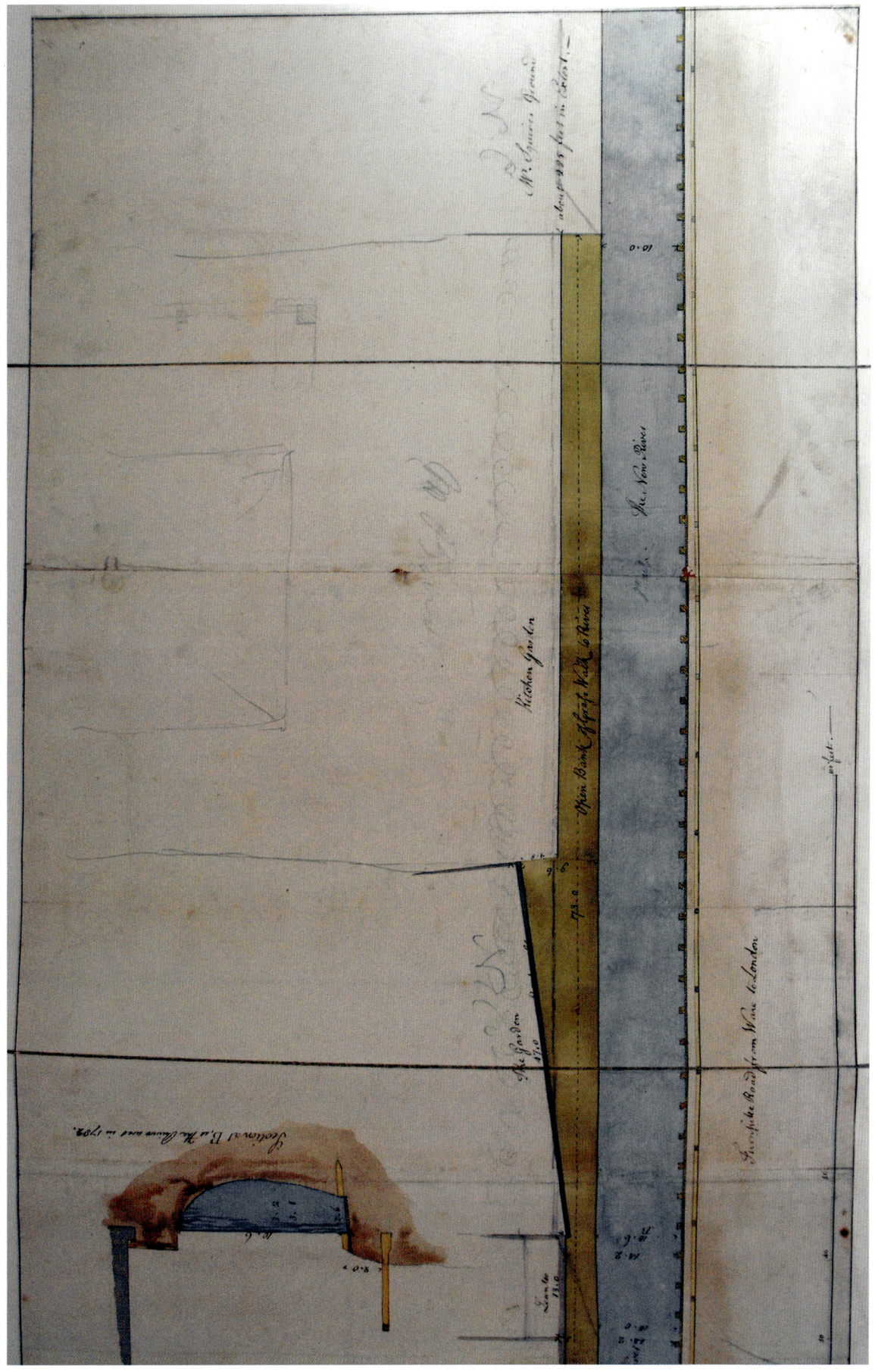

LARGER 2 of 2: **1782 New River at Mr Prior's Dwelling House,** Ware (TW Archive; MFK photo).

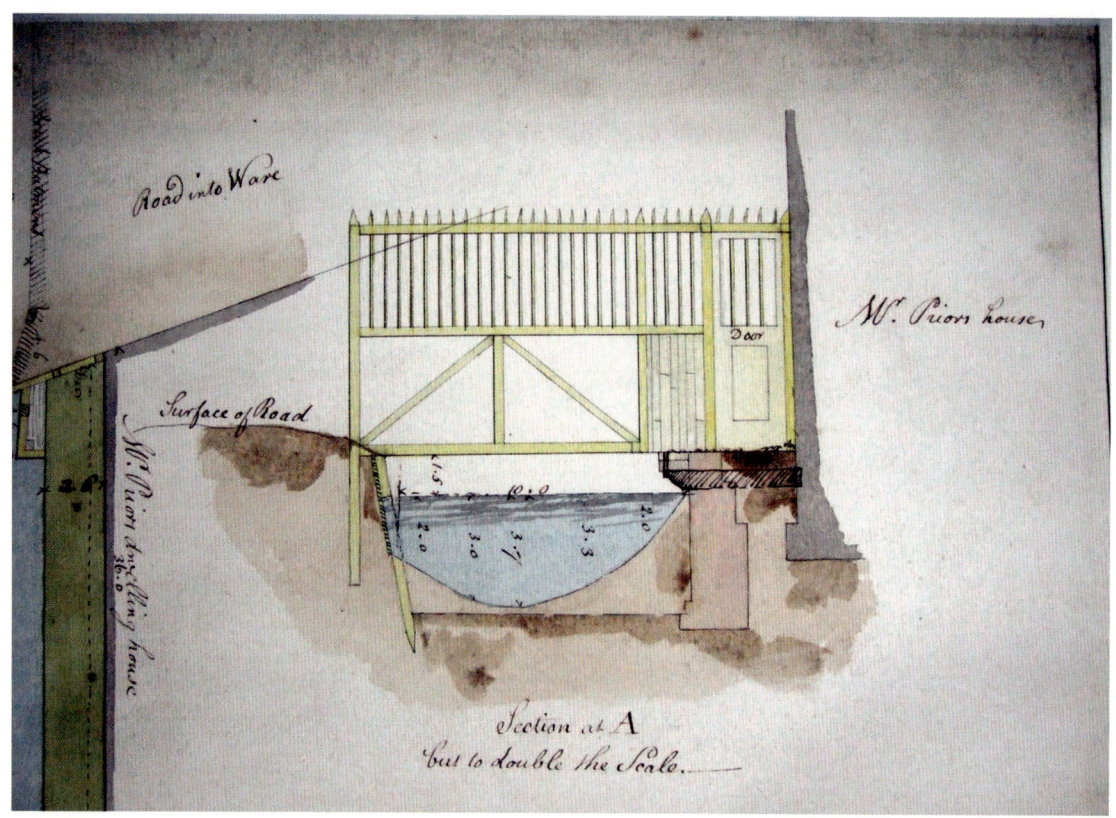

LARGER 3 & 4: **1782 New River at Mr Prior's Dwelling House**, Ware (TW Archive; MFK photos).

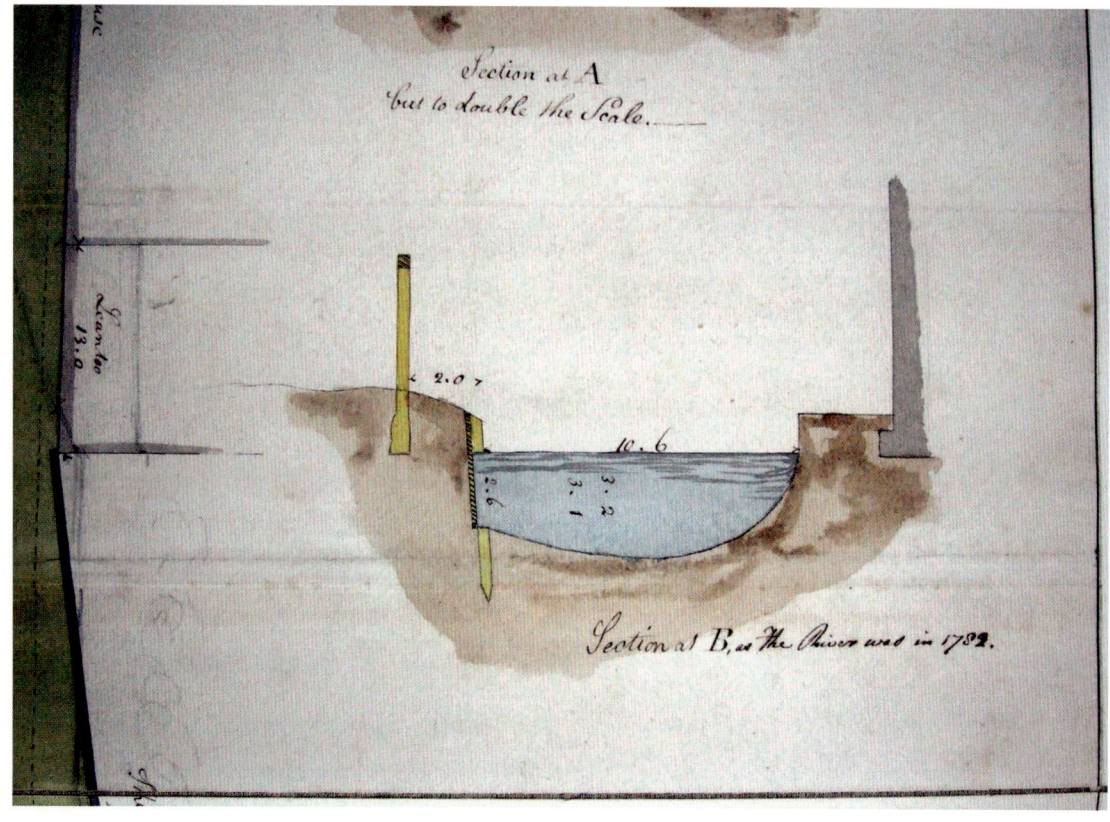

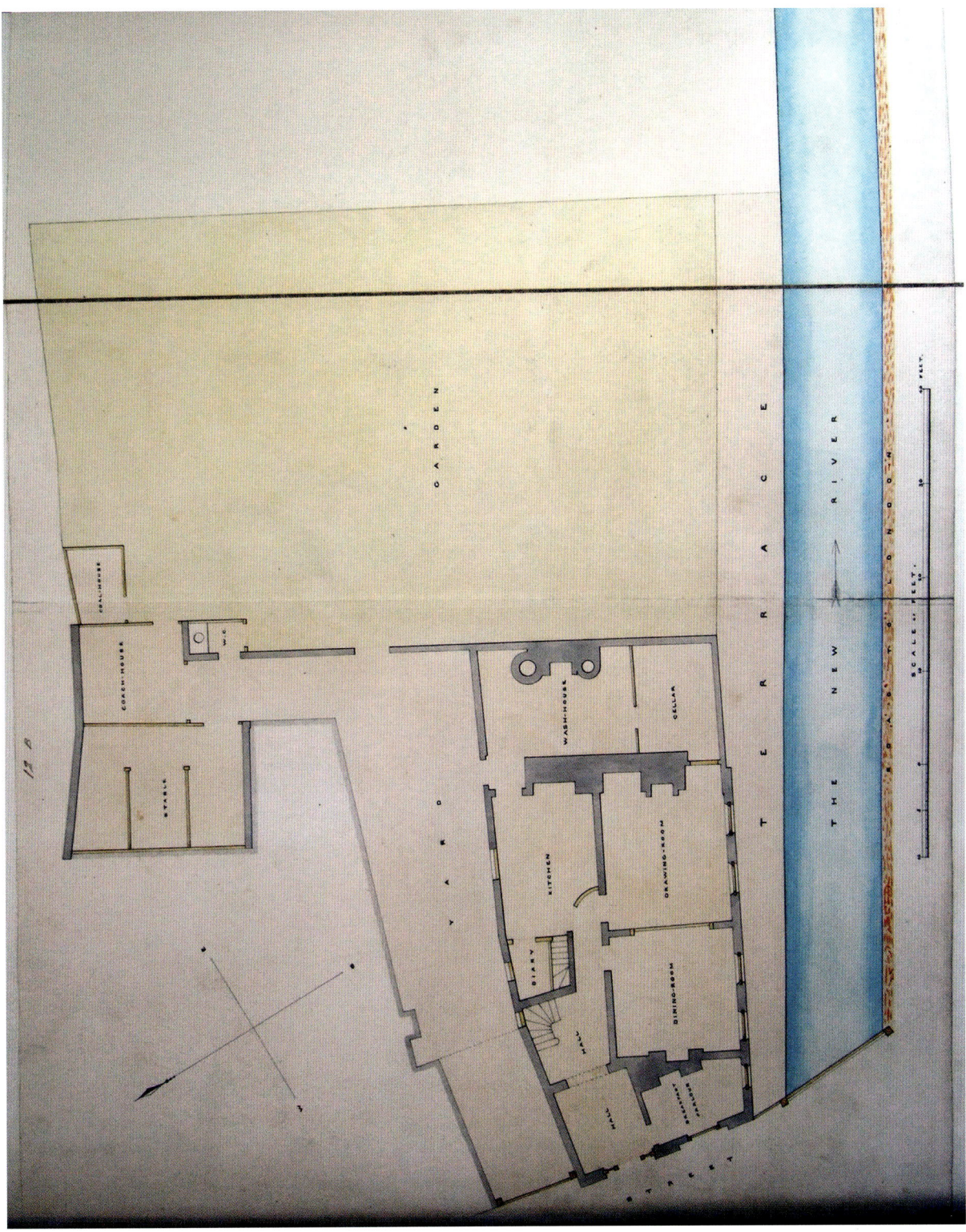

Prob. 1800s (Undated) NRC Plan: Unspecified location, but **probably at Amwell End** (TW Archive; MFK photo).

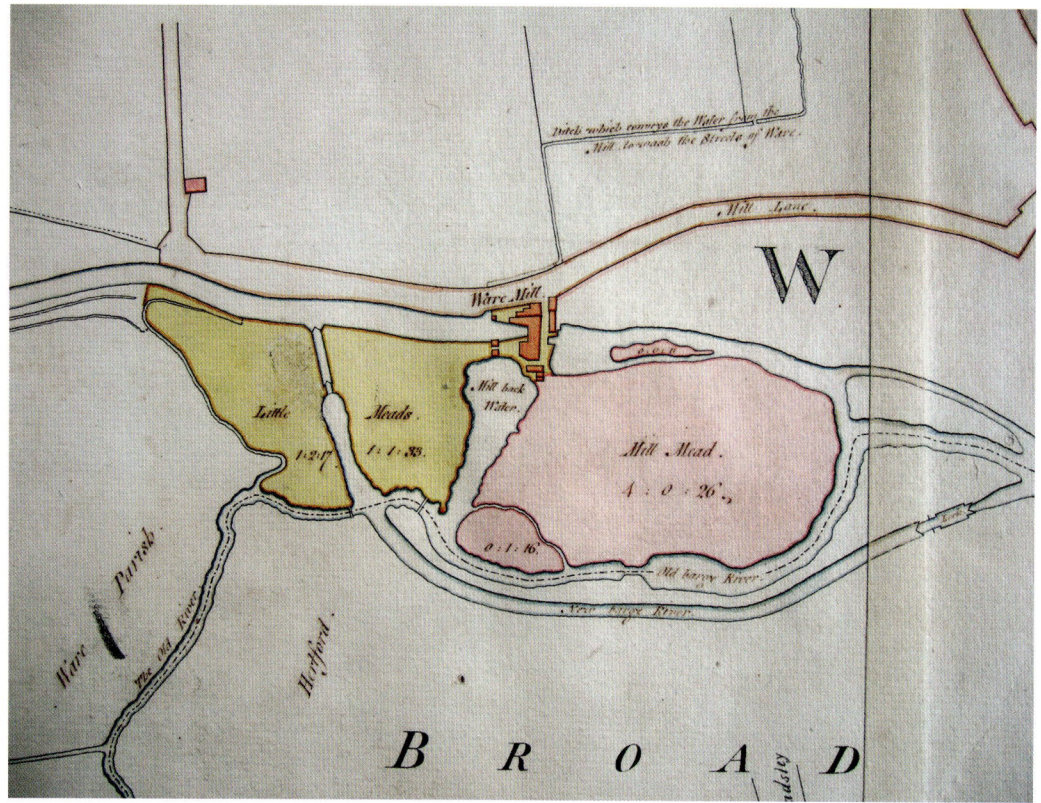

ABOVE: 1775-1809 Plan 1, **Ware Mill & channels** (TW Archive; MFK photo).
BELOW: c.1830-40 **Land at Tail of NRC Ware Mill**. Note the Privy in the corner of the Tail water (TW Archive; MFK photo).

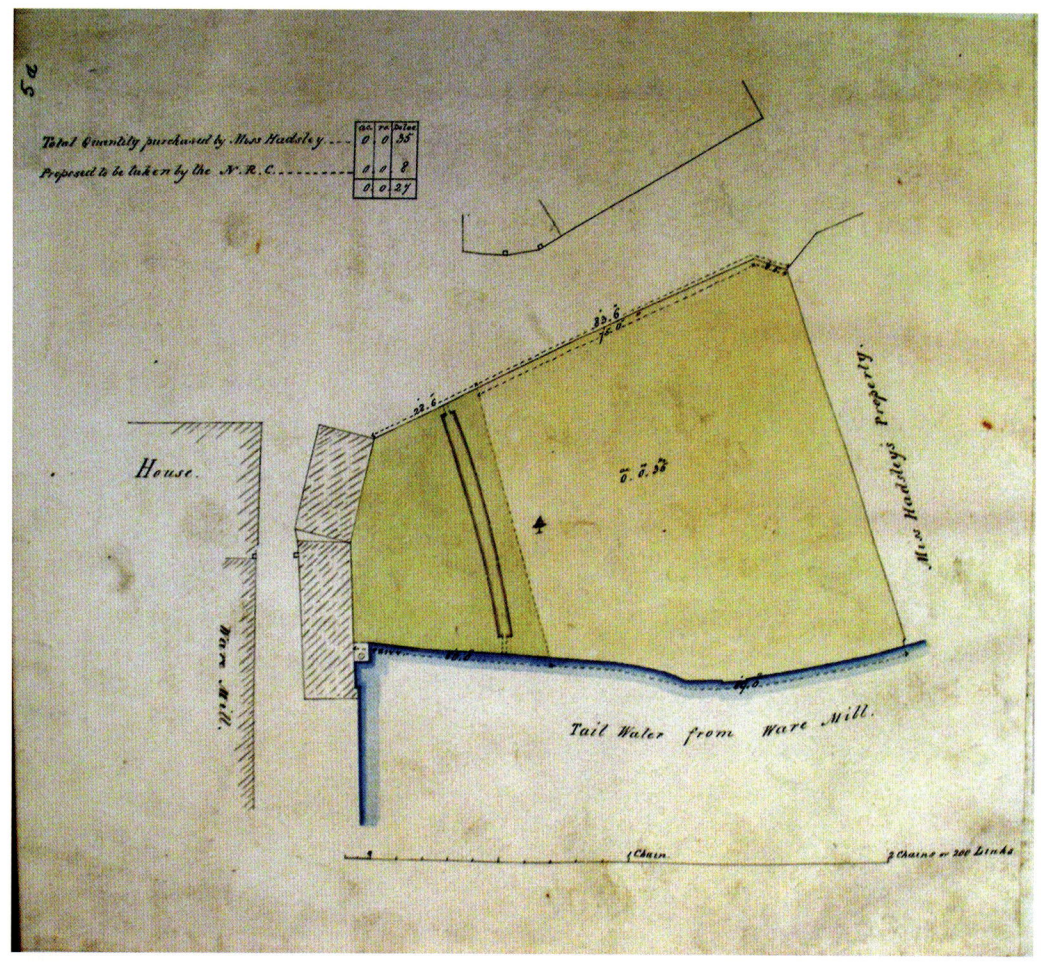

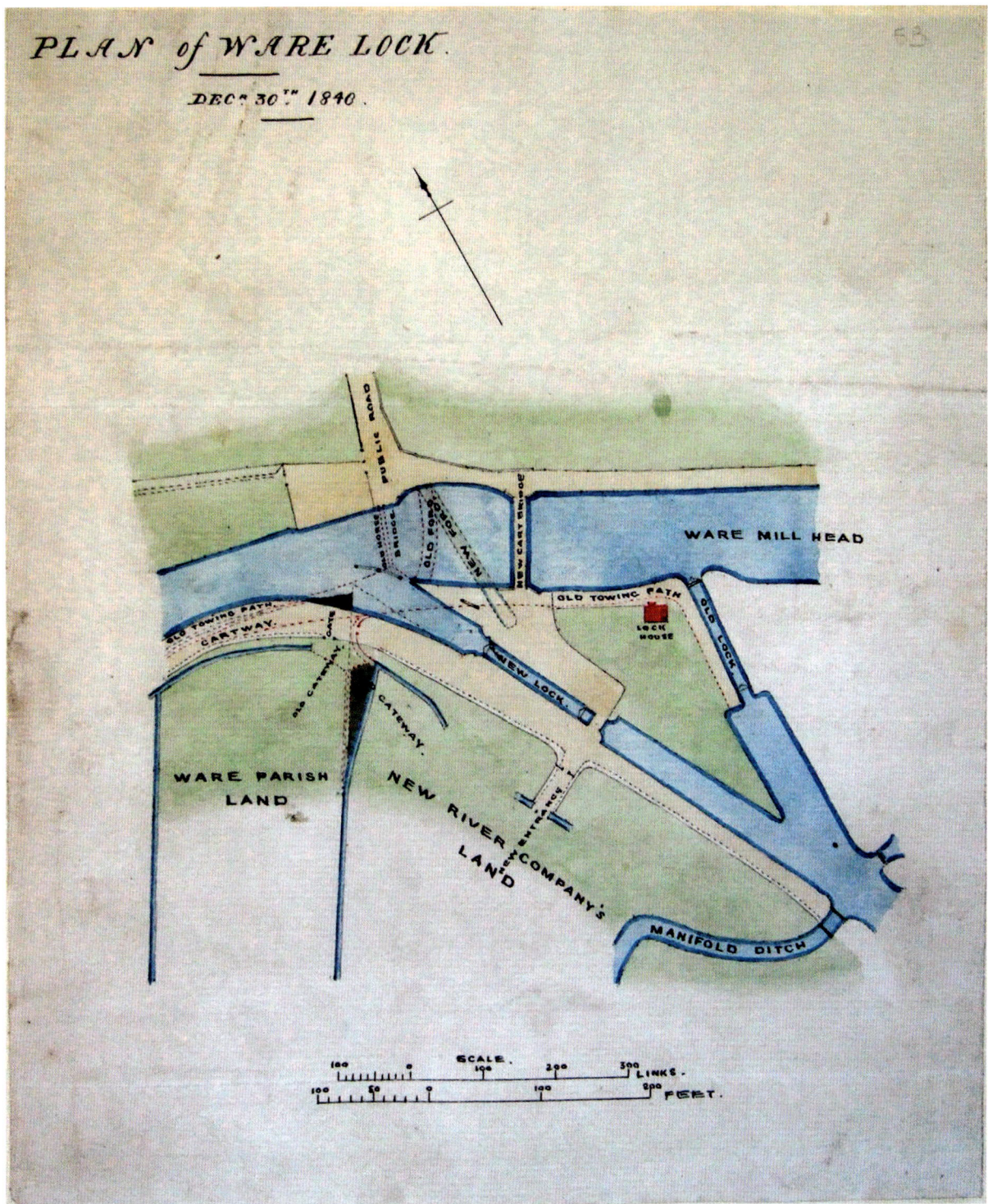

30 Dec. 1840 Plan of 'New' Ware Lock showing NRC Land (TW Archive; MFK photo). The Ford would suggest on the presumed line of the Roman 'Ermine Street'. Note the end of the Manifold Ditch (Old River Lee or Barge River).

1. Old Ware Lock: Cistern or Pound Lock built 1658 (also mentioned in 1669 agreement). In 1738-39 purchased by the NRC. Rebuilt 1741-2 by Henry Mill the NRC Surveyor.

2. New Ware Lock: Built 1831-2 by NRC, rebuilt 1922.

Off plan to the E, Portobello Turnpike (Lock, on Old Barge River) built 1740 by William Whittenbury for the Lee Trustees. Just E of this which was another Lock, 1766 Navigation Act for New/Ware Cut. There is a confusing array of names that most of the historical texts do not accurately identify.

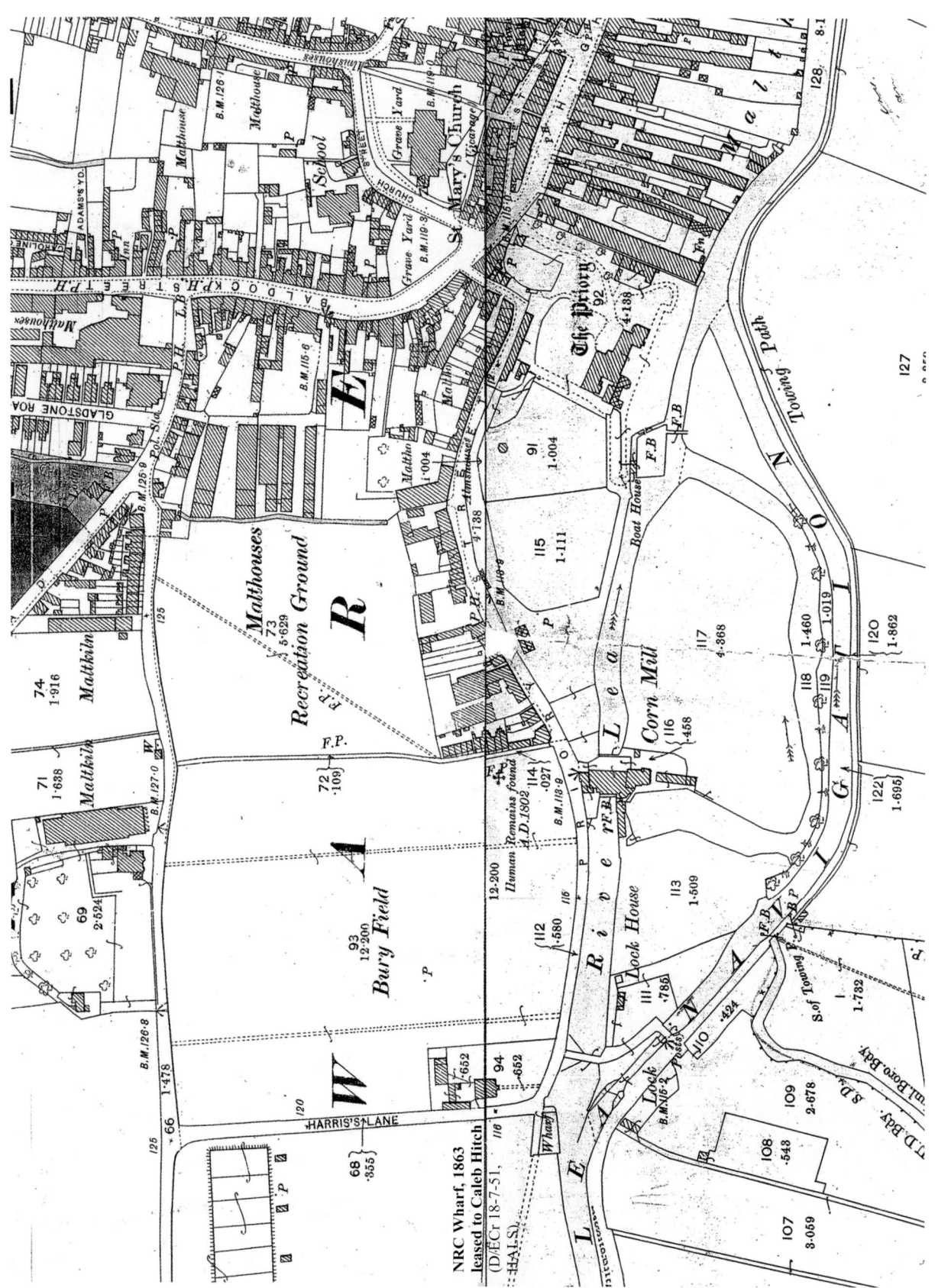

1898 OS Map: **Ware Lock & Mill property of NRC, and NRC Wharf** (OS map, HALS).

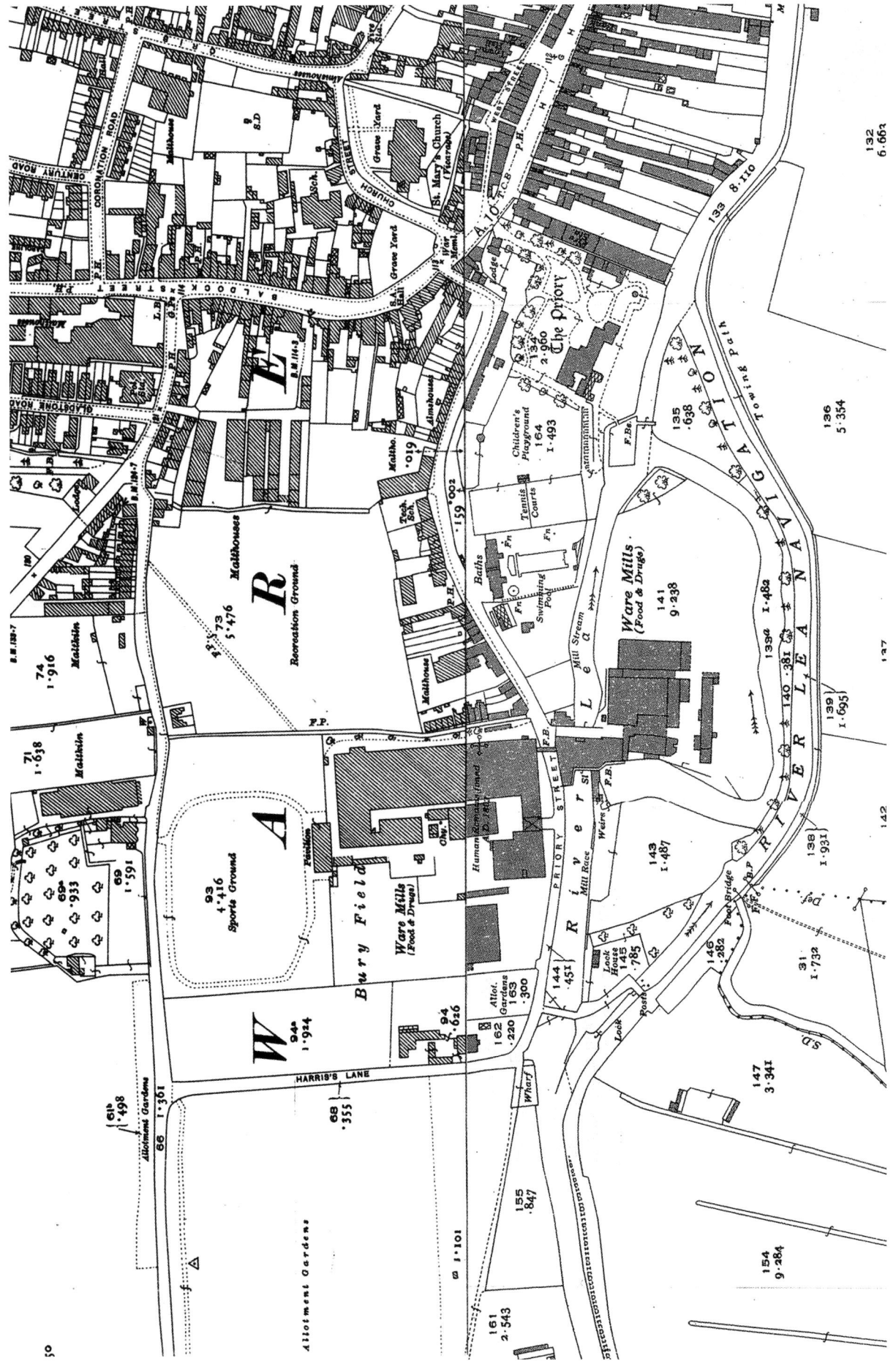

1923-38 OS Map: **NRC > 1904 MWB Ware Lock, & Ware Mills** expanded SE c.1900 by Allen & Hanbury > GlaxoSmithKline ((Above OS map 1923, below 1938) HALS).

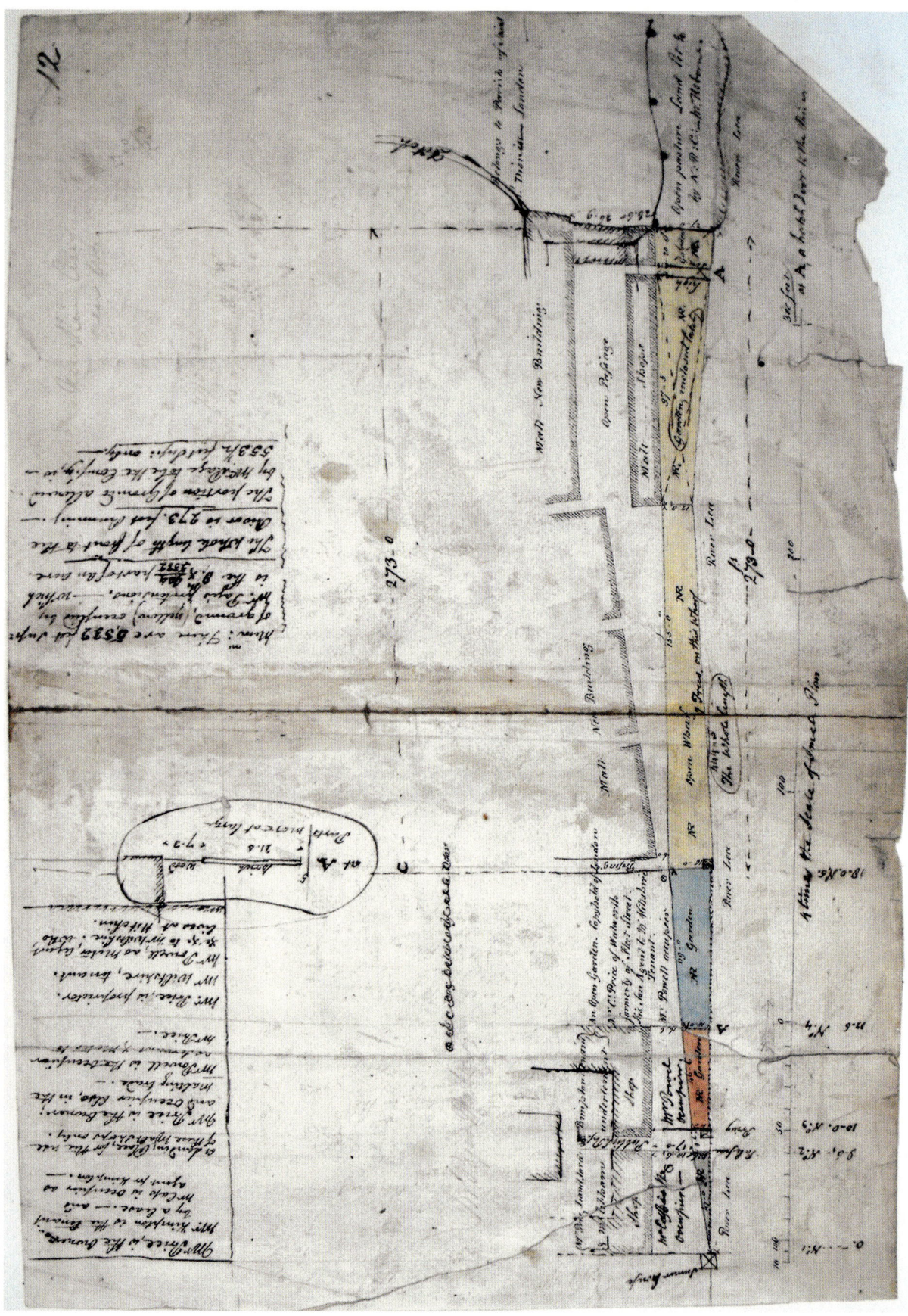

Prob. early-1800s (Undated): **NRC land presumably on N-bank of the River Lee at Ware** (TW Archive; MFK photo).

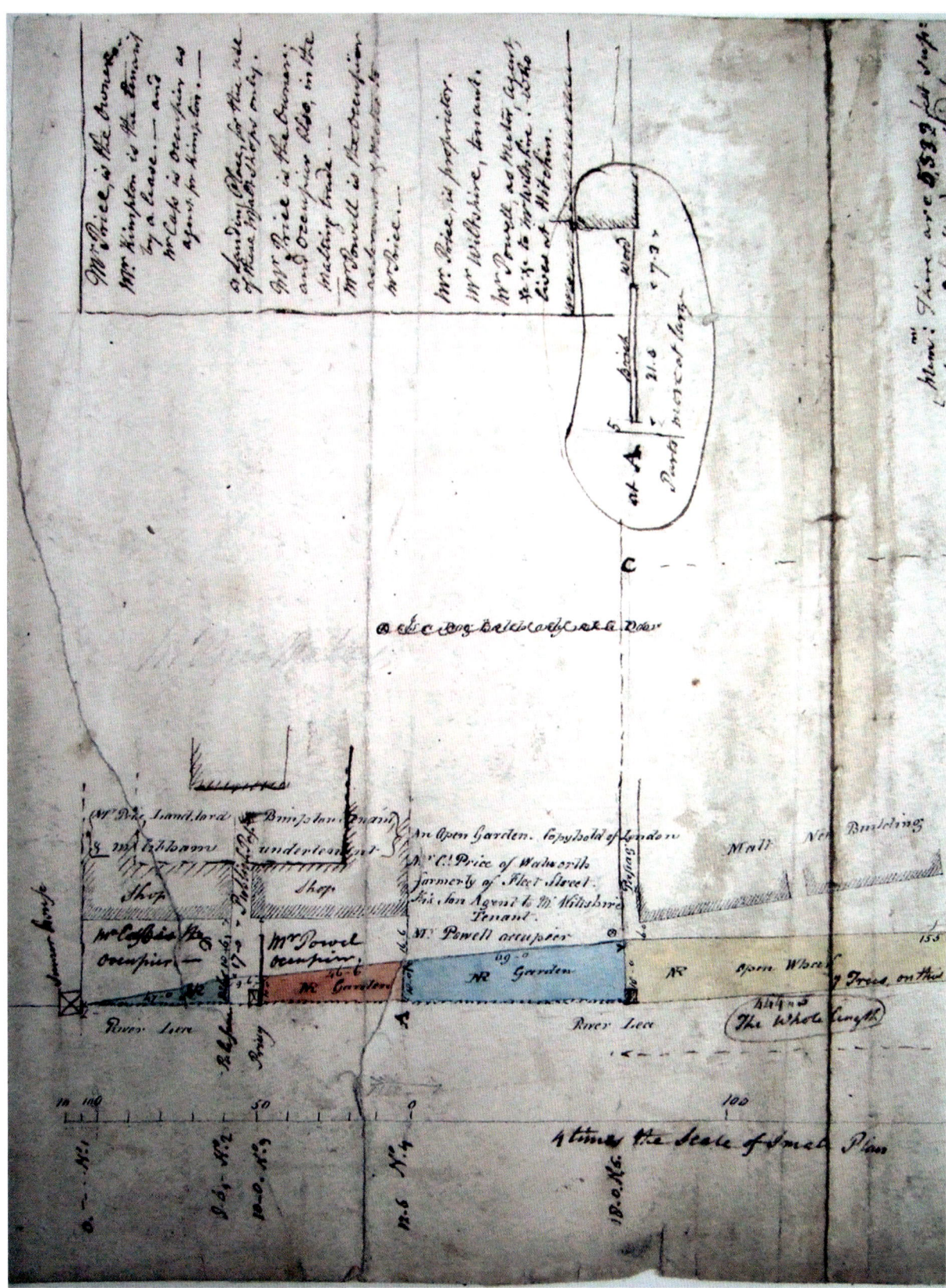

LARGER 1 of 2: Undated (Prob. early-1800s) NRC land presumably on N-bank of the River Lee at Ware (TW Archive; MFK photo).

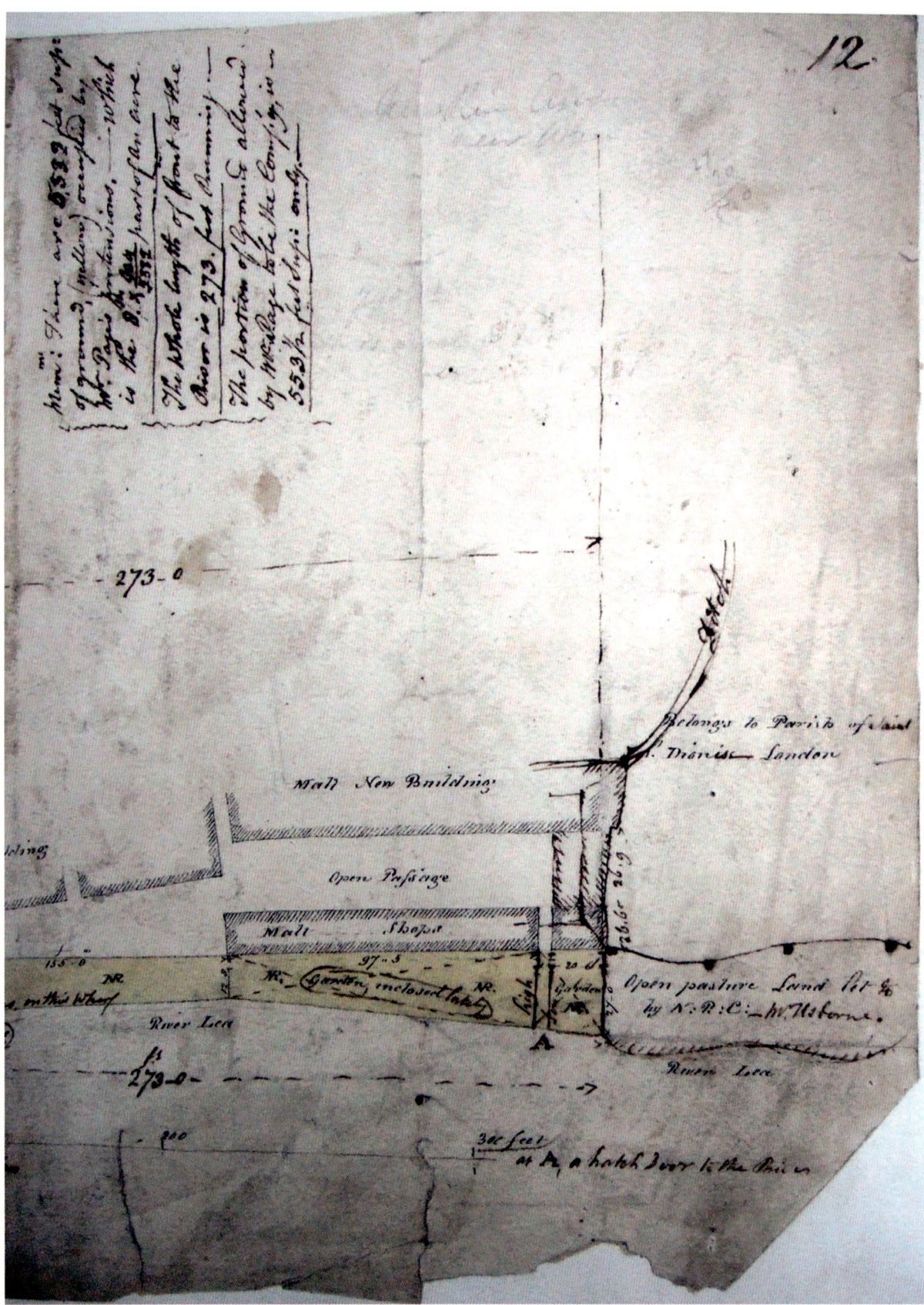

LARGER 2 of 2: Undated (Prob. early-1800s) NRC land presumably on N-bank of the River Lee at Ware (TW Archive; MFK photo).

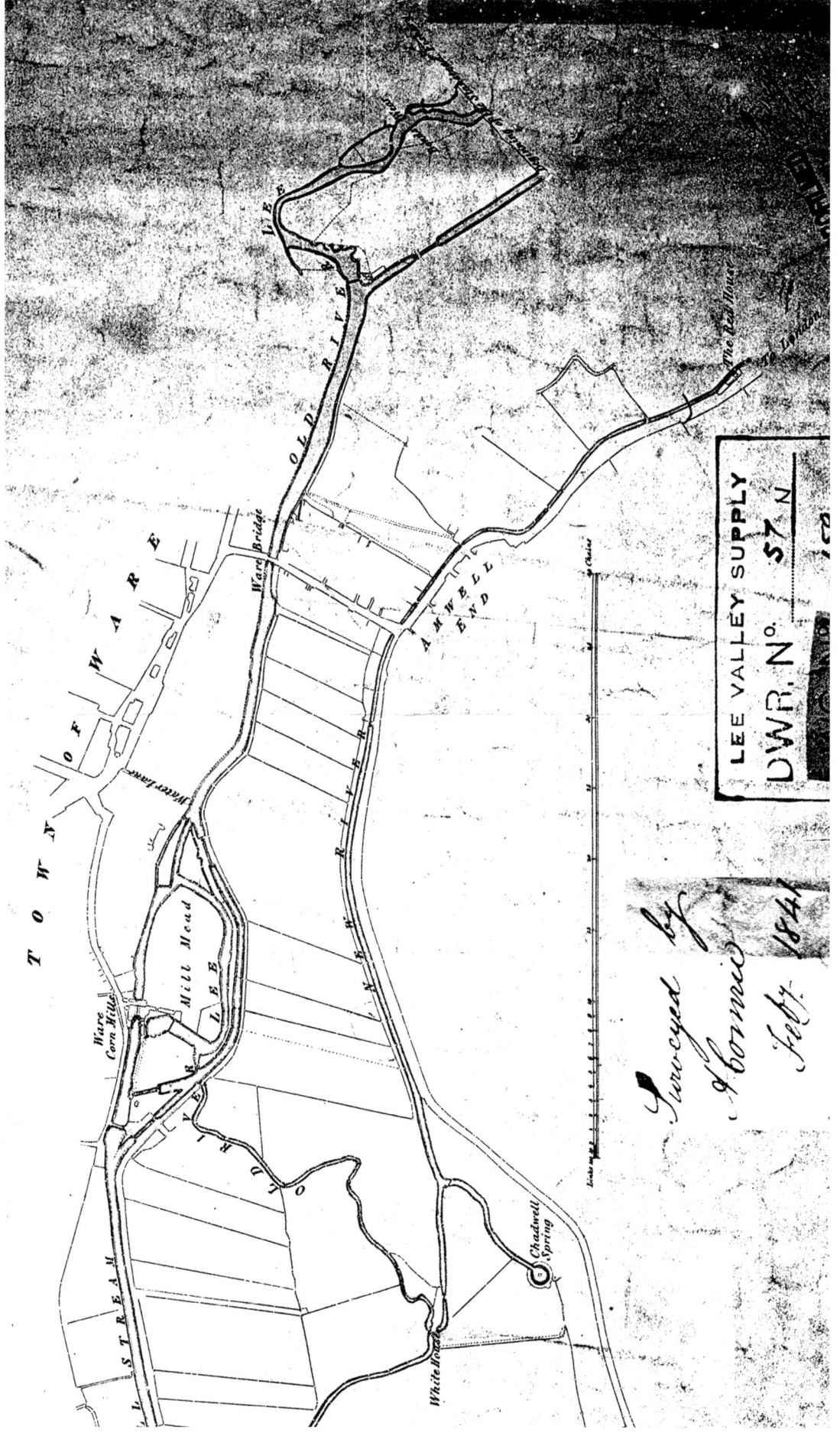

Feb. 1841 Plan: Course of the **River Lee (Old & New) & New River** (TW, Reading, Microfilm; MFK larger inset date).

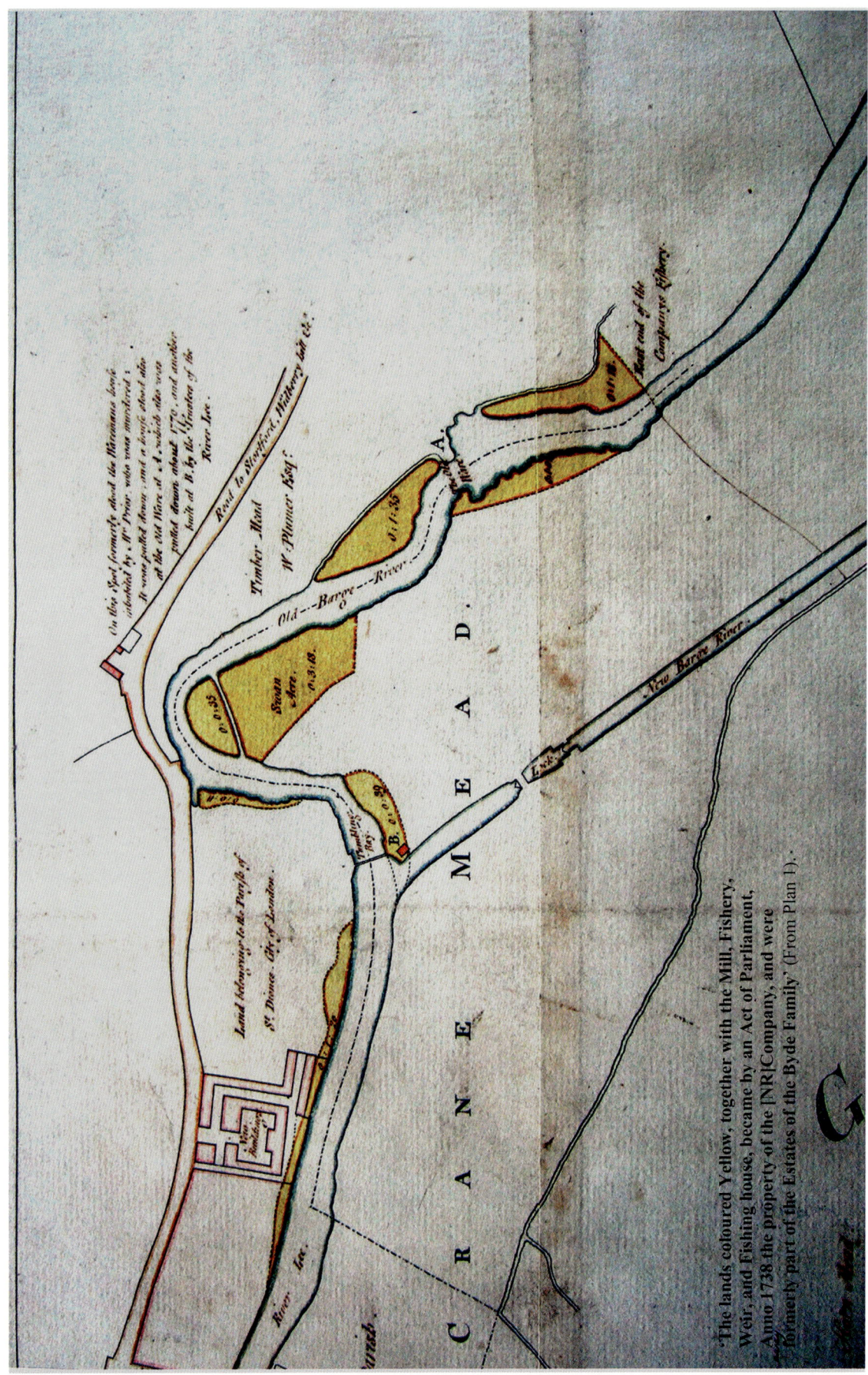

1775-1809 Plan 2: **Crane Mead**, E of Ware. **Yellow marked lands of NRC** (TW Archive; MFK photo). Also see page 163.

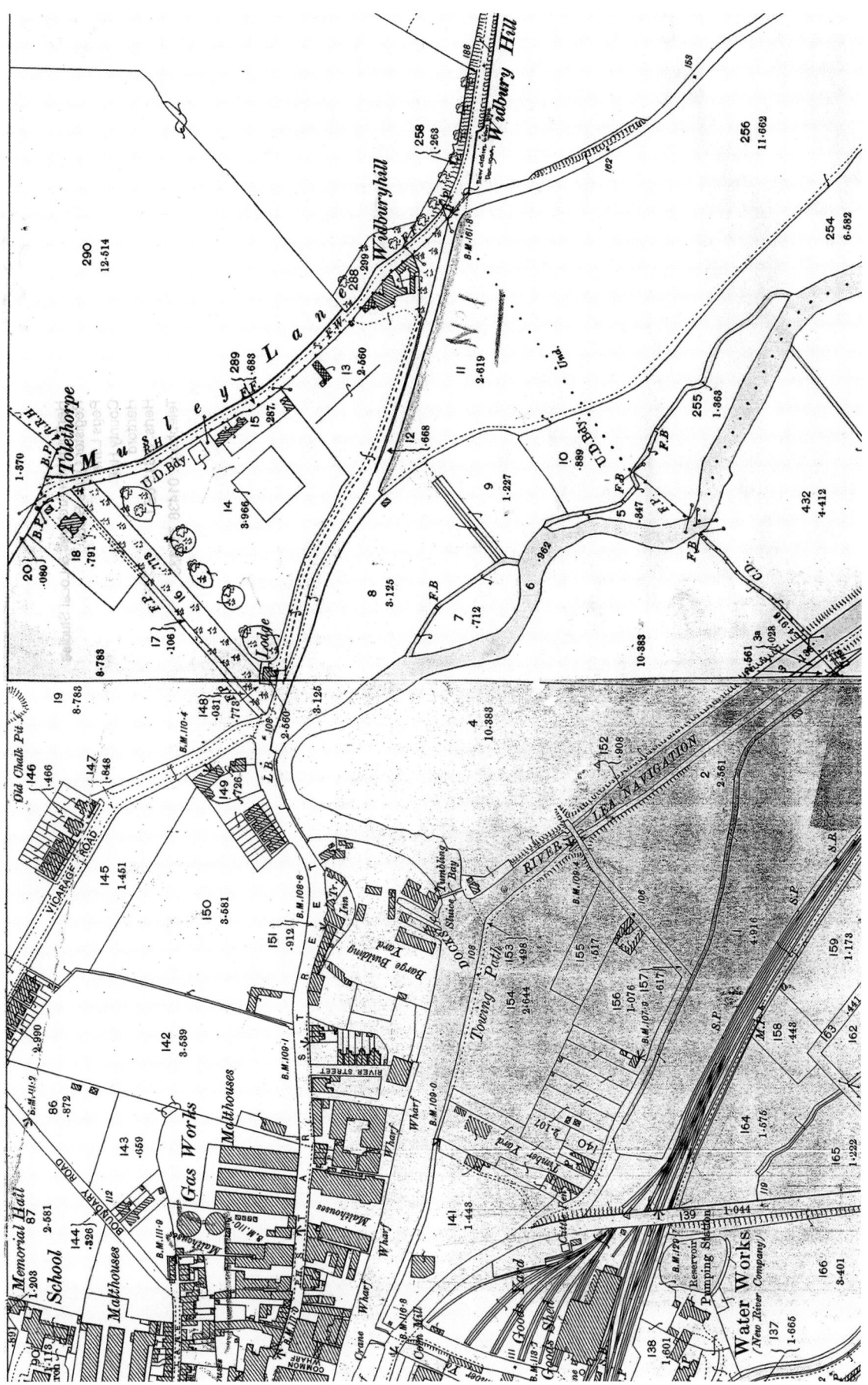

1898 OS Map: **River Lee & Navigation near Crane Mead**, Ware (HALS; MFK joined).

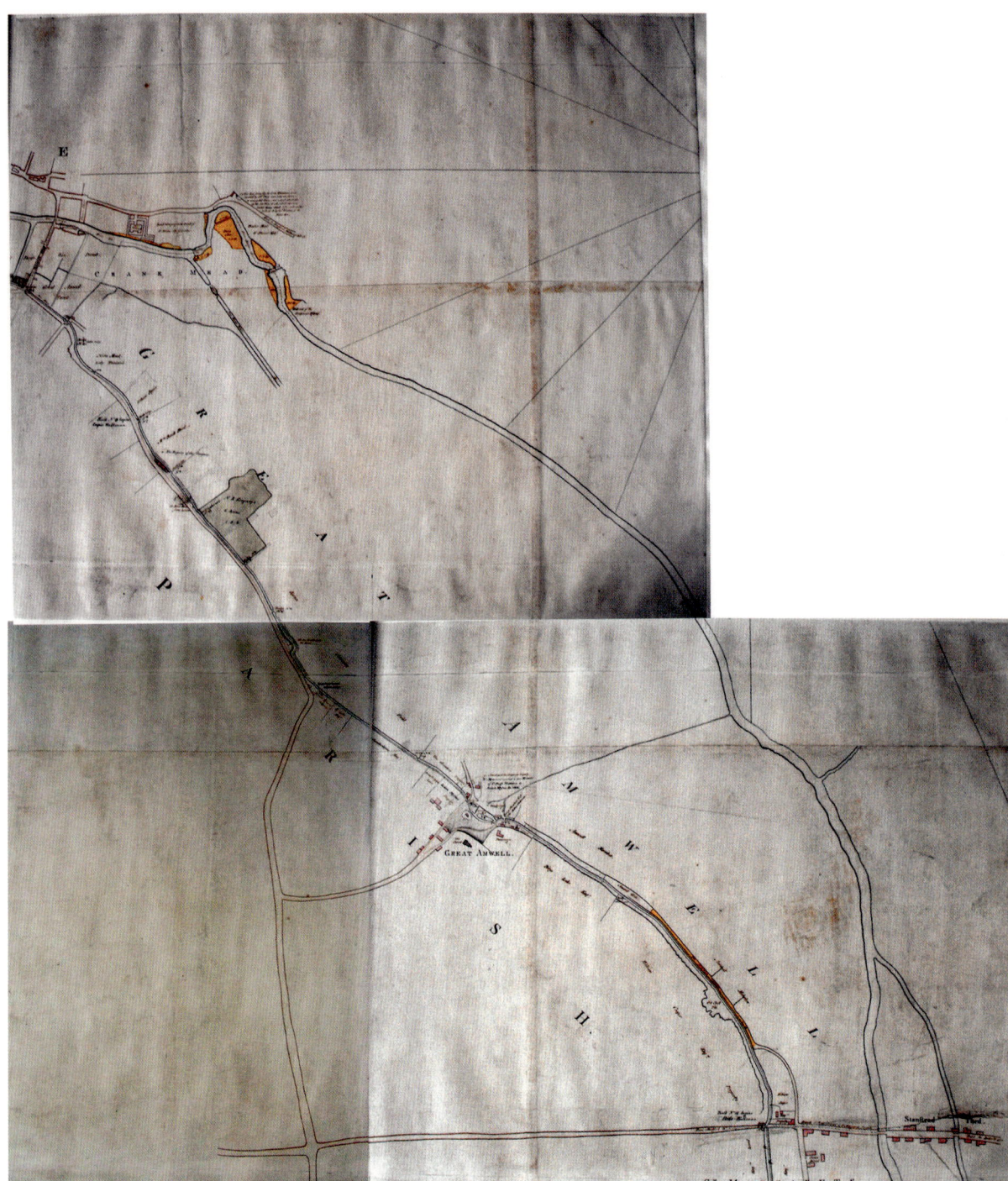

COMBINED Robert Mylne 1775-1809 Plans: **Plan 2 to Amwell Hill**;
Plan 3 Amwell Hill;
Plan 4 Gt. Amwell to Stanstead
(TW Archive; MFK photos joined).

1775-1809 Plan 2 (LARGE): **Amwell End, Ware to Lower Road, Gt. Amwell** (TW Archive; MFK photo).

1775-1809 Plan 2: **Ware, & New River from Amwell End to today's Viaduct Road,** with LHS larger at Amwell End (TW Archive; MFK photos).

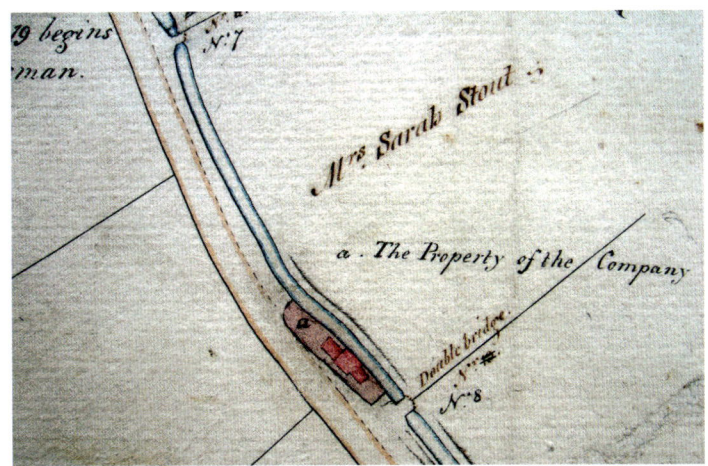

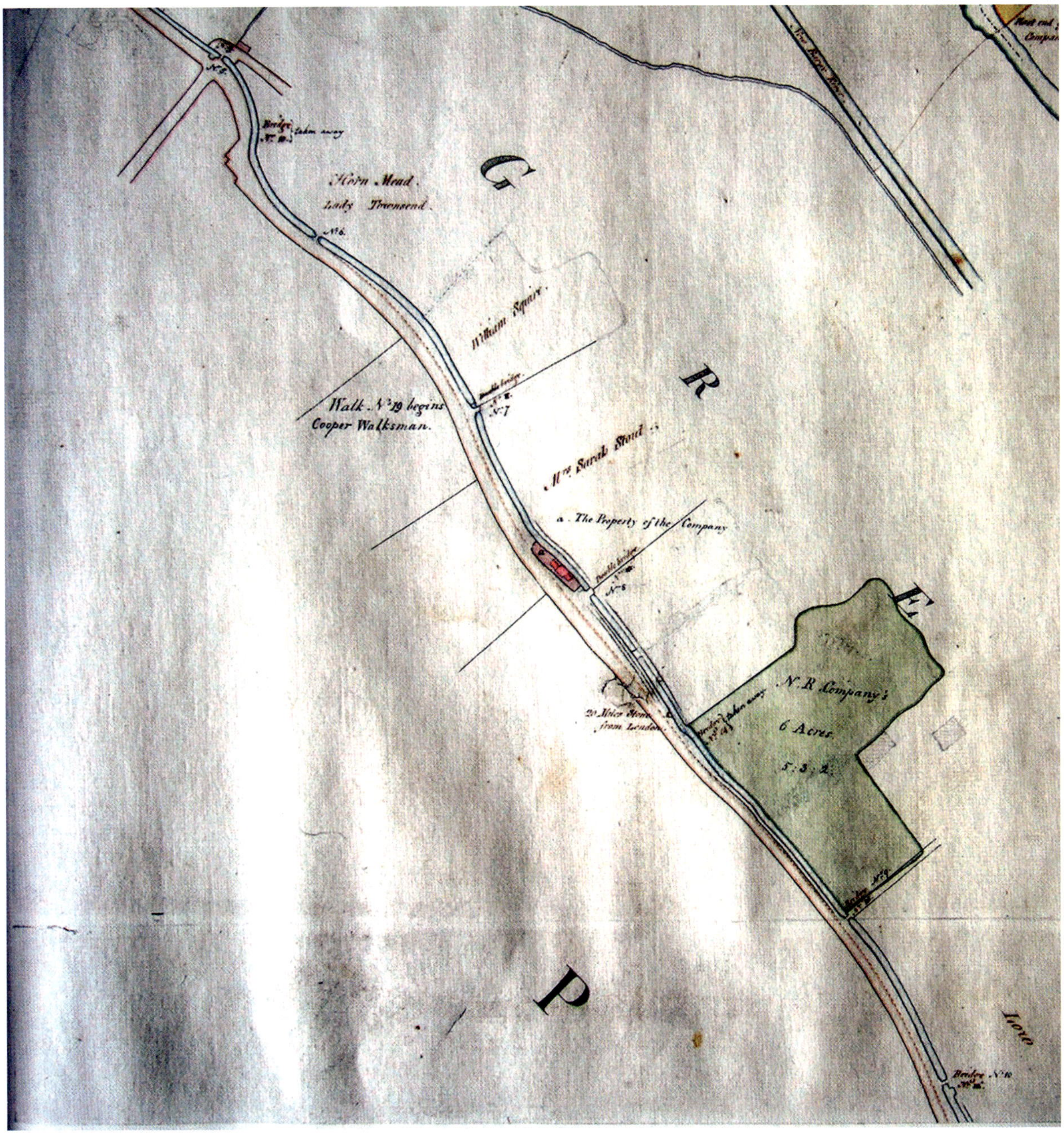

1775-1809 Plan 2: **New River near the Red House**, also shown above larger (TW Archive; MFK photos).

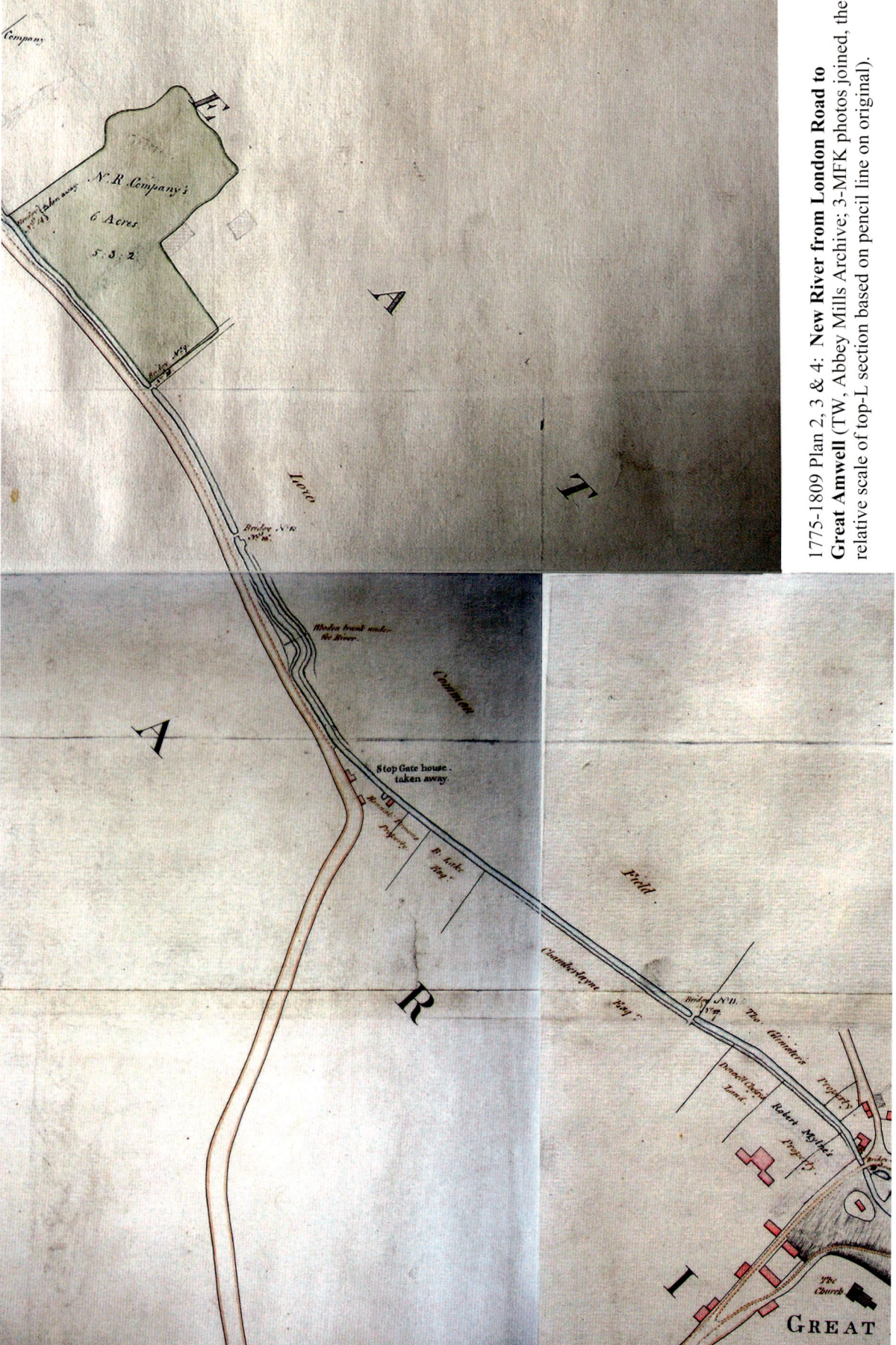

1775-1809 Plan 2, 3 & 4: **New River from London Road to Great Amwell** (TW, Abbey Mills Archive; 3-MFK photos joined, the relative scale of top-L section based on pencil line on original).

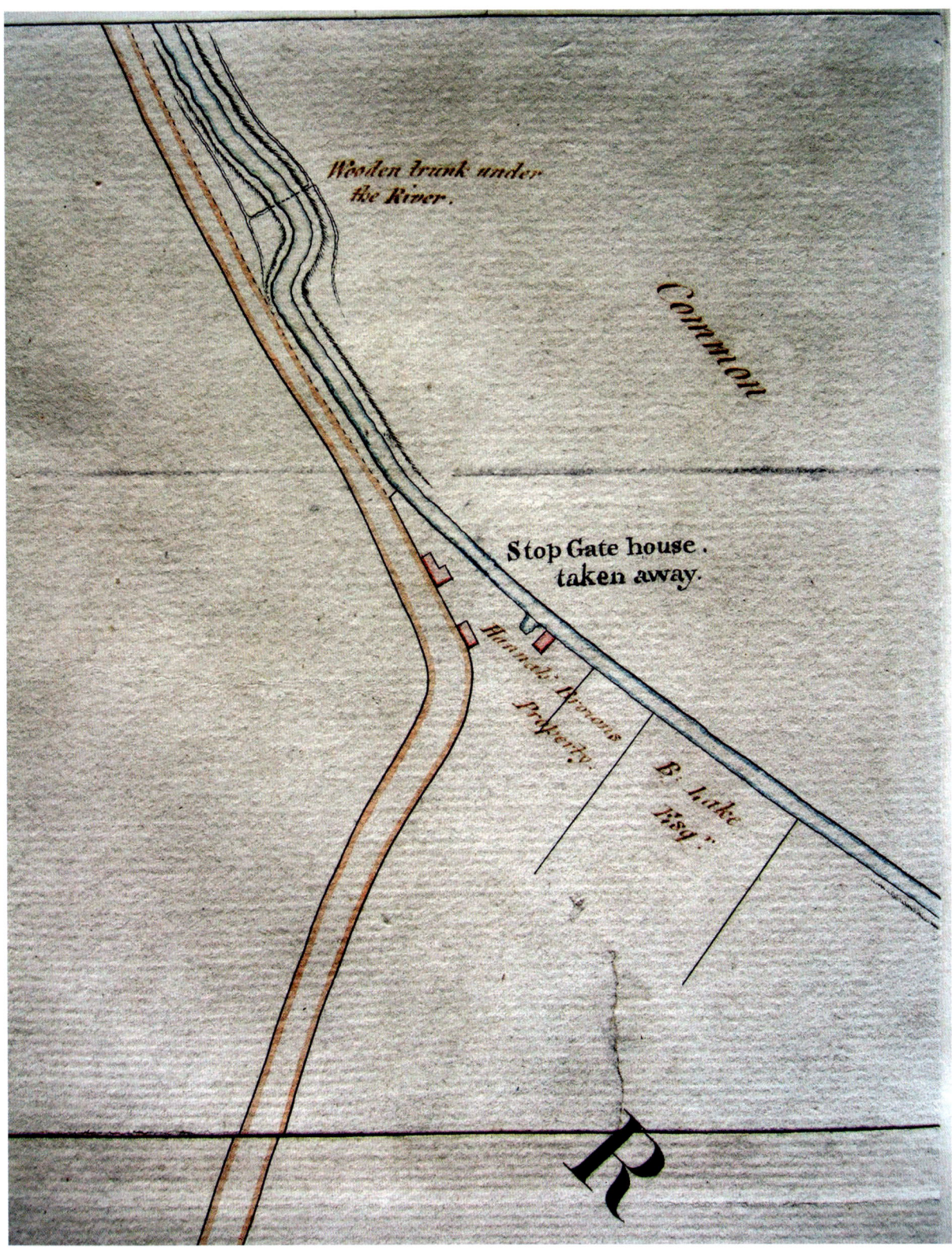

1775-1809 Plan 3: **New River at start of Amwell Hill** (TW Archive; MFK photo).

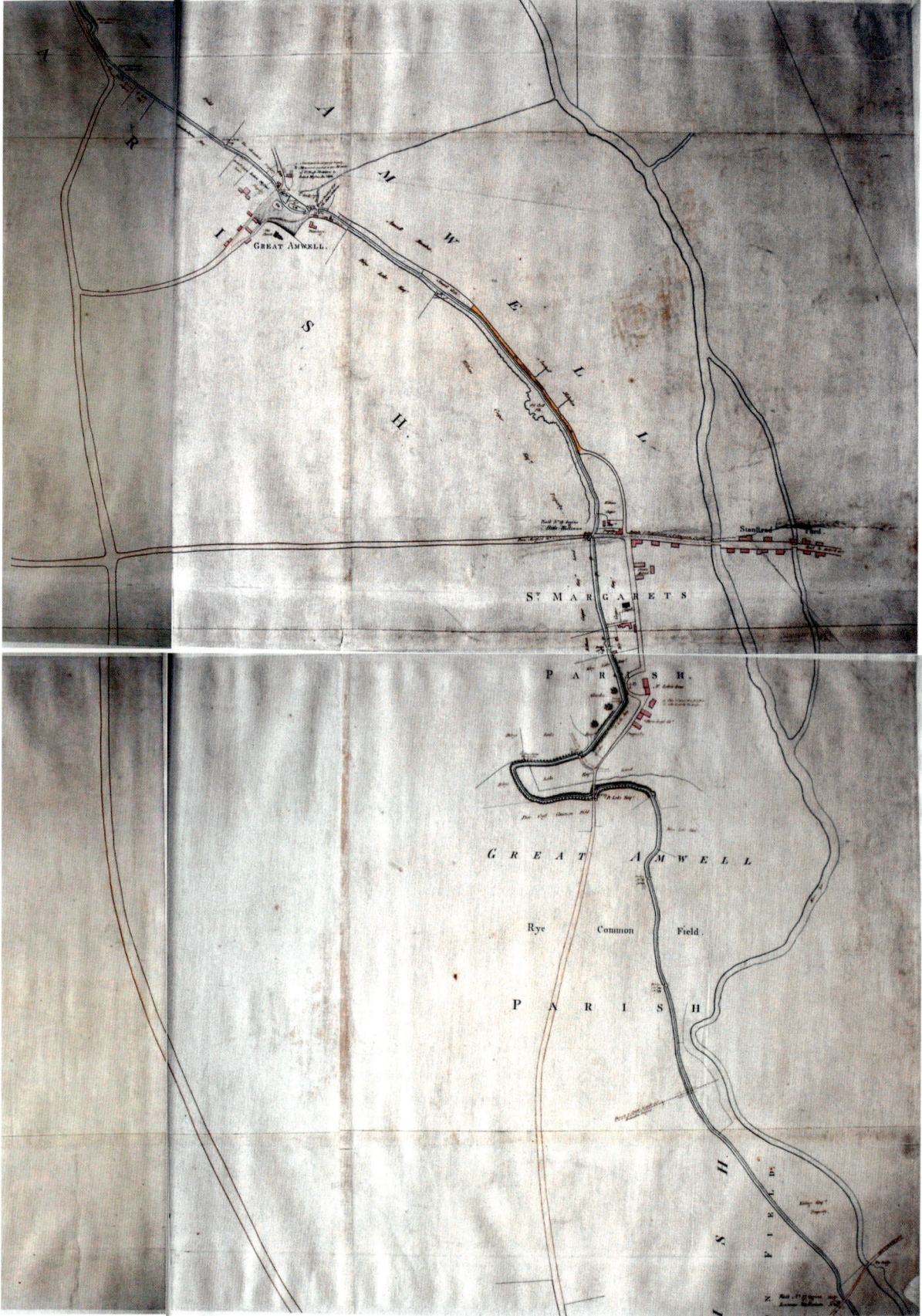

COMBINED Robert Mylne 1775-1809 Plans 3, 4, 4a & 5:
Plan 3 to Amwell Hill; Plan 4 Gt. Amwell to Stanstead; Plan 4a Road only; Plan 5 Stanstead Loop/s
(TW Archive; MFK photos & joins, lower join based on rivers not road).

1775-1809 Plan 4: **Great Amwell to St Margarets** (TW Archive; MFK photo).

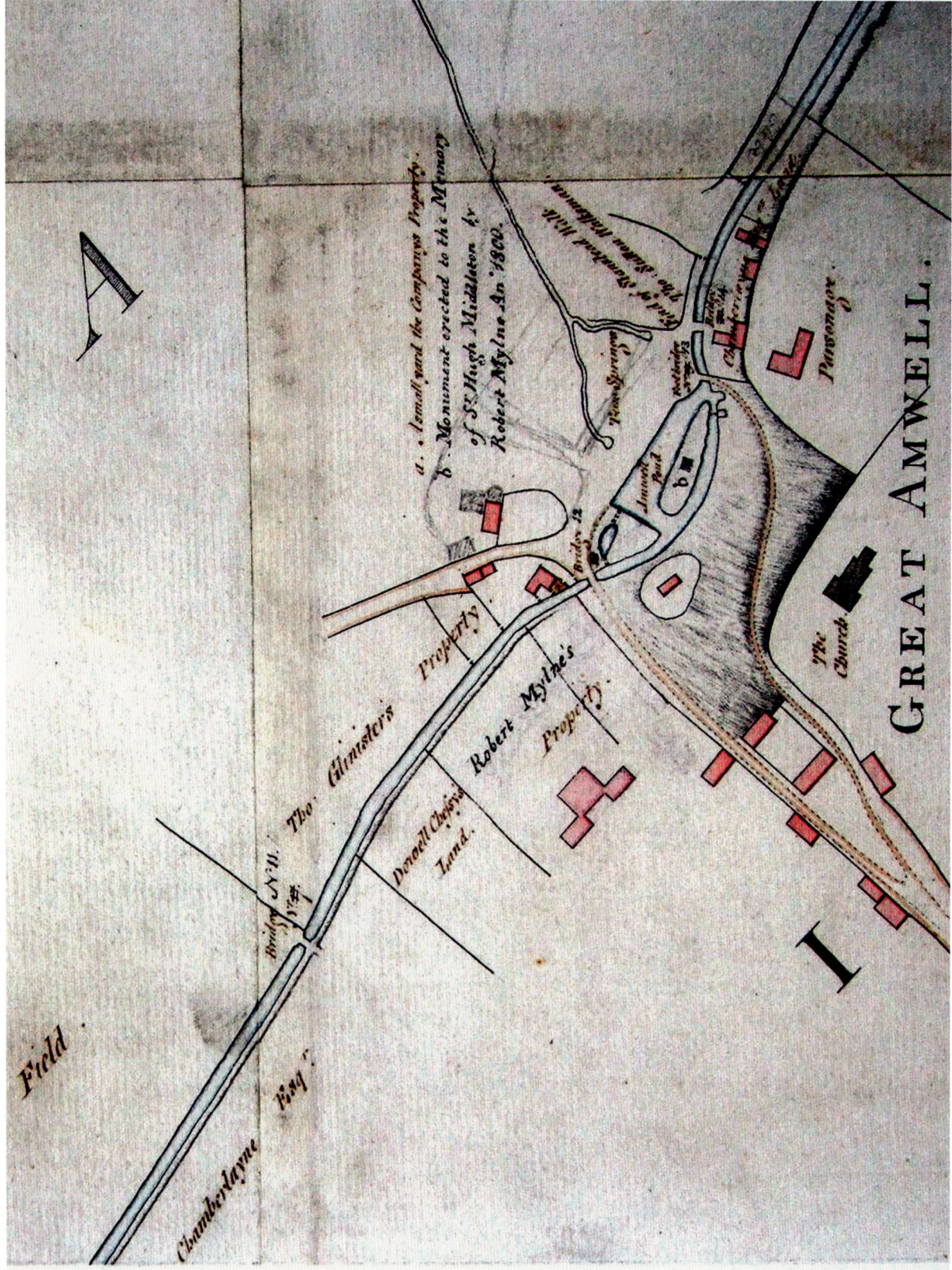

1775-1809 Plan 4: **New River through the village of Great Amwell**. Note as such there is only one island, whereas today there is two (TW Archive; MFK photo).

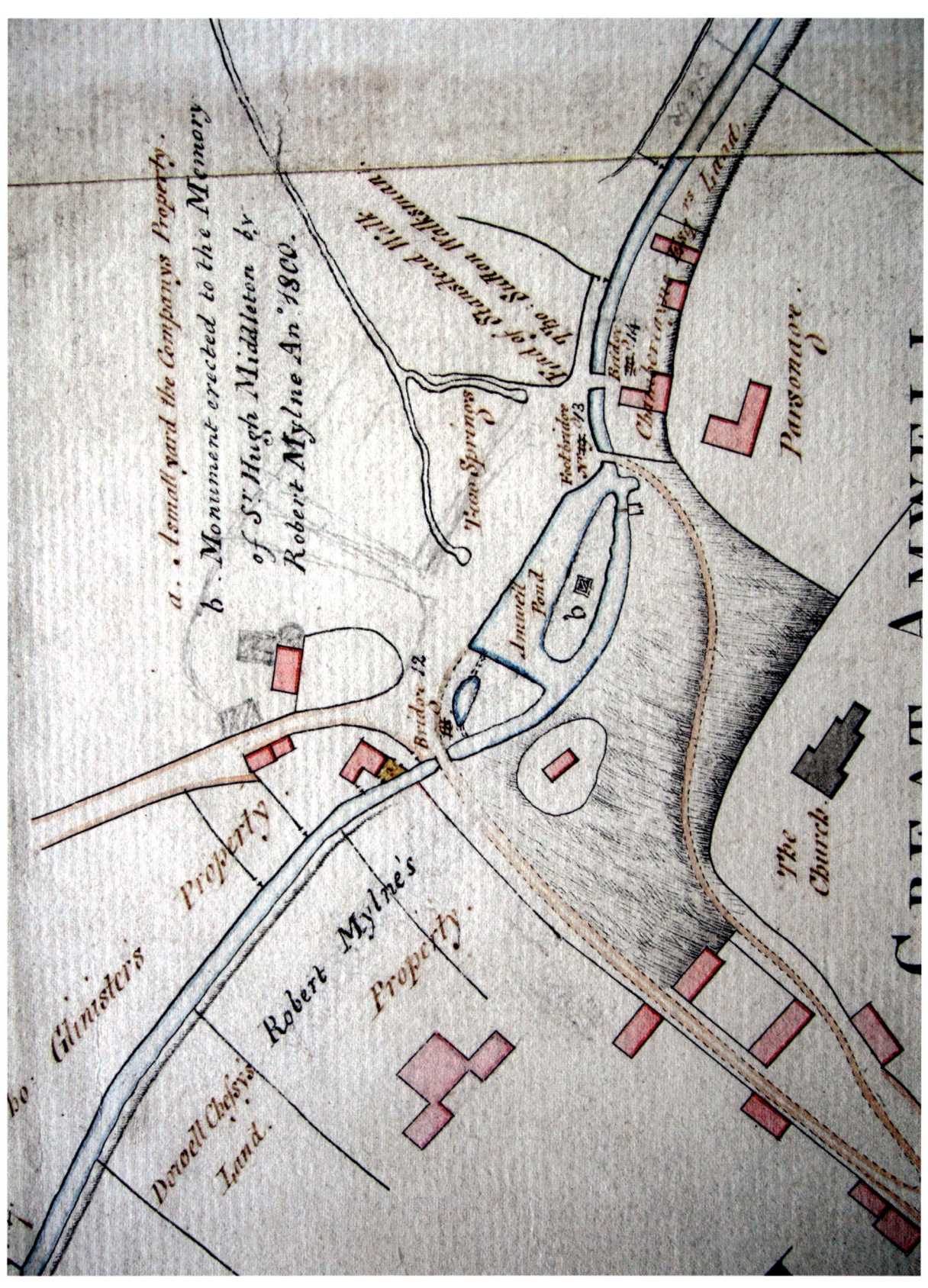

1775-1809 Plan 4 (LARGER): **Gt. Amwell Village** (TW Archive; MFK photo).

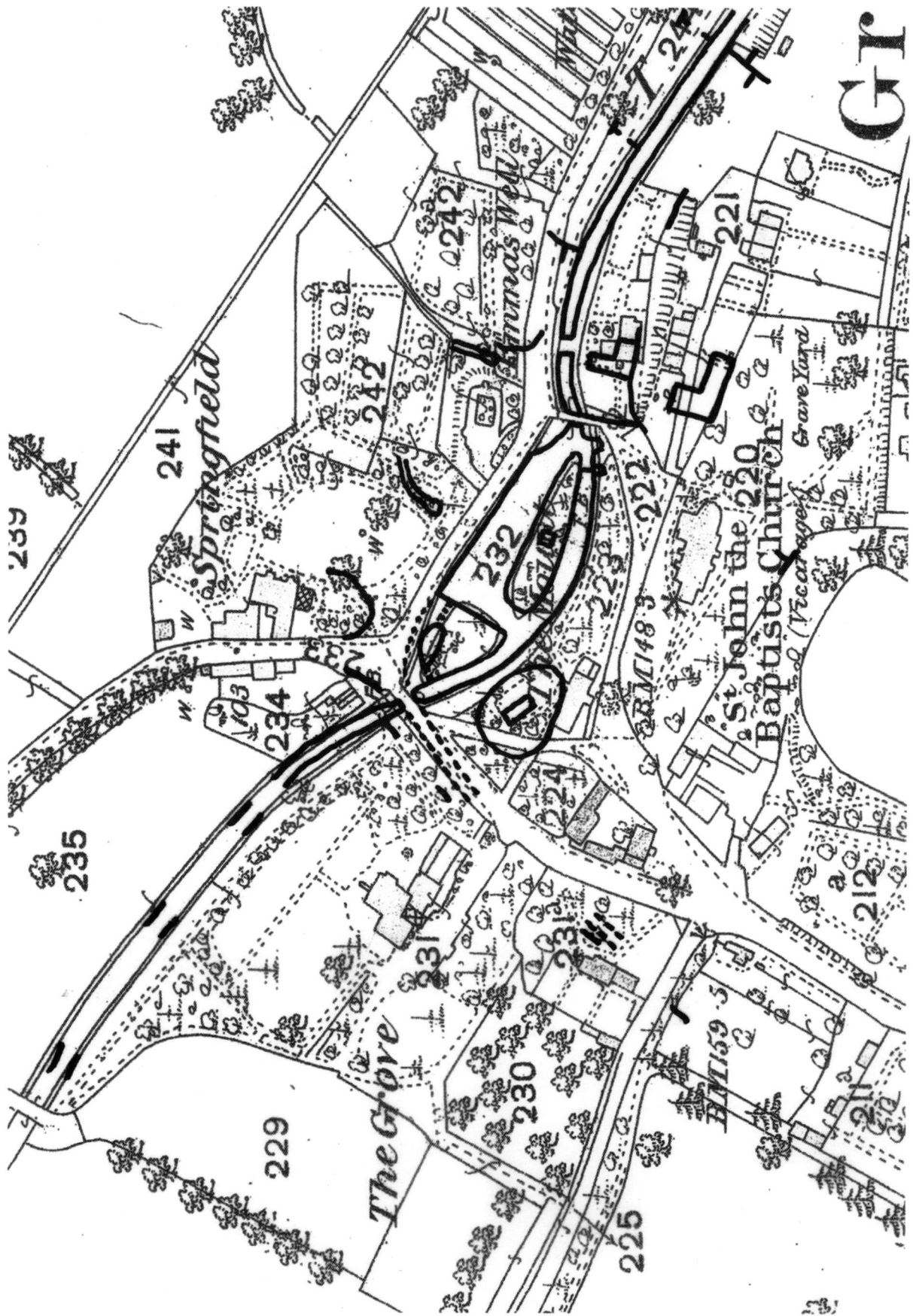

'Amwell Pond': 1775-1809 Mylne map overlaid on 1880 OS map (TW Archive; HALS; Overlay © M.F. Kensey). The very small pond with dotted lines into New River **probably the original Amwell Spring**, now part of a widened New River & extra island, & probable reason for creating today's 'easement' here.

ABOVE: Amwell Grove (Front Elevation). Built 1794-97 by Robert Mylne (NRC Surveyor) as his family's summer country house. Enlarged in the C19th when given extra floors, removing the unusual parapet, corner chimney stacks, and set-back wings (D/EX 440/P1-17, HALS).

BELOW: Prob. c.1770s, said to be **Washer-women aside New River before Cautherly Lane**, Gt. Amwell (Batty & Jukes Collection No. 25, HALS). But from maps not aware of any building on RHS.

AMWELL.

ABOVE: Late-C18th approaching Gt. Amwell, showing bridge to island from N-bank, bridge over New River to church, and former bridge at Thorpe's Farm > today's River Cottage (Batty & Jukes Collection No. 6, HALS).

BELOW: 1794 (Published) Thorpe's Farm, Gt. Amwell with former New River bridge S-side of church (Batty & Jukes Collection No. 7, HALS).

ABOVE: 1807 published print of **Lower Island** & Church, Gt. Amwell ((Drawn by Ellis & Engraved by Sparrow for Dr Hughson's 'London') ELSC&A).

BELOW: Probably c./1836, B & W photo of landscape of **Upper Island** & Church, Gt. Amwell (((Possibly G.S. Shepherd) Knowsley-Clutterbuck Collection) AM/GT/2, HALS). Assumedly the right way round (based on rectangular stone) but no RHS to New River!

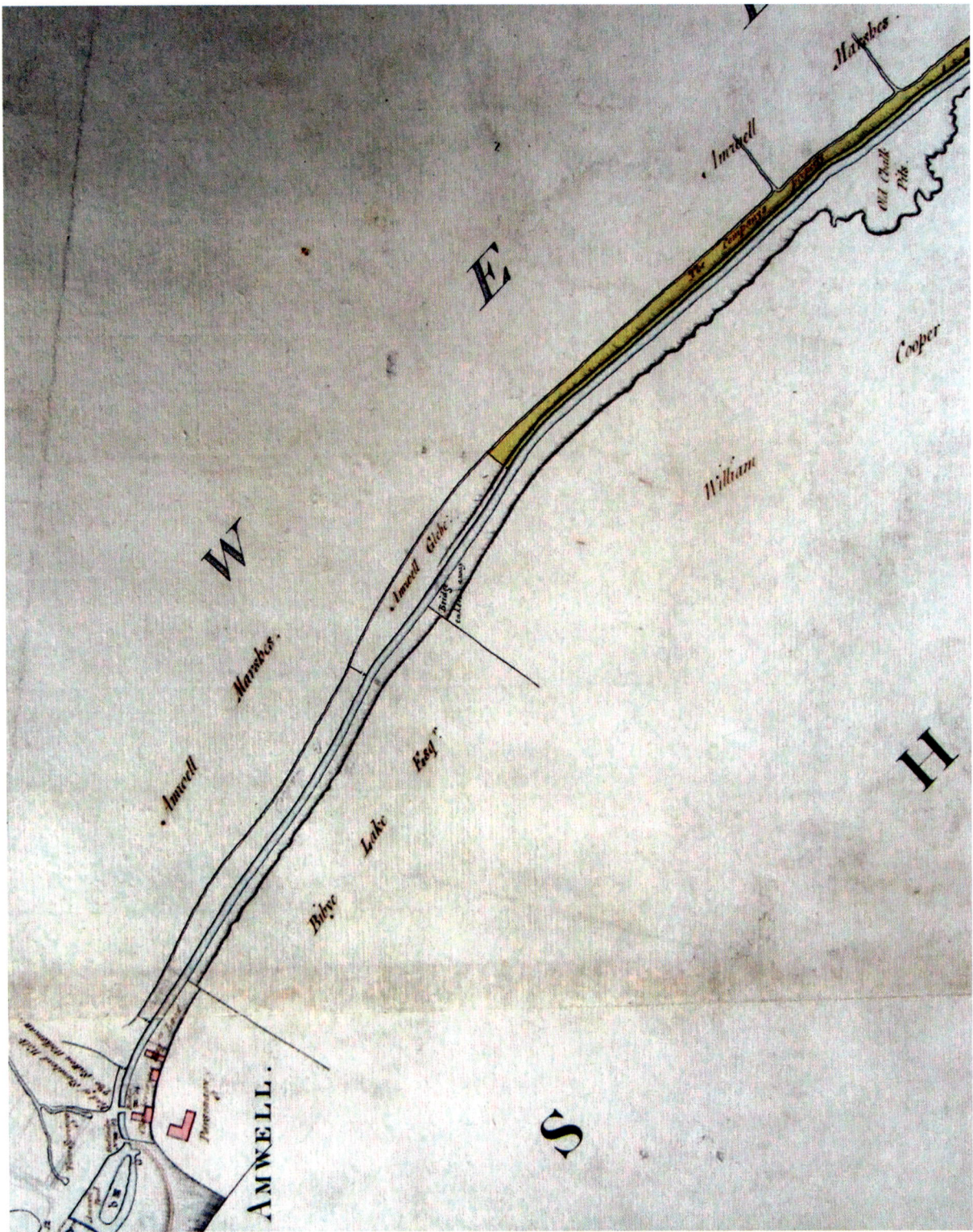

1775-1809 Plan 4: **New River SE of Gt. Amwell, approaching Amwell Marsh** (TW Archive; MFK photo).

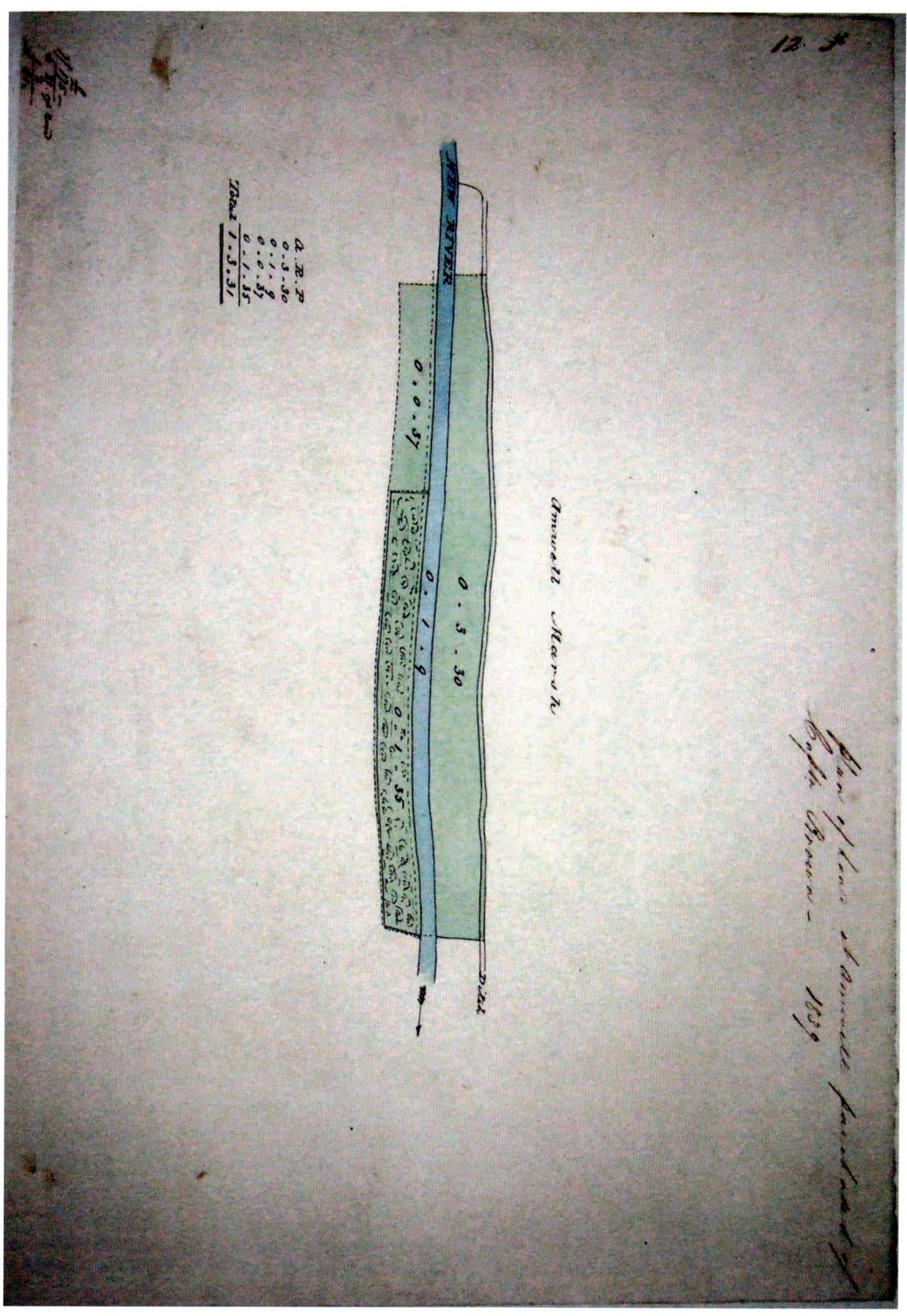

1839 Land at Amwell Marsh purchased by NRC from Capt. Brown (TW Archive; MFK photo).

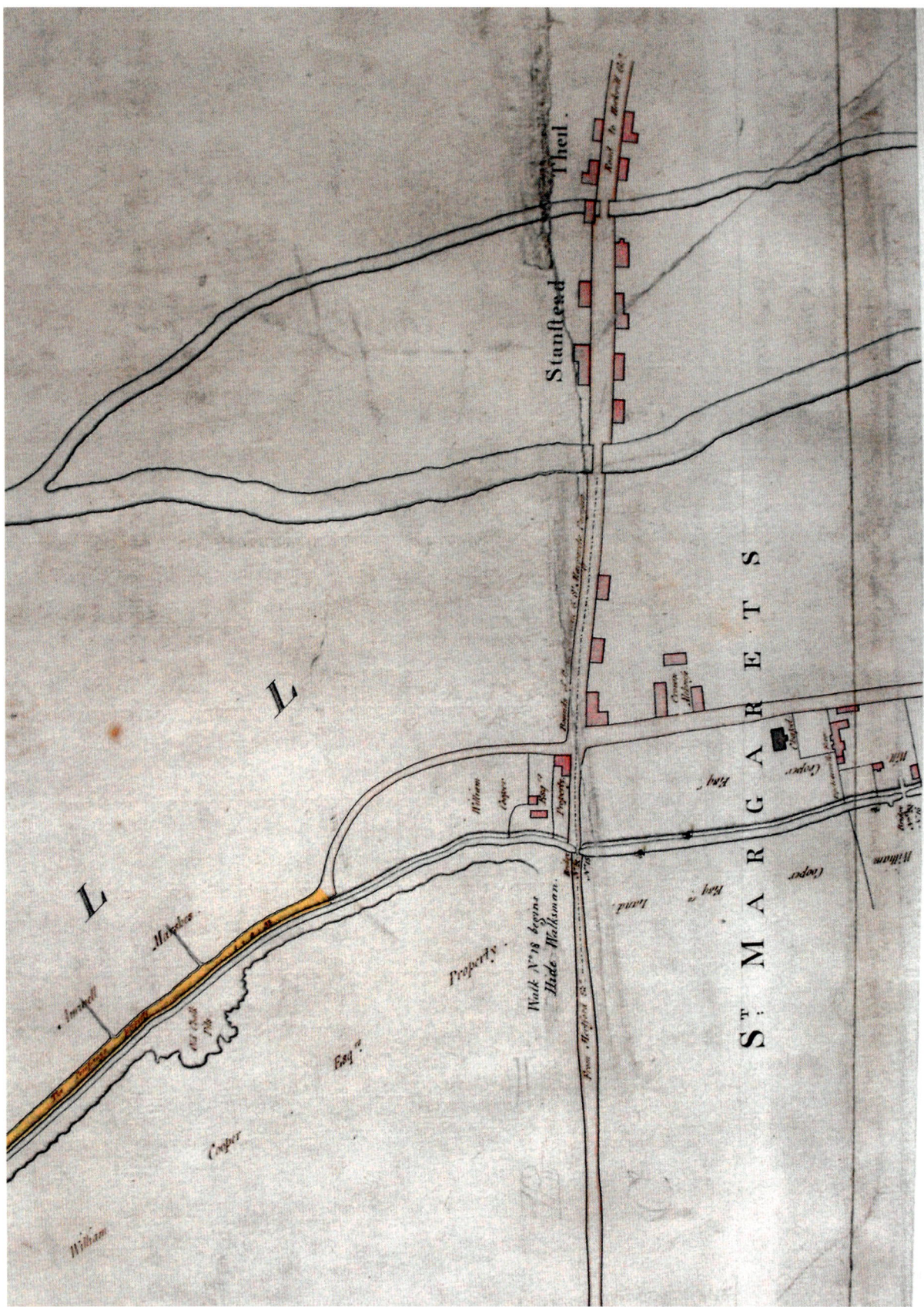

1775-1809 Plan 4: **New River SE of Amwell Marsh & St Margarets/Stanstead Therl** (TW Archive; MFK photo).

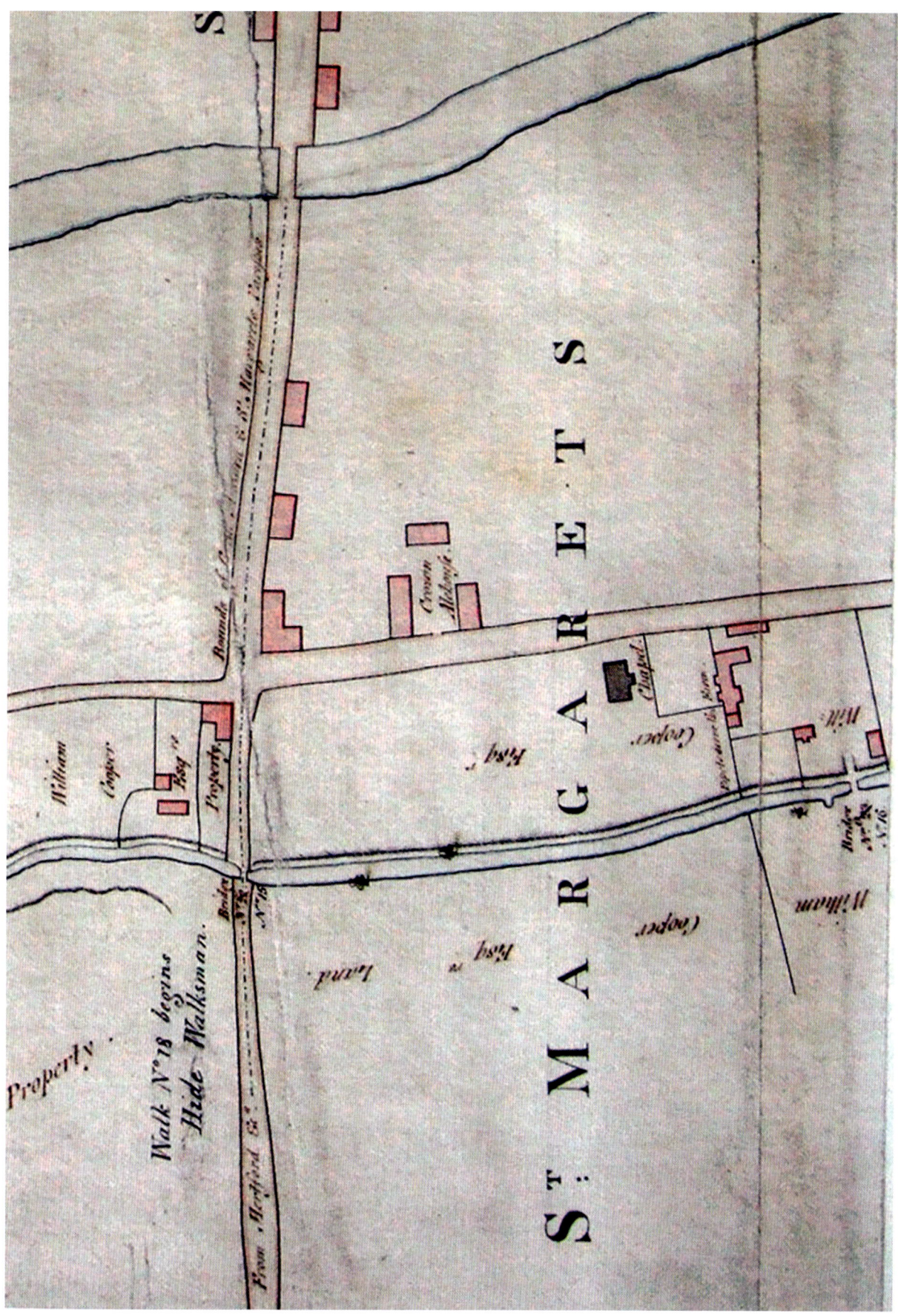

1775-1809 Plan 4 LARGER: **New River at St Margarets/Stanstead** (TW Archive; MFK photo).

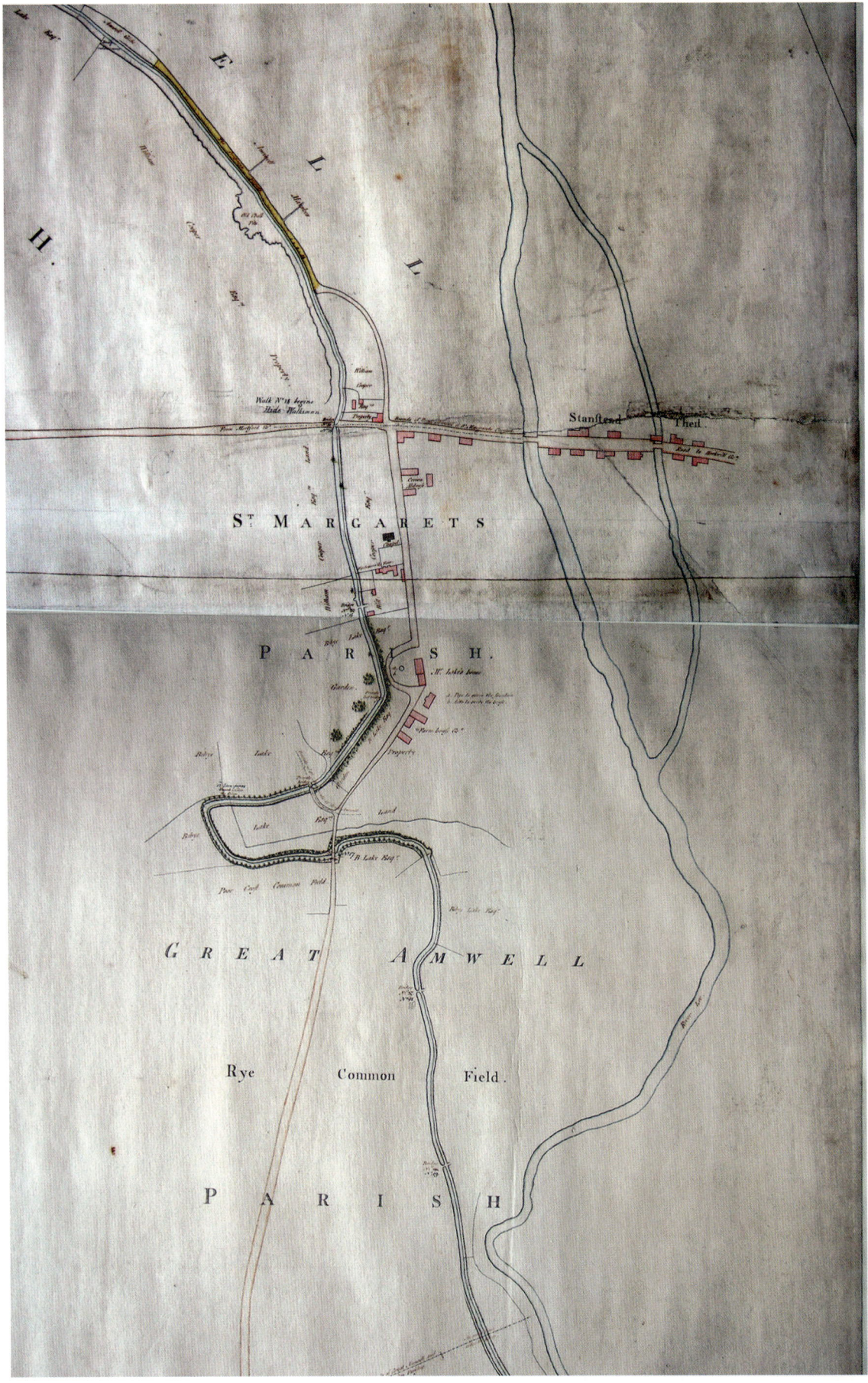

1775-1809 Plan 4 & 5: **New River at Stanstead St Margarets & Rye Common** (TW, Abbey Mills Archive; 2-MFK photos joined).

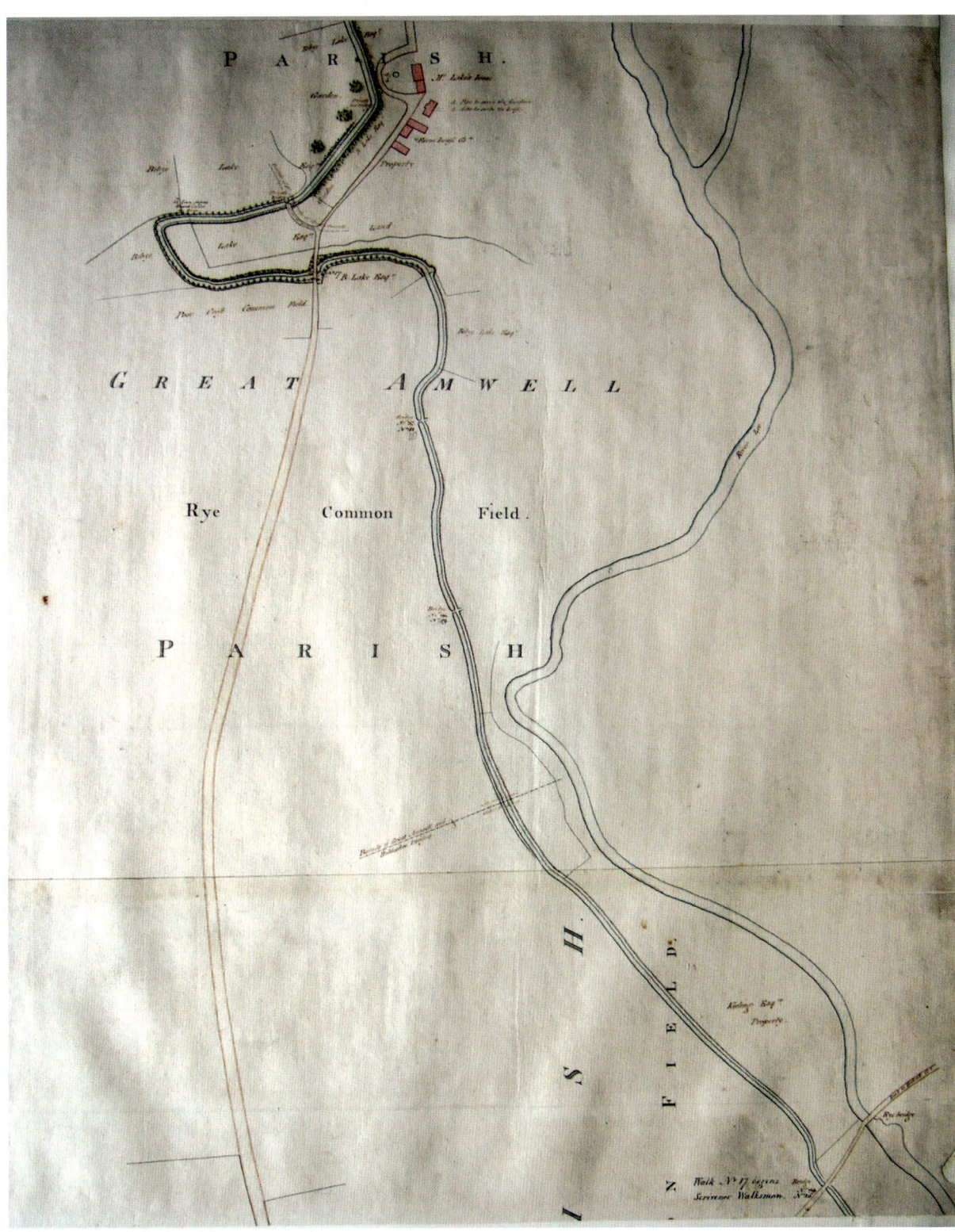

1775-1809 Plan 5 & 6: **Stanstead Loop/s to Rye Bridge** (TW Archive; MFK photo).

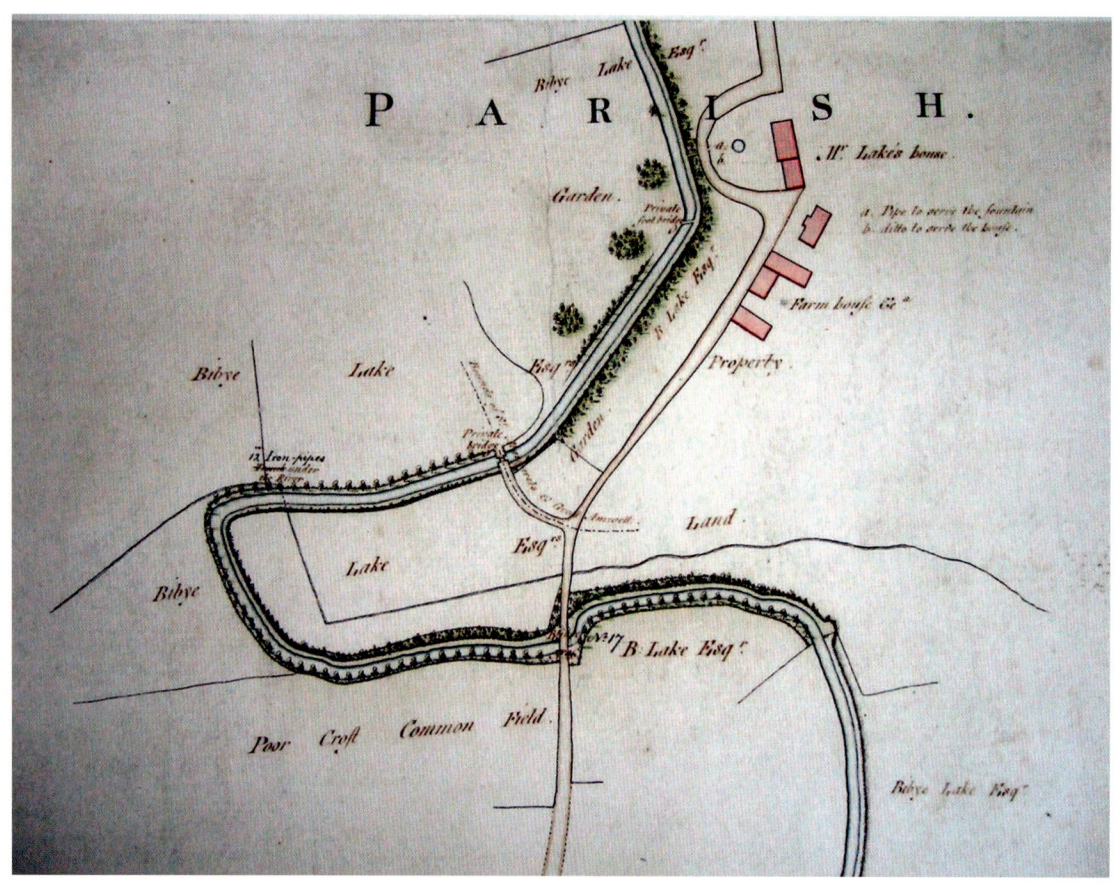

1775-1809 Plan 5 & 6 (TW Archive; MFK photos).
ABOVE: New River at Stanstead Loop/s.
BELOW: New River at Rye Bridge.

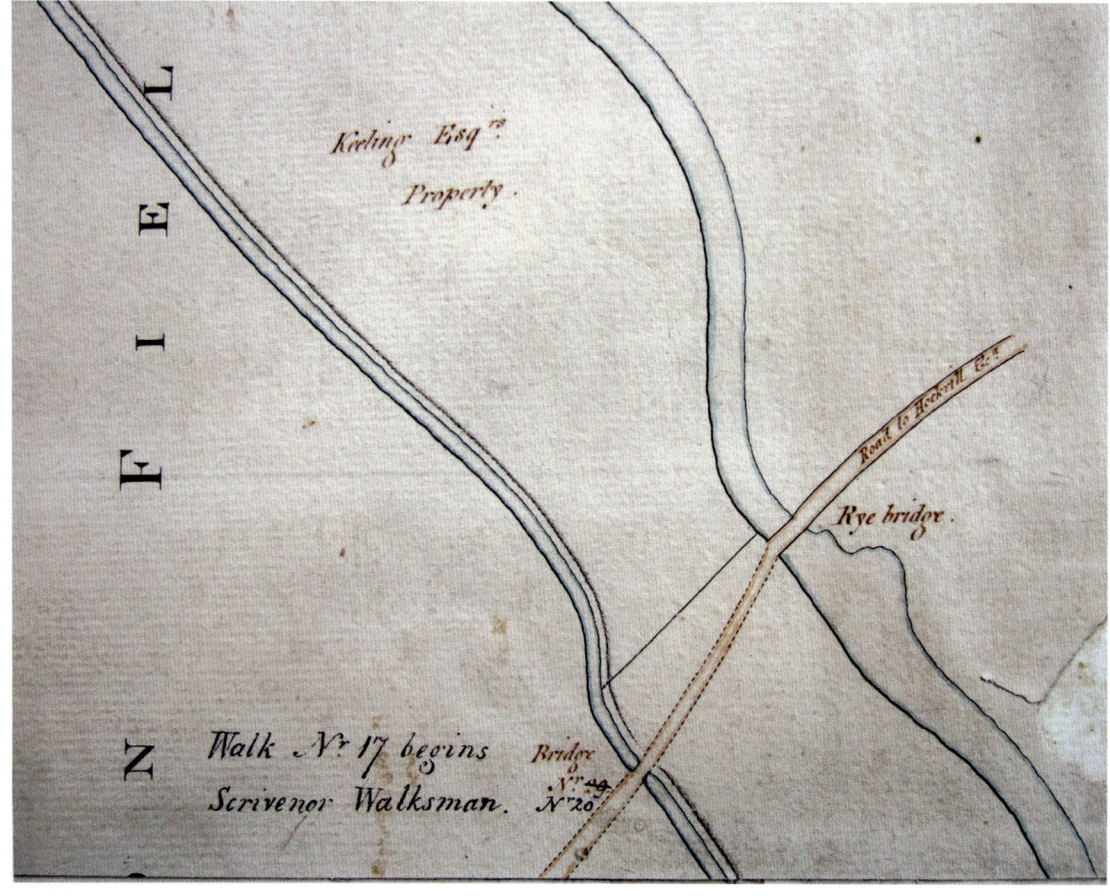

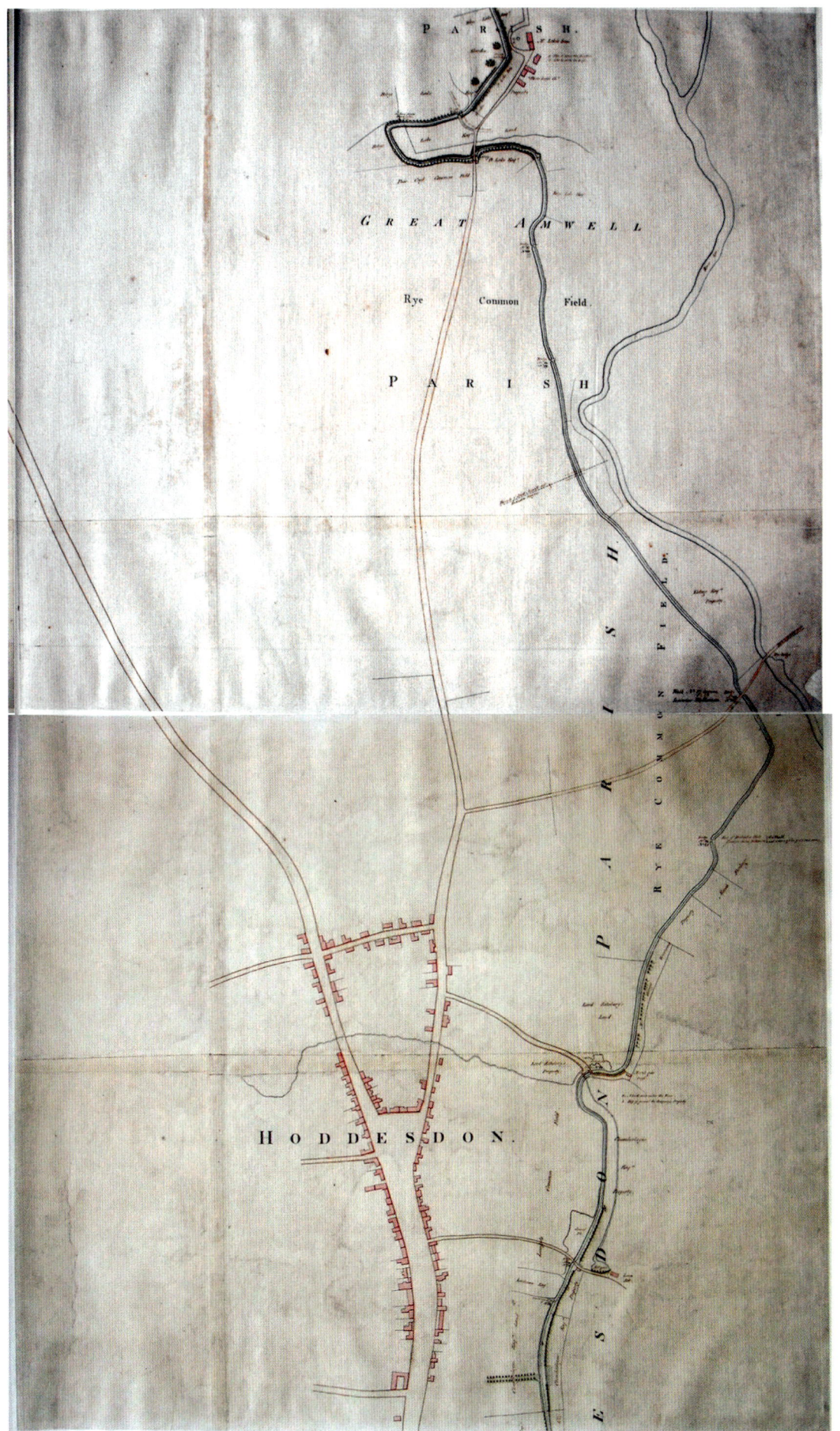

COMBINED Robert Mylne 1775-1809 Plans: **Plan 5 Stanstead, & Plan 6 Hoddesdon** (TW Archive; MFK photos & joins).

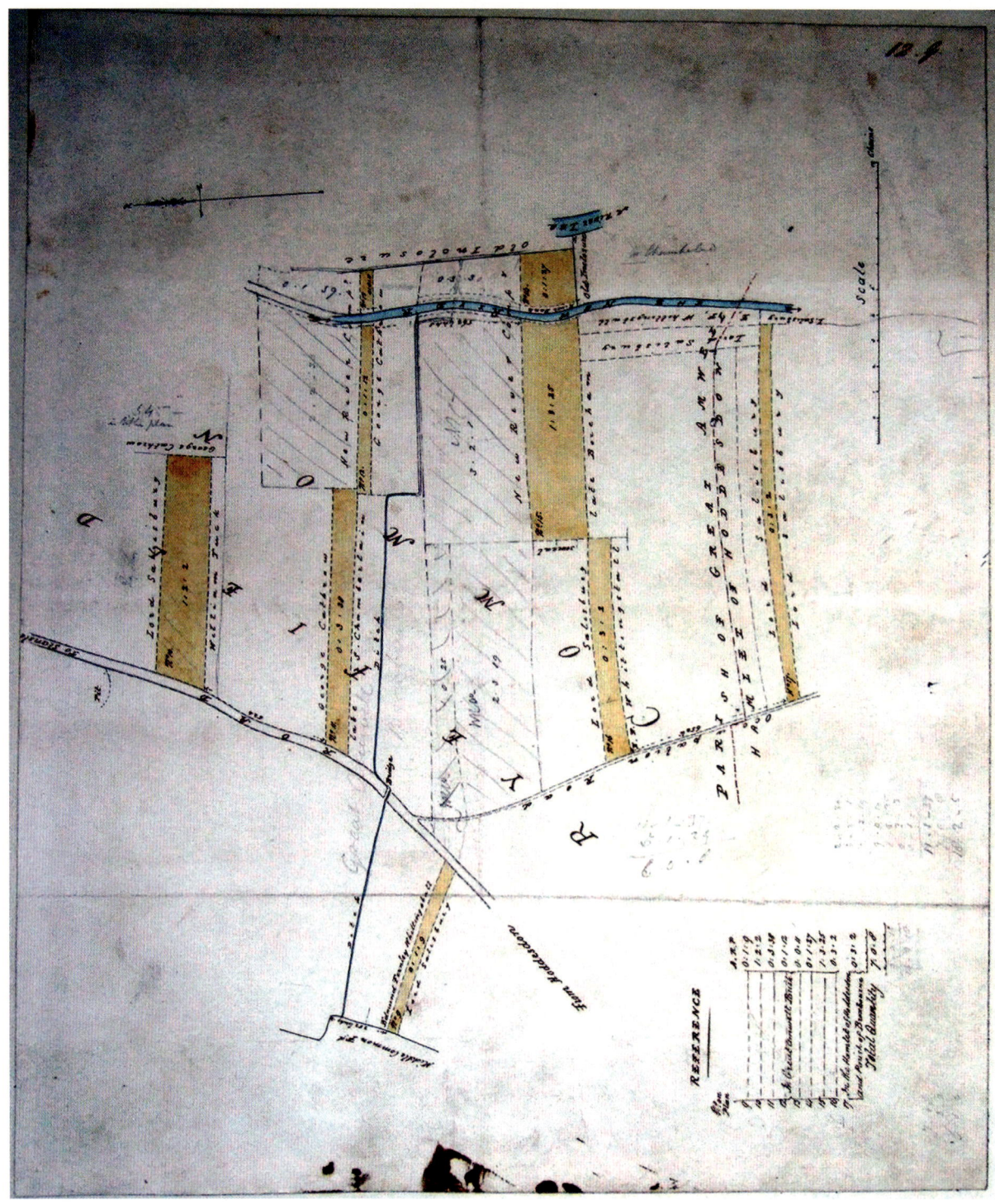

Undated (Prob. early 1800s): **NRC Land at 'Rye Field Common'** (TW Archive; MFK photo).

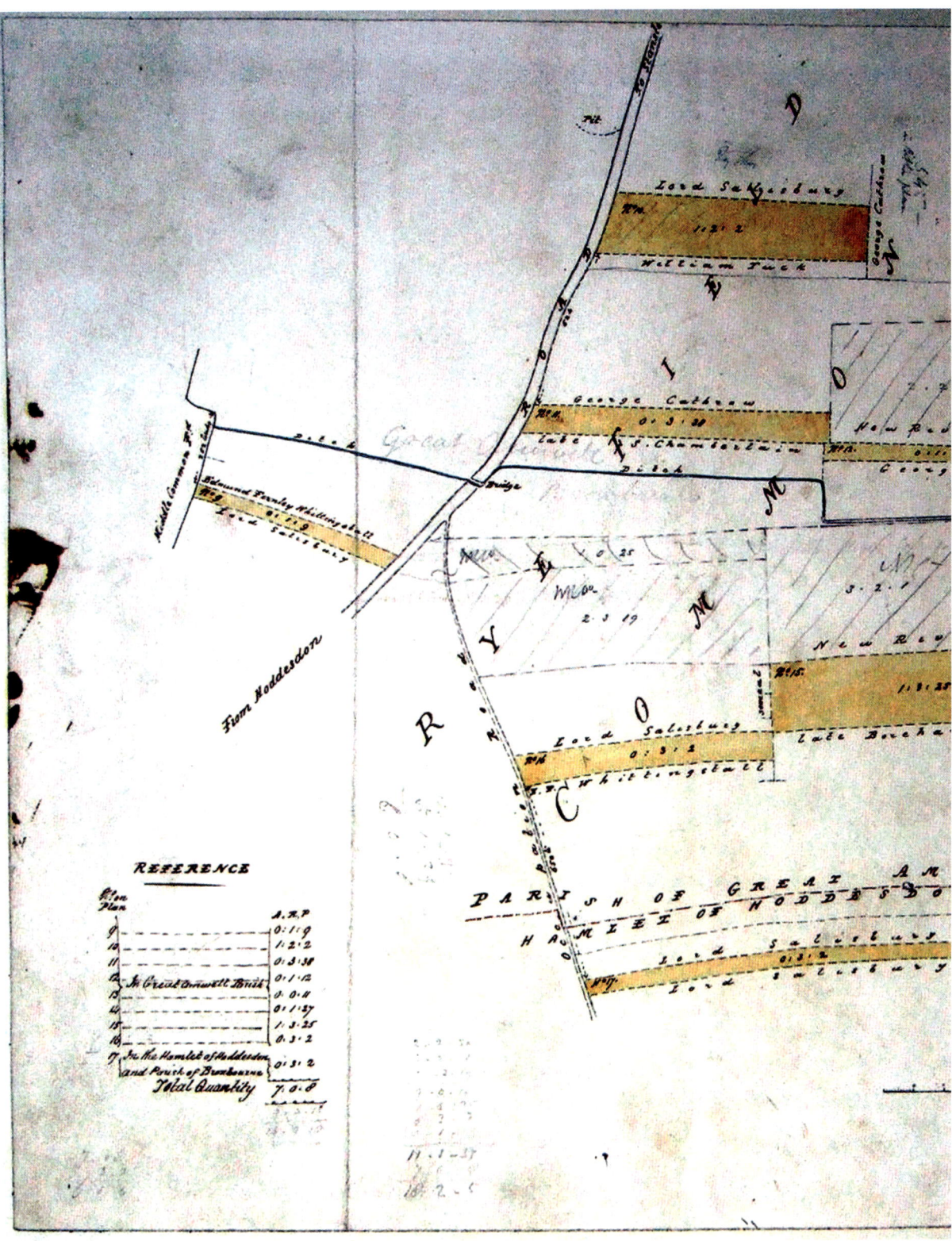

LARGER 1 of 2: Undated (Prob. early 1800s) **NRC Land at 'Rye Field Common'** (TW Archive; MFK photo).

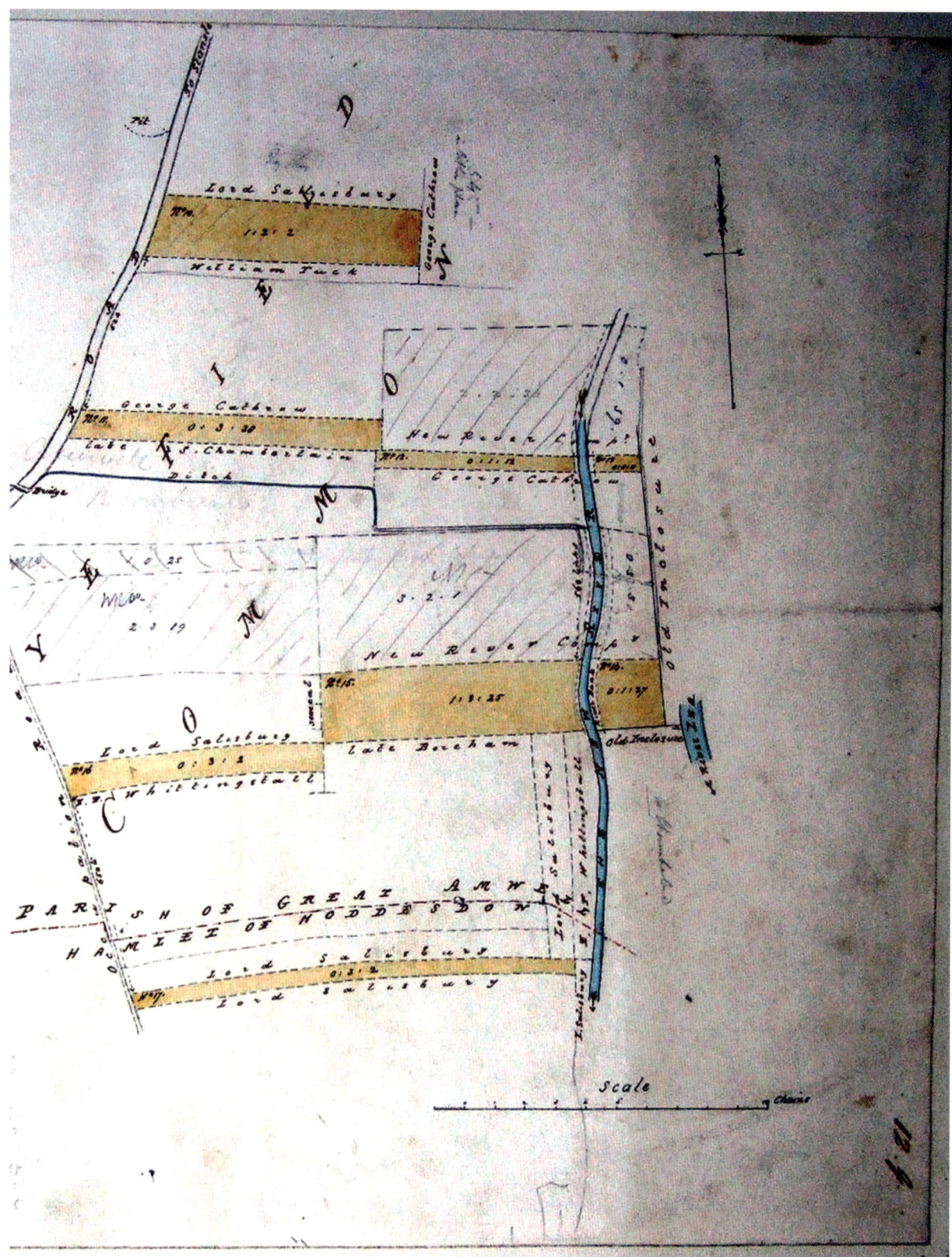

LARGER 2 of 2: Undated (Prob. early 1800s) **NRC Land at 'Rye Field Common'** (TW Archive; MFK photo).

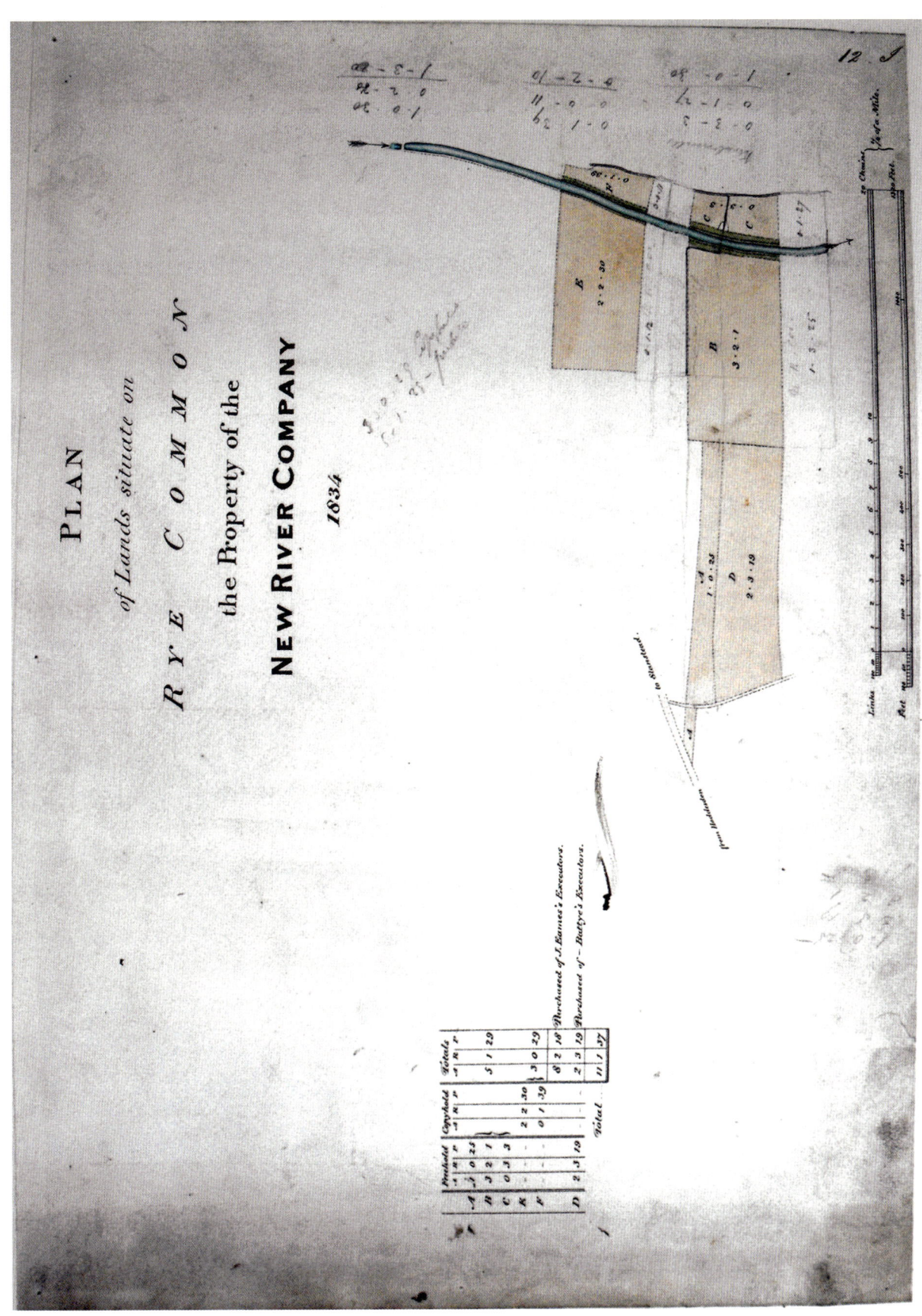

1834 NRC Land at 'Rye Common' (TW Archive; MFK photo).

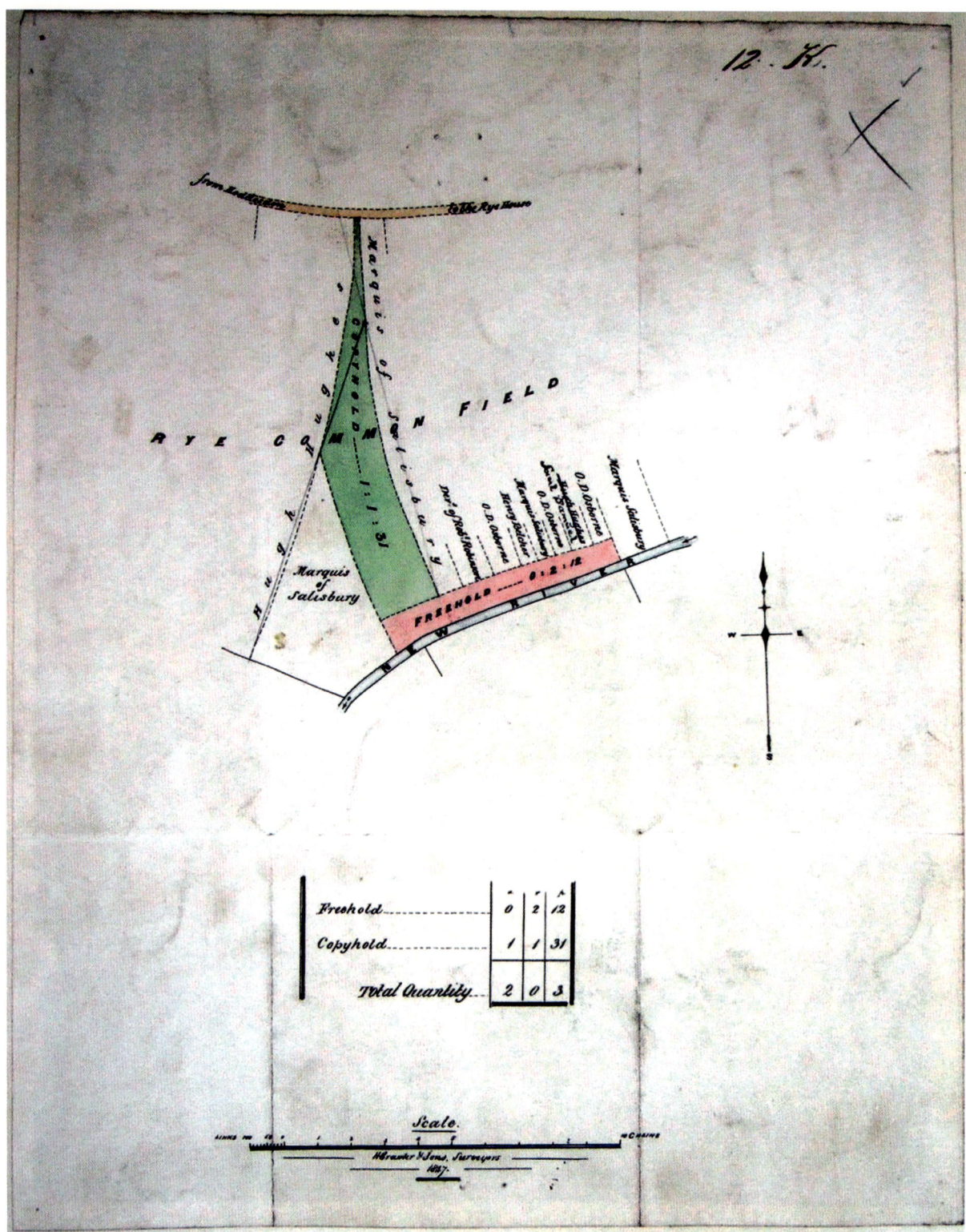

1847 NRC Land at Rye Common Field (TW Archive; MFK photo).

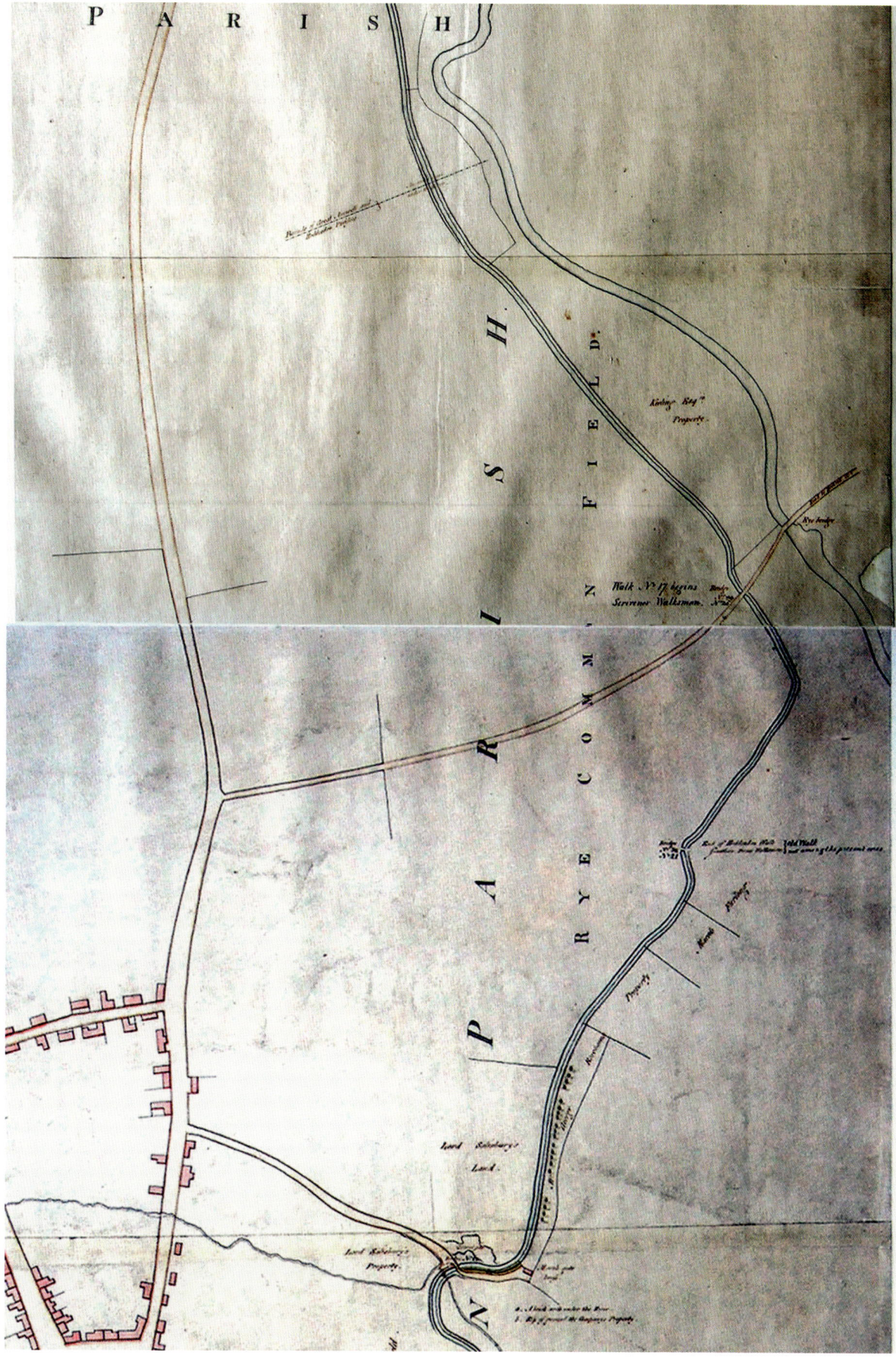

1775-1809 Plan 5 & 6: **New River approaching Hoddesdon** (TW, Abbey Mills Archive; 2-MFK photos joined).

1775-1809 Plan 6: **New River through Hoddesdon** (TW Archive; MFK photo).

1775-1809 Plan 6 LARGER: **New River through Hoddesdon** (TW Archive; MFK photo).

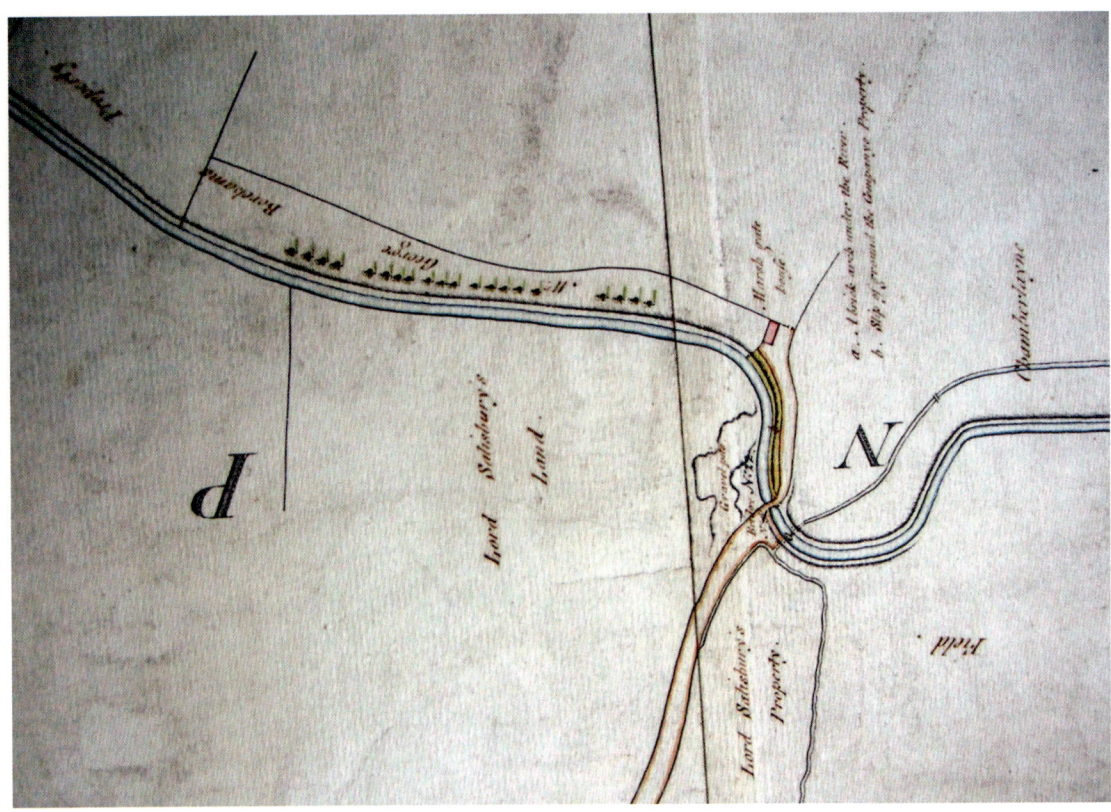

1775-1809 Plan 6 (TW Archive; MFK photos).
    ABOVE: New River near today's Hoddesdon Pumping Station.
    BELOW: New River through Rye Common, N of Hoddesdon.

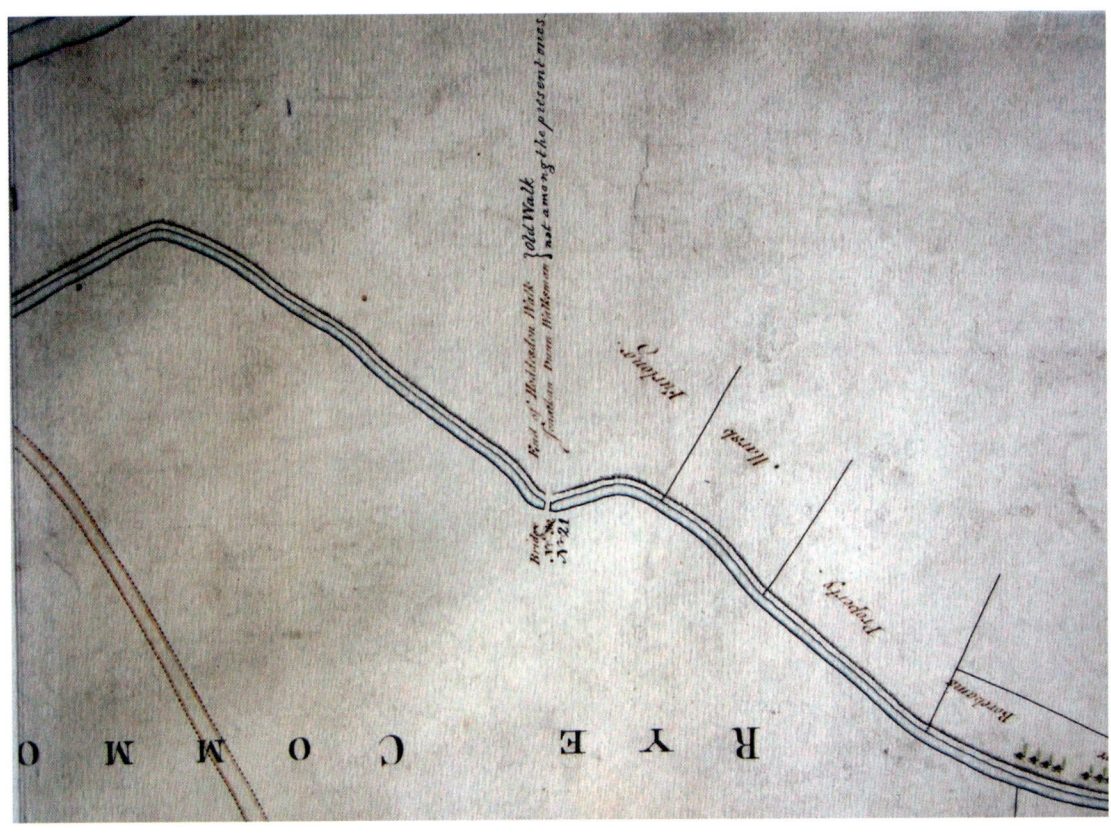

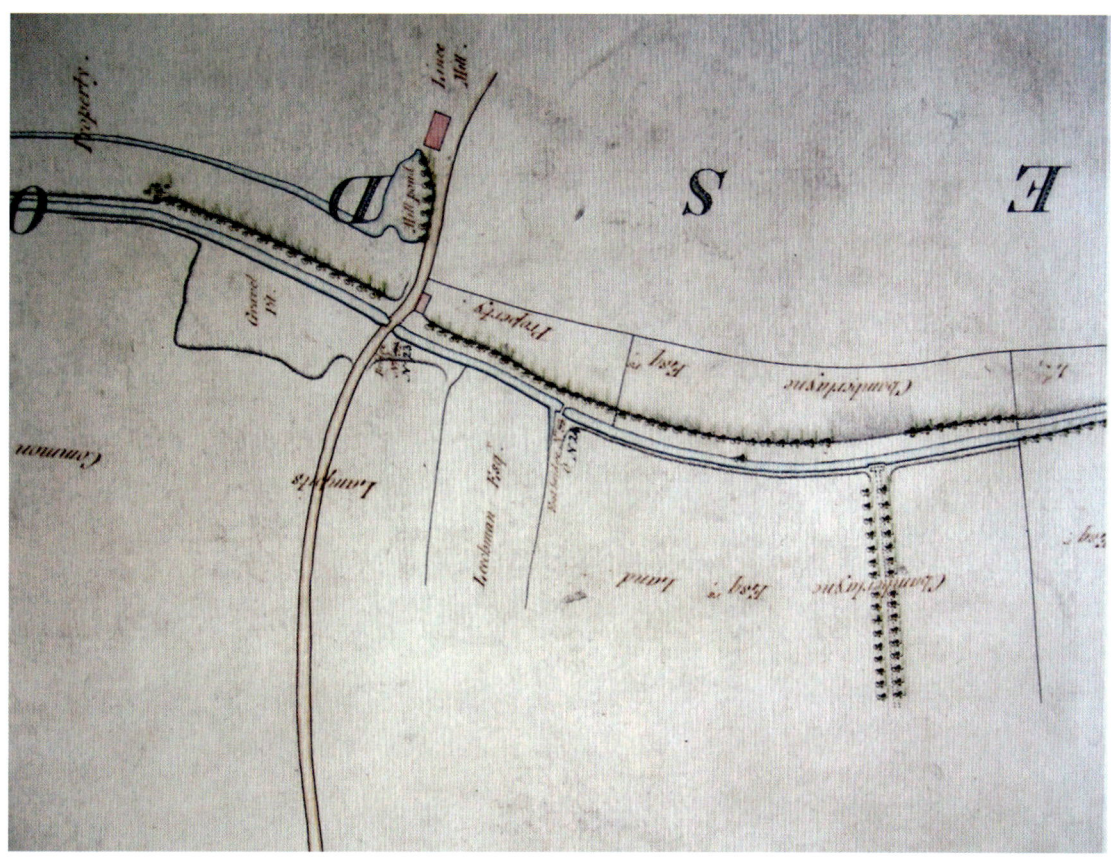

1775-1809 Plan 6 (TW Archive; MFK photos):
  ABOVE: New River S of today's Conduit Lane (& The Lynch) Hoddesdon.
  BELOW: New River near today's Conduit Lane (& The Lynch) Hoddesdon.

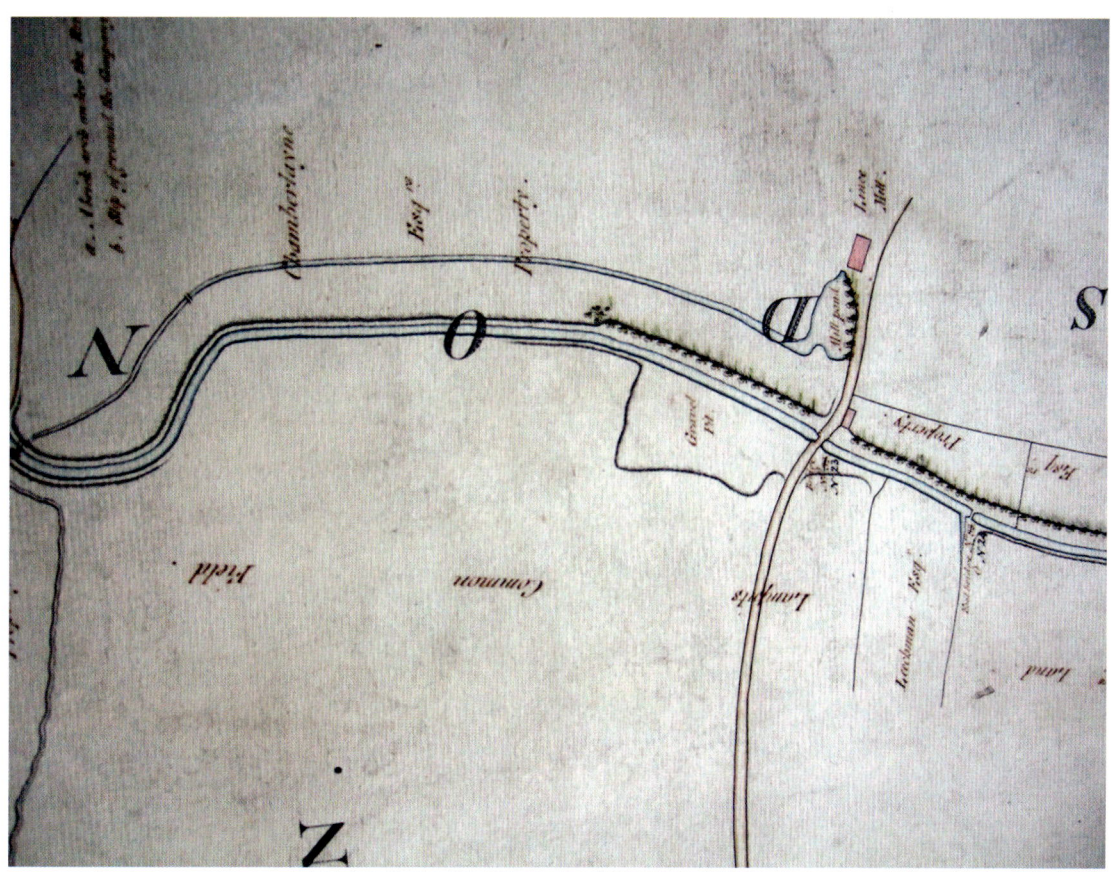

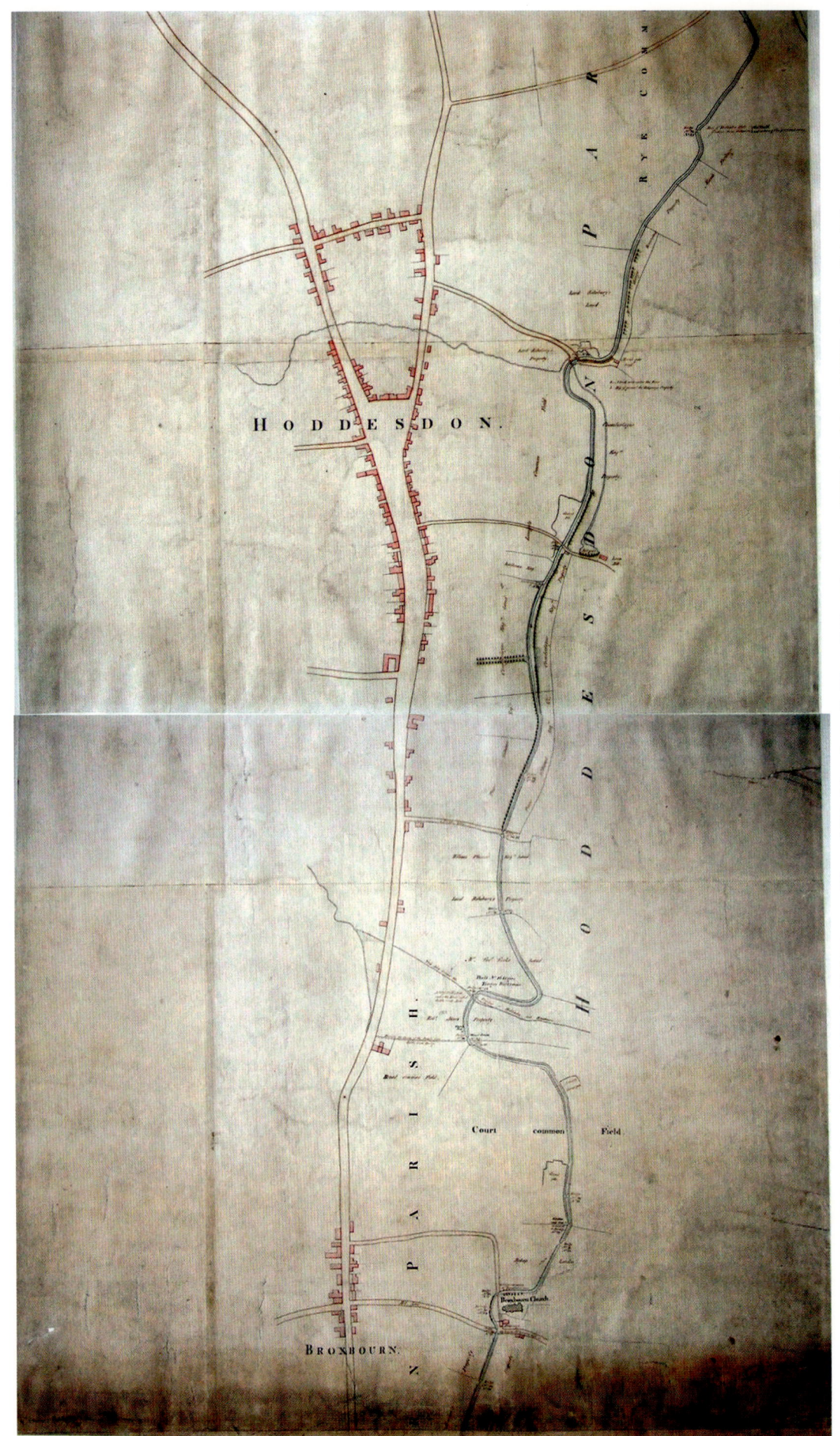

COMBINED Robert Mylne 1775-1809 Plans: **Plan 6 Hoddesdon, & Plan 7 Broxbourne** (TW Archive; MFK photos & join).

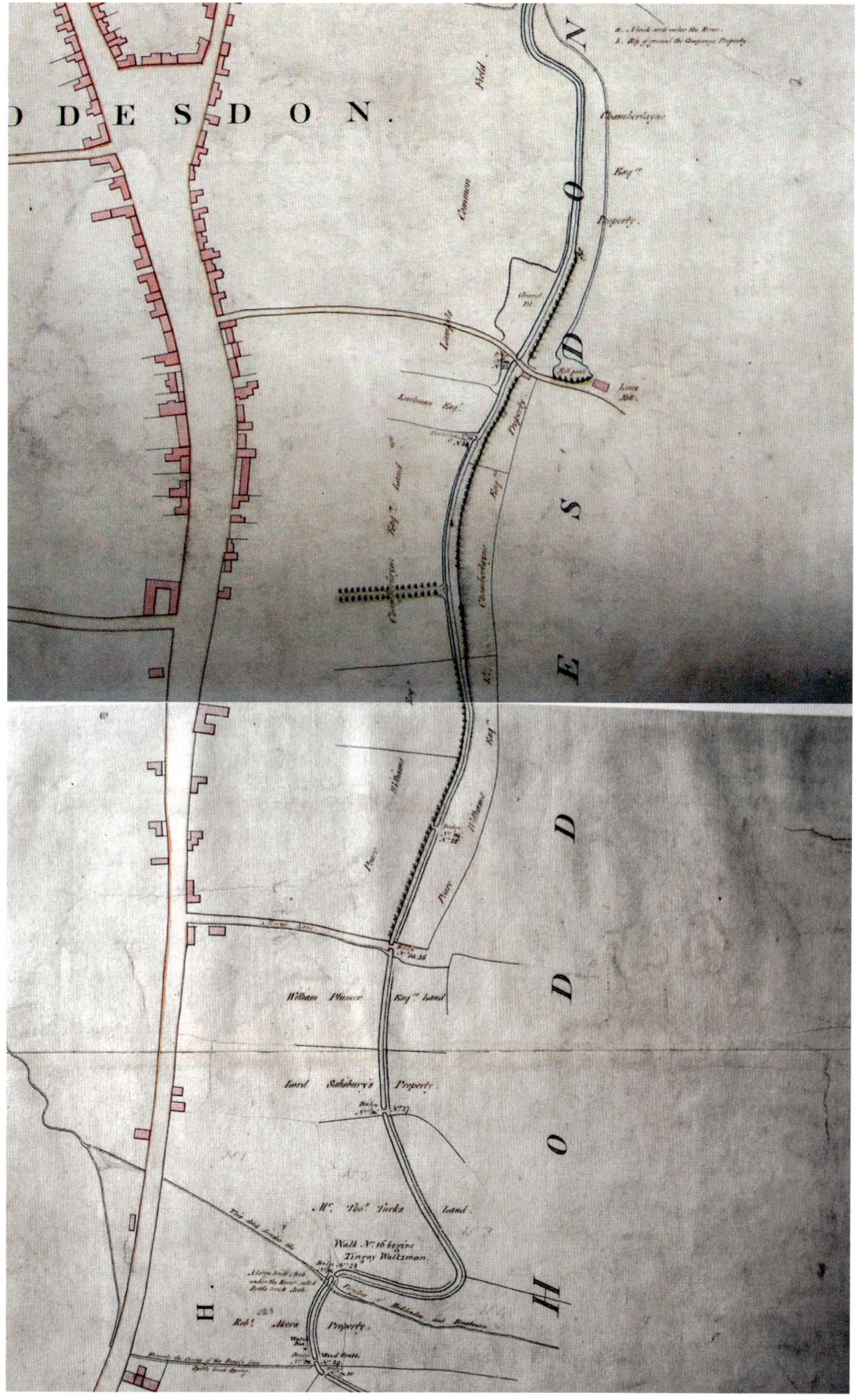

1775-1809 Plan 6 & 7: **New River between Hoddesdon & Broxbourne** (TW, Abbey Mills Archive; 2-MFK photos joined).

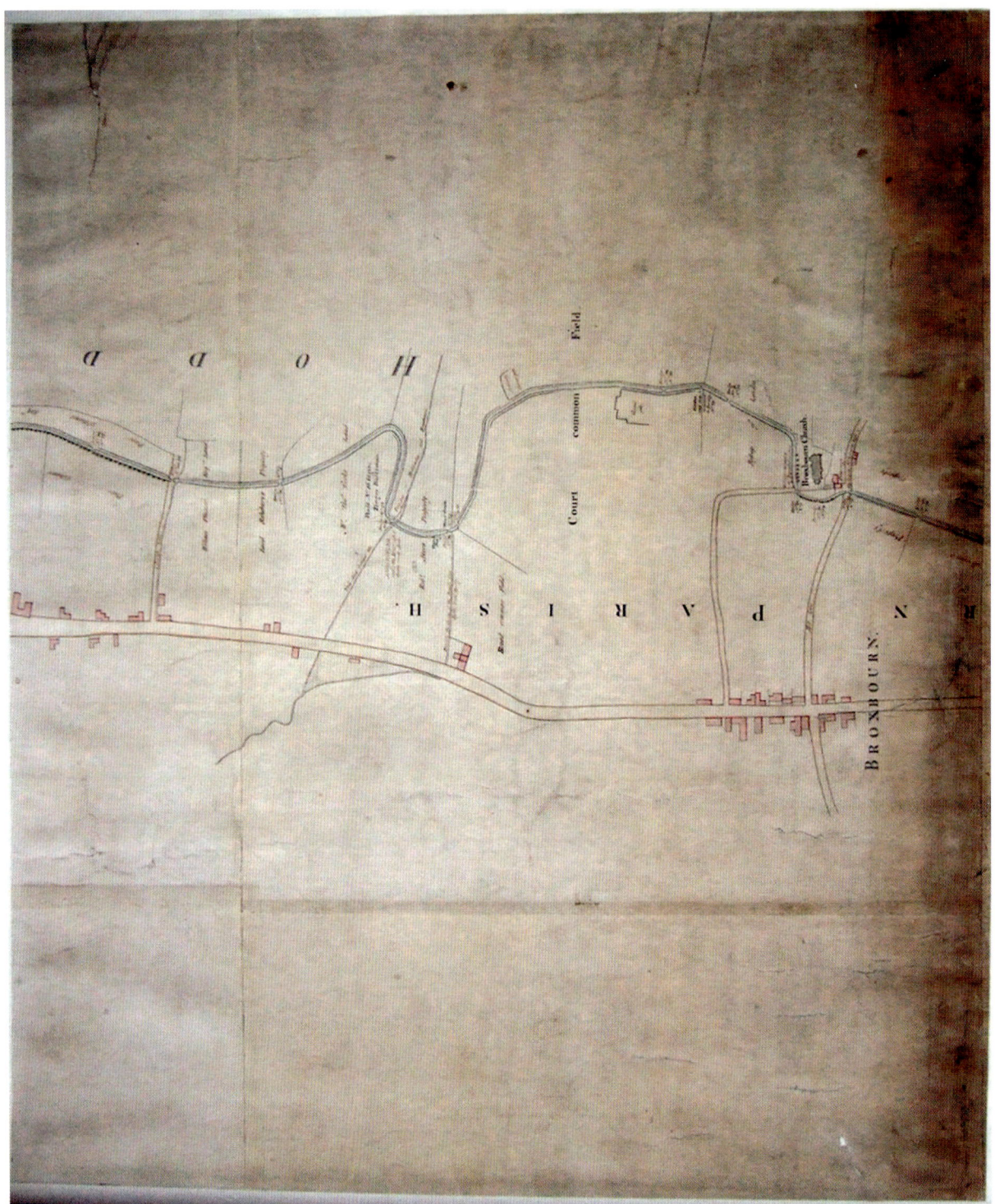

1775-1809 NRC Plan 7: **New River through Broxbourne,** Herts. (TW Archive; MFK photo).

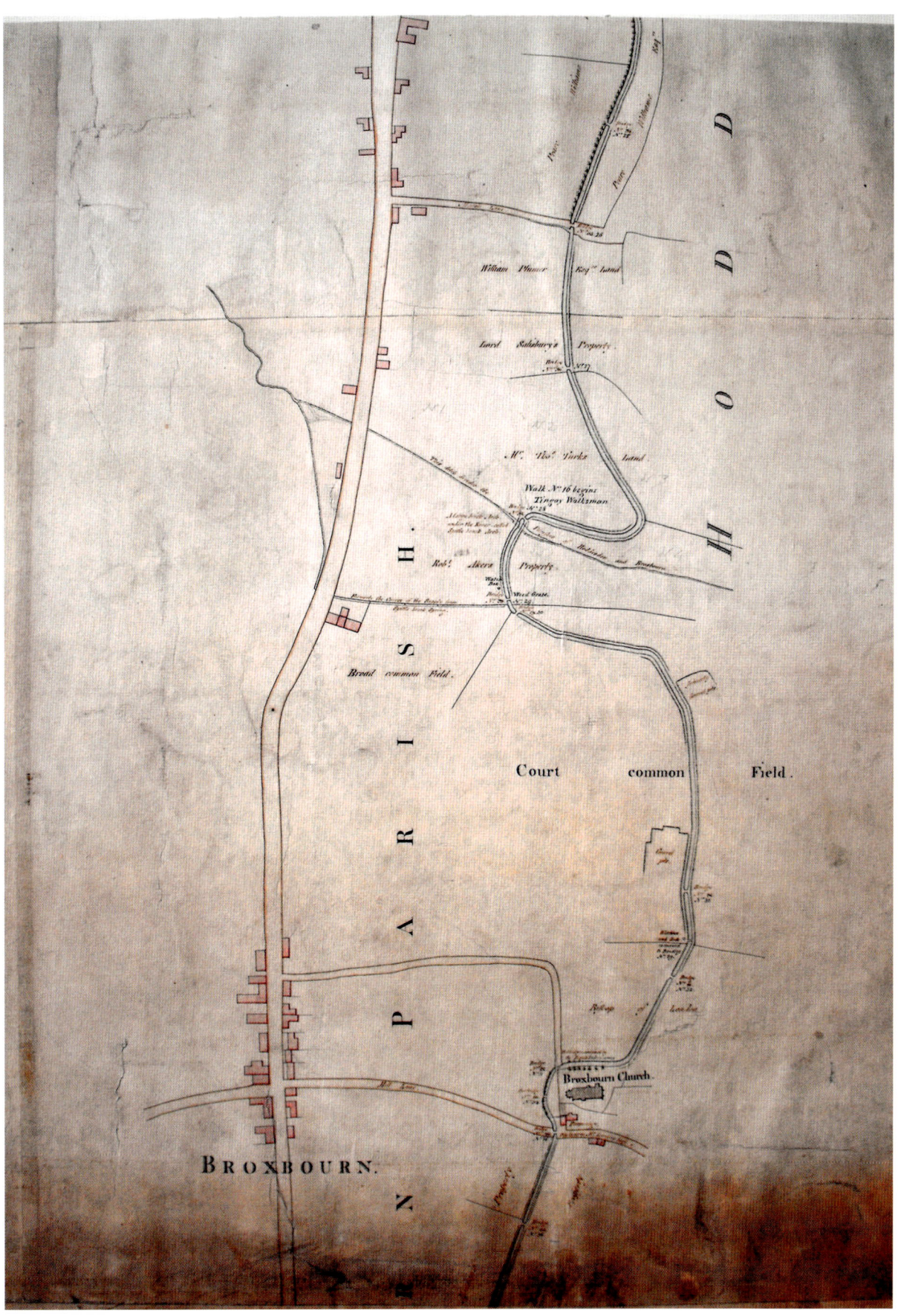

1775-1809 NRC Plan 7 LARGER: **New River through Broxbourne**, Herts. (TW Archive; MFK photo).

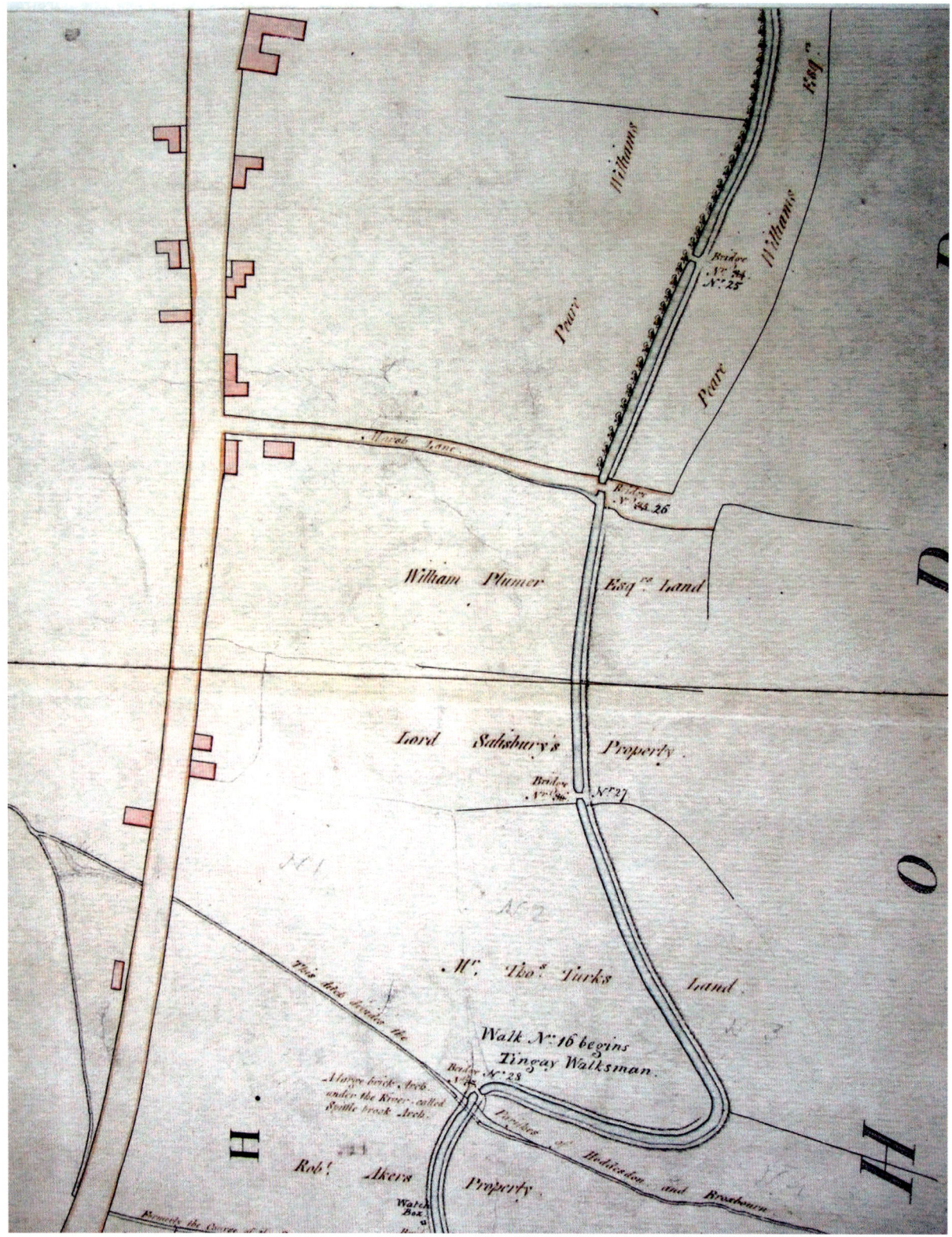

1775-1809 NRC Plan 7: **New River approaching the Broxbourne Loop** (TW Archive; MFK photo).

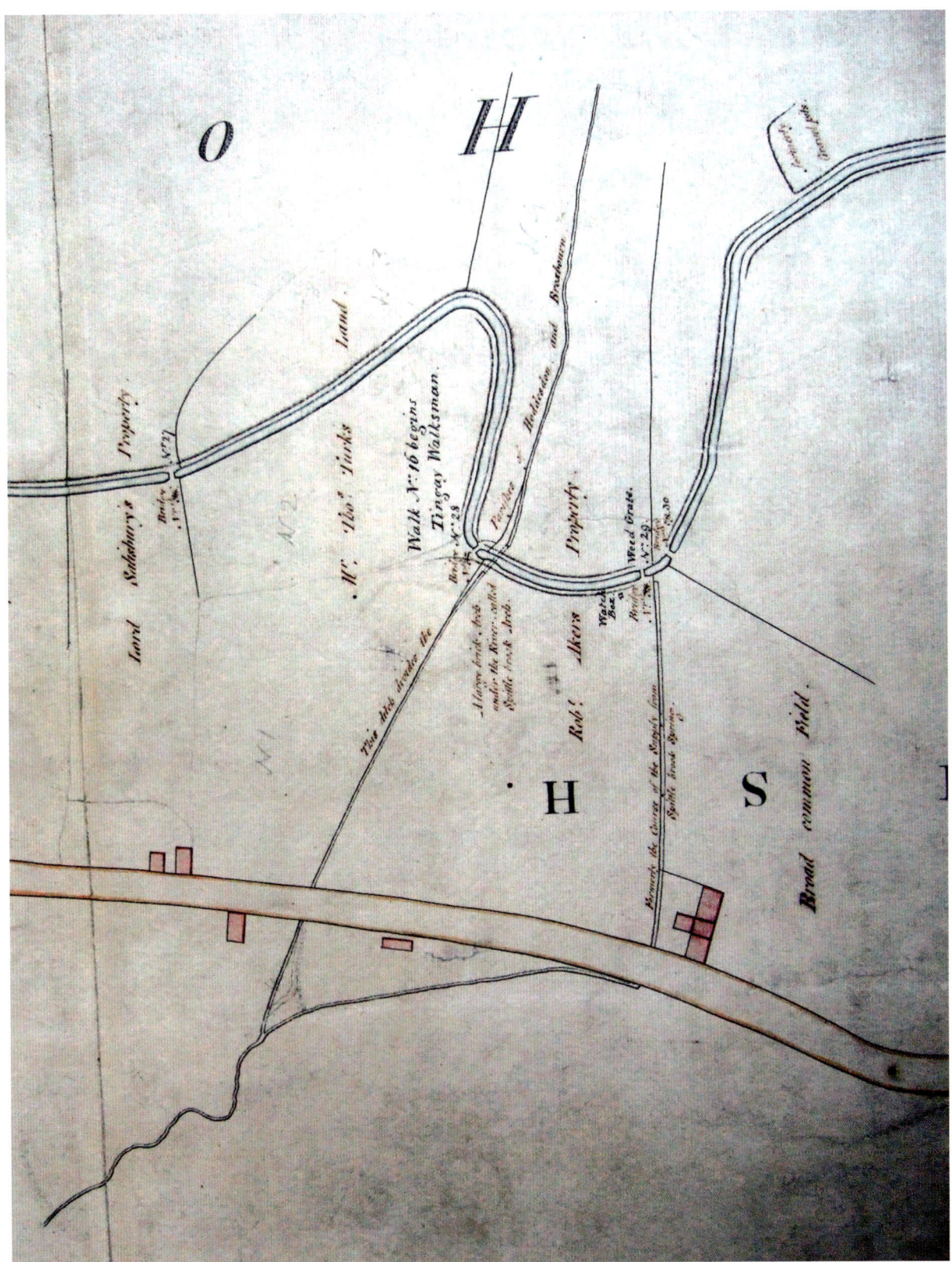

1775-1809 NRC Plan 7: **New River at the Former Broxbourne Loop** (TW Archive; MFK photo).

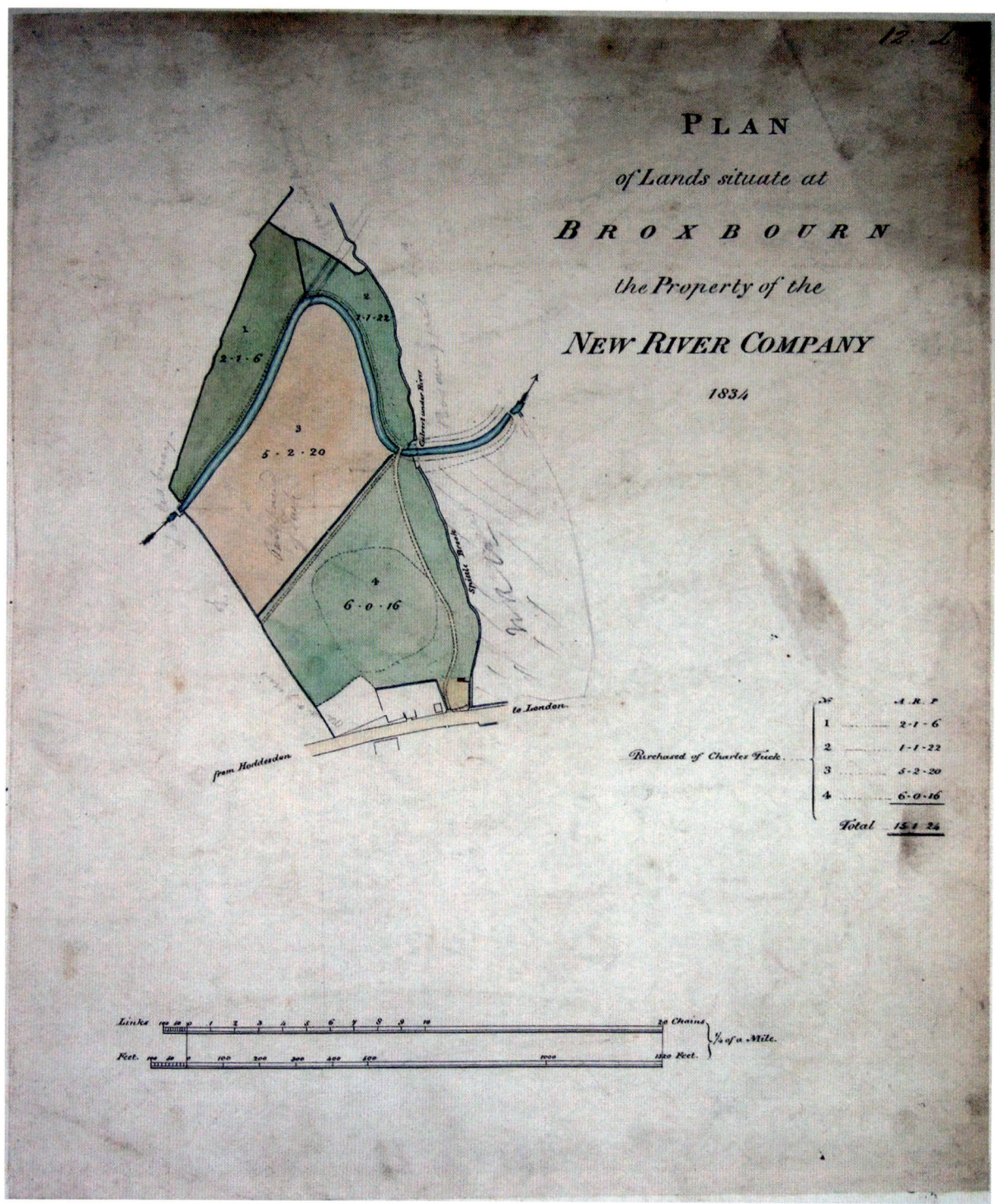

1834 'Plan of Lands situate at Broxbourne the Property of the NRC'. At the start of the former small Broxbourne W-Loop (TW Archive; MFK photo).

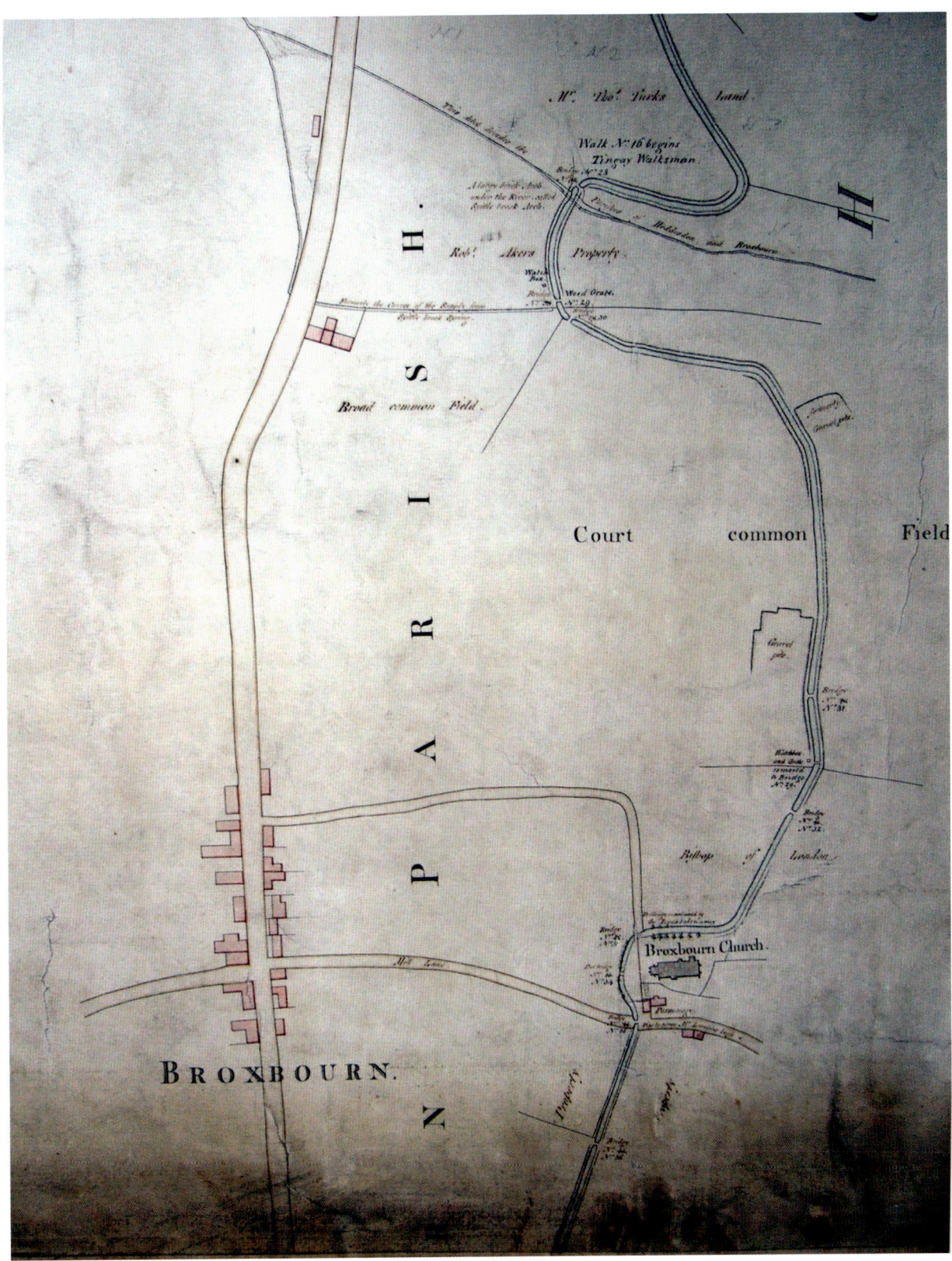

1775-1809 NRC Plan 7: **New River approaching Broxbourne Church** (TW Archive; MFK photo).

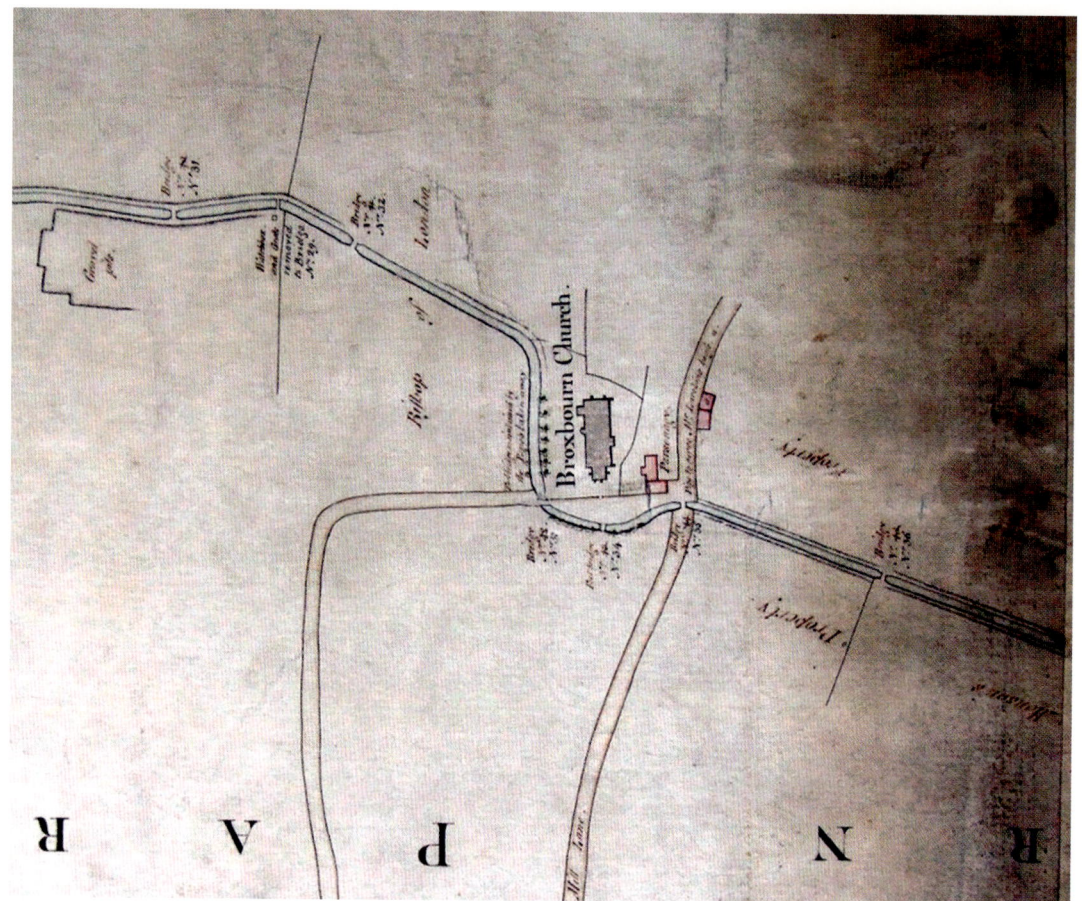

ABOVE: 1775-1809 NRC Plan 7, New River former course at Broxbourne Church (TW Archive; MFK photo).

BELOW: 1794 former course of New River almost reaching Broxbourne Church (Published 6 April 1852, Rock & Co., London, County Views, HALS).

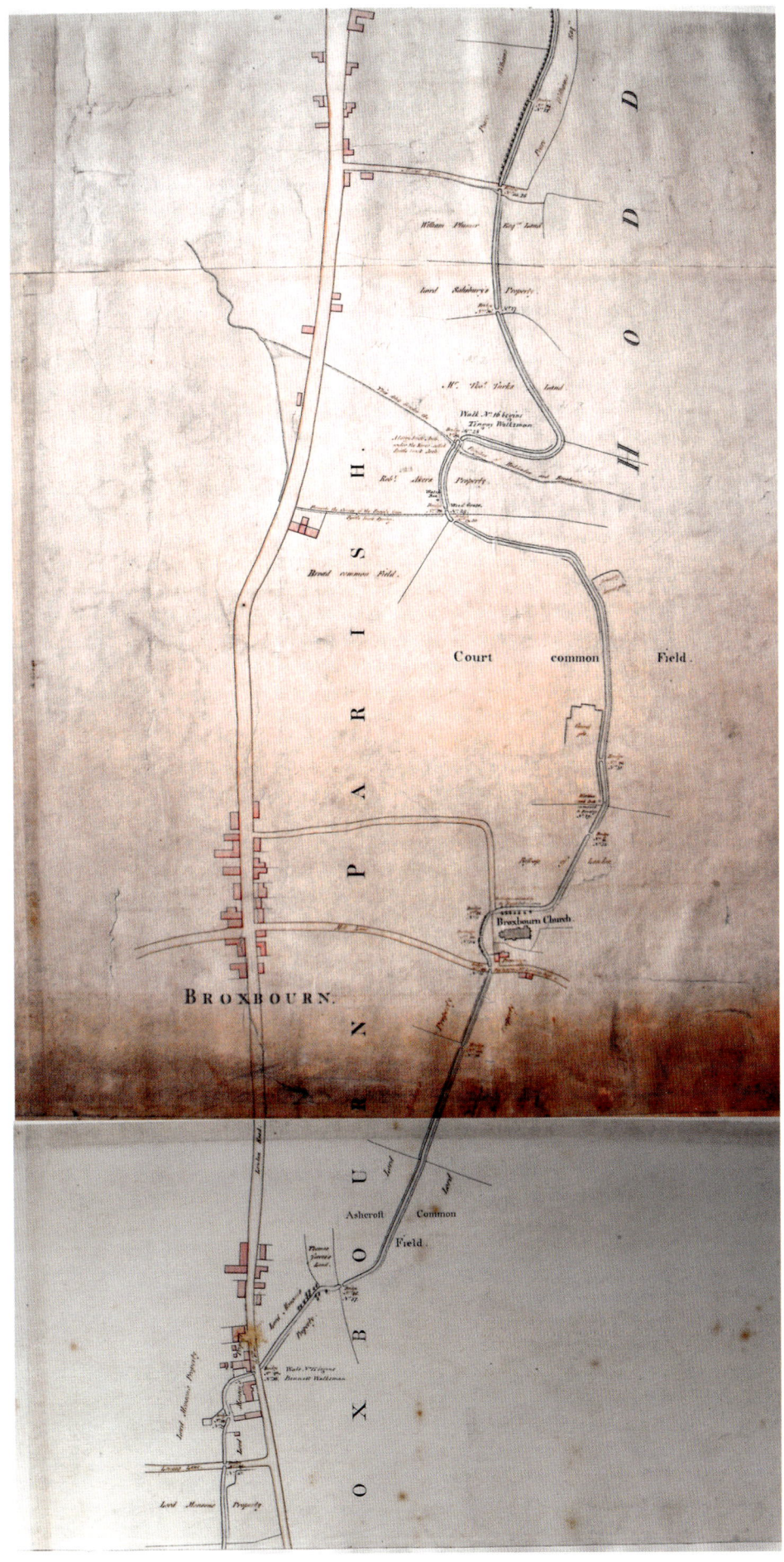

COMBINED Robert Mylne 1775-1809 Plans: **Plan 7 Broxbourne, & Plan 8 Broxbourne High Road** (TW Archive; MFK photos & join).

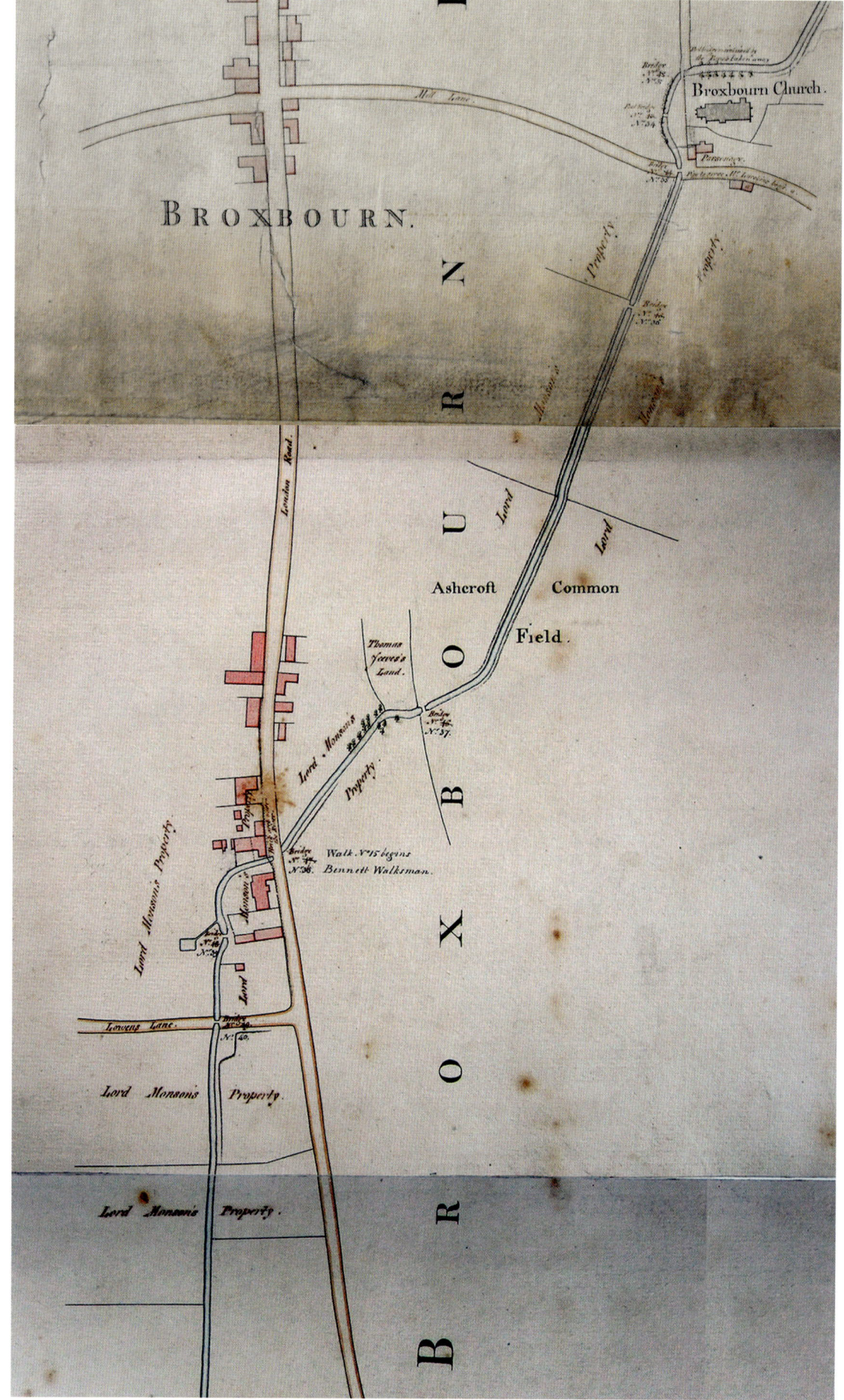

1775-1809 Plan 7, 8 & 9: **New River at Broxbourne High Road** (TW, Abbey Mills Archive; 3-MFK photos joined, the original top map grubby).

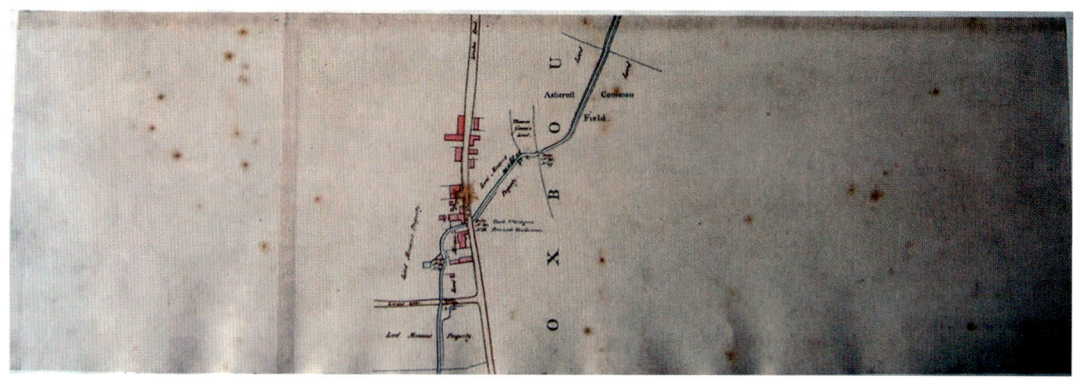

1775-1809 Plan 8: **New River at Broxbourne High Road** (TW Archive; MFK photo).
    ABOVE: Details on small plan 8.
    BELOW: LARGER.

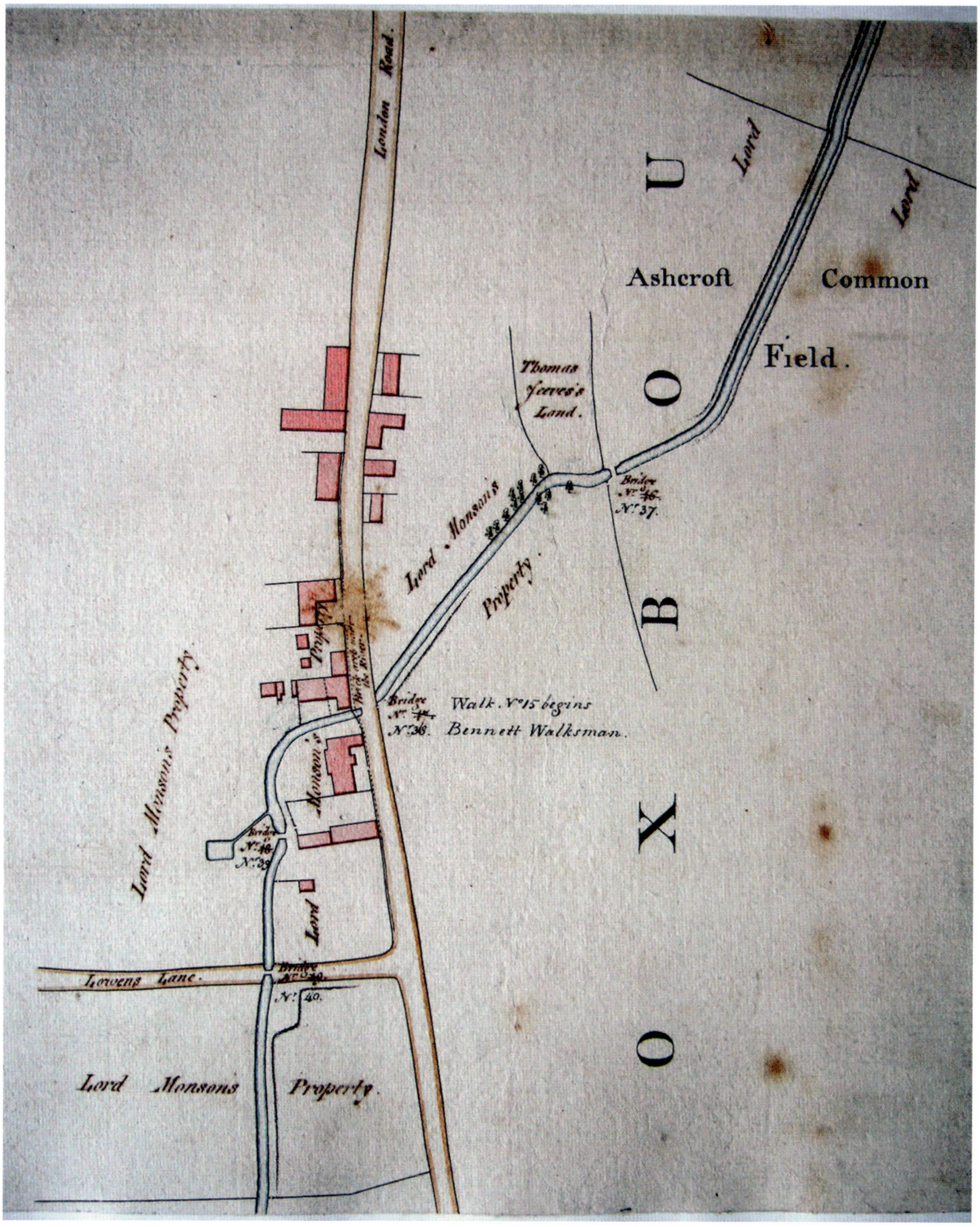

254

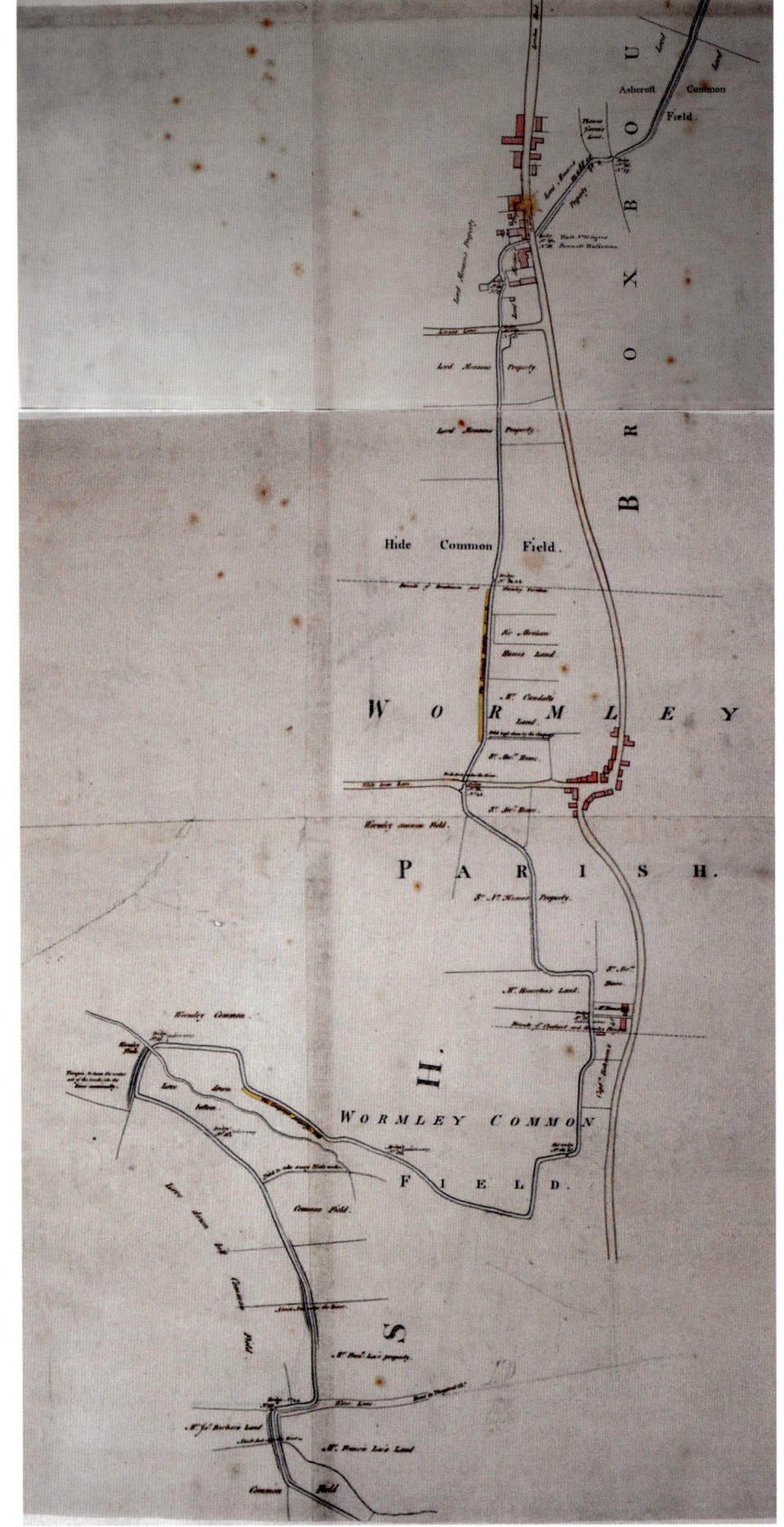

COMBINED Robert Mylne 1775-1809 Plans: **Plan 8 Broxbourne High Road, & Plan 9 Wormley Loop** (TW Archive; MFK photos & join).

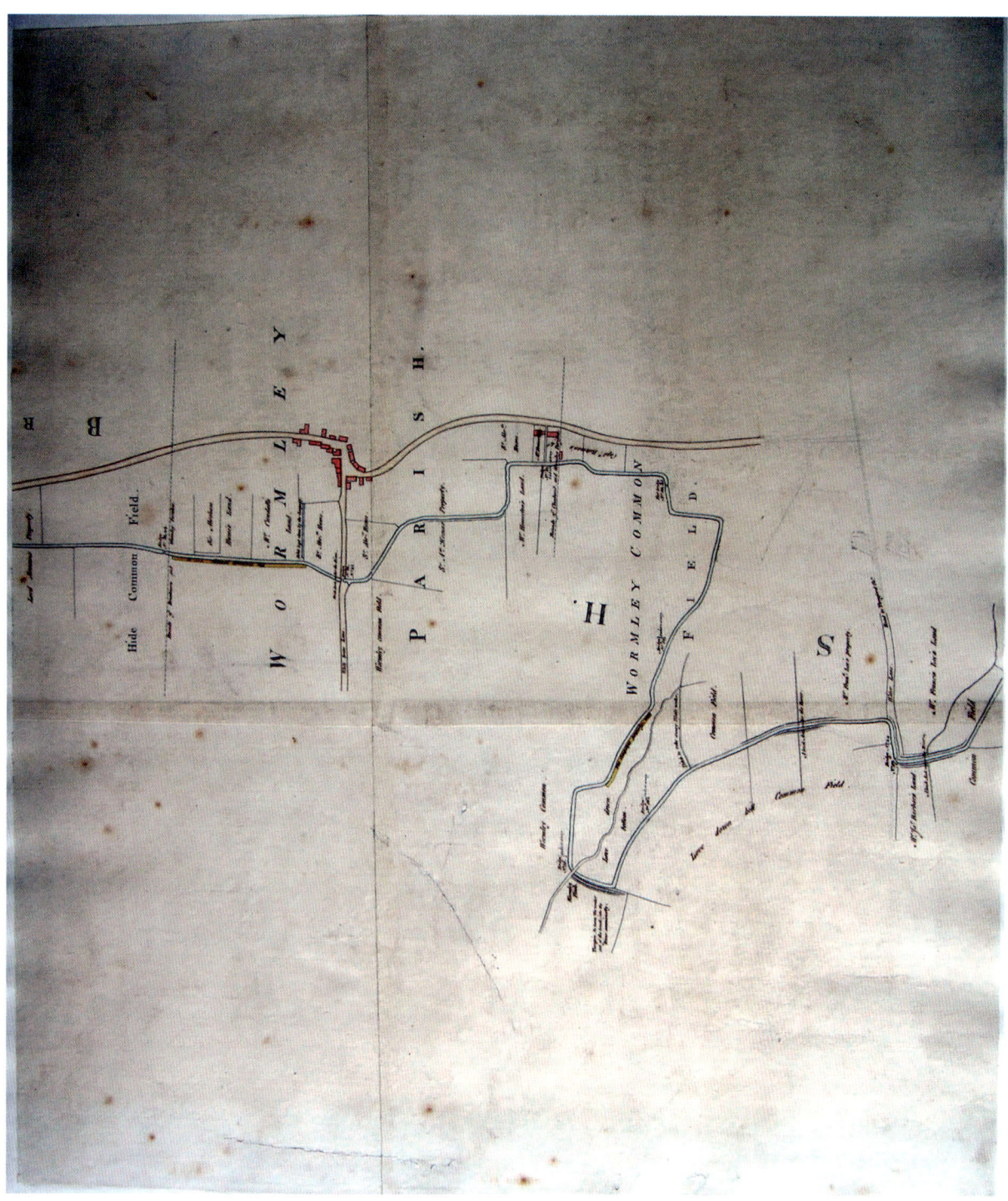

1775-1809 Plan 9: **New River through Wormley** (TW Archive; MFK photo).

1775-1809 Plan 9: **New River course at Church Lane Wormley** (since straightened), **former E-loop Wormley, & start of former W-loop Wormley** (TW Archive; MFK photo).

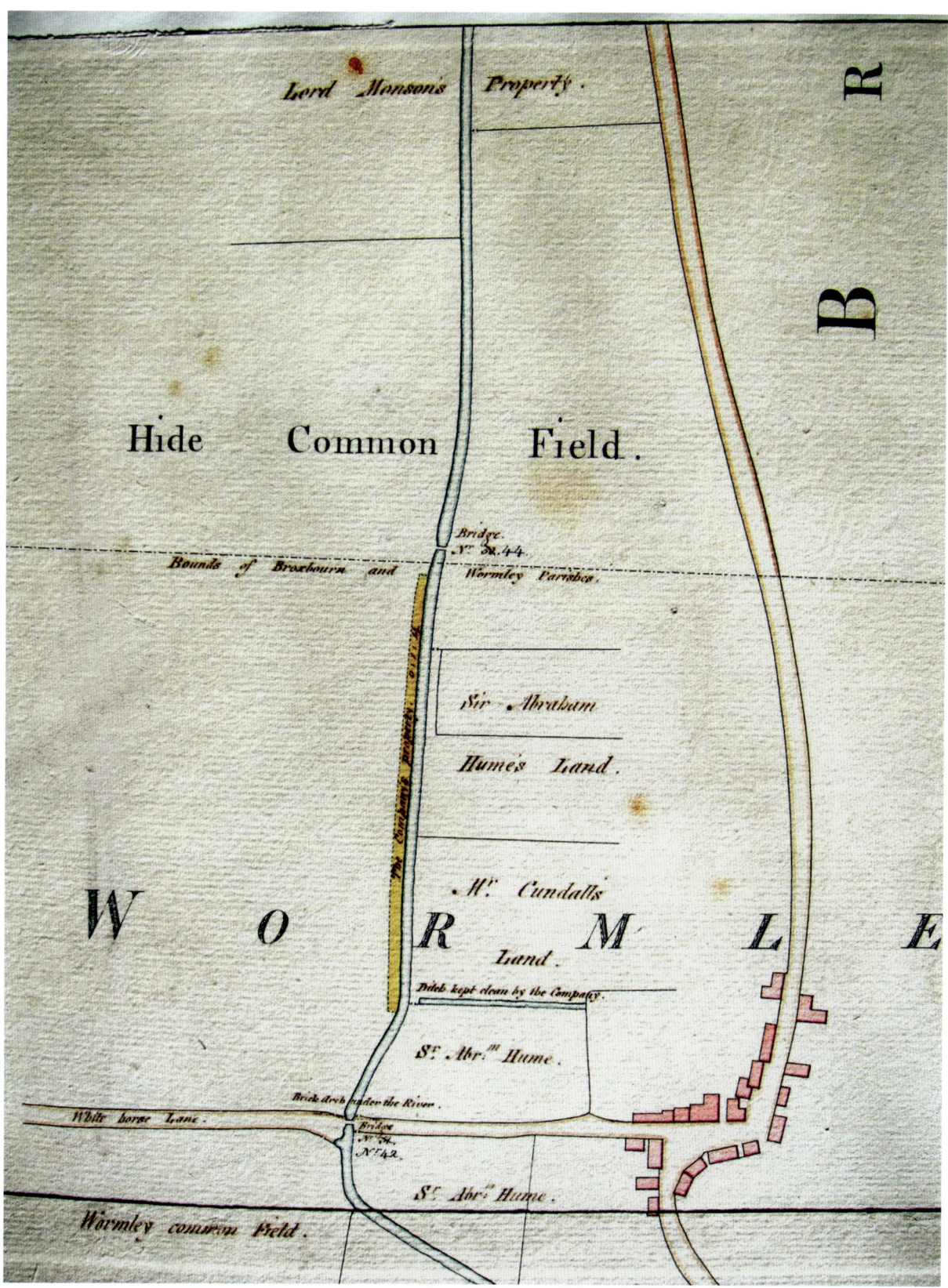

1775-1809 Plan 9: **New River to former course at Church Lane, Wormley** (TW Archive; MFK photo).

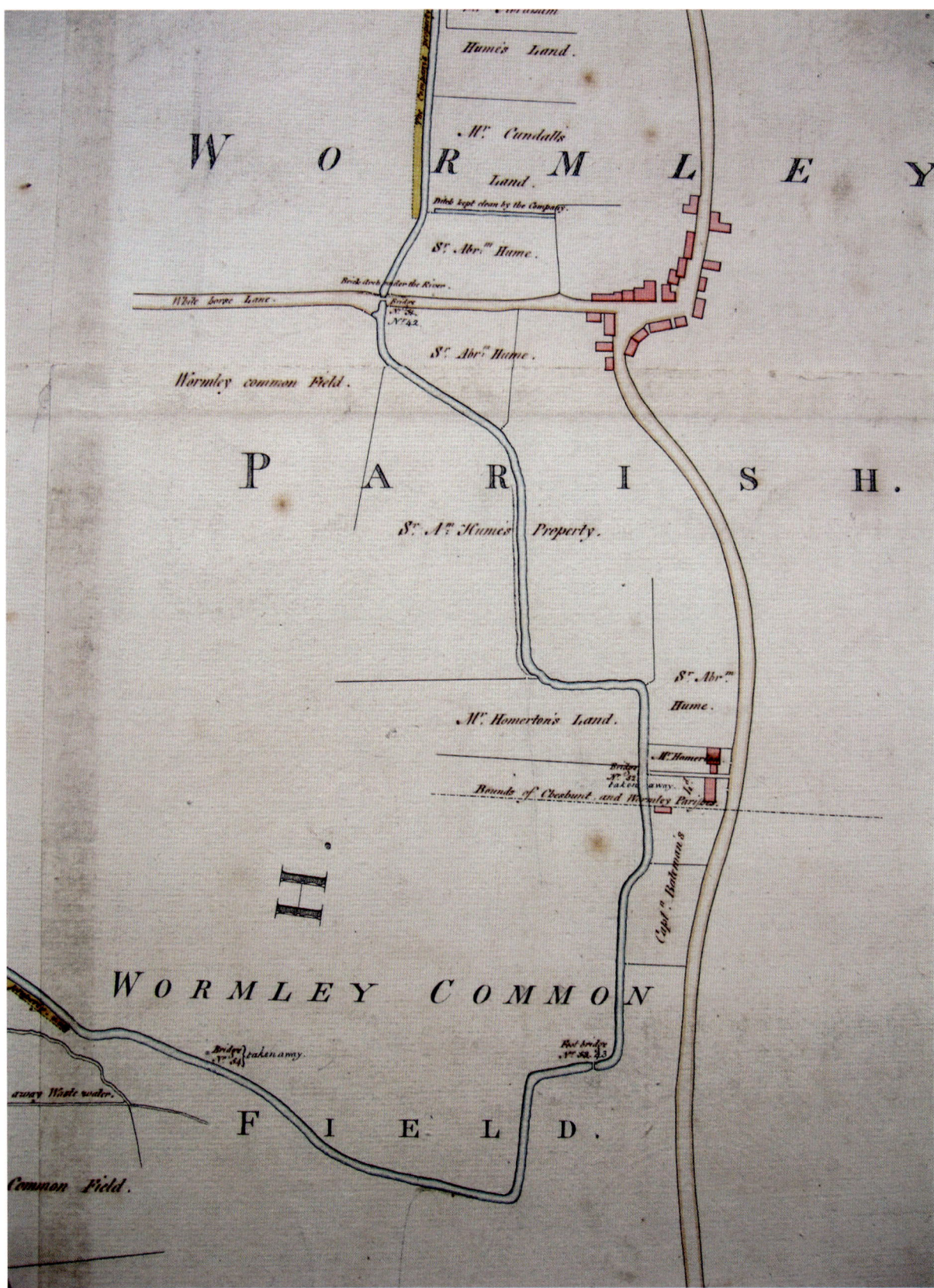

1775-1809 Plan 9: **New River former course at Church Lane, Wormley; former E-loop Wormley, and start of former W-loop Wormley** (TW Archive; MFK photo).

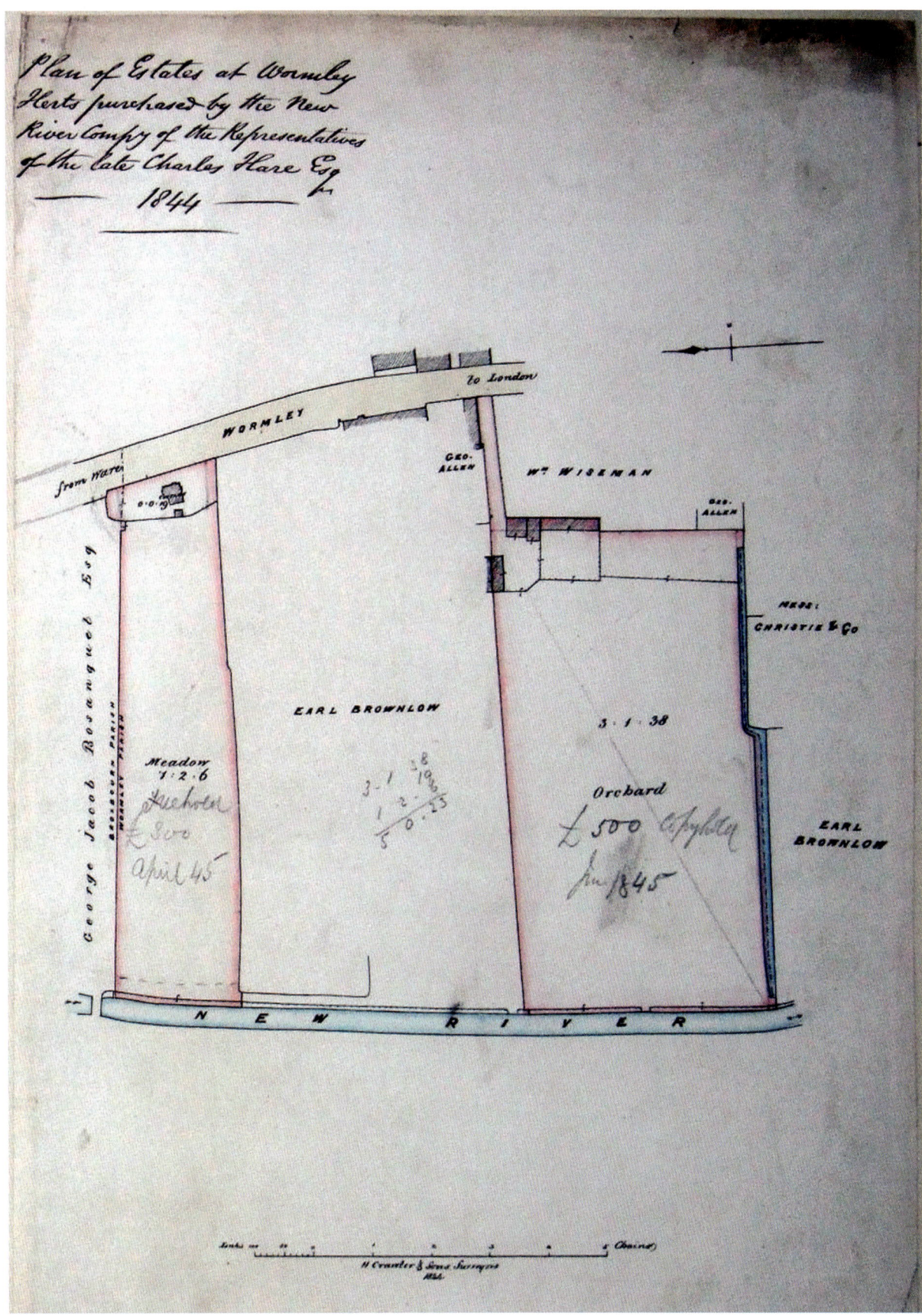

1844 'Plan of Estates at Wormley, Herts., purchased by the NRC of the Representatives of the late Charles Hare Esq.' On S-side of Broxbourne-Wormley Parish border, probably showing Wormley Lodge in NE-corner (TW Archive; MFK photo).

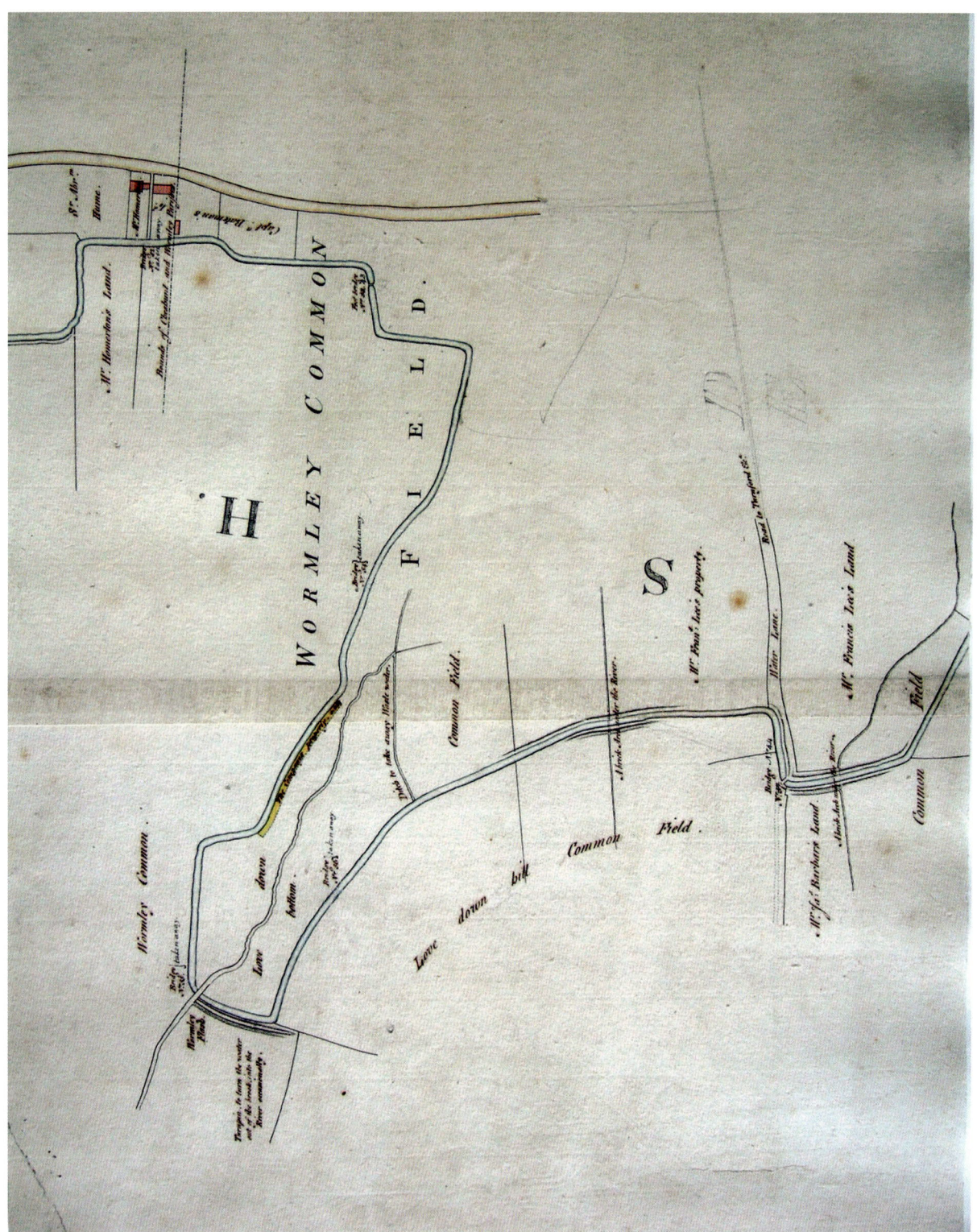

1775-1809 Plan 9: **New River former E-loop Wormley, and former large W-loop Wormley** (TW Archive; MFK photo).

ABOVE: 1806 print of 'Wormley Bury seat of Sir Abraham Hume, Bart.', 'a Chinese bridge over a sheet of water ... adds to the beauty of the scenery' ((Drwn & Engr. by Ellis for Dr. Hughson's 'London') ELSC&A). 1734-dated rainwater heads from earlier John Deane built house (SITE OF) on lawn opposite portico.

BELOW: Wormleybury House (Grade I Listed) Private Apartments (MFK 2004 photo). The house built 1767-69 by Robert Mylne (NRC Surveyor) for Sir Abraham Hume (d.1772), and further work by Mylne on grounds or within house 1773, 1775, 1777, (1777-79 the main staircase decorated by Robert Adam), 1787, 1794, 1798-9.

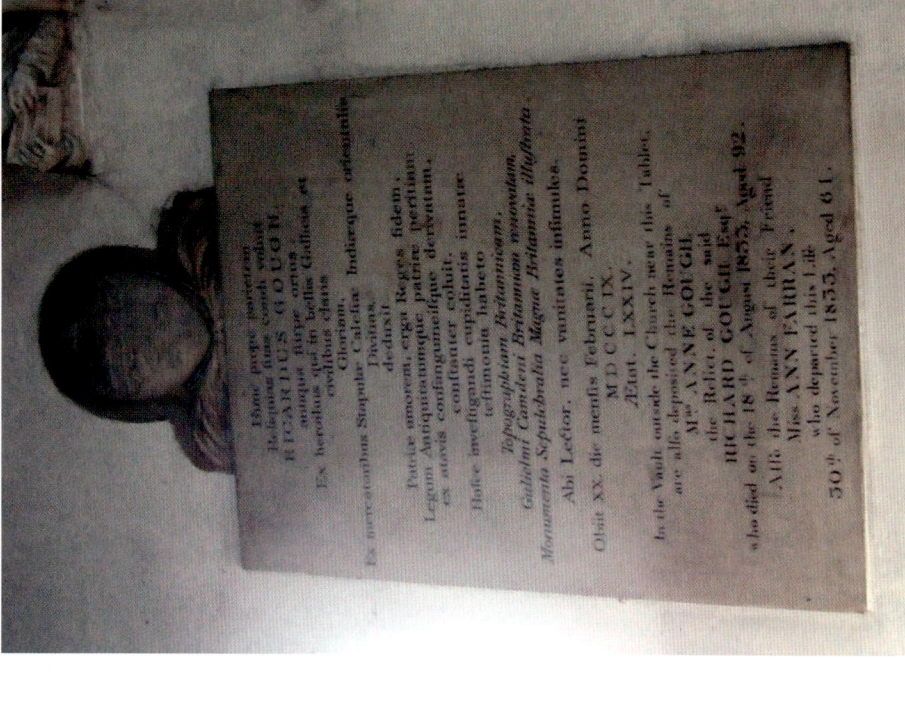

LEFT: William Purvey Tomb (Wormley Church). The spectacular William Purvey (d. 23 Aug. 1617, aged 59-years) & wife Dorothy (nee Denny, 2nd husband George Purefoy) alabaster monument probably by William Cure the younger, S-side chancel/SE-wall, Wormley Church. Purvey 'One of his Majesty's Auditors of the Duchy of Lancaster' and local landowner, one of the three main opponents (with Henry Atkins - Dr. to King James I & King Charles I, & another) **attempting to stop the construction of the New River when it reached Wormley** (MFK 2008 photo).

RIGHT: Richard Gough Wall Memorial (Wormley Church). Further to R on the S-wall, memorial wall tablet to the celebrated antiquarian writer Richard Gough (d. 20 Feb. 1809) & Anne his wife (their **Gough Park house aside the former course of the New River at Enfield**), their vault in the graveyard near the wall where his monument is fixed (MFK 2008 photo).

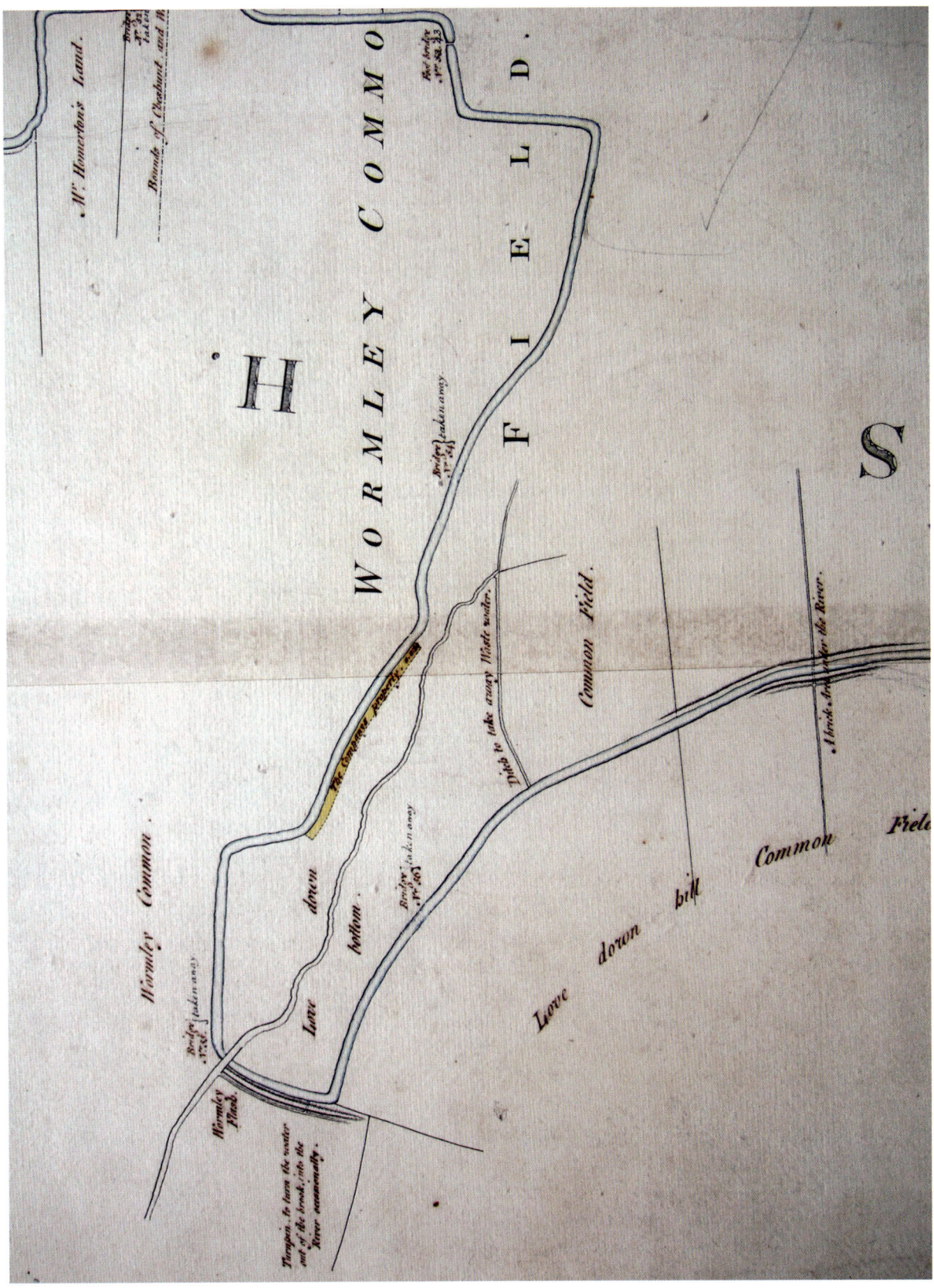

1775-1809 Plan 9: **New River former W-loop Wormley at Wormley Flash** (TW Archive; MFK photo).

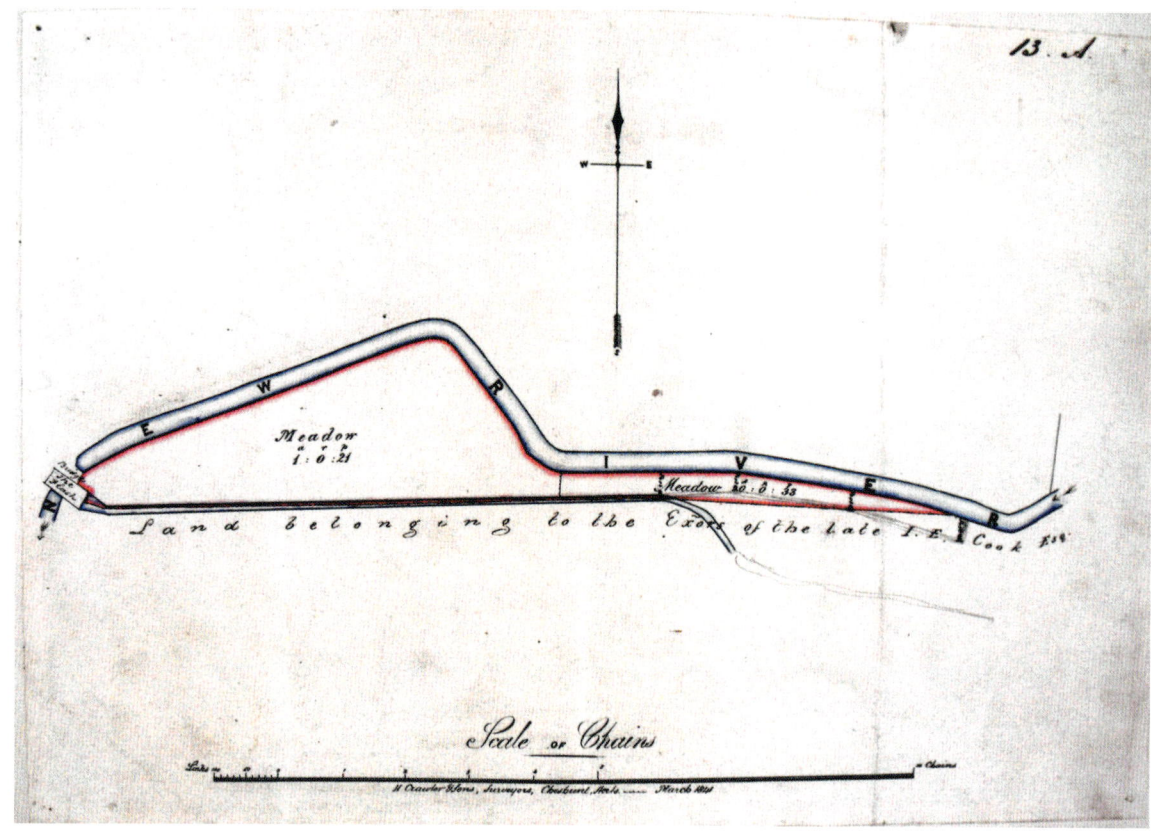

ABOVE: c.1834 Plan of NRC purchased land before Wormley Flash on the former Loop to W (TW Archive; MFK photo).

BELOW: 1775-1809 Plan 9, **New River at end of former W-loop Wormley**, into Turnford (TW Archive; MFK photo).

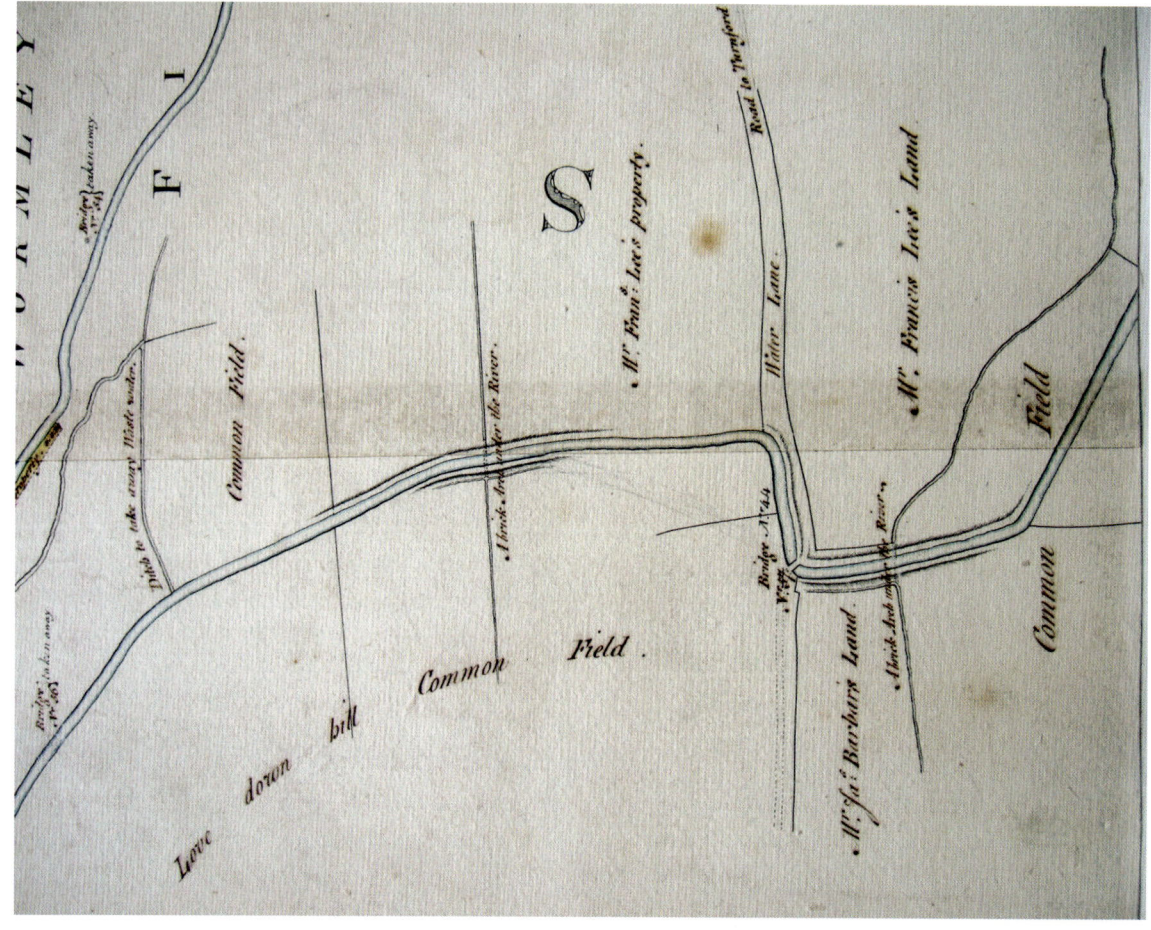

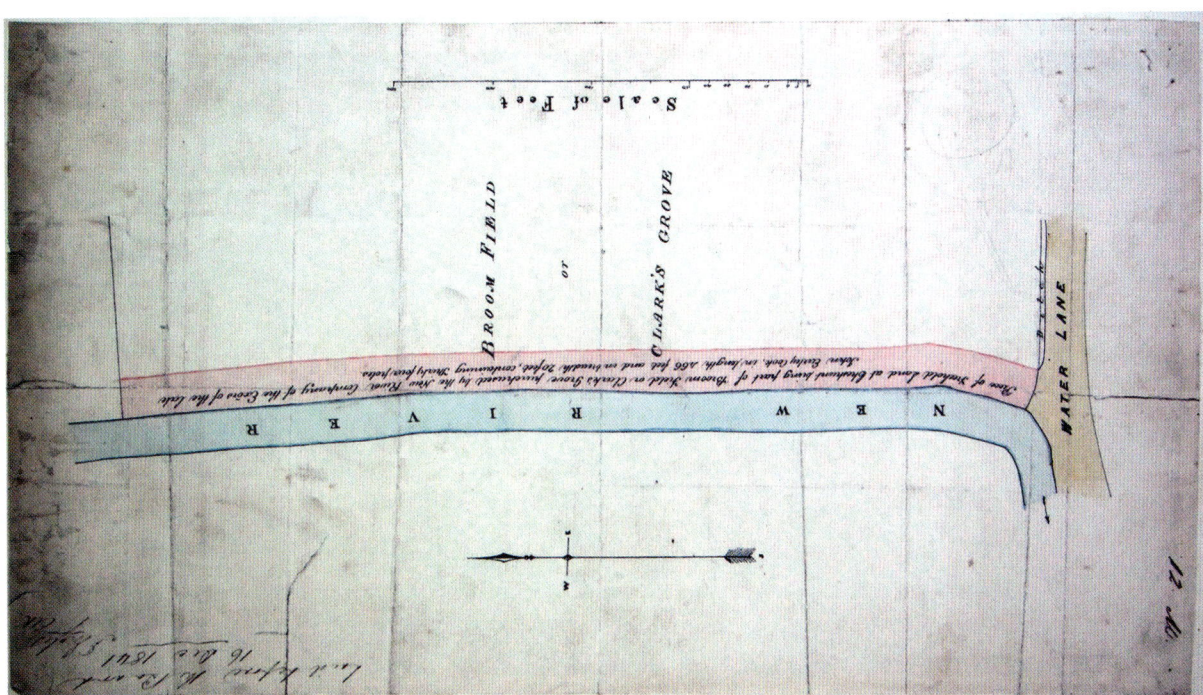

ABOVE: 16 Dec. 1841 Broom Field or Clarke's Grove, mentions Cheshunt, Water Lane & the late John Earley Cook.

Both probably the **same piece of land at Water Lane**, N-side of Turnford Brook on former W-loop Wormley, on a section probably now beneath the A10 bypass.

BELOW: Probably pre-dates Above. 'Land near Turnford' (Index), mentions Mr Cook's & Sr. Abrm. Hume's land (TW Archive; both MFK photos).

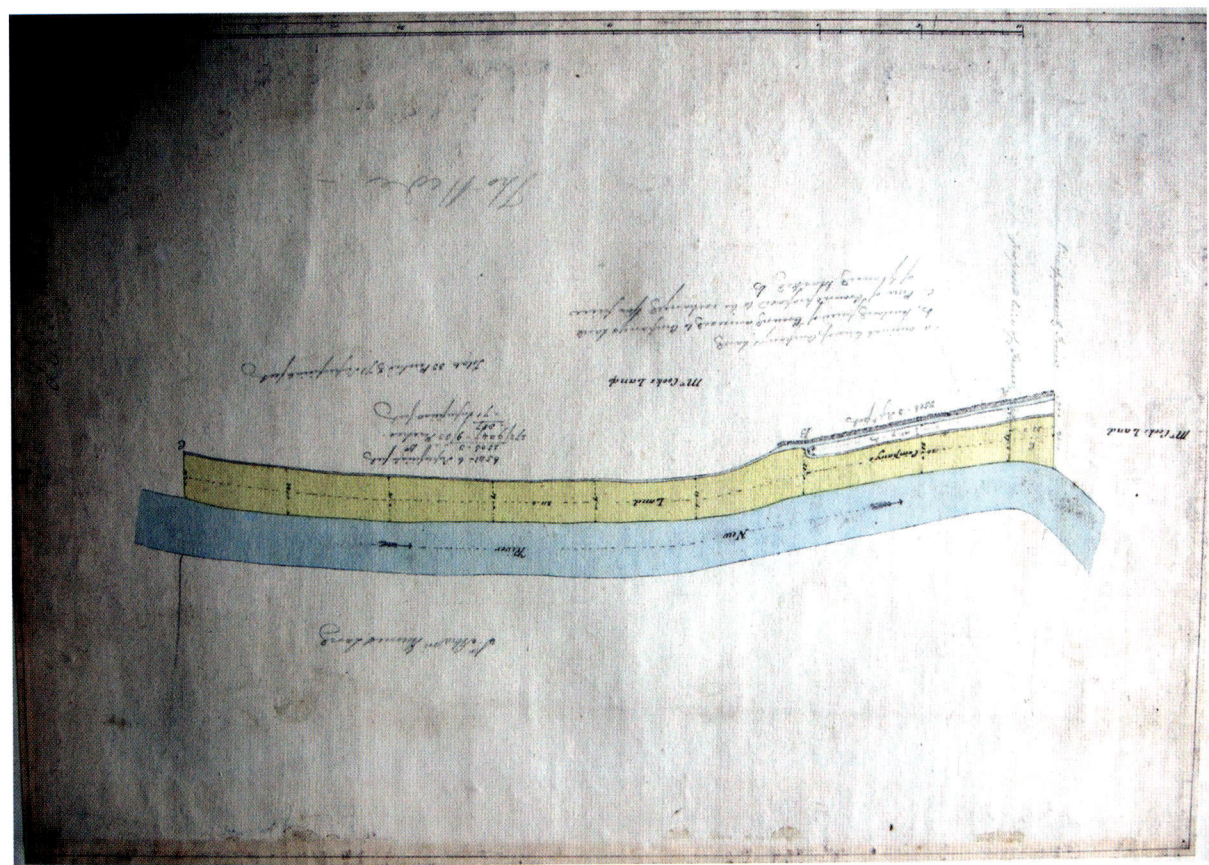

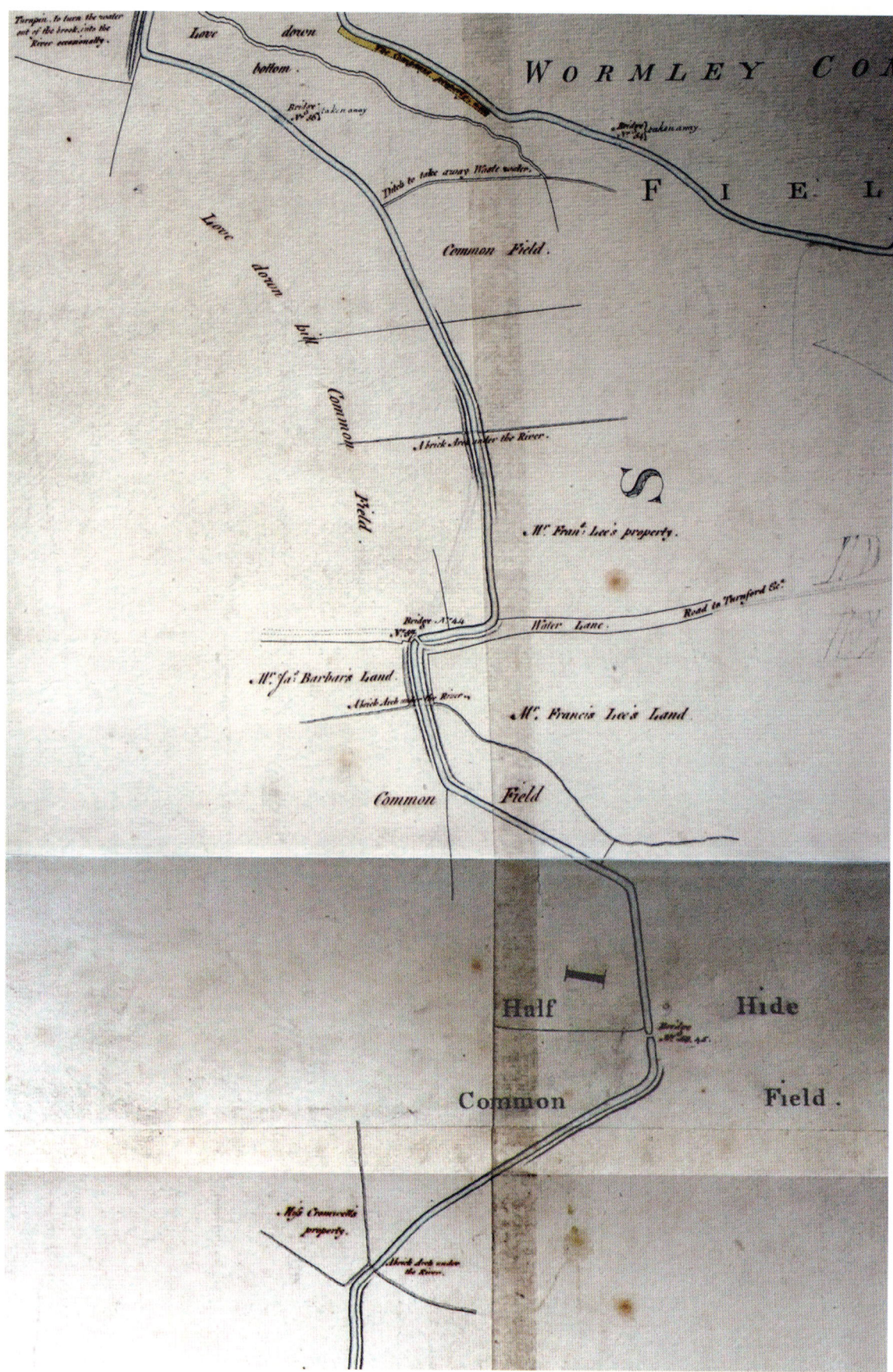

1775-1809 Plan 9 &10: **New River at Turnford** (TW, Abbey Mills Archive; 2-MFK photos joined).

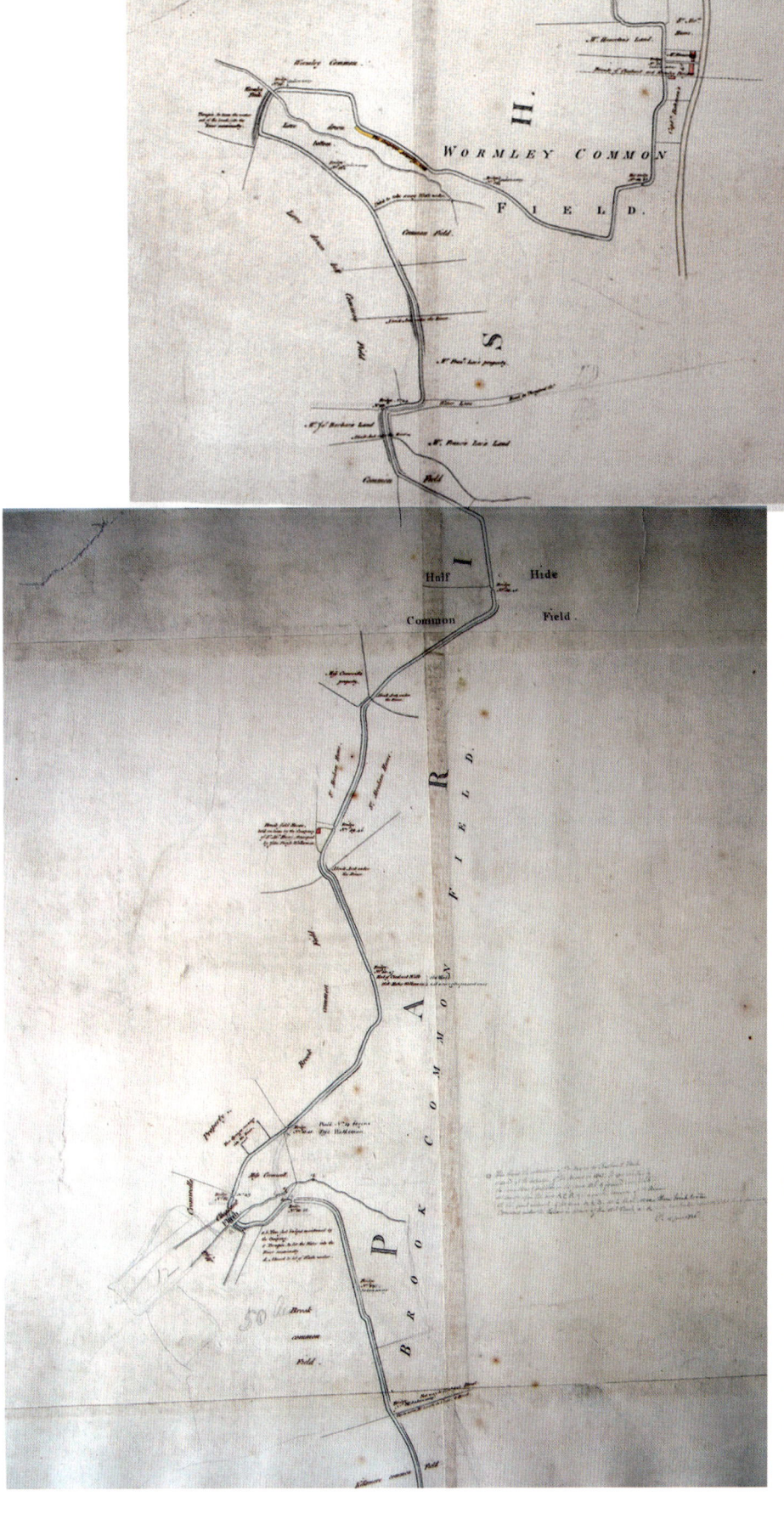

COMBINED Robert Mylne 1775-1809 Plans: **Plan 9 Wormley Loop, & Plan 10 North Cheshunt** (TW Archive; MFK photos & join).

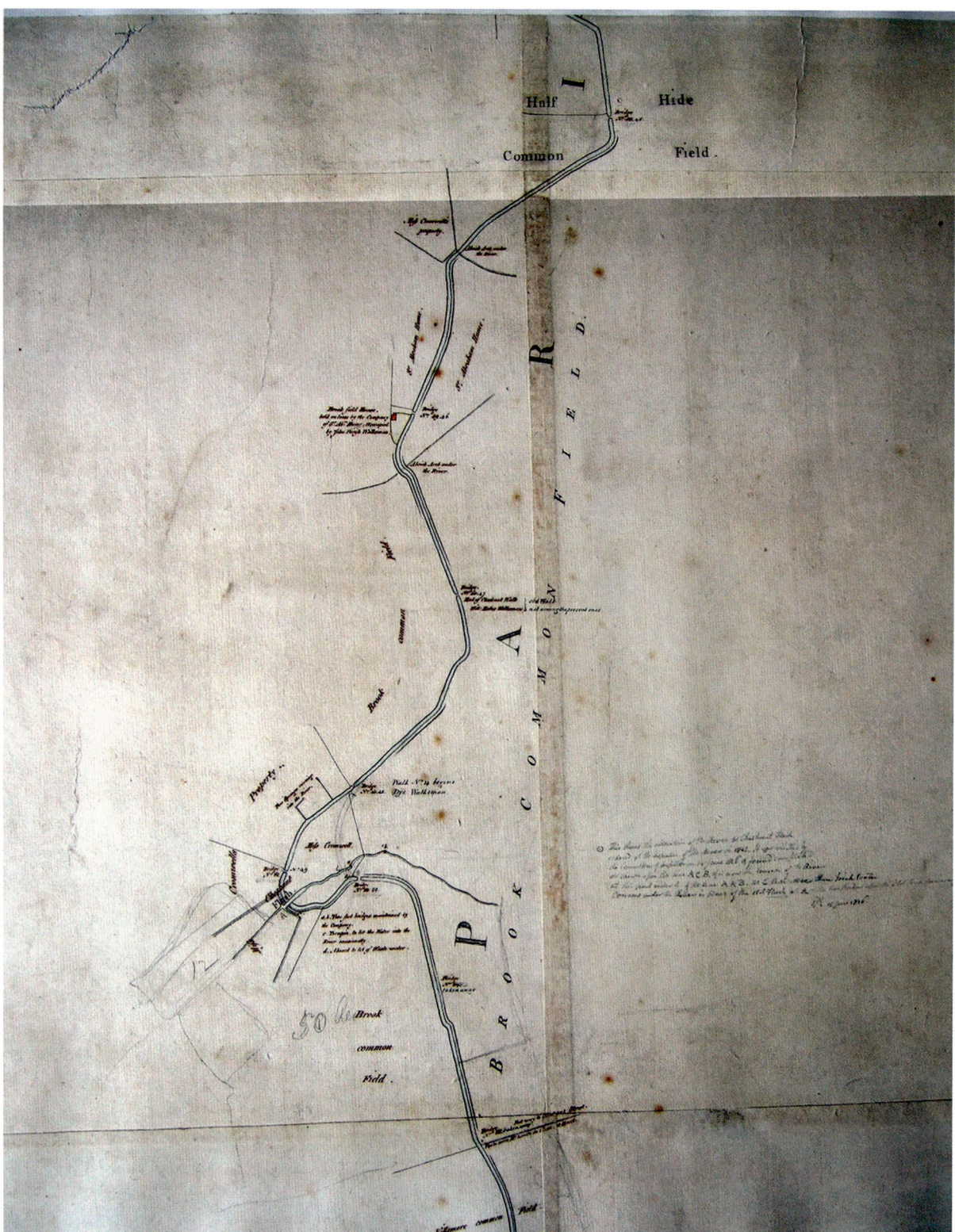

1775-1809 Plan 10 LARGE: **New River through Turnford & N Cheshunt** (TW Archive; MFK photo of centre of plan - since both sides blank).

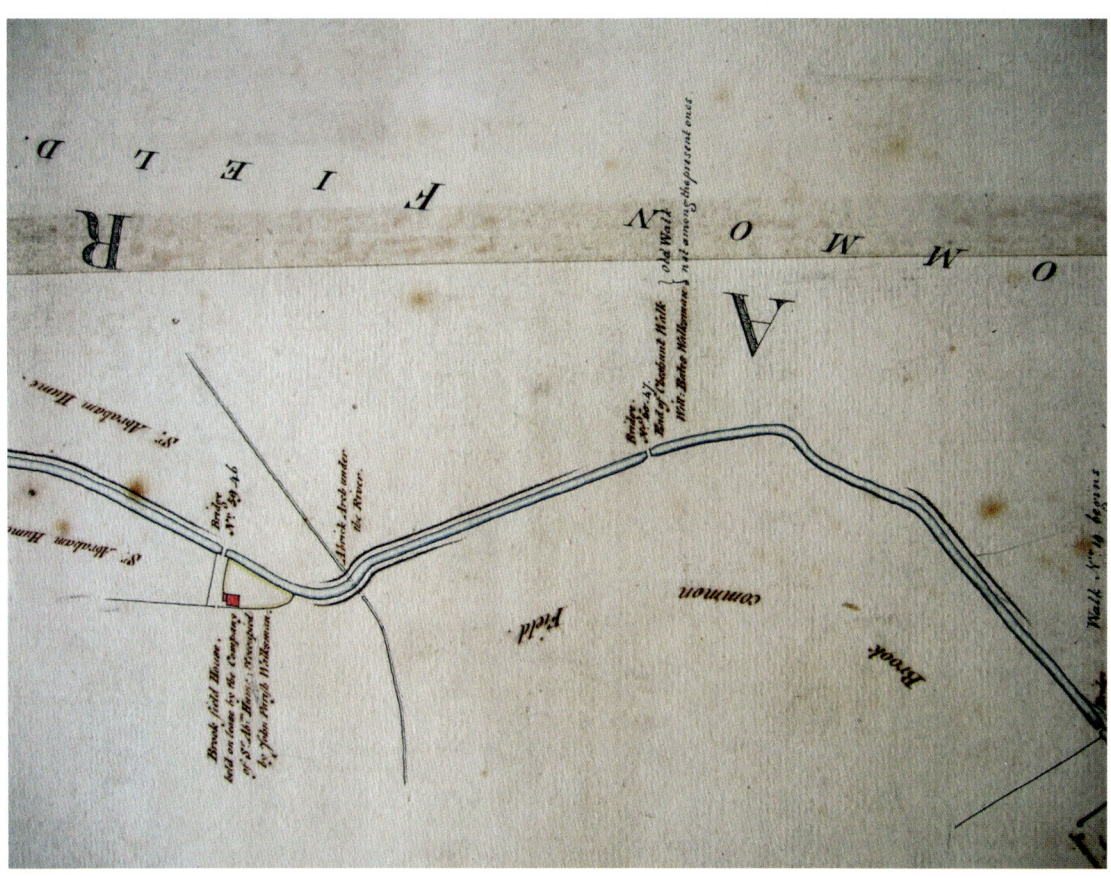

1775-1809 Plan 10 (TW Archive; MFK photos).
ABOVE: From N of Brookfield Shopping Centre to N-side of North Cheshunt Reservoir.
BELOW: New River from today's Turnford PS to N of Brookfield Shopping Centre.

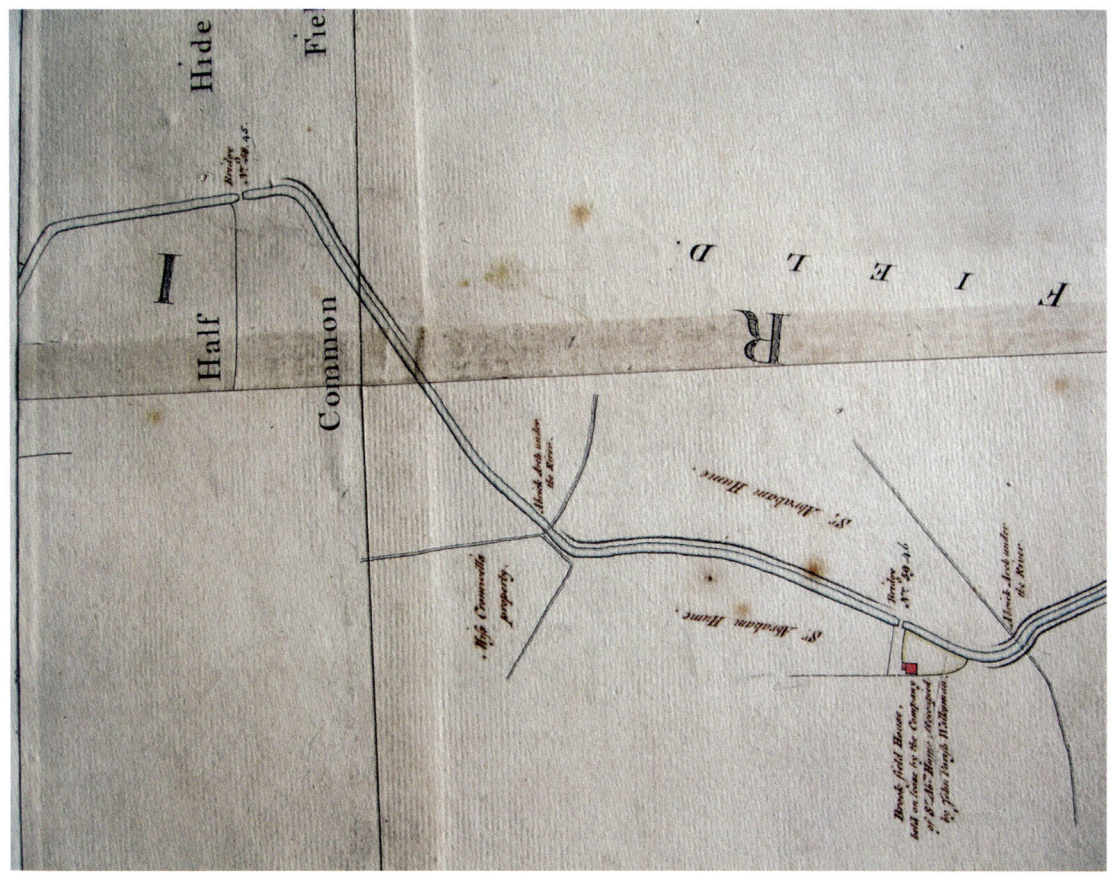

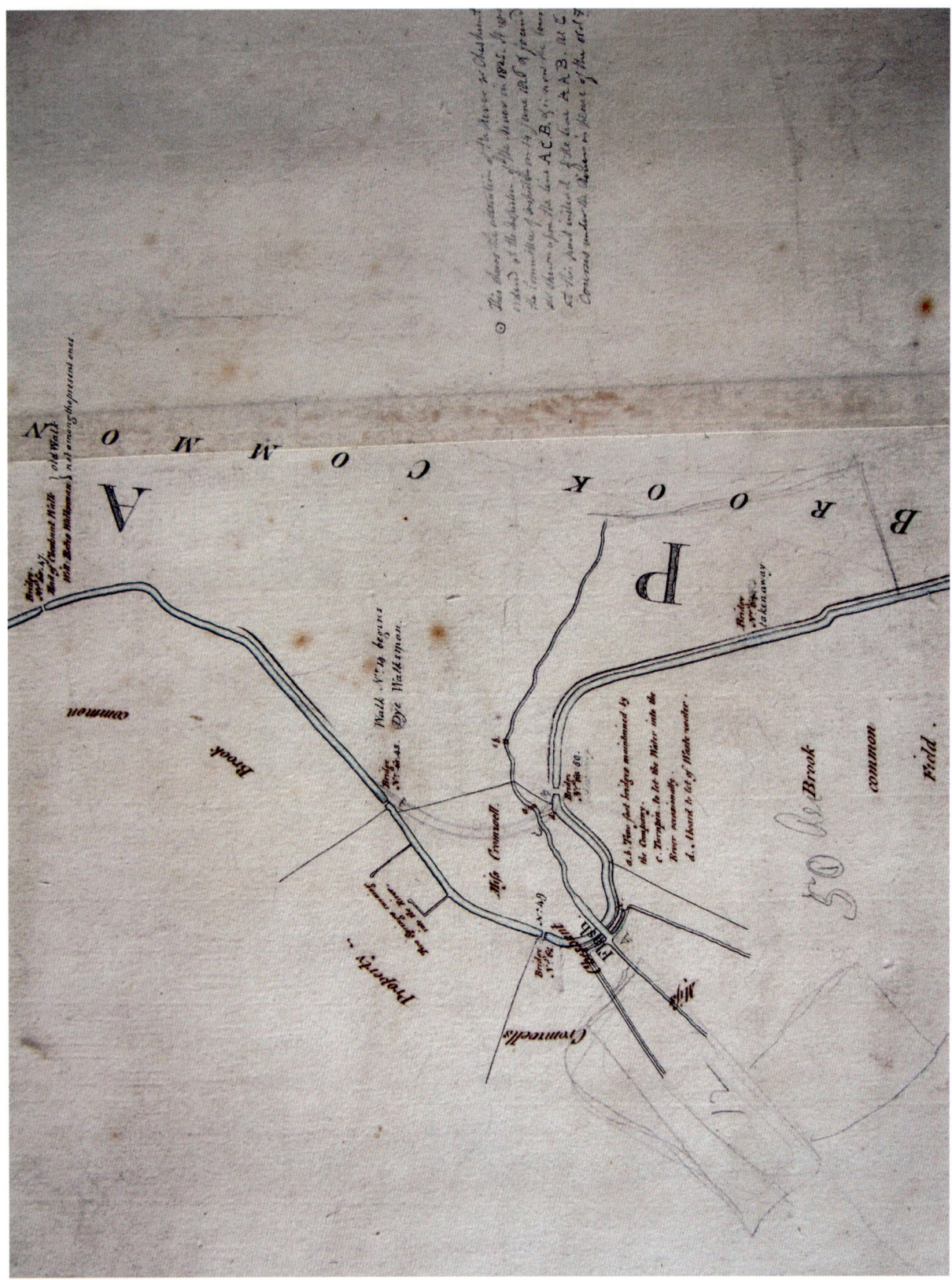

1775-1809 Plan 10: **New River at former Cheshunt Flash** (TW Archive; MFK photo).

1775-1809 Plan 10 (TW Archive; MFK photos).
    ABOVE: At today's former South Cheshunt Reservoir southwards.
    BELOW: LARGER former Cheshunt Flash.

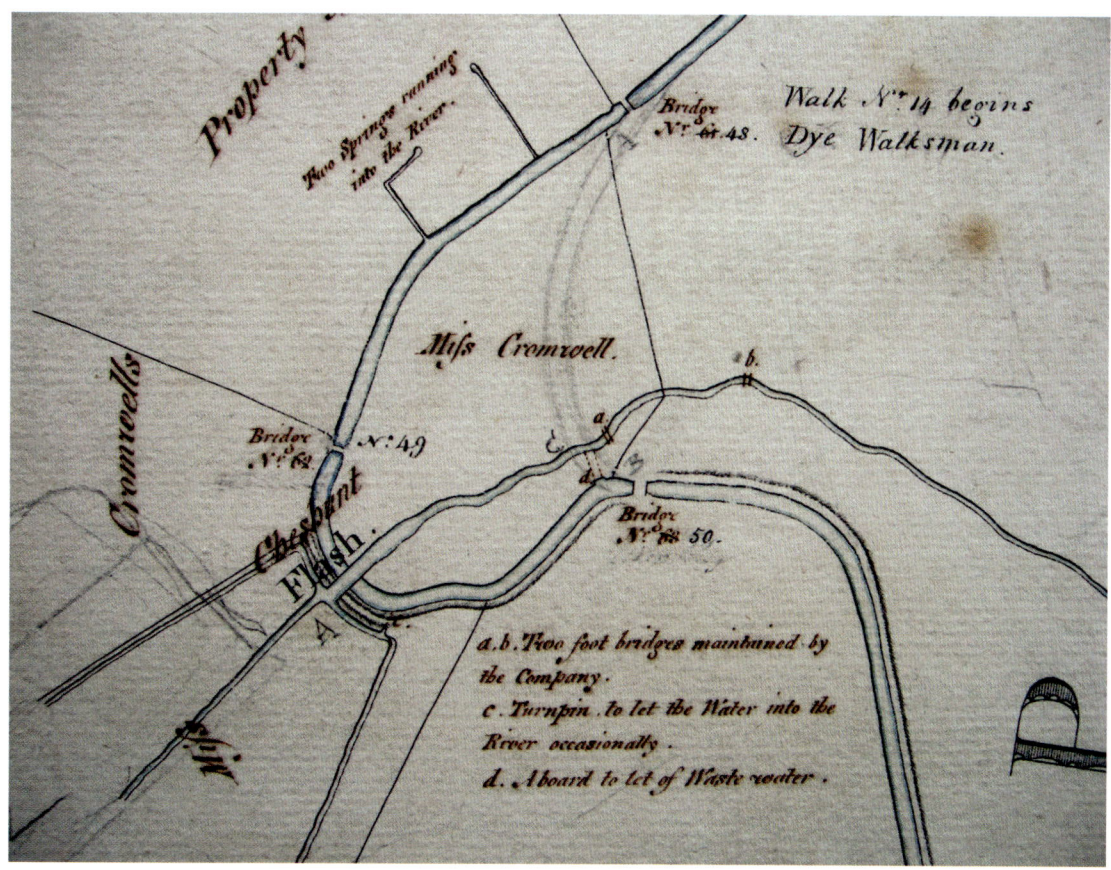

272

ABOVE: Later 1826 note.

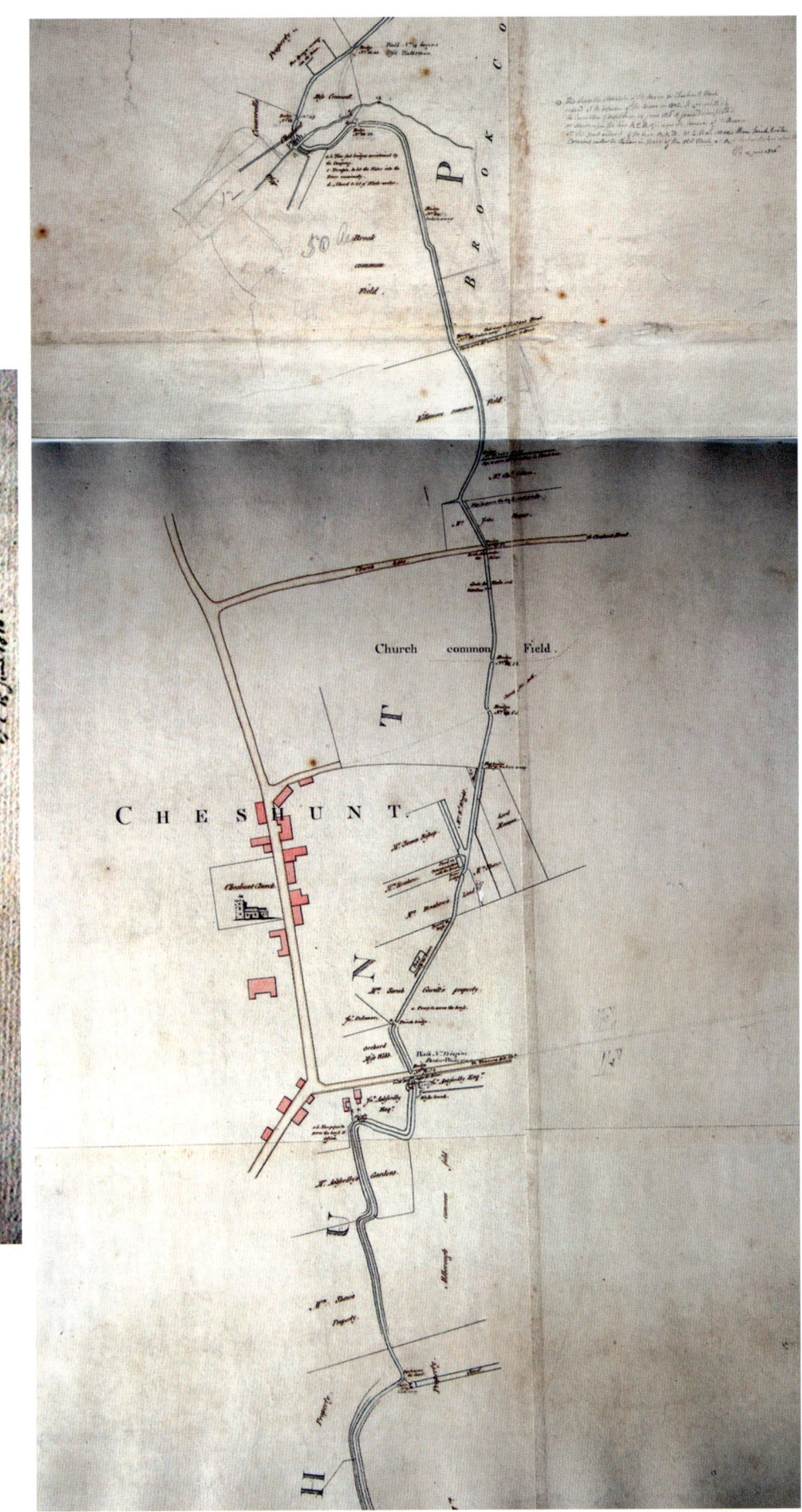

COMBINED Robert Mylne 1775-1809 Plans: **Plan 10** North Cheshunt, & **Plan 11** South Cheshunt (**Bury Green**) (TW Archive; MFK photos & join).

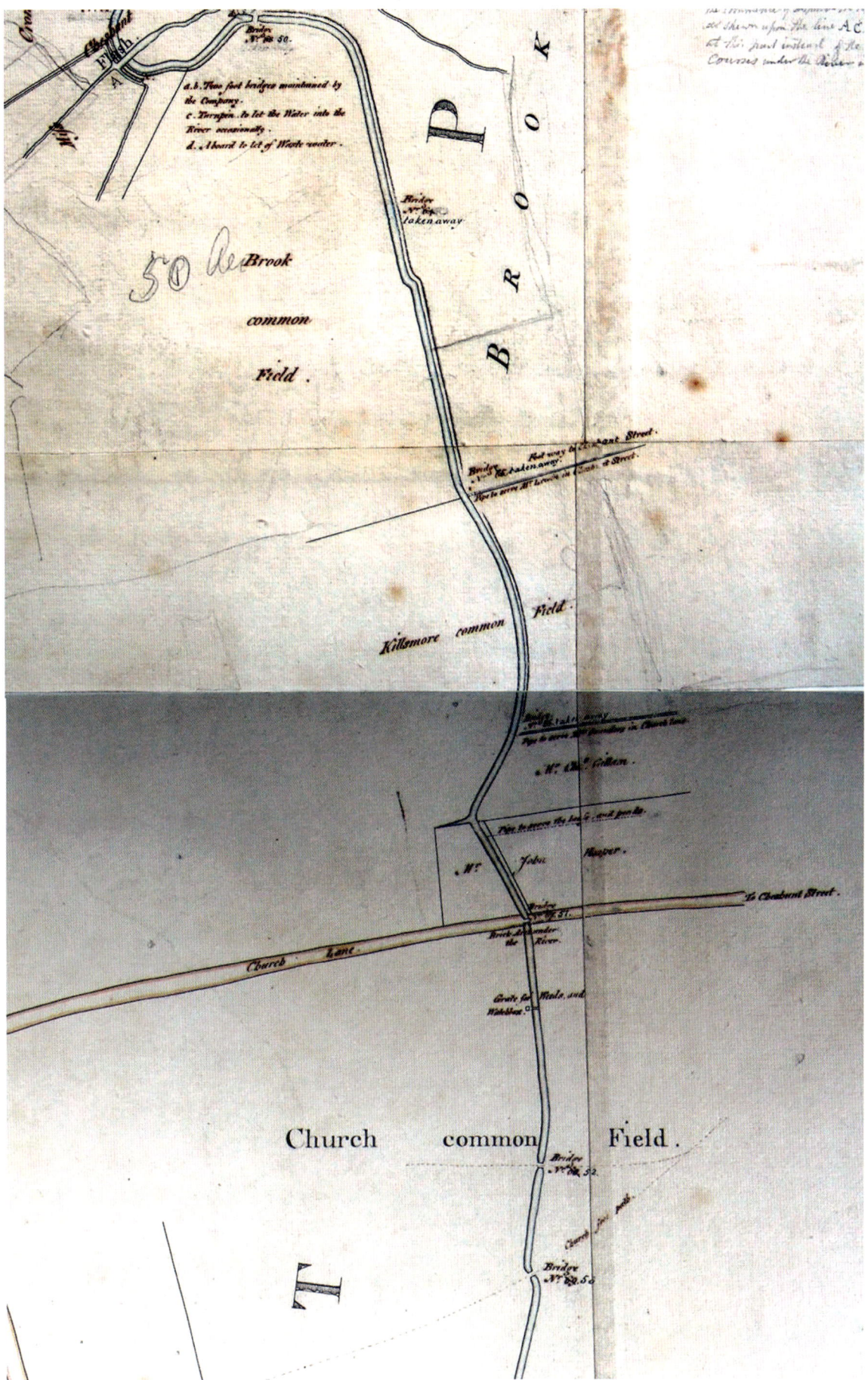

1775-1809 Plan 10 & 11: **New River approaching Church Lane, Cheshunt** (TW, Abbey Mills Archive; 2-MFK photos joined).

1775-1809 Plan 11: **New River from Church Lane to College Road, Cheshunt** (TW Archive; MFK Photo).

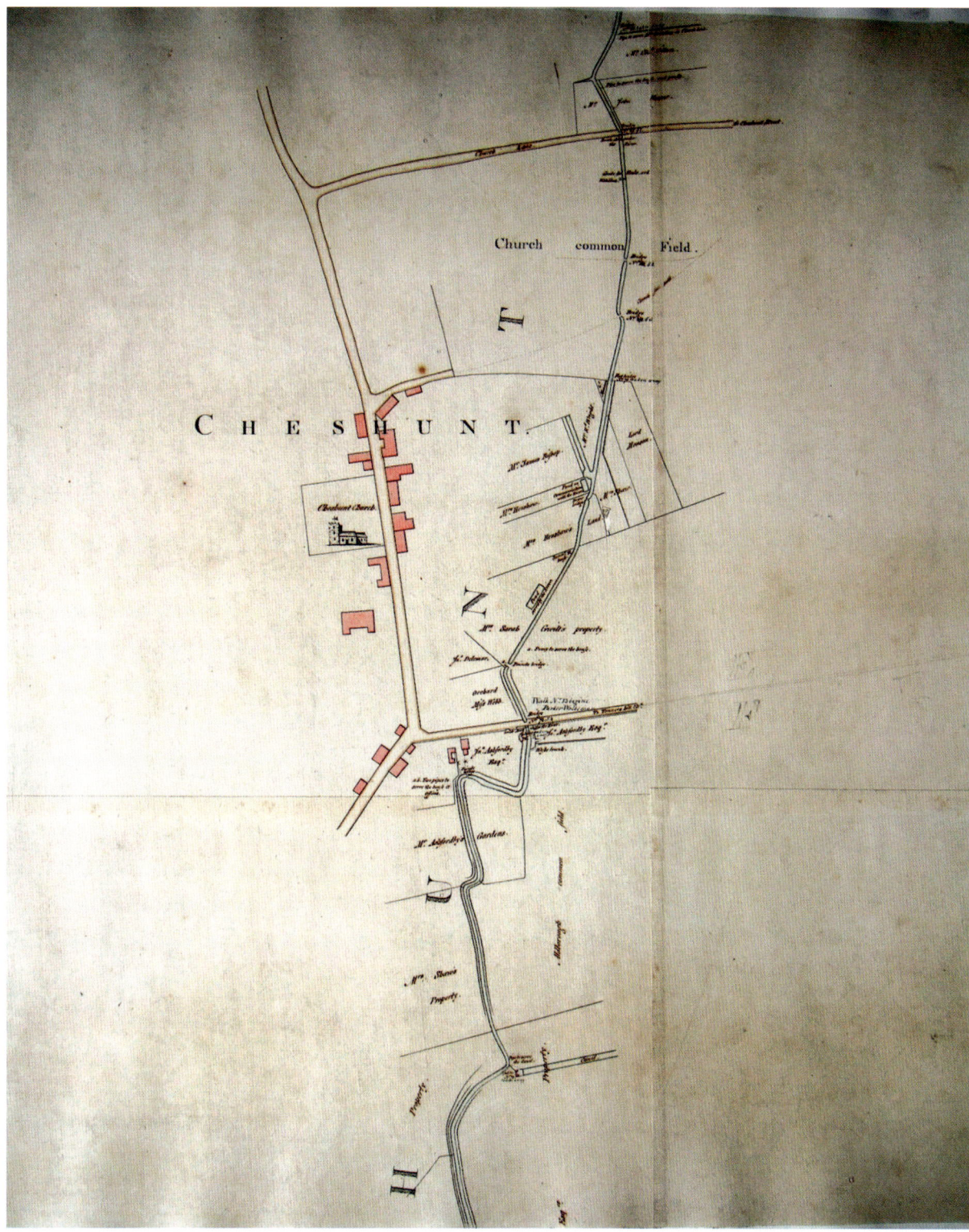

1775-1809 Plan 11 LARGER: **New River from Church Lane to College Road, Cheshunt** (TW Archive; MFK photo).

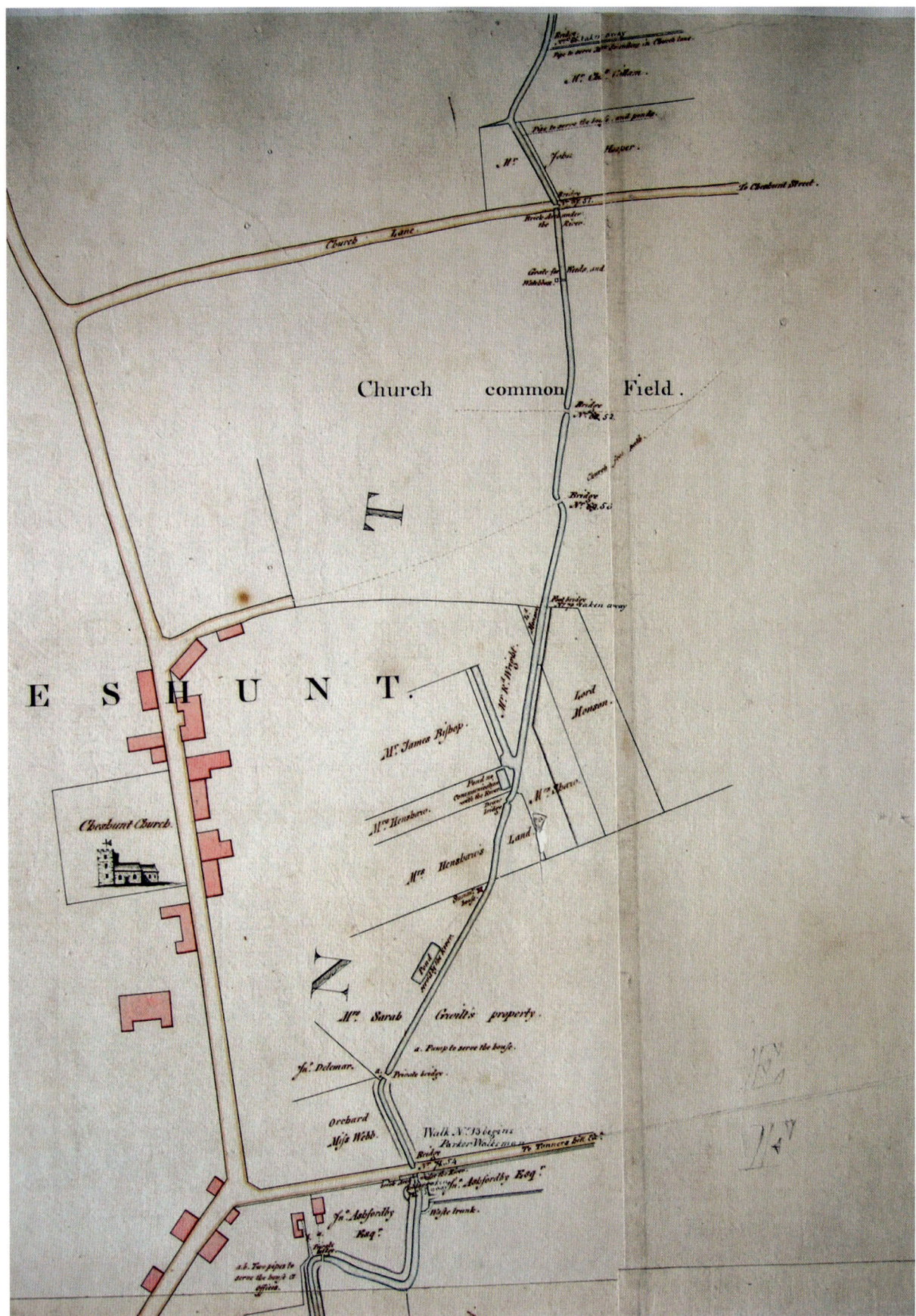

1775-1809 Plan 11: **New River from Church Lane to College Road, Cheshunt** (TW Archive; MFK photo).

A SOUTH EAST VIEW OF CHESHUNT CHURCH
Pub.d by J Sewell 32 Cornhill Aug.1.1800.

ABOVE: 1800 print of Cheshunt Church, Churchgate showing the Church Gates long since gone ((Shirt del., Ridley sculp., publ. by J. Sewell) Country Views, HALS).

See later for following:

'Theobalds Park' House/Mansion: Central part built c.1763 for George Prescott (d.1801) an M.P. and son of a wealthy Chester merchant. c.1820 the estate leased to the London brewer Sir Henry Meux, and later in 1888 purchased. His son also Sir Henry adding the two side-wings.

Today a Grade II Listed Building, 2006 owned or leased by 'Verve Venues' for Conferences & also catering for weddings etc.

BELOW: 1806 print of Theobalds Park, prior to the c.1854 creation here of an island in the New River ((Drawn & Engraved by Ellis for Hughson's 'History of London') ELSC&A).

THEOBALDS, Herts.

ABOVE-L: Henry Atkins Tomb, inside Cheshunt Church (MFK 2010 photo).

Henry Atkins one of the three main opponents (with William Purvey of Wormley & another), for a time halting the completion of the New River. 'In a recess in the [S-]wall, under the east window of this aisle, is a small altar-tomb under a canopy representing curtains drawn aside and looped up to the columns which support the cornice above. On the front of the cornice are these three shields of Arms: 1. Azure; three Barrulets argent, and in chief as many Bezants, for Atkins; impaling, Sable; three, Mill-picks or, for Pigot. 2. Atkins; impaling Quarterly of 4: I. and IV.; Sable; a Lion passant or; in chief on the Waves of the Sea proper, three Bezants, for Hawkins: II. Paly of 6 or and gules, on a chief of the last three Escallops of the first. 3. Azure; a Bend plain, cotised indented or. At the back of the recess on an oval tablet is this inscription: Henry Atkins Dr. of Physiq physician in ordinary for the space of 32 years to King James and King Charles was the son of Richard Atkins of Great Barkhamsted in ye county of Harford Gentl. and dyed Ano. 1635, aged 77, and lieth heere entered in this vavlt, which hee cavsed to bee made Ano 1623 for himselfe and his only wife Mary (whome he then bvryed heere aged 56) whoe was davghter of Thomas Pigot of Dodershall in the covnty of Bvcks Esqr. they had issue only one son Sr. Henry Atkins knight whoe dwelling at Clapham in the covnty of Svrrey died Ano. 1638 aged 44 lyes there bvried by his owne appointment' (E9-2, pp224-225; (Salmon's 'Hertfordshire', 1728, p12) 8A1, 3/3-2; E8-2, p115 aged 77; E10, p589 'on South Side of the Chancel').

ABOVE-R: Ashfordby Tomb, outside Cheshunt Church (MFK 2010 photo).

1775-1809 (Robert Mylne's Survey of New River): 'a. b. Two pipes to serve the house & offices' of Jno. Ashfordby's premises on N-bank of Former NR-Loop at Grove House, Bury Green, Cheshunt.
1 & 1/12 (2/6, ¼, 1/3, & 1/6) NRC Adventurers' Shares, 1739 (John Mitford > John Ashfordby Snr.), from1765 used to borrow money from Peter Holford, 1774-5 (John Ashfordby Jnr. > Peter Holford). On the N-side of Cheshunt churchyard, probably near the chancel, published 1874-8 'On a pyramid, resting on a heavy square pedestal, are these arms. In the centre:- A Saltire engrailed; over all, on a Shield of Pretence, an Inescutcheon within nine Cinquefoils in orle, for ASHFORDBURY. On the dexter, ASHFORDBURY; impaling, A Pelican in her piety: and on the sinister, ASHFORDBURY, impaling the Arms on the Shield of Pretence. On the sides of the pedestal are inscriptions which may be thus summarized:- John Ashfordbury, late of this parish, Esq., died 25th Feb. 1747, aged 70. Mary, his first wife died 17th April 1717, aged 39. Frances relict of John Ashfordbury died 17th Feb. 1774, aged 86. John, son of John Ashfordbury died 30th Sept. 1778, aged 52. Mary, daughter of John and Frances Ashfordbury, was unfortunately burnt to death 17th Feb. 1796, aged 68. Also two infant children of John and Frances Ashfordbury' (E9-2, p233).

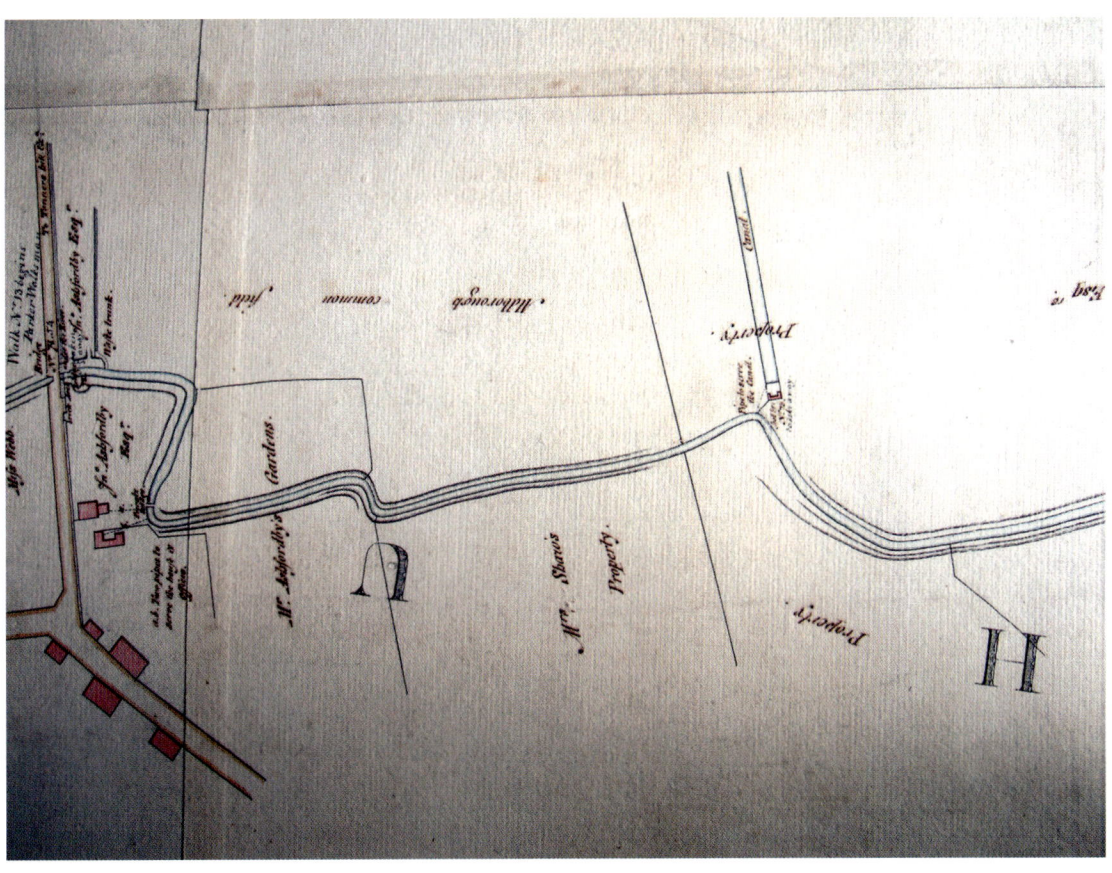

1775-1809 Plan 11 (TW Archive; MFK photos).
    ABOVE: S of today's College Road, Cheshunt. Showing former 'Bury Green' W-loop.
    BELOW: N & S of today's College Road, Cheshunt.

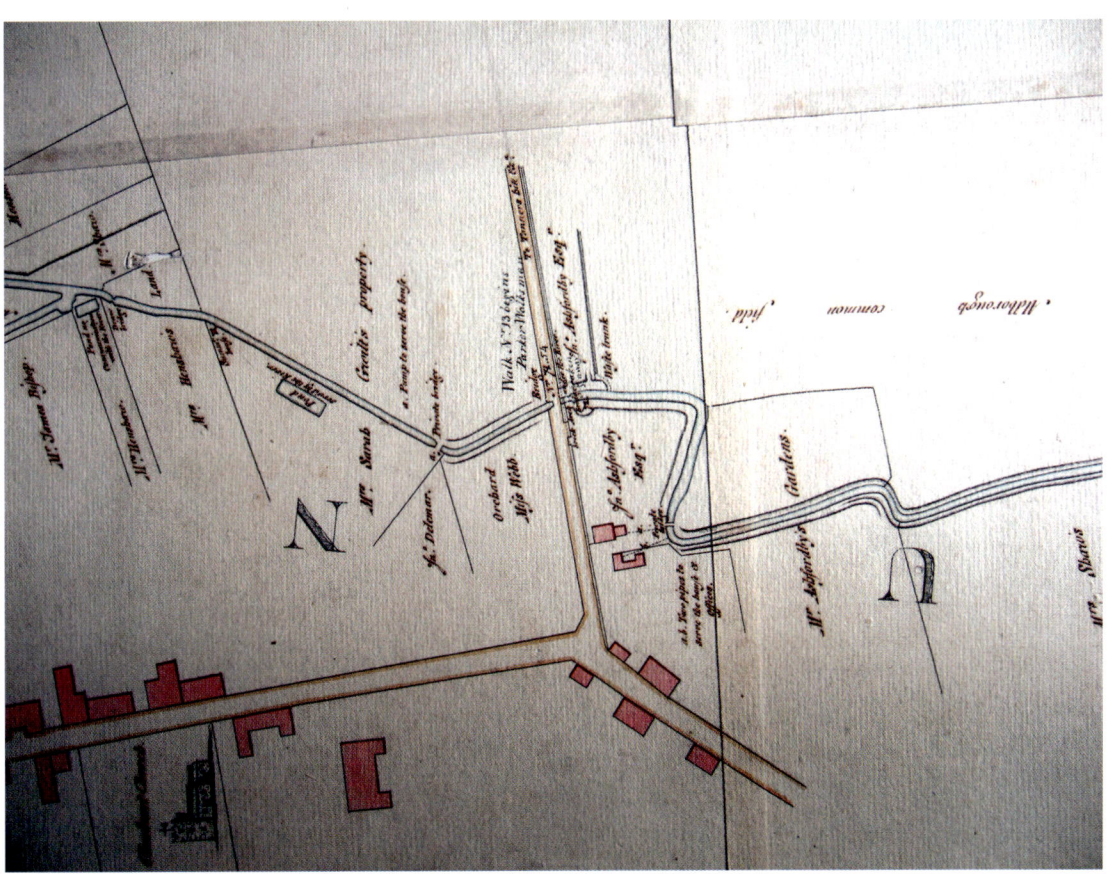

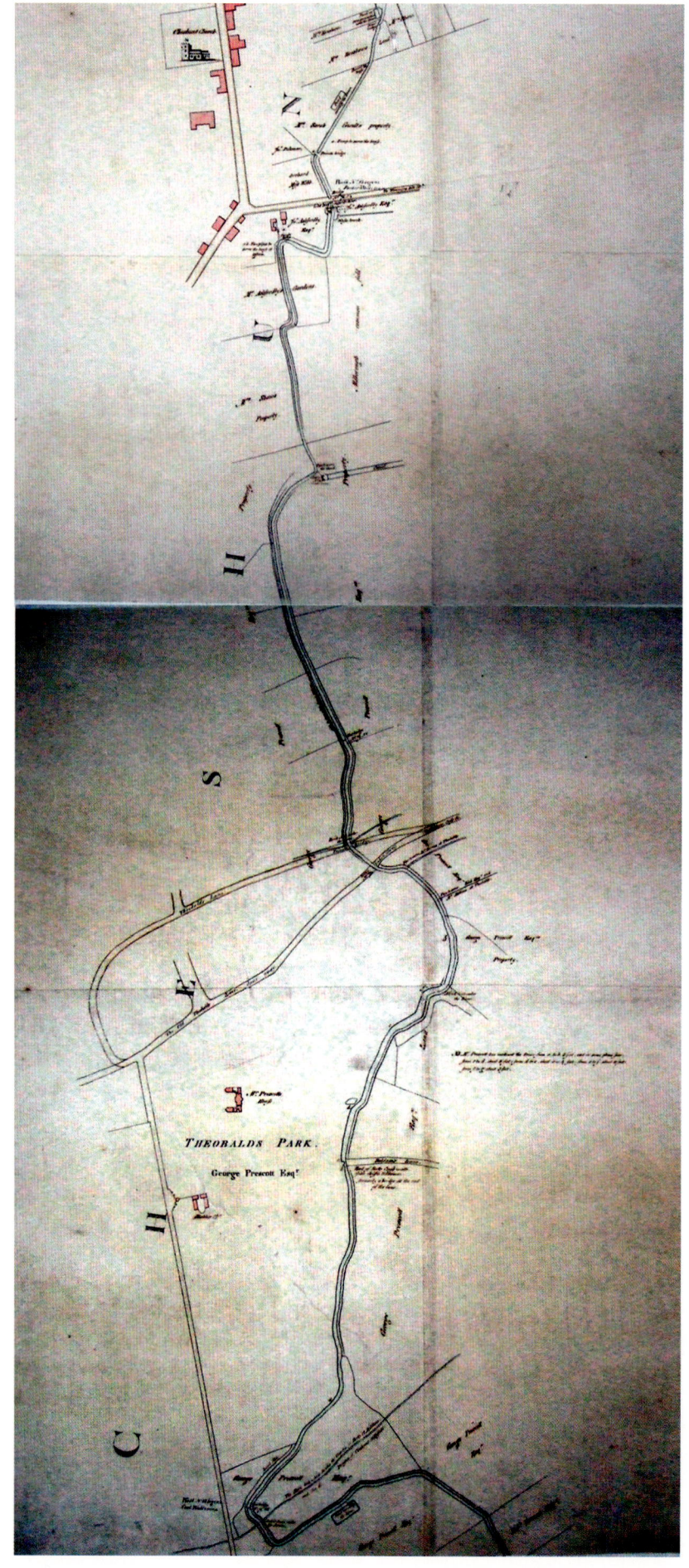

COMBINED Robert Mylne 1775-1809 Plans: **Plan 11 South Cheshunt (Bury Green), & Plan 12 Theobalds Loop** (TW Archive; MFK photos & join).

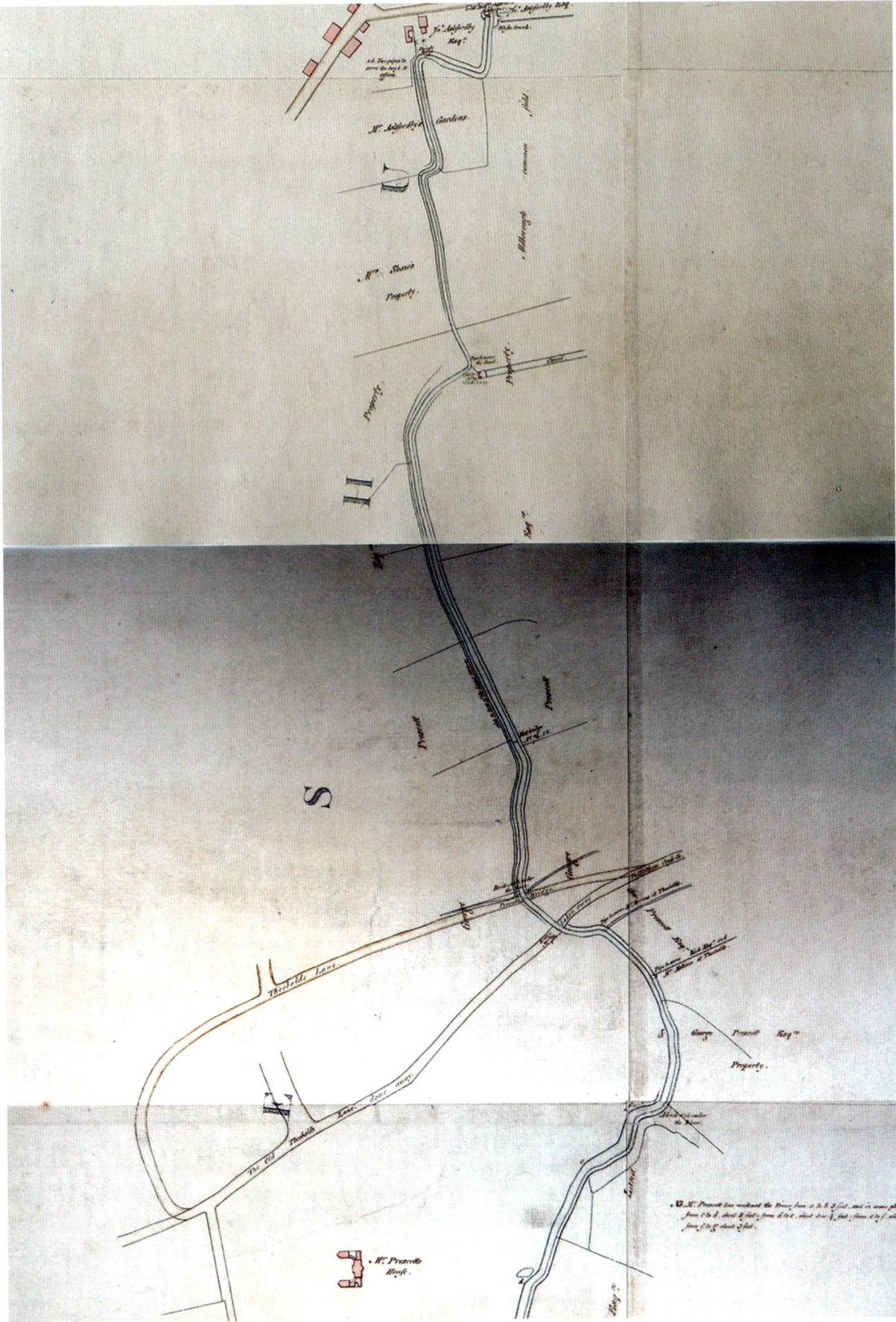

1775-1809 Plan 11 & 12: **New River from College Road to Theobalds** (TW, Abbey Mills Archive; 2-MFK photos joined).

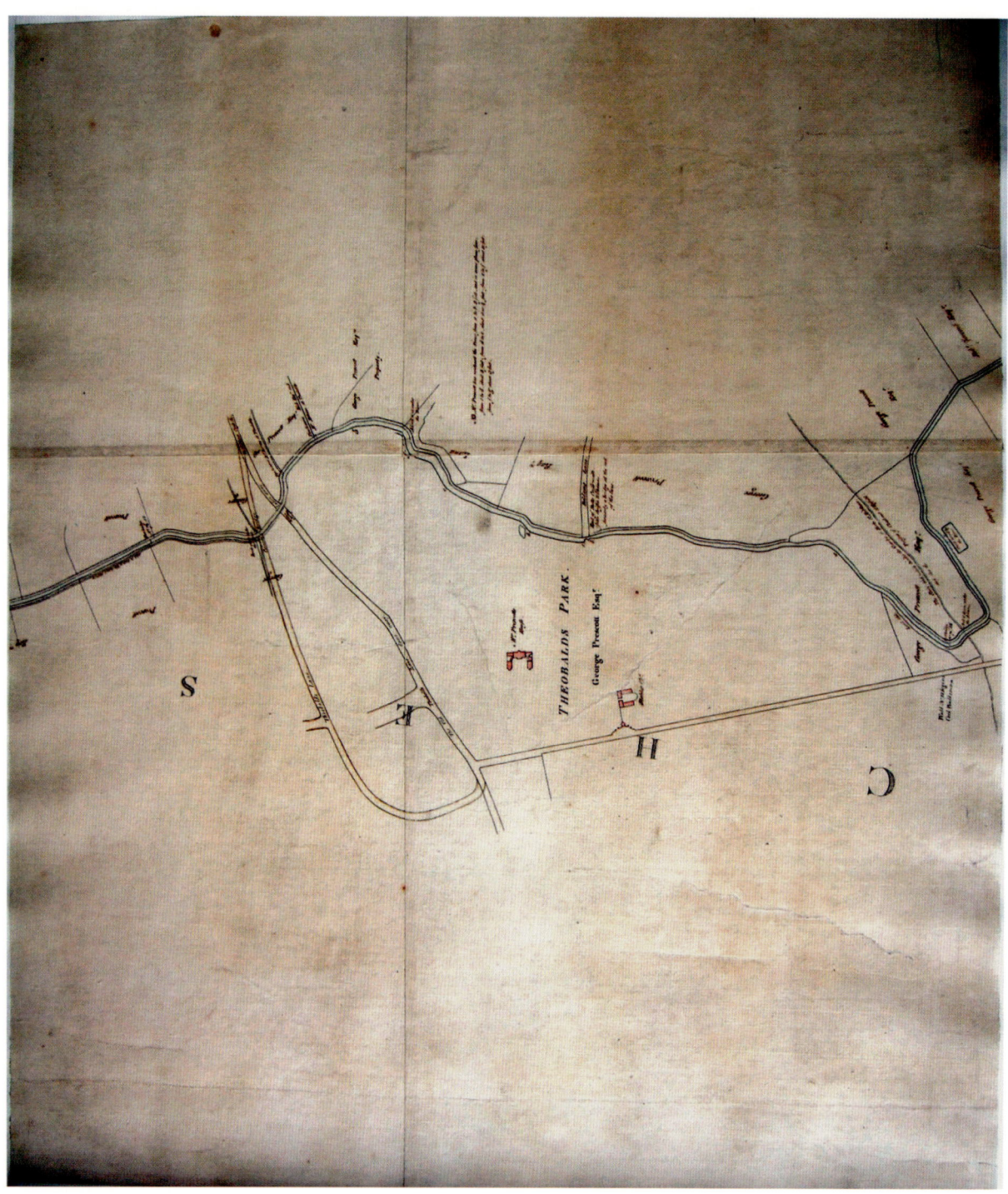

1775-1809 Plan 12: **New River through Theobalds, Cheshunt** (TW Archive; MFK photo).

1775-1809 Plan 12 LARGER: **New River through Theobalds, Cheshunt** (TW Archive; MFK photo).

284

'Theobalds Park Wall' by Maberly Phillips, F.S.A., J.P., pp248-262, 1915 (ELSC&A; MFK improved).
East Herts Arch. Soc. Trans. Vol. V, Part III.

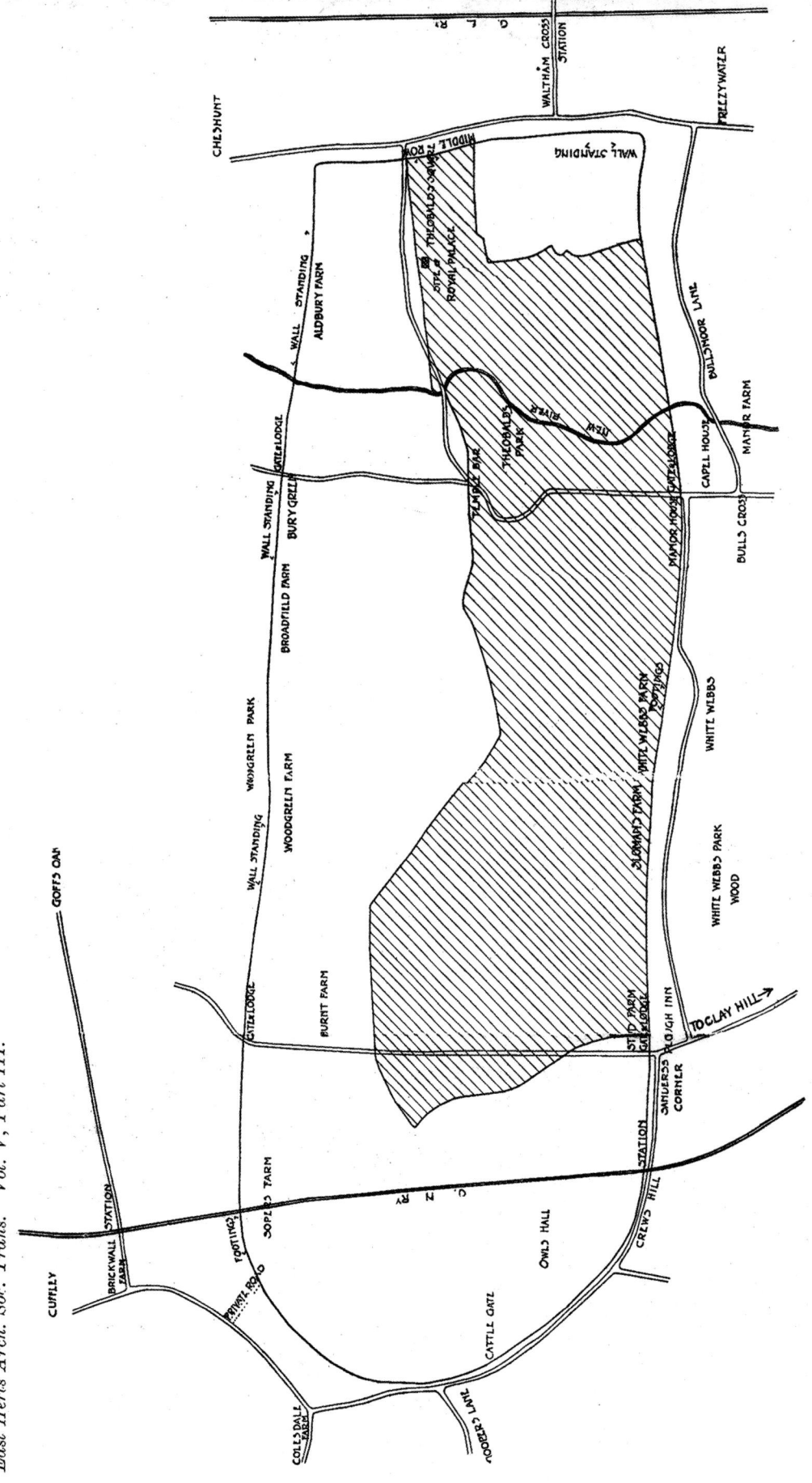

PLAN OF WALL BUILT BY JAMES I AROUND THEOBALDS PARK *(circa 1620)*.

1620-1623 approx. 9.5-mile long red-brick wall (9-10ft. high by 2ft. 6-inches wide with heavy coping) erected around Theobalds Park with six main gateways & lodges for park-keepers. Visit Cedars Park Cheshunt for the best viewable equitable remnants, since virtually all of the outer wall is now just foundations.

Photo from 'Theobalds Park Wall' by Maberly Phillips, F.S.A., J.P., East Herts. Archaeological Society Transactions, pp248-262, 1915, ELSC&A).

DATE STONE IN WALL AT ALBURY RIDE, CHESHUNT.

In 1923 "A good view of this remnant is **obtained from the banks of the New River, looking eastwards**, and a close inspection reveals a tablet, about 2 ft. square, bearing the inscription 1621, …" (C4, p66). Which because it was a danger to the children in the playing fields of Riversmead School, was demolished, the tablet given by Ian Gilmore to the local council, and is now displayed at Cedars Park (C2, p28).
1935 Cheshunt School (Grammar), Windmill Lane (dem. post-1992). Cheshunt Sec. Mod. School > Riversmead School > 1988-closed old Bishopslea School, College Road. 1990-Sept. 1992 Cheshunt Grammar > Bishopslea site new Cheshunt School.

BELOW: '1621' stone re-erected in Cedars Park (MFK 2010 photos); RHS enlarged plaque.

1896 OS Map: **New River near Theobalds Palace (SITE OF)** (OS Map, ELSC&A).

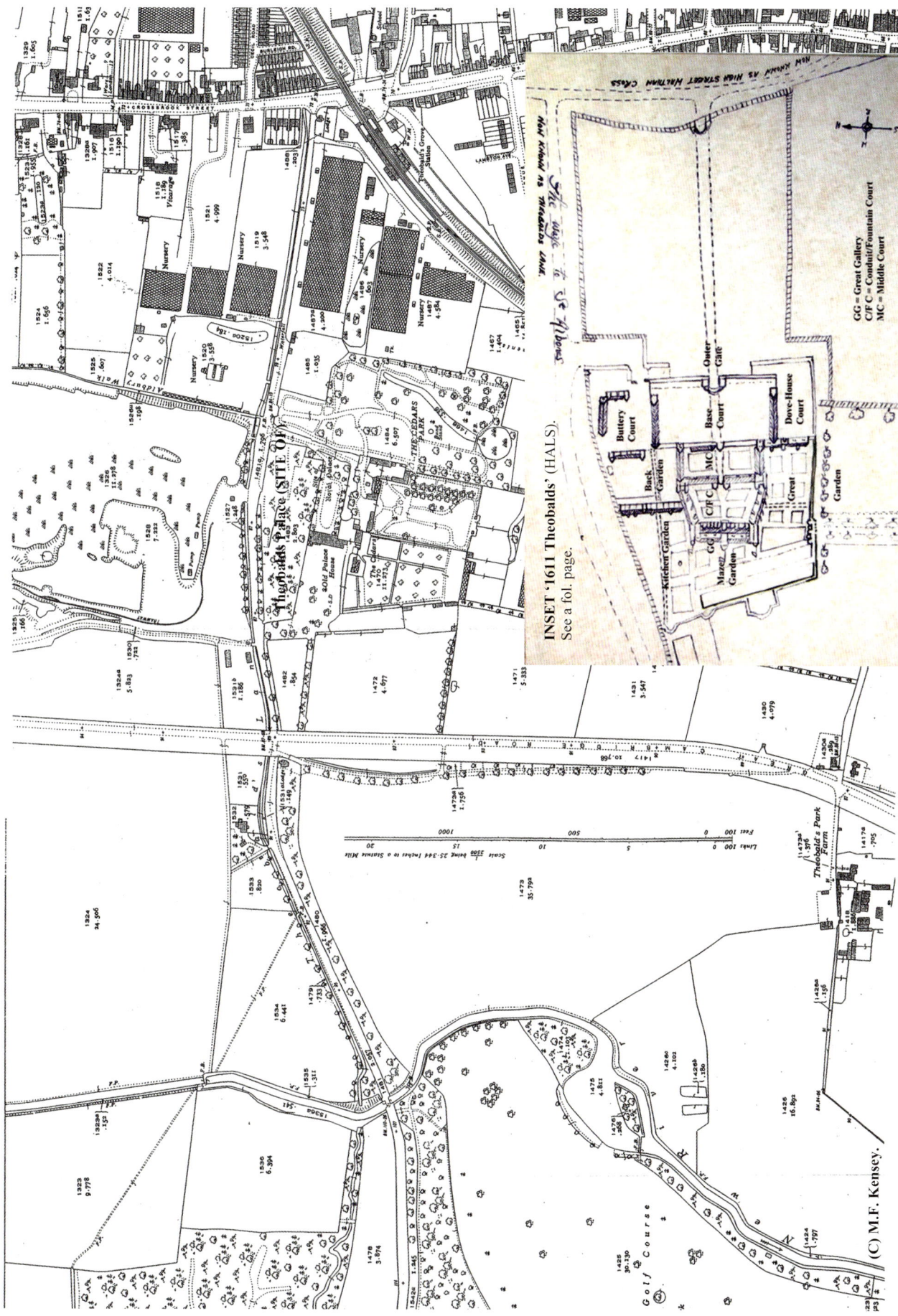

1935 OS Map: **New River near Theobalds Palace (SITE OF)** (OS Map & inset, HALS; MFK annotated).

PREVIOUS NOTE: Cheshunt Flash (1775-1809 R. Mylne plans).
Pencilled note: 'This shows the alterations of the River nr. Cheshunt Flash ordered at the Inspection of the River in 1825. It was visited by the Committee of Inspection on 14 June 1826 & found completed as shown upon the line ACB & is now the course of the River at this point instead of the line AAB. At C there are three brick water courses under the River in place of the old Flash at A & the two bridges upon the old line done away. [Initials] 15 June 1826'.

THEOBALDS 'PALACE'
Associated details of 1935 OS map with John Thorpe's sketch; and portraits of owners of Theobalds 'Palace':

1611 Survey of Theobalds: 'THEOBALDS: Part of survey of the [Cheshunt] Park, made by John Thorpe 1611, showing the house & surroundings' said to only show the Inner & Fountain Courts (((Original on vellum & tinted, Cotton MSS (Aug.1, i.75), British Museum; also Sir John Soane's Museum) 1959 'The Buildings of Theobalds 1564-1585' by [Sir] John Summerson, Archaelogia Vol. 97 (XCVII), London Society of Antiquities) D/EHw/Z10, HALS). MFK version of NPG portrait of Lord Burghley, Robert Cecil (B1, p41), King James I (1K10F, p3), King Charles I (1K10F, p22).

1689 (William Bentinck, Earl of Portland): The park and house remained with the Crown, until King William III bestowed the estate on one of his favourites, a Dutchman William Bentinck, Earl of Portland (E8-2, p95 2 Pars Orig. 1 Will. & Mary, rot. 53, in scacc.). He quite ruthlessly for more adequate returns, forced ejectment on the pretext of sueing one of his tenants called Philip Mitchell who was leasing a farm called Queen's Lodgings, a house called Whatleys and a meeting house and tenement called Prickmans House. The old Duke had permitted Mitchell to **lay six-inch pipes to his land from the New River** at a cost of £300 to Mitchell, the Duke allowing him £200 then charging him £12 a year, but because the NRC in 1686/7 had replaced the pipes with ones of one-inch which were inadequate, Mitchell refused to pay the £12 per year; the court only permitting Mitchell to carry off his crop and use the barns until Christmas ((King's Remembrancer Bills & Answers Henry VIII-1841, 582. 22, and 582. 36) B10, p144). The property transferring to his son, created a Duke by George I (C7A, p11).

Theobalds House/Palace (SITE OF) > Cedars Park, Cheshunt, Herts.: 2002 (Golden Jubilee of Queen Elizabeth II) installed main gates to Cedars Park, that incorporate bronze roundels designed by the 22 winners of a competition open to residents, who were also presented with framed-certificates whilst their photographs were taken. List of winners as follows:

	Date & Description	Entry Name
1	1560 William Cecil (simplified Head)	**Mr. M.F. Kensey**
2	1563 Theobalds Palace (workshop entry + Borough Choice)	Swash & Holy Trinity School.
3	1564 John Gerard (Herbalist to W. Cecil/Lord Burghley	C. Howell
4	Maze & Tree, 2 workshop entries.	Holy Trinity School
5	Fountain	K. Heller, St. Clements
6	1571 Queen Elizabeth 1st visit	T. Johnson, Holy Trinity School.
7	1598 Robert Cecil (picture from Borough of Broxbourne).	-
8	1603 King James 1st (falling into the New River).	**Mr. M.F. Kensey**
9	Menagerie (combine monkey & elephant + workshop)	Stoddard & Holy Trinity School.
10	1623 Brick wall around park (workshop entry)	Holy Trinity School.
11	1625 King James death.	T. Marlow
12	1625 Charles 1st being crowned.	Amanda (School)
13	1642 Civil War	A. Sexton Holy Trinity School.
14	1650 Palace damaged	J. Page (School).
15	1661 George Monk, coat of arms (Borough of Broxbourne).	-
16	1763 Prescott Family, coat of arms (Borough of Broxbourne).	-
17	1820 Meux Family - brewers & owners.	Megan, Holy Trinity School.
18	1910 Admiral Sir Hedworth Lambton. (workshop entry)	Holy Trinity School.
19	1921 World War One Tank.	Lucien Bonefonte
20	Cheshunt U.D.C. - coat of arms (Borough of Broxbourne).	-
21	Cedar Tree/Icehouse/Dovecote.	Mr. Smart
22	2002 Queen Elizabeth II's Golden Jubilee.	Holy Trinity School.

Roundel 8 should read fell into the New River 9th Jan. 1622 (Borough of Broxbourne's Cedars Park leaflet has pictures of all the roundels, labelling roundel 8 as 1598 when the roundel itself shows 1603, although refers to 1622).

ABOVE (TOP): Sept. 2002 (Golden Jubilee of Queen Elizabeth II) installed main gates to Cedars Park (SITE OF Theobalds Palace), Cheshunt. The £31,000 gates incorporate 22 bronze roundels (winning designs from over 150-entries into a competition, roundel details of all winners listed in main text) depicting a timeline of historic milestones, famous people, and enduring features of the gardens.
MFK the only person to design two winning roundels, as shown above with details below.

BELOW (LEFT): 1st roundel from L to R, Sir William Cecil (1520-1598), Lord Burghley, Secretary of State to Queen Elizabeth I, who from 1564-1585 built the palatial Theobalds House (often visited by Queen Eliz. I). In 1607 King James I exchanging Old Hatfield Palace (& other properties) for Sir Robert Cecil's (Earl of Salisbury, younger son of Lord Burghley) Theobalds House, which was converted into a country residence Royal Palace, where he could indulge in his passion for hunting. In 1609 impaling Theobalds Park, and there-after greatly enlarging the park (incorporating parts of or all of, Cheshunt Common, Cheshunt Park, Northaw Common, and Enfield Chase; by 1650 some 2,508-acres with 6-lodges or gates). From 1620-1623 enclosing the park with a 9.5-mile circumference, 9-10ft. high red-brick wall, 2ft. 6-inches wide with heavy coping.

BELOW (RIGHT): 8th roundel from L to R, King James I falling from his horse into the New River ('Myddelton's Water') on 9th January 1622 (MFK 2006 photos).
Theobalds Palace where King Charles I set out at the start of the Civil War (1642-1651), so pulled down 1651.

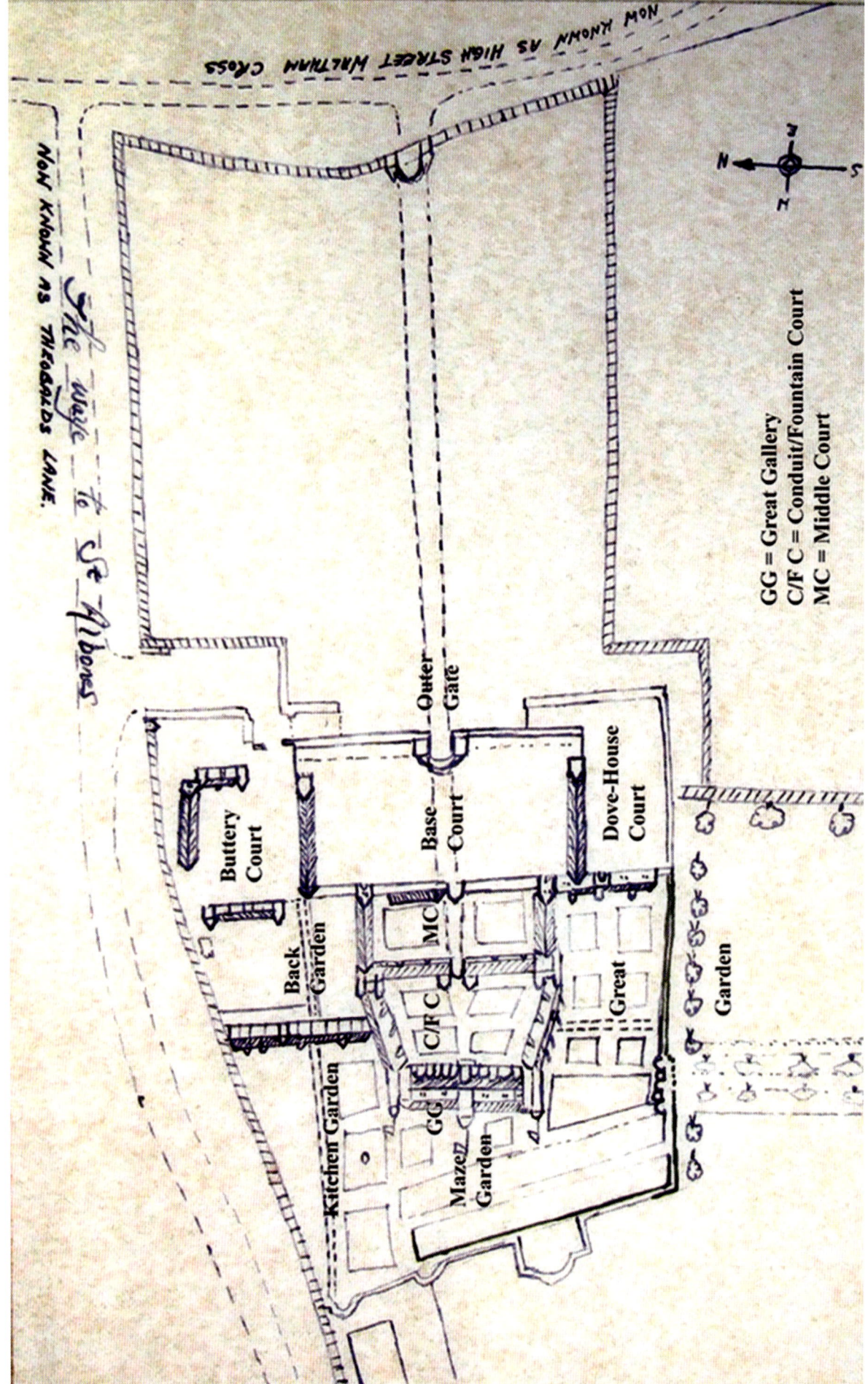

LARGER 1611 Theobalds Palace (SITE OF): 'THEOBALDS Part of survey of the [Cheshunt] Park, made by John Thorpe 1611, showing the house & surroundings' ((Sketch based on British Museum, Cotton, Aug. 1, i. 75/Sir John Soane's Museum, in Summerson's article Archaeoligia Vol. XCVII, 1959), Misc. photos, sketches & notes on Theobalds, D/EHw/Z10, HALS; MFK annotated).

ABOVE: Front of Old Palace House (demolished 1970) built from the remains of Theobalds Palace (MFK 8 Aug. 1970 photo). MFK when a young lad helping as a baker's boy on a Co-operative Society delivery round, the then still standing house being the first call of the day.

BELOW: View from inside (MFK 8 Aug. 1970 photo).

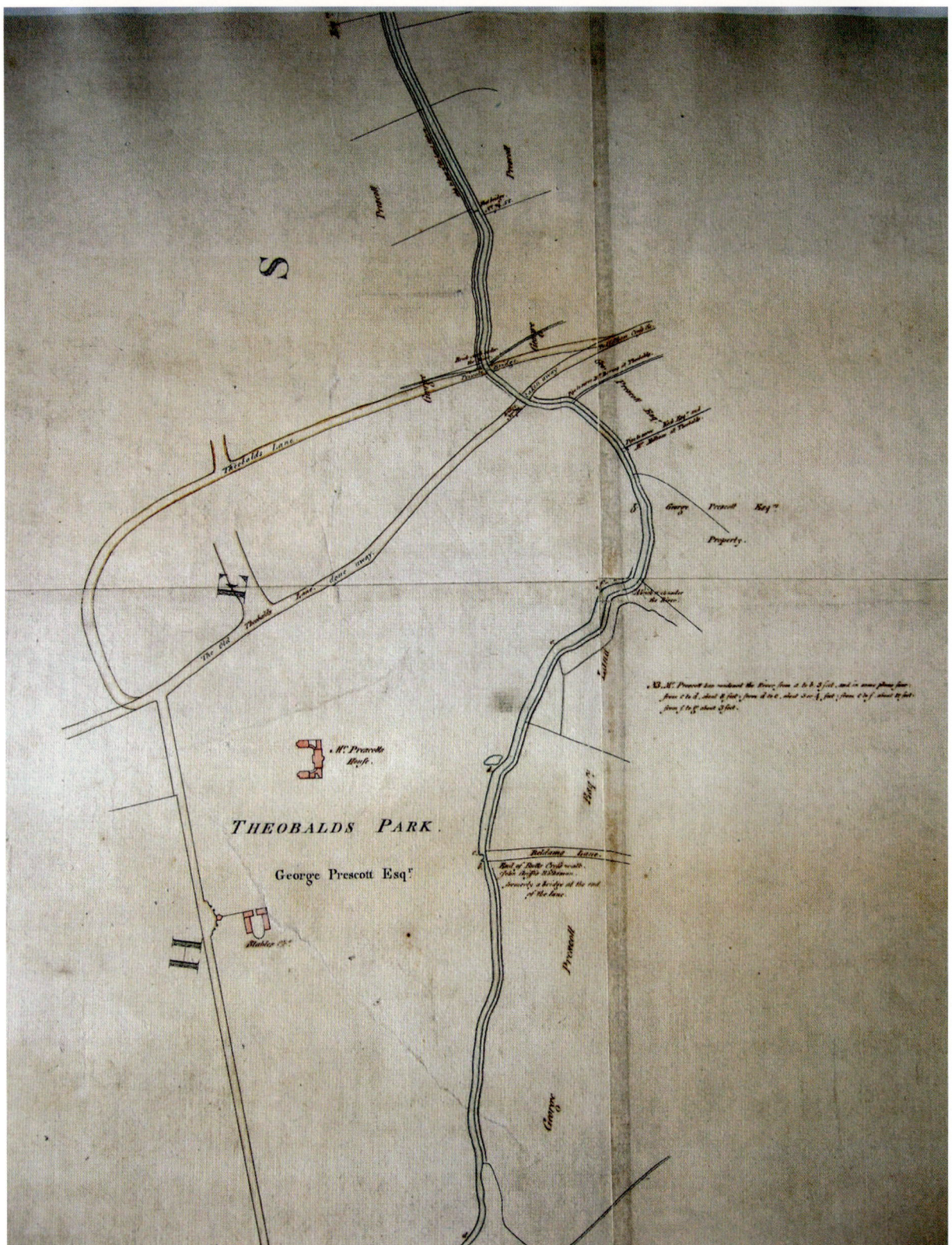

1775-1809 Plan 12: **New River over Theobalds Brook & past Theobalds Park, Cheshunt** (TW Archive; MFK photo). **ABOVE:** Enlarged mid-page note.

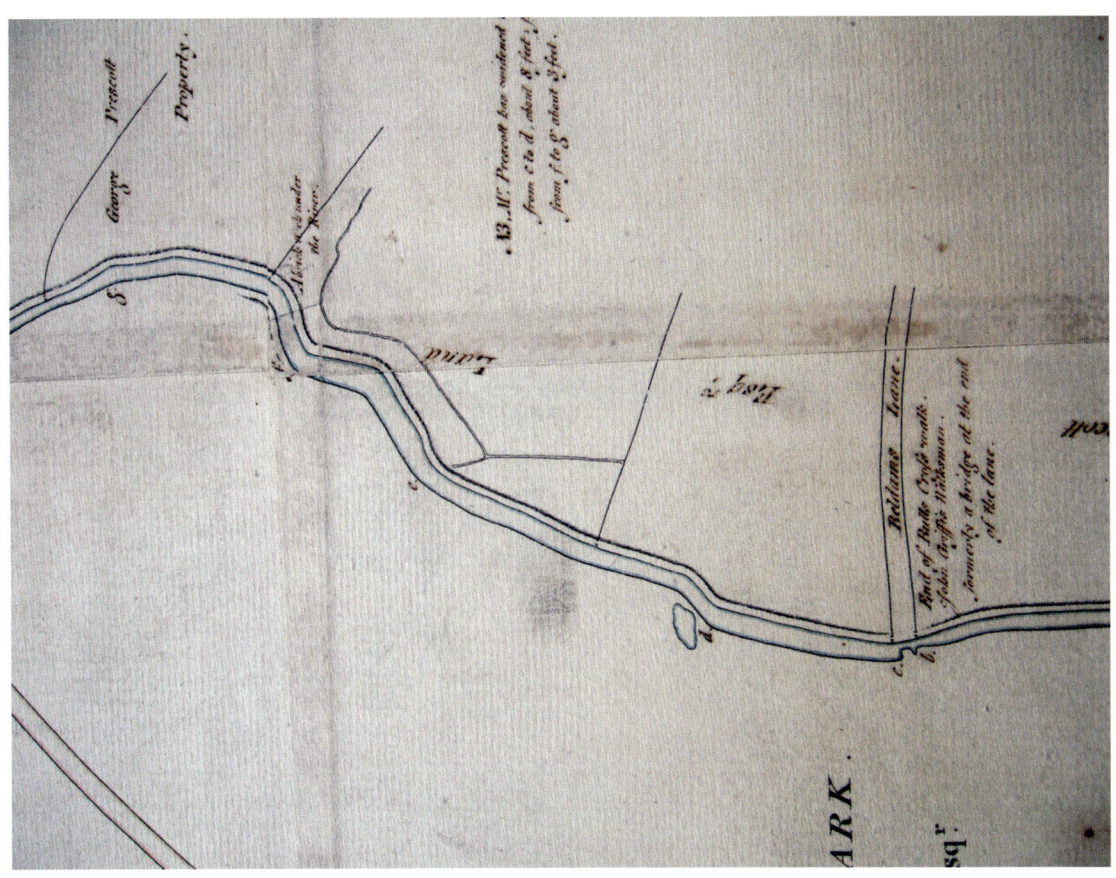

1775-1809 Plan 12 (TW Archive; MFK photos).
ABOVE: New River through Theobalds Park, Cheshunt.
BELOW: New River over Theobalds Brook.

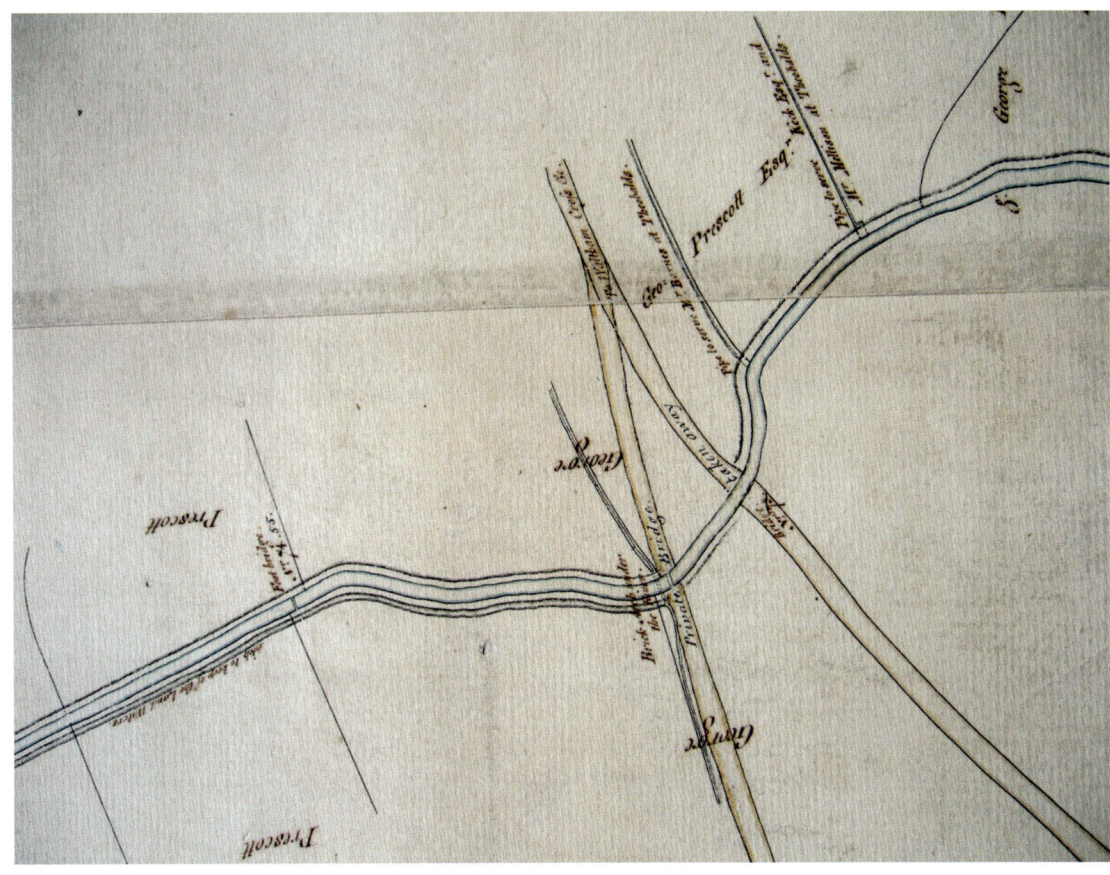

1775-1809 Plan 12: **New River former Theobalds W-Loop** (TW Archive; MFK photo).

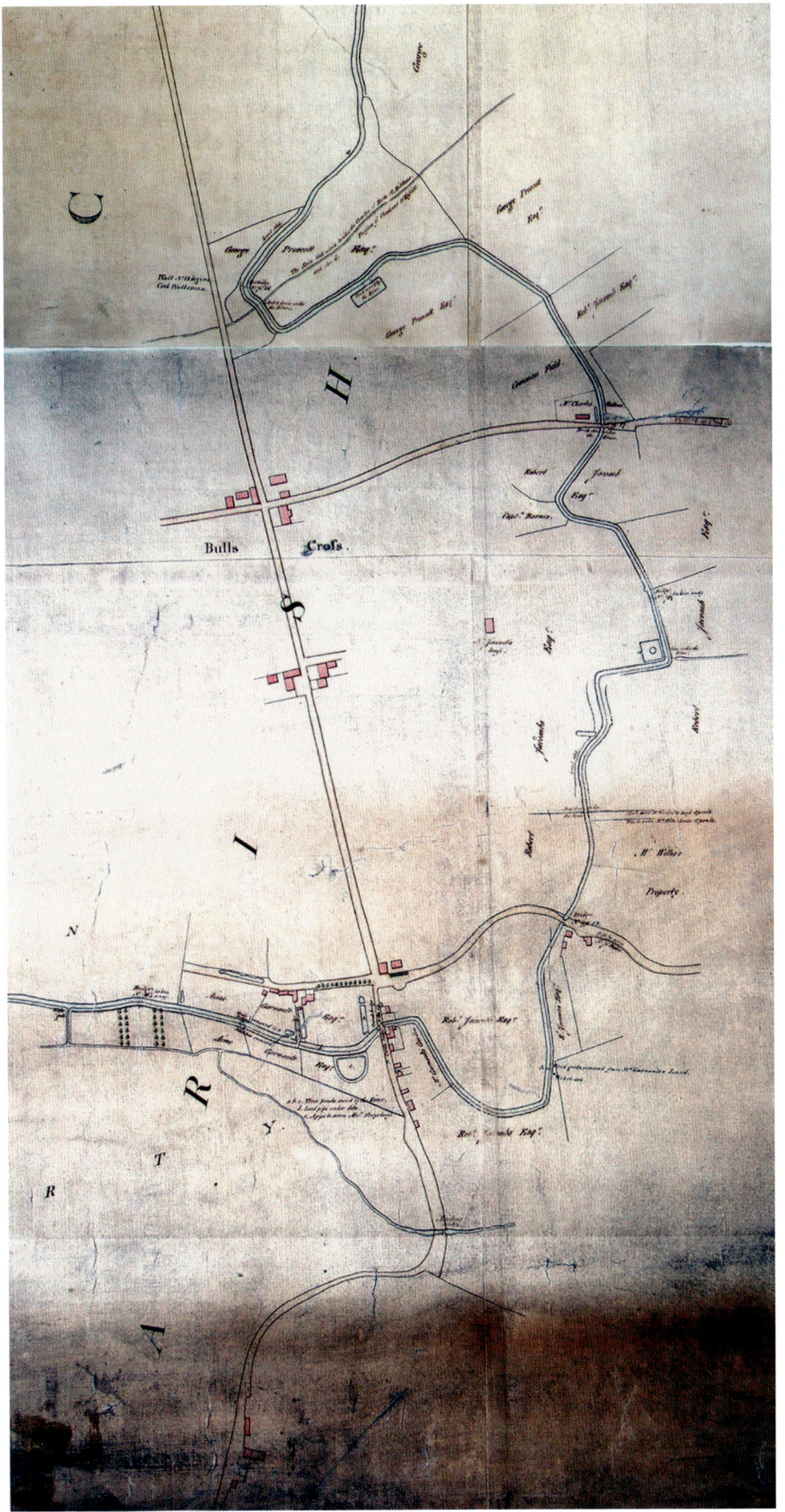

COMBINED Robert Mylne 1775-1809 Plans: **Plan 12 Theobalds Loop, & Plan 13 Turkey Street & Myddelton House**, Enfield, Middx. (TW Archive; MFK photos & join, bottom horizontal line across when adjusting darkness).

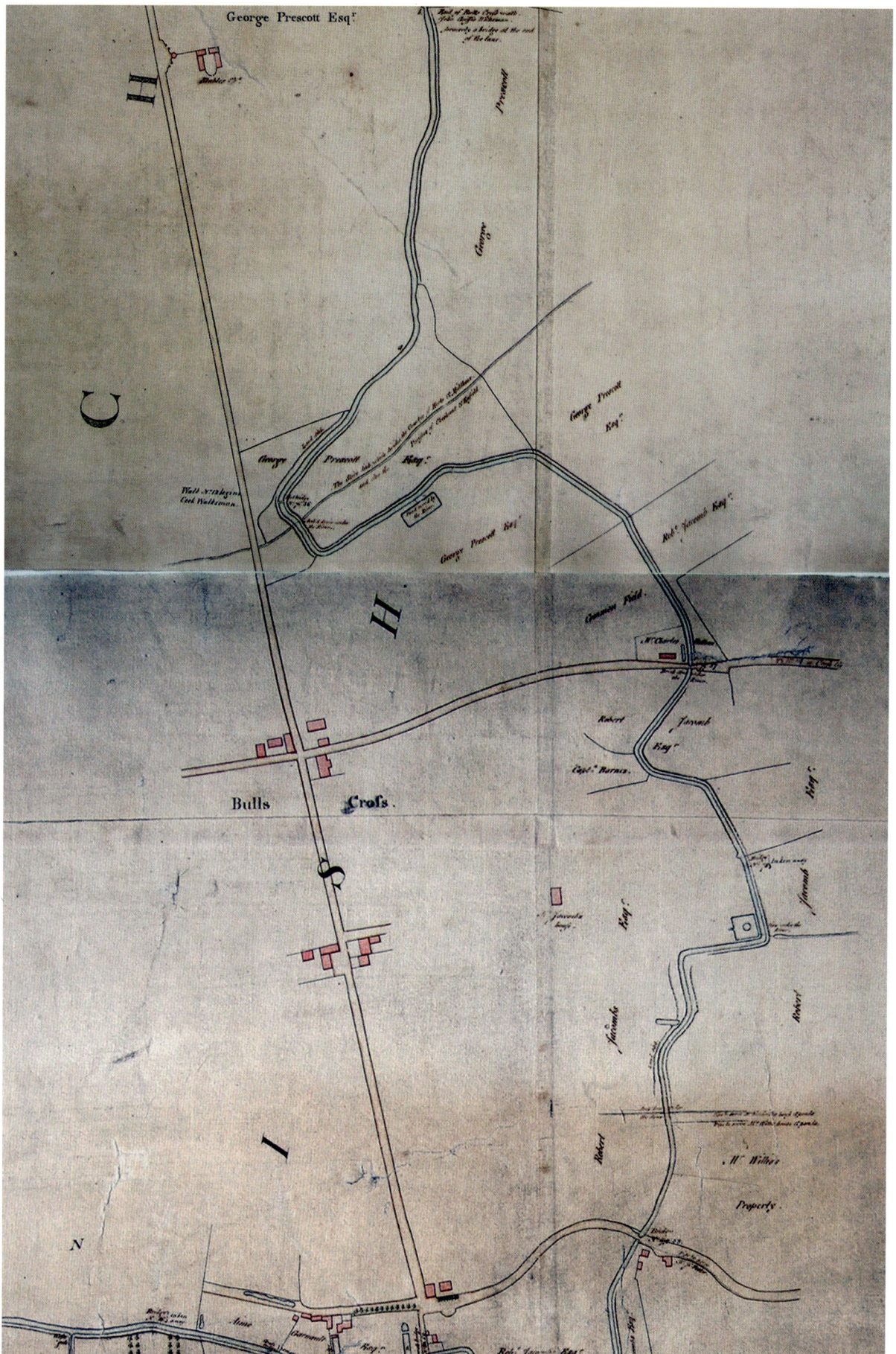

1775-1809 Plan 12 & 13: **New River from Theobalds to Bulls Cross**. Note the former course of Bullsmoor Lane, prior to the construction of today's Capel House (TW, Abbey Mills Archive; 2-MFK map photos joined).

Note Mr. Jacomb's House on previous page, lower mid-page:
ORIGINAL Locations of Honeylands Manor House, 1ˢᵗ Capel House & Bullsmoor Lane: See the 1775-1809/1866-67 Overlay (in Vol. 2), which shows an attempt to find the location of the original Honeylands Manor House (**No. 1**, Manor Farm) and also on the same basis the 1ˢᵗ Capel House (**No. 2**), today's Capel House (**No. 3**), and the Original line of Bullsmoor Lane. Also see p3 sketch map of 'The Story of Capel' by Jack Edwards (Copy at ELSC&A).

First of all the New River was drawn exactly to scale from Mylne's 1775 map and proportioned to the 1866-67 OS map (Mylne probably surveyed the NR). Knowing that Mylne's diagonal to the former crossroads at Bulls Cross is inaccurate (something he probably would not have surveyed, but approximated), his map has been proportioned horizontally to project the relative position of Jacomb's house on the 1866-67 OS map, and similarly for the relative position of Mylne's location for today's Capel House. The results are good enough to show the relative positions of all three houses, and mainly confirming that the original Honeylands Manor House (**No. 1**) was sited approx. on W-side of Manor Farm > Capel Manor Primary School (also see the NRC c.1856 Overlay, Vol. 3).

PROBABLY N-side Turkey Street?

> **SHORTENING (MYSTERY LOCATION) near Enfield**
> **1728 (Minus ?-miles) Shortenings:** The New River also called Middleton's Water 'ran formerly two miles farther about, near Enfield and Hornsey **[both at unknown specific locations]**, which is now saved by finding a more commodious channel' (('History of Hertfordshire' by N. Salmon, LL. B., 1728, p20) 8A1, 2-8; may have been included in Henry Mills 1722 measurement of river; 15J, p180 (Salmon, 1728) Enfield & Hornsey improvements). Awaits finding maps of Enfield with reliable further information.
>
> **NOT THE FOLLOWING**
> **Prob. c.1769 (Abortive Attempt) to Bypass Enfield Parish:** 'About the same time another report prevailed in ye neighbd. [neighbourhood] the proprietors of ye New River had for contemplation a scheme for shortening its course in ye parish of Enfield wch had it been carried into executn. wd. **have deprived ye town of their greatest benefit**' ((Handwritten letter of the antiquary Richard Gough) D1624 No. 8, ELSC&A).

1866-67 OS Map (Before Turkey Street) the Even Previous NR-Course?: Just to the SE a curving watercourse with a strange shape (annotated '**X**'), filled from local ditches, there being a known watercourse just to NW (going beneath the New River, although not as such shown on OS maps). If it was ornamental why is it in the middle of a field and not embellishing the grounds of Roselands? Since 'X' is not on the 1775 & 1803 maps presumably not a possible remnant of an earlier course of the New River! But the land it encompasses was **probably the property of John Grene (NRC Clerk)**, and as such could have been purchased at cost from the NRC! Without copies of earlier surveyed maps it is impossible to prove.

ABOVE: Capel House (Grade II Listed), Bullsmoor Lane, Enfield. 1804 print ((Drn. & Engr. by Samuel Rawle 1771-1860) ELSC&A); 2009 a copy for sale at $50. The following sited on the W-side of the New River.

1. **Honeylands Manor-house, near Bull's Cross (DEMOLISHED Pre-1793):** Honeylands mentioned 1275, 1486-1546 held by the Capels, 1562 leased by the queen to Robert Wroth, in 1572 comprising 17-acres > 1745 Robert Jacomb, who built a new house, so demolishing the Manor-house, presumed sited on the W-side of Capel Manor Primary School. The 1775-1809 Mylne plans shows the Manor house to the S of the original Bullsmoor Lane as **'Mr. Jacomb's house'**; SITE OF shown on 1804 Enf. Encl. Map (Edwards).

    1754-1803 Bullsmoor Lane diverted to present course (Edwards).

2. **Late-C18th the Said 1st 'Capel House' built near 'North Field' (DEMOLISHED Post-1803):**
Built as a new house by Robert Jacomb. In 1783 to William Hart > 1793 Rawson Hart Bodham (Edwards). Demolished post-1793 by Rawson Hart Boddam. Said to be shown on 1754 Tithe Map, 1754 Rocque Map, and on 1804 Enf. Encl. map Edwards calls 'Probable site of first Capel House' (Edwards).
The 1775-1809 Mylne plans show this as the house of 'Mr Charles Bottom' [pos. Boddam see fol. Rate Book].

    1794 (Bulls Cross Quarter, Rate Book): '14, Captain Boddam for **Bulls moor place**, 1. 1. -'. (ELSC&A).

    3 April 1800 (Auction) Bullsmoor Place & Messuage Adjoining: At the decease of Thomas Boddam, freehold for sale with 'A pleasure Ground, Lawn, and Garden, neatly laid out, and chiefly bounded by the New River' (ELSC&A).

3. **(c.1750/1750s/c.1760?) 2nd/Today's CAPEL HOUSE (New Manor-house N of Bullsmoor Lane):**
Built c.1750 by Alexander Hamilton who d. 1761. The name Capel House transferred by Rawson Hart Boddam when it became his main residence that was 'greatly improved' (Edwards). Said to be shown on 1754 Tithe Map, 1754 Rocque Map, and 1804 Enf. Encl. Map ('Story of Capel' by J. Edwards' pp3-5; VCH Middx. Vol. 5, 1976, pp. 224-229, Ref. 67, 68, Robinson, European Mag.; www.capelmanorgardens.co.uk). The 1775-1809 Mylne plans show a cluster of buildings at the former western crossroads.
   a) 3-buildings on NW-corner, the **site of the so-called 'Old Manor House'** (1866-98 Edelston family), some time after 1920 'falling down', today the site an open field by stables.
   b) 2-buildings NE-corner, the northern one likely today's Capel House, the **southern one since demolished**.
   c) Building on S-frontage of previous Bullsmoor Lane, **since demolished**.

Remains of small cottage found in the flower-bed near SE-corner of the car park (Edwards). Name changed to Capels after 1803. Pony raised water from a well (E-wall of house) with water gauge, well in yew garden, and a pump with planted horse trough (Edwards). The house & grounds today run as the Capel Manor College for Horticulture, Arboriculture (Tree Surgery), Garden Design, Floristry, Animal Care, Saddlery & Environmental Conservation, with grounds open to the public.

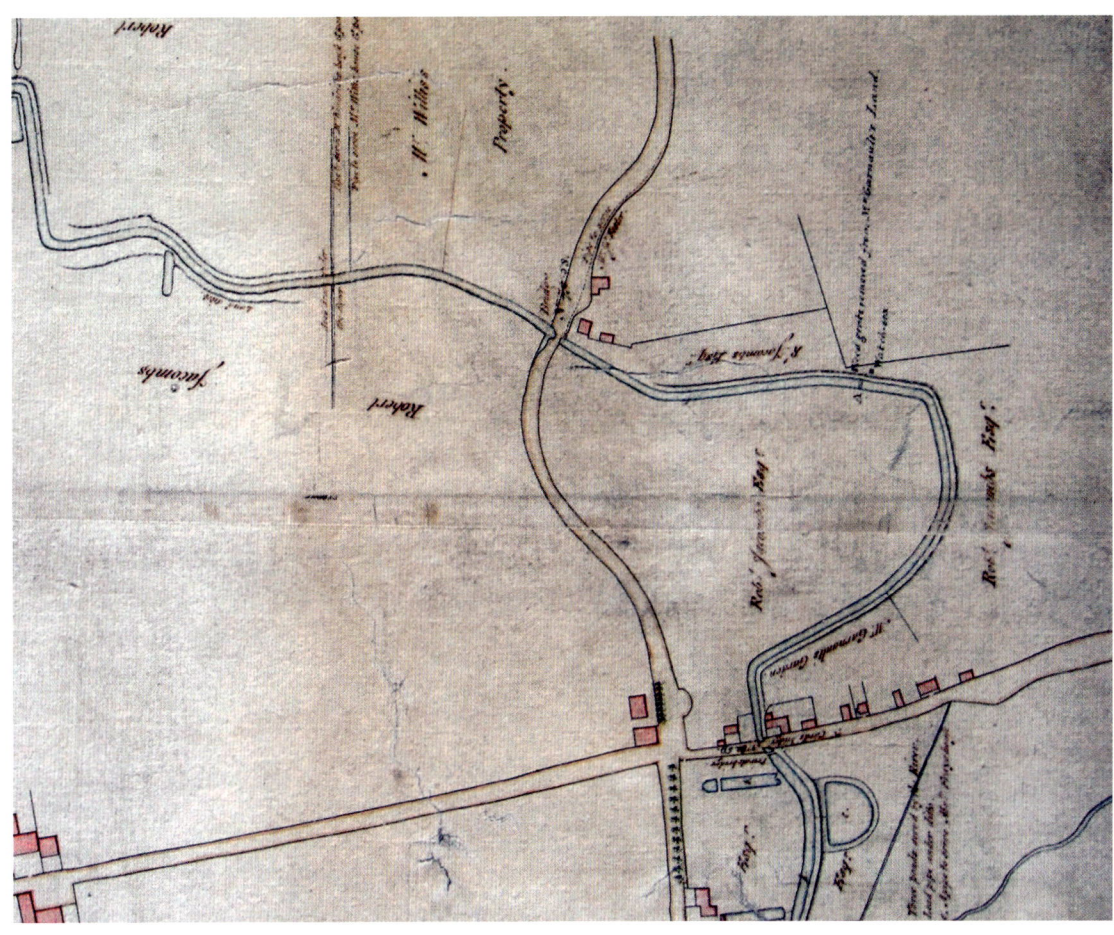

1775-1809 Plan 13 (TW Archive; MFK photos).
ABOVE: New River from previous line of Bullsmoor Lane (former W & E Bullsmoor Loop/s).
BELOW: Past Turkey Street, into grounds of Myddelton House (former Whitewebbs W-Loop), Enfield, Middx.

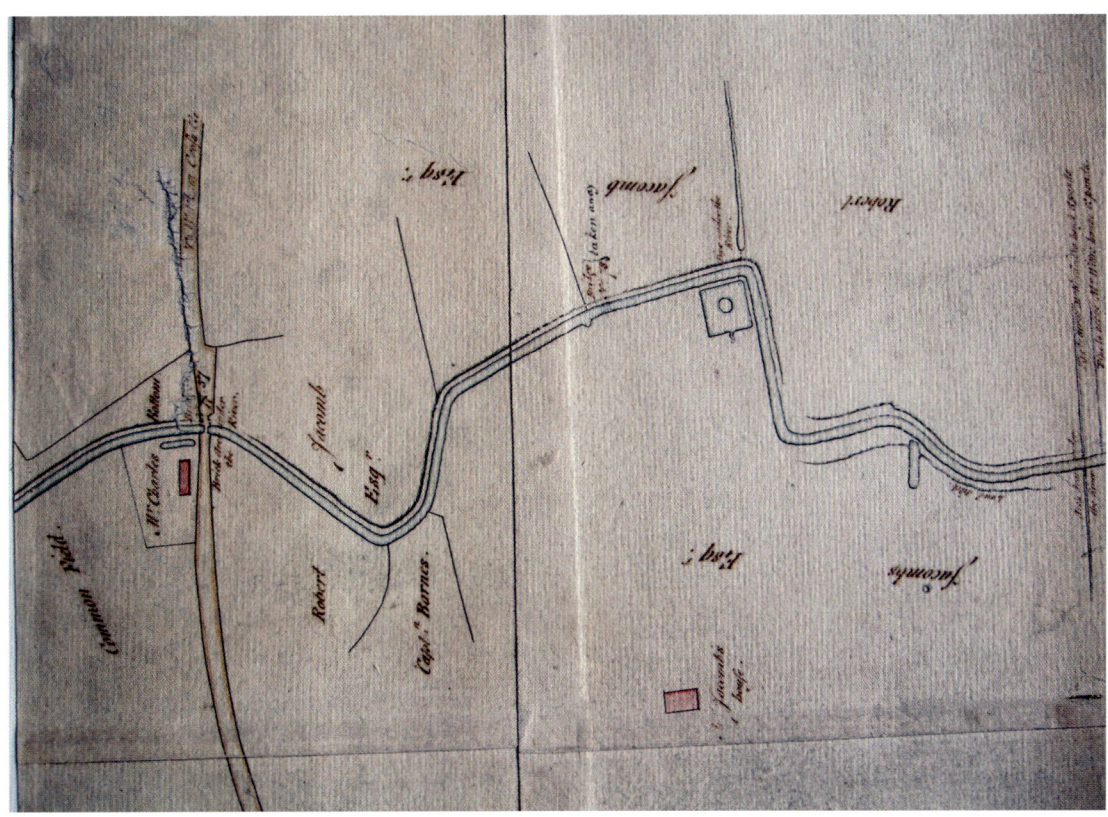

1775-1809 Mylne Plan 13, 14 & 15: **New River through Bulls Cross, Turkey Street, Myddelton House, Dickinson's Trough, Whitewebbs, Enfield Flash, Bull Beggars Hole, Gough House & Forty Hill**, Enfield, Middx. (TW, Abbey Mills Archive; MFK photos joined).

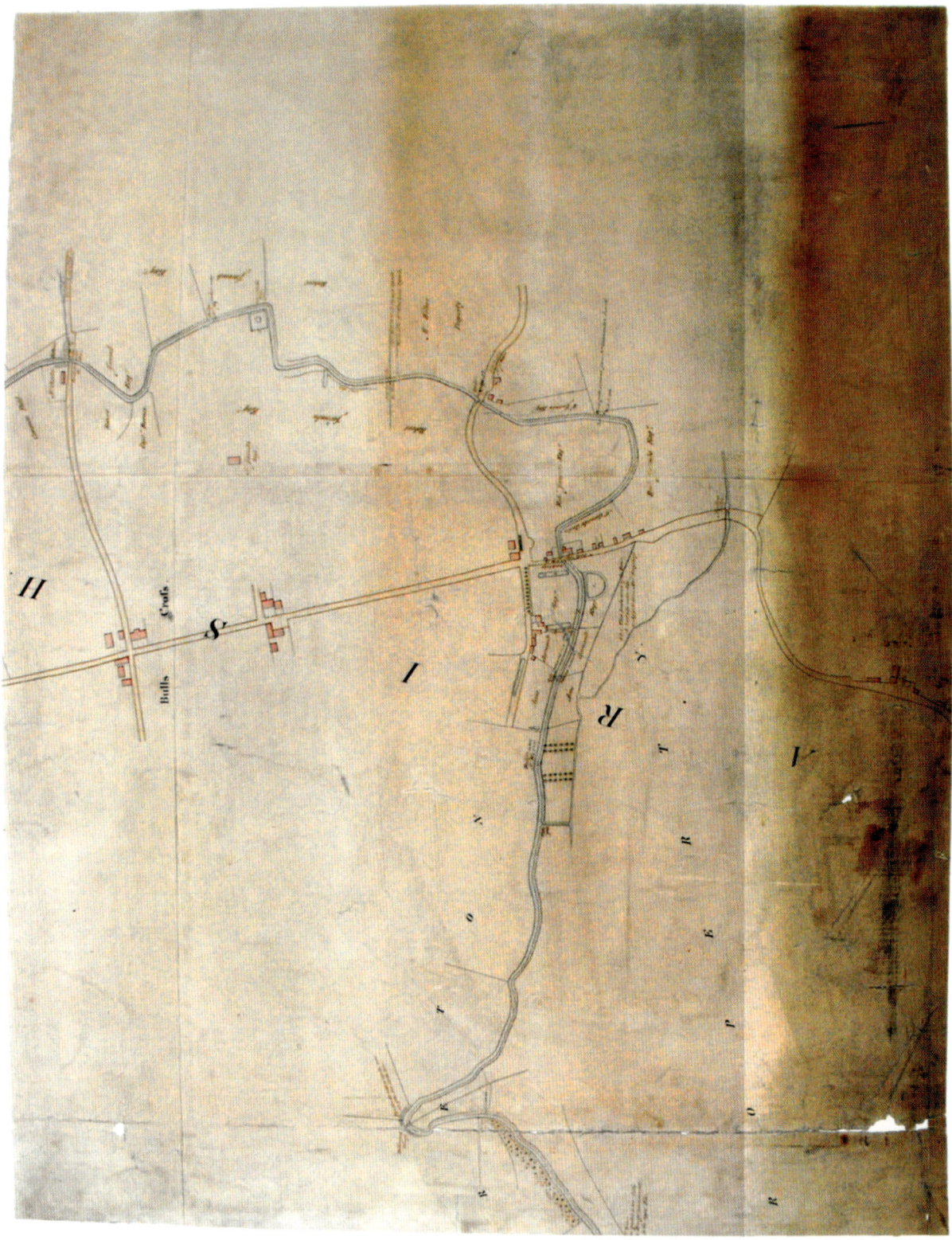

1775-1809 Plan 13: **New River from Bullsmoor Lane, past Turkey Street, through grounds of Myddelton House to Former Dickinson's Trough,** Enfield, Middx. (TW Archive; MFK photo, bottom line result of enlightening lower part).

1775-1809 Plan 13 LARGER: **New River from N of Turkey Street, through grounds of Myddelton House**, Enfield, Middx. (TW Archive; MFK photo).

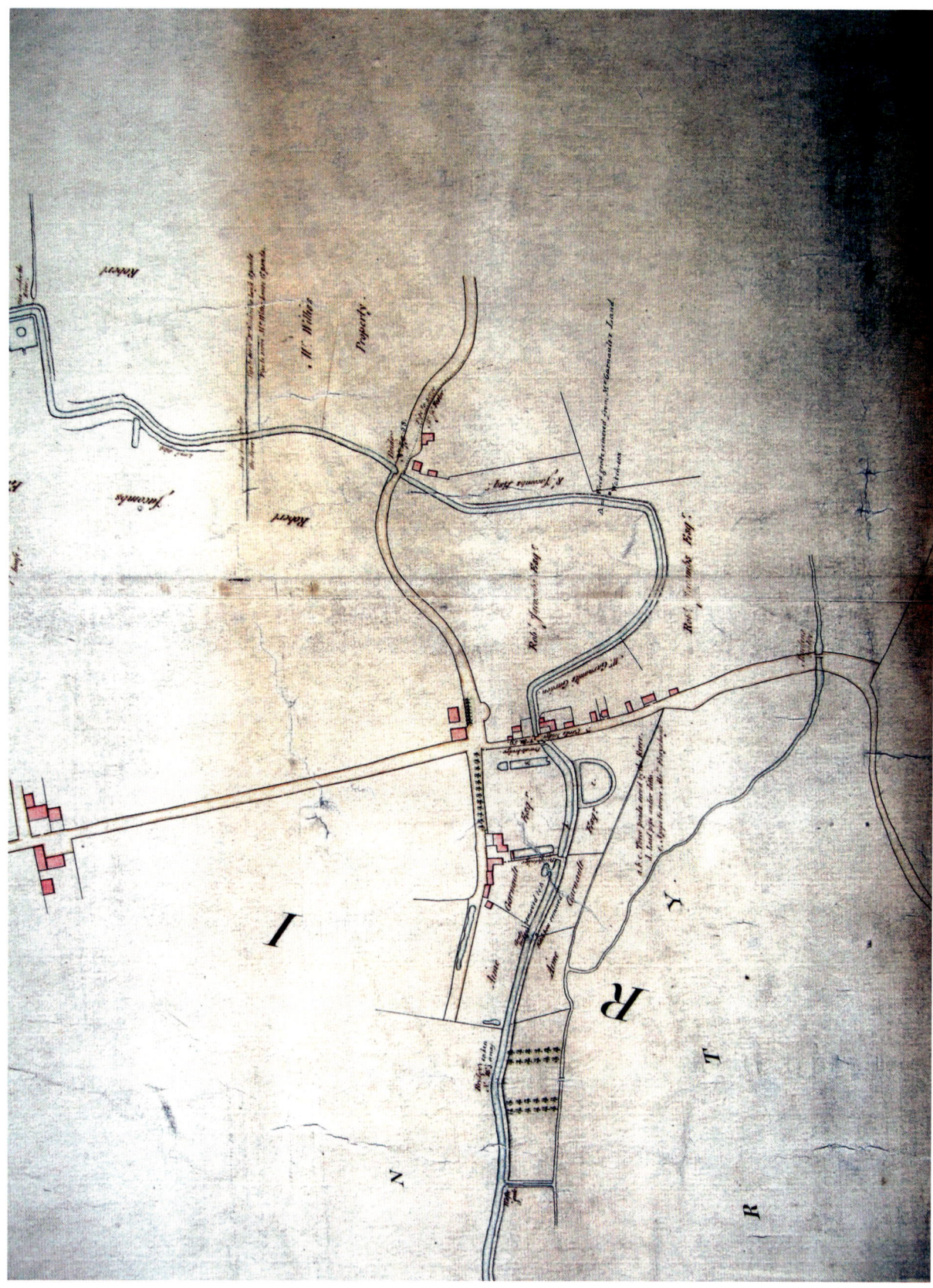

1775-1809 Plan 13: **New River from former Bullsmoor E-Loop, past Turkey Street, through grounds of Myddelton House on former Whitewebbs W-Loop**, Enfield, Middx. (TW Archive; MFK photo).

**Elizabeth (Sir Hugh's Granddaughter) & John Grene's (NRC Clerk)
Property at Turkey Street, Enfield.**

John Grene's property on N-side (probably at the W-end near the New River) Turkey Street, Enfield. John Grene Clerk to the NRC 1667-c.1697, died 29 March 1705 (15J, p80/87; 12, p8). He married Sir Hugh Myddelton's granddaughter Elizabeth, his main residence from 1667-97 was probably at the Water House, New River Head, London.

The following incorporates a chronological summary of the contents of a complex Court Decree:

Brown paper cover titled '**24th Novr. 1757, Ibbot v. Tuckfield, Copy Decree**', 134pp handwritten original (D2322, ELSC&A), transcribed 2009 by Michael F. Kensey. The surname as listed by ELSC&A is **NOT Groom, BUT GREEN**. This document unlocks the history of the legal transactions & proceedings between those involved over a near 50-year time span, such that were many complications between the two families often caused by the many deaths of those involved over this period. With some additional helpful notes, the page numbers (p001 etc.) referring to the Court Decree itself.

1 July 1641 Order for Earl Rivers to answer a petition from a John Green, clerk, as administrator for the late Edward Wymarke; with an annexed answer ((HL/PO/JO/10/1/64) Parliamentary Archives; assumedly our one). Draft order made 27 July 1641 in a cause of a John Greene against the Earl of Rivers ((HL/PO/JO/10/1/68) Parliamentary Archives).

In 1655 John Grene supposedly returning from Spain, in 1656 marrying Elizabeth Myddelton and getting only £1,500 by her (Berry Archive, Science Mus. Lib.).

Might be related, at Tottenham Church 'Thomas Grene, son of John Grene servant, of Sir Thomas Barnardiston, knight, baptised 1st March, 1593' (B75-6, p77).

Elizabeth Myddelton (1st Sir Hugh's Granddaughter): The granddaughter of Sir Hugh Myddelton (who built the New River), being the eldest daughter of Sir William Myddelton, Sir Hugh's third son. She inherited **3-Adventurers' & 1-King's Shares** in the NRC and became the 1st wife of John Green (Senior), having four children viz. **Giles, Elizabeth, Catherine & William**.

The eldest son Giles married a Mary Soame but died before his father without Issue (p018 Mary; Berry Archive, Science Mus. Lib., **nee Soame**).

Elizabeth probably married a John Hunt, and Catherine probably Thos. Atkins (p069).

William the second son d.1738.

NRC Shares (Myddelton > Green > Ellicombe/Ellacombe)

William Green (married Jane, pos. the daur. of Hamey Burwell?) died 1738 leaving a daughter Jane who married the Rev. Richard Ellicombe Clerk, such that it was **she who inherited the 4 NRC shares via the 21 & 22 July 1674 Settlement & 25 Nov. 1746 Court hearing**. Jane's rights not being affected by the 1685 Decree (p120; 'Sir Hugh Myddelton' by J. W. Gough, Rev. Richard Ellicombe of Stoke Cannon near Exeter).

1665 (5-year Maintenance Contract) at £1,000 per Annum: John Greene to manage the 'country work' of the New River from Ware to Islington at £1,000 a year, including all country troughs, flashes & bridges but excluding the Essex Road, Islington tunnel.

19 Sept. 1667 (Royal Command) from Whitehall: After the death of Gregory Hardwicke, **recommending John Grene in his place as Clerk to the NRC** ((CSP Dom. Charles II 1667 April-Oct, Vol. CCXVII, SP 44; Ent. Book 25, p23) Berry Archive, SML). Such that at a Nov. 1667 NRC Board Meeting voted into that position at £100 per annum until c.1697 (or his death in 1705), and thus probably living at New River Head, Islington where in 1693 he is said to have remodelled the Oak Room & 2-side rooms, although having a family home at Turkey Street, Enfield.

12 Oct. 1670 (Decree Against Mr Avery) Prob. of Capel Manor: John Grene's letter regarding a Mr Avery living near John Grene at Enfield, stopping New River workers passing by the river through his grounds, and obstructing the stream by throwing in logs to preserve the fishing, and stopping the workers from cleansing the stream, after the General Court ordering an action in Council, suspended after promising would not do again, but lately assaulting me and two workers shedding my blood, when using a net to draw out the matted weeds from the mud where no scythe will cut, upon the reproachable words of my wife did arrest him. As a deterrent for such others in future, the Governor ordering a Company suit against him (decree in the Exchequer), for obstructing cleaning, placing the logs and his fishing with nets prejudicing the banks. Avery a drunk, beats his wife and is abusive to all his neighbours (adding one my uncle Simon may side with), such that when you see Mr Mytchell, tell him that's the reason Mr Avery befriends him. Signed J. Grene, 12 Oct. 1670 (((3rd part or 3 letters mentions recipient as person who had previously surveyed the River, signed and dated at end 12 Oct. 1670) 3-typed sheets headed 'Sr., since May last about my uncle') 8A1, 2-8).

9 Dec. 1673 (DEATH) ELIZABETH MYDDELTON in childbirth: Probably 1673 as her epitaph, and not 1675 as per Gents. Mag. article, and was re-interred 1674 in a Pew & Vault, N-aisle/wall inside Enfield Church.

13 April 1674 (John Grene's Pew & Vault) SITE OF: As from 1 Feb. agreed that John Grene to be given 7ft. 4ins by 6ft. 3ins adjoining the N-wall for the erection of a pew and vault beneath, for £3pa from a brick messuage in Turkey Street and 2-acres of arable land in Dung field for disposal to the local poor. His late wife re-interred in new vault ((Indenture with John Grene's large signature at bottom) D715, ELSC&A).

21 & 22 July 1674 (Settlement) Lease & Release: At his 2nd marriage 1674 to Joanna his servant, having four more children viz. **John Green Junior, another two sons and a daughter**, John Green Senior settling his estate that included a property at Enfield and **Four NRC shares** viz. 3-Adventurers' & 1-King's shares (p065/077/117 **22 & 23 July 1674**/118/119/120/121; Berry Archive, SML, July 1674).

One son called **Robert** serving an apprenticeship when his father died (Berry Archive, SML).

1682 (Preparing New Settlement): John Green Senior to defeat the original Settlement preparing a new one (p118).

1684 (Bill) Court: For revising the previous Settlement of his estate (p069).

8 & 9 Sept. 1685 (Trust) Lease & Release: New Trust (p073). After Bill & Answers in 1685, the 1674 Settlement ordered to be delivered up to the new 1682 Trustees, in 1685 making a New Settlement (p118/120; Berry Archive, Science Mus. Lib., 9 Sept. 1685 Indenture).

10 April 1686 (Decree): For New Settlement & Trust (p071).

4 & 5 July 1694: 'purchased in all the sums of money secured by the said first Settlement' (p074/119 Conveyance/p120; Berry Archive, Science Mus. Lib., 1694).

13 Dec 1697 (New River Shares): John Greene's Bill for Draft Act for disposing of four NRC shares (HL/PO/JO/10/1/493/1177, Parliamentary Archives).

12 Jan. 1698 (Select Committee): Taking evidence & adjourning but not meeting again (Berry Archive, SML).

22 Mar 1700/1 Lewis Price, cordwainer of Clerkenwell, bond to John Grene of Enfield to perform covenants in an assignment (Acc 2558/NR13/159/1, LMA).

1 Dec. 1702 (Deed) Trusts: (p050).

3 & 4 Dec. 1702 (Marriage Settlement Trust) Lease & Release: Intended Marriage Settlement for John Green Junior & Mary Lockwood. Annuities from property in Enfield & 4 NRC shares to John Green Senior for Life > Joanna his Wife for Life > John Green Junior for Life > Mary Lockwood his intended Wife for Life > Sons 'In Tail' Male > Daughters (pp004-005/pp021-022/035/078/116).

4 & 5 Dec. 1702 (Deed of Settlement/Trust) Lease & Release: (p022/052/053/130/130).

29 March 1705 (DEATH) JOHN GREEN SENIOR: 27 Jan. 1702 Will, buried in the same vault as his first wife inside Enfield Church. In June the NRC Shares devised to his Widow Joanna ((House of Lords) Berry Archive, SML; 15I, p69 John Green died 1705; 15J, p80 John Grene d.29 March 1705).

1709 (Court) Hearing: Declaring that William Green could not be bound by the 1685 Decree or Settlement, his Interest remained in the 1674 Deeds, until execution of the 1694 Deeds (p119/120). The terms applying to William Green regarding the 1694 Settlement were upheld in an 11 Nov. 1709 Chancery Bill, and the Appeal dismissed Thurs. 25 Jan. 1711 ((Brown's Cases in Parliament; House of Lords) Berry Archive, SML).

MYSTERY GOLD RING (Difficult to Attribute because of Date of Death?)
Inscribed Gold Ring Found 1789 (J. Greene d. 2 Oct. 1710 aged 74): 'In 1789, a gold ring was found by a shepherd at Durance [not far from Turkey Street], within which was engraved, **I. GREENE, OB. 2 OCT. 1710 ÆT. 74**'. A long footnote saying: 'J. Greene in a house, afterwards Mr Collins's, in which there was a portrait of him in the dress of the time. His daughter married Mr North, a brewer, who had by her a son, and two daughters; the eldest married Mr. Spence, a brewer, and the other the late Mr Charles Hunt ['an attorney, and vestry clerk of this parish'], who died suddenly, Sept. 9, 1789, leaving a son seventeen years of age, and a daughter. Mr Greene had a faculty pew to his house, to continue in force while any of the family resided in the parish'. 'Mr Hunt built a handsome house in Silver-street, now in the occupation of Mr Strainage. His widow resides in Bath' (B3, p51; J's then written as I's, OB. = died, ÆT. = aged; B3-2, p61).

In Jan. 1711-12 at the death of his mother, Robert Paltock (1697-1767) the later romance writer, left in the care of her "loving friends", Robert Nightingale and John Grene or Green of Enfield (B24-1v1, p215); if so possibly our John Green Junior.

22 March 1711 (First Loan): John Green Junior borrows £600 from George Bourne secured on the property at Enfield (p009/035).

25 & 26 July 1712 (Further Loan) Lease &Release: John Green Junior borrows a further £400 secured on the property at Enfield, totalling £1,000 (p009/034/126).

25 & 26 Dec. 1712 (Mortgage) Lease & Release: On the aforementioned premises (p021/033/034-035/036/038-039/049/060/108/110/112/127). After the last Trustee Roger Tuckfield's death, vested in his Eldest Son & Heir John Tuckfield (p115).

Pre-1717/1717 (Comment): The late NCR Clerk John Green [Snr.] had 3-Adventurers Shares, encumbered by two annuities, the first of £100 p.a. to his son William for life, the second for £250 p.a. to his son John forever. By his will the remainder assigned to his wife & her assigns forever, but the widow ignoring the above annuities when assigning one share each to **John Green [Jnr.], William Talman & John Matthew** (Case of Ephraim Green, 111.a.64., British Library).

12 & 13 March 1717 (Further Loan) Lease & Release: John Green Junior borrows a further £600 (with another £400 on call) secured on the property at Enfield, from which date the £100 p.a. annuity to George Bourne unpaid (p015/037/039/048/111/112-113/127). Interest unpaid from 24 June 1718 (p049).

Late-1719 [prob. 1718] (Commission of Lunacy): His mother Joanna Green issuing a Commission of Lunacy against her son John Green Junior (p017).

Feb. 1719 (Declared a Lunatic): John Green Junior declared a 'Lunatick' ('and to have been a 'Lunatick' for two years & six months before that time') his mother granted custody of his person, then later Roger Tuckfield (p018/020/031/p112 2-years & 6-months). Mention of an Agreement dated 10 Feb. 1719 (p126).

21 March 1719 (Spousal Maintenance) Court Order: £100 p.a. from the estate to Mary Green the Wife of John Green Junior (p032/034).

In 1724 1r. of land and 3-acres of pasture in the Enfield common field **Ashdownes** [near Turkey Street] in the occupation of a John Green (D166, ELHU).

Nov. 1726 (DEATH) JOANNA GREEN: Death of second wife **Joanna Green** who bequeathed £1,000 plus the interest to her godson Henry Tuckfield (pp029-030/031-032).

Only two shares held by 'Johan Green's Exrs.' in 1751, but only showing a total of 28 Shares, the list continued 1763 only showing 25 Shares; some probably held by Trustees (Gents. Mag.; Berry Archive, SML).

1727 (Legal Proceedings): George Bourne v. John Green Junior & his Wife Mary (p002/020/107). And soon after a Cross Bill against George Bourne (p040).

18 Feb. 1729 (Agreement): Between John Green Junior and his Wife Mary (p045/110/131).

1729 John Grene assignment of mortgage on a house at Two Bridges [probably Turkey Street since has Turkey Brook], Enfield to John Elwick for £95 for 500 years (Acc/0801/0118, LMA).

13 April 1730 (Hearing) & Decree: Referred to Masters of the Court, the Court confirming the 18 Feb. 1729 agreement, and that the aforesaid premises should be sold (p048/050/088/102-103/104/126/127).

20 Oct. 1730 (Property Sale) Turkey Street: 'To be peremptorily sold before Anthony Allen, Esq. one of the Masters of the High Court of Chancery, at his House in Cursitors-street near Chancery-lane, on Wed. the 18th day of Nov. next, at four of the clock in the afternoon, a Freehold Messuage, with Coach-house, Barn, Stables, Gardens, Fishponds, and several small parcels of land, in Tucky-street, in the Parish of Enfield, in the County of Middlesex, and a cottage near thereto adjoining, and a Rent Charge of £250 per annum forever, **payable out of Four Shares in the New River Water-works**. Particulars may be had at the said Master's House' (www.london-gazette.co.uk).

10 July 1732 (Report): Court Master's Report that from 23 Oct.1732 George Bourne was due £2,983. 15s. 3d. and [presumably Henry] Tuckfield £1,824. 16s. 1d., such that a Receiver appointed for recovering the same. The Master offering the said property for sale, but having **no bidder whilst John Green Junior & his Wife remain alive** (p054/055/058).

27 April 1734 (DEATH): Of **John Pitkin** a Trustee of the 4 Dec. 1702 Trust (p107).

1738 (DEATH): Of William Green (p076; Berry Archive, SML, **d. 1738**).

Soon after a Bill by Richard Ellicombe & Jane his Wife against George Bourne, Mary Green and others (p076).

9 & 10 Jan. 1738 (Loans) George Bourne (Lease & Release) > Henry Garbrand > Roger Jonyns: George Bourne borrows £600 from Henry Garbrand upon security of the Enfield estate, and afterwards another £500 (Released to Roger Jonyns for £500 paid to Henry Garbrand and £500 to George Bourne), then a further £800 from Roger Jonyns, after whose death this amount claimed by John Harvey Jonyns his Heir at Law (p061/080-081/086-087/096).

25 & 26 March 1740 (Loans) Bourne > Garbrand > Roger Jones (Lease & Release): By Deed Poll or Indorsement (p095/099/127).

May 1740 (DEATH): JOHN GREEN JUNIOR without Issue, 30 Aug. 1737 Will, naming a John Green his Heir at Law, likely a relation (p058-059/092).

Earliest Enf. Rate Books for Bulls Cross, 1st Rate Enclosures June 1740 (2b-c) the churchwardens summons to render 1746-7 accounts (DRO4/D1/2a-ac, LMA).

19 Jan. 1741 (PROPERTY SALE) TURKEY STREET: 'To be sold, pursuant to an Order of the High Court of Chancery, before Anthony Allen, Esq. one of the Masters of the said Court, at his house in Cursitor-street, London. A Freehold Messuage, with Coach-house, Barn, Stables, Gardens, Fishponds, and several small parcels of land, in Tuckey-street, in the Parish of Endfield, in the County of Middlesex; and a cottage near thereto adjoining: And also a Rent Charge of £250 a year for ever, **payable out of four shares in the New River Water Works**. Particulars whereof may be had at the said Master's House' (www.london-gazette.co.uk).

8 June 1742 George Bourne vs. Elizabeth Tuckfield & others; and Mary Green vs. George Bourne & others. Regarding rent charge from New River shares ((T85, RB11) ACC 2558/NR13/158 repaired March 1993 (originally part of Acc 2558/NR13/157/1-13), LMA).

17 Oct 1743 letter to Jasper Bull from Harrey Burwell, grandfather of Jane Ellicombe, summarising the case and asking the NRC to proceed quickly to settle the case (Acc 2558/NR13/159/2, LMA).

22 Jan. 1744 (Report): Court Master's last Report saying £3,581. 2s. outstanding to George Bourne, who died before execution of the Bill, his Will dated 2 March 1742 (p057/060/063-064/126/127/128/129 29 Jan. 1744 Master's Report).

c.1740-46 Rev. R Ellicombe & Jane his wife vs. John Grene, an infant, and others, March 1993 repaired case papers ((T84, RB4) Acc 2558/NR13/157/1-13, LMA; and Acc 2558/NR13/159/6-8, LMA).

c.1740-1747 (Protracted Legal Case): Ownership of the four NRC shares recovered by the Rev. Richard & Jane Ellicombe (nee Green, only child of William Grene, the only surviving son of John Grene Snr.) from the descendants of John Grene's second marriage, but subject to a perpetual £250 annuity, that was **sold to William Jennens and inherited by Earl Howe** (No date or ref., Ellicombe Family Papers, Acc 2558, 1582-1974, 371 series, LMA).

25 Nov. 1746 (Court) Hearing: Regarding the 21 & 22 July 1674 Settlement, **Jane Myddelton** (daughter of William Green) married to Richard Ellicombe Clerk, **was intitled to the 4 NRC Shares** (p077/121/122).

31 Jan 1746/7 attorney's opinion on the settlement to be made ((1863 copy of Mr Ellicombe's case (Acc 2558/NR13/159/3, LMA).

4 > 2 NRC Shares

9-10 June 1769 Richard Harrey Burwell Ellicombe & Mary Brown abstract of marriage settlement (Acc 2558/NR13/159/4, LMA).

July 1771 - June 1883 £250 annuity paid to **Earl Howe**, 1837 election of Richard Rous Ellicombe to the NRC Board, dividend payment, and a financial assistance claim from one of Sir Hugh Myddelton's descendants ((T84, RB4)) Acc 2558/NR13/160/1-21, LMA).

1787-1788 the Rev. William Ellicombe **sold two NRC shares** (No date or ref., Ellicombe Family Papers, Acc 2558, 1582-1974, 371 series, LMA).

Oct 1782 - Oct 1830 Rev. William Ellicombe's notebook listing the diners at Alphington Parsonage on every Fair Day, including other events and the weather ((T84, RB4) ACC 2558/NR13/162, LMA).

3 Dec. 1788 copy of appointment relating to the sale of **two New River shares**, subsequent to the marriage settlement of William Ellicombe & Hannah Rous (Acc 2558/NR13/159/5, LMA).

Nov. 1805 – Mar. 1825 Rev. W. Ellicombe's correspondence with son, Hugh Myddelton Ellicombe, regarding New River shares, annuity paid to **Lady Howe**, payments due under the marriage settlement of William Ellicombe, and family coats of arms ((T84, RB4) Acc 2558/NR13/166/1-43, LMA). c.1805 - Feb 1831 Rev. W. Ellicombe's account book, including from Xmas 1785 (previous to his mother's death) the two Adventurers' shares half yearly dividends, after which falling to his eldest brother, but **inherited by him in Aug 1804**; plus rent receipts and memoranda regarding the Benbow Estate & Walronds 1811-1825 ((T84 RB4) Acc 2558/NR13/163, LMA).

Apr. 1831 – Aug. 1852 Hugh Myddelton Ellicombe correspondence with his son Richard Rous Ellicombe, concerning New River shares, annuity to **Lady Howe**, registering Ellicombe coat of arms and other family history ((T84, RB4) Acc 2558/NR13/167/1-33, LMA).

24 Aug 1831 probate copy of Rev. William Ellicombe's (of Alphington, Devon) 12 Jan. 1822 dated will with 16 Apr. 1831 dated codicil, **settling the New River shares on his son, William** ((T89, RB7) Acc 2558/NR13/161, LMA).

Feb. 1861 – Sept. 1886 mostly letters of the Rev. Henry T Ellacombe (the uncle) to Richard Rous Ellicombe, regarding New River shares, impending take-over of NRC, family history, and H. M. Ellicombe memorial window to be placed in Alphington Church (T84, RB4) Acc 2558/NR13/168/1-56, LMA; also see Acc 2558/NR13/306-308).

From 1753 Richard Ellicombe incumbent of Stoke Canon until he died 1778, having two sons William b.1754 (Rector of Alpington having 8-sons) and **Hugh Myddelton** Ellicombe b.1747 (Rector of Bridford died without Issue). **In 1763 only two shares held** by the Revd. Mr. Jno. Ellicombe.

July 1771 - June 1883 (NRC Shares) Ellicombe Family: £250 annuity paid to **Earl Howe**, 1837 election of Richard Rous Ellicombe to NRC Board, dividend payments, and claim by descendant of Sir Hugh Myddelton for financial assistance ((T84, RB4) Acc 2558/NR13/160/1-21, LMA).

In 1831 a Col. Ellicombe on the NRC Appeals Committee. In 1835 & 1837 the Rev. W.R. Ellicombe holding 2-Shares (Berry Archive, SML; Jno. probably John; 'New River L5.72' both dates, Isl. LHC). In 1852 an Ellicombe on the NRC 'Finance & Rating' Standing Committee (Berry Archive, SML).

In 1836 H. T. Ellicombe changing the spelling of his own immediate family's surname back to its **original pre-1638 spelling of Ellacombe**. By 1862 the Rev. Henry Thomas Ellacombe, M.A., rector of Clyst St George, Devon from 1850-80. The last holder, his son Canon Henry Nicholson Ellacombe, Rector/vicar of Bilton near Bristol, where he had a celebrated garden. Such that when he visited Myddelton House, Enfield (the home of the last NRC Governor, Henry Carrington Bowles-Bowles) to attend NRC meetings, he encouraged E.A. (aka 'Gussie') Bowles in his horticultural interests. Canon Ellacombe holding two NRC Shares until being taken over by the MWB in 1904, after which becoming a board member of the New River Company Ltd. until his death in 1916. He had seven daughters and two sons ('Sir Hugh Myddelton' by J. W. Gough; 'E.A. Bowles & his Garden' by Mea Allan; 'Lives of the Engineers' by Samuel Smiles; also see 'Henry Nicholson Ellacombe, Hon. Canon of Bristol, Vicar of Bitton & Rural Dean, 1822-1916, A Memoir' edited by Sir Arthur W. Hill, Country Life Library, London, First edition MCMXIX/1919, and 'In a Gloucestershire Garden 1896' by Henry N. Ellacombe, based on papers written for the Guardian 1890-93, republished 1982).

18 Aug. 1748 (Spousal Maintenance) Annuity: Until this date £100 p.a. paid to Mary Green, then in arrears (p090).

9 June 1750 (DEATH): Of **John Hunt** the Court Receiver for the aforesaid property, claiming to be Heir at Law to John Green Junior and obtaining Letters of Administration for Real Estate not covered by his Will (p105/106).

24 Nov. 1757 (Court Decree): Administrators of B. Ibbot v. Mary Green & others.

20 June 1758 (SALE OF PROPERTY TURKEY STREET) with RENT CHARGE from Four NRC Shares: 'To be peremptorily sold, pursuant to a Decree of the High Court of Chancery, before Thomas Harris, Esq.; one of the Masters of the said Court, at his Chambers in Lincoln's Inn, on the 12th of July next, at eleven in the forenoon, the estates hereinafter mentioned, in the following lots, viz. Lot No. 1, A Rent Charge of £250 a year, **payable for ever out of four Shares in the New River Water-Works**, clear of all deductions whatsoever. Lot No. 2, A freehold messuage with stables, gardens, fish ponds, and several parcels of land thereto belonging, situate in Turkey Street in the Parish of Enfield in Middlesex. Particulars of-the said estates may be had at the said Master Chambers' (www.london-gazette.co.uk).

John Green Senr. (lived near a Mr Avery) > Sold by Heirs >
  Mr Collins > Mr Justice Coleman

John Green Junior: Married Mary Lockwood, squandered £1,600, a huge sum in those days, such that Feb. 1719 declared a 'Lunatick', 30 Aug. 1737 Will, died May 1740 without Issue. **His lunacy causing the forced Sale of the Green's property in Enfield to pay off creditors. The premises at Enfield**

presumably sold, and the money used to pay off the debts and annuities.
> **Mr. Collins:** 'J. Greene in a house, afterwards **Mr. Collins** ...' ('Hist. of Enfield' by Robinson Vol. 1, p51). Possibly the 1785 New River Walksman called Wm. Collins. Various Collins mentioned on index cards but none appear applicable (ELSC&A).

 c.1760 by the New River Bridge in Turkey Street lived Joseph Fisher a shoemaker and commercial grower of carnations, who was about to sell his brick tenement, garden, chaise-house, stables, hay loft and piece of pasture (B10, p229).

> **Justice Coleman**
3 Jan. 1778 (Manor of Enfield): Lease & release of property & moiety in Turkey Street, Enfield, Mrs Margaret Willis of Turkey Street to her nephew & heir William Coleman of Romford, Essex, John Jessop of Waltham Cross, Essex & Richard Harrison of Enfield ((2 items; marked 'No. 1') D4452/5/7/7/5, Staffordshire Record Office).
In 1783 reference to a William Coleman of Enfield (D 114/3/2, Nat. Arch.).
Described 1784, "Mr. Grene lived in a house on the N-side of Tuckey [Turkey] Street, Enfield, now inhabited by **Mr. Justice Coleman**, and great part rebuilt since it was sold by Mr. G.'s heir. .. ... In the house before-mentioned was a portrait of Mr. John Grene, in the dress of the last century. To this house was annexed, by faculty, a pew in Enfield church, to continue their property so long as any of the family remained in the parish" ('Gents. Mag. Oct., 1784, p723, the fourth number of vol. LIV. Part II; 'Hist. of Enfield' by Robinson Vol. 2, p60 footnote/p62).
24 April 1790 (Manor of Enfield): Thomas Robinson Hill absolute surrender to William Coleman of property & land in Turkey Street, Enfield ((2 items with copy of same) D4452/5/7/7/7, Staffordshire Record Office).
26 May 1790 (Manor of Enfield): On surrender of Thomas Robinson Hill, admission of William Coleman to property & land in Turkey Street, Enfield (D4452/5/7/7/8, Staffordshire Record Office).
26 May 1790 (Mr Coleman) Fine: 'Manor of Enfield. Received the 26 Day of May 1790 of Mr Coleman the Sum of 14 shillings being a fine the Lord of the said manor by me, Wm. George, Bailiff of the Manor' (D993, ELSC&A).
1794 Enfield Rate Book for Bull's Cross Ward, that incl. Turkey Street, lists a John & Edward Green (p12, ELSC&A).
9 May 1799 (William Coleman of Turkey Street, Enf.) Redemption of £4. 17s. 1½d. Land Tax: Paid by William Coleman for a garden and premises at Bulls Cross in the occupation of [blank] Smith Widow, garden and premises at Bulls Cross in the **occupation of William Coleman**, and premises at Bulls Cross in the occupation of George Gibbon (D991, ELSC&A).
2 April 1800 (Manor of Enfield): Property & land in Turkey Street, Enfield, £400 mortgage by demise for 500 years, William Coleman of Turkey Street, Enfield and his eldest son William Edward Coleman of High Holborn to John Smith of Waltham Cross, Essex ((Marked 'No. 2') D4452/5/7/7/9, Staffordshire Record Office).
1803 Encl. Map: Shows the fol.:

		Access to		
NR. '1622 [Rob's '1632']	'814	'1603 South	'839 [Rob's '834']	'843' prob. '848
NR. **W. Coleman Esq**.	**Willm. Coleman Esq**.	Field. Sold.	**W. Coleman**	**NOT** Coleman'.
NR. 2. 0. 35'.	4. 1. 2' with **2-buildings**.	8. 2. 34.'.	1. 1. 9'.	**Coleman** although col. Yellow.

------------------------------ Turkey Street ---

'833	'834	?838?
Willm. Coleman	0. 1. 35.'.	0. 2. 11?
1. 1. 13'.	**Prob.**	Has yellow
'835	**Coleman**.	marking, so
Willm. Coleman		**could be Coleman!**
2. 2. 35'.		

N. B. Robinson's 1803 copy simplified map (of Encl. map) shows two different plot Nos. Also called South Field on 1785 Breton plan (ELSC&A).

 Justice William Coleman's House probably the square building on N-side of Turkey Street (at bend before Turkey Street straightens) on S-side of field '814' (the only building shown on 1785 Breton plan), the other probably an outbuilding.

After W. Coleman's Death > William Edward & Mary Coleman

1803 (Heirs of William Coleman) Enf. Encl. Map: Two allotments of freehold land No. 1622, '2a. 0r. 35p.' in **'Post & Gate Field'**; and land on the Chase at Whitewebbs No. 1860 '0a. 0r. 20p' (Enf. Encl. Map, '1806 Enf. Award' Book p21/p57, Enf. Encl. Award Index by G. Dalling, all ELSC&A).

12 Sep 1806 (Manor of Enfield) Conveyance: For £21 lease & release in fee in trust, to discharge & sell the principal sum & interest due on the mortgaged property in Turkey Street, Enfield, William Edward Coleman of Stratford, Essex & his wife Mary, & (by the direction of John Smith) Edy Hutchins, to Israel Thomas Coleman of Clerkenwell ((2 items; marked 'No.3') D4452/5/7/7/14, Staffordshire Record Office).

1806 (Late Wm. Coleman Esq.) No. 1622 '2a. 0r. 35p.': Awarded two allotments of freehold land in Post & Gate Field containing 2a. 0r. 35p., on SE bounded by part of meadow land of William Coleman **by the New River & Turkey Street** ('1806 Enf. Award' p21 mention of 7s. quit rent paid by William Coleman to King/p57, ELHU).

> 17-acre Post & Gate Field came into the possession of R.H. Boddam of Capel Manor, now the sports ground of the Ferguson Radio Corporation ('Townsman's Notes' Enf. Gaz. & Obs. 23 Sept. 1966, p10, ELHU).

20 May 1807 (Manor of Enfield): Admission of Mary Coleman by her attorney Israel Thomas Coleman to premises in Turkey Street, Enfield (D4452/5/7/7/15, Staffordshire Record Office).

11 Sept. 1811 (Manor of Enfield): For £410 lease & release of land, messuage & premises in Turkey Street, Enfield, Israel Thomas Coleman of Clerkenwell, Middx. & William Edward Coleman of Stratford, Essex to Thomas Smith of Turkey Street ((2 items; incorporated Enfield plan marked 'No.3') D4452/5/7/7/18, Staffordshire Record Office).

9 June 1813 (Manor of Enfield) Copy Admittance: William Edward Coleman to messuage in Turkey Street (**formerly called Salmons**), Enfield (P23/5/7/1/7/24, Staffordshire Record Office); **for Salmons also see** 1833 (P23/5/7/1/7/43); 22 Oct 1853 Mrs Caroline Giesler (P23/5/7/1/7/48, Staffordshire Record Office).

25 Feb. 1815 (Manor of Enfield): Counterpart lease of 4a. 3r. 15p. of land in Turkey Street, Enfield, for 13¼ years at £45 p.a., William Edward Coleman linen draper of Stratford, Essex to **Charles Frederick Giesler** furrier of Cheapside, London (P23/5/7/1/7/27, Staffordshire Record Office).

17 May 1815 (Manor of Enfield): William Edward Coleman granted licence to lease or demise premises, messuage, & two crofts of pasture in Turkey Street, Enfield to Charles Frederick Giesler (P23/5/7/1/7/28, Staffordshire Record Office).

> **For the Giesler's also see** (1812, P23/5/7/1/7/20 & P23/5/7/1/7/23; 1814, P23/5/7/1/7/26; 1815, P23/5/7/1/7/27 & 28; 1817-1849, J.P. Jones re. **Mrs Caroline Giesler**, P23/5/7/1/7/42; 1825, P23/5/7/1/7/34; 1833, P23/5/7/1/7/46, 47 & 48). 26 July 1859 the representatives of the late Charles Frederick Giesler sell Roselands to John Pateshall Jones (D4452/5/7/5/7, Staffordshire Record Office).

24 May 1820 (Manor of Enfield): **At the death of William Edward Coleman** the admission of Israel Thomas Coleman & Thomas Kinnard to copyhold in Turkey Street, Enfield ((2 items; with Coleman & Kinnard copy admissions) P23/5/7/1/7/29, Staffordshire Record Office).

19-21 Nov. 1827 (Manor of Enfield): Regarding Mrs Giesler & Enfield property, parish register copies of marriage (2 June 1799 entry of William Edward Coleman & Mary Lancaster at St George's church, Hanover Square) and baptism entries (6 Aug. 1800 William Whitsed, son of William Edward & Mary Coleman of Craven Street, St Leonard's church Shoreditch) ((2 items) P23/5/7/1/7/38, Staffordshire Record Office).

14 March 1828 (Manor of Enfield): William Whitsed Coleman of Ryde, Isle of Wight & Mrs Fanny Coleman of Hornsey, to the Rt. Hon. Lady Laura Tollemache of Hanworth Park, Middx., copyhold land & messuage in Turkey Street, Enfield, release in respect of claims & covenant for the title of same premises (P23/5/7/1/7/39, Staffordshire Record Office).

28 May 1828 (Manor of Enfield): Land & messuage in Turkey Street, Enfield, admission of Lady Laura Tollemache on surrender of Israel Thomas Coleman & Thomas Kinnard (P23/5/7/1/7/40, Staffordshire Record Office).

1 April 1833 (Manor of Enfield) Endorsed **'Salmons-Coleman's devisees'**: Out of court surrender for £700 by Lady Laura Tollemache of land & messuage in Turkey Street, Enfield, to Mrs Caroline Giesler (P23/5/7/1/7/43, 44 & 45, Staffordshire Record Office).

An MFK transcription of the full text of the 24 Nov. 1757 Court Decree itself (too lengthy to repeat here) has been deposited at the ELSC&A.

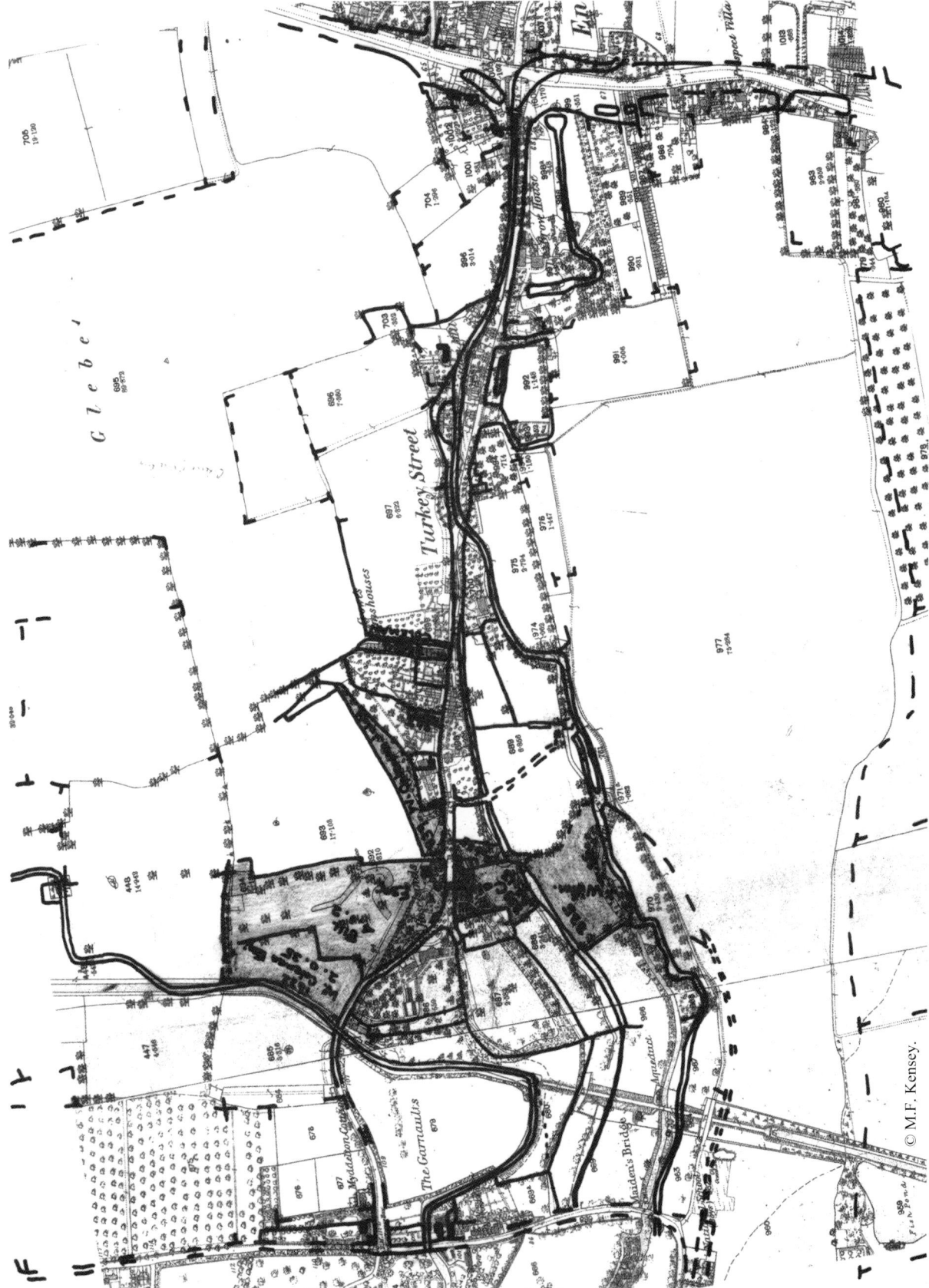

By 1670 John Grene's House (NRC Clerk) > Mr Collins > By 1784 Justice William Coleman (SITE OF), N-side, Turkey Street, Enfield. 1803 Enfield Enclosure Map overlaid on 1866 OS map, shaded area offering reasonable accuracy for location. Shows the diversion of Turkey Street fol. the 1860 Quarter Sessions Order for Roselands (Enf. Encl. & OS Maps, ELSC&A).

ABOVE: 1803 Enf. Encl. Map, showing lands of William Coleman, Turkey Street, Enfield.

BELOW: 1803 Enf. Encl. map overlaid on 1935 OS map. 'Y' prob. outbuilding, **'X' prob. SITE OF** Mr/Justice William Coleman's house (**former property of John Grene NRC Clerk**; only 'X' shown on Breton 1785 map of Forty Hall estates). If so, **obliterated by later c.1860 line of Turkey Street** (Maps, ELSC&A).

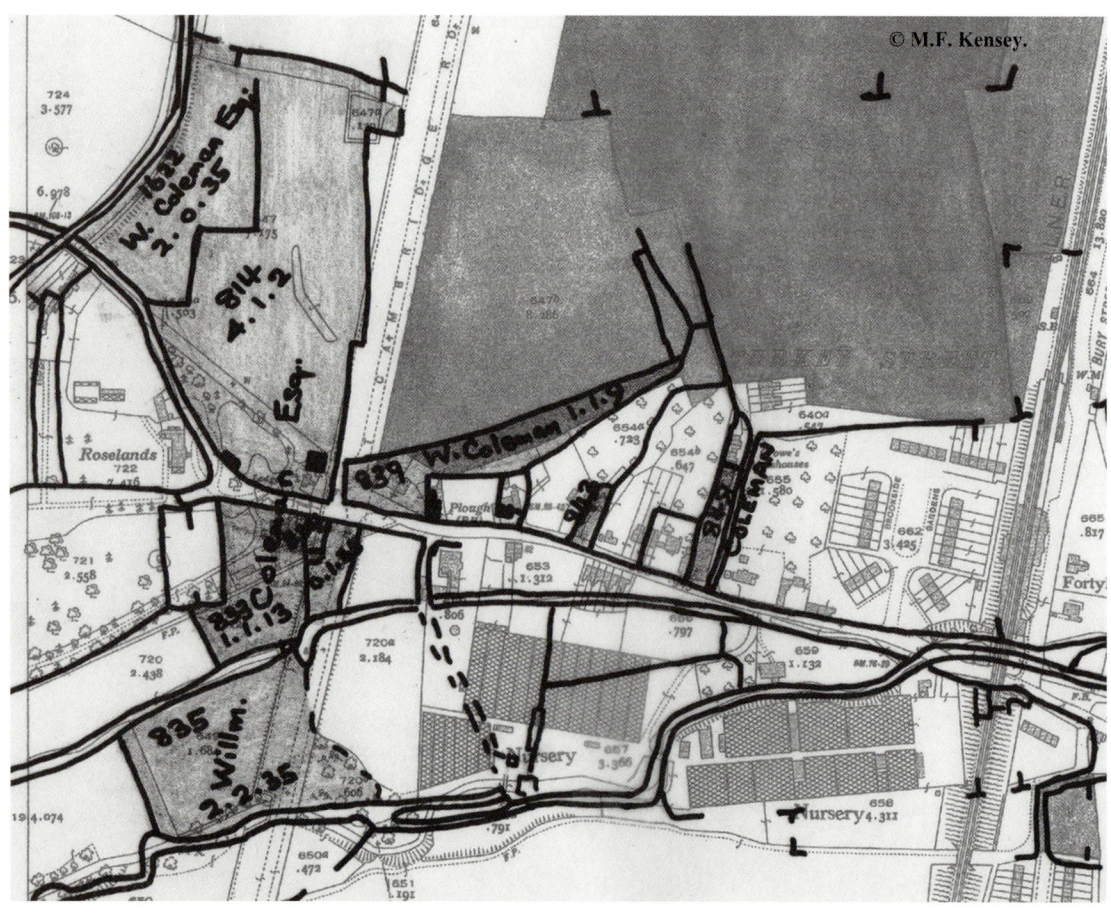

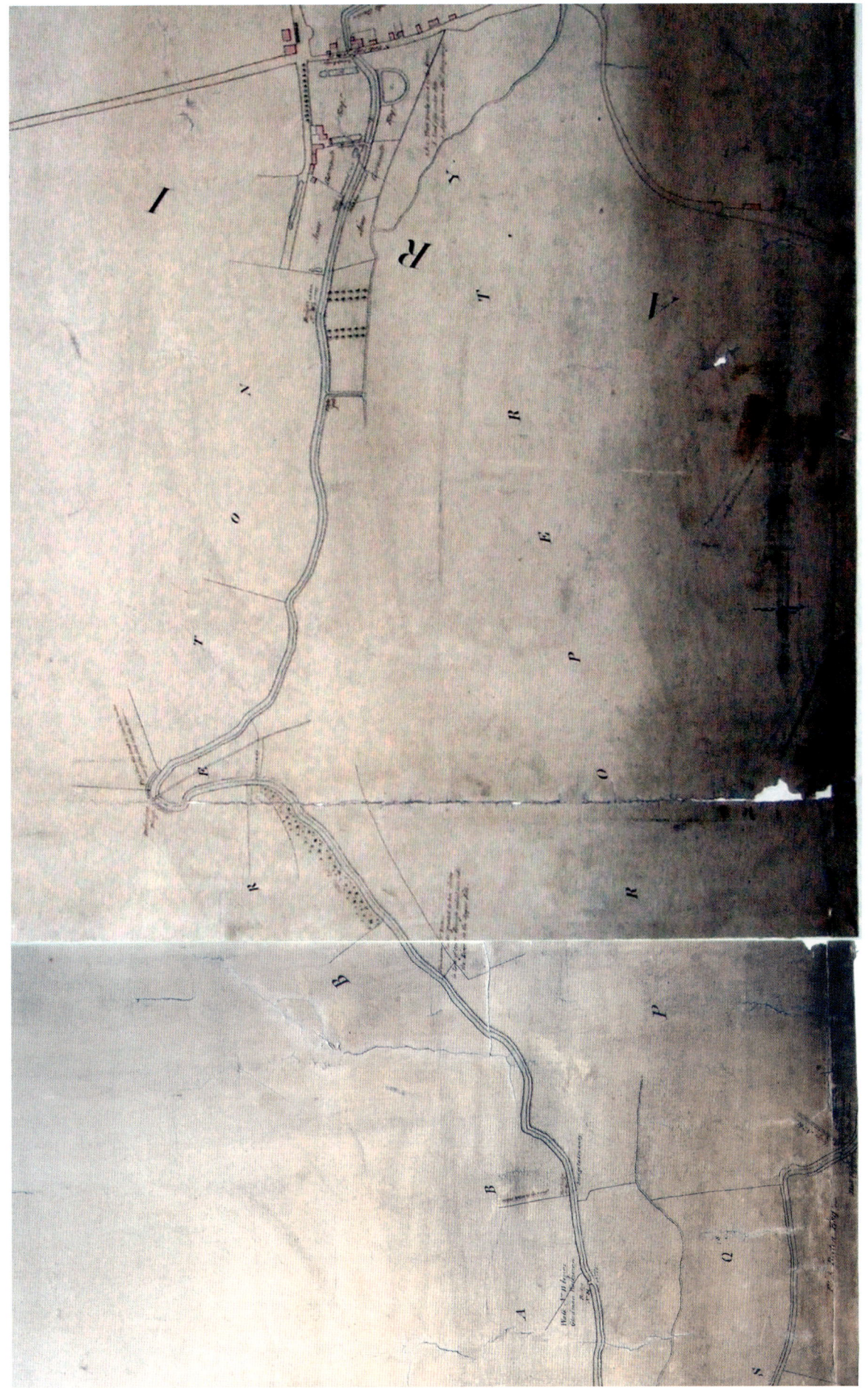

COMBINED Robert Mylne 1775-1809 Plans: **Plan 13 Myddelton House, & Plan 14 Enfield Flash**, Middx. (TW Archive; MFK photos & join).

1775-1809 Plan 13: **New River through grounds of 'Bowling Green House' > Myddelton House**, Enfield, Middx. (TW Archive; MFK photo).

Card's Bridge (Bulls Cross) over New River: Mentioned 1686/1771, the **location finally identified by MFK** on Mylne's 1775-1809 map, 1799 rebuilt & widened by Mr Garnault (Robinson's 'Enf.' Vol. 1, p67).

ATTEMPT TO IDENTIFY LOCATION OF FORMER Bowling Green House

1754 Trinity College Estate plan shows two buildings ((Thanks for the permission of 'The Master and Fellows of Trinity College Cambridge') ELSC&A).

See the 4-OVERLAYS, described as follows:
1. 1773 Eliab Breton Estates plan overlaid on 1935 OS map (Maps ELSC&A).
2. 1775-1809 Robert Mylne Survey overlaid on 1935 OS map (TW Archive; MFK photo; ELSC&A).
3. Oct. 1818 NRC Plan overlaid on 1935 OS map (TW Archive; MFK photo; ELSC&A).
4. **Probable Centric Location:** 3-versions overlaid together on 1935 OS map, such that **thought located immediately south of today's Myddelton House**.

Elizabethan 'Bowling Green House'
> c.1812-1818 **Myddelton House & Gardens**, Enfield, Middx.

The house since 1967 the headquarters of the Lee Valley Regional Park Authority, with the famous 4-acre legacy gardens of the botanist E.A. Bowles (1865-1954, dubbed 'The Crocus King'), M.A., F.L.S., F.R.E.S., V.M.H., **OPEN TO THE PUBLIC FREE OF CHARGE**. Relies on its past for its future, and is restoring the gardens back to Bowles' original scheme, **but not how Bowles all through his life remembered the New River through its grounds?**

Its gardens mainly created from the family's wealth from being jewellers, then print sellers, investing in and reaping the considerable dividends from NRC shares for nearly 180-years!

18 April 1612: Had reached Garnaults, where the river makes a horseshoe before crossing the road to the grounds of Myddelton House. "Shrubbs"; "Ashdowns"; "Bowleing Hill" presumably near Bowling Green house the predecessor of Myddelton House (8A, p15 quote).

28 Aug. 1613 (Consolidating New River) Between Theobalds Park and the Trough at Gyrton Park: The original New River channel cleared and bottomed between Theobalds Park and the Trough at Gyrton Park (15J, p42). John Gyrton the keeper of Little Enfield Park (Whitewebbs), the trough probably Dickinson's Trough.

1724 Michael Garnault (1669-1746) purchasing 100-acres that included the red-brick Elizabethan Bowling Green House (B3, p269; 'Gents. Mag.' Vol. II, p927).

7 Feb. 1726 (Michael Garnault's Agreement) with NRC: "… there is an agreement between Michael Garnault and the company made in Feb. 1726 when he was about to effect certain improvements to his recently acquired property, Bowling Green House, viz. building a cart bridge over the river from his orchard to his courtyard, laying a leaden pipe under the river to drain the water from his cellars, making a canal or fishpond in his garden to be supplied with water from the New River, and building a brick wall to the upper bank of the river. In order to avoid any damage to the company he undertook that the works, which were to be built at his expence, should be done at such times and in such manner as Henry Mill, the Engineer and surveyor to the company, should direct, and that they would be properly maintained. If they should prove detrimental they would be removed. He was already a member of the company anyway, owning **one Adventurers' and one King's share**. With him started that long association between the Garnaults, and subsequently the Bowles's, and the company" (8A, pp28-29 quote; (266) 8A1, 3/3-1). Shares said to have been purchased from the Duke of Montague, this title long extinct (Newspaper cutting, Myddelton House archive).

> **1 King's Share & 1 Adventurers' Share** purchased from **John Mitford** (the King's Share via his 1 March 1743 will to his nephew).
> **1-Half King's Share & 2-Half Adventurers' Shares** purchased under the Commission of

Bankruptcy from the Assignees of **Thos. Darwin** who went bankrupt c.1693 (15F, #53; 15J, p79 bankrupt 1696; also see B11, p26, B11A, p15, B11B, p319).

New River shares passing to his three nephews, the sons of his brother Aimé Garnault I:

1) Peter inherited the 2-Half Shares (Thos. Darwin) but died without issue, so passed to Daniel ['I'].

2) Aimé ['II'] (born c.1717) married Sarah and also died without issue. Aimé II inherited the 1-Half King's Share (Thos. Darwin), became a **member of the New River Board, and was proposed Treasurer 31st Jan. 1782, elected 7 Feb. 1782, but died 23 Feb. 1782**. Under his will passing to Daniel's son.

3) Daniel Garnault ['I'] who had three sons, presumably died pre-1769.

Daniel ['I'] Garnault's sons:

1) In 1781 Daniel ['II'] Garnault (d.1785-6) proposed as **member of NRC Board. In 1785 when NRC Auditor, presented with Silver 'Loving' Cup engraved with NRC Arms** ('Gents. Mag.', 9/7/1781, p95).

2) Samuel (c.1751-1827), after his brother Daniel II's death, proposed as a **member of the New River Board on 22 Feb. 1786, from 1804-1827 NRC Treasurer**, died aged 76 on 11 March 1827 according to his tombstone in Enfield churchyard, 'near the south door of the church, under a sarcophagus of white marble, which was afterwards erected to his memory' (14B2, p397 quote). **Probably always living in London** but buried near his next of kin at Enfield. Died aged 77 unmarried, 'Left his property to his grand-nephew, the son of H.C. Bowles, esq. F.S.A. of St Paul's Church-yard and Myddelton House, Enfield' ((Gents. Mag.) B24-B, p14).

Daniel [II] Garnault's son, Daniel ['III'] (1772-1809) of Bulls Cross, **from 1794 on NRC Board**, sold one of the Adventurers' Shares ('Gents. Mag.' Vol. 79, p582). His daughter Anne Garnault (d.1812), 1799 wife of H.C. Bowles (1763-1830) **inheriting the dividends from Three Fourth Parts, prob. of King's Share** ('Gents. Mag.' Vol. LXIX, p251).

In 1810 H.C. Bowles purchasing NRC Shares, prob. 2 x ½ Adv. Shares plus 1½ King's Shares (('Extracts from Mins. of NRC') 8A1, 2-8), and from c.1812-1818 built the white-brick Myddelton House. Their son H.C. Bowles ['II'] (d.1852) leaving these shares to nephew H.C. Bowles Treacher (> name change to H.C.B. Bowles) whose initials/monogram appear on the restored main gates, the previously fixed central pillar having been cantilevered, so that it can be swung open for wider vehicles ('London Gazette' 21 May 1852; ('Extracts from Mins. of NRC' and Shares held by H.C.B. Bowles, Governor) 8A1, 2-8; ('Gents. Mag.') NRAG News #53). H.C.B. Bowles became a **NRC Director, 1865 Auditor, 1866 Treasurer, 1884 Deputy Governor, 1886-1904 last NRC Governor. At his marriage 1889 given a King's Share (from his father), sold in 1898 for £115,000, and when relinquishing the NRC governorship was presented with a Silver 'Loving' Cup, a replica Silver Cup of 1785**, heirlooms passed on to E.A. Bowles the younger son and gardener. The eldest son Henry Ferryman Bowles (1858-1943, Baronet 1926) **in 1897 vesting the single King's Share to Mrs J.S. Nicholson, the Adventurers' Share purchased 1904 at MWB takeover**.

H.C.B. Bowles as the last NRC Governor holding NRC meetings at Myddelton House, and after the 1902-4 MWB take-over was elected the 1st Chairman of the New River Lands Company.

1968 (New River Filled-In) Myddelton House: After 350-years the former course of the New River through the grounds of Myddelton House filled-in 1968. And ever since **forgets it's past regarding its 350-year New River glory. NEVER TO BE A UNIQUELY BOWLES GARDEN AGAIN UNTIL A VESTIGE OF THE NEW RIVER RETURNS, in some form!**

Reproduction 'Watch Box'?: It would be a uniquely novel idea if they could build a full-size reproduction Watch Box (with its two poles), located in its original position beside the New River, luckily it would be in a contained area, which would not be so practical elsewhere on today's open River. Basically it is a timber sentry post, so should cost no more that around £300. It is not so much how accurate any reproduction Watch Box might be, **it is the unique fact that one was sited within the grounds of Myddelton House**, and if given a full-size reproduction would be the only place to have one today, thus a major visitor attraction. For Watch Boxes see the notes within the Tottenham section.

Walksman's Cudgels?: According to Brian Hewitt, A.E. Bowles had a NRC's Walksman's cudgel! Like gamekeepers the NRC Walksman would have needed to protect themselves, the NRC head office even having a collection of guns. Although I have found no references to them using cudgels in my researches, there is no reason to believe they did not have them.

London's New River in Maps Vol. 1, Part 1.   Garnault & Bowles Family Tree, Bowling Green House > Myddelton House & NRC Shares Inheritance

---

Pierre ———— Aime [I] ———————— Samuel ———————— **Michael** ———————— James ———— Jean ———— Marie ———— Judith ———— [Loimer (Berry Archive)].
Garnault   Will proved = Margaret Benoist   **of Bull's Cross** = Madeleine ??? d.1743 buried at Enf.
                    1740   b.1669 d.1746. **1724 purchasing Bowling Green House.**
                                                                                 Said to have possessed **2-Adventurers'** & **½-King's NRC Shares**, at his death allotted to 3-nephews.

Peter ———— Daniel [I] ———— Mary ???   **Aymé [II]** ———————— Margaret.
           b.1712 d.1758 = Mary ???   **of Bull's Cross**
                                               Born c.1717 = Sarah Arnold d.1790.
                                               **Proposed NRC Treasurer 31 Jan.
                                               1782 but died 25 Feb. 1782.**

           Daniel [II] ———— Mary Magdalen ———— Elizabeth ———— Aimée ———— Six d. in infancy ———— **Samuel** ———— Joseph
           of Bull's Cross   (girl)   b. 16 Oct. 1750
           b.1737 d.1786 = Sarah Paul d.1797.   John Bowles b.1701.   d. 11 Mar. 1827.
                                                Henry Carrington.   **22-years NRC Treasurer,**
                                                                                                       buried at Enfield.

           Daniel [III] ———— Sarah ———— **Anne** (*)
           b.1773 d.1809. b.1770 d.1771. b.1771 = Henry Carrington Bowles [I], F.S.A.
                                           d.1812. | b.1763 d.1830. **Built Myddelton House.**

Henry Carrington Bowles [II] ———— Anne Sarah Bowles ———— Jane Mary ———— Francis ———— Francisca ———— John ———— Garnault [Bowles].
of Myddelton House.   b.1800 d.1856 = Edward Treacher
b.1801 d.1852. | b.1792 d.1861.
                Others ———————— **Henry Carrington [Bowles] Treacher [> Bowles-Bowles] of Myddelton House** (for inheritance **1852 surname change**)
1866 NRC Treasurer,   / b.1830 d.1918 = Cornelia Kingdom b.1824 d.1911.
1886 LAST NRC Governor.
1895 purchases Forty Hall Estates etc.   (Sir) Henry Ferryman Bowles ———— John Treacher B. ———— Edward Augustus B. ———— Cornelia ———— Henry Carrington [III].
                                                later of Forty Hall   b.1860 d.1887.   **of Myddelton House**   Anne Medora.   b.1857 d.1858.
                                                b.1858 d.1943 = Florence/Dolly Broughton.   'Gussie' b.1865 d.1954. b.1868 d.1887.
                                                              | b.1866 d.1935.   **Myd. House purchased by**
                                                                                                     London University & Royal
                                                Wilma Mary Garnault Bowles = Eustace Parker b.1884 d.1952.   **Free Hospital.**
                                                b.1890 d.1928. | **(1920 surname change > Bowles)**   **1967-8 purchased as headquarters**
                                                                                                                    for Lee Valley Regional Park Authority.
                                                            Derek Henry ———————— Daphne Wilma Kenyon Bowles
                                                            Parker Bowles b.1915 d.1977.   b.1917 d.1995.
                                                            1951 sells Forty Hall to Enf. UDC.

(*) Inherited Bowling Green House (after her death replaced by Myd. House) estates, Whitewebbs House & NRC Shares. Based on 1916 'Pedigree of Garnault' by H. Wagner, F.S.A., & 'Pedigree of Ferryman's of Sileby, Leicester 1600-1900', Berry Archive, SML; 'Garnaults-Bowles Family' Berry Archive, SML; 'The Crocus King …', by Bryan Hewitt, p17. © Copyright M.F. Kensey.

ABOVE: 1821 print of Myddelton House, Bulls Cross, Enfield, soon after erection. Built c.1812-1818 for Henry Carrington Bowles (1763-1830) to replace Bowling Green House. The grounds from 1613-1968 intersected by the New River. The house later given a N-wing (RHS), and subsequently became the home of E.A. (aka 'Gussie') Bowles the famous Plantsman. Now used as the headquarters of the Lee Valley Park Authority, and the gardens open to the public (ELSC&A; MFK revised).

BELOW: Large bell inscribed '1775' on short swinging beam at front door of Myddelton House, said to have summoned the Enfield Parish horse fire engine, until replaced by mechanisation and preserved here (1 of 4 M.F. Kensey April 1969 photos). The bell was 'appropriated' by a LVPA executive for his estate near Ware. He and his wife died in a plane crash, and his son when much later contacted, said the bell passed on when the estate was sold off.

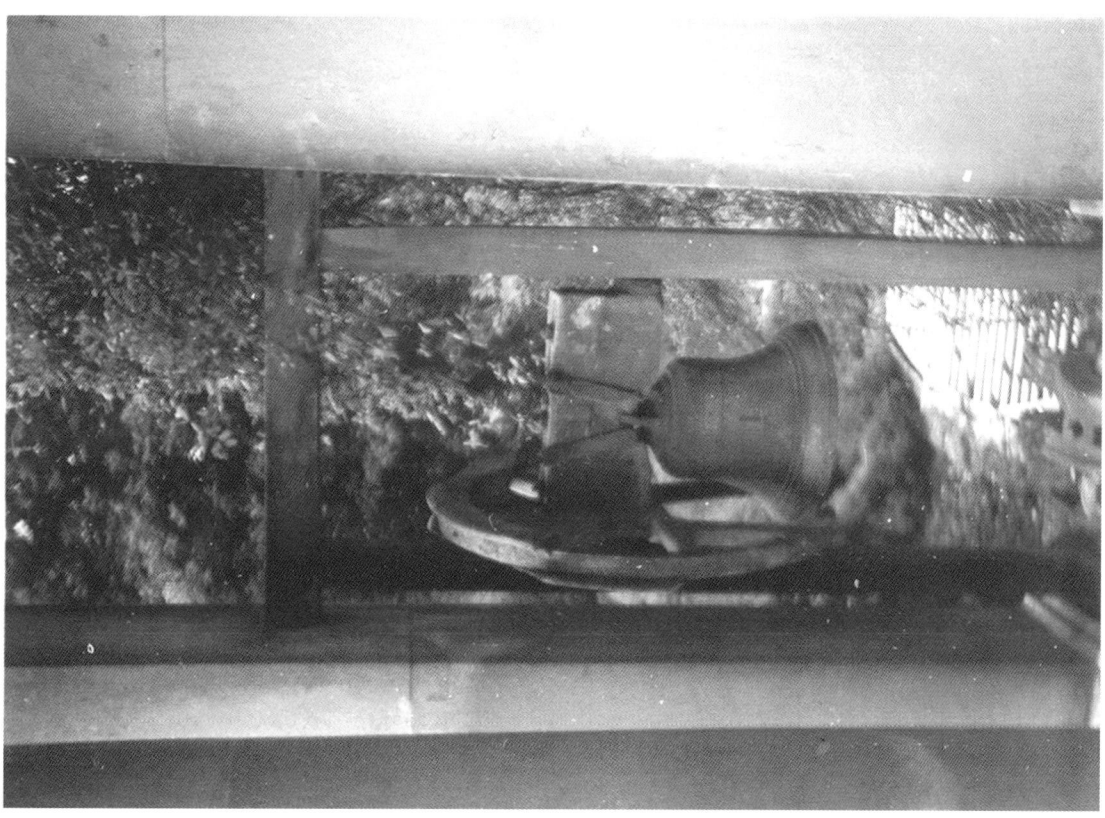

Portrait of Henry Carrington Bowles, F.S.A. (1763-1830) who married Anne Garnault. She inherited Bowling Green House & NRC Shares but d.1812, and he not wishing to live in a house that they both shared, from 1814-18 built the replacement Myddelton House, seen in the background ((C. Smith photo) Portrait by kind perm. of Lee Valley Regional Park Authority; MFK patched).

1884

Later inherited by a **nephew H.C. Bowles (Treacher >) Bowles, J.P., D.L. (1830-1918)**, who married Cornelia Kingdom. **1866 NRC Treasurer, last NRC Governor**, after the 1902-4 MWB takeover elected first Chairman of the New River [Lands] Co. Ltd. ('Elliott & Fry, 55, Baker St, W' photo, ELSC&A).

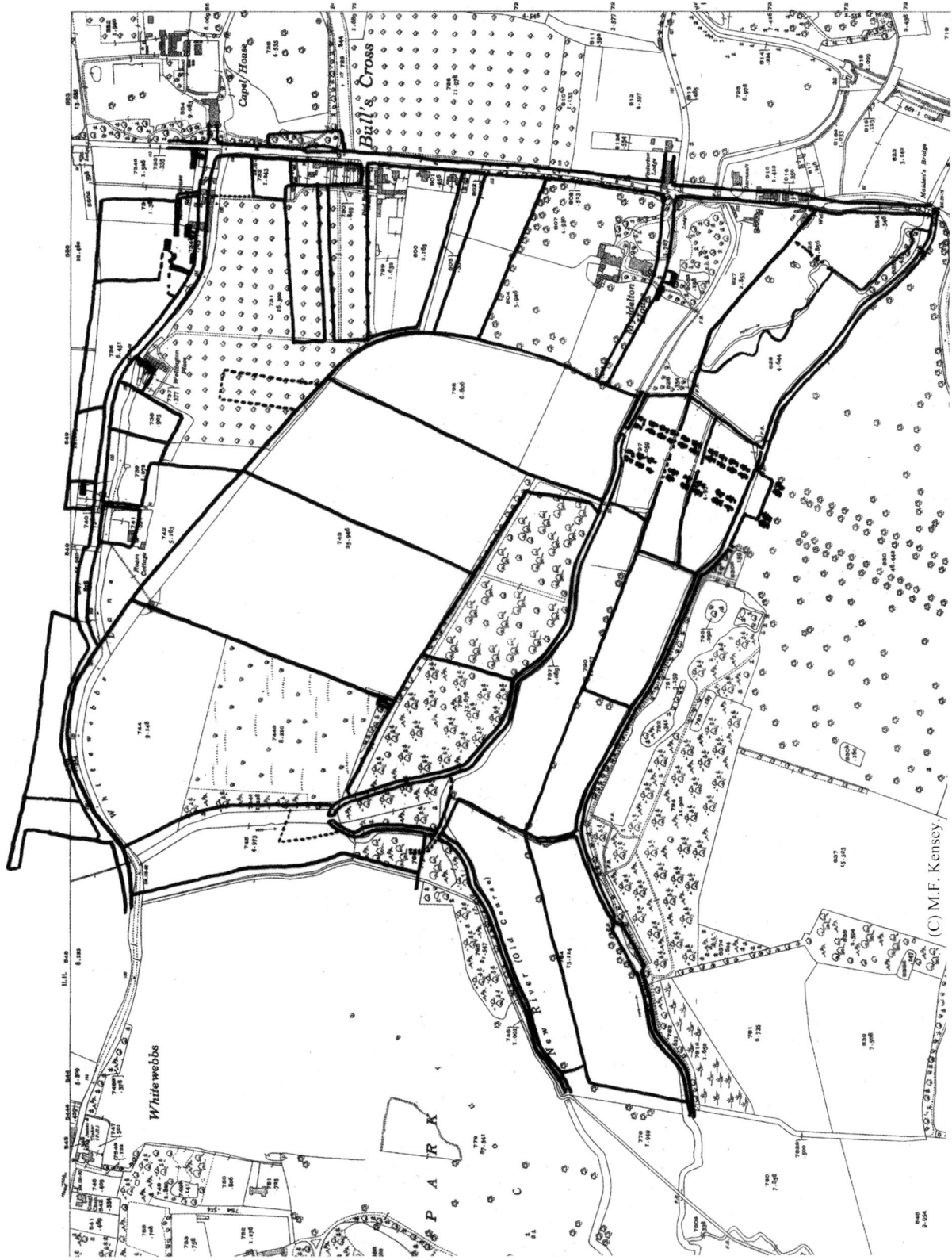

Version 1 of 3: 1773 Location of Bowling Green House ('Mr Garnault') > Myddelton House, Bulls Cross, Enfield. 1773 Eliab. Breton Estates plan [note Surveyed reasonably accurately] overlaid on 1935 OS map (Both maps, ELSC&A). For greater accuracy the Lower part of 1773 map used for alignment.

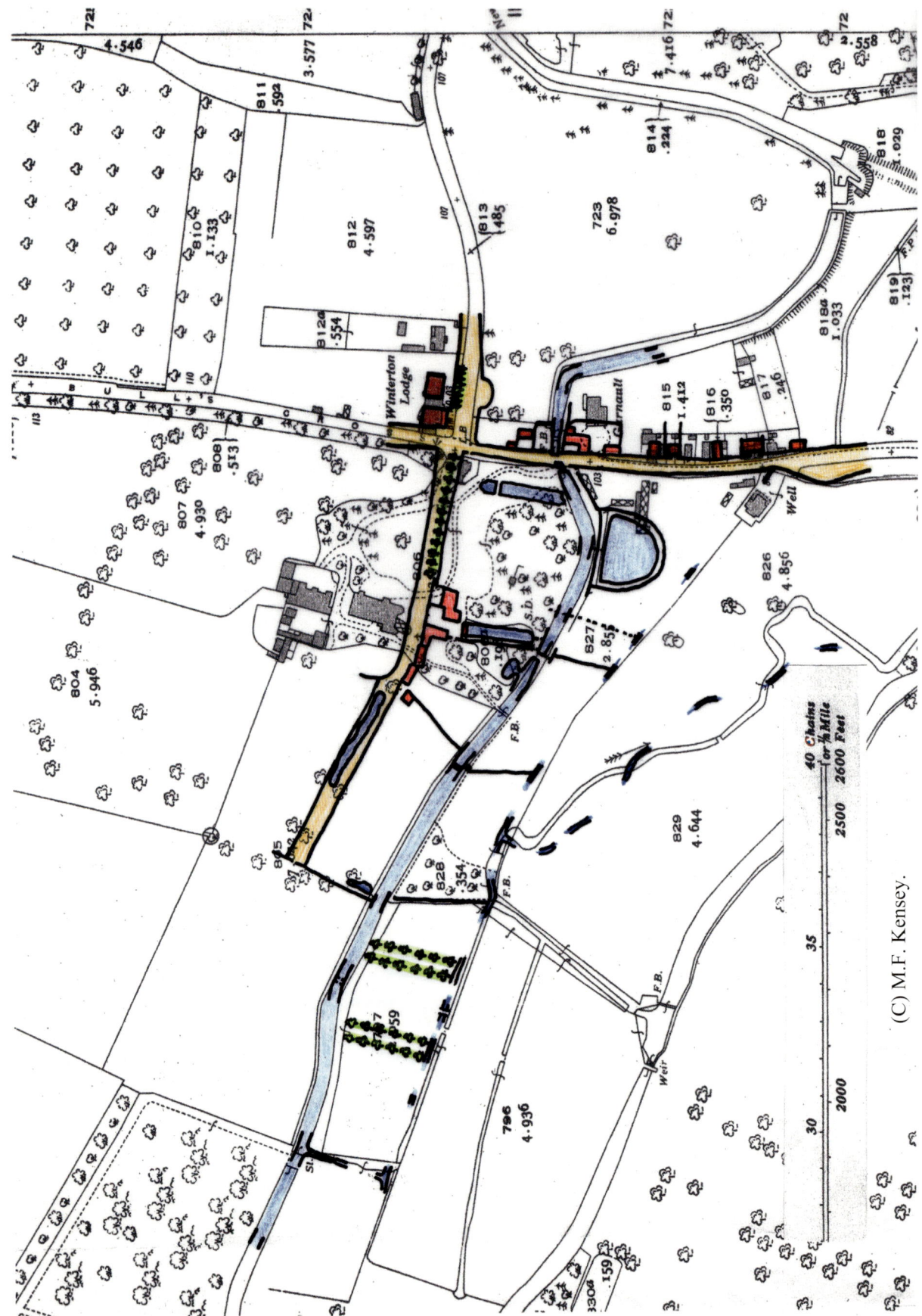

Version 2 of 3: 1775-1809 Location of Bowling Green House ('Mr Garnault') > Myddelton House, Bulls Cross, Enfield. 1775-1809 Mylne map (Bowling Green House Pre-1678, dem. 1814-1818) overlaid on 1935 OS map (ELSC&A). For text & specific details see separate 1775-1809 plans.

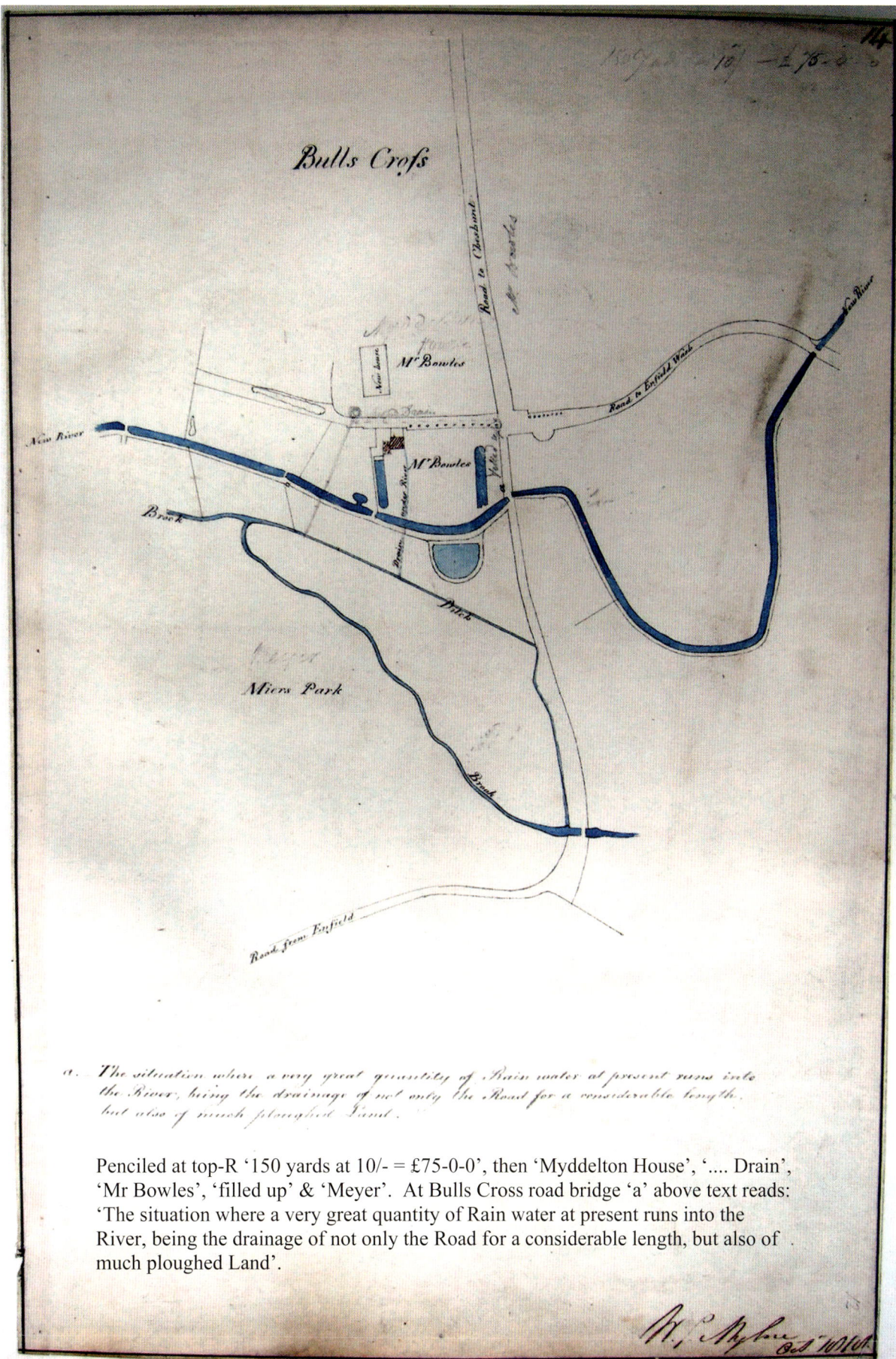

Oct. 1818 NRC (W.C. Mylne signed & dated) Plan of Bowling Green House & Myddelton House: Probably the only known plan showing both together (TW Archive; MFK photo).

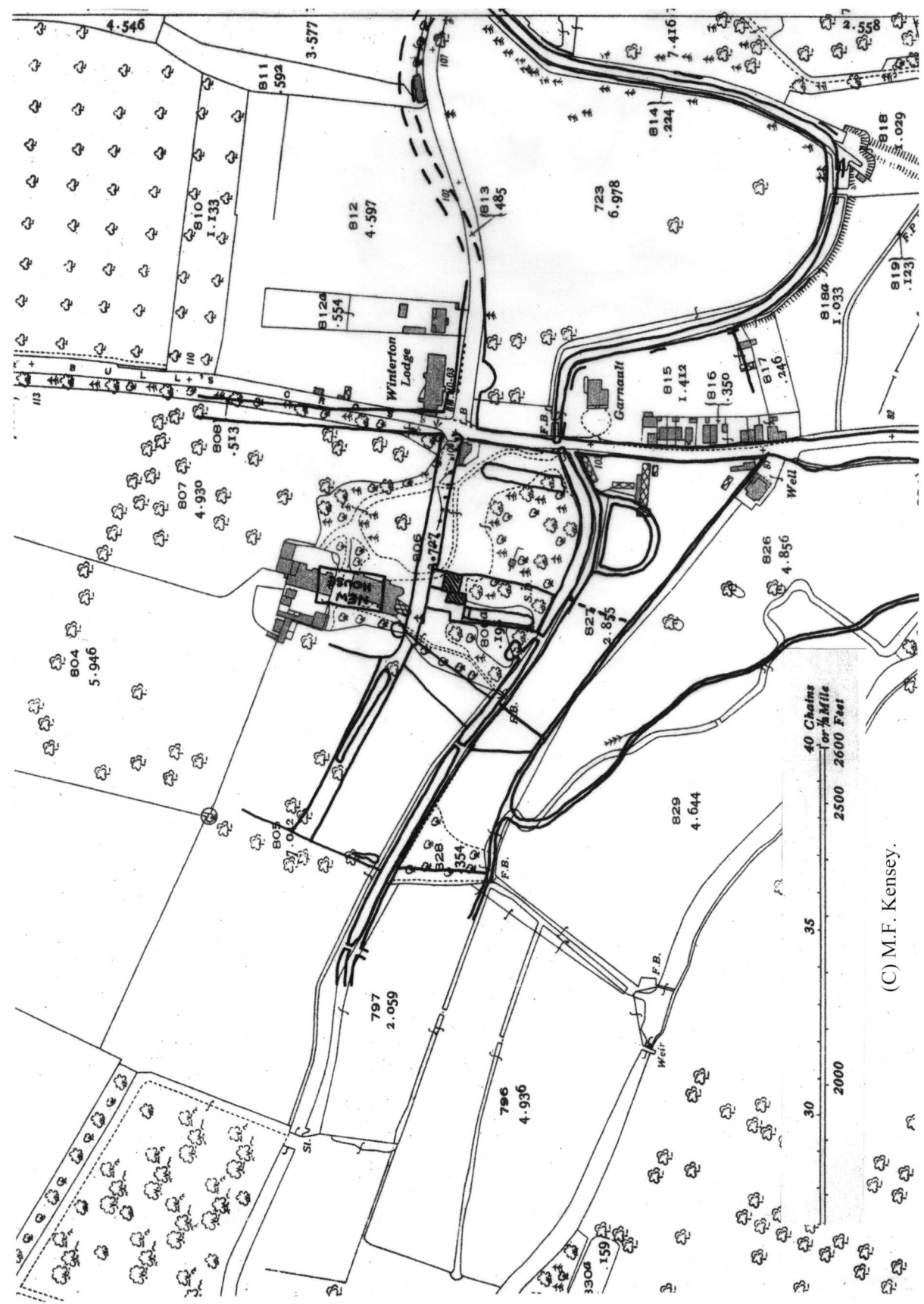

Version 3 of 3: 1818 Location of Bowling Green House ('Mr Garnault') > Myddelton House, Bulls Cross, Enfield. Oct. 1818 W.C. Mylne plan overlaid on 1935 OS map (OS map, ELSC&A). For text & specific details see separate Oct. 1818 plan.

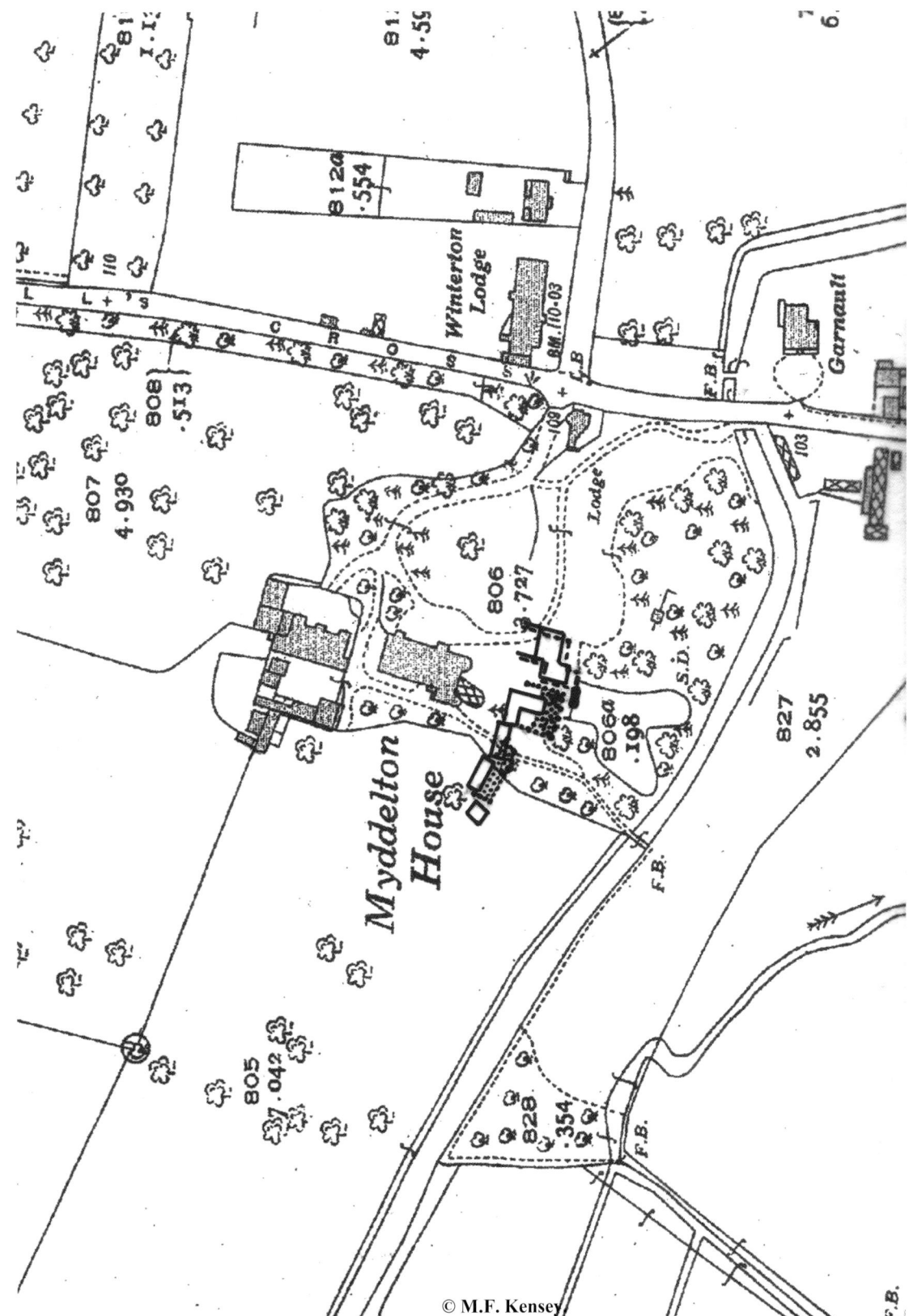

1773, 1775-1809, 1818 POSSIBLE SITE of the Pre-1678 Red Brick Gabled BOWLING GREEN HOUSE (Demolished 1814-18): Previous OVERLAYS enlarged & combined, overlaid on 1935 OS map (ELSC&A). 1773 Eliab. Breton Est. plan (**DOTS**). The 1785 Forty Hall Est. plan virtually identical, but to a larger scale. 1775-1809 Robert Mylne plan (**BOLD OUTLINE**). 1818 W.C. Mylne plan, probably used his father's original plan, hence the similar result (**DOTTED LINES**).

Probable centric location between the two indicated locations, such that just SOUTH of Myddelton House. This is the best probable location, unless further archaeological excavation proves otherwise. May have had shallow foundations, robbed for other building work, but there were various outbuildings.

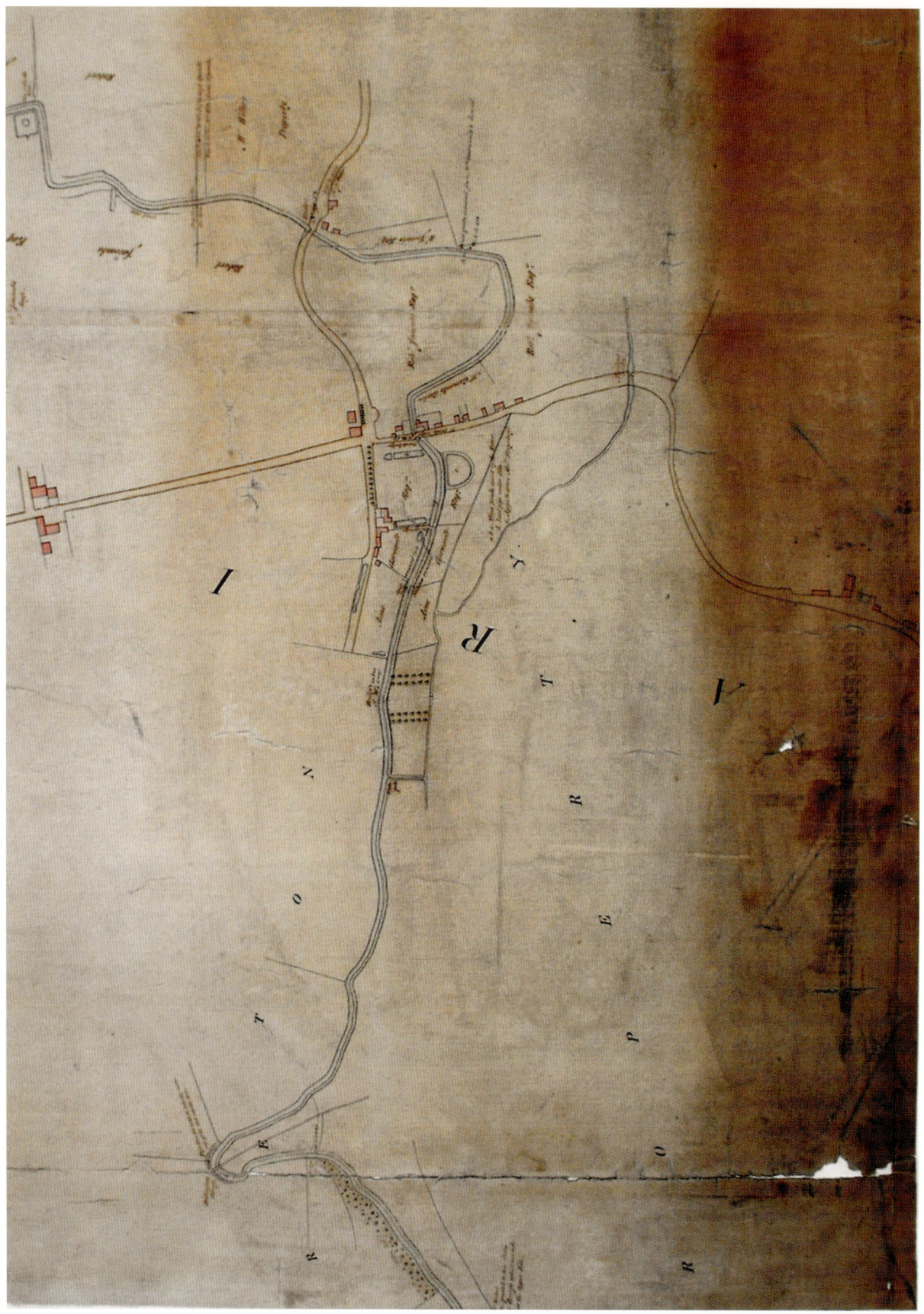

1775-1809 Plan 13: **New River from Turkey Street, through grounds of Myddelton House to former Dickinson's Trough**, Enfield, Middx. (TW Archive; MFK photo).

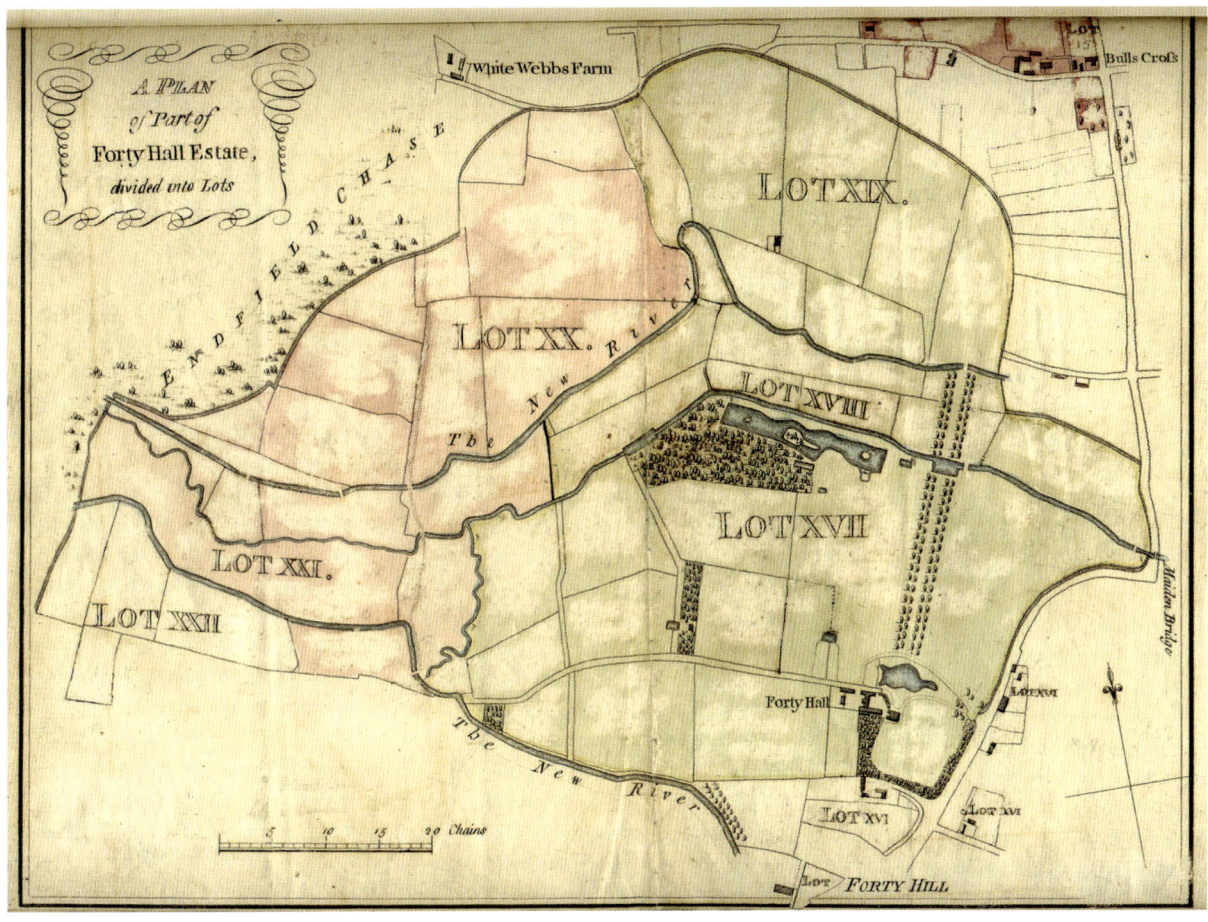

1773 Forty Hall Estate Plan (ELSC&A), showing the extent of New Park approx. 375-acres. At the building of the New River in the hands of King James I.

Mid-1500s to Mid-1600s 'New Park' (aka 'Little Park') SITE OF former Deer Park
> By 1656 part of Forty Hall Estate:

A deer park enclosed pre-1540, said to be a former part of Enfield Chase. Deer parks were normally securely enclosed by banks topped with quickset hedges or paling fences, to enclose the deer so that venison was always available especially for salting for winter months. 1540 Grant of Elsyng Hall by the Earl of Rutland to Henry VIII, becoming the home for his children (Lyson's 1810, Vol. II, p195). Diagrammatic representations of park shown on 1579 Saxton, 1593 Norden & 1608 Speed maps. In 1613 when constructing the New River, for **'altering the Cutt in John Gyrton's Parke which his Majestie found fault withal' £5. 4s.** John Gyrton the keeper of New Park for King James I. (J. W. Gough, p44, 1964; also mentioned in 1612). 1635 Survey of Manor of Enfield, the encroachment by Sir N. Raynton on his Majesty's New Park, covering the boundary fences of Enf. Chase, when he only had to repair the 'decayed' fences near Flash Road (DL 42/125/pam. 25, & item 16, & para. 10, PRO), 1641 Deed of Elsyng Hall (dem. soon after 1656) from the Crown to the Earl of Pembroke, included the Warren & 375-acre New Park (Lyson's 1810, Vol. II, p195). By-1656 part of Forty Hall Estate, shown on 1667 Blaeu's Middx. map, and in 1686 Manor of Enfield & Enf. Chase Survey, Enf. Chase adjoining the W-boundary of New Park (2 Jas. II, PRO). Shown on 1773 Breton plan (with probable fences), 1754 Rocque's map, and 1785 Thomas Bainbridge plan (with probable fences), and in 1787 Auction details, when Mrs Breton was forced to sell because of her son's gambling debts. In 1969 archaeological excavations of banks on the **NE & E-side of the 1820 NRC cast-iron aqueduct**, said to be the boundary banks of New Park, not saying why they should only be here (when the major part was fenced with paling), ignoring the above 1613 re-cuts of the New River, and only finding a 'ditch … re-cut a number of times', and banks 'almost entirely of rammed clay', which all better **suggests it was work due to the New River which was normally puddled with clay** (EAS News, No. 33, June 1969). Not to be confused with the inappropriately named aka 'Little Park', at the S-end of Gentleman's Row, Enfield.

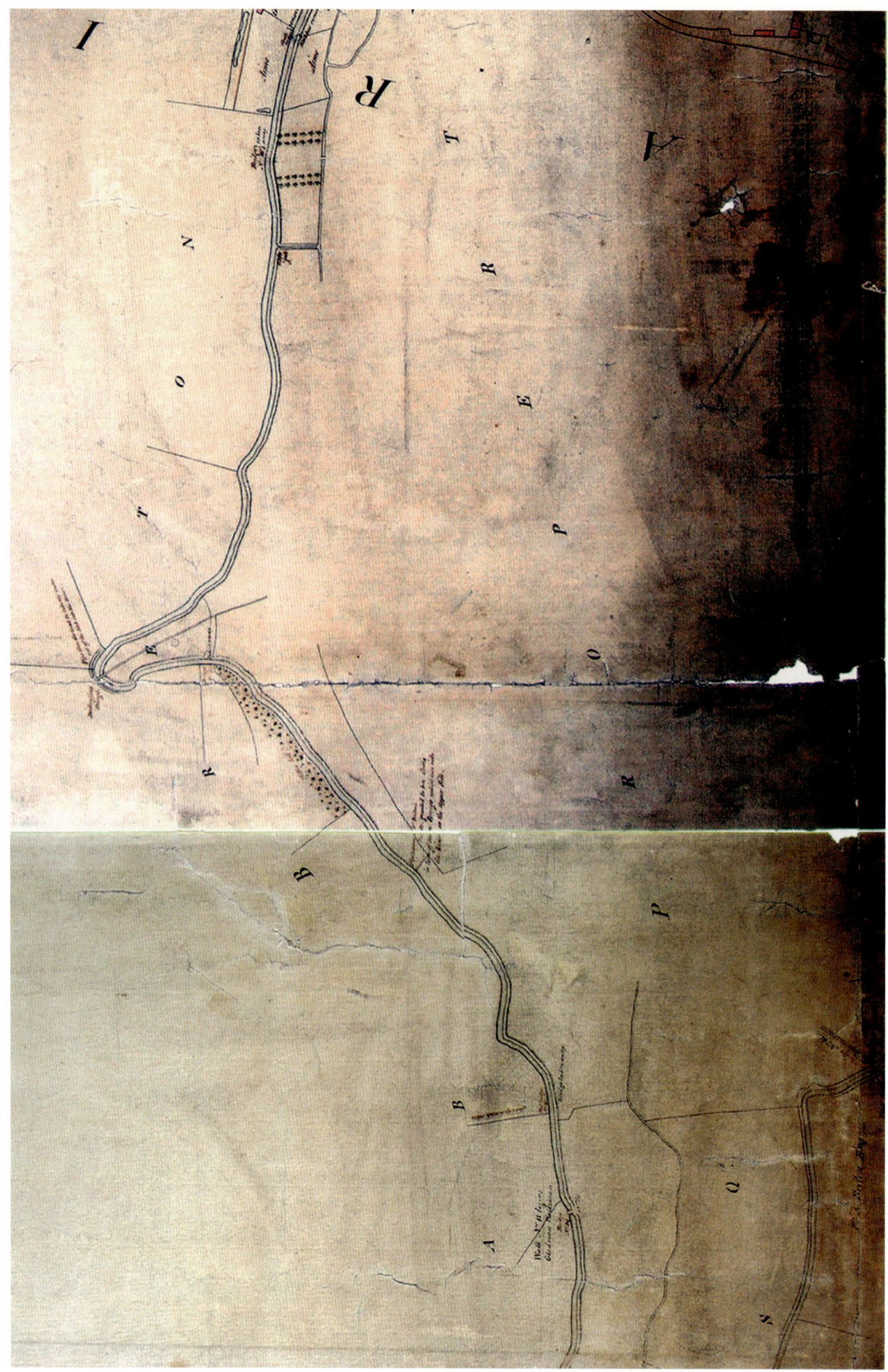

1775-1809 Plan 13 & 14: **New River at former Dickinson's Trough, Whitewebbs**, Enfield (TW, Abbey Mills Archive; 2-MFK photos joined, parts of original maps very grubby).

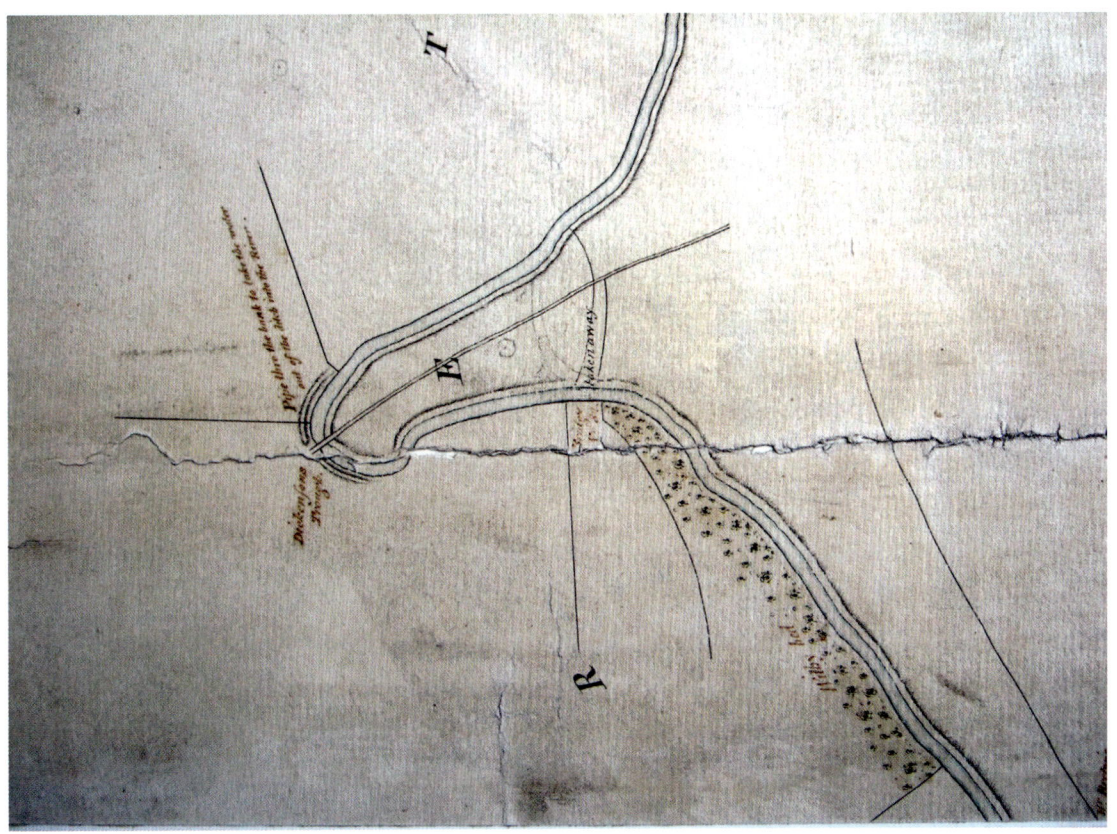

1775-1809 Plan 13 (TW Archive; MFK photos).
    ABOVE: LARGER Dickinson's Trough, 1613 mention of Trough at 'Gyrton' Park.
    BELOW: New River from grounds of Myddelton House to former Dickinson's Trough.

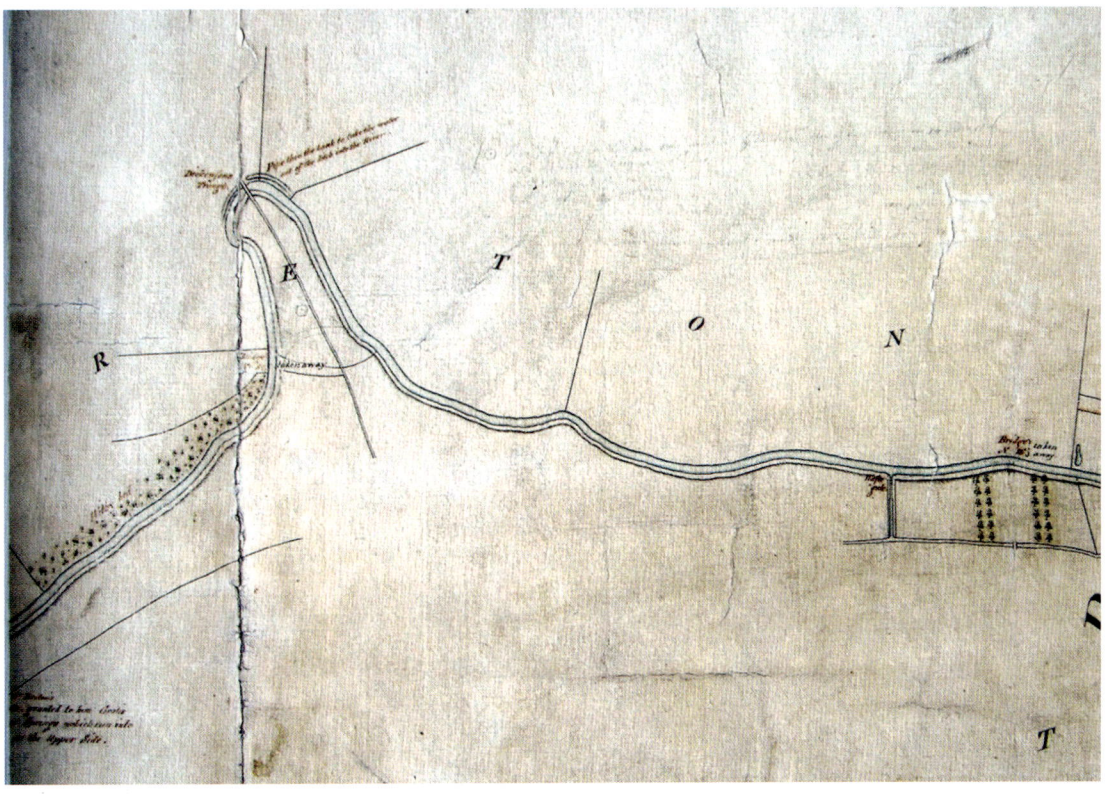

1775-1809 Plan 14: **New River at Enfield Flash**, Middx. (TW, Abbey Mills Archive; MFK photo).

1775-1809 Plan 14 (TW Archive; MFK photos).
ABOVE: New River continuing through Whitewebbs to Flash Lane & Clay Pit Piece.
BELOW: Through Whitewebbs.

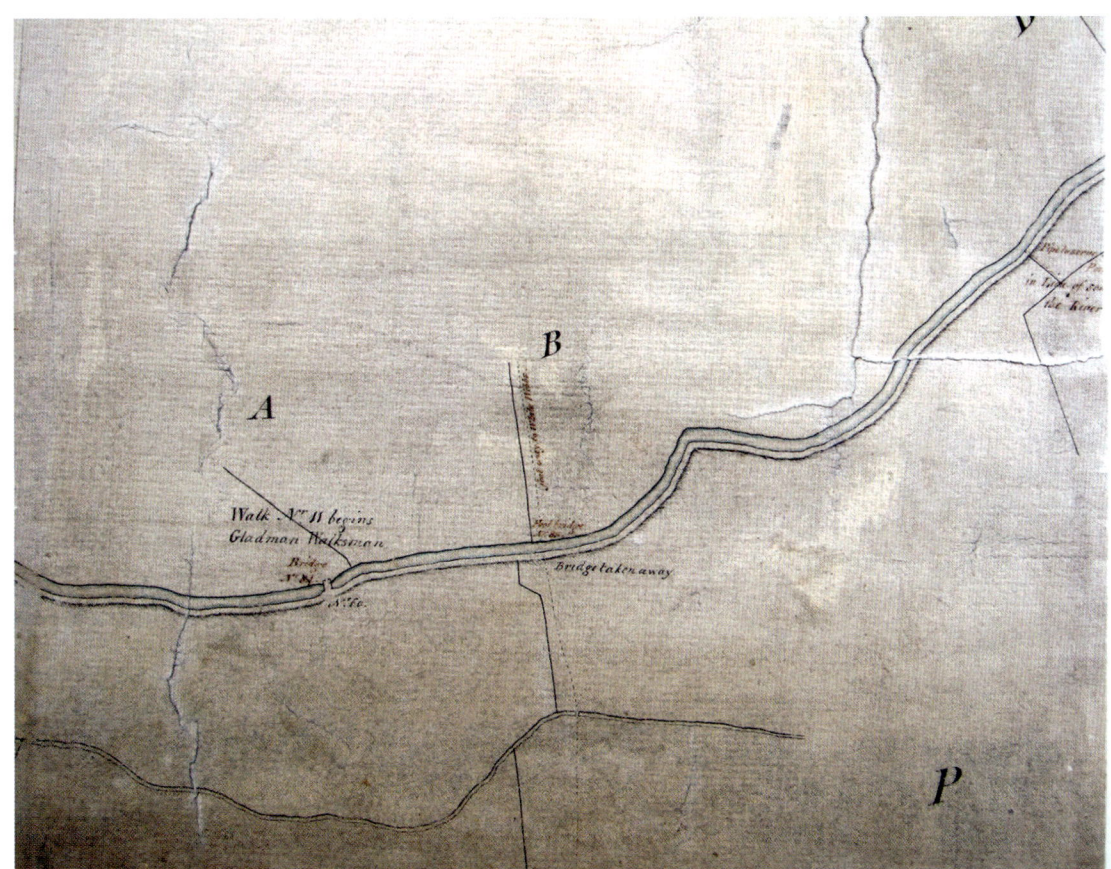

London's New River in Maps (Vol. 1, Part 1) by Michael F. Kensey

This is the end of Volume 1, Part 1.

See Volume 1, Part 2 for the continuation of Robert Mylne's 1775-1809 NRC plans from Enfield Flash to New River Head, Islington.

Vol. 1, Part 2 consists mainly of detailed coloured plans (MOST NEVER PREVIOUSLY PUBLISHED BEFORE, augmented by text), including plans of the former:

Enfield Flash,
Bull Beggar's Hole,
Gough Park/Ansell Green,
A detailed Enfield Town Loop,
Bush Hill Park house,
A detailed **Bush Hill Frame/Trough**,
Fords Green,
Palmers Green,
Hamilton Crescent Loop,
Southgate/Arnos Park Loop,
Edmonton/Tottenham/Wood Green Loop,
Hornsey Village Loop,
Hornsey Station Loop,
Haringay House Loop,
'Stamford Hill' Loop,
Holloway (> Highbury Sluice & Frame > Highbury Bank) Loop,
Clissold Park Loop,
Canonbury Loop,
'Horse Shoe Point' Loop,
Green Man Cistern,
Thatched House Sluice,
Essex Road tunnel,
Colebrooke Row,
Sadlers Wells,
A detailed New River Head (**Round/Outer Ponds, Water House; Windmill > Waterwheel > Smeaton's Engine House**), Islington **with associated cistern houses, reservoirs, and plans of New River Company wooden water mains**.

For Bibliography see Volume 3.

Index (Vol. 1, Part 1 & 2)

1775-1809 Large Robert Mylne Plans of New River (MFK Nos.).

1. **Balance Engine (River Lee) to Broadmeads** approaching Amwell End.
   Plans, **1-1**, 158-200 interspersed.
   Text, **1-1**, 132-134.
2. **Amwell End to today's Lower Amwell Road**
   Plans, **1-1**, 208-214 interspersed.
   Text, **1-1**, 134.
3. **To Start of Amwell Hill**
   Plans, **1-1**, 214-215. Text, **1-1**, 134.
4. **Great Amwell to St Margarets**
   Plans, **1-1**, 217-228 interspersed.
   Text, **1-1**, 134-135.
5. **FORMER Stanstead Loop/s (Bypassed by Embankment)**
   Plans, **1-1**, 228-237 interspersed.
   Text, **1-1**, 135.
6. **Hoddesdon**
   Plans, **1-1**, 237-243 interspersed.
   Text, **1-1**, 135-136.
7. **Broxbourne**
   Plans, **1-1**, 243-251 interspersed.
   Text, **1-1**, 136-137.
8. **Past Broxbourne High Road**
   Plans, **1-1**, 251-254 interspersed.
   Text, **1-1**, 137.
9. **Through Wormley**
   Plans, **1-1**, 254-266 interspersed.
   Text, **1-1**, 137-138.
10. **Turnford into Cheshunt North**
    Plans, **1-1**, 266-273 interspersed.
    Text, **1-1**, 138.
11. **Church Lane to S of College Road, Cheshunt**
    Plans, **1-1**, 273-280 interspersed. Text, **1-1**, 138-139.
12. **Theobalds, Cheshunt**
    Plans, **1-1**, 282-292 interspersed.
    Text, **1-1**, 139-140.
13. **Bullsmoor Lane to Dickinson's Trough, Enfield**
    Plans, **1-1**, 293-327 interspersed.
    Text, **1-1**, 140-141.
    Mystery Shortening, **1-1**, 143, 295.
    Older NR Course?, **1-1**, 295.
14. **Former Whitewebbs Loop, Enfield**
    Plans, **1-1**, 328 to **1-2**, 338 interspersed.
    Text, **1-1**, 141.
15. **Bull Beggars Hole to Tenniswood Road**
    Plans, **1-2**, 338-350 interspersed.
    Text, **1-1**, 141-142.
16. **Tenniswood Rd. to Enf. - Bush Hill, Edm. Boundary**
    Plans, **1-2**, 350-372 interspersed.
    Text, **1-1**, 143-145.
17. **Bush Hill to S-side of Ridge Avenue**
    Plans, **1-2**, 374-415 interspersed.
    Text, **1-1**, 145-146.
18. **Fords Green to Hedge Lane**
    Plans, **1-2**, 418-425 interspersed.
    Text, **1-1**, 146-147.
19 Part 1. **Hazelwood Lane to Oakthorpe Road**
    Plans, **1-2**, 427.
    Text, **1-1**, 147.
20. **Former Southgate/Arnos Park W-Loop**
    Plans, **1-2**, 429-448 interspersed.
    Text, **1-1**, 147-149.
21 Part 1. **Sidney, Wood Green High & Woodside Roads**
    Plans, **1-2**, 450.
    Text, **1-1**, 149.
19 Part 2. **Edmonton & Tottenham**
    Plans, **1-2**, 453-469 interspersed.
    Text, **1-1**, 149-150
21 Part 2. **Wolves Lane (S-end) to Wood Green**
    Plans, **1-2**, 476-481 interspersed.
    Text, **1-1**, 150.
    Mystery Shortening, **1-1**, 150.
22. **Former Hornsey Village W-Loop**
    Plans, **1-2**, 484-494 interspersed. Text, **1-1**, 150-151.
    Mystery Shortening, **1-2**, 483.
23. **Former Hornsey Station & Haringay House E-Loops**
    Plans, **1-2**, 496-498.
    Text, **1-1**, 152.
24. **Finsbury Park, & Stoke Newington**
    Plans, **1-2**, 500-509 interspersed.
    Text, **1-1**, 152.
25. **Highbury, & Clissold Park to Canonbury**
    Plans, **1-2**, 517-531 interspersed.
    Text, **1-1**, 153.
26. **Canonbury to Essex Road** Plans, **1-2**, 533-556 interspersed. Text, **1-1**, 154.
27. **Colebrook Row to New River Head**
    Plans, **1-2**, 563-600 interspersed.
    Text, **1-1**, 154-155.

A

Aden Terrace, Stoke Newington,
   1775-1809 plans, **1-2**, 530.
Amwell, Herts., **1-1**, 6.
Amwell End, Herts.,
   1773 plan, **1-1**, 192-193.
   1782 Mr Prior's house, **1-1**, 195-198.
   1800s later at Mr Prior's house, **1-1**, 199.

Amwell (Great), Herts.,
> Amwell Grove, **1-1**, 221 print.
> Approaching Gt Amwell, **1-1**, 222 print.
> Island/s & Church, **1-1**, 223 prints.
> Mylne estate, **1-1**, 131.
> NR Island (1775-1809), **1-1**, 218.
> NR Islands **Overlay**, **1-1**, 220.
> Thorpe's Farm, **1-1**, 222 print.
> Washer Women aside NR, **1-1**, 221 print.

Amwell Hill,
> 1775-1809, **1-1**, 214, 215.

Amwell Marsh,
> NRC land 1839, **1-1**, 225.

Ashfordby,
> John (1775-1809), **1-1**, 139, 278 Ashfordby tomb Cheshunt churchyard.

Atkins (Dr. Henry), **1-1**, 10, 278 tomb in Cheshunt Church.

B

Backhouse, **1-1**, 29, 38, 40.
> Backhouse (Sir William), **1-1**, 39-40, **1-2**, 613.
> Backhouse (Dame Flower, Countess of Clarendon), **1-1**, 39, **1-2**, 613.
> Backhouse (Sir John), **1-2**, 612, 613.
> Backhouse (Samuel), **1-2**, 612.

Ball (Edward) representing King James I, **1-1**, 12, 29.

Bateman (Robert), **1-1**, 35.

Bath & Wash Houses 1846-7 Act, **1-1**, 56.
> Public baths (NRC), **1-2**, 532.

Berners (Robert), **1-1**, 35.

Blagrave (John) who assisted later Surveyor Edward Pond on original NR course, **1-1**, 6, 12.

Boone (Stephen) original bricklayer, **1-1**, 15, **1-2**, 612.

Bowes Farm (1775-1809), **1-1**, 148.

Bowles family, Myddelton House, Enfield, see Myddelton House.

Bridewell Precinct/Hospital (NRC), **1-1**, 47-48, 66, 69 1667 map, 70 Bridewell bridge print & NRC Bridewell Precinct building print.

Broad Mead, Ware, Herts.,
> 1809 land, **1-1**, 191.

Blackfriars Bridge (First), **1-1**, 71.

Bridges (New River),
> Card's Bridge, Myddelton House (1775-1809 Mylne plans text), **1-1**, 141, 313.
> Cast Iron private bridge (1775-1809), **1-1**, 152, **1-2**, 498 map.
> Draw bridge (1775-1809), **1-1**, 139, 276 plan.

Broken Wharf, **1-1**, 52, 67, 69 1667 map, 73 c.1872 map.

Broxbourne, Herts., **1-1**, 12.
> 1775-1809 Mylne plans, **1-1**, 243-250.
> Broxbourne Church,
>> 1775-1809 Mylne plans, **1-1**, 249-250.
>> 1794 NR at Broxbourne Church, **1-1**, 250 print.
> Broxbourne High Road (1775-1809), **1-1**, 251-254.
> Former Brox. NR Loop (1775-1809), **1-1**, 246-249, 248 1834 NRC land.

Bullocks Cistern (> Lane's Garden Cistern) > St John Street Reservoir, **1-2**, 589, 630.

Bullsmoor Lane, Enfield,
> Former NR Loop (1775-1809), **1-1**, 294, 297.

Bulmer (Bevis), **1-1**, 53.

Bush Hill, Edmonton, Middx.,
> Amwell Close Former NR Loop, Bush Hill, 1775-1809 plans, **1-2**, 377.
>> Additional plan (Mellishes), **1-2**, 378-381.
> Bush Hill Basin,
>> 1775-1809 plans, **1-2**, 387.
> Bush Hill House/Red House (Sir Hugh's former country residence > Halliwick House), **1-2**, 393.
>> 1812 rear of house, **1-2**, 390.
>> c.1900 rear of house, **1-2**, 390.
> Bush Hill Park House/Mansion,
>> 1775-1809 plans, **1-2**, 382-383.
>> Pre-1809 plan bridge & ditch, **1-2**, 384.
>> 1813 plan bridge & ditch, **1-2**, 385.
>> 1834 Stables & NR bridge, and N-side view of NR bridge, **1-2**, 386.
>> Myddelton's Sun-Dial, **1-2**, 393.
> Bush Hill Sluice House,
>> Pre-1796 plan, **1-2**, 388.
> Elmscott Gardens (NRC River Surveyor's House), **1-2**, 389.

C

Calendar (Modernised), **1-1**, 5.

Canonbury,
> Balls Pond Road NRC 7-inch main (Early-1800s), **1-2**, 539.
> Canonbury Former NR Loop (1775-1809), **1-2**, 532-533, 538.
>> New River itself called **'The Gap'** at SE-end of Canonbury Loop, **1-1**, 154, **1-2**, 533.
> Horse Shoe Point Former NR Loop, **1-2**, 542-545, 553 text.
>> After bypassed, **1-2**, 543 print.
>> c.1823 NRC plan, **1-2**, 544.
>> 1819 from Canonbury Tower, **1-2**, 543 print.
> 'The Two Sisters' trees near Islington (c.1810 print), **1-2**, 532 plus Bathing in NR.
> Willow Bridge (c.1840), **1-2**, 541 print.

Capel Manor/House, Enfield,
> Avery, **1-1**, 302-303.
> Capel House 1804 print, **1-1**, 296.
> Charles Bottom's house (1775-1809), **1-1**, 140.
> Bullsmoor Place (Capt. Boddam), **1-1**, 296.
> Robert Jacomb's house (1775-1809), **1-1**, 140, 295.
> Honeylands Manor House, **1-1**, 295.

Chadwell Spring, Ware, **1-1**, 40, 172, **182-185**.
> 1773 plan of area around Chadwell Spring, **1-1**, 180.
> Ceasing to flow, **1-1**, 185.
> Christening 1769 in a boat at Chadwell Spring, **1-1**, 183.

C13th monks using Chadwell Spring, **1-1**, 182.
Hassall's 1631description, **1-1**, 183.
Pedestal stone Chadwell Spring, **1-1**, 109, 185
dates when rebuilt, 187 **photos**.
    Other marker stones & Gauge/Capstone/s, **1- 1**, 188 **photos**.
Re-wharfed, **1-1**, 185.
Richard Gough's 'Genius of Chadwell Spring', **1- 1**, 184.
Scott's 1776 poem mentioning Chadwell Spring, **1-1**, 184.
'Slipe' land near Chadwell Spring, **1-1**, 190.
Stones 1773 near Chadwell Spring, **1-1**, 183.
Vallens 1589/90 poem, **1-1**, 182.
Widened from Chadwell Spring 1613, **1-1**, 182-183.
Chambers (John) nephew of 1st Sir Hugh, **1-1**, 35.
Cheffins (R) Clerk of the NRC Yard, **1-1**, 41, 42, 52.
Cheshunt, Herts., **1-1**, 12.
    Aldbury, **1-1**, 12.
    Cedars Park 2002 Gates Competition, **1-1**, 288, 289.
    Cedars Park (Site of Theobalds Palace), **1-1**, 288-289.
    Cheshunt Church, **1-1**, 277 1800 print, 278 tombs in churchyard.
    Cheshunt village (1775-1809), **1-1**, 272-276.
    Church Lane (1775-1809), **1-1**, 273.
    Former Bury Green NR Loop (1775-1809), **1-1**, 279.
    Former Cheshunt Flash NR Loop (1775-1809), **1-1**, 270-272, 288 note.
    Killsmores, **1-1**, 12.
Cheshunt Park, **1-1**, 12.
Chigwell, Essex (last Sir Hugh), **1-1**, 46.
Cholera, **1-1**, 56.
City Road & Goswell Road, Islington,
    1775-1809 plans, **1-2**, 568.
    Angel Inn (1775-1809 plans), **1-2**, 568.
    c.1720 Old Street Cistern > 1787 Goswell Street Road Cistern > 1775-1809 Dalby's Cistern, **1-2**, 568 plan, 574 text.
        1787 Goswell Street Road Cistern plan, **1-2**, 575.
        c.1805 plan of Cistern House at City/Goswell Street roads, **1-2**, 576-578, 579 another c.1805 or later plan.
    Dalby's House, **1-2**, 574 text.
    NRC Wooden Trough Lined with Lead, Sadler's Hollow/The Hollow, Jack Plackett's Common, **1-2**, 574 text.
Clarendon,
    2nd Earl, **1-2**, 613.
Clay Hill, Enfield,
    Patten's/Pettin's Ware Lane, **1-1**, 142, **1-2**, 349.
Clissold Park,
    1791 NRC plan, **1-2**, 526-527.
    Clissold House/Paradise Row (1775-1809), **1-2**, 524, 530.
        Clissold House NR bridge (1804), **1-2**, 528 1804 print.
        NR at Paradise Row (c.1750), **1-2**, 528 print.
    'Coffee Pot' Sluice House, **1-2**, 515.
Colebrooke (Sir George) land near Essex Road, Islington, **1-2**, 550, 569 Colbrook.
Colebrooke (James), **1-2**, 555.
    Burton's Brewhouse near arch end, Essex Road, **1-2**, 555.
Colebrooke Row, Islington,
    c.1800 plan, **1-2**, 569.
    Camden Street (> Camden Walk) New River Bridge 1819, **1-2**, 572.
    Charles Lamb's house (c.1845), N-end Colebrooke Row, **1-2**, 564.
    Cistern House (NRC), Hattersfield, **1-2**, 555.
    Elizabeth Pullen's Pond & Samuel Pullen's Pond (1775-1809 plans), Colebrooke Row, **1-2**, 563, 568. Mr Pullin, **1-2**, 569. Later called Rhode's Pond (1827 plan), **1-2**, 571, 573 Early-1800s plan.
        Mr Rhodes, **1-2**, 569; Mr Rhoades, **1-2**, 570.
    Islington Tunnel (Regent's Canal) beneath New River, **1-2**, 571 text, 572 E-end of tunnel 1835.
    Looking N from Duncan Street 1825, **1-2**, 572.
    S-end of Colebrooke Row (Early-1800s), **1-2**, 570.
    Starvation Farm of Baron d'Aguilar (c.1800) N-end Colebrooke Row, **1-2**, 564.
Colthurst (Edmund), **1-1**, 2, 3, 4, 8, 12, 15, 38, 95.
Cornbury, **1-1**, 40.
Crane Mead (1842) Ware, **1-1**, 163.
Crown & Horseshoes pub Enfield,
    '3 Horseshoes Alehouse' (1775-1809), **1-1**, 144.
    1775-1809 plans, **1-2**, 367.
    Pre-1840 NR bridge at later Crown & Horseshoes, **1-2**, 368.
Cudgels (NR), **1-1**, 315.

D
Dorset Yard/Gardens/Pipe Wharf (NRC Offices), **1-1**, 49, 66, 69 1667 map, 71 NRC plan of Dorset Stairs offices, 72 1771 front elevation.
Drownings & suicides/New River Drag Stations, **1-1**, 16 Sadlers Wells, 59 Enfield.
Dunster (Edward), **1-1**, 133.
    1811 Dunster family land > NRC, **1-1**, 189, 190, 191 Barrow Common Field.

E
Early London water supply Schemes, **1-1**, 1.
Edmonton,
    Edmonton Church (All Saints), **1-2**, 391 1793 print.
    Edmonton Church/Latymer Trust (Sir Hugh), **1-2**, 393.
    Tile Kiln Lane > Tottenhall Road/N-end Wolves Lane (1775-1809), **1-2**, 453-454.
    'Toads Hole' today's Chequer's Way (1775-1809), **1-2**, 456.
Ellicombe's (inheriting Elizabeth Myddelton's NRC

shares), **1-1**, 39, 80.
Enfield, **1-1**, 12.
   Ansell's Green,
      1775-1809, **1-2**, 346.
      1818 NRC plan, **1-2**, 348-349.
   Bull Beggars Hole,
      1775-1809 plan, **1-2**, 337-339.
   Chase Side/River View/Gentleman's Row,
      1775-1809 plans, **1-2**, 369-371.
   Church Street,
      1775-1809 plans, **1-2**, 371-372.
   Clayesmore (NR) crescent lake, **1-2**, 334, 335
      1834 plan.
   Enfield Chase, NRC master carpenter found not
      guilty of rape, **1-1**, 45, 57.
   Enfield Church (St Andrew's), **1-2**, 359.
   Enfield churchyard, **1-1**, 40.
   Enfield Court, **1-2**, 366 1843 NRC pipe.
      c.1829 Summer House, **1-2**, 366.
   Enfield Flash, **1-2**, 330.
   Enfield Grammar School, also see Enfield Court.
      1775-1809 plans, **1-2**, 365-367.
   Enfield Town,
      1775-1809, **1-2**, 358-365.
   Enfield Town Park/Carr's Basin,
      1775-1809 plans, **1-2**, 372.
   Gough Park,
      1775-1809 plan, **1-2**, 341-343.
      1834 plan at Gough House, **1-2**, 344.
      1841 print of Gough House, **1-2**, 344.
   Man blown into NR at Enfield after explosion at
      Waltham Abbey, **1-1**, 60.
   Southbury Road,
      1775-1809 plan, **1-2**, 355.
      1834 NRC plan, **1-2**, 356.
Essex Road, Islington,
   Green Man Cistern W-side of Essex Road, **1-2**, 553 text.
      1775-1809, **1-2**, 545.
      1784 NRC plan, **1-2**, 546.
      1828 NRC plan, **1-2**, 548.
      1834 NRC plan, **1-2**, 549.
      Undated NRC plan, **1-2**, 547.
   Green Man Lane/Frog Lane 7-NRC Mains
   (c.1770) > Today's Greenman Street to Rosemary
   Street, **1-2**, 550-552.
      'Rosemary Branch Alehouse', **1-2**, 552.
   Thatched House Sluice (N-side of Today's
   Pleasant Place) W-side Essex Road, **1-2**, 549
   1834, 553 c.1790 print.
Essex Road arch/tunnel (1650-Post1851), Islington,
1-1, 39, **1-2**, 553-554.
   1775-1809 plans, **1-1**, 154, **1-2**, 556.
   Early-1800s X-section, **1-2**, 560-562.
   1816 X-section, **1-2**, 557-559.
   'Arch of brick'/'Dark Arch', **1-2**, 554.

F

Filtration (Chelsea Waterworks), **1-1**, 53.
Finsbury Park,
   1775-1809 plans, **1-2**, 500-502.
Fire hydrants/plugs, **1-1**, 39, 56, 57.
Fogwell Spring (to Sir Hugh Myd.), **1-1**, 19.
Ford (Sir Edward) Waterworks > 1667 NRC, **1-1**, 40, 48.
Forty Hall Estate, Enfield,
   Deer Park > New Park aka 'Little Park', **1-1**, 325.
Forty Hill,
   'Four Tree Hill' (1775-1809), **1-2**, 340.

G

Garnault (Aimé/Aymé II), **1-1**, 46, 314, **1-2**, 359 Enf. Church.
   Feb. 1782 NRC Treasurer but died the same month, **1-1**, 81.
Garnault (Ann) wife of Henry Carington Bowles, **1-2**, 359-360 Enf. Church.
Garnault (Daniel II), **1-1**, 314.
Garnault (Michael), **1-1**, 313, **1-2**, 359 Enf. Church.
Garnault (Samuel) NRC Treasurer 1804-27, **1-1**, 81, 314, **1-2**, 359 & 361 Enf. Churchyard.
Garnaults (Myddelton House), **1-1**, 313-314.
   Family tree, **1-1**, 316.
Gauges (NRC, other),
   Gauge (Amwell End), **1-1**, 134.
Goldsmiths' Company,
   NRC share to charity, **1-1**, 35, 36, 53.
   Sir H. Myddelton, **1-1**, 4.
      Prime Warden, **1-1**, 10.
      Portraits, **1-1**, 37, 38.
Goswell Street road, **1-1**, 46, 49.
Gough (Richard) historian, **1-1**, 262 memorial tablet.
   Richard Gough's 'Genius of Chadwell Spring', **1-1**, 184.
Grant (Capt. John), **1-1**, 39.
Grene/Greene (John) married to 1st Sir Hugh's granddaughter, **1-1**, xiii, 39 river maintenance, 41, 48, **1-2**, 359-360 Enf. Church.
   Arms of Grene & Myddelton, **1-2**, 360, 613.
   Grene v. Grene, **1-1**, 43.
   John Grene Junior, **1-1**, 303.
   Turkey Street, Enfield property, **1-1**, 302-308, 309 1866 overlay, 310 1803 Enf. Encl. Map & 1935 overlay.
   William Grene 2nd son (> daughter Jane who married Rev. Ellicombe), **1-1**, 302.
Gyrton Park Trough, Enfield, see Dickinson's Trough.

H

Hampstead Aqueducts/Water Company > 1861 NRC, **1-1**, 56.
Highbury Frame/Boarded River, **1-1**, 38, 131, **1-2**, 513, 514 described 1784, 520 plans.
   3,000 loads of earth & 20,000 bricks, **1-2**, 513.
   c.1650 lined with lead & later sale of lead, **1-2**, 513.
   Crown of Arch falls into Brook (1787), **1-2**, 514.
   Flooded (1670) John Grene & Simon Myddelton, **1-2**, 513.

Highbury Bank (1812), **1-2**, 521, 522 plan.
Highbury Frame > Highbury Bank (1775-1809 plans), **1-2**, 518.
Throughput measured (1704), **1-2**, 513.
Watch House, **1-2**, 513.

Highbury,
Arsenal Tavern NOT site of Sluice House, **1-2**, 512.
Former Highbury NR Loop, **1-2**, 511-512.
Highbury Bank (Bypassing Highbury Frame), **1-2**, 513-514.
    Iron Pipes Green Lanes (Bypassing Highbury Bank), **1-2**, 515.
Highbury Park Tavern, **1-2**, 515.
Highbury Sluice House (1st & 2nd), **1-2**, 511.
    Archaeological Watching Brief, **1-2**, 512, 519 Pre/1834 plans.
    Pre-1809 Horse machine > Dec. 1819 Waterwheel with 1834 Steam Power backup, **1-2**, 511-512.
    Gordon Riots (1780), **1-2**, 511.

Hinde (Peter), **1-1**, 35.
Hoddesdon,
1775-1809 Mylne plans, **1-1**, 231, 237-243.
Lince/Lynch Mill (1775-1809), **1-1**, 241.
Hollar (Wenceslaus), **1-1**, 48 map of New River.
Holloway/Ring Cross, **1-1**, 13.
Former Holloway NR Loop, **1-2**, 511 text, 516 Overlaid on 1871 OS map.
NRC > MWB Pipe Track, **1-2**, 511.
Holloway Waterworks bankrupted 1815 by NRC, **1-1**, 49.
Hornsey,
'Five Elms Alehouse' (1775-1809), **1-2**, 489.
Haringay House former NR Loop (1775-1809), **1-2**, 498.
Hornsey Flash & Grate (1775-1809), **1-2**, 489.
Hornsey Village Sluice House, **1-2**, 490 c.1810-17 print, 490-491 1834 plan.
Hornsey Station former NR Loop (1775-1809), **1-2**, 498.
Hornsey Village (1775-1809), **1-2**, 487-494.
Mr Gould's estate, Hornsey (c.1800), **1-2**, 488.
'Three Compasses Inn', **1-2**, 493 c.1830 print.
Water Supply, **1-2**, 483.
Hughes (Edward) NR Clerk, **1-1**, 9, 12, 82.

I
Inglebert, **1-1**, 3.
Iron Water Pipes,
Outward Leakage Enforced, **1-2**, 626.

J
Jolly Butchers pub, Wood Green,
Three Jolly Butcher's Alehouse (1775-1809), **1-1**, 150.
Jones (Howell) measurer/ganger, **1-1**, 15, 34, **1-2**, 612.

K

King Charles I, **1-1**, 286.
Royal Moiety sold to Myddelton, becoming the 36-King's shares burdened by the **Crown Clog**, **1-1**, 29, 40.
King James I, **1-1**, 10, 23, 48, 286.
Buy out the NR Adventurers (Abortive), **1-1**, 27.
Half costs & half profits to King James I, **1-1**, 11.
Edward Bull inappropriately called the king's 'Surveyor of the New River', **1-1**, 23.
King James falls into New River, **1-1**, 26-27, 104, 289 bronze roundel.
Sir Giles Mompesson the king's 'surveyor of the [New River] profits', **1-1**, 23.

L
Lamb (Charles & Mary) essayists, **1-2**, 391 grave.
Lane's Garden Cistern (Former Bullocks Cistern) >
St John Street Reservoir, **1-2**, 589, 630.
Pre-1805 Section of ground from Lane's Gardens Cistern, **1-2**, 590.
Pre-1805 Sketch of Lanes Gardens Cistern, **1-2**, 591.
Lewis (William), **1-1**, 35.
Lewyn (William), **1-1**, 12, 15, 35, 82.
Lloyd (John), **1-2**, 614.
Lockmead (Early-1800s), Ware, **1-1**, 163.
London Bridge Waterworks (LBWWs) > 1822 NRC, **1-1**, 52, 67.
Broken Wharf, **1-1**, 52, 53, 67.
Morris family, **1-1**, 53.
Richard Soames, **1-1**, 52.

M
Mantles (Commandery), Islington, **1-1**, 40, 42.
Metropolitan Water Board (MWB), **1-1**, 58.
Coat of Arms, **1-1**, 58.
Compensation for NRC shareholders, **1-1**, 59.
WW1 damage to New River, **1-1**, 60.
WW2 damage to New River, **1-1**, 60.
Middleton (Thomas, no relation to Sir Hugh) dramatist, **1-1**, 14, 15, 16.
Mill (Henry) NRC Surveyor, **1-1**, 25, 43-44, 45, **1-2**, 613.
Breamore Church near Salisbury where buried (memorial epitaph), **1-1**, 44-45.
Myddelton (Sir Hugh 1st Baronet),
Addresses in London, **1-1**, 4, 5.
Baronetcy, **1-1**, 16, **27**.
Bush Hill House (Myddelton's country house), **1-1**, 10.
Churchwarden of St Matthew's, **1-1**, 32.
Coat of Arms (1st Sir Hugh), **1-1**, xiii, **27**, **1-2**, 404.
Dame Elizabeth Myddelton 2nd wife of Sir Hugh 1st, **1-1**, 32, 34, 35, 36, 37 portraits, 38 death, **1-2**, 391.
Daughters (of Sir Hugh 1st baronet),
    Anne, **1-1**, 35.
    Elizabeth, **1-1**, 34, 35, 36.
    Elizabeth M., **1-1**, 36.

Hester, **1-1**, 34, 36.
Jane, **1-1**, 32, 34, 36.
Mary (6th daughter & 12th child), **1-1**, 36, **1-2**, 391.
Death & Will, **1-1**, 32.
St Matthew's church (location plan & print), **1-1**, 33.
Did not die in reduced circumstances, **1-1**, 36.
Tributes to Sir Hugh, **1-1**, 36-37.
Failed to find coal, **1-1**, 5.
Family tree, **1-1**, xiii, 2.
Goldsmiths, **1-1**, 4.
Great jewel from City of London, **1-1**, 27, 35.
Knighted myth, **1-1**, 16.
Marriages, **1-1**, 4.
Mining silver in Wales, **1-1**, 21.
Estimated mining profits, **1-1**, 23.
Map & plan, **1-1**, 22.
Richard Newell, **1-1**, 34.
Trial in front of umpires, **1-1**, 23.
Myddelton brass Whitchurch porch, **1-1**, xiv.
Myddelton's house Galch-Hill, **1-1**, xv, 2.
Myddelton Name (used for Roads, Schools, Pubs Railway Engines etc.), **1-1**, 113.
Myddelton's native district, **1-1**, xv.
Not a pipe smoker, **1-1**, 5.
Not a Clothmaker or Merchant Adventurer, **1-1**, 5.
Portrait (Sir Hugh), **1-1**, frontispiece, 3, 37.
Reclaiming Brading Haven, Isle of Wight, **1-1**, 26, 28.
Ruthin, **1-1**, 4.
Signature, **1-1**, xiii, 12.
Silver Cups donated by Sir Hugh, **1-1**, 19.
Sons (of Sir Hugh 1st baronet),
Myddelton (Bartholomew), **1-1**, 36.
Myddelton (Henry), **1-1**, xiii, 34, 35, 36.
His son Henry (& Starkey's), **1-1**, xiii, 46, 53.
Myddelton (Hugh), **1-1**, 36.
Myddelton (James), **1-1**, 36.
Myddelton (John), **1-1**, 36.
Myddelton (Robert), **1-1**, 36.
Myddelton (Simon) youngest son & his family, **1-1**, 29, 34, 35, 38, 39, **1-2**, 391.
Elizabeth (daughter of Simon Myddelton, wife of John Lane, leaving one son), **1-2**, 391.
Hezekiah (son of Simon Myddelton), **1-2**, 391.
Mary Soame (2nd wife of Simon Myddelton who had 8-children by him), **1-2**, 391.
Rebecka (daughter of Simon & Mary his wife, **1-2**, 391.
Sarah (2nd daughter of Simon Myddelton) who married the Earl of Oxford, & died without issue), **1-2**, 391.
Simon's son Hugh created **Baronet of Hackney** 1681, **1-1**, 35, 38, 42 died in poverty 1702.
Myddelton (Thomas), **1-1**, 36.
Myddelton (William, 2nd Baronet), **1-1**, 32, 34, 35, 36, 38.
Myddelton (Sir Hugh [2nd] 3rd Baronet, 1-1, xiii, 29.
Myddelton (Sir Hugh [5th] the 6th/LAST Baronet of Ruthin), 1-1, 46.
No fortune for later heirs, **1-1**, 53.
Myddelton (Elizabeth) granddaughter of 1st Sir Hugh married to John Grene, **1-1**, xiii, 39, **1-2**, 359-360 Enf. Church.
Statues of Sir Hugh, **1-1**, 38.
Myddelton (Richard) nephew of 1st Sir Hugh, **1-1**, 35.
Myddelton (Captain Roger) nephew of 1st Sir Hugh, **1-1**, 34.
Myddelton (Sir Thomas) elder brother of 1st Sir Hugh, **1-1**, 15, 34.
Myddelton (Sir Thomas) nephew of 1st Sir Hugh, **1-1**, 35.
Myddelton (Timothie) nephew of 1st Sir Hugh, **1-1**, 35.
Myddelton House (former site of Bowling Green House), Enfield,
1775-1809 Mylne plans, **1-1**, 312.
1775 former Enfield parish fire bell, **1-1**, 317.
1821 Myddelton House print, **1-1**, 317.
Bowles family, **1-2**, 362 Enf. Churchyard.
Family tree, **1-1**, 316.
H.C. Bowles, **1-1**, 314, **1-2**, 359-360 Enf. Church.
H.C.B. Bowles (last NRC Governor), **1-1**, 314, **1-2**, 359 Enf. Church.
New River filled-in Myddelton House, **1-1**, 314.
Original location of Bowling Green House, **1-1**, 313.
1818 NRC plan, **1-1**, 321.
Version 1 overlay, **1-1**, 319.
Version 2 overlay, **1-1**, 320.
Version 3 overlay, **1-1**, 322.
Optimum of 3-overlays, **1-1**, 323.
Myddelton (Sir Hugh) Tavern, almost opposite NRH, **1-2**, 585 print, 596 called Alehouse on 1775-1809 plans.
Mylne (Robert) NRC Surveyor, **1-1**, 25, 38, 43, 49, 66, 71, 72, 131-132.
Silver Cup (NRC), **1-1**, 131.
Turnpike Trusts & Toll Roads incl. Toll Bars, **1-1**, 132.
Wife (Mary Home) & Family, **1-1**, 131.
Mylne (William Chadwell) NRC Engineer, **1-1**, 49, 67, 132.
Sons,
Robert William Mylne, **1-1**, 132.
William Chadwell Mylne (2nd), **1-1**, 132.

N

Neville (Sir Henry), **1-1**, 12, 13.

New River,
    Accounts (Original), **1-1**, 3, 11, 12, 17, 47.
    Bathing/Washing in New River, **1-1**, 45, 99-100, **1-2**, 532.
    Bed of New River,
        Concreting the Bed, **1-1**, 108.
        Pumps & Dams (When Originally constructed), **1-1**, 9, 26, 85.
        Temporary (Troughs & Bypass Pipes), **1-1**, 85, 108.
    City of London Acts, **1-1**, 3, 6.
        Attempt to repeal Acts, **1-1**, 10.
    Compensation Commission, **1-1**, 9.
        Compensation, **1-1**, 18, 47, 48.
            Bush Hill, **1-1**, 19.
            Edmonton, **1-1**, 13.
            Islington, **1-1**, 13.
    County Vote, **1-1**, 9.
    Drum, **1-1**, 12.
    Expenditure (Original), **1-1**, 16, 17
        £500,000 +/- myth since 1734, **1-1**, 16, 17.
        Costs (Original) including Distribution Pipework with today's equivalent, **1-1**, 17.
        New River itself up to Sept. 1613, **1-1**, 18, 19.
    Extension of time, **1-1**, 11.
    First survey, **1-1**, 6.
    Formal opening ceremony, **1-1**, 13. Public Pageant & Parade, **1-1**, 14-15.
    Giant Plough, **1-1**, 9.
    Great Hold-up, **1-1**, 10.
        Work resumed, **1-1**, 12.
    Historical Features (NR), **1-1**, 85.
        Aqueducts (NR), **1-1**, 94-95.
            Flash Lane, Enfield, 1820 cast-iron aqueduct, **1-2**, 333.
        Artists depicting the NR, **1-1**, 113.
        Augmenting supply,
            Surface water/Common sewers, **1-1**, 90-91, 92.
        Boat hoists/Davits/Python Rigs, **1-1**, 101.
        Boats/Punts for river maintenance, **1-1**, 101.
        Boundary markers (NRC Stone & Iron) & other markers, **1-1**, 98-99, 109, 133, 183 stones said put down c.1728.
            Capstones, **1-1**, 133, **169**, 171 location of one SE-side WH Sluice, 172.
                Capstone SE-side WH Sluice, **1-1**, 176 **photo**.
            Round Pond (NRH) marker on arch of bridge, **1-1**, 109.
            Stone just before WH Sluice, **1-1**, 176 **photo**.
            Stone N-side of WH Sluice, **1-1**, 175 **photos**.
            Wooden post, **1-1**, 98-99.
        Bridges (Original), **1-1**, 13.
            Earlier Number of bridges, **1-1**, 88-90.
            Iron bridges, **1-1**, 89, 90.
            Relocated bridges, **1-1**, 90.
            X-sections at bridges, **1-1**, 90.

        Cattle Troughs (Cast-iron), **1-1**, 100.
        Cistern Houses (NRC), **1-1**, 93.
            Bullocks Cistern (> Lane's Garden Cistern) > St John Street Reservoir, **1-2**, 589.
            Dalby's Cistern (1775-1809), **1-1**, 154.
            Green Man Cistern (1775-1809), **1-1**, 154.
            Hattersfield Cistern (N-end of Colebrooke Row), **1-2**, 555.
            'New Cistern' Stoke Newington (1775-1809), **1-1**, 153.
            Newington Green (1775-1809), **1-1**, 153.
            NRC Cistern Houses South of Clissold Park, **1-2**, 525 text.
        Cutting the Grass Banks (Scythes > Lawnmowers), **1-1**, 102.
        Cutting water weeds, **1-1**, 19, 100-101.
        Drainage Pipes & Brick Culverts, **1-1**, 88.
        Easements, **1-1**, 94.
        Fences along NR, **1-1**, 13, 27, 60, 104 **c.1840-50 cast-iron**.
        Filtration (Filter Beds & Chlorination etc.), **1-1**, 95.
            Purity/Quality of water, **1-1**, 90, **1-2**, 615.
                Dogs & Filth, **1-1**, 90.
            Sampling, **1-1**, 106.
            Screening rubbish, **1-1**, 53, 90.
        Flashes/Troughs/'Chutes'/'Pysher' & Frames, **1-1**, 91-92.
            Bush Hill/Great Frame, **1-1**, 131, **1-2**, 392 1775-1809, **393-396**, 397 1686 plan, 401 before & after, 402 1784 print of Frame, 403 col. Painting, 405 diagrams of trough, 406 X-section of impending embankment.
                1725 inscription stone (since lost), **1-2**, 404.
                c.1783 plan, **1-2**, 398.
                1786 inscription stone (now faces road), **1-2**, 410.
                Clarendon Arch prob. built 1682, **1-2**, 394, 395 1784 moved 80ft. to E, 396 1794 rebuilt after settlement, 394 **inscription amended & restored 1780**, brook at the arch mainly bypassed 1967 by new parallel tunnel, 404 1784 print of arch, 410 post 1786 arch, 414 c.1800 print of W-side of arch & 2008 photo.
                Embanked (Frame replaced), **1-2**, 395, 396 costs, early-1900s enlarging channel, 409 shown embanked 1775-1809, 411-412 1789 plan of embankment, 413 c.1789 plan.
                Gordon Riots, **1-2**, 395.
                Lined with lead, **1-2**, 394 c.1650, 396 timber sold for £93-99, lead for £974, 407 Sale of timber, 408 schematic of various phases.
                Lordes Pond/Tillstones Park, **1-2**, 393.
                Raised 1ft. higher 1725 & 1775, **1-2**, 394.

Dickinson's Trough/Trough at Gyrton
Park (Enfield), **1-1**, 141, 311, 313.
Haw/Hawe Mores (Cheshunt?), **1-1**, 13.
Enfield Flash (1775-1809), **1-2**, 330.
   c.1820 NRC plan of Enfield Flash, **1-2**, 333.
Frames, **1-1**, 93.
Geddings ('Gyddinges'), Stanstead **1-1**, 92.
Hornsey Flash & Grate (1775-1809), **1-1**, 151.
List of NR flashes, **1-1**, 92.
Newman's Flash Southgate (1775-1809), **1-1**, 148, **1-2**, 441 1599.
'Pysher' (For land water), Wood Green, **1-1**, 92.
Sadler's Hollow/The Hollow, Jack
Plackett's Common (Wooden Trough Lined with Lead), **1-2**, 574 text.
Schematic of NR Trough/Flash, **1-2**, 332.
Tarred & sealed with oakum (Caulking), **1-1**, 91, **1-2**, 394.
Wild's/Mincing Flash, Arnos Park (1775-1809), **1-1**, 148, **1-2**, 438.
Wooden Trough under NR (1775-1809), **1-1**, 146.
Gradient/Fall/Level, Width & Length of NR,
   Depth, **1-1**, 107.
   Gradient/100ft. contour, **1-1**, 107, 108.
   Length (Original), **1-1**, 108-111.
      Reductions & Increases in length, **1-1**, 109-111.
      Myths on length, **1-1**, 109.
      Opposing Streams, **1-1**, 108-109.
   Width, **1-1**, 107-108.
Grates (Waterweed Removal) manual, **1-1**, 101.
   Autogrates, **1-1**, 101, 63 list.
Islands (New River), **1-1**, 93.
   Bowes (1775-1809), **1-1**, 148.
   Broxbourne, see Vol. 3.
   Theobalds, **1-1**, 277.
Notice Boards (MWB), **1-1**, 105.
Piling & Wharfing, **1-1**, 85.
Piped sections & Culverting, **1-1**, 94.
Plugs (Drains), **1-1**, 85.
Poaching/Fishing in NR, **1-1**, 100, **1-2**, 581, 614-615.
Puddled clay to prevent leaks, **1-1**, 85-87.
   Clay Pits/piles, **1-1**, 86, 87, **1-2**, 331.
   Leakage, **1-1**, 87.
Seats (inscribed NRC) along NR Path, **1-1**, 101-102.
Sluice Houses,
   Arnos Park (1775-1809), **1-1**, 148.
   Clissold Park, into (1775-1809), **1-1**, 153.
   Highbury (1775-1809), **1-1**, 153.
   Thatched House (1775-1809), **1-1**, 154.
   White House Sluice (1746), Ware, **1-1**, 173, 177 **photo**, plus sluice inside, 178

inside Sluice Gate.
      1746 7 1823 stones at Weir & footbridge, **1-1**, 179 photos.
Sluices/Weirs, **1-1**, 88, 89, 90, 98, 104.
   Stone Sluice, Green Lanes Stoke Newington (1775-1809), **1-1**, 152, **1-2**, 509 plan.
Tunnels, **1-1**, 93-94.
   'Stamford Hill' Loop bypass tunnel (1775-1809), **1-1**, 152.
   Also see Essex Road, Islington.
Verse & Literary Mentions of the New River, **1-1**, 113-129.
Valve-plates/stopcocks (NRC) Street Mains, **1-1**, 105.
Watch Boxes/Houses, **1-1**, 100, 314, **1-2**, 470, 651 adjacent to Old Toll House Coppice Row.
Water-level gauges, **1-1**, 98.
Waterwheels on NR, **1-1**, 96.
      Highbury, **1-1**, 96. Hornsey, **1-1**, 96.
      New River Head, **1-2**, 629.
Inspections of NR, **1-1**, 48.
Length of New River, **1-1**, 45.
Loan myth (Myddelton), **1-1**, 10.
Loan from City (Myddelton), **1-1**, 19.
Myddelton's opponents (Purvey & Atkins), **1-1**, 10.
Myths, **1-1**, 16.
Outside Capital, **1-1**, 9.
   New River shares (Original), **1-1**, 13.
   NRC shares,
      Ashfordby's, **1-1**, 278.
      Elizabeth Myddelton > Ellicombe's, **1-1**, 302, 304, 305, 306.
      Garnault shares, **1-1**, 313, 314.
Places reached (when first constructed),
   Additional Cuts, **1-1**, 13.
   Amwell Spring, **1-1**, 9.
   Broxbourne, **1-1**, 12.
      Broxbourne Church, **1-1**, 9.
   Chadwell to Amwell, **1-1**, 13.
   Cheshunt/Park, **1-1**, 12.
      Aldbury, **1-1**, 12.
      Killsmores, **1-1**, 12.
      Theobalds/Park, **1-1**, 12, 13.
   Edmonton, **1-1**, 13.
   Enfield, **1-1**, 12, 13.
      Hatchmore Grove, **1-1**, 13.
   Holloway, **1-1**, 13.
   Hornsey, **1-1**, 13.
   Islington, **1-1**, 13.
      Mantells, **1-1**, 13.
   Only death, **1-1**, 9.
   Rye Field, **1-1**, 13.
   Southgate, **1-1**, 13.
   Spital Brook, **1-1**, 9.
   Stoke Newington, **1-1**, 13.
   Ware (land), **1-1**, 19.
   Wood Green, **1-1**, 13.

Wormley, **1-1**, 12.
    Watery Lane, **1-1**, 13.
Proclamations on merits of NR, **1-1**, 40.
Sights & sound over 400-years, **1-1**, 52.
Start date (Original NR), **1-1**, 6.
Stealing NR water, **1-1**, 99, **1-2**, 554.
Statutory powers transferred to Myddelton, **1-1**, 11.
Surveying original route, **1-1**, 6.
Trumpeter, **1-1**, 12.
Vandalism on NR, **1-1**, 21, 38.
Water tenants (NR customers), **1-1**, 20, 23, 40, 49.
    21-year supply agreement 1616, **1-1**, 20-21.
    Water lease, Fleet Street main, **1-1**, 21.
Workforce (Original), **1-1**, 6, 7 chart, 8, 12.
    Main body of workers, **1-1**, 9.
X-section (Original NR), **1-1**, 8.
New River Artificial Recharge Pumping Stations, **1-1**, 60. 63 **List with dates**, 97.
    Bat bricks, **1-1**, 97-98.
New River (Wildlife), **1-1**, 106.
New River Company (NRC),
    Accounts (Original), **1-1**, 11, 27, 29.
    Crown Clog benefits, **1-1**, 29-32.
        Adair Case 1799, **1-1**, 29, 49.
            Charles I > John Robinson > John Buckworth > Silvester Dennis > Dennis Cooling > 1st Earl of Albermarle > 1737 William Adair > Alexander Adair > Sir Shafto Adair > 1956 MWB, **1-1**, 30-32.
        Adair 1911, **1-1**, 59.
    William Bishop & Flower Backhouse (later Lady Cornbury), **1-1**, 29.
    Land Tax, **1-1**, 30, 31.
    Simon Myddelton & Sir Hugh [2nd], **1-1**, 29.
    Clarendon family, **1-1**, 29.
Failure to get NRC recognised by Parliament, **1-1**, 26, 27, 38.
Great Fire 1666, **1-1**, 39.
Incorporation 1619, **1-1**, 23.
    Chest for NRC charters, **1-1**, 38.
Legal proceedings, **1-1**, 40, 42, 49, 56, 57, 59.
Myddelton's management fee of NR, **1-1**, 26, 48.
NRC Acts, **1-1**, 49, 53, 54, 56, 57, 58.
NRC Capital, **1-1**, 42, 52, 56.
NRC charges,
    Net rateable value, **1-1**, 57.
NRC Clerkenwell Estate, **1-1**, 49, **1-2**, 614.
    Myddelton Square, **1-2**, 615.
NRC Clerks/Secretary, **1-1**, 82-83.
    Beadle beneath Clerk, **1-1**, 82.
    Jasper Bull, **1-1**, 39, 41.
    Charles Rivington, **1-1**, 82.
NRC Collectors, **1-1**, 45, 83.
    Aquila Garfield, **1-2**, 618.
    John Lloyd, **1-2**, 618.
    Heathcote, **1-2**, 619.
    Identification Tag (NRC), **1-2**, 619.
    Rules for NRC Collectors, **1-2**, 619.

NRC Courts/Board meetings, **1-1**, 38, 39, 48, 66.
NRC Dividends,
    First dividends, **1-1**, 38.
    1663-1903 dividends, **1-1**, 73-77.
NRC drinking fountains, **1-1**, 112, **1-2**, 642- 643.
NRC Fishery/ies, **1-1**, 133, 134.
NRC filters, **1-1**, 53.
    Kempton Park (MWB), **1-1**, 55.
    New River Head, **1-2**, 642.
NRC fire 1769 Bridewell Precinct, **1-1**, 47-48.
NRC Former Headquarters & Thames sites, **1-1**, 66-67.
NRC Governors (& Oath) & Deputy Governors, **1-1**, 79-81
    Holford, **1-1**, 66, 99 1771 Secretary.
    Memorial rings, **1-1**, 46.
    Smith (Robert Percy), **1-1**, 78 portrait.
NRC Limited 1904 (Property Company), **1-1**, 59.
    H. Stoddard, **1-1**, 59.
    London Merchant Securities, **1-1**, 59.
NRC mains,
    Cricklewood to Fortis Green (MWB), **1-1**, 55.
    Kempton Park to Cricklewood (MWB), **1-1**, 55.
    Kempton Park to Hampton (MWB), **1-1**, 55.
    Littleton to Kempton (MWB), **1-1**, 54.
    Willesden to Fortis Green (MWB), **1-1**, 55.
NRC Main sites, Geographical list, **1-1**, 62, 64.
NRC Minutes, **1-1**, 48, 49.
    NRC Board minutes 1769-1904, **1-1**, 48.
NRC Officers & Staff, **1-1**, 48, 83.
    Auditors, **1-1**, 83.
    Engine workers, **1-1**, 83.
    NRC Secretary/Clerk,
        Rowe, **1-1**, 67.
NRC Offices, **1-1**, 66-67.
NRC Pumping Stations & Wells, **1-1**, 56, 96 List.
    Amwell End well, **1-1**, 96.
    Amwell Hill well, **1-1**, 96, 97.
    Amwell Marsh well, **1-1**, 96.
    Betstile/Colney Hatch well, Southgate, **1-1**, 56, 57 1871 NRC, 96.
    Broadmead well, **1-1**, 96.
    Broxbourne well, **1-1**, 96, 97.
    Bush Hill Park Estates Co. well etc., > 1887 NRC, **1-1**, 57.
    Campsbourne (Hornsey) well, **1-1**, 96.
    Cheshunt well, **1-1**, 96.
    Coal bunkers, **1-1**, 97.
    Furnace refuse, **1-1**, 59.
    Hadley Road well & P.S. (Local Authority > MWB), Enfield, **1-1**, 56, 96.
    Hampstead Heath well, **1-1**, 57.
    Highfield well, **1-1**, 96.
    Hoddesdon well, **1-1**, 96, 97.
    Hoe/Goat Lane well, **1-1**, 96, 97.
    Hornsey P.S., **1-1**, 97.

Hornsey well aside NR (1775-1809), **1-1**, 151.
Kempton Park P.S. (I & later II by MWB), **1-1**, 54-55.
Rye Common well, **1-1**, 96, 97.
Standpipes, **1-1**, 97.
Stoke Newington P.S., **1-1**, 97.
Turnford well, **1-1**, 96, 97.
Weigh Bridges, **1-1**, 97.
Whitewebbs well, **1-1**, 96.
NRC records, **1-1**, 59.
   1686 inventory, **1-1**, 49.
   Pre-1769 fire, **1-1**, 47-48.
NRC Reservoirs, **1-1**, 56.
  Covered (Reservoirs), **1-1**, 55.
    Bourne Hill, Palmers Green, **1-1**, 55.
    Cricklewood balancing reservoirs, **1-1**, 54, 55.
    Dartmouth Park Hill/Maiden Lane, **1-1**, 55.
    Fortis Green, **1-1**, 54, 55.
    Hampstead Grove/Heath, **1-1**, 55.
    Highgate, **1-1**, 55.
    Hornsey Lane/Archway, **1-1**, 55.
    Southgate/Oakwood, **1-1**, 55.
    Stroud Green/Crouch Hill, **1-1**, 55.
  Open (Reservoirs), **1-1**, 54-55.
    Abortive reservoirs, **1-1**, 54.
    Amwell End, **1-1**, 54.
    Camden Park Road, **1-1**, 54.
    Cheshunt, **1-1**, 54.
    Hornsey Basin, **1-1**, 54.
    Kempton Park, **1-1**, 54.
    Staines Open reservoirs & **Staines Aqueduct** (with Joint Committee), **1-1**, 54, 58.
    Stoke Newington, **1-1**, 54.
    Tottenham Court Road-Hampstead Road, **1-1**, 54, **1-2**, 630, 637-639 with X-section & plan.
      Well (R.W. Mylne), **1-1**, 132.
NRC Seal, **1-1**, 24.
NRC Shares, **1-1**, 57-58.
  Income Tax, **1-1**, 40.
  Land Tax, **1-1**, 40.
  Local Rates/Poor Law, **1-1**, 40.
  Poll/Income tax, **1-1**, 40.
  Socage tenure/realty (real property), **1-1**, 23.
NRC Silver cups,
  Daniel Garnault, NRC 1795, **1-1**, 314.
  H.C.B. Bowles replica silver cup NRC 1903, **1-1**, 314.
  Robert Mylne (NRC 1806), **1-1**, 131.
NRC Surveyors/Engineers, **1-1**, 83.
  William Grace, General Surveyor, **1-1**, 83.
  Henry Mill, **1-1**, 39, 43-44; also see under Henry Mill.
  Robert Mylne, see Robert Mylne.
  William Chadwell Mylne his son, see W.C. Mylne.
  John White (River Surveyor), **1-1**, 40.

NRC Takeovers, **1-1**, 65 list.
NRC Treasurers, **1-1**, 81-82.
  Simon Myddelton, **1-1**, 29, 39; also see Simon Myddelton.
NRC Turncocks, **1-1**, 45-46, 57, 83, **1-2**, 619 photo.
  Aquila Garfield, **1-1**, 40.
  MWB (NR District) Turncock plates, **1-2**, 619.
  NRC Turncock's business card, **1-1**, 45.
  NRC Turncock's key, **1-1**, 45.
NRC & Grand Junction Water Co., **1-1**, 58.
NRC & W. Middx. Co., **1-1**, 58.
NRC water fittings, repairs & stamping, **1-1**, 57, 58.
NRC as water & land company, **1-1**, 23.
NRC water rent receipts, **1-1**, 40, 42 Pepys, **1-2**, 618 two Water Rent Receipts.
Tapping the River Lee, **1-1**, 25.
  4 times the water for only double the cost myth, **1-1**, 26.
  20-inch extraction pipe (& other pipes), **1-1**, 25, 172.
  1737 & 1738 Acts, **1-1**, 26.
  Balance Engine & Timber Gauge, **1-1**, 25, **161-163**, 164 Illustrations, 172.
    Ditches pos. used, **1-1**, 172-173.
    Old/Timber Gauge or Trough, **1-1**, 133, 163, **169-170**, 171 location of Old Gauge, 172.
    New Gauge (aka Marble Gauge 1773-76), **1-1**, 133, 163, **170**, 173, 181 May 1830 sketches.
    New Gauge (1856 > Today's), **1-1**, 163, 170, 173.
  Dams/2-jetties at Ware, **1-1**, 25, **1-2**, 393.
  Great pipes to Lesser pipes, **1-1**, 25.
  Lee Trustees & cost of water, **1-1**, 26.
  Limited to the 1670 outtake, **1-1**, 25.
  Manifold Ditch,
    1738-9, **1-1**, 173.
    1856 bypassed, **1-1**, 173, 174 plan.
    Ancient or new, **1-1**, 25.
  River Lee, **1-1**, 56.
    Acts, **1-1**, 56.
    Hertford sewage & NRC, **1-1**, 56.
    Sewage, **1-1**, 57.
    Ware Lock (NRC), **1-1**, 26.
    Ware Mills (NRC), **1-1**, 26.
  Tapping subsidiary streams, **1-1**, 25.
  Thefts from NRC, **1-1**, 45, 46.
  Trees not within 5 yds of NR, **1-1**, 23.
New River dog patrols, **1-1**, 60.
New River Football Club (MWB), **1-1**, 59.
New River Former/Loops, geographical sequence,
  Manifold Ditch, **1-1**, 165, 173, 174.
  Stanstead, **1-1**, 230.
  Broxbourne, **1-1**, 247.
  Broxbourne Church, **1-1**, 250.
  Wormley-Turnford, Herts.,

Wormley Church Lane straightening, **1-1**, 257.
    Wormley Church Lane E-Loop, **1-1**, 258.
    Wormley Flash & Turnford Loop, **1-1**, 260.
Cheshunt Flash, **1-1**, 271.
Cheshunt (Bury Green) W-Loop, **1-1**, 279.
Cheshunt (Theobalds) W-Loop, **1-1**, 292.
Enfield (Bullsmoor E-Loop), **1-1**, 300.
Enfield (Whitewebbs/Enfield Chase) W-Loop, **1-1**, 311 to **1-2**, 351.
Enfield Town loop,
    1775-1809, **1-2**, 355-374.
    WW2 bombing of bypass pipes, **1-1**, 60, 111.
Bush Hill (Amwell Close), **1-2**, 377-382.
N-side Ford's Green (Minor Loop), **1-2**, 418 see later Vols.
S-side Highfield Row (Minor straightening), **1-2**, 422 see later Vols.
Barrowell Green (Minor Loop), **1-2**, 422-423.
Hamilton Crescent W-Loop, **1-2**, 427.
Southgate/Arnos Park Loop, **1-2**, 429-446.
Edmonton-Tottenham-Wood Green Loop, **1-2**, 449-481.
Hornsey Village Loop, **1-2**, 486-494.
Hornsey Station & Haringay House Loops, **1-2**, 496-498.
'Stamford Hill' Loop (1775-1809), **1-1**, 152, **1-2**, 504-507.
Holloway/Highbury W-Loop, **1-2**, 511-522.
Clissold Park W-Loop, **1-2**, 523-529.
Canonbury W-Loop, **1-2**, 533.
Horse Shoe Point W-Loop, **1-2**, 542-545.
Map overlays (MFK) of former NR Loops, **1-1**, 112.
New River Head, Islington,
    1667 John Jennings plan, **1-2**, 594.
        Overlay of 1667 plan on 1775-1809 plans, **1-2**, 595.
    1743 William Gardiner plan, **1-2**, 586-588.
    1775-1809 plans, **1-2**, 592, 596 onwards.
    1805 W.C. Mylne plan around NRH, **1-2**, 601-603.
        'New Prison', **1-2**, 602 plan.
    c.1820 Laying out streets around NRH, **1-2**, 604-606 plan.
    Archaeological Excavations (NRH), **1-2**, 615.
    Bagnigge Wells, **1-2**, 599 plan.
    Brayne's/Briants/Bryant's/Pantheon Row, **1-2**, 597 1775-1809 plans, 648.
    'Bull in the Pound', **1-2**, 599 plan.
    Butchers Mantles, **1-2**, 600 plan.
    Canaletto the artist, **1-2**, 614.
    Chimney aka Devil's Conduit moved to NRH, **1-2**, 615.
    'Coach & Horses', **1-2**, 596 1775-1809 plans.
    Cold Bath/Fields, **1-2**, 598 plan, 652-655.
    Coppice Row, **1-2**, 648.
    Dobney's, **1-2**, 600 plan.
    Elm Street, **1-2**, 648.
    Fishing, **1-2**, 614, 615.
        Carp (& Eels) in the Wooden Pipes, **1-2**, 625.
    Goose Yard, **1-2**, 600 plan.
    Gordon Riots, **1-2**, 614.
    Hanging Field, **1-2**, 599 plan, 614.
    Hollar's 1665 prints around NRH, **1-2**, 617.
    Islington Spa or Tunbridge Wells, **1-2**, 596 1775-1809 plans.
    'Kings Arms', **1-2**, 596 1775-1809 plans.
    'Low Pond', **1-2**, 598 1775-1809 plans.
    Mill Field, **1-2**, 600 plan.
    Mill Yard, **1-2**, 596 1775-1809 plans.
    Mount Pleasant, **1-2**, 648.
    MWB headquarters building, **1-1**, 60, **1-2**, 615.
    MWB Laboratories (NRH), **1-2**, 615.
    Myddelton Street, **1-2**, 607 S-side c./1812 plan, 608 1813 plan proposed houses, 609-610 c.1825 houses in Myddelton Street area, 611 c.1830 alterations to mains near Myddelton Street.
    Northampton Field, **1-2**, 597 plan, 648, 649 plan.
    NRC Offices, **1-2**, 615.
    'Old London Spa', **1-2**, 598 plan.
    Pennies Folly, **1-2**, 600 plan.
    Pipe Yard, **1-2**, 596 1775-1809 plans.
    Pumping (also see New River Head),
        Smeaton's 1767 'Fire-Engine', **1-1**, 131, **1-2**, 614, 646 prints.
        Waterwheel, **1-2**, 513 lead from Highbury to NRH, 629 Low Pond.
    Round Pond,
        Cleaning, **1-2**, 612 text, 615.
        Ducking Pond, **1-2**, 612.
        Filter Beds, **1-2**, 615, 642.
        Grating, **1-2**, 612.
        Maximum Size, **1-2**, 614.
        Outer Cistern, **1-2**, 613.
        Outer Pond/s (> 3 filter beds), **1-2**, 615.
        Representations, **1-2**, 612-615 text.
        Semi-circular brick cistern into Round Pond (1774), **1-2**, 614.
        Waste Ditches, **1-2**, 612, 626.
        Wall surrounding, 1-2, 612.
        Waste Ponds (> Outer Ponds), **1-2**, 612, 613.
        Water House, **1-2**, 612, 614 1782 encased in brick, 616 1689 depiction, 622-623 Pre-1820 plan.
    Sadlers Wells Field, **1-2**, 600 plan.
    Sir Hugh Myddelton's Glory print, **1-1**, 14, **1-2**, 616.
    Small Pox Hospital, **1-2**, 598 plan, 648.
    Smock Field, **1-2**, 600 plan.
    St. John's Street Turnpike, **1-2**, 597 plan.
    Tent Field, **1-2**, 600 plan.
    Tile Kilns, **1-2**, 599 plan, 632.
    Toll House (Cobham Row), **1-2**, 648, 651 Old, 652 New.
    Upper Pond, **1-2**, 600 1775-1809 plan, 626-627.
        c.1752 perimeter **shown fenced**, **1-2**, 632 print, 642.
        Post-1767 perimeter **shown walled**, **1-2**, 632 print, 642 Brick wall > Iron Railings.

Claremont Square Covered Reservoir, **1-2**, 642.
NRC Drinking Fountain, **1-2**, 642.
Pumping (High Service), **1-2**, 640-642 text, 644 print.
    Boulton & Watt Steam Engines, **1-2**, 641-642.
    'Fire Engine' (Smeaton's Atmospheric Engine), **1-2**, 641, 646 Smeaton's drawings of Eng. House & section, 647 1818 chimney.
    Square Horse Works, **1-2**, 640-641, 645 1753 print.
    Steam > Electricity, **1-2**, 642.
    Triple Expansion Engines, **1-2**, 642.
    Waterwheel, **1-2**, 641 text, 645 **schematic**.
    Windmill, **1-2**, 640 text.
Standpipe, **1-2**, 642.
Upper Pond Cistern House (1730), **1-2**, 627.
Water Distribution from NRH (via Cistern Houses & Small Storage Ponds), 1-2, 624-630.
    Cistern Houses (Gravity), **1-2**, 624.
        Crown Alehouse/Tavern Cistern, **1-2**, 630.
        Cube/**West Cistern**, **1-2**, 627, 635 c.1800 West Cistern plan.
        Jerusalem Tavern Cistern, **1-2**, 630.
        Middle Cistern House (S-side Outer Pond), **1-2**, 626, 633 Post-1730 plan, 634 Post-1782 plan.
        Out/Outer Cistern House (S-side Water House, E-side Outer Pond), **1-2**, 627.
        'Water House' Cistern, **1-2**, 626.
            c.1741, 31-Leaden Distribution Pipes, **1-2**, 631 print.
    Small Storage Ponds, **1-2**, 624.
        West Pond, **1-2**, 627-628, 636 1819 plan.
        Mill/Low Pond/Reservoir, **1-2**, 628-629.
    Waterhouse Field, **1-2**, 597 1775-1809 plans, 650 plan.
New River Path, **1-1**, 60-61.
Nightingale's Alehouse, Southgate (1775-1809), **1-1**, 147.
Northampton (Water Supply), **1-1**, 43.

O

Owen's Row (Formerly Aside New River), Islington.
    1839 Lady Owen's Free School, **1-2**, 580 print.
    Post-1840 Rebuilt Lady Owen's Free School, **1-2**, 580 print.

P

Palmers Green,
    Former NR Loop N-side Barrowell Green (1775-1809), **1-2**, 422.
    N-side Barrowell Green (Post-1809 & 1834), **1-2**, 423.
    Hamilton Crescent Former NR Loop (1775-1809), **1-2**, 427.
    Hedge Lane (1775-1809), **1-2**, 425.
Parnell (William) supplier of timber, **1-1**, 9, 12, 15.

Plague, **1-1**, 3, 27.
Poems,
    New River, **1-1**, 49-52, 113-129.
Pond (Edward) later Surveyor of original course, **1-1**, 6, 12, 15.
Puddle Dock (NRC offices), **1-1**, 48, 66, 69 1667 map.
Purvey (William), **1-1**, 10, 262 memorial tablet.

R

Ranger Mead, Ware, **1-1**, 133.
Red House (NRC), SE of Ware, **1-1**, 213 1775-1809. NRC Balance House also called Red House on a map, **1-1**, 163.
Rival schemes to New River,
    Chelsea School, **1-1**, 9, 10.
    Edward Hayes scheme, **1-1**, 12.
    Hoddesdon Springs, **1-1**, 27.
    St. Albans/River Colne, **1-1**, 45.
    Tyburn, **1-1**, 38.
Rhodes, **1-1**, 100.
Rye House, Herts.
    'Rye Common Field' (1847 NRC land), **1-1**, 236.
    'Rye Field Common' (Early-1800s NRC land), **1-1**, 232-234.
    'Rye Field Common' (1834 NRC land), **1-1**, 235.

S

Sadlers Wells Theatre,
    1803 New River water to Stage, **1-2**, 581.
        Archimedes Wheel, **1-2**, 581-582.
        Water tanks described, **1-2**, 582.
    c.1808 print of water scene on stage, **1-2**, 581.
    1823 alterations to speed of water to stage, **1-2**, 582.
    1891/2 48-inch pipe replacing open New River, **1-2**, 585 print.
    Edward Sadler's Music House, **1-2**, 581.
    Robert Boyle, **1-2**, 581.
    Miles's Music Hall, **1-2**, 581.
    Well itself, **1-2**, 582
Seven Sisters, trees at Enfield (1775-1809), **1-1**, 145, **1-2**, 377.
Sewers, **1-1**, 49, 57.
Shire Ditch (1775-1809 Herts.-Middx.), **1-1**, 140.
Smith (Robert Percy), **1-1**, 78 portrait.
Southgate, Enfield, Middx.,
    Broomfield House,
        1800 print, **1-2**, 433.
        Lanscroon 1726 murals c.1975, **1-2**, 433.
    Former Southgate NR Loop (1775-1809), **1-2**, 429.
        Arnos Park,
            Alderman Wild's House (1599), **1-2**, 436.
            Beaver Hall (1804 print), **1-2**, 440.
            Former Sluice House, **1-2**, 435.
            Minchenden House (Post-1843 print), **1-2**, 440
            Private NR bridge (just inside park), **1-2**, 435.

Summer House, **1-2**, 435.
  Wild's Flash (1775-1809), **1-2**, 438.
  Bowes Farm/Manor 'steps' (1775-1809), **1-2**, 448.
  Bowes Road (1775-1809), **1-2**, 446-448.
  Newman's Flash, **1-2**, 441 1599, 442 1775-1809.
  Powys Lane NRC bridge 1819, **1-2**, 434.
  Seafield Road private bridge (1784 print), **1-2**, 443, 444 Late-C18th painting, 445 viewpoint.
  Green Lanes (1775-1809), **1-2**, 430-431.
  Nightingales Alehouse (1775-1809), **1-2**, 432.
St. Mark's Church, Clerkenwell, **1-2**, 615.
Stamford Hill,
  Former 'Stamford Hill' Former NR Loop (1775-1809), **1-2**, 504 text, 505 plan, 506-507 c.1830 plans.
Stanstead NR Loop/s, Herts.
  1775-1809, **1-1**, 228, 229, 230.
Stoke Newington,
  Bailey's Wharf on River Lee (NRC c.1830 Abortive), **1-2**, 506 plan.
  Lordship Road (1775-1809), **1-2**, 508.
  NRC Stoke Newington Pumping Station, 1775-1809 plans, **1-2**, 509.
St. James' Palace NRC supply, **1-1**, 41.
St. John Street Reservoir completed 1805 (Former Bullocks Cistern > Lane's Garden Cistern), **1-2**, 589, 630.
St. Margaret's, Stanstead Abbots,
  1775-1809 Mylne plans, **1-1**, 227, 228.
St. Paul's Cathedral (NRC cisterns & engines), **1-1**, 53.
Summer Houses,
  Cheshunt (1775-1809) Site Of, **1-1**, 139.
  Arnos Park (1775-1809 Site Of, **1-1**, 148.

T
Thames Water,
  London Ring Main, **1-1**, 60.
  Thames Water Authority 1974, **1-1**, 60.
  Thames Water Plc. 1989, **1-1**, 60.
    German RWE Group 2000, **1-1**, 60.
    Australian Macquarie Bank Group 2006, **1-1**, 60.
Theobalds, **1-1**, 10, 12, 26, 27.
  Former Theobalds NR Loop (1775-1809), **1-1**, 292-294.
  Theobalds (1775-1809), **1-1**, 139, 281.
  Theobalds Palace (Site Of), **1-1**, 286-289b.
    John Thorpe 1611 survey, **1-1**, 287, 288 NRC pipes (c.1690).
    William Bentinck, Earl of Portland, **1-1**, 288.
    Robert Cecil, **1-1**, 286.
    William Cecil, **1-1**, 286, 289.
  Theobalds Palace Wall, **1-1**, 284-285.
  Theobalds Park, **1-1**, 12, 140, 277 1806 **print**.
    1775-1809 Mylne plans, **1-1**, 290, 291.
  Old Palace House, **1-1**, 289b **photos**.
Tottenham,

1619 map of Tottenham showing NR, **1-2**, 467-468.
Clay Hill House/Green/Farm (1775-1809) >
Devonshire Hill Lane, **1-2**, 457.
  1837 NRC plan of Clayhill Farm, **1-2**, 466.
  Louisa Powys' land > 1839 NRC, **1-2**, 474.
  Northumberland's land > 1837 NRC, **1-2**, 471 map, 472-473 text.
  'Watch Box Field' NRC bridge, **1-2**, 470 1818 print.
White Hart Lane,
  1829 NRC Iron Pipes, **1-2**, 459.
  C15th Crook's Farm > White Hall, **1-2**, 459, 465 plan & print.
  Serles Grove (1840), **1-2**, 475.
  White Hart Lane from Clay Hill (Post-1809 NRC Watercourses), **1-2**, 460-464.
Trihurst (Richard), **1-1**, 35.
Turkey Street, Enfield,
  1775-1809 Mylne plans, **1-1**, 297.
  John Grene's & Elizabeth Myddelton's (Sir Hugh's granddaughter) property, Turkey Street (> Collins > Coleman), **1-1**, 302-308.
  Salmons, **1-1**, 308.
Turnford, Herts.,
  1775-1809 Mylne plans, 266.
Two Sisters trees, Canonbury (1775-1809), **1-1**, 153.

U
Upper/High Pond > Claremont Square Reservoir, Islington (NRC), **1-1**, 42, 56.
  Soho Square, **1-1**, 42.
  Islington village, **1-1**, 43.

W
Walksmen (New River), **1-1**, 10, 83, 102-103.
  Walks (Gate Keys), **1-1**, 103.
Walpole (Sir Robert) Houghton Hall, Norfolk, **1-1**, 43.
Ware,
  NRC land aside River Lee, Ware early-1800s, **1-1**, 204-206.
  Crane Mead, Ware 1841, **1-1**, 207, 208 1775-1809, 209 1898.
  Ware Lock (I > II) 1840, **1-1**, 201, 202 1898, 203 1923-38.
  Ware Mills, **1-1**, 200 1775-1809 & c.1830-40.
Waterbearers/Tankard bearers, **1-1**, 1, 42.
  Water carrier, NR water, **1-2**, 618.
Water Companies (London), **1-1**, 49.
  Failed merger of W. Middx. with NRC, **1-1**, 49.
  Intense Competition 1806-15, **1-1**, 49.
  Metropolitan Water Companies 1850 plan, **1-1**, 68.
  Metropolitan Water Examiner, **1-1**, 57.
Water supply,
  Constant, **1-1**, 57, 58.
  Intermittent, **1-1**, 12.
Waterwheels (NRC Pumping),
  Highbury (Horse Machine > Waterwheel, **1-2**,

511-512).
New River Head (Covered Overshot Waterwheel), **1-2**, 640-641.
Waterwheels near Rosoman Street, **1-2**, 629.
Waterworks Acts, **1-1**, 56 1847 & 1852, 57.
Winchmore Hill, Enfield, Middx.
   Ford's Green,
      1775-1809 plans, **1-2**, 418, 421-422.
   Green Dragon pub (1st), **1-2**, 402 print, 408 & 415 maps.
   Highfield Road,
      1775-1809 plans, **1-2**, 422.
   Oliver's Farm (1838), N-side Firs Lane, **1-2**, 416.
   Ridge Avenue,
      1775-1809 plans, **1-2**, 415.
White (John) NRC River Surveyor, **1-1**, 40-41, 86, **1-2**, 359 Enf. Churchyard.
Whitacres (Miles) representing King James I, **1-1**, 12.
Whitewebbs/Enfield Chase Former NR Loop, 1775-1809 Mylne plans, **1-1**, 298.
Wilkinson (Alexander) original costs of NR, **1-1**, 17.
Wooden Water Mains (NRC), **1-1**, 12, 46, 49, **1-2**, 624-626.
   1st & 2nd line of NR pipes, **1-1**, 19, 43.
      Gray's Inn, **1-1**, 19.
      Shoreditch, **1-1**, 19.
      Ludgate, **1-1**, 19.
      Soho Main, Grosvenor Main, Oxford Main & Portland Main, **1-1**, 19.
      St Mary le Bonne, **1-1**, 49.
      Wood > Cast-iron mains (NRC), **1-1**, 49, **1-2**, 625.
   c.1800 line of pipes NRH to Mount Pleasant, **1-2**, 648 text.
      Names of Mains, **1-2**, 648.
   City's Green Yard, Bear Quay near Tower, **1-1**, 12.
   Dave Allkins with Wooden Main, **1-2**, 624.
   Bartholomew (John) pump maker of Ware, **1-1**, 12.
   Elm trunks, **1-1**, 12, 41 'Firr' pipes.
   Horne (Thomas) paviour, **1-1**, 15.
   Horse/Boring engine, **1-1**, 41-42, **1-2**, 624.
   Iron mains, **1-1**, 52 1817 Act.
   Lacey (Avery), **1-1**, 12.

Parkes (Richard), **1-1**, 12, 15.
Paviours, **1-1**, 46, 83.
Pipe borers, **1-1**, 83.
Pipe-borer's wharf Bridgehouse yard, **1-1**, 12, 41, 67, **1-2**, 624.
Quills & swan-necked cocks, **1-1**, 19, 20.
River Fleet,
   Farringdon Road/Mount Pleasant line of NRC Wooden Pipes across Fleet, **1-2**, 625 print, 656 plan.
   Tile Kilns/Bagnigge Wells, line of NRC Wooden Pipes crossing the Fleet, **1-2**, 625-626 print, 632 print of location.
Stack of Wooden Pipes, **1-2**, 624.
Testing wooden pipes, **1-1**, 41.
Wood Green,
   Duckett's Manor/Moat/Farm House > Dovecote Farm > Dovecote House & Villas, **1-2**, 478 text, 479 1840 print & plan.
   High Road (1775-1809 with small kinks straightened), **1-2**, 450.
   Chitts Hill & Roundhouse (Post-1822), **1-2**, 451.
   'Pysher' (1775-1809 for land water), Wood Green, **1-1**, 92.
   Upper Wood Green (1775-1809), **1-2**, 477.
      Irelands & Perrie Field (1840), **1-2**, 478.
   Wood Green (1775-1809), **1-2**, 480-481.
Wormley, Herts., **1-1**, 6, 10, 12.
   1844 NRC land, **1-1**, 259.
   Former Church Lane NR Loop (1775-1809), **1-1**, 254-258.
   Former Wormley-Turnford NR Loop (1775-1809), **1-1**, 260-266.
      Pre & 1841 Broom Field & Clarke's Grove (Water Lane), **1-1**, 265.
   Wormleybury Church, **1-1**, 262 **photos**.
   Wormleybury House, **1-1**, 261 **print & photo**.
   Wormley Flash (1775-1809), **1-1**, 260, 263.
      c.1834 NRC land before Wormley Flash, **1-1**, 264.
Wright (Edward) earlier Surveyor of original NR course, **1-1**, 6, 9, 12.

Y

York Buildings Waterworks > 1818 NRC, **1-1**, 52.